1965
157

—·5

THE COMMUNISTS AND PEACE

JEAN-PAUL SARTRE

The Communists and Peace

WITH AN ANSWER TO CLAUDE LEFORT

TRANSLATED FROM THE FRENCH BY
IRENE CLEPHANE

HAMISH HAMILTON

LONDON

The Communists and Peace (*Les Communistes et la Paix*)
was first published in *Les Temps Modernes*, Nos. 81,
July 1952; 84–85, October–November 1952; 101, April
1954. Reprinted in *Situations*, *VI*: 'Problèmes du Marxisme', 1, Gallimard, 1964.

Answer to Claude Lefort (*Réponse à Claude Lefort*) was
first published in *Les Temps Modernes*, No. 89, April
1953; reprinted in *Situations*, *VII*, Gallimard, 1965.

Printed in Great Britain by
Western Printing Services Ltd, Bristol

Contents

THE COMMUNISTS AND PEACE

WHEN the Compagnies Républicaines de Sécurité were making charges against the miners, the press of the Right proclaimed a victory: which made me think that *Le Figaro* had no liking for the workers. But I was wrong. I apologize all round, and in particular to M. Robinet. For M. Robinet in fact adores the workers. He did not want to express his affection—through shame, I take it. But after the set-to at the Renault factories, he has expressed his nice feeling. At first, I must say, I was surprised to read this heading in large capitals: 'Workers' Victory.' I could not help wondering over whom the workers had gained this victory, unless it was over the employers and the security police: that is to say, the readers of *Le Figaro*. But I was quite wrong: no, the proletariat had not beaten the 'coppers'. Nor the middle classes either: it had triumphed over the Communist Party—the one political group which represents it in the Assembly—and the Confédération Générale du Travail, the oldest and largest of the trade-union federations.

In short, the workers had disarmed themselves, thrown down their weapons. Only one more effort was necessary: they must dissolve their unions, vote Independent at by-elections, and thus gain the most satisfying victory of all: victory over themselves. That, indeed, is the condition in which the workers are lovable: without weapons, their hands bare, their arms open. The people at Fourmies on May Day 1891 were splendid: they had no shock troops, no paramilitary organization: just people in the streets, lots of people, milling about. Children, lilies of the valley, a young girl carrying a bough of mistletoe. Major Chapuis's troops were able to take aim carefully and fire point-blank.

Such convenient occasions may occur again, and I appreciate that we should congratulate ourselves if they do: the massacre

of Fourmies certainly is the type of spectacle called by
M. Mauriac 'scandalous, but in the best sense'. But the imbecile
satisfaction expressed by certain journals 'of the Left' passes
my comprehension. Unhappy people: once again the CP has
done the trick: they loved it, they left it regretfully, it has
smothered them in filth, they loathe it. A love affair. I meet
them sometimes, these outsiders. They still smile tenderly, but
they are rather drawn about the eyes. They embody the contradiction of our time. How can you *at the same time* believe in
the historic mission of the Proletariat and in the perfidy of the
Communist Party when you notice that the one votes for the
other? They can be disentangled, but with difficulty. Each one
goes, more or less rapidly, through four predictable stages.
Stage one: 'The CP is certainly wrong, but *all the same* we
can't go against the proletariat.' Stage two: 'I have always loved
the workers; but *all the same* it can't be denied that they are not
very far-sighted. Look at the German workers: they allowed
themselves to be taken in by Hitler's claptrap.' Stage three: 'I
stopped being interested in the workers when they failed to
express any indignation over the Soviet concentration camps.'
Stage four: the Apocalypse: 'We've made an alliance with the
United States. Stop. We'll smash Russia with atomic bombs.
Stop. We'll hang all Communists. Stop. And on the ruins we'll
build real socialism, international, democratic, reformist.' There
can be no doubt that the finest working-class victory will be
won by American troops over those of the USSR; but he who
dares to say this aloud must be either a traitor or maddened by
disappointment, which comes to the same thing. Generally
speaking, these persons stick to half-tones and, in order to study
the enemy more closely, visit reactionary drawing-rooms to
throw stones. Or they make distinctions: they are for the Indo-
Chinese and the Spanish Republicans, against the Chinese and
the Greeks; for Lenin, that great liberal, and against Stalin the
autocrat. They know that's preposterous, and they mutter
softly to themselves, 'If only this damned working class would
make up its mind once for all to drop the CP.' Consider, for
example, M. Altman. I know him well; he is no traitor, not even
a bad man. But the Communists have treated him according to
the technique used by Charles Boyer in *Gaslight*: by repetition
of the same trick, the patient is made to believe that he is mad

and wicked. After three years of this treatment, M. Altman is already more than half convinced. And this is what he wrote on May 29 in *Franc-Tireur*: 'The agitation against everything "American" seems to have taken the form of maniacal and murderous rage. A man has a perfect right to criticize American policy, if he thinks that a good thing to do. But has he the right to show, by every means from slander to sabotage, that only those men, those allies are to be tolerated who stand at our side ready to ward off eventual aggression? ... Has he the right to throw into the street men, women, and children at watchwords which call to mind racism pure and simple? In this context it is no longer a question even of Communism, but of Russianism.... Everything that does not contribute to Stalin's Russia ... everything that is for liberty, so far as it still exists on this side of the iron curtain, everything of that sort should be annihilated before being exterminated. ...'

Have you observed?—'if he thinks that a good thing to do'. What subtlety, what implications in that brief phrase, and how willingly a man would die for the language and the culture which permit these fine shades! 'If he thinks that a good thing to do': this seems no more than a paraphrase of, 'If that is your opinion.' But to accept that would be to forget the very slight discredit attaching to the expression. 'Since you thought well to pledge me without asking my opinion....' You follow?: criticize your American allies if you think it a good idea; M. Altman does not think it is, and if he leaves you free to do so, he gives you a discreet warning that you are going to commit follies. Alas, I am afraid these subtleties are lost: the Americans who read the article haven't the basic teaching to relish them as they properly should. Besides, they are our *allies*: M. Altman tells us that straight out. Moreover, he is right, absolutely right: the French government—which one, by the way?—has signed the North Atlantic Pact. In short, the worker enjoys democratic liberties: he can think, speak, vote. So why need he brawl in the streets, like a hooligan? But of course, it is the Stalinist who pushes him on. This Stalinist, his evil genius, the everlasting agitator, Russian today, Boche yeserday, scattering English gold in 1789, Russian gold in 1840, fanning the discontent of the masses and turning it to account to throw them into politics. Made fanatical by his treacherous diatribes, the workers, no longer law-abiding, are the first victims of their own violence. As we know today, it was this agitator who rushed the mob into its attack on the Bastille; who took advantage of the resentment of a few black slaves, perhaps punished too harshly, to deprive us of Haiti; who financed the conspiracy of the Four Sergeants, the days of June 1848, the endless strikes at the end of the century, and, to finish up, the mutinies of 1917. How can his tricks be thwarted? How can he be finally reduced to impotence? M. Altman knows: 'If a daring social democracy could wrest from the Stalinists the monopoly of defending the workers, we should not be in this situation.' Here is a man who doesn't make us feel any younger: in a hundred and sixty-two years, neither the cure nor the evil has changed. And in M. Altman's democratic daring there is perhaps some resemblance to the wise progressivism of that Comte de Morny who as early as January 1898 wrote in the *Revue des Deux Mondes*: 'Communism secretly saps the foundations of societies and of governments. Will the evils that threaten us be prevented by moderate concessions, intelligent reforms, careful study of financial and social questions, devoted zeal of the rich for the poor, coupled with courageous resistance to factions? That is the real question.'

Go for daring social democracy: moderate concessions to the trade unions; devoted zeal of employers for their workers; bold resistance to factious *separatists*. But where is the basis for such a course? Where is the political team that will apply it? Where is the majority that will carry it into power? M. Altman is no dupe; he is well aware that it takes years for a political group to gain enough influence to secure representation in the Assembly. Now he is convinced that it is war *tomorrow*, war provoked by the Russians and a war lost if we cannot manage *this very day* to draw the masses away from the influence of the Party. Poor M. Altman: you would suppose that after thirty years he might know these Communists; he must be well aware that they won't let go of the morsel. So sometimes his favourite argument turns over on itself in his mind, and he says to himself: since the daring social democratic party is not yet in power, must we not recognize that, at the present moment, only the CP is a *possible* representative of working-class electors? I wish I could say that M. Altman sleeps lightly these days! For he is one of a sufficiently large group, the *Amicale des Futurs Fusillés* which is to the next war what the *Association des Anciens Combattants* was to the war of 1914–18. They have often invited me to their feasts, but I have been unable to persuade myself to go and share their virile and funereal jollity. 'Come, come,' they say, 'you're one of us!' But, if the next war does break out, I see so many reasons for believing we shall none of us survive that I am not going to waste my time enumerating those peculiar to me.

As to that, the golden sound of a thousand trumpets on June 4: the proportion of strikers was about two per cent! M. Altman is exultant, he felt alive again. Two per cent. At last the working man understood: he was tired of pulling the chestnuts from the fire for the USSR and indicated his mistrust of the Party which aims at setting him against republican institutions; satiated with violence, he went back to his little suburban garden, to his much-praised gentle manners. At once everyone offered him guidance. Force Ouvrière opened its arms to him; M. Altman began to wonder seriously if he could not work off his daring social democratic party on him.

Beautiful children, dear slimy rats, you are running to war! Believe me! It is a slimy rat who is speaking. You are running to war and you are carrying us along with you. The workers' indifference is no brake on the landslide to massacre: it accelerates it; if it is bound to be decisive, you may as well polish your boots. By dint of looking for lice on the Communist Party, you have become near-sighted; and you so often lament that the CP 'has the monopoly of defending the workers' that you have come to believe it acquired this privilege by chance. You call it the party of the hysterical, of assassins and liars; it rouses hatred and its tricks are so glaring that day after day your newspapers have no difficulty in frustrating them. The whole proletariat must therefore be criminal, mendacious, and hysterical. Otherwise, how explain that it is still Communist? Stalin's nose, perhaps? If it had been shorter . . . ?

Even if we poison their cowardly comfort, these troubled souls must be recalled to decency and reminded of certain disagreeable truths: that it is not possible to fight the working class without becoming the enemy of man and of oneself, but if the CP wishes and without your raising even your little finger, the working class will be against you; that to become a traitor, it is not necessary for the Communists to accuse you of treachery; but that it is therefore necessary to keep a clear head, for spite, hatred, fear perhaps, and the smiles of the Right may lead you from one day to the next to fall into treason; that, in fact, there is no need to count on the liquidation of the CP. Certainly the proletariat is rather sullen about it at the moment, but that is of little account and will remain among themselves— the central committee has already learned its lesson. That is the position; you can do nothing, neither can I. If it is more than you can bear, turn on the gas, or go fishing. But don't begin to cheat—otherwise you will end, as did one man I know, by preaching war in Carnegie Hall and disgusting even the Americans. When you heard of the demonstration against Ridgway, you displayed boundless indignation: that covered absolutely everything! All the intolerable faults of the Communists; their lawlessness, their violence, their disastrous craze for mobilizing the workers in trade unions with political watchwords. Well, I am afraid you may cheat; that incurable vice with which you reproach the CP—I wonder if it is not simply the peculiar nature of the proletariat.

The facts are there: the manifesto, the abortive strike which followed, the by-elections at Renault's, then at the Assembly. Lines a little crossed, apparently conflicting. No matter: let them talk. They will perhaps tell you if you are traitors or just simply slimy rats.[1] They will tell you, in other terms, in what degree the CP is the *necessary* expression of the working class and in what degree it is the *exact* expression.

I. THE DEMONSTRATION OF MAY 28, 1952

(i) *Pulling the chestnuts out of the fire for the USSR*

'The worker is tired of being the plaything of Moscow. He would not take part in the demonstration because he disapproved of the principle of it.' What do you know about that? Have you heard him *with your own ears* complain about it? It is *we* who see the hand of Moscow everywhere: I don't say we are always wrong; but the worker is not made like us. Like the middle-class man, he is great at interpretation: but his Manichaeism is the reverse of ours: at the back of all our actions, he discovers American gold. To say he has noticed that we misuse him is to suppose our method of interpretation substituted for his. Has M. Robinet noticed that he is the plaything of the United States? And M. Altman? Besides, the French CP has never hidden the fact that it aligns its policy with the general policy of the directives worked out by the Comintern and then the Cominform. In the resolutions passed by the Third World Congress of the Third International, it is stated that 'the Party as a whole is under the direction of the Communist International'. And that 'the decisions of the Communist International are binding on the Party and on each of its members'. Now at that time (1921), of the five members of the 'Presidium of the Executive Committee' three were Russian, one was German, and one Hungarian. That did not prevent 130,000 French Socialists, after the Congress of Tours, from forming the [French] Communist Party, while 30,000 continued to follow Blum. Besides, the profound differences which separate the Italian CP from the French Party prove that a large degree of initiative remains with regional leaders. You claim that this policy serves the interests of the USSR exclusively. But now's your chance to prove it. It is clear, in fact, that the Third International was born of the need for authority.

The failure of the pacificist movement in 1914, the helplessness
of the workers, and the collaboration of leading Socialists in
the bourgeois government of national unity led militants to
favour complete discipline. The congresses of the Second International 'were simply academic assemblies resulting in value-
less resolutions'; at all levels of the SFIO, there was anarchy.
Most of the militants were convinced that 'the class struggle
was entering on a period of civil war'. They wanted therefore
to forge a new party which would be a weapon. Authority,
efficiency, ordered command: that was what they asked of the
Third International; and without any doubt they would rather
follow the directives of foreigners who had defeated the middle
classes of their own country than obey Frenchmen who had
collaborated with the French middle classes. What the 130,000
adherents of the CP wished for, what they achieved, was *democratic centralization*, a kind of total and permanent mobiliza-
tion which would insure the maximum efficacy of each member.
From that time, the leaders defended themselves against two
reproaches continually made against them: 'Centralization must
be carried out in such a way that it strengthens the members of
the Party . . . in their activity. . . . Otherwise, it will seem to the
masses simply like bringing the Party under official control.'
And 'the outcry about the dictatorship of Moscow is a trivial
means of distraction'.[2] But the organization so conceived is, in
its essence, ambiguous. For if working-class action is conceived
and led at international level by a centralized party, its watchwords, whatever their aim, will appear in this or that local
sector to be abstract commands; each regional proletariat will
be treated as the means to that inevitable end which is World
Revolution and, in the absence of a highly detailed and total
knowledge of events—which can be attained only by the
historian, and in retrospect—faith alone will convince the led
that they are not being played with, and that the sacrifices they
accept are legitimate. As always, facts say neither yes nor no:
after Pearl Harbor, the Communist Party of the United States
asked their Negro members to put a damper on their anti-racial
campaign: no point in feeding Nazi propaganda. Many Negroes
had become members of the Party because it was the only one
that supported them: they felt they were being let down, and
they left it. They cannot be blamed: but what was the final

object of the watchword? Did it envisage the interests solely of the USSR, or those of Europe and the world?

To decide this point, it would be necessary first of all to maintain the view that the conflict of 1940 was simply an imperialist war. That is the Trotskyite view, and the Trotskyites were consistent since in 1942 they condemned the Resistance. But left-wing members of the Resistance would have been unwilling to follow them. In any event, the question can be settled only after taking up a position on much vaster questions and, finally, on that of the value of the Russian Revolution and of Marxism.

The matter was seen correctly in 1921. After the war, French Socialists were inclined to return to that absolute pacificism which, in spite of its failure in 1914, remained in the French tradition. Lenin wanted them to make a distinction between imperialist wars and revolutionary wars. The anarchists of the extreme Left refused for a long while to accept this distinction: as wholehearted pacificists, they claimed the right to shout, 'Down with all armies, including the Red Army.' Who was right? That evidently depends first on the *value* of the USSR in relation to Revolution, secondly on the value of the Revolution in the USSR. And, in accordance with your convictions, you could show that the demand made by Lenin broke a deeply felt tradition of French Socialist life, that it introduced by force an absurd exception at the heart of a coherent system; or that the situation which made pre-war absolute pacificism legitimate had to a large extent passed away after the October Revolution. People seemed to be engaged in one of those interminable debates between the optimistic *philosophes* and the disciples of La Rochefoucauld: human actions are passed in review, and each person explains them according to his own lights; this man on altruistic grounds, the next by interested motives. If these debaters cannot understand one another, it is because they have decided *a priori* on human worth. And if you cannot get on with the Communists, it is because you have got *a priori* an opinion on the value of the Russian experiment.

In January 1918, Lenin wrote: 'The Soviet Republic will remain a living example before the eyes of the peoples of all countries, and the strength of revolutionary penetration of this example will be stupendous.' And in March 1923: 'What

concerns us is not this *inevitable* ultimate victory for Socialism;
it is the tactics we must follow, *we, the Communist Party of
Russia*, we the might of the Russian Soviets, to prevent the anti-
revolutionary states of the West from crushing us.' The whole
problem is contained in these two texts. For a convinced Communist, in fact, Socialism must necessarily triumph because
capitalism carries within itself the seeds of death. That is to say,
Russia is not the one way of reaching the final solution. Born in
the antagonisms which provoked the war of 1914–18, it could
disappear: the antagonisms will survive it, and the capitalist
nations will in the end collapse. In this precise sense, the safeguarding of the USSR is not the *necessary* condition for world
revolution. But these considerations are not *historical*: histori-
cally the opportunity of the proletariat, its 'example' and the
source of 'the strength of revolutionary penetration' are in the
USSR. Besides, it is *in itself* an historical value to be defended,
the first state that, without yet actually representing socialism,
'contains its premises'. For these two reasons, the revolutionary
living in our era whose job it is to prepare for the revolution
with the means at hand and in the historical situation which
has devolved upon him, without losing himself in those
apocalyptic hopes which will end by deterring him from action,
must link the cause of the USSR indissolubly with that of the
proletariat. At least, that is what Lenin thought and what
stands out clearly from the texts collated. But, on the other
hand, the USSR appears to be the *historical chance* of Revolution and not its *necessary condition* (in the mathematical
sense); so that it seems in any event that it might be other than
it is without the future of Revolution being in danger, that it
could, for example, exact *fewer* sacrifices in the democracies of
the East. The more dangerous its situation, the more the aid it
will demand from the proletariats of Europe will be necessary
for itself. But the harder its exigent demands, the more they will
tend to appear in the eyes of the people's democracies and the
proletariats to be simply for one particular nation. So that in
the most favourable circumstances the identification of the
USSR and the revolutionary cause will never be complete, and
anti-communists will always be able to point out to the French
worker that he is 'pulling the chestnuts out of the fire for
Moscow'. But, conversely, he can prove this *in only one case*:

if he can show that the Soviet leaders no longer believe in the Russian Revolution or think the experiment has been liquidated by failure. From which it is clear that, even if the fact were true —which I very much doubt—the proof would not be possible today. In every other hypothesis, the Politburo may be mistaken, take a false road, commit deadly errors (Revolution is inescapable, but the USSR might disappear); whatever it does, it does not sacrifice the worker to the *Russian nation*.

In the demonstration of May 28, we find a perfect illustration of the conflict of opinion that makes anti-communists and communists irreconcilable; both are impervious to experience because they have already taken their stand, but the first, sensitive to the blood that has been shed, see only a kind of cruel and warlike violence; the second may judge it inopportune and clumsy: it nevertheless remains, in their eyes, a moment in the great game of chess which the proletariat plays against international capitalism.

(ii) *'Moscow wants war.'*
Undoubtedly the real problem is different, and those who talk of Moscow wish to mislead us. For it is by no means certain that Moscow ordered this demonstration. It certainly inspires the policy of national parties, but on a very large scale. Billoux,[3] on his return from Moscow, wrote an article to proclaim the rupture of the CP with 'the middle classes who deliver up the country to the new occupier'. But even admitting that it had been dictated to him—which appears to me to beg the question —the actions he announced were serious otherwise than as a simple march past, even if accompanied by brawling; the demonstration must have been decided on in relation to current affairs by the political bureau, and under its responsibility.

And what was its object, in fact? For the press reports disturbances, disorder, hatred, without giving any reason for all this to-do. 'Its object?'—the anti-communist will be amused by my ingenuousness—'Come, come! but to prepare for war!' Obviously! I hadn't thought of that: the Communist Party and the *Combattants de la Paix* bid the people of Paris demonstrate against war: a blinding proof, this, that the USSR wants to attack us. Blinding, indeed, for him who agrees with the doctrine of our ministers: *si vis pacem para bellum*, from which it is to be logically deduced: *si vis bellum para pacem*. Since the signing of the North Atlantic Pact, notions of rural tranquillity are commonly associated with the sight of military garb; and a sudden encounter with a tank has, on the most nervous, the effect of a tranquillizing draught. By contrast, the civilian is suspect, since he does not wear a uniform. Doesn't he want peace? Certainly he clamours for it: even more dubious: he is a sedition-monger. Clearly he had chosen his dress to suggest the discouraging idea of disarmament; and the only obect of his appeals for harmony is to disorganize defence. You remember how uncomfortable we were when the cold war allowed us from time to time a little respite? We asked ourselves, what does this conceal? And only yesterday, General Clark was overcome with anguish when he realized that fighting had stopped on the Korean front; five heavy bombardments were necessary to calm him. In the same way, strange silences have for some while made the world tremble. Communist or not, the man who wants peace remains for us tied up with these feelings of uneasiness; he must be in the pay of the enemy. What will happen if his behaviour takes its pattern from the violence which he rejects? And I agree that the CP has a loud voice: it shouts its will to peace so loudly that each man believes his last hour has come.

But you, you who play at indignation, what else do you do? Don't you too pretend to wish for peace? I look for your olive branches and I see only bombs. You show, you say, your strength so that you will not have to use it? But to demonstrate strength is already to do violence. To secure submission from a Negro kinglet, you cover the sky of Africa with your bombers; this white violence is worse than the other: he will bow down without your firing a shot, but you have broken his will by terror. Consider besides the result of your very peaceful menaces: they beget very peaceful answers, that is to say, massacres. You publish the results of your atomic experiments and you boast of your power to raze Moscow in twenty-four hours: in the interests of peace, of course, and to discourage the eventual aggressor. But the Soviet government too is anxious to discourage the aggressor: it brings down a Swedish aeroplane to show that its air space is inviolable. From one discouragement of aggression after another, in Greece, in Berlin, in Korea, even in Paris, men are dying every day. That is your Peace: Peace through fear. If the USSR was as afraid as you are, your peace would already have become war.

For the USSR wants peace and proves it every day. Your American allies repeat that conflict can be avoided only by being armed to the teeth. 'The USSR will not make us uneasy once we are stronger than it is.' Stronger: capable of crushing it if it moves. Let us suppose you have reached this degree of power: who will decide that it has stirred? What are the limits of your patience? Must it invade an allied country, or is it enough for a satellite state to imprison a cardinal? The American government declares that it will not attack except for very grave reasons. I should like to believe that. But the Russians? How can you hope they will believe it? How trust the promises of a Democratic government which is not even able to control its generals and which, in six months, will perhaps give place to a Republican government? I have no doubt, you may be sure, of the purity of American intentions, but I unfortunately know that a change of military potential necessarily produces a change in feeling. There is no need to resort to Marxist analyses to know that a nation, any nation, has the foreign policy of its armaments: that much to be regretted era, when the Americans detested war because they had no cannon, is still very near. Now, you pretend that the Soviet leaders are monsters who consider human life of no account and can unleash war by a snap of the fingers. Then *why don't they attack?* Why don't they attack while there is still time, while their fighter forces are superior to the enemy's, while their armies could overrun Europe in a week? 'Because,' you say, 'they are afraid of our atomic bombs.' I quite understand: so they are waiting until the stock has been tripled and the Atlantic army is ready. O wonderful calculation! The USSR wants to make war, in three years it is bound to lose, and it doesn't make war while it can still win. The Russians must be mad. Unless they do quite simply want peace.

Peace? I see you suppress a smile: still another neutralist, a believer in Father Christmas.—Fine: you yourself are a realist. During the war of 1940 those Frenchmen who collaborated with the German army were called *realists*; today a *realist* is a Frenchman who believes that the USSR is the devil and who takes refuge, weeping, in the skirts of America. Besides, *you know* the members of the Politburo are mad dogs. And who told you that? What proof have you? I pick out the subtlest of *Le Figaro*'s reporters, M. Raymond Aron, and this is what I read: '[the neutralist] ... likes to imagine a Soviet - Union strictly on the defensive, uneasy over American preparations, anxious only to be sure of its safety. To understand the illusion on which this neutralist attitude is based, it is enough to recall the diplomacy pursued by the Soviet Union from 1943 to 1947 when the Western nations multiplied their efforts at collaboration.'[4] It *is enough*: you have read correctly. Such are the arguments against us. It might be supposed that Aron is not speaking seriously: for, in fact, as he suggests, I have looked at Soviet 'diplomacy' in vain: I do not lose my illusions. There is no courtesy in this diplomacy; it is rough, unscrupulous, exhaling distrust and hatred. Clearly the USSR, undoubtedly ill informed, has not taken European attempts at collaboration seriously. It seizes pledges whenever it can, sometimes at the risk of dangerously increasing international tension.[5] No, I will not award the USSR a prize for virtue. But it was invincible in Europe; American rearmament—even on Aron's admission—had not begun, and it *never* made a move likely to unleash war. Moreover, the Communist Party collaborated with the bourgeois parties of the Western democracies, and its watchword was: *produce.* If you accuse the USSR of having, *from 1947*, sabotaged European reconstruction, at least acknowledge that *before that* it stimulated this process. And if you see a proof of warlike intentions in this sabotage, then, for the love of logic, see a proof of pacific intentions in the Stakhanovism of Marcel Paul.

It seems to me, on the contrary, that the present attitude of the USSR, its hesitations and its ambivalent diplomacy were precisely defined thirty years earlier in an article by Lenin dated March 2, 1923:[6]

> It is not easy for us, however, to keep going until the socialist revolution is victorious in more developed countries. ... The system of international relationships which has now taken shape is one in which a European state, Germany, is enslaved by the victor countries. Furthermore, owing to their victory, a number of states, the oldest states in the West, are in a position to make

some insignificant concessions to their oppressed classes—concessions which, insignificant though they are, nevertheless retard the revolutionary movement in those countries and create some semblance of 'class truce'.

At the same time, as a result of the last imperialist war, a number of countries of the East, India, China, etc., have been completely jolted out of the rut. Their development has definitely shifted to general European capitalist lines. The general European ferment has begun to affect them, and it is now clear to the whole world that they have been drawn into a process of development that must lead to a crisis in the whole of world capitalism.

Thus, at the present time we are confronted with the question—shall we be able to hold on with our small and very small peasant production, and in our present state of ruin, until the West-European capitalist countries consummate their development towards socialism? But they are consummating it not as we formerly expected. They are not consummating it through the gradual 'maturing' of socialism, but through the exploitation of some countries by others, through the exploitation of the first of the countries vanquished in the imperialist war combined with the exploitation of the whole of the East. . . . The East . . . has been definitely drawn into the general maelstrom of the world revolutionary movement.

What tactics does this situation prescribe for our country? Obviously the following. We must display extreme caution so as to preserve our workers' government and to retain our small and very small peasantry under its leadership and authority. . . . We are labouring under the disadvantage that the imperialists have succeeded in splitting the world into two camps; and this split is made more complicated by the fact that it is extremely difficult for Germany, which is really a land of advanced, cultured, capitalist development, to rise to her feet. . . . On the other hand, the entire East . . . has been forced into a position where its physical and material strength cannot possibly be compared with the physical, material and military strength of any of the much smaller West-European states.

Can we save ourselves from the impending conflict with these imperialist countries? May we hope that the internal antagonisms and conflicts between the thriving imperialist countries of the West and the thriving imperialist countries of the East will give us a second respite as they did the first time, when the campaign of the West-European counter-revolution in support of the

Russian counter-revolution broke down owing to the antagonisms in the camp of the counter-revolutionaries . . . ?

I think the reply to this question should be that the issue depends upon too many factors, and that the outcome of the struggle as a whole can be forecast only because in the long run capitalism itself is educating and training the vast majority of the population of the globe for the struggle.

In the last analysis, the outcome of the struggle will be determined by the fact that Russia, India, China, etc., account for the overwhelming majority of the population of the globe. . . . In this respect there cannot be the slightest doubt what the final outcome of the world struggle will be. . . .

But what interests us is not the inevitability of this complete victory of socialism, but the tactics which we, the Russian Communist Party, we, the Russian Soviet Government, should pursue to prevent the West-European counter-revolutionary states from crushing us. To ensure our existence until the next military conflict between the counter-revolutionary imperialist West and the revolutionary and nationalist East, between the most civilized countries of the world and the Orientally backward countries which, however, comprise the majority, this majority must become civilized. We, too, lack enough civilization to enable us to pass straight on to socialism, although we do have the political requisites for it. . . .

(Then follows a general plan for the internal economy of the USSR.)

What changes have there been since this text, wonderful in its lucidity, was written?

—The USSR has become industrialized. But the immense exertion of the USA tends to maintain the difference between production in the West and in the East.

—The revolutionary movement in China has been fulfilled in a revolution. But the industrialization of China has not even begun. India remains outside the movement: conflicts which will benefit the USSR may develop there from one day to the next. But we haven't reached that point yet.

—It is not possible in 1952 to talk of 'prosperity' as it was after 1918. Nor of social peace either. But the working class is on the ebb, and middle-class governments have firmly decided to use every means to suppress social troubles. For the moment, the centralizing effect of American imperialism prevents national and international clashes from growing worse. It would seem that the Russians counted on an economic crisis in the USA which has not yet occurred.

As a whole, there is a real disproportion between the Eastern *bloc* and the Western *bloc*. Although the USA and China are virtually in a state of war, this war between a country still very backward economically and the most 'civilized' of the capitalist states is in no way like the war predicted by Lenin which he, expected to deliver a mortal blow to capitalism. In a word, if it were possible to imagine, by reference to this article, what its author might write on the policy the USSR should adopt today, it seems obvious that he would have repeated the key phrases: 'We must display extreme caution. . . .' 'Can we save ourselves from the impending conflict with these imperialist countries? May we hope that' their 'internal antagonisms . . . will give us a' third 'respite. . . ? The issue depends upon too many factors' for 'the outcome of the struggle as a whole' to be forecast. But 'there cannot be the slightest doubt what the final outcome of the world struggle will be. . . .'

It does not seem to me that Stalin has followed a different policy. It is clear that, to begin with, the Soviet government despised the League of Nations as an instrument of middle-class imperialism; then, from the moment Japan and Hitler's Germany began to cause Russia disquiet, it drew near to the League of Nations, upheld at Geneva the thesis that peace is indivisible, and ranged itself on the side of the 'conservative' nations against the 'proletarian' nations. This was the era when Stalin declared: 'We do not want an inch of territory belonging to others and we will allow no one to seize an inch of our territory.' The USSR went so far as to sign a pact of mutual assistance with France. Until Munich, it played the game of the democracies, restricting itself to recommending them to exercise greater firmness. The attitude of the French CP, considered in relation to the foreign policy of the USSR, is very significant. From 1928 to 1930, fearing that the capitalist powers might launch an attack on Soviet Russia, it set out its programme for the struggle against imperialist war and decided on the principal measures to be carried out in the event of a conflict. From 1935 and until 1938, faced with the menace of internal and external fascism, unity of action with the Socialists was considered, then carried into effect. The USSR's anger and apprehensions after Munich are well known, 'that attempt of the reactionaries in Britain and Rome [sic] to unite with the fascists of Germany and Italy against the Soviet Union'. The USSR certainly feared encirclement and war. In vain, confronted with urgent danger, the British and French governments in 1938–39 urged a Russian alliance. The distrust of the Soviets was not to be laid: they were convinced that Germany was at the parting of the ways and that, according to the gamble of alliances, it would throw itself on its neighbours either of the West or of the East. Ribbentrop and Molotov signed the Russo-German pact. Enough has been said about this proceeding, and it certainly lacked delicacy: but who can deny that Russia, in default of world peace, meant to preserve *its* peace? Germany was to be forced to attack it in 1941, and the opening operations seemed to indicate that the Soviet army was not altogether prepared for the shock. After 1944, the downfall of Germany re-awakened the obsession of an anti-Soviet crusade. The USSR, by all possible means, by its policies, tried to protect itself. From 1947, the European Communist Parties were eliminated from control posts; new Soviet stiffening. I have sought in vain, but in the course of these three decades have found no will to aggression among the Russians; I see a distrustful and encircled nation which still remembers the Allied intervention of 1918 and its subsequent quarantining, a nation that would prefer anything, even a world war, to being overwhelmed, but that seeks by every possible means to save itself from this war. It is brusque certainly, and contemptuous, and touchy, and on occasion dangerous. But if it is true that revolutionary parties, in complaining of Russia, hardly help to calm feeling, on the other hand the wrongs they have suffered in middle-class democracies from police repression and, in fascist countries, from the systematic extermination of Communist leaders have served only to increase tension. For it is, at the same time, the USSR which the middle class detests in the Communists and the Communists which it detests in the USSR. What is not in doubt is that our obsession with Russian aggression corresponds exactly to the Russian obsession with encirclement.

Do not be deceived: if there came a day when the USSR lost all hope of avoiding war, it would unleash the conflict itself.

And who could blame it? But its leaders are as divided as ours. Since 1946, Molotov has believed war inevitable. The Yugoslav business showed that he had not altogether convinced his colleagues, certain of whom, it would seem, thought that the conflict could be delayed until a decisive crisis occurred to shake the Western world; German resistance, British reticence, fluctuations of opinion in France and in Italy, the bogging down of the Americans in Korea, unrest in the Arab world, the Viet-minh war—so many cards remained to be played. According to international circumstances and also, perhaps, to the balance of forces within the Politburo, one or other of these concepts prevailed, always tempered by the view of the minority.

These alternations were reflected in the policy of the CP, and it is in this climate that the demonstration of May 28 must be set. It has frequently been linked with the article published by Billoux after his journey to the USSR. Now, this article, as Gilles Martinet clearly showed in *L'Observateur*, rather than being a 'turning point' for the party, proclaimed a return to the line of 1950. That year, at the XII Congress of the Party, Thorez denounced 'Marshallized rulers enfeoffed to American capitalists . . . and . . . having recourse to methods of assassination and terror against the working class'. In September 1951, on the contrary, Jacques Duclos declared at a session of the Central Committee: 'Employers and workers may certainly find themselves in the same camp for the reconquest of French independence.' And, in May 1952, Billoux took up Thorez's themes: 'The defence of French industry cannot be undertaken in a "national union" of workers, the middle classes, and the industrialists.' Thus we are back again simply to the intransigence of 1950, to return a month later, with Fajon's report to the Central Committee (June 19, 1952), to the Duclos trend: the employers are not homogeneous; many French industrialists are threatened with ruin through the arms policy. Billoux's article had not been understood: sectionalism must be abandoned, a hand must be held out to the peasant masses, the middle classes, the intellectuals and 'to those among the employers who suffer from American domination'. This time the swing was quicker and wider: Billoux had gone further than Thorez, Fajon went further than Duclos. The pendulum seemed to have gone mad. It was said that these periods corresponded to the rhythm of the international situation; but that is not quite correct: in April 1950, it is true, Thorez declared that 'peace hangs only by a thread'; but the war in Korea had not yet broken out (did he know it was near?), and American re-armament began in the following autumn. In September 1951 a slight relaxation could be chronicled compared with the month of January although the same threats weighed on the world: German rearmament had been decided on, the armistice negotiations in Korea dragged on, a Conservative victory in the British election was considered certain, the Ottawa conference was about to open. As to the last two swings, they took place in the same menacing and tense atmosphere, and this double sensation was unaccompanied by any noticeable modification in the Soviet attitude which remained ambiguous enough. Besides, no analogy is to be found in Italy at the same period, and it is striking that Togliatti, some days after the publication of Billoux's article, got Nenni to propose to De Gasperi a common front against the monarchists and neo-fascists. That alone is enough to preclude the idea of any orchestration in national Communist movements.[7] The swings of Communist policy in France are characteristic of the French Communist Party which, for reasons I will explain later, reflects and at the same time amplifies Russian alternations: their rhythm, their periodicity, their extent depend on at least three factors: inter-national circumstances, the internal life of the Politburo, the internal life of the French Central Committee. The demonstra-tion of May 28 was decided on in a climate of pessimism. It was a supreme effort in favour of peace; but in advance no one believed in it: that explains the will to failure and the recourse to violence. The Communist Party expected the worst: 'No capitalist country,' said Stalin in 1927, 'would knowingly throw itself into a widespread war without first having guaranteed its rear, without having "checkmated" its workers and "its" colonies'. Persuaded that it would be dissolved, the Party already saw itself forced to go into hiding. Fajon's report makes an explicit allusion to this defeatism: 'All party activities among the masses must be carried on in broad daylight,' he said, as though he wanted simultaneously to reassure the militants and to disclaim over hasty conclusions. When the political bureau decided on this demonstration, it mattered little to him whether the people of Paris would attend it; he knew in advance that the order would not be obeyed:[8] 'This was,' said Pierre Thibault in *France-Soir*, 'an action planned by commandos going into a battle lost in advance'. A battle lost in advance: that is true, the demonstration was *bound to fail*. But it is also true that proletarian victories are long term victories and are often born of battles lost at the moment. What we middle-class persons can hardly understand, we who want to remember only our semi-victories, is the long patience of the worker and this mixture of fatalism, despair, and courage which, under pressure of an intolerable situation, induces him at times to enter into a fight in which he knows in advance that he will be beaten. In deciding against fate on this absurd 'day', the Communist Party was in fact acting under the inspiration of working-class tradition.

But above all it *interpreted* the deep-seated pacificism of the masses, and you lie knowingly when you congratulate the worker on not allowing himself to be mobilized in support of interests which are not his own. One of the deepest and simplest feelings of the proletarian, one of the direct and fundamental ideas of his class consciousness, is this realization of himself as simply existing and having no sense of solidarity with society as a whole. He is not integrated in society, he *lives beside it* in a semi-segregation which is imposed on him and which in the end he claims. In times of international tension, his social ties are still relaxed when everywhere else they are tightened; how could he identify himself with the psychic and social tension of the lower middle class which surrounds him? This contrast between lack of interest and general over-excitement inclines him to pacificism. And this pacificism is inversely *first* the re-affirmation of working-class isolation in the midst of a society of exploitation, then, *only after that*, a declaration of solidarity with the working class of the enemy nation. While the other classes contemplate their own society across the frontier, but changed into a diabolical reflexion of Society, the worker also sees himself there, exactly the same, for the middle class of his own country is the negation of his own class. So that the simplest attitude, closest to spontaneity, that which best expresses his feelings, is internationalism. The oldest of the workers perhaps remembered the appeal launched in January 1906 by the federal committee of the C.G.T.: '*War on war*. Workers . . . war is at the mercy of the slightest incident. The press knows all about this . . . and it is silent. Because the object is to oblige people to march, on the pretext of national honour, war is inevitable because it is defensive. Now, the people don't want war. . . . The working class has no interest in war. It alone pays all the expenses, pays with its work and its blood. That is why it is incumbent on that class to say very loudly that it *wants peace*.'

As we have seen, the constitution in *Nation* of the Russian Revolution has complicated things a little. In asking the proletariat to make one exception in its anti-militarism, the CP introduced a contradiction which must, in the end, shuffle all the cards and deprive spontaneous feeling of its expression. Since the 28th, people have wanted to divert to the profit of the USSR the *sacred* power of certain words, certain situations. Instead of explaining to the worker the ties of real and indissoluble solidarity which bind him to the USSR, the USSR is said to be the socialist fatherland of the worker, and the worker is said to be the soldier of the USSR, fighting behind the lines. At the same time, the techniques of the struggle against war were perfected and militarized: for the solemn and vague 'general strike', the CP, taught by the failure of 1914, wanted to substitute sabotage, defeatist and illegal propaganda, etc. Already, about 1928–30, the working class seemed to be out of tune and the 'Red International day against war' (August 1, 1929) was a failure very like that of May 28, 1952. Today, as we might expect, internationalism, which assumes the inorganic juxtaposition of the masses (they stand *one beside the other*, separated by frontiers; no one commands them, their representative gatherings are parliamentary) broke up under the effect of *centralization*. The principle of the 57th 'resolution of September 1921': 'The directive committee of the Party is responsible to the Congress of the Party *and* to the direction of the Communist International' might be expressed symbolically by this phrase: The worker has two fatherlands, his own and the Republic of Russian Soviets. Basically, the introduction of fatherlands completes horizontal partitioning. Internationally the utterance of the CP is as strong as it is in each particular country: like cells, nations communicate with one another only through the intermediary of the superior rung. But beyond these partitions intended to tighten bonds and secure the authority of the central power, the interest of the Proletariat and that of the USSR remain identical: we deny ourselves Greffuelhe's arguments which go right to the heart of trade unionists. ('Defend the soil of the Fatherland? I see nothing against that, on condition that the defender is the owner of that soil.' Socialist movement enquiry, August 1905.) But it must be recognized also that the new propaganda aims at emancipating the worker, at providing him at once with a means of getting outside himself, a transcendent link with the Other—unhappily in the form of the Kantian imperative and military duty. The language adopted is itself military: '[This day of 1929] will mark the transition of the proletariat to the counter-offensive on the international front. . . .' But behind this communiqué-like language and through words borrowed from nationalist propaganda, a kind of sub-conversation continues between a proletariat still basically pacificist—simply because that is its natural situation—and the militants who, behind their ideological and verbal apparatus, are perhaps also the same. In short, it is one of the serious symptoms of *aphasia* as an international phenomenon: communication is through language; but against that, to restore the truth the cadres and the troops make use of words which lie, but which are tacitly understood. Speak to old trade unionists of the counter-offensive of the proletariat, and they hear an old voice from before 1914 which whispers: 'Workers. . . . In Germany as in France community of ideas is precise on this point: the proletariat of the two countries refuses to go to war. Hence, by our common and simultaneous action, we shall force our respective governments to take our will into account.' Up to a point, the demonstration of May 28—which was far more the act of militants carried away than a spontaneous demonstration—was intended to give to the masses a tragic representation of their deep aspirations, rather as, according to Nietzsche, the 'figurative' representation in Greek tragedy reflects the deepest instincts of the chorus.

In short, our fine gentlemen must be persuaded that the proletariat has no reason to fight. You explain daily to the worker that the USSR has betrayed the Revolution; he is surprised at this, he cannot believe it worries you much; and whatever you say, he doesn't believe a word of it. When *Le Figaro* publishes tittle-tattle about the Rumanian embassy, undoubtedly that amuses the dowagers; but then dowagers love valets. The workers have no particular liking for them. Even if, by some stroke of folly, a worker happens to read this paper regularly and allows himself to be persuaded of Soviet treachery, that might be a reason for not fighting in the ranks of the Red Army; it certainly wouldn't be a reason for fighting against it. But you will say: in order to free the unfortunate Russian proletariat. Yes. Well, well, I am under the impression that that propaganda is not yet altogether to the point; and I don't think you will enroll many people if you ask them to take up the anti-Bolshevist crusade preached by Hitler and to range themselves alongside Chiang Kai-shek against the Chinese of Mao Tse-tung, alongside Franco against the Spanish Republicans, Syngman Rhee against the whole Korean people, beside Beloyannis against the fathers and brothers of the deportees of Makronissos, beside an oligarchy of *colons* against the Tunisians, the Malagasies, and the Vietnamese.

You have noticed, I believe, that there were many unreasonable demands; and you have renounced indoctrination. When, in spite of everything, for conscience's sake, you want to produce reasons for dying for the United States, you arrange art exhibitions, conferences and concerts: in short, you take part in what has for some little time been called a 'cultural battle'. But you are careful to double the price of entry: so as to ensure that at least you will be 'among yourselves'. Or perhaps you send from Paris to London and Berlin a skewerful of intellectuals, wan and sweet as young ladies, who recite compliments they have learned on culture and liberty. But whom do you want this feminine orchestra to persuade, apart from the readers of *Annales*? Culture is certainly dead when writers set out to *defend* it instead of *creating* it. As for the worker, he doesn't give a damn. To interest him in it, it must first of all be presented to him, and then it must concern what interests him. A woman sugar block loader working in a refinery has charge of a group of four machines, and each machine fills thirty units in two-and-a-half minutes; each unit weighs a pound and a half so that the worker carries nearly two hundredweight every two minutes, about twenty tons a day. Go and talk to her about her

son and her husband, explain to her that it is to free the poor
sugar block loaders in Soviet refineries who haven't the
right to express their opinion on abstract painting or the theories
of Lysenko; make her understand that the United States has
perfected a hydrogen bomb and is quietly preparing the admission of Spain to the United Nations, just simply so that the
sugar block loaders of the Western democracies can continue to think and to express their thoughts in complete independence. Do not be afraid: she will not strike you: she is too
tired. But you will wax indignant with her and go away bewail-
ing that the meaning of freedom has been lost in Europe. Yet
she too longs to be freed. But the freedom she craves is not like
yours; I fancy she would willingly renounce the freedom of
expression of which such good use is made at the Gaveau
gallery if she could be freed from the shooting pain of the
rhythm of the machines, the heteronomy of tasks, the cold, the
depressing decoration of the factory. To give her a sense of
freedom, more freedom than she has ever known, all that
would—provisionally—be necessary is that, in the same time
and for the same wage, she should have to move ten instead of
twenty tons. What do you expect? You would have wanted
culture. You say you can't stand it, that patience is necessary,
that the grandchildren of today's sugar block loaders will be
released by technical progress? Fine: then if you want to make
war, wait until they are born. And don't expect to convince
their future grandmother by extolling high American wages and
the superiority of material life in the USA. What do these continual comparisons between the USSR and the USA matter to
her? So far as she is concerned, it is not a question of whether
she works in Stalingrad or in Chicago, but in a France that is
either at peace or at war. You simpletons are so afraid of the
Soviet régime that you do everything you can to bring it on
yourselves. For today there is peace; the Americans are among
us and the Russians are in Russia; but if it should be war tomorrow, the Americans would be in America and the Russians
would be among us. The workers know that from the beginning
of hostilities, they will lose even that wretched wage called the
'minimum living wage'; they don't want to be 'occupied', even
by the Red Armies: they want the Russians to be in Russia and
the Americans in the USA. If they did not move on May 28, it

was because they judged—for reasons I shall examine later—
that the game wasn't worth the candle; but there was no disagreement over the principle of the demonstration. And do
believe that they have no special affection for Ridgway, or for
any other American. For you know, slimy rats—and even *Le
Figaro* is beginning to suspect this—the Americans are wonderful propagandists; but their best propaganda is made for the
Russians.

(iii) '*The CP and CGT weary the workers by forcing
    political demonstration on them.*'
But here is a new argument: the workers would blame the CP
for having perverted their sole weapon of defence by diverting
it to uses for which it is not designed; they should have been
wise and shown the 'Russian' agitators that they meant to keep
politics and economics apart.

If you are right, they have given the employers a very handsome present: for the employers believe in this separation; more
perhaps than the men of 1789 believed in the separation of
powers. When the Puritans secularized commerce and industry,
God in this sector had to be replaced by a brazen law of wages:
inflexible, this law delivered up the innocent to the exploiters;
divine, it justified success; thanks to it, it was possible to prove
that the rich were good and the poor wicked.

This was the law of supply and demand, 'true regulating
mechanism, adjusting price, eliminating certain aspiring sellers
and certain aspiring buyers, . . . stimulating production in the
event of a shortage, discouraging it in the event of a glut'.[9] It permits a return to optimism, proves that riches are proportionate
to social usefulness, and that the best businessman is he who
sells in the best market and is thus the chosen of God and the
benefactor of the human race. The law fitted relations between
employer and employed admirably: labour was a commodity,
a wage its price. No one could blame the employers: wages were
what *was possible* at each moment, neither more nor less since
the regulating process was automatic. Thus the economic
province became that of necessity while the political province
remained that of freedom. So long as the two provinces were
kept separate, all went well. That the economic influences the
political must be admitted, but the intrusion of politics into

economics disturbs consciences and causes offence: the action
of the politician tends to prove that economic necessity is not
perhaps autonomous and that the effect of other factors may
modify its course. Some theorists proposed to reduce the political to the economic: but the middle classes would not accept
this; they preferred division into compartments. Divide and
rule. It simply became the practice to call demagogic every
concession made by the politician to the poor classes without
its having been extorted from him. Generosity is on principle
false generosity. 'This reform, generous in appearance. . . .'
That means that every attempt to substitute a humane order
for the mechanical order is bound to fail. There is only one way
of being good: to adapt oneself to the natural order, obey the
law, make each man work as hard as he can and pay him as
little as possible; the whole of society will benefit by production
at the lowest price. This praiseworthy concern to justify profit
is at the base of a truly comic theory: that of *terrible goodness*
to be found in Claudel and among followers of Hitler. If the
worker uses his trade-unionist rights to mix up the economic
and the political, he will in the end disturb the whole harmonious mechanism. All will be well if he reserves trade union
action to defend his interests. At bottom, it has to be recognized
that the fluctuations of the market tend to push the average
wage a little to one side of what, in the eighteenth century, was
reverently called the *natural* wage, which Turgot defined thus:
'what is necessary to provide a worker with subsistence.' The
trade union will interfere only by substituting a single contracting party for several sellers. It cannot modify the eternal laws
of economics; but a certain power has devolved on it from the
fact that, quite simply, it functions as a monopoly. It will thus
profit from this to parcel out the crude wage, due to the simple
play of economic forces, and to bring it as near as possible to
the natural wage.

Thus classical economics described what would happen if
relations between men were strictly comparable with the relations of things among themselves. Or, if you prefer it, it established the laws of a universe in which man is perfectly without
humanity towards man. The trade union is tolerable if it puts
itself, as a particular instance (that of a single seller and several
buyers), within the framework of these strict laws. It cannot be

tolerated if it proposes to humanize them. But, although the middle-class point of view is clear enough in itself, I can no longer understand it if I try to look at things from the point of view of the wage-earner; and the distinction between the economic and the political becomes so shifting and so vague that I can hardly believe it exists. First of all, I am not at all clear what is meant when the worker is admonished to confine himself to defending his interests. Has the worker any interest? As Marx put it: 'The real task of the proletariat is of necessity to revolutionize the conditions of its existence.' Already I can see the anti-communist shrug his shoulders: it would seem that I am not serious, and that such ill-timed jests lost France in 1939. Good. So let us be serious. The worker has an interest in so far as he is a worker. That is to say, he must *to begin with* accept his condition as a whole. This done, his right to ameliorate the details may be conceded. So the middle-class thesis (under both the rather worn form of classical economics and the modern form of collaboration between classes) is that the worker must remain a worker. Nothing surprising about this since he is created to be that as the employer is created to be an employer. It will be said that a strike is subversive when the claims of the strikers draw their inspiration from the concept of man. When the employer proclaims that the proletarian is a proletarian by birth and should so remain, he is not playing politics: he is laying down the principles of management. The worker, on the other hand, does the same when he wants to do away with the proletariat. The whole history of labour legislation reveals the preoccupation of the middle-class magistracy with distinguishing good from bad strikes. As early as 1872 Depeyre, in defending before the Assembly a proposed law which punished affiliation to the International, declared that the intention of the legislators was 'to protect the working population' against every attempted strike that 'should be the result of bad thought, of a plot against the social order'. And still today, in weakened terms, the Conciliation Board of the Seine (decision of March 26, 1947) picks up again on its own account the theory of the 'improper strike': 'It is expedient to apply this right [of striking] while taking into account the absolute principle that the exercise of a right is limited by the misuse that could be made of it; that, in fact, in organized society, a right is never unlimited;

that it finds its natural limit, in the absence of special regulations, in the rights of others and of the community. . . .' Fine
and just words: the trouble is that the 'organized society' in
which the worker lives and whose rights he ought to respect is
precisely that capitalist society which oppresses him. So that
the middle-class decision to limit the right to strike to industrial
claims is *already political* and rests on a total concept of the
world and of man.

Well, even in accepting this concept, even in defining *with*
the employers the interests of the workers, I do not reach an
understanding of what they are. This factory with a lavatory
for the use of its staff: the *interest* of the staff is that the drain
pipe should not be stopped up. The country of these workers is
carried along towards war by a stupid policy: their *interest* is
that the war should not take place. Between these two examples,
there is room for the whole of social life. You say that the
second is of a *political* order? Is that so certain? In the event
of a conflict, the peasant class provides the 'human stock', and
benefits in return by the rise in price of food products; in short,
quarts of blood are bought from him. The situation of the
proletariat is exactly the reverse: its losses in human lives are
less: he suffers *economically*. Not at first, but later when the
excessive production of heavy industry and the difficulties of
reconversion lead to crises and unemployment. In 1938, the
aggregate of wages was worth twice that of taxes; in 1950
the aggregate of taxes equalled the aggregate of wages. The
worker could declare with good reason that military conflicts injured him in his material interests. More than that: if you declare
that war is a political fact you reject the socialist explanation of
war and the infernal circle: over-production—search for outlets
—conflict. I do not say you are wrong or that this theory is true:
that is beside the point here. I only say that you are introducing
into your definition of what is political and what is not judgments of value, presuppositions, an ideology. Certainly the
Marxist theory of cyclical crises, Lenin's theses about capitalist
imperialism are either true or false. But proof devolves on the
specialists. Most people deny or accept them without being
even acquainted with them and would be greatly put to it to
discuss them. Yet Merrheim in an item on the agenda which he
put to the vote at Marseilles in 1908 declares that 'all war is

nothing but an assault on the working class, a bloody and terrible means of diverting that class from its claims', and all those associated with him repeat the formula after him *as if they understood it*. And nationalists retort by accusing these 'defeatists' of having sold themselves to the enemy *as if they were sure of it*. Here are two concepts of the world confronting one another, lived and felt rather than thought. Any reconciliation between the two seems impossible: in particular 'reformism' puts an abrupt and voluntary stop to working-class claims which seems to have no justification whatever. This can be judged by what happened in 1908: two years earlier a congress had passed a resolution advocating 'anti-military and anti-patriotic propaganda'. Niel, reformist trade unionist and minority leader, expressed his point of view at Marseilles: he was against anti-patriotism which groups the militants *politically*. Janvion supported the same point of view: a victorious Germany would have no difficulty in imposing a penalty the greater part of which would be paid by the workers. It is therefore tempting to believe that the two speakers declared themselves against anti-militarism *for the same reasons*. Not at all: anti-militarism, according to Niel, is within trade union territory since 'it has as its aim a struggle against the intervention of the army in strikes'. This will not seem either abstract or absurd to those who call to mind the massacres of Fourmies, 1891; of Martinique, 1900; of Châlons-sur-Marne, 1900; of Raon-l'Étape, 1907; of Draveil-Vigneux and Villeneuve-Saint-Georges, 1908. It is necessary to fight against the army because the army represents repression. But this reasoning is just as untenable: to incite the soldier to disobedience is a political act. And, if the current of anti-militarism is strong enough, there is a risk that national defence will be enfeebled, victory will be given to Germany, and the workers will be exposed to the payment of this heavy penalty from which Janvion wanted to save them.

No, we must accept it that trade unionism has only two coherent positions. Either it confines itself to maintaining immediate demands, or it will defend the workers in every sector of national activity. But the worker who sticks to elementary claims has, it must be understood, *already* taken up a political position: he rejects not only the Revolution, but also, for example, solidarity strikes; he resigns himself to his fate, and betrays the working class.

The truth is that it is *impossible* to stick to immediate demands. Marx put it very well: 'A struggle for a rise of wages follows only in the track of *previous* changes, and is the necessary offspring of previous changes in the amount of production, the productive powers of labour, the value of labour, the value of money, the extent or the intensity of labour extracted, the fluctuations of market prices, dependent upon the fluctuations of demand and supply, and consistent with the different phases of the industrial cycle; in one word, as reactions of labour against the previous action of capital.' But in that case the workers take action *too late* and 'in 99 cases out of 100 their efforts at raising wages are only efforts at maintaining the given value of labour'.[10] In order that the proletariat can defend itself, it is therefore necessary that the trade union should be able to work *on the causes* rather than on the effects. If you refuse it the right to influence the *circumstances* with all their political and economic implications, national and international, you cut back its claims to the level of blind impulses, you deprive it of the *human* possibility of foresight and prevention. You reduce the worker to a hungry belly and a protesting mouth. In a word, the trade union 'must have as its real task' to exact and secure the right, on the ladder of a business, of administration, on the national ladder the right to control the economic consequences of government policy. And that, whether it be reformist or revolutionary, is the only point of view of the interests 'of the worker qua worker'.

Economic fact, like *homo oeconomicus*, is a creation of the mind. Or rather it symbolizes correctly certain limited situations in which the oppressor is in a position to treat the oppressed like a moron. In French West Africa for example, racism and the inadequacy of black trade unionism create a native sub-proletariat which is systematically kept in all ways to a level of life below that of the least favoured whites.[11] Here, 'in practice, payment tends to be determined by the play of supply and demand'.[12] To put it another way, racial ideology allows the native worker to be reduced to the level of a pure economic fact. Not altogether, however: for understandable reasons, the administrative authority actually fixes the minimum wage rate. So that the political ideology of racism (with its economic infrastructures) and the political ideology of paternalism (bureaucracy in the home country) unite to determine the level of life considered 'fair' and 'adequate' for a black. Now it rightly happens that, in the mother country, middle-class economists have ceased to base the theory of wages on the law of supply and demand. 'Labour,' writes Mossé, 'is not a commodity. Wages are not a price regulated by the market. . . . It is impossible to state if there is a relationship, and what it is, between the wage of a worker and his productivity, between the general level of wages and employment, production, prices, money, etc.' They consider today that the problem of wages has become a problem of the distribution of the national income between persons and social groups. And what is to fix the rates? A complex collection of factors into which enter collective representations and values, ideologies, ratios of strength between groups, and data that are properly economic. 'Rather than a price,' writes Mossé, 'the wage is a *share* in a global result at the heart of which apportionment between elements attributable to such or such factor is impossible. Or perhaps it is a *levy* comparable to a tax by the way it is established and by its incidence. Or again it is the *spring* which supplies individual and family needs. If that is so, the problem of wages becomes a problem of human reactions, of psychology, or relative strength: *in a word, a political problem, ruled by ideologies, by beliefs concerning justice, equity, social hierarchy.*'[13] The economists are growing soft-hearted: one of them says, 'We have passed from neutrality to humanism.' And another: 'From objective economics to normative, political economics.' What has happened? Simply that, by forcing its way in, the proletariat has become part of mankind. Up to 1848, the factory worker, in his isolation, was not ripe for a trial of strength. *Then* he was simply a beast; his connexion with the employers tended to identification with a purely economic relationship. During the second half of the nineteenth century, the proletariat formed itself into an independent social force. Now at last, the middle classes *acknowledged* that labourers possess the dignity of man. From that moment, the *humanism* of which they were so proud was invested with a contradiction: the worker is a man because he causes fear, but the social order makes it necessary that he should be kept in his animal condition. The contradiction lived in and suffered by the proletariat became the contradiction of middle-class thought. Everybody put forward a solution. And everyone, in the name of humanism (from which sprouted reformism, collaboration between the classes, corporativism, radicalism, Christian socialism, etc.) sought ways that would allow middle-class society to digest its proletariat. The problem was simple, but difficult to solve: to what conditions ought a creature of human appearance to respond so that we could at the same time call him a *man* and treat him like a beast? The solution has not yet been found. So that by their mere silent presence, by the weight on the established order of the cold threat of their harsh and voluntary orderliness, by their glance, these men, appearing suddenly to be a society within a society, promote trouble in paradise and cause humanism to explode: here surely is a *political action*, the most important, perhaps, since 1789. It is not difficult to understand that all action in common by the oppressed, even if it is kept strictly within the limits of industrial claims, is *in itself*, and as an event of a certain kind which occurs in society, a political action: for it reveals the degree of cohesion of the working-class troops, their moral climate, the strength and extent of the claim-making movement, and, according to the result of the battle, that strength will either grow as it attains self-realization, or diminish; the ties which unite trade unionists will tighten or relax, the relationship between employers and wage-earners will evolve in one direction or another. The workers are deeply aware of this connexion in depth which attaches them to the whole working class and puts them in opposition to the middle classes. Also a strike, whatever it is about, is always something more and something other than a strike. A large working-class society does not limit itself to confronting the leaders of industry: it pays attention also to the consumers, the *public*. It is a question of getting the public into play, of the workers' not making themselves unpopular, of winning an appreciation of their importance in the national economy, of persuading public opinion to bring pressure to bear on the employers. Very often the bettering of their conditions of life is not *in itself* the aim of trade union action: its aim is to gain prestige, to keep members, to increase membership. As for the striker himself, for him it is *always* a question of something more and other than his immediate interest: anger rather than want, rather than misery persuades him, confidence in his leaders, his need to assert that he is a man in the face of those who treat him like a thing. Let us put it that trade unionism is *one way of being a man*.

Objectively, trade unionism is political. In itself it covers the whole extent of *working-class being*; without exception, the limits imposed on it have their source in a political ulterior motive. Very evidently, the reformer is timid, conservative, secretly attracted to the middle class: the frontiers he prescribes for trade union activity must arise from secret compromises since they can never be explained by the objective situation; and it is clear that Niel's dislike for all anti-patriotic demonstration is rooted in unacknowledged jingoism. But it must be added that trade-union militants are always aware of the *political* importance of the trade union. Certainly, in the heroic days of anarchic trade unionism, they showed distrust of parties, but that was 'from a feeling of brutish opposition to the middle classes'. Greffuelhe tells us that they 'wanted *fiercely* to be led by workers'. They wanted this precisely because to them reactionaries and socialists were barkers of the same kidney; they would *carry out the Revolution themselves*. The same congress in 1888 pledged the workers to 'separate themselves from the politicians who betray them' and to put their hopes in the general strike which alone could 'carry them on to emancipation'. Later on, there is to be noted at the heart of the CGT a certain alternation between reformism and revolutionary trade unionism. But the militants on both wings are in agreement that trade-union action should be developed *in every direction*. To the revolutionary, the worker is in himself the major contradiction of middle-class society, he is the negation of the system of ownership. His claims have a double aim: satisfied, they would improve his fate by bringing about the progressive downfall of the capitalist order. The general strike will finish the job. The reformer, at bottom, has the same final aim in view, to be attained, however, by continual progress. Anyhow, he will be 'wherever the interests of the workers are under discussion' and will call for 'direct and general participation on the economic plane'.

Both tendencies would *unreservedly* have approved the programme of the CGT, called 'Programme de 1949', in which it
is said, notably, 'The basic condition is dictated by experience
of the first plan of modernization and of equipment, and of
what has happened as a result of the intervention of the
Marshall Plan. [We must] get rid of the Marshall Plan, denounce
the military agreements of the Western *bloc*, re-establish normal relations between states, demand release from repara-
tions. . . . *So many resolutions which condition the carrying
into effect of the confederal programme of economic and social
recovery, which in its turn conditions their complete realization. . . .*'

For your hatred of Communism, dear slimy rats, has made
you forget that it is *in retreat* in relation to the agitations of this
era. Between 1905 and 1910 your fathers lived in fear of a feat
of strength. As May 1, 1906, came nearer their assets flew away
to the same place yours fly to today. To restore gold and confidence, it was necessary to invent a conspiracy and lock up a
few trade unionists. Our Communists are nationalists, don't
forget that. They are against *a certain policy*, but not against
national defence. Henri Martin, guilty of distributing leaflets
denouncing the abject folly of the [French] war in Vietnam,
was sent to prison for five years: but he was not inciting soldiers
to disobedience. During the early years of the century, on the
contrary, anti-militarist propaganda was of daily occurrence.
There was a great outcry when certain leaders of the Communist Party declared publicly that the proletariat would not
fight against the USSR. But French trade unionists, believing
themselves to be in agreement with the workers of Germany,
publicly declared, and spread the information over the country
by means of posters, that they would resort to the general strike
to prevent war. And, although this kind of fantasy is of hardly
any interest, if we imagine for a moment the Greffuelhes and
the Merrheims placed in a situation similar to our own, there
can be no doubt that they would have carried the Federal
Congress with them to condemn in advance any anti-Soviet
crusade. So, when our fine newspapers speak nostalgically of a
golden age when trade unionists presented their claims to the
employers as though they were New Year greetings, they are
dreaming. They want to cover up the fact of exploitation, of

which trade-union militants never lose sight; to them trade unionism is a weapon which the employers have freely given to the workers so that discussions can take place on an equal footing. But the workers themselves are well aware that their organizations have been forbidden and hunted down; they know that the original aim of the trade union, with or without the help of the CP, is to 'change the world'. It is this apparent misunderstanding which gives the fact of trade unionism its ambiguity. But the employers are in no doubt and they know very well how to sing two different tunes. When working-class organizations appear to oppose rearmament or a war policy, they raise their eyebrows in grieved astonishment. 'How,' they ask, 'can you behave in this way to us? Politics has nothing to do with trade unionism.' But when a strike upsets or hampers them, even though purely economically, they claim that they break it in the name of politics. In 1910 the railwaymen stopped work. Briand had the strike committee arrested. Interpellated by the Socialists, he declared: 'There is one right above all others: the right of a national community to live freely and proudly. Now a country cannot be left with open frontiers; that is impossible. . . . If, in order to maintain safety, it had proved necessary to resort to unlawful action, I should not have hesitated.' The principle is laid down: every strike can be prohibited in the name of superior interests. Trade unions have no right to resist war; but in the name of the necessities of war, trade unions may be suppressed. On January 13, 1915, Millerand declared to a delegation of metalworkers: 'Working-class rights, social laws no longer exist; there is only the war.' In this way trade-union rights were suppressed in the name of a war which the trade unions had no right to reject.[14]

'They are in the right,' says the indignant anti-communist. 'They are in the right. Did they vote, yes or no?' The argument is taken up in all good faith, I am sure, by M. Thibault, political commentator on the paper *France-Soir*: 'Free elections, very different from anything known in the paradises of Moscow, have been held in all the countries of Western Europe since the signing of the North Atlantic Pact. Everywhere the majority of the electors has clearly given its verdict, and it is an imposture for Communist agitators to pretend they speak in the name of the French people who have clearly determined their position.'

It is hard to decide whether these dialogues of the deaf which have been carried on for seven years by groups and classes, and which nearly every man finds at the back of his mind when he has shut his newspaper, are encouraging or sinister. For after all M. Thibault cannot hope to upset a Marxist by this evocation of universal suffrage. If he really believes his argument unanswerable, I would remind him of a text of Lenin's, chosen almost haphazard among a hundred similar texts: 'The more developed a democracy, the greater the dependence of middle-class parliaments on the Stock Exchange and the bankers. It does not follow that there is no need to make use of middle-class parliamentary institutions, and the Bolsheviks have successfully made use of them in more than one part of the world. . . . But it does follow that only a liberal is capable of forgetting the *limitations* and the *relativity* of middle-class parliamentary institutions. In the most democratic bourgeois state, the oppressed masses every time come up against a glaring contradiction between *formal* equality, proclaimed by "democracy", the capitalists, and the thousands of restrictions and the *real* guile which make wage slaves of the members of the proletariat.'

Between 1944 and 1947, the CP helped the middle classes to reconstruct their organization under state control: the Party hoped to make use of parliamentary institutions to seize power and, at the same time, transform it; but they remained true to the Leninist doctrine according to which working-class power is truly expressed only in the domain of the class struggle. Since 1946, it has found itself torn between its parliamentary policy and social struggles: in the bourgeois state, its ministers played the part of hostages and the Party recognized at its heart, in the shape of growing tension between its deputies and its militants, the conflict of the possessing classes and the proletariat. After its expulsion from the government, the state apparatus fell altogether into the hands of the middle class which, at every control lever, replaced Communists by its own creatures; all republican institutions worked against the Party. The Party therefore transferred its interpretation of the will of the people to another field, that of demonstrations in the streets.

That at least is what a Communist would reply. But this reply would not satisfy M. Thibault any more than his question would trouble M. Fajon. I will try to state the facts without pig-headedness and to explain as simply as possible that, today, a worker, if he votes for the Communists, is right to regard his ballot paper as wasted.

I recall in passing what you have made of him: a second-class citizen. Scarcely had he decided to vote for the CP when his vote underwent a mysterious diminution of value; *ipso facto*, it was worth less than that of his neighbour. To send 103 Communists to the Chamber of Deputies required five million votes like his; to send 104 Socialists, only 2,750,000 votes were needed, and for 95 MRP, 2,300,000. By losing 400,000 votes, the Party lost 79 seats; the Socialist Party lost 600,000 votes and gained five seats. Roughly, only roughly, the vote of the docker is worth half that of the chemist or the sacristan, or half that of his brother-in-law, the secretary of the town hall. It must be acknowledged that the RPF is not in good shape either. But with 900,000 fewer votes than the CP it secured 15 more seats: not too bad a position; the transaction against the two extremes was brilliantly carried out, but one of them is more extreme than the other. 'So,' says our docker, 'am I sub-human?' Yes: he is 'politically weak'. And, altogether by chance, it happens that he is a working man. Yes, I know: it is legal; no doubt of that. There has to be an electoral law, certainly. And then, after all, the CP has only to enter into an alliance. The last motion passed by the MRP Congress declared in full: 'Those who reject respect for democratic rules and for the different political families exclude themselves of their own will from this union and themselves bear the responsibility for this.' In short, if someone hangs back, so much the worse for him. Only *with whom* do you want the CP to enter into an alliance? With the MRP? With the RGR? And so far as there is some drawing together with the SFIO, M. Guy Mollet has said straight out: With a *French* Communist Party, united action. And at once. With the Russian Party, never! In short, the die is cast: within the framework of world-wide institutions of democracy, an anti-democratic law concerning a particular party has been quite legally passed. Between ourselves, it is something which, broadly, might lead people to go out into the streets and break a few windows or bash in a few faces. Just a century ago, on May 31, 1850, the dockers of the era were deceived by an analogous arrangement. Universal suffrage was not abolished, no: the elector simply must have lived in the *commune* for three years. As during the crisis years of 1847–49 the workers were moving about a great deal in search of work, this measure came to the same thing as depriving industrial workers of their right to vote. By a stroke of the pen, 2,600,000 electors were disfranchised. The method of 1951 is much more developed: 2,500,000 electors were disfranchised because it took 5,000,000 Communist votes to elect 103 deputies. But no one knows which among these five million men were condemned to a blank voting paper. Of two Communist electors, there is always one who is allowed to play without reference to the rules, but nobody knows which one. Besides, the proletariat is not rudely indicated by external characteristics: the CP stands out as the Party of the wicked by its refusal to enter into an alliance, and the elector in voting Communist stands out as a proletarian.

The docker clings to a little hope. After all, the CP is the first party in France. Perhaps these 103 deputies will carry through a good piece of work. They will never, certainly, enter a government coalition. But the opposition has a part to play: it criticizes, it moderates or provokes, it influences. It will perhaps give the government the courage to say 'No' sometimes to Washington. Unhappily it is with the opposition as with the members of the CP: there are two oppositions in the Chamber, one of which counts and the other of which doesn't. The RPF works at a distance—on policy in Indo-China, for instance; the CP does not. The votes of its elected members are virtually neutralized: in calculating its majority, the government treats them as a constant negative. They complicate the parliamentary game a little, and it is necessary to be careful before asking for a vote of confidence, but that is all: instead of playing the classic game of billiards, our champions play French billiards. Also, when M. Brune upbraids Duclos for having recourse to agitation instead of expressing his opinion in the Chamber; when M. Bony loudly proclaims in *L'Aurore* that every French citizen has the right of persuasion, I believe they are joking. Let them tell me, in fact, *with whom* Jacques Duclos could have a discussion in the Assembly! Suppose some inspiration of genius carries him to the rostrum. He speaks, he grows enthusiastic, he lashes out, he makes the galleries weep. And after that? He will gather in the monotonous applause of his followers, and the even more monotonous abuse of his opponents. Hasn't he moved the deputies then? Not one: they weren't listening. It has happened in parliamentary history that a minister has fallen as the result of an opponent's speech. But that is because people still believed that an opponent could speak the truth. Today we *know* that the opponent is a liar: because, of course, he is a Communist! The largest party in France is separated from the other parties by an invisible barrier: the workers' deputies never omit to give their opinion on the subject in question, but this is pure ceremonial. Of two dockers walking together on the quays of Le Havre, one hasn't the right to vote and the other has voted in vain. Do you think the Communist Party was so far from expressing the opinion of its electors when, on the day after the elections, it announced the demonstration of May 28, saying explicitly: 'The Party must have recourse to other forms of action essential in the struggle against a fiercely reactionary majority.' To punish these deputies of the second class, the majority decided that they should be deprived of their parliamentary immunity.

But he has not yet reached the end, our docker. Fifteen years earlier, he could still hope that his government, by an abrupt involuntary jump of independence or of pride, would for a moment cease to follow in the wake of the British. Today he has the certain knowledge that the 'continuity of our policy' is the calm continuity of slavery. We are stiff-necked only with the Malagasies and the Tunisians. Sold? No, not even that: it is worse. The Americans have got us for nothing. If, at that moment, he remembers Lenin's expression: 'In the most democratic bourgeois state, the oppressed masses at each step run into a flagrant contradiction between the *formal* equality proclaimed by capitalist democracy and the thousands of restrictions and *real* guile which make proletarians into wage slaves;' and if he then says, 'Once more, Lenin is right', whose will be the fault, great family of Petsche, Bidault, Lussy, Pinay, and those in alliance with you? One day he will have had enough of it; and his pal too. This pair, instead of discharging American tommy-guns, will chuck them into the sea. And the 'coppers' who arrest them will say to them indignantly, 'You dirty bastards! If you were against the North Atlantic Pact, couldn't you say so? Instead of spoiling equipment. In this country everyone is free. Everyone has the right to vote.'

(iv) '*The CP leads the workers into illegality and violence.*'
The demonstration of May 28 was deliberately, impudently illegal: proudly, disdainfully, no permission was asked. On Wednesday, the Prefecture sent an official statement to the papers: 'As permission has not been sought, any gathering on the public highway is forbidden.' At the same time, by means of posters, the CP calmly called on the people of Paris 'to respond in a body to the appeal of the Peace Council'.

Shall I admit that this placarded contempt of the law hardly bothered me? This confession, if they read it, should grieve certain professional thinkers in the United States. 'Weakening of the democratic conscience among European intellectuals' will be their diagnosis. It would be in poor taste, however, to insist that French intellectuals should express surprise at the illegal doings of the CP since, as long ago as 1920, in the 'Address of July 26 to Members of the French Socialist Party', the Third International proclaimed that propaganda, 'where it is difficult on account of discriminatory laws, should be carried on illegally'. The text went on: 'To refuse to do so would be a betrayal of revolutionary duty.' At that time, the Socialists were afraid of neither the word nor the thing. And Léon Blum, at the Congress of Tours, made a curious distinction on the subject: 'Certainly no Socialist would allow himself to be caged in legality.... But illegality is one thing, and clandestinity is another.'[15] So far I see no problem: a party declares that it will, if necessary, act illegally. Democracy tolerates this in the name of liberty of thought. This party organizes a forbidden demonstration. The police oppose it by force and arrest such demonstrators as offer resistance. All that is *normal*, and the first collision between demonstrators and 'coppers' of the Second Republic happened before M. Cachin was born. On the other hand it would be difficult for me to deplore the illegality of the Communist demonstration without at the same time denouncing the capriciousness of its repression, which is also very evident. What justification is there for Duclos's arrest? Was he caught in the act in a conspiracy against the safety of the state? There was no such conspiracy. And if it is conceivable that there was one, how could he be caught in the act two hours after the demonstration? Carrying weapons without a licence? What an avowal: a deputy has a club and a revolver in his car: for this offence you arrest him in spite of his parliamentary immunity, you throw him into prison, and you keep him there without letting him out on bail. Nonsense! M. Duclos was arrested because he was secretary general of the Party, and the Party had organized the demonstration. In order to rationalize public vengeance the government threw over all the precautions accumulated in a century and a half by magistrates and lawyers, and reverted to the grossest notion of responsibility. The slight trouble it took to justify its actions is even more disquieting: it was well aware that public opinion would be an accessory. No, it is not the Western intellectual who has lost his taste for the Republic; it is the whole of society. That the Communist Party has for thirty years been asserting its contempt for middle-class legality, and has done this with impunity: this proves the strength of our institutions. In this, according to your taste, you may find reason to admire the greatness of democracy or to denounce its contradictions. That a certain M. Pinay trifles rather harshly with Republican institutions and runs the risk of throwing them out of gear is no great evil: this gentleman is a nobody; he emerged from the shadows a week or two ago; the machinery of government will be mended as soon as he is lost in darkness again. But that France should have surprised its President of the Council in the very act of violating the law and did not flinch: that surely suggests that the Republic has been winged. And the arguments adduced to justify this arrest! Consider MM. Robinet and Brisson: in *Le Monde*, M. Duverger calmly declared that perhaps the dissolution of the CP was not a matter of urgency. At this, these two gentlemen lost their patience and bit him: 'A conspiracy? What conspiracy? The whole CP is a conspiracy! That has been its boast for thirty years! What more do you want?' But, you will say, these high-ups are bound to practise the anti-sovietism of shock. Perhaps. But M. Duverger, as he tells us in a new article, has received a great many letters which prove that the average opinion of the peaceable readers of *Le Monde* is utterly anti-democratic. 'What are you complaining about? Don't hinder the government from carrying out its policy. It has taken Duclos off our

hands.' Or: 'The officers as well as their troops must pay.' Or
again: 'Pinay was right, for the Communists have sat tight.'
Or: 'There can be no question of illegality where those outside
the law are concerned.' To tell the truth, M. Duverger does not
cite letters in *these* terms: it is *I* who wrote them out, for such
comments have been made to me, and in running through his
article I recognized them. Stern warning to the Communist
Party: all this proves that it has frightened the shopkeepers and
the middle classes. We may think, in fact, that the heads of
industry feel very little concern for democratic liberties: what
do you expect them to make of liberty of thought? If they had
it, they would enjoy it little more than a sugar block loader
from a refinery: they pay certain jesters to enjoy it in their
stead. The liberty, the one liberty, they insist on is that of leading as they like the battle for production: this is called liberalism. For them, the advantage of Pinay over de Gaulle is that he
juggles away liberties without touching liberalism, whereas, if
we may believe M. Vallon, the Gaullists dream of 'substituting
a self-conscious for a blind economy'. Between the upper
middle class, which lays claim to the concrete power of making,
acquiring, allotting to itself profit, on the one hand, and the
proletariat, which above all lays claim to the right to live, on
the other, only the lower middle class commonly defends the
formal liberties of our democracies. Certainly these are negative
and limited; they separate more than they unite men; but for
that very reason they protect the *status quo* and allow a certain
foresight, establish a sort of ventilation at the heart of a society
becoming every day more closely integrated. It is the lower
middle class which pushed forward the advent of universal
suffrage; the majority of the same class formed both the framework of opposition to the Second Empire and the personnel of
the Radical and Radical Socialist Parties after 1880. This class
made the Republic; Republican institutions are violated under
its very nose, and it is silent. Is it so frightened? We shall come
back to that. But what in any event seems clear is that today the
democratic régime is no more than a façade: all real conflicts
develop outside it. In his last article Duverger propounds the
question very well: in terms of statistics. After the CP, he tells
us, has won a fifth or even a quarter of the electorate, its
antagonists can still follow the fascist system: we can rub along

as a republic. But if they gathered up 50 to 51% of the votes, 'It is not a question of holding on to democracy but only of choosing between the régimes that will follow'. The CP, in France, gathers in the majority of working-class votes: the nature of the political régime thus depends solely on the importance proletarian organizations may take in the life of the nation. Here is a game of bridge with dangerous zones: beyond a certain limit lie reaction and fascism. But if the 'dangerous zone' is rapidly cleared, working-class parties take power and form a 'people's democracy'. As can be seen, the reproach of illegality doesn't go to the root of the matter. We are simply on the threshold of the dangerous zone, and these skirmishes around the old legality are at the same time the first annunciations of a new legality founded on the sovereignty of the masses, of the eminent, or of the Party.

The reality hidden under these expressions of contempt is the class war. If you have understood this, you will perhaps be constrained to reproach the Communist Party for its violence and the illegality of its doings: today, all violence, directly or indirectly, comes from the proletariat which gives back to us what we have given it. All workers' rights, even those which have been freely agreed, have been snatched in the height of the struggle; in the midst of the tidy rights of a bourgeois system of law, these rights have the appearance of upstarts; they are kept in quarantine; and, although the Constitution of 1946 expressly recognizes it, purists handle the right to strike cautiously. On what do you want to found it? On the excellence of human nature? Then there would be no need for it. On liberty? But the striker is using coercion. On equality, then? But, on the contrary, it is the implicit recognition of inequality. 'By definition even, the strike is a right to be hurtful; it is a weapon rather than a right.' And you would give certain men the right to injure others? 'It is the right of legitimate defence applied to a group.' So a contract is an act of aggression? Our society cannot justify the strike without recognizing first and foremost that it is a society of oppression. 'For half a century, the rules of the right to strike have been related to actuality at the time of each wave of social conflict.' Why, of course! this practice is recognized the better to canalize it, to limit it. To end, a jurist acknowledges with a sigh that 'the fact of the strike is a phenomenon similar to a volcanic eruption ... by its nature rebellious against appearing as of the order of the rules of right'. Strange function of the worker: he is the illegal source of legality. In May 1936 Blum declared, 'I do not consider occupation of factories legal.... It is not in conformity with the rules and principles of French civil law.' In fact, it was an attack on the right of property. To which Thorez very justly answered, 'They say "illegality". Not at all: it is a new legality which is developing.' It could be objected that this new legality is inconceivable under any régime: it contradicts the fundamental principle of middle-class society and, in a socialist society, would be unnecessary. Irrational, prematurely sanctioning working-class *practice*, it makes sense only in our intermediate and contradictory world; it is actually the reflexion of the worker, the negation of himself and of society, whose *real* function is, in destroying his own proletarian condition, to destroy the order which crushes him. Even when he has no intention of staying off work, a worker knows that he *can* go on strike and that this constant threat has a regulating effect on wages. He himself is this threat and he feels its violence; in a society based on oppression, violence is, by a crowning injustice, first of all a result of the fact of oppression. How much simpler everything would be if it were possible to summon the oppressors before their own justice. But no: the oppressor is strong and unruffled; he places his strength at the service of the law; if he kills, he does so legally. Naturally: he made the laws. And then, as Engels pointed out, 'the middle classes created the proletariat by purely economic methods and with no occult help from violence'. And he added: 'Even granting that all individual ownership rests originally on the personal labour of the owner, and that, in the later course of events, he has changed nothing except equal values for equal values, we are, nevertheless, by the progressive development of production and exchange, bound to arrive at the current method of capitalist production, at the monopolization of the means of production and sustenance in the hands of a small class, at the reduction of the other class, forming the vast majority, to the condition of propertyless proletarians.' In short, the worker is in great danger of being duped. He is oppressed, he is overworked; and yet if he goes over in his mind the sequence of causes, he finds neither theft nor coercion: it has all happened delicately. Better still, he has even *accepted* his condition, at least for some time: 'So long as a method of production continues to be on the upward grade in its evolution, it is applauded even by those to whom the corresponding method of distribution is disadvantageous. That is the story of the English workers at the time of the industrial revolution.' When the crisis occurs and the method of distribution suddenly appears to be unjust, *who* is responsible? However far back he delves into the past, the worker finds himself already caught up in a society which has its code and its system of law, its government, its idea of what is just and what unjust; more serious still, whose ideology he shares spontaneously.[16] A destiny, limits are imposed on him; he is condemned to fragmented and semi-automatic tasks whose meaning and purpose escape him, and to industrial diseases. Forced to repeat the same gesture a thousand times a day he is discouraged by weariness and poverty from exercising his human qualities, he is shut up in a dull world of repetition; little by little, he becomes a *thing*. But when he tries to find those who are responsible for his condition, there is no one; everything is in order: he has been paid what is due to him. In 1930, many American workers refused to sign on at the hastily improvised unemployment pay desks: they were ashamed of being out of work and felt a sense of guilt. The European worker, sharper, sees the ambiguity of this intolerable situation; he certainly rejects it with all his strength, but in spite of himself he accepts it because he has been born into it, and simply seeks to better it. The conveyor-belt operative forces the rhythm in order to catch up with the profits of the professional man, to offset humiliating inequalities and to give himself the sense of being more of a man; but all he achieves is to make himself more of a thing. Perhaps he prefers flow-production, refuses to support the trade-union groups which attempt to limit or regulate the rhythm. And when he finds himself back at his work, exhausted, enslaved by laws outside his control, his spontaneous, unformulated but perpetual refusal to be reduced to a mere mechanism runs counter to his willingness to maintain a method of production whose yield to him is greater. In short, he is not at first sure whether he is not himself responsible for this society into which he has been born, which has no rules to protect him nor a name for the wrong he has committed. The other classes put up with his poverty bravely, and explain to him that it is essential to the equilibrium of society as a whole. He is the object of the state's solicitude: a supplementary wage, and various allocations are showered on him; and yet he cannot be persuaded that he is totally bound up with a community which, for economic reasons, daily delivers secret sentences of death and allows two of a poor man's youngsters to die against one of a rich man's.[17] Part accomplice, part victim, jointly responsible and a martyr, he wants what he does not want; his whole body rejects what his will to live accepts. He detests this monster which mechanization has made of him, and yet he knows that, without changing the universe, he cannot be other. The contradiction is not in him only; it is imposed on him; mass production requires that he be contradictory, man and machine at the same time. His services as a man are called on whenever it is too difficult or too costly to construct an automatically controlled machine; improvements in cybernetics will render him useless. Thus he is asked to add to steady attention a certain diffuse vigilance, to be at the same time present and absent: a man *up to a certain point*; for manufacturers will not hesitate to tell you that general education is harmful to the output of the conveyor-belt operative—but his man's eyes cannot yet be altogether replaced by photo-electric cells. So that the original violence is not oppression: this is in fact mixed up with justice and order; it is the inward oppression, the oppression *lived* as an internal conflict, a restraint exercised by one half of himself over the other half. The first violence is that which the worker exerts against himself by the extent to which he turns himself into a worker. Hunger and the distress of unemployment are not yet violences submitted to; they become that when he *accepts responsibility* for them, and he makes himself their abettor when he forces himself to accept work at a wage below the trade-union rate. An employer needs a typist; it is a period of crisis: thirty young women offer themselves, all equally capable, all with the same diplomas. He summons them all at the same time and asks them simply what pay they want. A horrible Dutch auction begins: the employer has only—apparently—allowed the law of supply and demand to operate; but each typist, in asking a lower wage than the next, does violence to the others and to herself, and contributes, in humiliation, to lowering a little further the working-class standard of living. In the end the one engaged, taking advantage of some slight income (a widow's pension—or perhaps she is a young girl living with her family), will ask a rate of pay below the minimum living wage: that is to say, it is she who puts into effect against herself and all the others the act of destruction which the employer is far from carrying out himself. To get work, the worker has to force himself to make the condition of the working class more and more unlivable for himself and for all the rest. People pretend to believe that violence is born suddenly, at the moment a riot or a strike occurs. Not at all: in moments of crisis it comes out into the open, that is all. The contradiction is reversed: docile, the worker rejects what is human in himself; insurgent, he rejects what is inhuman. This rejection is itself a humanism, it contains the exigent demand for a new justice. But since oppression is not a visible offence, since the ideology of the ruling class defines what is just and what unjust, since nothing can be got unless an order that is sacred is smashed by force, the worker sees the affirmation of his own reality as a man in a manifestation of violence. Besides, hardly has he raised a finger than society mobilizes its police forces. His environment is changed: he is prepared for violence, society makes sure he pushes it to extremes. His discontent *must* be transformed into a strike, his strike into a brawl, the brawl into murder. When he has walked into the trap and asks himself in amazement how the political claim of his rights as a man carried him along to hit and kill men, then repression starts. And the return to calmness is not pacification but a return to the original violence. The primitive contradiction re-appears, but magnified: the striker has experienced the counter-violence of society, it still acts on him, and he reacts to it through two contrary feelings, fear and hate. At the same time, he has discovered himself and he knows that for the present violence is the law of his action. The middle class views with fear and disgust this sudden explosion which in fact reflects back the oppression that class exerts; it seems to this very shrewd and very civilized class that violence *has its source* in those who are oppressed and is due to their barbarism; to this class, the worker becomes fathomless violence *made objective*. The worker is not unaware, he knows, that he makes middle-class people afraid, and, by a new reaction to the 'projective personality' conferred on him, he lays claim to this violence which is held as a grievance against him. These remarks are intended to show the ambiguity of the workers' state: for the proletariat is amenable to an historic right which does not yet exist and perhaps never will exist. Seen from the point of view of a future society which will be born thanks to his efforts, his violence is positive humanism;[18] considered in our present society, it is partly a right (to strike) and partly a crime. In fact, humanism and violence are the two indissoluble aspects of his effort to get out of his oppressed condition.

The slimy rats are amiable by nature and violence horrifies them: not surprising, since they belong to the middle class. The trouble is that they have a marked liking for the working class. To get over this difficulty, they have invented the myth of working-class suffering: violence made its bow to the world with the Third International. Strange perversion: for the evidence is that working-class violence is the very substance and strength of the CP; it has taken it over, it feeds on it, and if the leaders have understood the workers, it is because they speak the same language. Certainly, with the Party this violence loses its character of an *immediate* eruption: it is 'mediatized', conscious; it is determined by its own self-image; the CP is the revealed, hypostatical will. No matter: when there should be a certain lag between the manifestation of violence and the original violence from which it proceeds, nevertheless the working class *recognizes itself* in the trials of strength which the CP initiates in its name.

What am I trying to prove? That the demonstration of May 28 was clever, effective, praiseworthy? No. Simply that it again falls into the framework of demonstrations by the people. 'If only the Communist Party had been dissolved,' you may say, 'in place of it we should have a "genuine left", amiable, polite, ready to make distinctions, subtle reservations, which would fight capitalism but would be just to persons, which, without rejecting violence, would not make use of it except as a last resort, and which, while knowing how to stir up the generous enthusiasm of proletarians, would if necessary protect them from their own excesses.' Splendid programme: only if this 'left' were called up for you by the touch of a magic wand

(I still cannot see how you could come by it otherwise), I wouldn't give it a week before it split: you would re-discover some of its members in the socialist group of the Assembly or at the publishing office of *Franc-Tireur*, while the others would be in the streets demonstrating against Ridgway.

'Your line of argument,' you will say, 'is all very well. Only it has a weak spot because, on May 28, the working class didn't move, and the mass demonstration took place in the absence of the masses.' A laugh for the slimy rats! Well, let us go back a bit and see.

II. THE STRIKE OF JUNE 4, 1952

ON May 28 and June 4, the Communist Party organized two demonstrations. What did it expect from them? What was their real significance? If it is true that they were flops, why did they miscarry? What meaning must be read into this double defeat? What were its consequences? And if they would seem to have been ill-omened for the working class, for the whole French community, and for peace, is there any way of putting things right? That is the skein of questions I would like to try and unravel.

On May 28, what might the Communist Party have achieved? When the police are out in numbers, what can the crowd demonstrate except its *passion*, in all senses of the word? Since the powers-that-be forbad a procession, how could a procession be held except by seizing power? That is obvious. Great indignation brought the Parisians into the streets, they were walking along and sometimes took possession of a house as they passed. As a result of the February Revolution, government was put back into the hands of a middle class mad with fear. Today precautions are taken to avoid fortuitous events: political life has become so serious that no party can allow itself to be carried into power in its own despite. In 1952, a demonstration in the streets could *at a pinch* be the signal for insurrection—on condition that it had been agreed to in advance—but it could not be launched without warning. Always half-way between a disturbance and a ceremony, martyrdom and challenge, these banned processions demand violence: that is, to suffer it. They are the outcome of failure, gestures not intended to be effective, and the inefficacy of which *is evident*. The masses are made aware of their immense power and their provisional powerlessness. In giving them a respite from the patient work of *organization*, these explosive festivals make clear the need for

organization. In short, this is the 'theatre of the street' longed
for by Artaud: the rôle of the Parisian people in these shows is
generally taken by the Parisian people themselves who undertake to raise up before their own eyes a picture of their glorious
destiny and, above all, of their lost spontaneity: everything is
done to ensure that they have the illusion of being still that
antique crowd which rolled and danced from end to end of the
boulevards of last century; and it is that crowd, in fact, except
that the demonstrators are summoned, officered, and led, and
are prohibited from touching the shop windows or taking anything as they pass, even the Bastille.

A banned demonstration must be a flop: that doesn't mean
that it must start as a flop too. But the organizers foresaw a
bitter, and not at all a symbolic, defeat: they knew the masses
would not stir. *They knew it*: for two years, from dailies to
periodicals, from great organs of the right to the sheets put out
by the working-class opposition, the whole press had reported
and commented on the 'discouragement of the workers'—and
had the political bureau alone failed to notice this? Glance
rather at Jacques Duclos's notebook: to be sure, nothing is
spelt out; but you will find the word 'explain' repeated a
hundred times: *explain* to the dockers of Marseilles; *explain* to
the workers; there has not been enough *explanation*—you will
sense growing disquiet and a wish 'to intensify the struggle'
against certain working-class hesitations. Note how they come
back again and again to the same preoccupations, the same
themes; these people are very well aware of their difficulties. In
that situation, you will ask, why choose this moment to invite
the Parisians to a political demonstration? I reply: because they
had to. When a procession is announced a long time ahead, a
festival committee finds it very difficult to call it off if the
weather breaks up. Now, the demonstration against Ridgway
had been announced months before: to be precise, since the
demonstration against Eisenhower. In protesting against that
general, the Party had tacitly committed itself to protesting
against all his successors. A mass party cannot be content to
sound public opinion: it must develop its uncertain trends,
define them and bring them out into the open; it must also
reflect them back to the public: and what better resonator than
the masses themselves? It will inveigle them into making an

objective exhibition of their will, push them all into actions which exceed their intentions and drag them on still further. If the people of Paris are against the North Atlantic Pact, they must be made aware of their hostility. But only violent and hazardous action can do that. The Parisians aren't very zealous at the moment? All the more reason for deciding on a popular demonstration. Like all *actual* relationships, the link between a party and the masses is ambiguous: on the one hand it is guided by them, on the other it 'organizes' them and attempts to 'educate' them; and as it is not a question of changing them but of helping them to become what they are, it is at the same time a simple expression of what they are and an example to them. When it addresses them in its manifestoes, sometimes it uses the imperative, sometimes the future, sometimes the present indicative to designate the same reality, the movement which is deed and valour at the same time: 'French workers will know how to remember ... the labouring masses do not allow themselves to be misled by this gross manoeuvre. . . . Workers, demand your freedom', etc. In their eyes this represents their aspirations, their inclinations, their wishes, but *made red hot*: that is to say, at the highest level of *efficacy*. Sometimes they follow the Party, sometimes even they drag it along, but they may also stay behind. No matter: if it is sure that it speaks in their name, if it judges that only an accident hinders them from following it, it goes on: it acts for them and in their name. The masses are action and passion at the same time: in the end they will change the world, but for the moment the world crushes them; their pressure could be irresistible; but for the time being cold, hunger, police repression can get the better of them. The Party itself is *pure action*; it must go forward or disappear; it is the strength of workers who are at the end of theirs, and the hope of those who despair. To have called off the demonstration of May 28 would have been 'to move a step backward': it could not take into account the weariness of the workers without running the risk of increasing that weariness and inclining them to resignation. Perhaps from this moment the political bureau appreciated that it would soon have to change its tactics: but, anyway, that could be done only *after* the demonstration. The masses will not realize their weariness: they will bear witness through third persons; their failure will be covered by the violence of brawls, their action will be shown up *as it ought to have been*. Special gangs will be engaged to make gestures of violence in front of them—their own violence which they will see alive and detached from themselves; from their suburbs and their working-class neighbourhoods they will be present at the fight between demonstrators and 'coppers', facile symbol of the class war.

In short, what did the Party want when it sent its militants in to the attack on the Place de la République? To seize power? Kidnap Ridgway? Cause the government to fall? Not at all: it wanted simply to point something out. What risk was it running? If things had gone off as usual, the bourgeois press would have commented dispassionately on what happened and everything would have returned quickly to normal.

M. Pinay didn't see things that way. Did he then believe in a conspiracy? What an idea! He followed the example of those great ministers who have upset the nation with no good reason in order to bask without trouble in the glory of reassuring it. To launch the Loan, the government resorted to a classic proceeding: it diverted its competitor's propaganda to its own profit. See how it enlivened the debate, how it gave a tone to the discussion by prohibiting Valliand's paper for no reason. This climate of violence was created by mysterious persons with American knuckle-dusters who came along to knock up the actors. Immediately it was whispered that the minister had given way to pressure by the American embassy: splendid publicity. Future participators in the Loan liked to see the finger of God in these details: if the United States, in such a small affair, condescended to defend us in spite of our culpable tolerance, what wouldn't it do in a real emergency? Emotion tended to calm down when Ridgway's visit provided the theme of the second publicity campaign. To begin with, André Stil was arrested. How artful! This arrest was so obviously arbitrary: the great French middle class hates the republic and distrusts fascism, but it dotes on the arbitrary which it finds aristocratic and which offers it the image both of the anarchy it enjoys and of the authority it dreams of for others. It lifts up its head and wonders thoughtfully if it has not got its hand on that rare bird, a liberal with a grip of iron.

The day of the demonstration arrived; M. Baylot and the

government organized a panic: the one guaranteed that the masses would not stir, the other that it was on the track of a conspiracy the importance of which we were invited to gauge by the number of 'coppers' charged with its suppression. The aim of the conspirators? How do you expect anyone to know that since the ministers' vigilance had thwarted their plans? Fortune smiled on M. Pinay. Everything served his turn, even the blood shed. The police, as we know, fired in the air. A bullet ricochetted from the sky and fell into the crowd: did it hit a Frenchman? No: the hand of God deflected it just in time on to an Algerian. You know how that was turned to account: so there were some foul Arabs in the ranks of the separatists! And what were they doing there? It's all very well to use African regiments to checkmate the Malagasies—splendid: that's native against native. But only an enemy of France would mix the Arabs up in the quarrels of Frenchmen. In short, when evening fell, the forces of order had won the game. A very small game, a very small victory: a single corpse and two priests beaten black and blue—not nearly enough to launch a loan.

The demonstration ended; the people went home, angry, tired, vaguely disappointed. The news had already reached the working-class neighbourhoods: another flop. People were silent, hiding their bitterness and sadness under bad temper. At that moment M. Pinay had a leading Communist picked up in the open street. We all know the hypothetical legend put out by the press next day: Duclos put his hand in his pocket; terrified for a moment, the police foresaw the perhaps incalculable consequences of his arrest; then good citizenship, disinterested love of law decided them to arrest him. That might have passed, if there had been laws to defend, but actually there weren't: here was a citizen returning home in a car whom circumstances made *legally* immune from arrest. Strange love of law which subjected him to the last outrages under the pretext that the law was about to be violated. You don't understand, someone breathes: it was a situation of extreme urgency; and legality had been given a holiday because the Republic was in danger. A conspiracy! You think M. Pinay believed in this conspiracy? And M. Pleven, too? And the press of the Right? Wait: put the question to them: ask *what* conspiracy was in question, insist on proof, or at least some clues: you will be told loftily

that the Communist Party is a *permanent* conspiracy and that
it ought to have been dissolved immediately after the Congress
of Tours. No; the manoeuvre stinks in one's nostrils: unlike
Lyautey, the Government made use of its strength simply to
demonstrate it. And to whom did it demonstrate it? Why, of
course: to its future investors.

If you consider it without prejudice, the Pinay operation is
disconcerting. That it was an act of violence which must compromise the cause it was supposed to save, no one can doubt:
the middle class puts all its propaganda into supporting formal
liberties; if it destroys them with its own hands, what will it
claim to be defending? But if we examine in detail the circumstances of the arrest, the whole thing grows confused. It might
be taken for a scenario written in collaboration by two authors,
one cunning, the other a fool. If the Government wanted to
show its strength, what hindered it from liberating Duclos at
once after the failure of the strike? Was it really necessary for
all Europe to hear the slaps administered to ministerial cheeks?
Why lie about the time of the arrest? On the radio? Why this
nonsense about carrier-pigeons? And this hoary twaddle about
a conspiracy: it is a hundred and ten years old—why resort to
it again? The liberal press did not seem to notice these contradictions: at that time it still regarded M. Pinay as Parsifal. But
if you didn't share this opinion, you may have had the feeling
that some Machiavelli had whispered to the ministers, that
they hadn't understood him very well, had had no luck in acting on his advice, and in the event had found themselves faced
by consequences beyond their capacity. As for the Machiavelli,
I can't vouch for his existence: in this clever and harebrained
operation, the ministers provided the blundering and others the
cleverness; but this may have been due simply to circumstances.

M. Pinay kept to his idea—the idea of the Loan. A few days
later, a newspaper carried this heart-warming note: 'The demonstration was a failure and the Loan is said to be a success: on
which side are good Frenchmen?' This is clear: good Frenchmen subscribe to loans and don't trail about the streets.
M. Pinay expected his reward not from the street, but from
trade, the banks and the Assembly. What he was preparing so
earnestly was not the dissolution of the CP, but the break-up of
the RPF; if he tried to checkmate the Left opposition, it was the

better to muzzle that of the Right; and if he kept his embarrassing captive under lock and key, that was simply to blackmail
his colleagues: this became clear when he demanded a vote of
confidence in an Assembly frozen with fright: 'My office is at
your disposal. But whoever takes it must take over my prisoner
too.' That day, M. Duclos saved the government.

In short, the red peril stunt was played on us: a stunt which
wasn't tried for the first time yesterday, but which still takes us
in. Only M. Pinay did not give it its classic form and, according
to the experts, it was even heretical to attempt it in the circumstances: for if the trick is to succeed, it is generally considered
indispensable that there should be no red peril. Consider the
Americans: what inborn feeling for propaganda, what wonderful knowledge of the heart they must have to have carried to
perfection this rather worn process which reached them from
Europe! And do you believe they could have produced that
marvellous propaganda weapon, *anti-communism*, if there had
been any Communists in the USA? If you meet CP militants
every day, or even every month, how can you believe that they
eat children? But if you have never seen one, how prove they
don't eat them? And then think of the economy in personnel:
if no one is a Stalinist, everyone is suspected of being one; the
average man plays two rôles: denouncer in the mass, denounced
when alone. Of course the victims can never prove their innocence since the charge doesn't state of what they are accused.
Because he applied the process without discrimination, M. Pinay
was in danger of noticing to his cost that *there are* Communists
in France.

Well, no: everything went off as if there weren't any. Must
we really believe that a Machiavelli advised the government?
That is a plausible but not a necessary explanation. This short-
term operation came to a head in a battle which has lasted since
the Liberation and in which the French middle class has known
how to conquer and to keep the initiative. The Machiavellian-
ism is in things: whatever M. Pinay did, his action, born,
served, surrounded, nourished by other manoeuvres less obvious
and deeper, must have reflected a borrowed intelligence. At a
certain moment in battle, if one of the adversaries has the
advantage, everything is to his benefit, even chance works in
his favour. M. Pinay, unthinking, arrested Duclos at the

moment when it became clever to arrest him. There is an *objective* sense in the 'stroke of May 28' which *perhaps* was not apparent to any of those who were its authors but which sprang to the eye after the stroke: it became the symbol of a strategy which I shall try to define in the next chapter.

Considered from this point of view, the arrest of Duclos was illegal *because it had to be.* If it had been legal, the Party would have had a way out: it could protest through its press, at its meetings, against the *intent* while declaring that it bowed to the formal legality of the *act.* In taking up Duclos, the minister stopped up every outlet: he issued a public challenge to the Communists; he attacked them on *the failure* of the demonstration, and when they were in full retreat; he compelled them to accept a trial of strength at a moment and on a ground chosen by him, with the whole world as witness. Protest? Set the Constitution over against the government? That could be done, that was done: Duclos lodged a complaint of misuse of authority. Naturally our virtuous newspapers waxed ironical: 'If our laws are against you, why do you protest when they are disobeyed? By what right do you, who transgress them every day, cry out when we stretch the law? You are for or against the Republic according to your interest at the moment, and you do not appeal to our codes except to tie us up in rules which you do not obey.' The argument is worthless, and we shall have occasion to recur to the relations of the CP with democracy. But when the only aim is to destroy it, it is the middle class itself which has set the universality of the law against the particularisms of the Ancien Régime: why should the Communists abstain from indicting their enemy in the name of his own principles? Then you uphold Maurras? Not at all: Maurras was a member of the middle class who drew all his resources from middle-class society; he had the culture and the freedom which give a real content to formal liberties; he betrayed his class to the profit of a small minority of the middle class. The Communists speak in the name of the proletariat which shares in the economic life of the country without having any part in its social life: if a worker happens to draw some advantage from middle-class laws, all the same, they are not *his* laws, for they favour those who exploit him. Yet the Party could not be content with a legal action: for the government in violating the

law had gone out to meet the masses on their own ground,
which is illegality; in slighting their Party publicly, it challenged
them: 'Here's your leader, and that's what I do with him: if
you don't like it, that's all the same to me.' The masses therefore must reply *on this ground* to the challenge: in Henri
Martin's case, the Party may have found the reason for the
prosecution absurd, and the sentence delivered iniquitous; but
it did not dispute the right to arrest and punish a soldier or
sailor caught distributing leaflets: it restricted itself to demanding in its press, at meetings or by petitions, a review of the case.
Inversely, if a government of fascist leanings arrests a representative of a bourgeois party, this party can have recourse to
legal action: for it will wish to prove that democratic laws are
sufficient to protect us from dictatorship. But if violence is done
to a party of violence, the only answer is violence.

In our societies, government and assemblies hold their power
from institutions as much as from the will of the people, first
because it is the institutions which define the elector; then, and
above all, because power may continue legitimate when it does
not correspond to the wishes of the majority, on the one condition that it be backed by law. After the municipal elections of
1947, a government half repudiated by the country was able to
keep power, wait for the ebbing of the Gaullist movement, and
pass an electoral law which ensured the return of the same
majority in the next Assembly.

The CP enjoys an authority which resembles that of a government; but as it has no *institutions*, its sovereignty comes from
the masses themselves. You tell me it is enfeoffed to Moscow?
That there is no internal democracy in the movement? It may
well be: nevertheless, if the masses suddenly refused to follow
it, it would be lost; however powerful it may be, it resembles
Antaeus who had no strength except when he touched the
earth. The five or six million votes given every four years to the
Party sanctify its electoral importance without justifying its
revolutionary activity: the electors do not object to either
demonstrations or political strikes, but their voting papers do
not reveal whether they take part in them. It is in the street that
the CP measures its power; it is the size of mass demonstrations
which *legitimate* its authority. Here, then, over against an
abstract and very rational system of election, is a delegation of

public powers, clandestine, dangerous, questionable but which brings us back again to the springs of sovereignty. Only, with these plebiscites as with Descartes's divine creation, they are valid at the moment, but they must be continually renewed. If the whole of France had gone on strike yesterday, there is no guarantee that it would go back to work tomorrow; there is no *institution* to extend and prolong the result of these popular expressions of opinion beyond the day on which they take place: and that is understandable since, by its very violence, the torrent of demonstrators expresses a sort of constituent will which revokes the laws in being. The middle-class man is never deceived: his intrigues may re-shape ministries, but *true* power comes from the masses; what he dreads and hates in the 'populace' is its savage sovereignty. But since the relations between the crowd and its leaders are constantly changing, he does not hesitate to take the Communists at their word and compel them to take part in a plebiscite when circumstances are least favourable to them. If the result goes against them, it will be published. In vain they explain that it is a question of passing weakness: an electoral party can survive its defeats, but a revolutionary party cannot be distinguished from the revolutionary impulse of its troops. The minister pays the Communists back in their own coin: they appeal to the proper principles of the middle class; it is in their name that they are obliged to lay down their cards. The savage sovereignty of the people makes M. Pinay split his sides in soft laughter: he knows very well that he has not got the majority of the country behind him; but, until an electoral law determines it, the only right of the majority is to be silent. On the other hand, he also knows very well that a revolutionary party has no right to *submit*: he takes M. Duclos up and waits; the challenge will assuredly be accepted. In fact, the political bureau has seen the trap (and, if it has not seen it, the resistance and the excuses of the CGT would have made it clear), but it will go into it head-on: better leave the militant with the memory of a defeat than of a stealthy evasion of the enemy. The order for the strike was sent out, the government was ready: if the masses stirred, they would be crushed; but it was generally believed they would not stir. For June 4, as for May 28, the forecasts of the political bureau and of the government were completely in agreement.

In short, *nothing* was expected, *nothing* happened, and, on this morning, M. Pinay built his glory. The day of June 4 is historic in that it was like every other day; we read in the newspapers next day that the streets were looking as usual, that the underground railway was running as usual; it was one of those working days turned by a peculiar charm into high holidays in the eyes of friends of order.

I was abroad, my relations with the Communists were good but not delightful; they no longer said I put man on all fours, but they still accused me of having spied on the Resistance on behalf of the fascist middle class. In fact, the demonstration of May 28 had not seemed to me opportune, and I feared new riots, useless deaths. Plenty of reasons for learning with indifference if not relief of the failure of the strike. But the news produced in me the contrary effect: the protestations of worthy journals did not succeed in covering up the strange silence of France, and I had the feeling that I had just been informed of a small defeat of man. I did not know then that a great many other people saw things in the same way. Since, the middle-class press has written that we were in a funk. Why not, after all? Let it be funk, one of those rare words which our newspapers can understand. But funk *of what*? Of the police régime which was proclaimed? Of American ascendancy? Of the witch hunt? Of the war which threatened? All causes of disquiet which I find very reasonable. But I haven't got it: we were afraid because the working class had disowned the Communist Party. If it was only that, stop worrying; for we were very peaceful: the Party will not disappear so soon and it is not true that the working class demonstrated repudiation of it: on June 4 *nothing* was demonstrated and *there was no* working class. If you want to know, it was just that that made us afraid; and I am writing this article in order to try to understand why France was silent.

It would appear that it was not silent, that it shouted its contempt in M. Pinay's face; in short, the so-called failure of the strike would be disputed by the CP, and we were frightened without cause. I ought to rejoice, but I have simply changed my anxiety: at present, it is my deafness that distresses me. I see M. Caillois smiling: see what we come to if we amuse ourselves defending the Communists outside their principles. Does Sartre think he will please them by groaning aloud over a defeat which they don't admit?—No, I don't think that. Who then would be mad enough to want to please militants, communists or not? And why would he do it? If I took this trouble, what should I get out of it? A furtive handshake from a 'crypto'? A pallid smile from pursed lips? Nothing there to make my heart beat. No: a mass party is to be fought, joined, or agreed with from the outside on common objectives. So much the better if action decides feelings: middle-class individualism reduces them to moods, let us return to love or to hate the whole man through his works. It is true: the aim of this article is to declare my agreement with the Communists on certain precise and limited subjects, reasoning from *my* principles and not from *theirs*; why will become clear. Since the Congress of Tours, it has happened a hundred times that men or groups 'of the Left' have declared their actual agreement with the CP while at the same time underlining their differences of principle. And if their co-operation seemed desirable to the Party, it accepted their alliance *in spite of* the differences. It seems to me today that the situation, for the Party as for us, has changed in such a way that similar alliances ought to be desirable up to a point *because of* the differences.

As to the fact itself, can the CP be said to dispute it? Yes and no. It recognizes that the strike did not succeed, but its chief worry appears to be to exonerate the working class and, to succeed in that, it does not hesitate to take all the blame on itself. Precipitancy, poor transmission of orders, lack of cohesion, extravagant tone: we know all its self-reproaches. To tell the truth, this is to let the devil have his due. The enemy gives the events of June 4 an essential explanation: the evil nature of the CP must in the end disgust the working class; the CP recognizes the facts but explains them as accidental; the working class is still ready to fight; it is simply that *individuals* have committed errors and have not chosen the right time to summon it. This is what M. Duclos said at the last session of the central committee: 'The working class has been the determining element of victory. In its immense mass it has been with our Party against the schemers. But this does not mean that the adoption of a position is always and everywhere translated into

strikes, demonstrations, or petitions. The mistake of the government and its officials has been precisely to believe that unless
there is a strike or a demonstration, the working class is
apathetic. The workers realized that the anti-Communist plot
was the prelude to violent attacks on their conditions of life,
the rights they have gained, democratic liberties, and peace.
And there is no doubt that the action of the working class was
bound to develop very seriously if the people's movement had
not, with the liberation of July 1, given a first hard blow to the
schemers.'[19]

On one point I am in agreement with the CP: which is that it
is impossible to read acceptance of repression into the silence
of the masses. 'So be it,' you may reply. 'But for the same
reasons, you cannot represent it as disapproval.' I am not so
sure: of course, a negative indication is difficult to interpret.
But it is not easy to believe that violence practised on the leader
of a working-class party, following a demonstration—even if it
was not popular—could leave the masses indifferent. The
workers live under the constant threat of three scourges called
rising prices, unemployment, repression. Whatever the long-
term future of which they dream or for which they prepare,
their short-term future is always gloomy: they are well aware of
the hostility of the ruling classes, whom they know to be involved in schemes whose consequences are for the most part
disastrous to the proletariat, but they are ignorant of the details
of these manoeuvres, and their effects often reach them without
their having had any presentiment of the causes. In this uncertain half-light in which everything they undergo seems the
worst thing possible, abrupt changes are of bad omen. You
remember those eddying years when we knew that Germany
was preparing for war without being able to estimate its rearmament effort, you remember our continual disquiet and the
baleful flavour of those days: from time to time Hitler made a
gesture, delivered a speech, and on each occasion we felt war a
little nearer. Certainly the comparison is not reasonable: but
when I, a middle-class man relatively cushioned against crises,
want to understand the climate of the working-class suburbs,
the heavy atmosphere, the blocked future, it is to that period of
our history that I turn. In arresting Duclos, the middle classes
conveyed news to the proletariat, and the news was bad.

Without forgetting the age-long hatred of the workers for 'coppers', the difficulties of their daily life, the uncertainty of their budgets and their ancient, unhealed wounds, how can it be denied that they saw in the judicial action taken against the Communist Party the premonitory signal of new persecution?

At present, need this muffled disquiet be likened to a *movement*? Can this mixture of apprehension and resentment be accepted as *action*? I don't think so. According to M. Duclos, the government made the mistake of underestimating the resistance of the masses. Possibly; but if M. Pinay didn't notice their anger, on whom did this vain and mute resistance react? And how count the liberations of July 1 as a people's victory? If I were a Communist, it is to Montesquieu rather than to the proletariat that I should acknowledge my gratitude: for the middle-class principle of the separation of powers for some months acted as a brake on the government's repressive action. A scrupulous magistracy proud of its prerogatives quite simply refused to give up to the executive authority the independence which is its reason for existence and that degree of sovereignty which it possesses. The people's movement should have given new life to the judges? But where does that idea come from? And if it isn't expressed by strikes nor by demonstrations nor by petitions, how should middle-class magistrates know that it exists? In fact, France was motionless and mute, and it was in the midst of a great silence that the *Chambre des Mises* took its decision. And, so far as I can see, the government was not guilty of underestimating popular indignation; it was guilty of not having foreseen such a predictable arrest. Since the Third Republic,[20] the magistrature has never obeyed anyone: why should it be expected to accept any masters, above all when those masters are called Baylot and Pinay?

It is, then, equally false that the masses brought pressure to bear on the ministers and that they remained indifferent. The fact is they were disapproving and they did not make their disapproval clear; that is what appeared suspicious; why did they make no attempt to express their very real discontent?

'Because their rancour was too strong, because they condemned Communist policy, and because they were offered the opportunity to show it.' By this clever reversal, the bourgeois press converted the absence of reaction into the will not to

react. Suppose we admit this: but *what* are we speaking of?
Of May 28 or June 4? You may tell me it is all one, that the
second flop was only a confirmation and an aggravation of the
first. I am not at all convinced of this: in my eyes, there was a
profound difference between the two days.

  To be candid, I don't care a straw for the demonstration of
May 28: successful or abortive, it was simply a matter of
routine and of 'current affairs'. Above all, it had a *political*
character. The Communist leaders had studied the international
situation, estimated the available forces, and come to the conclusion that a limited operation would contribute in its weak
way to modify the linking of those forces. What they did, others
might wish to do on their own account: each one could appreciate politically a political action. And if I cannot believe you—
you will see why—that the *working class* demonstrated against
the demonstration, I willingly admit—why not?—that a good
many workers abstained from taking part through a kind of
hostility which conveyed a repudiation: 'What's the point of it?
We shan't get anything by it,' etc. Perhaps there were even a
few who wanted to show by their absence that they condemned
this prestige policy. As for the majority, it was even simpler:
and the militants know very well that demonstrations against
war are rarely a draw. The failure of the red day, in June 1929,
offers many analogies—at least superficially—with that of
May 28: the same call to the masses: 'Show that you have
decided to hinder the anti-Communist crusade;' the same 'very
noticeable' absence of the working class. Only one difference:
it was Thorez who was arrested. The Party thoroughly understood the problem: it knew well enough on each occasion that
it would have to support the political adoption of a definite
position on economic claims, it wished to be able to analyse the
local situation, to disengage general causes and show how
immediate interest tied in with class interests. But, as we shall
see, that is not always easy: a link is perhaps missing or the
leaders make mistakes: in that event only the political action is
exposed to view, and it does not always succeed in drawing the
masses. And that is certainly not because the workers judge
political action not to be in their line, or because they are confused by the use of their ordinary weapons to denounce
colonialism or imperialism: but quite simply because their

objective is presented in a form that is too abstract and too remote. They fight in better heart when they are shown, for example, that in defending their wages they endanger the policy of rearmament and, as an indirect consequence, the North Atlantic Pact. Because they are defending their own special interests? No: because their grasp of events remains direct, because they see the effects of action in detail, because all their 'political education' rests on the idea that world-wide events show themselves, on the scale of nations and towns, under the aspect of local concrete changes the course of which can be modified by local concrete action.

But, anyhow, the strike of June 4 *was not* political. Or must the rage that stirred the Italian workers when they learned some unknown man had fired at Togliatti be called political? Forestalling orders to strike, they rushed into the factories, occupied them, put the employers under lock and key: all were in agreement, Communists, non-Communists, anti-Communists; it was a tidal wave. For two days the government thought it had lost control of the situation. And what, political or otherwise, were the objectives of this demonstration? To protest? Against whom? Against a madman? For no one thought—even at the time—that the government formed by parties of the Right would have been stupid enough to have a Communist leader assassinated at a moment when the CP was in control of a good third of the country; as for the 'pressure' of the masses, on whom could they bring it to bear except perhaps God the Father? Yet the event had immense consequences: in an outburst of passion, the class had asserted itself *in action* in the face of the nation, of all Europe; *before* the outrage there seemed to be only a scattering of groups attractive or repellent to one another, standing side by side or interpenetrating one another, families, societies, undertakings, parishes, etc.; suddenly *after* it, the barriers were down, and the proletariat made itself *visible*. It was this violent jump, that and nothing else, which the Communists expected from the French worker; it was not a question of attaining more or less distant objectives in more or less indirect ways: the working class was attacked in its most everyday reality, in its elementary rights; the leaders it had chosen were taken to the Bastille under its nose and the political bureau demanded of them—without hope, as I have said—an immediate and passionate reaction. No one asked it to break the windows of the Presidency of the Council or to set fire to the Élysée: it was desired that the workers make themselves visible. They did not do so.

'That proves,' replies the anti-Communist, 'that they wanted to throw off the yoke of the CP. These mass demonstrations, you could say, are barbaric consecrations, and it is in the street that the proletariat renews its faith in its leaders. Conclusion, therefore: when the streets are empty, the leaders are disowned.'

Don't let us go so fast. In 1951 the masses were already showing signs of exhaustion, and yet five million electors voted for the Communists; since June 4, some by-elections have taken place which do not indicate a noteworthy retreat from the averages of last year; on the morrow of the abortive strike, FO carried off a success at Renault's which was seized upon by the best papers. This unquestionable gain *at least* testifies to the ill-humour of the working class. But what has rarely been underlined on the right, and seems to me even more significant, is that the CGT, less than a fortnight after its fiasco, retained 60% of the votes. There is therefore in the Renault factories a majority of workers who maintain their faith in it while at the same time reserving their right to disobey it; there are four or five million electors in the country who vote for Communist deputies but do not raise a finger to stand up for them when their parliamentary immunity is violated. It is true: the CP is in danger of losing that kind of sovereignty which is born of action; and these remarks seem at first sight to indicate a crisis in its *revolutionary authority*. But it is also a standard and parliamentary party; and since, in practice, it controls the CGT, it is a trade-union organization: from these two points of view, it keeps its prestige; 60 to 70% of the workers accept that it defends their material interests; 25 to 30% of the electors accept that it represents them in the Assembly. In spite of that, you come and tell me that the working class disowns Duclos: all right. Yet it seems clear to me that the working class cannot disown him without disowning itself; but wait a moment: I will admit anything you like—the workers are tired of Communist tutelage, of Party bureaucracy, of its submission to Moscow; they upbraid it heatedly and daily wax indignant against the

CGT. So what? No one wanted them to give a sweet pledge of love to the political bureau, but to react to a challenge, an insult, a threat. Yesterday, in arresting Duclos, the government annulled their votes by a stroke of the pen; in arresting Le Léap today, it tears up their trade-union cards. Disown Duclos *at such a moment*? And while they are about it, why not thank good M. Pinay for having delivered them from a tyrant? Or do you really think that a proletariat forged in a hundred and fifty years of struggle, conscious of its traditions and of its greatness, is going to declare to you with a smile: 'I am not very pleased with the leaders I have given myself; that's why I don't mind their being arrested and, while I keep my faith in them on certain points, I don't mind the law's being infringed a little, if necessary, so long as they are cleared out of my way'? That commentators in *Le Figaro* should take the working class for a foolish virgin is quite in order. But you 'anti-Stalinist' Marxist, you who count on its perspicacity to deliver it from its present leaders, how can you admit that it has quietly opened the door to police repression? You have said and repeated after Marx, after Lenin: the middle class has foisted on itself laws which strangle it; it is to the advantage of the proletariat that it should be compelled to respect them. We must, you would say, rise against every abuse of power. Are you going to add today: except when the Stalinists pay the price? I understand: you can do anything you like because your attitudes have no effect on the masses; you have made a pact of non-intervention with the facts: they happen without disturbing you, without cancelling or confirming your theories; on the other hand, you have undertaken never to interfere in order to modify their flow. But the reactions of FO and the CFTC seem more disquieting. Whether they are reformers or revolutionaries, independent or controlled, trade-union organizations have this in common: they have developed within the framework of middle-class democracy and make use of all the weapons provided for them under the law. If the government violates the law or changes it, all of them are touched: the working class can have confidence in its strength only if it sees it in broad daylight; the strikes of 1936, for example, took place in a gallery of mirrors. Imagine an abrupt return to clandestinity; action by partisans would continue to be possible, but not by the masses: the eyes of Samson would have been plucked out. You suggest we are not as far as that yet? No, certainly; but it is not so very long since we emerged from that condition, and we all have memories which ought to make us touchy on the subject of arbitrary arrests. 'That's all very well,' you say to me. 'You're quite comfortable: you may have been insulted, perhaps slandered, but not persecuted. An FO militant is the victim of systematic and continuous persecution: he is insulted, sent to Coventry, has his work botched, is from time to time knocked about. When the Communists are mentioned to him, do you suppose he thinks of separatism, of camps, of bureaucracy, of Titoism? Get away with you! He thinks: "They make me furious, the dirty dogs; but just wait a bit until things change, and I'll make them furious in my turn". All the same it would be too convenient if the CP had only to raise its little finger and all its victims would rush to its rescue.'

It is quite true that the divisions in the working class must make life impossible for many workers; those with a grudge do exist, certainly. But what is wanted of them? To let bygones be bygones? Restore trade-union unity? Hold out a hand to the CP? Not at all: but to take part in a strike of limited duration and symbolic scope to defend the working class and their own organizations. It was easy for them to make their reservations known and to declare, for instance: 'We have not forgotten our disagreements, but we have put them aside for once; however deep they are, we will never allow them to overflow the framework of the class, and we repudiate once for all the kind cooperation of the government and the employers in whatever form it is suggested: even if their intervention appears at first sight to favour us at the expense of our enemy, we know that in the end it will injure us all; whoever uses violence against a representative—any representative—of the workers, uses it against us all, and against him the oneness of the proletariat will be restored.'

Nothing happened. The leaders of Force Ouvrière would doubtless have associated themselves with a 'spontaneous' and irresistible movement lest their organization should fail to profit by it. But, foreseeing the failure of the strike, they hoped it would be a crucial experience and that it would bring into the open their disagreement with the Party. Was this a good bet?

The flop happened, and who profited by it? Our middle-class citizens and their ministers.

An 'inspired' item in *Preuves* accused me of causing a lot of embarrassment with very little reason: these events are ancient history and I am the only person in France who remembers them. My reply is that there are at least two of us who are still interested in them: I am reminded of them continually because every day M. Pinay makes it clear that he hasn't forgotten them. Had it been successful, the strike would have stopped him at once: he would have ceased to be minister and Le Léap would not be in prison (I am not going so far as to say that that would be the contrary). Abortive, it showed him 'just where he could go too far'. For this reason alone, which is evident, I say that the strike of June 4 served not only the interests of the Communists but also those of the proletariat and of the whole nation. Where do you find evidence that the *proletariat* reprimanded its Communist leaders? When, the better to oust a competitor, a workers' trade union acts as the tacit accomplice of the class enemy, I say: exit the proletariat.

Who, then, refused to go on strike?—Well, *individuals*, in very great numbers; put it, if you like, the great majority of the workers.—And isn't that what you call the proletariat?—No, it's not that. Look: after the strike, the non-Communist press published evidence as to the state of mind which had led to the flop; why didn't you give us this evidence? I believe it was trustworthy—at least in part—first because I was able to check some of it; secondly because the facts reported were almost exactly identical right across the gamut of opinion; finally, and above all, because they were obviously against the interests of those who cited them and because they showed the opposite of what people would have liked to prove. No one of these reasons by itself would have been convincing; taken together they are not without strength. The evidence adduced is striking first of all by what it lacks. If you look for clear and politically motivated refusals, you will be disappointed; in the pub, in lower middle-class districts, the first boozer regards himself as the electorate, as the nation; he takes sides for or against the North Atlantic Pact, he explains what a government 'worthy of the name' ought to do in Tunisia: his judgments have the force of law, he speaks in the name of all, and he insists that everyone should admit him to be right. In the instance we are considering, you will find nothing that resembles the agreeable certainty of the elector sure in his rights: the worker is content to refuse his *personal* participation; he does not pass judgment and far from wishing, like Kant and the drunkards of the Fourth Republic, 'to exalt the maxim of his action into a universal law', on the contrary he strives to preserve for himself a private character; on the understanding that if his comrades take him to task, treat him as 'yellow', in short if they try *first* to put him back into the historical circumstances, he will defend himself on the ground they have chosen, he will try to prove to them that he is in the right politically and that they ought to have acted as he did. But, on the other hand, if his circle hesitates and he feels that his decision might instigate a general movement of abstention, he takes fright and makes the point that other attitudes are possible, that his own commits only himself: it is above all on the *singular* aspect of his case that he insists. Fundamentally, did he refuse? He would say rather, it seems, that he *could not* obey: 'You haven't my family burdens, or you are sure to keep your job, etc., so of course you are free to do what you want; for me, it's not at all the same thing. . . .' Decide not to go on strike? Be unable to decide to go on strike? He swings between the two. He is not very sure whether he hopes that his example will be followed all over France or that his absence will pass unnoticed; he is equally afraid of a demonstration made without him and of a mass abstention which might have serious consequences. Yes, the dominating feeling is that of powerlessness. As a rule, trade-union orders are recognized as duties, and the shop stewards make every endeavour to persuade him that they are practicable: you must, therefore you can. Today he answers them: I must not because I no longer can. 'You know very well that we shall achieve nothing, that we shall lose our wages for nothing.' Or again: 'Force Ouvrière is not moving: we shall be alone.' Or again: 'Go and look for such bunkum as a month's paid holidays? That's easy!' Or still again: 'I can't because I've got three youngsters and my wife has just had an accident,' etc. Which of these arguments touches on class? Through so many dreary replies, we divine a return to that fatalism which ceaselessly threatens the oppressed, which the ruling classes seek ceaselessly to develop, and which revolutionaries have never ceased to fight. This discouragement is born of isolation, and in turn begets it: it is in shattering this ring that the working class asserts itself, and the rather forced optimism of the Communist militants expresses their will to save hope, the cement of the proletariat. How could those who say they will not move because FO refuses to move, declare more plainly that the working class is in shreds? And yet the non-Communist organizations count at the most a fifth of trade-union membership. At the heart of an integral whole, what is twenty per cent in opposition? Almost nothing: the bad hats, the waste material; the majority disregards them and declares its unanimity. If this 'waste material' were to organize itself, everything would change; that bumptious unanimity which considers itself the working class is only a majority trade union. Yesterday it still believed itself infallible, and its decisions the only possible decisions; from minute to minute the proletariat was only what it could and should be; 'Its aim and its historic action [were] irrevocably and obviously laid down for it in the very circumstances of its life;' each of its reactions expressed it to the full. At present the decisions of the CGT are *accidents*: hasn't it been proved that others are possible and, sometimes, better? It wasn't the proletariat which ordered this strike through the lips of its leaders: it was *a particular way* of answering the government's challenge. In a word, the resolution of the leaders was binding only on them; they might be *good* leaders but that too implies that they might be *bad*: the masses, without its being their fault and without their having changed, tend to regard them as enlightened monarchs who think for them. It will be understood that I am not questioning, for instance, the 'authoritarianism' and the 'bureaucracy' with which the CP is upbraided: I recall quite simply the effects of a trade-union split, *whatever it is*; working-class disagreements tend to produce a certain resignation in the masses which, instead of asserting themselves in an unanimous reaction, are led to choose between several probabilist policies. Engaged in an activity of which their comrades disapprove, the followers of the CGT have the feeling that they are fighting without protection; it is not only the conclusion of the operation that is uncertain; it is the operation itself: weakened, unsure, limited, it reflected the *opinions* of certain specialists; and if there are specialists of 'general interest', why be surprised that the worker tends to occupy himself with his 'special interest'?

For, after all, do people believe that the strikers of 1920, 1936, 1947 were all celibate and childless, marvellously ensured against unemployment, and provided with a savings-book? Or, conversely, do people believe that today's worker has totally forgotten the interests of the working class? Does capitalist exploitation seem juster and more humane to him? Does he accept colonialism, imperialist wars, and police repression in better part? Is he going to sacrifice his leaders in order to draw nearer to the employers?

Try to find out for yourself: accost one of those who refused to go on strike, speak to him openly, at random, and on the quiet slide into your remarks the odd poisoned arrow against Communist policy: who knows, perhaps he is of your opinion; that won't prevent him from breaking off the conversation abruptly, for he will have recognized the class enemy beneath your smiles. In short, today as yesterday the workers have the same cares, the same aims, the same loyalties. Yet a man risked death in 1942 who, ten years later, would not even risk his wage for a single morning. What has changed? His motives? The forces that drive him? No: their relationship, the method of appraising them. And what produces these changes if not the flow of the world: that is to say, history from day to day? The historic whole determines our powers from moment to moment, lays down their limits for our field of action and our *real* future; it conditions our attitude in relation to the possible and the impossible, the real and the imaginary, what is and what ought to be, time and space; from which point we in our turn decide on our relations with others, that is to say, the meaning of our life and the value of our death: this is the framework in which at last our *me* emerges, that is to say, a practical and variable relationship between here and there, now and always, the past and tomorrow, this world and the universe, a decision, incessantly revocable, on the relative importance of what are incorrectly called 'private interest' and 'public interest'. To take extreme instances, in so far as a community submits to the flow of the world or contributes to its movement, its members take refuge in the immediate present or have at their disposal a future extending well beyond their death, shrink within the little they have or chance everything for a cause the triumph of which they will not see, order their ventures to accord with their needs or determine their needs as a function of a venture. To one group history discloses outlets; the other it forces to mark time before closed doors. The worker of today is no more in possession of his working tools than was the worker of 1850, so that basically his claims do not change. But the organization of capitalist society has not stopped evolving nor has the position of the worker gone unmodified: it will be found that, according to the era, he 'sticks' more or less to political activity or is absorbed more or less in his industrial life; his ties with class organizations tighten or relax, the great aims suggested to him—it matters little whether reform or revolution—appear real to him, sometimes even close at hand, sometimes distant, sometimes imaginary. If he loses hope, no speech can give it back to him: but if action takes hold of him, he will believe: activity in itself is faith. And why does it grip him? Because it is possible: he does *not decide* to act, he acts, he *is* action, the subject of history: he sees the final aim, he touches it: in his lifetime, a classless society will be brought into being. The immediate reality is the Future; considered from the depths of the future, private interests are abstract shadows; death itself does not give rise to fear: it is just a very personal event that must happen to him in the environment of that Future which, in common with everybody else, he possesses.

Often action ends in disaster: then the workers, the collective subject of history, became once more its individual objects. The worker changes his skin, he sees the world with different eyes: the things that were clear yesterday have grown dim; others grow clear, close, everyday, disagreeable: why struggle if nothing changes? If there is hope of winning, if there is nothing more to lose: then it is worth fighting. But if there still remains something to lose—even only a paltry wage—and all hope of winning has been abandoned, the workers will lie low. Those who used to risk their lives without even thinking about it, today fear starvation, and they say: 'We don't want to die of hunger.' When Koestler, already nonsuited by the infinite, had not yet chosen to be a cipher, he told us the story of the Spanish shepherd who fought *in order to learn to read*: risked

his skin to educate himself, a perfectly reasonable thing to do—
on condition always that there is a chance of winning. When
everything is lost, when the victors decided to spread illiteracy
and to base their power on ignorance, hunger became their
accomplice: so long as a chance remained, people ate if they
could, ate to fight; in order to fight, people acquiesced in not
eating; when everything was over, people ate to live and lived
to eat.

But want may beget a will to unite, hunger is not always or
even usually the auxiliary of power: if it is to serve the turn of
power, an extra turn of the screw is necessary: it will be reduced
simply to pangs of hunger if the future is carefully stopped up:
the future is born of action and turns back on itself in order to
acquire meaning; reduced to the immediate present, the worker
no longer understands his history: he makes it. For the moment
he looks at it as if he had always put up with it and sees in it
one single riot, always beginning afresh, always crushed. Unite?
With whom? He is dedicated, after defeat, to this strange
encircling isolation which each one rejects and each one puts
up with as the recoil of the isolation of the rest: 'I, of course,
would certainly go, but the others wouldn't.' Reduced to his
worn body, to the gloomy everyday awareness of his exhaustion, death appears to him the more absurd the less meaning his
life has; it inspires him with a horror so much the stronger the
wearier he is of living: the employers have nothing more to
fear—neither rebellion nor man-power crisis—when the
worker's only reason for living is his fear of dying. If he wants
to turn aside from himself and look outside, he is expected:
everything is prepared to reflect his powerlessness back to him.
In the middle of a supervised crowd, he paces boulevards
tailored against riots; a landscape of factories and suburbs
offers him a picture of harsh and inhuman order; about him an
opaque setting of resignation has been arranged. Common-
sense, reasonable calculation of chances, all whisper to him to
let go, to give up the struggle against his enemies who have
weapons, troops, money, machines, and knowledge. His fate
has become no more just and his masters are no better: they are
the stronger, that is all. His defeat does not decide against him:
it proves simply that the world is bad. Doubtless there might
have been other hopes, another truth: bank notes suddenly

changed into dead leaves, and troops refusing to fire on the crowd; but these truths were living and concrete only in the struggle: action would reveal them; when action becomes impossible, only abstract recollections remain. One thing is especially evident to the defeated: it is that man is a mistake.

Such evidence explains the June flop as due to discouragement: the worthy newspapers tried to show us the proletariat drawn up against its leaders, and instead we had the feeling of being present at its inward collapse. In refusing to appreciate the political bearing of the strike, the worker voluntarily put himself *on this side* of the interests of his class; he redoubled his isolation for motives which he invoked to justify himself; he broke collective ties, he lost contact with his leaders; if the strike did not take place, it was not because it was condemned by an unanimous impulse but because it aroused reluctance among millions who wanted to remain individuals. Collective aims, values, ideals were not touched: but they withdrew, they put themselves out of reach. They refused the struggle because they were certain of defeat: the worker had lost confidence in the power of the working class; it seemed to him that his class had no grip on events and that history would go on without it. War? He is against it, certainly: 'But if the Americans want to make war, the French worker won't be able to hinder them.' Political action? Certainly, it would be right that the worker should make the most of his opinion: 'But, in five years, what have we got? We've demonstrated a hundred times against the war in Indo-China, against the North Atlantic Pact, against German rearmament. And what has been the result? We haven't succeeded even in our economic claims: prices rise and, in spite of our efforts, wages never catch up with them.' Revolution? Michel Collinet maintains that the new generations don't know the meaning of the word. This is hardly believable —above all for his readers, since he stoutly insists, elsewhere, on the volume of Communist propaganda. What seems truer is that the attitude of the French workers has changed profoundly in the course of this half-century. Before the First World War, many workers believed they were reaching the end: they *would see* the General Strike. The war and the policy followed by the Socialist leaders disconcerted the masses, but the days of October gave them back their confidence: the Third International was formed in an Apocalyptic climate: Revolution would start in Germany and spread all over Europe. The worker of 1952 is told and told repeatedly, with an insistence that is itself almost suspect, that he will see the advent of socialism: 'Not only our children, but we ourselves will enjoy socialism.'[21] But he no longer quite believes this: he knows that the dictatorship of the proletariat isn't just round the corner. Has he gone over to reformism? Not at all. Factory equipment dates and the employers continue to be Malthusian; our industry is in tow, rearmament and colonial wars ruin the national economy;[22] a flick of the finger is all that is needed to cause the machine, patched up a hundred times, to fall to pieces. In these conditions—and when there is no question of doing more in the immediate future than ameliorate his situation—how could the worker trust himself to a slow, measured, progressive action towards compromises? From foreign policy to economic ideas, if he wants to achieve the smallest reform, he must overturn everything: for everything is wrapped in this badly tied-up parcel. He knows this, he learns it every day: can this conviction, vague as it is, that it is necessary to go from the whole to the parts and from changes of structure to the reform of details be called revolutionary? Perhaps not: it exalts in activity but discourages during hard times; in any event, it is radicalism. To this, so far as the French proletariat is concerned, are added very special motives for rancour: once in its history, and only once, it put its trust in its employers and they, naturally, deceived it. It was at the moment when they were trying to acclimatize the 'second industrial revolution' in France: they disarmed trade-union resistance by promising to use the new techniques to increase production; the conveyor-belt operative accepted additional wear-and-tear in the hope of raising the standard of living. Who knows? If the promise had been kept, we might have witnessed the birth and prospering of a new reformism. Exhaustion at the factory and well-being at home: in the USA this hot-and-cold shower regimen is the employers' best auxiliary. French employers preferred to decrease their costs and maintain their prices: to keep order, they trusted to good old methods, that is to say, to rifle shots. Today, like a dunce his fools' cap, like a cuckold his pair of horns, they wear with sullen impudence the title of 'the most backward employers in the world', awarded to them by the Americans. As for the worker, his work is as hard as that of his American comrade, but his real wage is lower than that of 1938, hardly higher than that of 1920. An equivocal situation: he grows exhausted at his job but he *sees* the oppression. For him it is not only a question of increment value, overtime, etc., difficult ideas which do not always mean anything to him: but he knows that in other capitalist societies, in Scandinavia, in the USA, the conditions of work imposed on the worker correspond with a higher purchasing power than his: he is doubly robbed. That is why he would rather not talk of collaboration between the classes, of their mutual understanding, of the common interests of Capital and Labour. Duclos undoubtedly expressed the opinion of his working-class electors when he said of a certain union that it would be 'that of the traitors and the betrayed'. Besides, this 'rationalization', by increasing the number of unskilled workers and liquidating the last internal patterns of the proletariat,[23] had the effect of squeezing the masses, of screening them from the influence of the working-class 'élite', and made of them a relatively amorphous and perfectly homogeneous substance. It is one very sure way of pushing them into radicalism: they are no longer directed by a relatively moderate 'aristocracy'; henceforth they make the most of their own point of view, that is to say the arbitrary demands and claims of the *least favoured*, those who are the least compatible with our social régime.

For all these reasons, and others, the French worker keeps up a sufficiently uncommon intransigence. Perhaps he is not aware that this is Revolution: but what would you call this irreconcilable violence, this contempt for opportunism, this Jacobin tradition, this catastrophism which puts his hopes in disruption rather than in indefinite forward movements? For myself, I see here the chief characteristics of a revolutionary *attitude*.

But exactly: what is it except an attitude? Action outlined and held. If the working class is not expressed by acts, if it is not integrated in a collective praxis, if it is not inscribed in tangible things, what is left? Nothing: a negation. Today the future is blocked by a bloody wall; the worker remains faithful to his beliefs and his traditions: but he is a revolutionary without a Revolution. He does not hold that it can never happen or that it is a myth, as Sorel held the 'general strike' to be; all the same he makes of it neither a *value* nor a virtue. But he does not reach the point of seeing in it the necessary outcome of 'prehistory', still less the *reality* of the proletariat: in his eyes it is a partly accidental event which must arrive at some uncertain date after his death; others who will start again from zero will make it. The worker of 1952 no longer has the feeling that he is preparing the way for them; from time to time in history there are short-circuits; everything stops and nothing that is done has any effect so long as the current has not been restored: he must have been born during a breakdown. If he still happens to say to himself as he looks at the youngsters, 'They will see it—I shan't,' this is above all a way of thinking of his death—like the shopkeeper who dreams, 'We shan't go to the moon, but our children will.' In the great moments of working-class history, the Revolution was not a future event or an object of faith, it was the movement of the proletariat, the everyday *practice* of one and all; not the Apocalytic conclusion of an adventure, but simply the power to make history; not *one* future moment but, for these men exiled in the unbearable present, the abrupt discovery of a future; Revolution was a task, the 'unending task' of the proletariat, it was the justification of individual existences and the universal dimension of each particular item of behaviour: in short, an unchanging linking of the individual to the class and the particular to the general. Each episode of the struggle had a double significance, tactical and strategic, and related to a double system of reference: through the immediate objective could be seen the distant objective. For the worker of today, the tie between these two significances has been broken: he can still defend his interests, demand, secure an increase in wages, but he does not establish any relationship between this little everyday victory and the destiny of the proletariat, he does not lay hold on the 'revolutionary bearing' of his claims: on the contrary, it seems to him that he has lost the initiative and that he is defending himself foot by foot against reaction; inversely, whether he obeys or disobeys *political* orders, whether he should go on strike or not against the war in Vietnam or against the North Atlantic Pact, these demonstrations have in his eyes a kind of unreality. He has no doubt that peace in Indo-China will be good for the proletariat; perhaps he even sees a bond between world peace and the advent of socialism. But his activity appears to him tinted with ineffectiveness: he has lost his grip on history and cannot change its course.

Among the motives he invoked before the strike of June 4 to justify his refusal to take part in it, I have said that there were no general ones. That is not altogether true. From time to time attention is drawn to an announcement which could pass for a general appreciation of the situation: the worker recognizes it but he can't stand it any longer. What? The Communist Party? The CGT? Moscow? No: politics. And it is not the politics of *the CP* which disgusts him but every kind of politics. Today workers can be heard saying, 'Politics, I'm fed up with it,' and many of the women say to their husbands, 'You'd do better not to bother about politics: what's the good of it?' What's the good of it, *since we shall change nothing*? It is not even *political activity in general* which is blamed: in other countries or in other times or for other men, it is perhaps appropriate; for the French workers of 1952 it is forbidden: 'Politics isn't for children.' For the moment you will find these reflexions only in the mouths of women—and of some men. No matter: it is a symptom. First because the strike of June, rather than a manoeuvre, ought to have been a demonstration of solidarity: the working class ought to have gathered round its threatened leaders; the day the workers baptize as 'politics' everything that extends beyond the framework of their immediate interests will mark the end of the proletariat.

At those moments when the working class is aware of its strength, it does not occur to it to lay down a limit to its activity; rather the contrary, the narrowest watchword is radically changed of itself and local action re-makes the movement of the whole. But when the workers restrict themselves from day to day to defending their wages, the initiative passes to the employers; the workers keep on the defensive, renouncing the effort to win so as not to run the risk of losing; and for lack of immediate action on all the factors of human life, the lowering of nominal wages is perhaps prevented, but not the rise of prices. That is why the true, the only limit which the worker should recognize for his acts is that of their effectiveness: if today he shuts himself up in his personal interest, it is because he is hindered from getting outside it, and if he's no longer interested in politics, it is not that he obeys a theoretical concept of trade unionism: it is quite simply because he *can no longer* do it. It is normal for the middle class to triumph; but I am speaking once again to all those who maintain that they are at the same time Marxists and anti-Communists and who today rejoice because the working class 'is in the act of breaking loose from the CP'; I would remind them of this phrase of Marx's which they have read, re-read, and commented on a hundred times: 'The proletariat can act as a class only by forming itself into a distinct political party,' and I beg them to draw the consequences: whatever they think of the 'Stalinists', even if they deem the masses to be deceiving themselves or to be deceived, what then will maintain their cohesion, what will ensure the effectiveness of their activity, if not the CP itself? The 'proletariat formed into a distinct political party': what is that in France, and today, if it is not all the workers organized by the CP? If the working class wants to break loose from the Party, there is only one way: to disintegrate into dust.

It is to hide this disquieting truth from the masses that M. Robinet, rapidly followed by all the press, celebrated the *victory of the proletariat.* Wonderful precaution: in buying *Paris-Presse* or *France-Soir* on June 5, the worker learned the *opinion of the working class*: it had judged that the strike was contrary to its class interests and had disowned its leaders. Disconcerted, he puts down the paper and wonders if he did think all that on June 4. His recollection, however, is that he did not *really* refuse to go on strike or pass judgment on the policy of the CP, that he preferred his own interest for want of being able to recognize and prefer the interest of his class, and that he went home uncertain, neither very proud nor very happy. Now these ruminations, multiplied, change completely and become the sacred verdict of the proletariat. Strange virtue of statistics: the abstention of the workers of Picardy and Provence makes clear to him the significance of his own small solitary defection. He had believed he was just simply to walk in procession; *objectively* he was taking part in a plebiscite. He considers with amazement this opinion which he has just learned and which is, at the same time, his and that of everyone;

perhaps he is already asking himself what attitude to take up in face of 'a party which the working class has disowned'. But no: he won't march. He begins to suspect that they want to make him take chalk for cheese and the unorganized mass of non-strikers for that organized community which the proletariat ought to be.

Here we touch the root of the problem: if the class ought to be able to disown the Party, it must be able to remake its unity outside it and against it. Is that possible? According to the answer to this question, the CP will or will not be replaceable and its authority legitimate or usurped. The facts do not disclose a collective reality in the affair of June 4. But more than that: not only have we not *seen* the class stand up to the Party, but it can be shown that such opposition is not even conceivable. No one believes any longer in the proletariat-fetish, the metaphysical entity from which the workers could be alienated. There are men, animals, and things. And men are real and remarkable beings who are part of historical wholes and cannot be compared either with atoms or the cells of an organism. United? Separate? Both the one and the other. There is no separation which is not a kind of presence nor connexion so close that it does not admit of secret absence. If the class exists, it will be as a new closeness of one and all, as a manner of being present which is realized through and against separating forces: it will make the *unity* of the workers. The fallacy of the anti-Communist is that he calls simultaneously to his aid two contradictory processes: in order to take away from the Communists the merit of having unified the masses, he begins by making a sort of passive unity of the class; then, to set it against them, he endows it with an uncanny spontaneity. I think it necessary therefore to recall certain truths known to everyone which seem rather forgotten. You must be willing to think that I have no ambition to make or re-make a theory of the proletariat: I only want to show that class unity can be neither passively accepted nor spontaneously produced.

(i) *It cannot be imposed.*
The unity of the workers cannot be developed mechanically by the identity of their interests or their conditions.

As for their interests, the evidence shows that their identity begets competition and conflicts. As for their condition, that is another matter. Since I am not propounding theories, I take this word to indicate broadly the manner of work and of payment, the kind and level of life, social relations. In everyday practice, these criteria suffice: I will *place* this newcomer if I am told what he earns and what he does; shall we be content with that if it is necessary to establish the logical relationship between him and the class to which he belongs?

The sociologist would be content with it. He wants only facts; still, he does not accept them all; the days of June 1848, the Commune, the Decazeville strike were facts: he will take no account of them. There were some dead? And afterwards? Do people prove the existence of a class by dying for it? If the proletariat exists, it must be with an entire scientific objectivity, like an inert object which the scientist looks at from the outside. If you can prove that certain objective factors determine the condition of manual workers, if this condition is the same for all of them, and if each one reacts to it by similar behaviour, you will have established the reality of the proletariat. The same factors, the same situations, the same reactions: there you have the class.

After that, of course, some will prove that there are classes ('considering that we have established by strict methods the specific characteristics of the working class, we recognize in it the dignity of an actual object'), and others that there are not ('considering that strict enquiry has not made it possible to establish the objective characteristics which would be proper to it, we have come to the conclusion that the alleged working class is an illusion'). I exhibit them back to back: their courteous contests hide a profound collusion: some maintain that the proletariat is an actual *thing*, others that it is an imaginary *thing*; both agree in reifying it. And the most artful system is that which proclaims its existence very loudly in order afterwards to reduce it to the likeness of a sack of potatoes. Wait, let us consider the best; they have approached the problem without preconceived ideas and have recourse to statistics in order to determine class characteristics experimentally. Even outside activities prescribed by production and in the fields in which it seems to enjoy a relative independence, it will be noted that the proletariat is distinguishable from other men by its behaviour; its condition gives it a character, that is to say a 'first habit'; in Marxist terms, production produces the producer. For example, comparative study of household budgets brings to light certain specific constants in working-class consumption. By extending their researches to language, mimicry, sexuality, etc., the investigators will end by establishing with positive exactness ... what jumps to the eye. Let them bring these present constants of certain social constants closer together; let them establish functional relationships between these and those. Let them go further: let them pass from the static to the dynamic and bring to light the influence of social processes in the way of evolution on the behaviour of the proletariat. Will they have at last discovered class? They say so, but I believe rather that they will have transformed the proletariat into a zoological species. If the members of a social group are treated like passive and interchangeable products of universal factors and if to begin with all the influences which these individuals can exercise on one another are brushed aside, what is likely to be found at the end of the reckoning if not the species, that isolation without hope endlessly repeated? We thought we had to do with sociologists; a mistake: they were zoologists. I have known a few zoologists. One, especially, who had dedicated himself to crayfish. He neglected the peculiarities which were of interest only to the crayfish themselves, such as the relations of one crayfish to another; from that, he came with no difficulty to the conclusion that all representatives of the species had an absolute identity. After which, he constructed some ingenious contrivances in order to study the action of alternating currents on the psychism of the eternal crayfish. How be surprised at this since he had reduced his eighteen thousand individuals to nothing more than eighteen thousand reproductions of a single pattern?

All very well when it is a question of crayfish: there will be less indulgence for those who apply the same method to enslaved men and who replace the soldiers of a fighting unit by the inert products of objective factors. I begin to suspect that our sociologists have somewhat mystified us: for each idea, they have substituted an ersatz concept which resembles it and proves exactly the contrary of what it is supposed to demonstrate. In the name of objectivity, they have brushed aside all the proofs of a working-class *praxis*; in its place, they produce false events which fall to dust when they are touched, and the deceptive unity of their averages overlays the infinite dispersion of the occurrences which they have brought into it. The worker eats a lot of meat! and of indifferent quality! What then? At Vitry, at Saint-Denis, I think it probable that the same cheap cuts make their appearance on the table every day, but you would try in vain to make me accept these thousand meals as a collective happening: you have done nothing but add up some isolated reactions which perhaps have their cause in the same objective process, but which are scattered in the dust of the industrial suburbs like a thousand drops from the same cloud; you assert that you are showing us human facts and you slide physical facts into their place. Deprived of culture, you say, exiled from the exquisite heart of society, held in subjection to nature by fatigue and his large needs, the manual worker tends to prefer quantity to quality. Well, what have you done? You have defined men by a privative cause and by the mechanical action of need; it could be said that you were giving us the recipe for manufacturing them.

Will it be said that the analysis is not serious? That a plurality of causes with no link between them has been enumerated, that the worker has not been connected with the system of production? That is true. But it is not a question of changing the factors: the bias must be changed. Wait: here is a definition by Bukharin which I came across in M. Goldmann's book:²⁴ 'A social class is a community of persons who play the same rôle in production and who sustain the same relations to production as other persons taking part in the process of production.' The accent here is put on production, but what have we gained by it? To be precise, the definition is stupid and not very Marxist: it is in fact by the resemblance of people that definition of class is attempted: they play the *same rôle*, they have the *same relations* with other persons. Will it be enough to call them a 'community' for them to form in themselves a class? But this community— either it is an aggregate, and then we are back to the species— or it is a *totality*; but, in that case, it would be necessary to give the generative principle in the very definition. Yes, Marx said that production produced the producer. But when a productive process, a unique and unnatural cause which produces a

hundred thousand incarnations of the essential being of the
working class, is carried out, this unity of operation could not
guarantee the synthetic unity of the products. If the proletariat is
only the inert waste product of industrialization, it will break
down into a dust of identical particles. The living unity of the
capitalist 'process' may brand with its seal the workers whom it
creates: in suffering refraction in surroundings that are inert and
without cohesion, it multiplies itself and becomes the formal
identity of diversity. One moon cannot unite the waves; it is the
dispersion of the waves which scatters moons all over the sea. In
short, I should distrust Bukharin: his definition is mechanistic,
like those of MM. Sorokin, Gurevich and Halbwachs.

All these scholars have undertaken to demonstrate the unity
of a class, and they have shown us the identity of specimens in a
collection. Now, unity and identity are opposed principles of
which the first knots the concrete ties between the persons and
the second the abstract ties between the cases. Thus their
method, in claiming to reconstruct the proletariat, destroys all
possibility of a real link between its members: to remain unim-
paired, identity of essential being requires absolute separation
of existence. If a worker of Lens and a worker of Amiens were
in contact, if each, in developing himself, developed the other,
in short if they took part in the same struggle, each, in his living
reality, would depend on the other, and they would resemble
one another the less the more closely they were united; it is by
community of action and not in isolation that each would become a person, and the sociologist would no longer have either
the means or the pretext to study separately their individual behaviour since they would all be related to a collective venture
and would be clarified through it.[25] Inversely, if he substituted
identity of condition for unity of class, it would be in order to
persuade us that collective action is an impossible dream. If the
workers are *made* before they unite, union can no longer *make*
them; external factors have given them a *character;* henceforth,
whatever their human relationships, they will glide over them
without noticing them. One proletarian wrote of another a
month or two ago: 'He is recognizable among a thousand.
Everything about him is characteristic, his language, his walk,
his gestures, his unobtrusive form, his way of eating, drinking,
amusing himself, loving, hating.' Here is something that justifies

your statistics. With a single reservation: the worker here described was absolutely desperate. That is what I wanted to come
to: your sociology is applicable to the worker only if misery has
reduced him to despair; it reflects his resignation, his passivity,
his renunciation; and that also is what M. Robinet, sociologist
without knowing it, would like to reflect back to the proletariat.
This victorious class which he evoked by his clarion call was an
aggregate of despairs and isolations; what he offered us as a
collective reaction was an average of discouragements; and what
was *identical* in all these exhausted men was the will not to
unite. M. Robinet gave the working class the right to vote so
that it could declare publicly that it did not exist.

In point of fact, what did it cost him, at *Le Figaro*, to
recognize in the workers this kind of passive cohesion which
identity of condition confers? The middle-class press long ago
worked out that there was no *fundamental* unity. Inertia is
absence of ties, hence indefinite divisibility: it is necessary to
count, draw lines, hold together unceasingly the conjunctions of
disparate elements which tend to break up; in short, unity is
only the reverse of a unifying action. Look more closely at this
'class' which M. Robinet congratulates: it is breaking up. What
do you find in its place? Molecular whirlwinds, a multiplicity of
infinitesimal reactions which reinforce or cancel out one another, the resultant of which is a physical rather than a human
force. It is the mass. The mass, that is to say, *precisely* the rejected class: since the effects it produces always have their cause
outside them in a pullulation of Lilliputian points of behaviour,
the mass is *externality*; it can have no needs, feelings, will or
behaviour: for its individuals, in deciding each for himself,
have not foreseen or willed the public result of their hundred
thousand private wills. It is a fragment of nature which lingers
at the heart of our societies. Of course it is only destructive: in
order to build it would require if not the unity of a person, at
least that of an organization or an undertaking. In fact, it is
composed of irresponsible elements: literally, the workers do
not know what they are doing since their single acts are going
to swell up far away, add themselves to other unknown acts,
and reverberate at last in the form of absurd storms. Revolutionary days? They are only days of great panic: the animals,
driven from their holes by hunger or by fear, wheel about the

town, smash, burn, plunder, and return home. Class hatred? How could this chaos of molecules love or hate? Its mechanical condition and perpetual disintegration simply happen to make us see an enemy of man in what is only mechanical nature at the heart of the antiphysis.

We are asked to accept as a class verdict the working-class reaction to the strike of June 4. But, fundamentally, M. Robinet is convinced that it is a question of mass panic. Hasn't it all the characteristics? The total results were neither foreseen nor wanted by individuals. They were negative in character; they expressed no collective intention; they did not have the effect of bringing the workers together but on the contrary increased their isolation and the distances which separate them. What does that mean? That class does not exist? That certainly is what it is hoped we shall believe. But we know very well that the working-class world is not a saraband of atoms: even on June 4, on other points, in relation to other objectives, the workers performed certain actions in common. What we learned is that the mass is a condition limited by isolation and renunciation into which the worker has perhaps never fallen, but to which he gets close every time he disrupts discipline and escapes from his organizations. The simple objective condition of being a producer defines the concrete man, his needs, his vital problems, the orientation of his thought, the nature of his relations with others: it does not settle his relationship with the class. If the tie of solidarity is broken, the worker would continue to be a producer, a manual worker, a wage-earner, but he would no longer be a proletarian, that is to say, an active member of the proletariat. Classes do not exist, they are made.

Who makes them? Not I, says the middle-class man. And that is true. Under the Ancien Régime division into orders was maintained by the aristocracy and by the monarch; the classes were official institutions with statutes. Nothing was clearer: the privileged kept up a hierarchy which favoured them, and the oppressed wanted to jump over the walls that imprisoned them. But today, by a stupendous reversal, it is the privileged who deny that there are classes, and the oppressed who appeal to them. The middle class has never dreamed of imposing a statute of class on the workers: very much to the contrary, all such codes and constitutions as might seem to look like inequality of principle are quickly pushed out of sight by their jurists. 'The real classless society,' says the liberal, 'is capitalist society'. And I believe, in fact, that the bourgeois ideal would be a classless and oppressive society—that is to say, quite simply a society in which the oppressed would accept oppression. The procedure which the middle class has followed for two hundred years, with infinite resources, aims at preventing the worker from becoming a proletarian by taking away from him the means of being a man: individuals are to be kept in a state of isolation, and working-class crowds in a state of fluidity, so much is it true that oppression tends to become its own proof and to make the oppressed such that they must legitimate it: the middle class must be charged with devoting itself permanently to an attempt to 'massify' the proletariat. Inversely, it is against this attempt that class makes and re-makes itself without ceasing: it is movement, action, and its degree of integration is to be measured by the intensity of the struggle it conducts against the middle-class manoeuvre. Class, *real* unity of crowds and historic masses, is revealed in an epoch-making operation which reflects an intention; it can never be separated from the concrete will that animates it nor from the ends it pursues. The proletariat itself creates itself by its daily action; it exists only in action, it is action; if it ceases to act, it will decompose.

I am saying nothing new: you will find all that in Marx. He recorded firmly that identity of needs created opposition among individuals: 'The organization of proletarians into a class ... is continually broken ... by the competition of the workers among themselves.' What gives the workers the power to surmount their antagonisms is the struggle against their employers: 'The proletariat passes through different phases of development; its struggle against the middle class begins with its very existence. In the beginning the struggle is started by isolated workers. ... During this phase, the workers form a mass spread out all over the country and divided by competition. ...' How could Marx, in this text, speak indifferently of proletariat and of 'mass ... divided, spread out' to describe the same object? It is because he already found the workers surmounting the situation made for them, a pugnacity among them which must *necessarily* produce union. The worker becomes a proletarian according to the extent of his rejection of his condition. For

those whom misery, exhaustion, circumstances incline to resignation, Marx has some very hard words: these are 'beasts', 'sub-
men'. But he does not blame or condemn them: he passes a
judgment of fact on them. The worker *is* a sub-man when he
consents simply to be what he is—that is to say, when he identifies himself with this mere product of production. This sub-man
will become man only when he 'becomes conscious of his sub-
humanity'. His human reality is not therefore *in what he is*
but *in his refusal to be that*, that is in his 'revolt against the fall'.
Undoubtedly he can try on his own account to escape from his
condition, to cross the line and integrate himself in the middle
class; he will be a deserter. It was precisely the existence of
these deserters which led Marx to state that revolt must contain
the principle of union: the worker who wishes to secure a
change for all his fellows as well as for himself is the proletarian; only then will he have 'as his real task the revolution-
izing of his conditions of existence'. From this point, the phases
of the struggle merge with the stages of unification. The proletariat 'is kept on the move by the results of its actions'. It is this
movement which holds together its separate elements; the class
is a system in motion: if it stopped, its individuals would revert
to their inertia and their isolation. This directed, intentional,
and practical movement needs *organization*. That is why Marx
talked of 'an organization by class', a formula which carries us
far away from Bukharin's definition; a class *organizes itself*.
Not for it's own enjoyment but to attain certain concrete objectives. Marx's definition of communism could equally well be
applied to the proletariat: 'It is not a stable condition, an ideal
to which reality must be adapted. . . . [It is] the *real* movement
which abolishes the present state of things.' From that it is easy
to understand why he suddenly defined the class by its praxis:
'The proletariat will be revolutionary *or it will not exist*'
[author's italics], and why, in fine, he refused to distinguish between action, the totality of its agents, and the apparatus which
brings them together: 'The proletariat cannot act *as a class*
except by forming itself into a distinct political party.' Certainly
the industrial system is the necessary condition for the existence
of a class; the whole historical evolution, the way capital works
and the role of the worker in a middle-class society prevent the
proletariat from becoming an arbitrary grouping of individuals;

but this in itself is not enough: *praxis* is necessary. It matters little whether this *praxis* is or is not engendered *dialectically* from the proletarian condition: the attribute of the dialectic is that its stages run by but retain in themselves the anterior stages. In accomplishing his real task, the worker *reveals* the proletariat and becomes a proletarian: it is striking that Marx, when sketching a sort of phenomenological description of the fighting worker, found in him *entirely new* characteristics born simply from the struggle: the proletarians 'found the greatest joy of their lives in their revolutionary activity'; the economist would be making a grave mistake if he believed that the workers counted the cost of a strike: '[this would be to be unaware that] the workers have generous hearts. . . .' That is, they find their reality as men much more in collective *praxis* than in the satis- faction of their personal needs. 'When communist workers meet, their first aim is doctrine, propaganda, etc. But at the same time they acquire a new need, the need of society, and what appeared to be a means has become an end.' In passing from the mass to the class, the worker has sloughed his skin: if pressure of circumstances, defeat or exhaustion lead him back to consideration of his own interests, he falls back out of the class and becomes again what has been made of him. You say the working class has demonstrated its disapproval of the CP? What class are you talking of? This proletariat which Marx has just defined, with its cadres, its apparatus, it organizations, its party? It ought to have *affirmed its unity* against the Commu- nists, to have demonstrated *as a class* through its repudiation of the CP. But where find the leaders, the pamphlets, the watch- words; where lay hold of that discipline and strength which characterize a fighting class? Is it possible to imagine the sort of authority necessary to clandestine organizations carrying out such a task and, from Lille to Menton, setting all the workers against their leaders? To draw 'the masses' to a collective re- pudiation of the CP, nothing less than the Communist Party itself would suffice.[26]

(ii) *Working-class unity does not develop spontaneously.*
'Certainly. If this repudiation had been instigated, we should have been less pleased by it. Of what interest are instigated demonstrations to us? We don't want to provide the masses

with new tyrants; we want to give them liberty: in our eyes, the reaction on June 4 was all the more important because it was *spontaneous*.'

A rumour put it about that the anti-Communist had hit the bull's eye: ever since Rousseau's tears, spontaneity gets the benefit of prejudice in its favour: the first move is good; people always come back to first impressions. With unseemly pride, we spread about our most secret truth: 'Yes, it is I, it is certainly I, I'm like that'. In this proportioning of nature and of liberty, liberty gives way to nature: people discover themselves as they are. Breaking away from habit and rules, adapted to circumstances without being determined by them, spontaneous impulse is a beginning, a windfall which, however, reflects our peculiar essence. That comes back to subordinating doing to being, action to passion, the visible to the invisible; man at the 'first impulse' escapes from hard necessity to unite without ceasing what he thinks, what he feels, what he does: his individual unity is already there, it opens out like a rose in the dark; it is the secret convergence which will be discovered by historians in his actions. Instead of developing, he looks inward and becomes sufficient to himself. Enough: the subject has inspired a very important literature; it can be consulted not without distaste but fruitfully.

What is new—at least, not *very* new: a century old—is that spontaneity is used for political ends. That just happens; social facts used to be treated like things, then we began to treat them like people: and so we have the masses becoming impulsive! Their spontaneity, fine, right, genuine, moves everyone and against its verdict, as against that of dogs and children, there is no appeal; any government which offered to oppose it would be very mad and very bad. Look at Tunisia, to go no farther: if it had been proved that people *spontaneously* wished us to leave, you may be sure we should not have stayed another minute. But the sad truth is that the troubles were *stirred up*. Let us consider: organization stifles the free impulses of the heart, *therefore true* spontaneity cannot support organization. Thus a riot *cannot be* spontaneous: that is inevitable, since no riot starts without a leader. You ask was it spontaneous? Come, come! free consent to oppression. Besides, do not imagine that mass parties reason otherwise: what they prefer, in this range of

ideas, is guided spontaneity. At arranged, well-drilled demonstrations with no surprises, they willingly recognize a torrential
impetuosity; but they detest the unforeseen, and those crazy
tidal waves that well up and drown the leaders: these are
fomented by the enemy. Even today it is impossible to read the
press of July 1936 without amusement: as the victory of the
Front Populaire was being celebrated, the masses took it into
their heads to occupy the factories; people exchanged glances:
who's pulling the strings? Why, of course, said the employers,
it's the Communists. A Communist worker said to Simone Weil,
it's the employers. People spoke also of Hitler and of the fifth
column. *Le Temps* thought Thorez guilty; Thorez opted for
Trotsky; but no one, at that time, attributed the move to spontaneity among the masses. Imagine! a movement born of *itself*,
without leaders? There *must* be something behind it.

June 4, on the other hand, was completely reassuring: the
masses simply did not react. Splendid! Here in total apathy was
first-rate spontaneity. The anti-Communist press was exultant:
'Eloquent silence: the people have spoken.' It was vain to object
that a total of individual spontaneities does not add up to a
collective will. Ninety-eight per cent abstained: surely that tells
you something? Don't you feel the quality of this stubborn
silence? that it is a shattering cry, perhaps the most desperate
human ears have ever heard? There is a stiffening, a hardening
of working-class consciousness. Where does this erectile awareness live? In the unconscious, of course; that is where, turgid
and at first invisible, it arises to be dispersed later in thousands
of acts of rejection.

To produce a class without leaving your study, the recipe is
simple: take the mass—which is pure number—and treat it as a
crowd—which is a rudimentary organism; of the crowd, take a
single personality, for example an inspired beggar woman; all
you have to do then is decipher her message. And if she is
silent? Don't worry: there are ways of making her speak. In the
instance we have under consideration she seems inclined to
silence: none of the workers who had refused to go on strike
had any intention of avowing disapproval of the CP; that
need present no obstacle. The anti-Communist left reminds us,
in this connexion, of a thought of Marx: It matters very little
what a proletarian believes he is doing; what counts is what he is

constrained to do. Obviously it is possible to give a purely
objectivist meaning to this formula—and that indeed is what
Marx seems to have done: the ideas we form about our actions
do not modify their inward logic, their objective structure, or
their historical consequences. But this is a dangerous interpretation: it would tend to the conclusion that certain objective
factors kept the workers on June 4 in a *state of dispersion*,
augmented their 'massification'. If only actions and the contents
of consciousness are to be considered, what had become of the
revolutionary impulse of the proletariat? And what had happened to its pugnacity? Has anyone ever seen a proletariat
without pugnacity? And didn't Marx say that it would be revolutionary or it wouldn't exist? Hence a glow of enthusiasm
must live in it, imposed on, misled, perverted by evil persons.
No trace of it can be found? That is because it is not directly
accessible to our senses. It will be enough to consider Marx's
formula in the light of psychoanalysis: self-consciousness is a
lie, the reasons it uses to explain its actions are lies. Analysis of
actions and of their subjective meaning leads back to the deep
spontaneity which is their source. If you do not admit this spontaneity, you will simply conclude that abstention by the
workers, their hesitations, their uncertainties are to be explained
by their objective state of exhaustion; but, if you begin by thinking that at all times and in all places the proletariat *must be*
revolutionary and if you throw light on its attitude by its historic
mission, *then* the discouragement and the inertia of which it has
given proof *can only be* the superficial and lying aspect of a
deep enthusiasm; since it is *necessarily* active, its passivity is the
form of activity it has chosen because that is adapted to the
circumstances. In terms of spontaneity, abstention becomes disapproval. For an anti-Stalinist Marxist the revolutionary *praxis*
of the masses cannot be confused with the manoeuvres they
carry out under the leadership of the CP. And as these
manoeuvres are all they do, their *true praxis* appears in what
they do not do. W noted, just now, liberty mixing with nature:
in the same way, here objective and subjective mix together, and
in the end a strange reality appears which is at the same time the
objective and elusive unity of the masses in so far as it can be
inferred from their dispersion and their subjective and invisible
impulse in so far as it can be deduced from their temporary

immobility. This ambivalent concept is then offered to us under the name of *class*. Everything happens as if that subjective spontaneity of the masses were called class in so far as it is perceptible from the outside as their objective unity. As spontaneity lies behind individual consciousness, objective unity will embed itself behind dispersion. Naturally, experience serenely continues to offer us the same dust. No matter: intelligible character, choice before experience, the absolute which mints itself in multitude, unity in power and in right of plurality, principle of fire circulating across inert matter, it is class which produces men, not men who produce class. The target had been reached.

For it is the target. Some time ago with that candour sometimes produced by hate, M. Laurat wrote:[27] 'If [the Communist leaders] were isolated from decent people, cut off from the mass of the nation and from the working class, they would soon be reduced to impotence.' And the other anti-Communists smiled bitterly. 'Cut them off: that's soon said. Give us the knife.' Now, that is how, under the effect of small shocks, decent people work loose from the Party: it owes its empire over souls to their acquiescence, and one sign of the cross is enough to send it back to Hell.

Splendid. But let us be careful not to prove by absurdity the necessity of the CP. Suppose the working class to be possessed; it is exorcized, and at the moment its devil flies away it opens its eyes and breaks into a thousand pieces! You see us *without a proletariat*? If the truth must be told, this possibility is not intended to frighten the right wing of anti-Communism which goes on repeating that the worker is a fool in thinking of himself as a proletarian. But the left wing cannot bear the idea either: with the disappearance of his *belle Dame sans merci*, the non-Stalinist Marxist loses everything, to begin with the honour of being faithful without hope. It is for his use that this electric idea of class-impulse has been brought into focus. If you look at the world through those spectacles, you will see class everywhere, even if the proletariat is in smithereens; and since it is a question of depriving the Party of the merit of effecting unity of working-class activity, the magic principle of this unification will be somewhere between the objective rule of production and the subjectivity of the producer as individual spontaneity lies between being and doing, or the Freudian *libido* between the body and consciousness. Strong in its flexibility, this proletariat made of rubber can swell without splitting or huddle together without breaking down: it expands and grows thinner, slips through the slits in its cage and re-assembles outside it, or compresses itself, breaks formation, rolls between the bars of the enclosure and rebounds farther, into the midst of its true friends.

This sort of twaddle flatters socialist optimism as juggling with 'natural goodness' used to flatter middle-class optimism. One more reason for distrusting it: optimism and pessimism are the obverse and reverse of the same practical joke. When the price of voluntary death is raised, do we lament a hardening of 'the national will to suicide'? And when it is lowered, must we be thankful for the stiffening of the national instinct for life? Do not tell me that class exists and that the nation is only an imaginary being since that is just what would have to be proved. For you lean on the identity of class (that is to say, on identity of conditions) to prove its spontaneity and on its spontaneity to establish its unity. But putting that on one side, let us agree that the abstentions of June 4 expressed a collective repudiation and see where that leads us.

I opened a Trotskyite newspaper which carried a commentary on recent events.[28] According to M. Germain, one of its contributors, the origin of working-class disaffection goes back to 1944: between Liberation and the end of 1945, the masses had several opportunities of seizing power and were compelled to miss their chance; this was how the leaders of the CP did 'violence to the instinct and the revolutionary dynamism of millions of militants'. De Gaulle crushed the working class? Not at all, answers M. Germain, who recalls the 'complete paralysis' of the middle class at the time of Liberation. Besides, there was no question of setting up the dictatorship of the proletariat. It was necessary to sound the 'people's power of expression . . . create and develop the germs of a new power which the masses had themselves built up from another source (committees of liberation, factory committees, etc.)'. The political bureau of the French Communist Party missed its moment because Stalin sacrificed the workers of Europe to his resolve to collaborate with American capitalism.[29]

That explanation is as good as another. Let us note that there is nothing specifically Marxist about it. To tell the truth,

Trotskyism in spite of itself suffers the common fate of all oppo-sitions: the party in power is realist since it asserts and pretends to demonstrate that the actual is the only possibility; there is one policy to follow: the one I follow. The opposition declares that there was at least *one other* and that it was certainly the better, and this constrains it, in spite of everything, to take up an atti-tude more or less tinted with idealism: there are possibilities which have not been realized; the *actual* process ceases to be the measure of man since what is not is truer, more effective, more consistent with general interests than what is: systematic analysis of facts opens on to the non-existent (that which has not taken place) and in the end the explanation of history continually re-fers to missed opportunities which exist only because they have been *imagined*. That is precisely the situation here. When M. Duclos writes: 'The Communist Party ... is aware that it has allowed no historical possibility to escape.... If a different course had been followed ..., it would have given a pretext to the fascist de Gaulle to crush the working class with American help....'[30] M. Germain made easy fun of him: a *pretext*? What is that? 'For a Marxist, social classes do not act according to pretexts, but according to their interests and the balance of forces which permits those interests to be attained.' Yet it is Duclos rather than Germain who is faithful to the spirit of Marxism: Marx is very far from denying the existence of the *possible*, but by that he understands the stages of future activity as they appeared in the course of preparing for it. Leaders and militants must be able to say to themselves as they consider the past, 'We have done everything possible (that is to say, our activity has been as extensive as circumstances permitted); nothing except what we have done was possible (the event has shown that the solutions we discarded were impracticable).' This attitude tends to identify reality and activity. All that is actual is *praxis*, all that is *praxis* is actual. Without doubt, such principles also inspire Trotskyism; but M. Germain, in his capacity of opponent, aims at establishing truths which go to contradict this: (i) the masses in France could have seized power immediately: that possibility was the most consonant with their interests, the best adapted to the circumstances, that which followed from existing strength, the shortest route to world revo-lution: in short, the possibility which summed up in itself the greatest *actuality* and the greatest *effectiveness*; nevertheless, it was not carried out; (ii) if the workers had seized power, the middle class *would not have* stirred. His attitude is intermediate between that of the militant who analyses the present situation in the light of the decision to be taken and that of the theorist who disentangles the significance of past events. It is true that the first has the right to set out the inventory of possibilities: but his analysis is subject to the pressure of the moment, illuminated by events, modified by 'the historical process', continually recti- fied by experience and, in the end, put to the test by the *praxis* itself. The theorist can claim to deliver us to a certain truth on condition that he sticks to what is and pays no attention to *what might have been.*[31] M. Germain bases his opinion on a dead actuality; he cannot claim certainty when he attempts to set out the possible consequences of what never was. As for the end of his search, as it never actually existed, it will make an abstract of an idea; in a word, it will be because it has been imagined. So that the correct Marxist schema is abandoned for a probabilist idealism the inferences of which are most often based on simple extrapolations. Besides, what is to be under- stood by this ambiguous term 'the possible'? The working class *could* have conquered: agreed! But on *what conditions*? The balance of forces favoured it, its interests urged it to seize power, but its leaders prevented it from doing so. Let us admit this: but *couldn't they* have done it? What made them do what they did? Obedience to the Politburo? But you have been pro- claiming that for many years; according to you, it is this same relationship with Moscow which characterizes the French Com- munist Party. Could it have changed its basic structure in 1944? And what does that mean? I know you distinguish a left current in the Party—I don't say you are wrong—and that you uphold the agreeable theory of a CP that is revolutionary in spite of itself: but how would the left have taken the lead on the mor- row of Liberation when everything depended on the USSR, when the middle classes seemed reduced to impotence, when many people still believed in American pacificism, if it is true, as you say, that the leadership of the Party still today, in full retreat, succeeds in imposing silence on the disaffection at the base? The policy of the USSR? Would you say that this is the offender? Perhaps: but at what moment was it *possible* to change it? Does it not reflect a determinate society, with its economic and political structures, its social strata and its internal conflicts? Is it necessary to go back to the death of Lenin? There are some who go as far as that; the game could have been played and lost about 1923-1924: in the autumn of 1924, after the defeat of the German proletariat, for the first time Stalin talked of 'socialism in one country'. That day the angels wept. We seemed to be back with original sin and the discussions of Leibniz and the great Arnauld on predestination: Stalin becomes the little father Adam of the atomic epoch. It is an admissible theory: it may be admitted that historical circumstances sometimes, but *very rarely*, combine in such a way as to allow an effective human act which determines the direction of history. If the opportunity is allowed to slip by, patience will be necessary for twenty, perhaps fifty, years until it returns; Trotskyism is a waiting art. But what then becomes of the 'possibility' of 1944? The stakes were laid. And if a few enthusiasts could believe they were going to lead the working class to victory, that was because they had looked at the details of the situation without considering the whole.

Others, on the contrary, claim—and M. Germain is perhaps one of these—that, even in a counter-revolutionary period, it is possible to exercise a continuing action on the course of the world provided the actor remains ready to exploit every contradiction. On their side is the agreement of Marx and Engels which accepted the contingency of detail[32] and that of Lenin which refused to apply to the study of history day by day the principles and methods which served him in interpreting the great wholes of universal history. They are permitted to believe that the obscurities and wavering of history in the short view will disappear before the gaze of the future historian. Perhaps, one day, the place and the rôle of present events will be clearer; perhaps it will then be evident that they were the *only possible* events. But so long as history is incomplete, so long as the particular event is seen from a particular perspective, it is impossible to explain the detail of a policy in going back without transition to general considerations. If the universe is a dialectical process whose every local movement has its reason in the movement of the whole, Trotskyites could understand Stalin's policy, but how could they condemn it? It will have been for all time and in all circumstances what must be and what could be, neither more nor less. Perhaps, then, it will be necessary to state that the cards were so dealt *from the beginning* as to make socialism impossible. Or, on the contrary, as Merleau-Ponty says: 'The way that seems to us winding will, perhaps, in the fullness of time and when the whole of history has been revealed, appear to be the only possible way and *a fortiori* the shortest.' Anyhow, the French CP is irrelevant. There were not nor could there be *unrealized possibles* except at the level of this wavering history in which events always occur behind or in advance of the appointed time, remain partially indecipherable, where a struggle, however profound its reasons, can, in the absence of an activating cause, remain long buried, like a delayed-action bomb. In the event under consideration, the struggle is there: it is the class struggle; the balance of forces is clearly defined: in 1944, the working class had a solid possibility of seizing power. What was lacking? The activating cause: a different orientation of Communist policy.

Only there is this: the Marxist opponent straddles two arguments: to make the 'Stalinists' aware of their mistakes or their lies, he wants to be irrefutable: he will therefore make use of the methods and views of sweeping dialectical history; to establish, on the contrary, that another act would have been possible in such and such circumstances, he has recourse to probabilist inferences. When Duclos refuses to 'provide a pretext' for repression, M. Germain makes merry: a pretext! 'Since when did the fascists wait for pretexts to smite the working-class movement?' In short, the CP is naïve enough to believe that it was *possible* for de Gaulle to act otherwise than he did. And that action was not *carried out* for lack of opportunity! 'Once given the balance of forces,' answers M. Germain, 'a suitable "pretext" can always be found'. See how the argument runs: de Gaulle is visibly reduced and loses his special features; first he becomes the Fascist—and Fascism is nothing except the full use of the powers he has at his disposal in favour of the interests he serves. Then he is merged in his class, and it is the middle class itself which we enfold in our glance. Why doesn't this strike the working-class movement? Because it hasn't the necessary strength. Each force tends, of itself, to go to the limit of its effect, is restricted by the other forces acting on the same point:

the event, the result of diverse forces, is always all that it could have been. As for the factors of regional history, they have vanished: the origin and character of the team in power, the actual structure of the middle class in 1944, particular interests, prejudices, beliefs, ideologies, necessities of day-to-day politics—all are eliminated. In 1952 de Gaulle is considered a fascist, *therefore* he was a fascist in 1944. Could this general, certainly not very favourable to the Republic though he had promised to re-establish it, have entangled himself at that time in personal contradictions? That would have had no effect on the course of events. Would the middle class, on the morrow of the ruinous occupation, have found it less costly to temporize and to feel repugnance to violence while quite ready to have recourse to it? That is of no importance. Since the middle class did what it did, that was because it could do nothing else. Good.

I apply these principles to the working class: I am not sure that it could have seized power but I have been told—and I believe it—that it was in its interest to seize power, and that the balance of forces was favourable to its doing so: it must therefore have seized power without being aware of the fact. Not at all! says M. Germain. It *could* have seized it, and its leaders prevented it from doing so. Of course! And what are these leaders? 'They are the leaders of the CP who are in favour of what we call bureaucratic conformity; that is to say, are ready to move to the right or to the left in sympathy with the needs of Kremlin diplomacy, to which they are ready to sacrifice the basic interests of the masses.'[33] The wicked men! But *why* are they like that? The fascist, I understood just now, was the pure manifestation of his class and its anonymous instrument; Soviet 'bureaucracy', I note also, when I read Trotsky or *Vérité* expresses the interests of certain local strata and is conditioned by the same society from which it emanates. And I even find this remark in *Révolution trahie*, 'Present Soviet society cannot dispense with the State and even—up to a certain point—with bureaucracy. And it is not the unfortunate remains of the past but the powerful tendencies of the present which create this situation.' That is what totally reassures me about the Politburo: the individuality or the particular will of its members matters little; it is the USSR itself which, by and through them, provides itself with the apparatus it needs at the present moment.[34] But

whence comes the bureaucracy of the French CP? It does not
rest on the masses since you accuse the political bureau of
'sacrificing their basic interests, of doing violence to their
revolutionary instincts'. Nor on the structure of our society
since this is a middle-class society and the CP does not play the
rôle of a government party. Nor on the balance of forces since,
according to you, this relationship is favourable to action. And
as for enfeoffment to the USSR, one of two things: either you
will show that today this is necessary for a revolutionary party—
when everything 'possible' disappears, and with your own hands
you tie the fate of the proletariats to that of the Soviet republics;
or you will say, like Bourdet, that it is *possible* to withdraw from
this domination: if that is so, it is individual mistakes, misunderstanding of the situation, faults of character (conformism,
cowardice, etc.) which go to explain the inertia of the CP. He
to whom you appeal has written: 'A revolution cannot be
ordered, it is possible only to give a political expression to its
internal strength.'[35] Moreover you admit that, by their individual action, its leaders have been able to put the brake on a
working class in full surge and in a revolutionary situation; in
short, you reject activating causes for the middle class and concede them for the proletariat. For one reason only: that all guilt
is *necessarily activating*: it adapts itself after a fashion to the
fatality of antiquity; with the necessity of modern times, it must
disappear: therefore you need a culprit.[36]

From this compromise between necessity and contingency,
between discipline and irresolution, between what is and what
should be is born your concept of spantaneity; 'the revolutionary instinct' which you recognize in the masses has only one
function: to mark in the absolute what *ought to have been possible*. And you would even accept that an inflexible law has
ruled the course of events since October 1917—who knows,
since the first original sin—if it were conceded to you that,
among so many vicissitudes, the revolutionary instinct remains
steadfast. At the bottom of the hearts of the masses must remain
eternal availability obscured by circumstances, but which they
can neither destroy nor create since it is the profound actuality
of the proletariat, the sentence which capitalism carries against
itself, in short that arbitrary demand without mercy which is
expressed objectively in pressure exercised on the Party and the

leaders, and which has for its sole object permanent Revolution. In endowing the proletariat with revolutionary spontaneity, you pollute it by your opposition. You would in fact consider that the political action of the CP is neither right nor appropriate, that it could and should be otherwise. But, in looking round you, you would discover only relative strengths, interests, actions: in short, what is, never what *ought to be*. And to begin with, who set out the ends to be pursued? Only, you are not qualified to reproach the CP with having abandoned revolutionary objectives; condemnation must be supported in the name of the masses; but what proves that you are speaking in their name, you who have no access to them? It is just that, far from wishing to make them happy in spite of themselves, you restrict yourself to deciphering the messages of their revolutionary instinct. If that instinct exists, it will be the arbitrary demand which defines ends and the means of attaining them: objectively, in fact, its exigency is revealed only when it appears as *praxis*; the masses have a spontaneous power to create and organize which has the effect of hastening the advent of the proletariat: that is how in 1944 they themselves set up committees of liberation and factory committees: these first steps indicated the way, the CP had only to continue the movement. And since these spontaneous steps showed the direction to follow, you can condemn the leaders who did not follow it: the people's instinct *revealed* what was to be done, what, with other leaders, would have been done. Spontaneity begets possibilities: it is the masses with their intransigence, their pugnacity, their sharp claims who create the *possibility* of seizing power; its impossibility is due to the leaders. But the leaders are nothing; it would seem that they can be changed instantly; the masses are *everything;* and just try to change them. Their spontaneity has the inexorable strictness of the dialectic, since it is production which produces the producer; at the same time this spontaneity is free since it expresses the essential in the proletarian movement. For the second time in history, it marks—over against that original sin which we have all inherited—nature sustained by Grace. And this grace, it must be confessed, saves you Trotskyites; without it, I should see you on the wrong track: what would have happened if the 'dynamism' of the masses depended on external factors? Suppose it was regulated by the balance of forces, the degree of exhaustion of the combatants, the memory of previous struggles, recorded conclusions, the policy of leaders.[37] Suppose the spontaneous action of the masses, instead of taking aim at the future, comes to nothing more than a rebound from the past; suppose it hangs on their weariness, on a false hope: farewell lowly power of collective prophecy, farewell spontaneity; you could still oppose Marx to Stalin, you can no longer subpoena the proletariat to witness against its leaders: the policy of the leaders and the temper of the mass are, on this hypothesis, both functions of external circumstances; finally, one reacts on the other, they exercise a mutual modification, are adapted one to the other and, in the end, equilibrium, mutual accommodation is reached, *possibilities* fly away: like leaders, like mass; like mass, like leaders. The destiny of the proletariat? Perhaps the Marxist method will enable you to *foresee* it; not to make it: you will be augurs. Anyhow, you no longer count. 'But,' you will say, 'this concept is not dialectical'. Why not? In any event, it is Engels's: 'History is carried out in such a way that the final result flows from the conflict of manifold individual wills, each determined by a given quantity of particular conditions: thus there are countless forces which criss-cross, an infinite group of parallelograms, and the resultant, the historical fact, can be regarded as the product of a force which works, as a whole, unconsciously and without will. What each one wants is in fact thwarted by the others and what results is something no one wanted.' In that view, 'unconscious and involuntary force' is a convenient fiction; as for spontaneity, there is none.

Consider: you speak today to the CP and you notify it of an order to propose unity of action to socialist leaders. This political plan is—at the *present* moment—both totally reasonable and totally absurd. Reasonable: if it were followed, France and Europe would certainly be changed, and war would move further off. Absurd: you are well aware that the CP will take no such step (Lecoeur's speech is evidence of the temporary triumph of those who want to bury it in solitude); if it should favour the step, the socialists would reject it out of hand. But, you say, the failure of this attempt would open the eyes of SFIO militants: that implies small knowledge of them, an underestimate of their resentment against the CP: they will not forsake their party, they would congratulate their leaders on foiling the manoeuvre. If it were a question of considering simply what will actually take place, your plan would get by as a pious wish with no importance or basis. But on the contrary you insist: this 'common front . . . is neither Utopian nor venturesome'. Why? 'Because millions of working men, officials, craftsmen, petty tradesmen and small peasants want this change.'[38] In a word, it is in the will of the masses that Trotskyite reasoning finds its objective guarantee. 'For a Marxist,' every true idea must be practical since truth is action; the Trotskyite idea would remain a pure lifeless abstraction, an idealist contingency—since of itself it produces no effect, and it points a way that it knows will not be followed—unless the masses, by their action and their demands, undertook to begin the realization of these purely subjective concepts. Not that the idea acts on them: there is a pre-established harmony; the Trotskyite decides that his speech is the verbal expression of collective spontaneity. He is on one side, the proletariat on the other: they never speak to one another, but between the intellectual system of the first and the impulse which carries the second beyond his wretched condition, a deep and tacit agreement is set up virtually over the head of the militant Communist who is content really to speak to the workers and to direct their movement in earnest. The vital and scarcely perceptible impetuosity of the masses is the surety of a futile diagnosis; or, if you prefer it, Trotskyism bases an abstract rationalism of opposition on a pragmatic irrationalism. It goes without saying, of course, that the spontaneous hankerings of the working masses exist only to be violated. From this we revert to the schema previously described: the secret disapproval inflicted by a group on the leaders it has itself chosen is called spontaneity, the silent complicity of a society integrated with the opponents it has exiled.

Let us go back to June 4: did working class spontaneity disown the CP? I very much doubt it. First, neither Marx nor Lenin believed in the permanence of a 'revolutionary instinct' among the masses. As for Trotsky,[39] he on the contrary insists on their 'profound conservatism' which appears to him 'a factor in social stability'. Exceptional circumstances are needed to 'free the malcontents from the constraints of the conservative spirit and lead the masses to rise'. Then, their feeling is at first purely negative: the leaders have plans, programmes: but the masses simply feel 'that they can no longer put up with the Ancien Régime'. Drawn on by the event, only then do they *experience a sense of revolution* in 'finding their bearings actively by the method of continual approach', always more to the left. When their impulse is shattered on 'objective obstacles', that reflux begins which leads to reaction: 'Great defeats are discouraging for a long time. The elements lose their power over the mass. In its consciousness ill-fermented preconceptions and superstitions come up to the surface. At this time, those recently arrived from the fields coupled with mass ignorance water down the working-class ranks.' Briefly, the masses are revolutionary given the conditions for a revolution; their impulse and their powers must be appraised according to the concrete possibilities of the situation, instead of setting up these possibilities according to the strength of revolutionary 'dynamism'. In particular, if their alleged 'instinct' is the effect of circumstances, its violence does not prove that it must be acted on. It is Trotsky, again, who wrote, 'The masses intervene in events not according to instructions from doctrinaires, but in accordance with the laws of their own political development. Bolshevik leadership . . . saw clearly that it was necessary to give heavy reserves time to draw their conclusions from the adventure. . . . But the advanced strata rushed into the street. . . . (Now), independently of the will of the masses, the experience can be transformed into a decisive battle and, in consequence, a decisive defeat. Faced with such a situation, the Party holds back and remains on one side. . . . This party of the masses must, most certainly, follow the masses into the area in which they haven taken up their position, to help them but without in any way sharing their illusions.' Trotsky himself claims for a party the right to appraise the people's 'dynamism' in the light of the general situation; he does not hesitate, in certain instances, to call the reasons for such an abrupt outburst 'illusions'—and M. Germain, Trotskyite, blames the CP for having no confidence in the people's instinct. Because, he will explain, the situation is different. That is true: but if we refuse to believe in the infallibility of the masses, what remains? Two doctrinal concepts—that of the international Communist Party and that of the French Communist Party; two ways of reasoning and two 'scientific' interpretations of the situation.

This repudiation of June 4, now treated as a document, now as testimony: let us agree that it exists and that it is hidden under the weariness and the discouragement of the workers. Are we any further forward? *What has been repudiated?* The unhappy initiative of May 28? The policy of the French CP since 1948? since 1944? since the Congress of Tours? Bureaucracy? Enfeoffment to Moscow? Soviet policy? And why not Marxism itself? Who will decide? You say it is all there: when the disapproval aims expressly at only one detail, the strength and closeness of the chain are such that the whole is involved. But that is not true: we are concerned with local and everyday history, opaque, in part contingent, and the link between the items is not so close that some of them cannot be varied within certain limits without modifying all the rest. The other day I read that the proletariat is tired of the Soviet leaders' meddling in its internal affairs; not, it is said, that it directly condemns this meddling: actually, it does not notice it and doesn't care a rap about it; but, and this comes back to repudiating it, it cannot endure the 'bureaucracy' of the CP which is its obvious consequence. But I continue to be in doubt: to be convinced, I should have to be shown first of all that this bureaucracy cannot be fought without first breaking with the USSR; then, and inversely, that a revolutionary party not enfeoffed to the USSR runs no risk today of being brought under official control by the circumstances of the struggle. In the absence of these particulars, I do not know how to judge the implication of this alleged repudiation. I see clearly that the CP recognizes it made a mistake, and I see also that it localizes it in the moments immediately preceding the strike: because it wants to get out of the mistake in the best way possible. I see certain middle-class people persuaded that the masses have passed sentence on Marx: that they are anti-Marxist.

Then I don't know the reason for this sentence; but as if that were not enough, neither do I know who is the judge passing it. For I imagine two kinds of repudiation: that which a revolutionary class inflicts *in the name of the revolution* on the leaders who want to stop it; and that which a defeated, broken, resigned class inflicts *in the name of the ideology of the victorious class* on the revolutionaries who want to drag it into new adventures. As for the first, it is the subject matter of history which condemns a traitor, and his condemnation is written into the history he makes. As for the second, a class, feeling itself once more a mass, picks up with its old chains 'its badly fermented prejudices and superstitions' and uses them to condemn its own glory. With which of these two judges have I to deal? The Trotskyites assert that it is the revolutionary: 'The French working class . . . has been sacrificed. . . . In spite of all justifications, today's criminal mistake is obvious to everyone. Next time, no worker will start out.'

How believe them, without faith in the irrepressible spontaneity of the worker? And then, to speak truth, I find the reactions of that revolutionary a little thin: he has, and he knows it, sacrificed his class, and, as the only reprisal for this, he stands aloof from an ill-timed strike? It would need good sight to find his *dynamism*, even better sight to discover mass pressure in the events of June 4.

According to the newspapers, revolutionaries have ceased to exist. In fact, did they ever exist? History has simply drawn the necessary distinction, putting gangsters on the left, decent people on the right. It was the worker's *prudence* that kept him away: that is to say, his good principles. He is sated with these useless acts of violence, all he wants is to work in peace. He finds life difficult enough as it is, and is not inclined to squander money on idiocies. In short, it is the middle class itself which repudiates the Party through his person. I am prepared to believe that the employers are content: their good friend the worker is cured at last; it would seem that the outrageous rent which ripped modern society apart has been mended, definitely and invisibly. The classes? That was simply a nightmare: if, as is logical, every individual forming part of a middle-class society is called middle-class, there will be none but middle-class people in the West—some in despair, the rest not too discontented.

If that is the way of it, at a guess the French CP would be struck to the heart by the disaffection of the masses. But the reasons adduced for their repudiation would leave it cold.

The anti-Communist was waiting for me at the corner. 'So the masses cannot judge the set-up?' My answer is that, when they are on the move, they may push their leaders before them.[40] His retort is, 'But the *rest of the time* the masses can-

not judge them?' Ah, Socrates! I see whither you're dragging
me! Well, I agree: they judge their leaders when they follow
them, but not when they do not follow them. Socrates
triumphs: 'You owe your freedeom to write to the middle
classes and you use it to refuse freedom to think to the people.'
The verdict has been returned: contempt for the people, sophis-
tical moderation, shameful liking for autocratic forms of
power; in a transport of servility, I concede to the CP much
more than it has ever asked: it claims that it is guided by the
opinion of the masses; it doesn't want justification of the
absolute empire over them which it has acquired; it hides it.

When I am abused, I push masochism so far as to wish that it
should be for good reasons. I will therefore explain why those of
the anti-Communist are bad.

Firt of all, I am not considering what is to be desired or the
ideal relationship between the Party-in-itself and the Eternal
Proletariat. I am trying to understand what is happening in
France, today, before our eyes. Kind friends have been so good
as to point out to me the existence of Anglo-Saxon and Scandi-
navian trade unions: these organizations, 'according to all reports', are better adapted than our CGT to advanced forms of
capitalism.[41] Perhaps: but what does that prove? That we
should regret not being Swedish? I come back to my own
country whose reputation is not that of being among the most
'advanced' of the middle-class democracies. French employers
are the laughing-stock of the world: to push your argument to
the limit, we ought to ensure that we have the class struggle we
deserve.

In France, therefore, and today, since we must be precise,
actual conditions forbid the worker to use the formal rights
conceded to him. You are aware of this since it is you who have
so arranged things that he cannot make use of them within the
framework of our institutions: why wax indignant when he re-
nounces these mirages and turns militant? You who declaim
over the scandal when you are told that a trade union election
is made by a show of hands—it is you who have faked the law
so as to reduce to silence a good third of the electorate. You
have accused the CP, according to its interest at the moment,
of defending and attacking in turn democratic liberties, but in
what way do you act differently? When it is a question of

criticizing the Communists, you claim all liberties for the worker; you deprive him of them when he takes it upon himself to criticize you.

Nor is that the end of the matter: looked at properly, our liberties were conceived by the middle class for the middle class, and the worker seems to have no idea how to enjoy them without himself becoming middle-class. The liberties make no sense except in a system of private property, and the owner of goods takes precautions against the arbitrary actions of the group. The assumption is, therefore, that the group *already* exists. In point of fact, for two hundred years the middle classes have amused us with a something it calls 'social atomism'; but that is to mystify the poor: for it itself forms a strongly integrated community which exploits them. We should be born free and alone? We should form society by tying ourselves up contractually? We should bestow freedom so that it is returned to us a hundredfold without altogether renouncing our natal loneliness? Just look at us: lone beings? When do we sigh for solitude except in company? Free? Yes: free to carry on certain very concrete activities which have their source, as a rule, in our economic power or our social function. Free, the industrialist who can lay off a quarter of his work people without explanation; free the general who can decide on a murderous offensive; free the judge who can choose leniency or severity. *True* middle-class liberty, positive liberty, is the power of one man over another. Society decides this before we are born: it defines in advance our capacities and our duties: in short, it places us. It *ties* us to others. Finally, the most trivial of our gestures and the most unobtrusive trait in our character are in fact synthetic acts from which evolve in the particular circumstances the unity of the middle class; each instance of our behaviour reveals our logical relationship to a particular family or professional group; each conduces to integrate us the more closely within it.[42]

After which, what becomes of those unfortunate negative rights by which middle-class democracy claims to set such great store? If they hardly enrich us, there is no risk that they will impoverish us. They represent simply the safeguard of our concrete powers; they establish between each of us and the community an imperceptible distance, they prevent us from perishing by suffocation. But it is true that middle-class reality falls outside them: our industrialist does not dream of exercising only those rights he shares with everyone else: he uses the power which he alone can exert. *Habeas corpus?* He hardly gives it a thought: no one dreams of arresting him. His real freedom sails the seas: it is the machine he has just bought in the USA. Politics? He can amuse himself by voting for the radicals, abandoning them for the MRP, returning to them: he will not change his self. His self is his factory, his family, his plans. In our societies, in time of peace, the political bond is of the loosest, the most fragile: the slightest jolt breaks it. This is not surprising, if we criticize parties freely: to criticize is to step back, to get outside the group or the system, to consider them as objects; if we are members of a political formation, we are never *inside it.* But have you ever criticized to their face and in public your employer, your manager, your head clerk? Aren't you part of the undertaking, integrated into it? If you were to be expelled from it, you would lose at one stroke your means of livelihood, your credentials, your object in life. People talk freely about politics because it seems no more than a purely formal activity; on the surface, liberal government resembles the principle of identity: it allows each person to be what he is and to have what he has. But as soon as it is a question of work, of *praxis,* in short of a synthetic activity carried on by an inte-grated group, good-bye to freedom of thought. Now middle-class politics is *also* a synthetic action, a class action; in moments of crisis, when the middle classes are menaced by the people, this politics shows its true face: the sole aim of deputies' 'debates' is to amuse the public, and their pretended divisions mask the existence of a *single party,* a class party, as authori-tarian and inflexible as the CP, whose agents are the police, the civil service, and the army, and whose function it is to crush the resistance of the poor. In such moments, the bourgeois goes on until he has thrown his freedom of thought down the drain. What would he do with it? It is time to forget divisions, he is lost unless he thinks as everyone else does. Criticize? Nothing so foolish: to criticize is to run the risk of causing disunity, of hindering government action. He abandons his rights to a group of cleaners which in exchange guarantees him his real powers and his possessions.

But for the worker, politics cannot be a luxury activity: it is his sole defence, the sole means open to him of becoming integrated in a community. The bourgeois is integrated from the start, his loneliness is an affectation; the worker is alone from the start, and for him politics is a necessity. The first is a man who supports a party in order to exercise his right of citizenship, the second a 'sub-man' who joins a party in order to become a man. The one catches in flashes a glimpse of the *reality* of politics, that is to say, of the class struggle; the other from the beginning suffers from that struggle, he is the object of it, and he sometimes has a suspicion that he in his turn could take the lead. For the bourgeois, there is everything outside politics; for the worker there is nothing, nothing save that 'working-class melancholy' from which Navel said the only escape is through action. Melancholy, that is to say loneliness. Do not let us conclude, however, that this loneliness is *natural*: middle-class people, to persuade us that this is so, have focussed upon their 'social atomism'. But to understand the meaning of all this philosophy, it will be enough to glance at the preamble of Le Chapelier's law on the 'alleged common interests' of the workers. No: the loneliness of the workers does not come from nature; it is *produced*; work, weariness, wretchedness, the kindly care of the middle classes have, if I may say so, provided the workers with an artificial 'state of nature'; what is called *the mass*. Later I will set out in detail the processes of massification; what matters here is that they all aim at imposing loneliness—not the complete disappearance of social relations, but their mechanization. In this operation, democratic rights have an essential rôle: as we have seen, for an integrated middle class, they offer only advantages; for those who stand alone, ceaselessly exposed to the forces of disintegration, formal liberties are fetters. Look at the free contract, the master stroke of the mechanism, happily combining the threat of death with liberty to work; the worker signs the contract freely on pain of death. In this amalgam of need and independence, need prevents the wage-earner from discussing his price, freedom makes him responsible for what is imposed on him. What right has he to complain? He could reject the offer. In a general way, the free contract forces the worker to take on himself his appointed destiny: he consents to his fate, he accepts it. Did the employer look for him? Didn't he apply for work? Hasn't he accepted additional tasks? Hasn't he tried to improve his output? Doesn't he voluntarily increase the risk of sickness or accident? And isn't it he who, very criminally, lowered his demands in order to steal his neighbour's job? After that, who dare speak of solidarity?—it is the law of the jungle. Struggle of the classes? No, indeed: struggle for life. In short, he has done it all, is guilty of it all, this man who complains of wretchedness, loneliness, forced labour. Before the contract, he was only a victim; after signing it, he is an accomplice. Besides, he throws himself into irons in vain: no one owes him anything. The work once done and paid for, the two contracting parties are free again; neither has any recollection of the day before; the day after, they do not recognize one another. If a fall is recorded on Wall Street, a slight shock will be enough to shake off staff. The free contract transforms the worker into a detachable atom. When the British parliament, towards the middle of the nineteenth century, took it into its head to pass the first laws to protect the workers, there was only one cry: Protect the women and children, if you want to, but *not the men*! They are adult, rational, free: they can defend themeselves *unaided*. There is the word that counts: unaided. The freedom of the worker is his loneliness; no one can intervene in his favour without running the risk of enslaving him, and the government will ensure freedom to work so much the better as it strives the more to protect the workers against all protection, even that of their own trade unions.

The franchise will complete the matter: in these mechanical summonses called elections the worker finds no trace of the solidarity he seeks. It is a question of voting *in isolation*, for a programme he has not devised and of which he takes cognisance alone: the greatest number of solitary individuals carries him along: the majority. But the idea of winning does not unify: it is alike in each and every one; *identity* of opinion is brought no nearer. Will he allow himself to be persuaded that all politics can be reduced to this society game? Under the pretext of giving him access to culture, the middle class proceeds to infect him with individualism; with freedom of thought and expression, he will be put into touch with probabilism, tolerance, scepticism, objectivism: all opinions are worthy of respect, all have value; why choose one rather than another? He is

bewildered. Democratic liberties approve massification and give
the worker a legal *mass status*. The isolation of fact becomes the
loneliness of right.[13]

Liberty to criticize, to have doubts, to vote, to die of hunger:
do you believe that that is what he is looking for? He must
certainly be crazy to plunge into loneliness when what he wants
most is integration! Separate himself from his comrades and
take a step backwards in order to criticize their actions when
all he wants is to be confidently united with them? What about
the scepticism which confounds ideas and blows on the meanings of the universe when *precisely* everyday reality is absurd
and when what he passionately wants is that life and death
should have a meaning? It would seem that doubt and uncertainty are intellectual qualities; but he must struggle to change
his condition, and these intellectual virtues only paralyse action:
ask him to call in question the cause he serves or to die for it,
but not both at the same time. An action of some importance
demands unified leadership; and he, precisely, needs to believe
that there is a truth; as he cannot establish it by himself, he must
be able to have sufficient faith in his class leaders to agree to
take it from them. In short, on the first opportunity he will con-
sign to the devil these liberties which strangle him: not that he
does not want working-class power and independence; but he
places this independence, this power in the community; he
dreams of exercising it, but only in the name of the *proletariat*.

However, what can he do? Nothing: not even imagine this
fighting community in which he could take his place. Crushed by
middle-class strength, overwhelmed by the sense of his own
powerlessness, exhausted, where is he to find the germ of this
spontaneity which you demand of him? Action could take hold
of him, upset him, change his universe, but whence will such
action be born? For him, it is not a question of passing progressively from the less to the more; it is by an internal revolution that a man becomes a revolutionary. He will become a
different man only by a kind of conversion. And this abrupt
appearance of another universe and of another Me, the subject
of history, he cannot envisage it so long as he remains crushed
on his rock: how could passivity *imagine* activity? It is not difficult to be middle class: it is enough to choose the right uterus;
after that, just allow yourself to be carried along. Nothing more

difficult, on the other hand, than to be a *proletarian*: you simply assert yourself by thankless and painful action, passing beyond weariness and hunger, dying to be reborn. For action to be always possible, *praxis* must exist in the hearts of the masses themselves, as a call, an example, a kind of representation of what might be done. In short, an organization is required which shall be the pure and simple incarnation of *praxis*. Well, you will say, why not the trade union? I shall answer that question in the third part of this essay. But for the moment, trade union or no, what counts is that, by the very necessity of the situation, the organism which conceives, carries out, brings together, and distributes tasks—whether it be a revolutionary trade union or a party or both—cannot be conceived except as an *authority*. Far from being the delightful product of working-class spontaneity, it imposes itself imperatively on each *individual*. It must be an Order which imposes order and gives orders. 'Liberality', enthusiasm, if they do come, will come afterwards; but to begin with the Party represents for each one the most austere morals: it is a question of assenting to a new life, of casting off a present personality; weary, he is commanded to weary himself still more; powerless, to throw himself blindly against a stone wall. As long as he is still outside, the *praxis*, that is to say the approach to the class, appears to him to be a duty. But if it were necessary to justify the existence of a dominating and invariably over-exacting organization, I should base myself rather on necessity than on origin: if it were spontaneous, its authority would not be established; which proves that first impulses are the best? Instead of which the Party, wherever it comes from, derives its legitimacy from the fact that first of all it answers to a need. Without it, no unity, no action, no class. Naturally the great majority of workers do not go into it: who can be militant after ten hours of work at a factory? But they cause the class to be born when they obey all the leaders' orders. In exchange for the discipline which they observe, they have the right not to be bothered by 'debates'. Two trade union confederations, two or three working-class parties: each weakened by the others: when people are outside, what do they decide? They stay outside. You claim that the masses *do not demand* a single Party? You are right: the masses demand nothing at all, for they are only a dispersion. It is the Party which demands of the masses that, under its leadership, they should gather together into a class. And the watchword, 'single party', was launched not by the French CP, not even by Lenin, but right outside Marxism—by Blanquists like Vaillant. The first National Congress of socialist movements put forward as its aim, in 1899, the realization of 'the political and economic Organization of the Proletariat in a class party for the Conquest of Power'.

If the class is neither the total of the exploited nor the Bergsonian impulse which stirs them up, whence would you expect it to come if not from the work men carry out on themselves? The unity of the proletariat is in its connexion with the other classes of society, it is its *struggle*, but this struggle, inversely, has a meaning only through unity; each worker, through the class, defends himself against the whole society which crushes him; and conversely it is by this struggle that the class is created. The unity of the working class is therefore its historical and moving link with the community, in so far as this link is realized by a synthetic act of unification which, necessarily, is distinguished from the mass as the pure action of passion. When it was a question only of transforming opposition and rivalry into community of interests, it was certainly necessary—unless we are to suppose all the workers to be touched at the same time by grace—that a principle of linkage should act simultaneously in many places and guarantee to each one the sincerity of all. That does not mean, of course, that the militant does not come from the mass: but if he does come from it, he is marked off from it. The man in the mass is still weighed down by his special interests, the man out of it must tear himself away from them, the organ of linkage must be pure action; if he admits the least germ of division, if he still preserves in himself some passivity—sluggishness, interests, divergent opinions— who then will unify the unifying apparatus? Ideally it should be a pure linkage, the relationship which arises when two workers are together.[44] In a word, the Party *is* the very movement which unites the workers by drawing them on towards seizure of power. How then can you expect the working class to repudiate the CP? It is true that outside the working class it is nothing, but if it were to disappear, that class would fall back into dust.

Is it to be understood that the worker is passive? Quite the contrary. He transforms himself into action when he enters the class and can assert his freedom only in action. But this freedom is a concrete and positive power: the power of finding out, of going further, of taking the initiative, of putting forward solutions. It is only by *going beyond* the immediate situation through movement together that this freedom can enrich it; freedom to criticize, by contrast, not only causes the leader of the cell or the trade union delegate to frown; it also makes each individual afraid *of the others*, recalling as it does previous loneliness and dissension. It must at least be understood that criticism, when it is tolerated, cannot spring from spontaneity or the 'revolutionary instinct': the worker, transformed by the organization into its subject, finds his practical reality from the time of his metamorphosis; whatever he thinks or does is from the time of his *conversion*; and that, in its turn, takes place within the framework of Party policy. His freedom, which is simply his power to go beyond what is given him—in other words, to act— is shown therefore at the heart of the essential reality which is the organization; he forms his thoughts on the problems presented to him by the Party in accordance with the principles given to him by the Party. In short, he does not judge the Party in the light of a policy whose principles, produced by his spontaneous reaction or by the contradictions of middle-class society, are engraved on his unconscious; drawn on, formed, raised above himself by the Party, he finds his freedom only in the power to go beyond each particular situation by acts within the organization and towards the common aim. In a sentence, it may be said that the Party is his freedom. In France today, a worker can express and realize himself only in class action led by the CP; he is formed by the reasoning of the CP, by its ideology and its principles; if he wanted to turn against Communist policy, they would in themselves tend to justify that policy. If a serious mistake is made or a defeat endured, he has no tools with which to understand its meaning, no forewarning of it; he simply loses his hold, his effort wanes, he falls back into the field of middle-class attraction; the class disintegrates. But having fallen back, he re-discovers, in the action of enemy forces, his despair, his ignorance and the sense of his powerlessness. The Party is formed anew, far from him, inaccessible, an imperative not to be judged, simply found *too hard*, inhuman, in the sense in which it could be said that Kant's ethics were inhuman. Which comes back to declaring that all class action has become impossible.

'To sum up,' says the anti-Communist, 'we said the working class repudiated the Party; you say that the Party has reduced the workers to despair. We don't feel inclined to continue these useless and protracted discussions.'

I concede nothing. Like everyone else, I notice the discouragement of the masses; but I am not yet sure that it is due to the policy of the CP. And then, between our two interpretations, I see an abyss; if you find only a verbal difference, that is because you look down on the working class. A proletariat, healthy and cool, which would repudiate the CP and immediately form a new party (you know, that famous truly French Communist Party, which would be distinguished from the actual French Communist Party by its independence, and would reveal its national character by restoring to life true internationalism): if such a proletariat existed, cognisance would have to be taken of its wishes: who could decide if not it? A proletariat returned to its natural standing of atomism, but still impetuous and always ready to re-form, to take up the struggle again, you could, at the worst, hope to fob it off with your rubbish, and, who knows, offer it a change of Party. But you know very well that the working class is breaking down, that it feels the measure of its own powerlessness, that it is in danger of delivering up its millions, defenceless, to the power hammers of the middle class; you know that, in the coming months, everything that will increase loneliness, resignation, and the distance between men will be brought into play against it, in order to turn the proletariat into an archipelago. When the workers have touched the bottom of bitterness and disgust, do you really believe you could put about your claptrap? I have already told you: if they lose confidence in the CP, they will distrust all politics; the universe will be bourgeois. And if you hope they will climb up the slope again, only the CP can help them to do so; if they rejoin their union, it will be to gather again round the CP; their pugnacity will be used in obeying its orders. Already it is whispered, 'Are you mad! To want an independent left linked with the Party! Do you want the Party to recover its influence over the masses?

If not, let well alone, quietly; leave the disintegration to go on; one day the Party will fall to pieces.' Fortunately things have not yet reached that point: but when they are at their worst and if you are the irreconcilable enemy of the Party, I cannot prevent myself from finding despicable those who wait for Communist collapse through the workers' despair. I am told that the worker will pull himself together, that I have not appreciated the French proletariat's powerful drive; upon my word, it should have a psychological outline: it should be known for its hibernations followed by abrupt awakenings. Look at 1848, 1870, 1936, 1948. I look: but rather than the violence of an explosive disposition, I discover in these battles the effect of definite factors; and in the 'sleep' which followed them, I see the effect of defeat and the Terror; working-class strength, on each occasion, has been overwhelmed, and it took long years to build it up again. If you are to be believed, there is no occasion for anxiety. In twenty, fifty years, we shall see arise a new reborn proletariat. In short, patience is the thing: after all, life is not so bad, and anti-Communism pays.

Good. Let us wait then. Twenty years, if you like. Unless, in six months, the Third World War breaks out. In which event it may well be that there will be no one at the meeting place: neither you nor I, nor a liberated proletariat, nor France.

III. THE CAUSES

I have shown that the discouragement of the workers should not be taken as even an implicit condemnation of Communist policy. It remains to discover the reason for it. That is my aim now.[45]

It is possible to evade the question in two ways both of which proceed from the same fallacy. The anti-Communist 'of the left' will not even hear of working-class lassitude: he depicts for us a proletariat of steel plunged to the hilt in middle-class carrion. The anti-Communist 'of the right' depicts the middle class as a young giant carrying in his arms a dying proletariat. Both pass over in silence anything resembling reciprocal conditioning: in short, they deny the class struggle.

The anti-Communist 'of the left' is on visiting terms with the French middle class; he willingly agrees that its national character has been produced by circumstances. As for the French proletariat, he simply denies its existence: there exists only the proletariat-in-itself, to be observed simultaneously in all capitalist countries. How could this proletariat be wearied? And what connexion could this distinct product of capitalism-in-itself have with our regrettably empirical middle class? The one is formed little by little by the action of accidental and therefore negligible factors. (We may cite, among other things, the Revolution of 1789.) Determined exclusively by the contradictions of capitalism, the history of the other is confined to reflecting successive changes in manufacturing industry. Our middle class stampedes and recovers its courage, makes mistakes and repairs them, manages its affairs well or ill; the proletariat never loses or gains the battle, never makes a mistake and never discovers individual truth. Irresistible, incompressible, everlasting, it ripens. Relentlessly. It is the most terrible enemy of capitalism-in-itself. It is impossible to see what harm it could do the French middle class: they will never meet.

This concept would permit some saving in historical explanation—and perhaps in all explanation—if its advocates had not taken it into their heads to denounce, over and above it, the crimes of the CP. Without the CP the French proletariat would have no empirical history: the Party has embedded itself in the working class like the grain of sand in Cromwell's bladder. What then? A disease of the proletariat-in-itself? The answer to that is that the proletariat-in-itself has no disease: it can neither restrain nor accelerate the movement-in-itself which animates it. No: its misfortunes spring from a very historical failing of its leaders. Had Stalin's heart been softer, it would have changed the face of the world. And don't ask how the empirical militants of the CP can throw out of gear the mechanism of an intelligible proletariat: through starting to hunt history, the anti-Communist is compelled in the end to re-introduce it in the most absurd form, as a succession of accidents, so as to account for the distance separating reality from his expectations.

As for me, I hold that the development of capital, taken as a whole, accounts for the features common to all working-class movements. But these considerations of principle will never in themselves explain the particular marks of the class struggle in France or in England between such and such dates. A concrete fact is, in its way, the singular expression of universal relationships; but it can be explained in its singularity only by singular reasons: to want to deduce it from an absolute but empty knowledge or from a formal principle of development is to waste time and labour. Actually, there are dialectics and they are in the facts; it is for us to discover them there and not to put them in. I have spoken of discouragement: if you want to prove that I am deceiving myself, you must establish by evidence that the workers have retained their 'pugnacity'. And when that has been established, this sustained courage would remain a particular mental state and, like discouragement, would require a particular explanation. The French proletariat is an historical reality whose singularity is shown, in recent years, by a certain attitude: I do not have to look for the key to that attitude in the universal movement of societies, but in the movement of French society, that is to say in the history of France.

The anti-Communists 'of the right' reach the same conclusions by inverse reasoning: over against the workers of flesh and blood they place eternal France, the one, you appreciate, which leaps forward so splendidly, which a heaven-sent man always saves at the last moment; sprightly, alive, alert, always busy, always running, it resembles the Magdalen. Knights and captains of industry, merchants, black-coated workers and country people: they all sing, they all work, they all take part in the bustle. Just one dead weight: the proletariat. France looks round: 'What prevents my workers from following me?' And what do you suppose it to be if it isn't the Communist Party? Since it has our destruction in mind, there is no need to be surprised that it has undertaken to brutalize the French worker. He, certainly, is not altogether a dupe: in flashes he recovers the good sense of his fathers, and appreciates that his interests are bound up with those of his employers; all he really wants is to work in order to skim off his just share of the national income. But the Communists have thrown his mind into confusion: though they do not succeed in setting him against his worthy masters, they retain enough strength to hold him back from joining forces with them. Divided between the distrust inspired in him by the CP and by his employer, he grows rigid, like a victim of tetanus. How far we could go, how much we could do if the virus filtering from Stalinism had not infected our proletariat!

Beautiful rats, do you hope to make us believe that France is immortal? Do you think you can long hide from us that it is dying? The evil which paralyses the proletariat started by striking the whole of society. You who are talking, are you so much alive? Your tail still moves when the word 'Communist' is pronounced in front of you but your body is flabby and cast down; everyday it grows colder. And the others? All the others? Where are our great hopes, our great ambitions, our great ventures? The peasant scratches the earth with his hands, the manufacturer stagnates, the banks have converted themselves into savings banks. We live badly, very badly: the pay of one out of two Frenchmen does not exceed the minimum living wage; the young suffocate or go abroad, saying there is no longer anything to do in France. And the government? Does it govern? Keeping up dissension by lies, faking the electoral law, imprisoning opponents, forbidding their sons entry to higher education, establishing over our divisions the crafty and hypocritical dictatorship of weakness, putting off indefinitely the passing of social laws, making promises to state employees and officials, then refusing to keep them, crushing the country under the weight of an absurd financial system: can that pass for an internal policy? To carry off the Malagasy chiefs by aeroplane in order to drop them on the roofs of their villages; to sprinkle the Vietnamese with napalm and to pillage in Vietnam; to impale Tunisians on bottles; to fire point blank on Moroccan workers: can that pass for a colonial policy? Swallowing milliards in a war which is known to be lost, continued in default of daring not to end it, and passed from one minister to another like the pox, faking French sovereignty, accepting domination by the United States over half the world and German supremacy in Europe: can that pass for a foreign policy? Are they statesmen, these Catholics with girls' nerves who swoon when they address parliament, roll under banqueting tables and take themselves for Richelieu because they have blood on their hands? These socialists who order miners on strike to be fired on; these great patriots who traffic in piastres; these illiterate and bloated flunkeys, always ready for boot-licking or putting up their backsides at an adequate price. . . . If they remain in power, no one in middle-class France will take any further interest in politics. Remember, in 1952, how the newspapers shouted 'Victory' because only five million electors abstained from voting at the elections! You speak of apathy when the workers stand aloof from a demonstration: what do you say when the electors stand aloof from the ballot box? In the France of today, the only class with a doctrine is the working class, the only one whose 'particularism' is in full harmony with the interests of the nation; a great party represents it, the only one which has included in its programme the safeguarding of democratic institutions, the re-establishment of national sovereignty, and the defence of peace, the only one which pays attention to economic rebirth and an increase in purchasing power, the only one, in fact which *is alive*, which crawls with life when the others are crawling with worms; and you ask by what miracle the workers follow most of its orders? For myself, I pose the inverse question, and ask what prevents them from following it always. There is no doubt about the reply: if the proletariat gives signs of exhaustion, it is because it has been overcome by the national anaemia. To struggle against this evil which enfeebles France and preys on us all, it is not enough to range ourselves beside the working class; it is necessary also to understand the disease from its causes. Leaving eternal France at grips with the Proletariat-in-itself, I propose to explain certain events, strictly defined in time and space, by the peculiar structure of our economy, in its turn defined by certain events of our history.

We live badly because we produce too little at too high prices. You ask whose fault this is? Well, you could blame Germany, which declared two ruinous wars on us; Russia which, from Moscow, puts the brake on reconstruction; those who opt out of birth and, by refusing to be born, deprive us of their future custom; the backward peasants who don't make up their minds to consume; in fact, the subsoil which has betrayed France by sliding away under its feet. In short, everyone is guilty with the exception of the ruling class.

This, indeed, is what bothers me: too many traitors. So many causes, so badly linked: a concurrence of chances. Is France dying by chance? We will return at leisure to the Muscovite and the worker. But is it conceivable that our stagnation is due to the two world wars? From 1913 to 1929, in spite of fifty-two months of devastation, French production increased by thirty per cent; since then it has remained stationary up to today, that is to say, for a quarter of a century: in the same period [1939–1952] Britain increased its production by half. So what? It is said that we have been marking time since 1929: whatever the evils that overwhelm us, is it not absurd to seek the reason for them in a disaster which occurred ten years after their first manifestations? The origin of such a continuous deterioration must have been due to a structural flaw, to bad workmanship.

The subsoil, then? No. Let us leave that to the speleologists and the potholers. Blame coal, petroleum, non-ferrous metals for concealing themselves abroad like vulgar capital when, for our merits, it was their duty to bury themselves under our feet: you will be no further. Nature has betrayed us? That's too bad; only at the same time it betrayed the whole of Europe, and consider: equally betrayed, the Belgians, the Swiss, the Scandinavians live better than we do. As for the British, at the end of the other war, they had good reason to raise the cry, 'Traitor!'

While their backs were turned, their ungrateful customers left them in the lurch: they bought American coal, Japanese cottons, German steel. If Britain ought to have done then what we are doing today, it would have fallen back on its dunghill, helping on its own ruin, prophesying meanwhile, but without lifting a finger in exorcism. It had every excuse: its old, splendid industry seemed the very bones of the nation: is it possible to change one's bone structure? Britain did change it: since the old foundations of its industrial preponderance had been sapped, it made up its mind to change in order to remain the same, to maintain production by turning its production topsy-turvy; in twenty years, it visibly transformed its anatomy and its physiology, reversed its demographic trends, regrouped and redistributed its man-power, abandoned its mine shafts and its mining villages, and turned deliberately to the manufacture of high quality products. Is our problem so different? For us too, it was a question of working on a problem that could not be attacked frontally, and of intensifying production by recasting our economy. But we are persuaded by inspired propaganda that our make-up is unalterable so that we may be diverted in advance from modifying it: France has soft bones, Pott's disease; above all when lying down: the least effort made by the invalid, and its vertebrae break. In short, we are required to believe that the moon is made of green cheese and to accept Nature as Destiny. Don't let us believe anything of the kind: Nature shuffles the cards and deals them, gives each one his hand but not the way he plays it; Nature puts questions but does not know the answers, indicates the direction of the economy but does not govern it. Even better: the economy creates Nature quite as much as Nature creates the economy. Industrialization can take many forms and paucity of natural resources does not *a priori* exclude them all: to begin with, we know that France, unlike Victorian Britain, could never begin to base its whole production on its mining industries; but was there any prohibition against the promotion of processing industries? Could it not have specialized? Developed at the same time the import of raw materials and the export of finished products? The problem was swiftly declared insoluble; but how do we know that since, until these last few years, this has very carefully not been stated? We can acquit the mineral kingdom: men have made the French economy, are making it day by day; our downfall, like our ancient greatness, is a human venture and we are at the same time its victim and its makers.

Suppose we heap everything on to the consumer's back? On this side, the narrowness of our internal market should keep down production to a certain threshold beyond which disposal of products could not be assured. Good idea! Its principal merit is that it leads us back to the human kingdom. The peasant consumes little: that's a fact, at least in the southern half of the country. But barring faith in eternal France and belief in the perpetuity of the French 'character', I do not see that the shrinkage of our markets can be treated as a first cause. We should be a nation of skinflints? You want a laugh. If the farmers fulfil badly their 'social duty as buyers', is it not, perhaps, rather that they live on the products of their land? What constrains them to that? Why, of course, continual diminution in their purchasing power. You want to know whence, in its turn, comes this progressive impoverishment? From the fact that, quite simply, working the fields no longer pays. Here we are sent back from consumption to production. Will you say that it is their fault and that, instead of buying tractors, they are obstinately set in their habits? That is true. But, in societies as in reciprocal machines, conditioning is reciprocal; in the stagnation of consumption must be seen an effect as well as a cause, or rather a cause which is at the same time the effect of its own effects. Let us reason in a clockwise direction: farmers buy few tractors, therefore few are produced; and since the market is too limited to redeem the costs of re-equipment, factories making agricultural machinery have no interest in modernizing themselves. Conclusion: tractors cost a lot because the farmers eschew mechanization. The reasoning is correct and, into the bargain, wonderfully adapted to encourage inertia: by choosing the farmer straight away as independent variable, you deprive yourself of all means of acting on him. Let us in passing bow to this fine example of reactionary pessimism: niggardliness and habit are part of peasant nature; therefore our economy will not change.

Now let us reason in the inverse direction: as long as the index of industrial prices remains above that of agricultural prices, small rural proprietors will not have the means to mod-

ernize their methods of cultivation; if they stand aloof from
mechanization, that is because it stands aloof from them, and
their habits will never be changed unless, to begin with,
machines are put within their reach. This second conclusion, as
legitimate as the first, has the additional advantage of being
practical: it opens the outlet which the other closed. But, you
will say, isn't the peasant himself held up by constriction of the
agricultural market? Yes, certainly. But we find again, on this
new ground, the same circularity of effects and causes. In the
clockwise direction, it is never possible to dispose of the harvest:
therefore France produces too much corn; in the inverse direction, the French are underfed, therefore France does not produce enough. Since it is necessary to change, let us change. But
where to begin? Is primacy with the offer or the demand? That
depends on what is understood by 'consumer'. Are our producers thinking of yesterday's customer or of tomorrow's? And
who are these exasperating buyers who are evading their duty:
is it the close-fisted rich, or the poor who cannot pay? Last
century, the manufacturer boasted that he created needs in
order to satisfy them. 'In a competitive system,' he used to say,
'production is increased to reduce costs. The narrowness of
markets is only a provisional accident: a market can be conquered, or created. Since there are forty million Frenchmen, we
have forty million customers. It is true that most of them are
consumers who don't know it. That is of no consequence: we
shall make them conscious buyers. If necessary, we shall go and
seek them out at home and, however little they can spend, we
shall ask them to spend still less.' In short, production depended
on the provision of tools and governed consumption; demand
varied in terms of supply. And it was on the continuous enrichment of the nation that capitalism based its sole justification, on
the great myth of progress. In other countries, the movement of
a competitive economy had to find its logical outcome in mass
production aimed at a mass market, the market being in theory
identical with the whole nation.[46]

Good. But what about today? In the France of 1954, demand
should condition supply? That was true in the days of the
Crusades: a stratified society whose economy was dominated by
agriculture offered a fixed and customary circle of buyers to
artisans who worked in traditional ways. Have we got back to

that? And can it be that our employers no longer believe in progress? In that event, how can they justify their privileges in their own eyes? Each year, for the last twenty-five years, they have lamented that consumption remains stationary. The fine excuse: we are living on what there is. When we are all dying of hunger, how could we eat more since we are not given any more to eat? It is true that children will not leave the hovels their parents lived in. But where could they go, since no one will build? Neither destiny nor human nature is responsibe for the strangling of the market; and production, whatever may be said, has not ceased to regulate consumption: but, with us, instead of stimulating it, it applies the brake. Everyone has heard of those night clubs where champagne costs a mint of money because the management wants to 'keep the clientèle select'. France has come to resemble them: it is the élite who consume, and prices are all specially studied so that we continue to be among ourselves; housing is refused to the homeless, food to the starving, footgear to the barefoot. The time is near when notices will be put up in the windows of bakers' shops: 'If you want to buy bread, correct dress is essential.' This at least seems clear: if consumption, half strangled, turns on production to stifle it in its turn, it was production that started the process; therein dwells the underlying defect of our economy.

This defect stares you in the face, provided you look for it where it is: it is called decentralization. In the United States, since 1930 factories employing more than 260 wage-earners have represented four per cent of the total number of undertakings and absorbed more than half the labour force. Among us, in 1953, managements which gave work to more than 100 wage -earners absorbed only forty-six per cent of the total labour-force and represented only a hundredth of French industry. Around several giants, micro-organisms swarm: in Paris, for metal processing alone there are 18,000 firms which together employ 400,000 workers. In trade, decentralization is even more marked: establishments with more than 100 wage-earners employ 12 per cent of the workers and represent 0·1 per cent of the total. Everyone knows these facts; from them it can only be concluded that France is a museum piece, contemporaneous with the Moral Order that went with gas lighting: this mechanism with its numberless wheels would seem to survive by a whim of history and to continue to obey the laws of last century. From which some are of the opinion that we shall suffer the fate of Athens, others that God is French.

They are all mistaken: our economy belongs to its own era, and the nineteenth century could not have produced it; to give it its wrinkles and its rather old-fashioned appearance, nothing less would suffice than the powerful devices we possess today. Certainly at first sight some 500,000 French firms with their eight to ten million wage-earners conjure up the palmy times of liberalism; but that is only an illusion. The liberal economy was determined by competition, which normally leads to concentration, rather than by diffusion. In order to preserve the archaic decentralization of our shops and factories, competition has therefore had to be suppressed: mining operations could not continue to exist if the manufacturing industries did not hold themselves aloof from absorbing them. In short, large firms have agreed to sell as dear as small ones. In this situation, small businesses are forbidden to enter into competition with one another: a truce *sine die* and peaceful cohabitation are imposed on them. From Dunkirk to Menton, prices are controlled by more or less secret groups which gather together a multitude of petty tradesmen and shopkeepers round a few large mounds of tinned food. To drive its tiny rivals to ruin, big business need only increase production a little. It takes good care not to, and if it sometimes decides to freshen up its equipment, that is not in order to produce more and sell more cheaply, but to increase profits by reducing manufacturing costs.

Whatever trouble it takes to spare its neighbours, this is useless unless it protects them effectively against crises: the least puff of wind will sweep them away. It therefore feeds them by the beakful—at the expense of the consumer: there is no doubt that a factory in Lyons could decrease its costs appreciably if it had the weaving and throwing done in its own workshops: it prefers to put out these processes to scattered firms which depend entirely on this work. But that is still not enough: the State must come in on these good works, increasing tax reliefs and subsidies, strengthening customs control. The State, that is to say the taxpayers and, to put it shortly, the whole of France.

The financial system has as its principal function the redistribution of the revenue: but this redistribution, among us, benefits firms which the normal play of competition would have wiped out. The Frenchman pays taxes so that he can buy national products at an enhanced price. Over the money that remains to him—supposing that he does retain any after these various deductions in advance—a special providence watches. Like that angel of Claudel's who untiringly diverts the young Prouhèze from the young Rodrigue in order to return her to an old man's bed, the angel of Malthusianism never tires of diverting new investments towards the most decrepit firms. To discover this, try to finance a company about to be formed: you will be made to repent your pigheadedness. 'What's your idea? To take part in the development of production? But who asked you to do that? Are we going to develop production when manufacturing industries don't make any move for fear of crushing home industries? Fortunately manufactured goods are very dear; that's natural since they are produced at great expense. Better to patch up the old machines: they were there when we were born and are still usable.' If you insist, the banks take a hand: take them your savings and they will give them to the State which will swallow them up in the funds of the National Debt. In short, the money of the poor is stolen, and, not content with that, the money of the rich is sterilized. From that point, everything is in order: out-of-date machinery, high costs of production; industrial prices rise in a spiral, agricultural customers desert the market. Rustics in their turn, using decrepit tools, produce at great expense and the rise in agricultural prices deprives agriculture of customers in the towns. A fine circle—see how effects reinforce causes: one branch of industry cuts down its productive activity, thus depriving certain undertakings of their normal outlets and so instigates contraction of the market; if they are to survive, the undertakings affected retrench in their turn, and this will entail new contractions; this gyrating depression will in the end return to its point of departure, inciting the factories which started it to new restrictions. Thus consumption adapts itself to production and production, in return, adjusts itself to consumption. The motor turns; but there is one annoyance: it goes more slowly at each revolution, and in the end stops.

When a social system is the object of so much care and claims such sacrifices, can it be maintained that it is the fruit of chance? The heavy mechanism would have got out of order long since if some one had not kept an eye on it; the cumbersome multiplicity of its wheels would have been simplified in use without intervention by an invisible hand. Put in another way, the 'managed' decentralization of our undertakings assumes unity of intention and unity of policy, that is, the secret unification of our economy. In France as in the United States, big business controls all sectors of the national life. The difference is that the Americans have killed off their small employers while we preserve ours in chains. They live, but only just, and their submissiveness has been assured by persuading them that they are already dead and would fall to dust if their permit to live were not regularly renewed. For this reason our economic system presents a distant resemblance to feudalism. Against competition, harsher every day, against crises, against the savagery of the barons, an always denser crowd of petty tradesmen and shopkeepers seeks protection. They end by offering their goods to big business, receiving them back immediately in the form of fiefs in vassalage after they have in the meantime been branded. At present, they have no more than a life interest in their shops and factories. Or could you call them owners, these wretched vavasours who drudge hard, painfully cut down their expenses, are their own hirelings? What can they do? Expand? Renew their equipment? Rationalize their undertaking? Produce or sell more? Nothing of the kind. Yet these reprieved dead are the 'men' of the great lord of industry: in exchange for a protection which keeps them from falling in turn into the proletariat, they have to render services of a very special order: their function is to save the face of competitive capitalism by covering up monopolies. Anachronistic, our economy? Say rather that it is aberrant: this system, artificially created and maintained by the watchful care of our big capitalists, aims at the integration of productive strength: but for technical concentration it substitutes centralization hidden by controlling agencies.

Let us try to understand why our feudal grandees are so bent on ruining France. It may be noted that they have an answer all ready: 'It is,' they say, 'to limit waste. Suppose the "factory" had committed the mistake of opening weaving sheds. A crisis occurs: it would find it difficult to close them. On the other hand, it is easy to drop the suppliers: the small employers are the future victims of elastic defence.' But these remarks are not very enlightening. Could it be declared more ingenuously that we are throwing ourselves into the water for fear of the rain? In the event of a sharp shock, this encirclement gives large companies a certain liberty of manoeuvre, but if the circumstances are favourable, they cannot profit from it. Should demand grow tomorrow, the small business will be incapable of satisfying it: and big industry has linked its fate with them. On a steep gradient, the prudent motorist puts his motor into low gear: thus our wise producers, fearful lest production should run away, put a brake on it with their own machines. They find the future full of menace and never of promise: there will be crises, and more crises, catastrophes, and then the deluge; they shrink into themselves so as to offer a smaller surface to disaster. Increase the national income? You are quite right, they jeer at that idea: they dream less of increasing their own incomes than of preventing them from falling; they anticipate the worst. The Marxist explanation of over-production and periodical crises is well known: in a competitive system, invested profits work out as growing means of production, and consumption by wage-earners goes on decreasing. Have our leading capitalists read *Capital*? In order to avoid crises, they have twisted the neck of competition, organized underproduction, and re-invest their profits abroad. Thus they have produced a depressive economy through fear of depression.

The process has been successful thanks to the small employers' co-operation. They conceal from the consumer Malthusianism in high places. Compelled to pay their work people very badly and to sell their products very dearly, they must go bust or settle prices and wages. If the government aspires to regulate the market, one bureaucrat's stroke of the pen may well wreck 500,000 undertakings. Besides, these petty tradesmen have strong lungs: if a minister dares to tax them, they will cry murder; if their workers call for a rise in wages, they will prove, with figures, that they haven't the means to grant it. And that is not altogether false since they are always on the point of bankruptcy. They alone are seen, they alone are heard, it seems that the nation's one business is to occupy itself with them; these noisy persons at death's door provide us day by day with the proof that nothing can be changed in France for fear everything should fall to the ground. Meanwhile, sheltered behind them, the big employer proceeds to the scientific organization of his factories: if he were willing to push his machines to the limit, prices would immediately slump; but he finds it more to his advantage to ensure a profit without risk by increasing to the furthest limit the distance between his costs and market prices.[47] As to do this it is necessary to keep an important fraction of French industry at its lowest potential, he solemnly recognizes the nominal ownership by small operators of their undertakings, that is to say, he perpetuates their impotence and the fragmentation of our resources; in return the petty tradesmen comply with their function, which it to produce little at great expense: this unjustified excess profit thus has the character of an annuity paid by small industry to great.

In this way our middle class rises in the social scale: it prefers comfort and stability to an undefined increase of profits; our feudal grandees are just simply people living on unearned income. However, there must be some explanation of this conservatism. Is it possible that our distrust of the future is confined to fear of future crises? Of course, our evolution must be put back into the European framework: the period of expansion has come to an end, Europe is losing its markets one after the other, everywhere is to be observed the tendency to change profit for unearned income. But why has this general contraction reached, with us, such a marked point? How explain the Malthusian frenzy from which we are in process of dying? I believe our history provides the answer.

History moves forward masked: when it unmasks, it brands actors and witnesses for ever; we have never recovered from the two 'moments of truth' which France knew in the nineteenth century and our middle class is playing a losing game today because it caught sight of its true face in 1848 and 1871.

Under the July Monarchy, the French people was composed of middle-class persons and animals; the king was middle class, and the middle class was king, the bourgeois was man and man

was bourgeois. The animal was an animal; he was harnessed
to machines. Often enough, hunger chased him through the
streets: he was calmed by letting dogs loose. And then, one day,
everything changed; that was in June 1848. The government
heard a din and put its nose out of the window: instead of the
usual cattle, it saw an army; the proletariat was bursting into
official history and fighting its first pitched battle. What a
shock: these brutes were fighting like men; everyone was struck
by the evident coherence of their manoeuvres. Those in possession found themselves confronting man of a species strange to
them: there lay the origins of their great fear. Since that other
creature claimed to have become man, humanity as a whole
became something different, and the bourgeois recognized
himself, in the eyes of that other creature, as other than man.
If the wretched were part of the human species, they were
different only by the violence they were made to suffer; suddenly middle-class man was defined by those he rejected: in
arrogating to himself the right to lay down the limits of the
species, he had set his own limits; if these excluded creatures
were, in their turn, to make themselves the measure of man, he
would see his humanity in those others as an inimical force.
Rarely had a question been better posed: sub-men had infiltrated into the human race; they must be dislodged from it.
But how? By hanging the leaders? That would not be enough:
the middle class had lost its untroubled certainties and would
not regain them unless once again it found itself alone in the
world. And then, if a massacre had been begun, it would have
been dangerous not to carry it through to the end: the slaughterers would not be acquitted unless they took care to get rid
of all the witnesses. In short, the only thing to exterminate
the working class. The business augured well: mad with rage
and shame, the middle class stripped bare wanted to put out
the eyes of the proletariat; the National Guard made a point
of shooting the wounded. Unfortunately repression stopped
too soon. The élite was dismayed: with ten million dead it would
have recovered its innocence; 1,500 shot transformed it into a
band of assassins. When all was over, it was so very much
afraid to see itself and to be seen that it gave up its political
rights to a gang of cleaners which in return guaranteed it its
right of ownership. Atrocious crimes attributed to the dead

were clear evidence of their bestiality; the survivors were kept in their brutish condition. All those in possession conceived a strong aversion to capital: to purify it, it was cut up into pieces; a rise in rents was all that was necessary to drive the poor beyond the town walls. The workers disappeared from official history. Nevertheless, they continued to live, packed in shadowy areas surrounding the towns. From time to time, their eyes glittered: then, quickly, the pack was fired into. It was not enough to deprive them of speech; memory must be taken from them too. A vain hope: they preserved their recollections jealously, and that prevented the middle class from getting rid of its own: not for a moment did it forget its terrors nor the horrible vision it had had, nor the blood in which it had drenched itself. This was clear when, at the fall of the Empire, its representatives, obsessed by funk and resentment, refused to sit in Paris. The rising exasperated but did not surprise them: they had been expecting it. One moment obliterated the relaxation of twenty years; it came back to the question of principle: they or we? In the eyes of their prisoners—those steady eyes which the beautiful ladies of Versailles practised putting out with the points of their parasols—the sons discovered the unbearable truth that had maddened their fathers. The interrupted carnage was resumed: with 20,000 shot and 13,000 imprisoned, of whom 3,000 died in gaol, the French middle class demonstrated to the world at large the improvement in its techniques of extermination.

It has had cause to rue this: despite its performance, it had repeated the mistake of 1848 and, for the second time, had stopped too soon: instead of wiping out the enemy, it had only won a battle and was in danger of losing a war of attrition. However, Europe watched it with amazement: in the exploitation of man, foreign employers could give us points; only— was it skill or clemency?—they had, as a rule, avoided recourse to arms. British capitalists would never have consented to kill the working man with their own hands; they contented themselves with brutalizing him, and for the rest allowed natural laws to take their course; workers grow tired, and the trouble of wiping them out can be left to God. These people did not forgive France for having revealed the nature of capitalism and changed the class struggle into civil war. Their contempt made our middle class feel very much alone: it would gladly have boasted of having carried out in twenty-five years the two prettiest massacres in contemporary history, but the puritans of Germany and Britain treated it like a black sheep. When it cried, 'Let us make common cause,' they moved aside holding their noses. To crown all, life had to be lived from day to day mixed up indiscriminately with the victims: and these victims emancipated themselves in an odd way, thanks to the good offices of Cavaignacs and Galliffets. Fifty years earlier, the workers had besought the employer to lean down and see their wretchedness, certain that to see their troubles would be enough to make him wish to cure them; in 1848 they still believed Lamartine who had spoken of the 'tragic misunderstanding which separates the classes'. After 1871, they understood; so much the worse for the middle class. Besides, the masters knew how to remain invisible, to stand aside in face of what they called 'the hard necessities of a liberal economy'. That is why the worker does not really hate them—abstractions can be hated only with an abstract hatred. Besides, even when he would hate them, his hatred includes his own incapacity: he knows they regard him as a brute which pretends to be human and which must be kept perpetually under restraint, but he regards them as men who do not know themselves, or do not want to. However violent the Revolution for which he hopes, it has never been his purpose to exterminate his class enemies: liquidation of the middle class should free its members from their ignorance and from middle-class separateness so that they may recover their humanity. It is not the man in them that he detests, but the privative idea, the negation of man: so long as the struggle is carried out in the economic sphere, the hatred of the worker remains generalized.[48]

In 1848 and 1871, the French middle class, obviously stunned, emerged from the clouds. Certainly capitalism, like all forms of oppression, maintains itself by violence: but there was no need for *that* violence or *that* savagery in repression: in 1848 the rising of the wretched was not a danger to the employers; in 1871 negotiations had been started, conciliation remained possible: if the people of Versailles rejected all possibilities, if they were the first to pass to the attack, it was because they wanted to kill. In a word, they showed zeal. Our middle class allowed itself to be distinguished by the insolence and cruelty of its officials, by the timorous cruelty of its politicians, by the harshness of owners and manufacturers, by the abject terror it first exhibited after victory, by the vile glee of its charming newspapers and its upright ladies; its actions carved its face: it was incarnate. Suddenly, working-class hatred became incarnate in its turn: the object of this hatred was no longer capitalist separateness; the workers detested the man of the French middle class, the man of flesh and blood realized in his historical enterprise. To all the workers of the world, the middle class man is the product of capital; to ours he is also what he has made himself, a killer—and he is going to remain that for a long time. The young working-class generation which grew up in the stifling silence of the Second Empire was a helpless witness of the slaughter of the Commune. When its apprenticeship ended, the class struggle had moved to the economic sphere; but these newcomers never forgot what they had seen: when they wished to gauge the employers' reactions, they brought to mind Thiers, Galliffet, Schneider, and relied on ineffaceable memories when they judged the employer capable of everything; every day they expected to see the social conflict degenerate into civil war, or rather it seemed to them that the class struggle was in truth civil war. These young men were to be irreconcilable enemies of the middle class: they had learned the hard way that each class sought the death of the other and, above all, they had been wronged. Everywhere else, the working class was starved; only in France was it bled. The proletarian of 1886 sold his working strength to men who had killed his father or his elder brother; his attitude towards them came from that, this strange mixture of heated up hatred, of cold hardness, of contempt, of fear, and of explosive violence. Everywhere else, working-class leaders renounced revolutionary activity more or less openly in favour of exploiting to the limit the advantages of universal suffrage: the workers would have their representatives in parliament. That was to choose integration: *the fact* of capitalism was accepted and the interests of the nation were defended in return for improvement by social legislation. The employers, reassured, developed their undertakings; those happy enough to possess an integrated proletariat had no occasion to worry about concentration of the

workers. Social democracy served as guarantee and intermediary; its very ambiguity[49] made it a permanent link between
Capital and Labour; by its mere existence, it prevented working-
class secession. When the oppressed chose oppressors to give
expression to their woes, everything was in order, communication had been established, national unity was preserved; and
then, from the moment they made use of speech, speech could
be used to bamboozle them: it is when they are silent that they
are frightening.

In France, they were silent: the proletariat had seceded;
after 1871, this decimated, injured class took shelter from the
nation and formed a society within society. What was universal
suffrage to them! They believed they had learned the hard way
that electoral friends are as a rule class enemies. After all,
society had given power to its machine-gunners. The state—
whether democratic or not—is 'the concentrated body of the
employers carried to supreme power'. For this reason alone,
even if it had a chance of influencing the debates, the proletariat
would not agree to take part in public affairs. Send representatives to the Chamber? And who then could represent it? It
enveloped both Right and Left in the same contempt; in its
eyes all politicians were middle class: could it be believed
that one man of the middle class, whatever his label, would
defend the interests of the workers against those of the rest of
the middle class? At the end of the century, France was the
only country in which social democracy had no working-class
foundations. The worker voted, it is true, but slackly and as a
matter of duty; he did not connect his function as an elector
with his activity as a protester: he fulfilled the first as a disintegrated individual, a detached citizen lost in the crowd of
other detached citizens; he exercised the second as an *organic*
member of a closed community. In short, the working class
enclosed in its savage isolation, no longer depended on anyone but itself: it rejected M. Millerand's socialism and condemned social legislation when it was passed through the
initiative of parliamentarians; its leaders lost no opportunity
of asserting the autonomy of the working-class movement or
of proclaiming the hostility of the trade unions and of the
Party; in vain the SFIO multiplied its advances; all it gained
from that was to be accused of 'violating trade-union independ-

ence'. In face of these 'debates', the proletariat, with no experience except *its own*, found its own way; it kept up the struggle in the only sphere which belonged to it: that of work. Revolutionary trade unionism was the proletariat itself, exalted by its isolation and proud of its friendlessness: betrayed by the peasants, twice betrayed by the lower middle class, it decided to extract everything—even ethical values—from its own depths; the workers were alive to a very special moment in their history: the moment of separation. In 1871, the nation had rejected them: they accepted their exile and changed the negative into positivity; what has sometimes been called trade-union imperialism or working-class totalitarianism was only the wonderful revulsion of a pariah caste: they wanted only to be *something*, they were condemned to be *nothing*, so they claimed to be *everything*.[50]

Our middle class withdrew into its shell in terror: now that the proletariat disowned its would-be defenders, all bridges were down, a no man's land populated by corpses separated workers from employers. The middle class had no longer even the resource of regarding this silent crowd as a herd of brutes: since they had held regular troops in check, the proletarians were men. Not altogether, however: if they were to be prevented from becoming judges, it was very necessary that they should continue to be animals. Men and ants at the same time, the proletariat appeared to be both transparent and opaque: it used intelligence, energy, courage on behalf of a mysterious animal nature and incomprehensible instincts. The employers were bewitched by this obscure mass and could see in it only the reflection of their own violence. Nor were they mistaken: the secret of the working class was that it took the French middle class for a gang of criminals. By wishing to challenge these mute judges, our élite confirmed their sentence: the decent people, having continued the massacres long after victory, could produce no legitimate defence: they had therefore to prove that by their own nature their victims deserved death. They exerted themselves to this end. The proletarian, they said, is neither man nor beast; had he been man, we should have respected him; had he been beast, we should have put him in a cage without doing him any harm; but this is a human beast, that is to say, a beast which attacks men with human means, or, if you prefer, a man always led on by irresistible forces towards the worst; he is free enough to be rightfully punished, slave enough by his nature for his redemption to be despaired of: in short, it is necessary to keep an eye on him and to be ready to knock him down without notice. Thus, in order to wash away its crime, the middle class gave itself the right to repeat it at will. Perhaps, had it pleaded with some appearance of reason that fury and fear had rendered it mad, and that it was guilty only by chance; but no: it wanted to justify its mistake; in justifying it, it changed and made itself criminal by vocation.

As for the young employer who, about 1890, ensured the changeover of the generations, it seemed at first that there was nothing with which he could be reproached: he was the son of an assassin, doubtless, but he was too young to have taken part in the summary execution, and blood spilled by the parents should not fall down again on the heads of the children. He thus had a choice, and could, as he wished, disown his father or stubbornly persist. He chose, as we know, obstinacy. He was brought up in hatred. To prevent him from judging the executioner, he was taught to detest the victim. He accepted it all, the active and the passive, the factory and the paternal crimes. Suddenly, he was constrained to call it all in question. 'When I went into the factory,' he said, 'I found hatred, and I have done nothing to provoke it. Why do they reproach me? We young employers have as yet killed no one, and, so far as I know, no young worker has yet been killed.' The proof is complete: since the young bourgeois has not yet cut a worker's throat, the worker's hatred has no justification, it is *a priori* the basic relationship of worker to employer; the proletarian is full of hatred by nature, the bourgeois is the innocent object of his detestation. Poor middle-class man! Whatever he does, it will always be the *other* who began: since you have been told that the workers seek our death! Even today, the argument pleases the reactionary paragraph writers: it is over sixty years old, and hasn't a wrinkle.

Since 1890, there is no small employer who does not identify himself with middle-class society. His workers ask for a rise? They want to destroy the nation. A trade-union congress calls capitalism in question? They want to cut his throat and violate his daughters. Thanks to this conjuring trick, the middle class, at the end of last century, endowed itself with a supplementary

right which might be called perpetual self-defence. This exquisite class made the blood it had shed a pretext for imagining
that it was in a state of siege, invested by brutes in human form,
and that each of its members, from birth to life's end, was continuously in danger of death. In a word, the children of Versailles detested the French workers with all their heart, as the
German barons, thirty years after the Peasants' War, still hated
the sons and grandsons of the villains whom their fathers had
tortured. He who has killed will kill. A third generation of
slaughterers entered upon its career, found the dust of its elders
and traced in it their virtues; these younger men did what they
could to give to the class struggle something of the air of a vendetta; they showed their hatred so that the workers might make
theirs apparent: thus each enmity was reinforced by the other;
in fact, they tried to keep up social tension to the extreme in
such a way that the least incident might release a disturbance
and bloody repression.[51] Arms were polished up and justifications were to hand: beautiful youth prepared itself for songful
tomorrows. We may well ask what miracle saved the proletariat
from a new Saint Bartholomew.

What miracle? But quite simply the 'second industrial revolution': it came to birth in the United States, reached Europe
and France; our upper middle class was on the threshold of the
twenty-five years of fat kine which would double our production
of cast iron and triple our production of steel. That was something to rejoice over, naturally, but not without mental reservation: the trouble with capitalism is that it begets burying beetles;
and these burying beetles began to swarm. Not only did the
working class increase continually by the influx from the fields,
but into the bargain, in urban centres, that class produced most
children. The statistics for 1906 revealed the frightening truth:
for every 100 married office workers, 299 offspring; for every
100 employers, 358; for every 100 working men, 395. And it
must be added that the neo-Malthusian propaganda of anarchist
trade unionists had reached the 'upper strata' of the proletariat:
the manual workers were most prolific. As long ago as 1869,
Leroy-Beaulieu noted gloomily: 'The workers who occupy the
lowest ranks, those who follow the heaviest and least well paid
work, continue to have a numerous family, either because they
do not understand their interests or because of the impossibility

of continence.' Result: the working class represented 28 per
cent of the population at the beginning of the Second Empire
and 35 per cent at the beginning of the twentieth century. If it
were necessary to give a name to the miracle which safeguards
the proletariat, I should call it the multiplication of burying
beetles. The employers took fright: the traditional aspect of
France was changing. In 1850, one Frenchman in seven lived in
a town of 5,000 or more inhabitants; in 1900, one Frenchman
in seven lived in a town of more than 100,000 inhabitants.
Now, it was the 'countryfolk' who helped the people of Versailles in 1871 in their great labours of purification; leaning on
the countryside, the middle class was sure to be able to crush, at
the least outburst, the working-class minority: after all, a soldier
is a peasant. But what would happen if the proportion were reversed? Whose turn would it be to carry out a massacre? Hatred
is very catching; whether or not they were born in the working
class, the new arrivals appropriated its memories and took to
themselves the sufferings of the Federates. During this time certainly Paris was purified: people lived there in middle-class
style, they voted as they should, they tolerated only the deserv-
ing poor; but when the people of Passy raised their heads, their
favourite obsession seems to have taken bodily shape: an
enormous crowd gathered at the gates of the city and continued
to grow; the capital was in a state of siege. Our gentlemen
mounted the fortifications: as far as the eye could reach, there
was the proletariat, the proletariat without end, covering the
country and trampling down the harvest; meanwhile from the
four corners of France, miserable wretches set out on the road
to join this army of burying beetles. The people of Versailles
had assassinated only a handful of persons; their children had
suddenly discovered that those few dead had a numberless
posterity. It must be stopped.

How? There was already talk of integrating the working class:
easily said, but integration meant paternalism and the fusillades
of 1871 had destroyed paternalism. In the north, the Company
integrated busily; but after all it worked in a retort. In those
locked sections where no one went in and no one came out,
everything was ready: the inhabitants changed their occupation
often without changing their house: if they left their village, it
was to set themselves up in the workers' city built nearby: there

they formed a social structure and customs, a feudal hierarchy with their place already marked out; in brief, proletarians were manufactured by operating controlled levies on the native population. But in the suburbs of Paris? Of Lyons? How to manage the metamorphosis of peasant into working man? Unceasingly factories rose from the earth and others shut their doors; unceasingly the demands of the market made modifications essential in the technique of production. These disruptions meant continuing insecurity of jobs; the workers had no geographical tie with their place of work; at Levallois-Perret, at Charenton, each evening the working population burst out and scattered; another replaced it, returning from all over the place. Were these semi-nomads to be run after? Where to look for them? How to get them together again? And what influence to exercise over them? Competition was opposed to paternalism, and continually reshaped the appearance of the suburbs; it perpetually stirred up these heaps of men by swinging movements which effected the transformation of countrymen into proletarians. So what? Dispersal? Break into fragments this enormous mass in which the least murmur was amplified until it resembled thunder? This was no new dream and the employers loved it long before the French Revolution, when they gave work to peasants outside the walls so as to escape guild regulations. Dispersion, decentralization, decongestion: substitute for the great uncontrollable mass 'small masses' scattered about the country and easily kept under control! Unhappily the moment was not favourable; besides, an understanding, a guiding plan would have been necessary: competition once more went against this by sowing discord among the employers.

So, how to prevent the terrifying increase in the proletariat? After all, it was not possible to fire into the pack. The policy of extermination was all very well in times of unemployment; in 1848, it was obviously right to shoot down men who cost money and provided no return. Anyway the liberal economy, that wonderful machine, undertook of itself to re-establish stability; it was hardly possible to do anything except give it a helping hand, and no one should find fault with the good faith of those who shot the workers in order to prevent them from dying of hunger. But these same reasons, in a period of prosperity, forbad the hampering of the free development of economic

forces. Whatever the increase in the working-class population,
the labour offering itself remained less than the demand: to
shoot a man who was so valuable would be wasteful. Now and
then the government could, as at Fourmies, allow itself a local
adjustment of working effectives. Still it had to act with prudence:
if the working class reached the point of growing angry, we
should lose millions. Taine and Renan advised recourse to the
gentle strength of social Malthusianism whose effects are so
slow that, to begin with, they escape notice. Since—as Leroy-
Beaulieu pointed out—this manoeuvre took no account of his
true interests (which obviously would order him to die as soon
as possible, and without offspring), it would be possible to try
to open his eyes. Our government ought to have taken on two
tasks: to bind the peasant to the soil, and to promote continence
among the poor. A speaking campaign should be arranged: in
parliament, at conferences, at the Academy, there should be but
one cry: 'The soil is dying, the soil is dead, long live the soil!' It
should be shown how skilfully France had, hitherto, balanced
agriculture and industry: it was in this harmonious balancing of
productive vigour that the secret of our happiness and our virtues should be sought. Don't touch it, don't take away from God
His longing to be French. Which meant, of course, seeing to it
that country workers are more numerous than town workers.
'When the ruling class exercises absolute power,' wrote M.
Sauvy, 'it is in favour of increasing the population.... When
for any reason the ruled acquire rights and, as a consequence,
the rulers duties, the question takes on a different aspect....
Sovereignty being no longer absolute, a limitation in the number
of births becomes if not necessary at least advantageous.'

The father killed excess workers: the son is persuaded that he
ought to prevent them from being born; excellent counsel, but
how to put it into effect? In a time of industrial expansion, multiplication of workers serves the interests of production; at the
beginning of the century, proletarians were at first sight afraid
because they were too numerous; but the true source of their
young power was that there were still not enough of them; the
call for man-power raised their value, led to an increase in
wages, limited the actual rights of the employers: between 1871
and 1910 the number of strikes annually rose from 267 to 1,073,
between 55 and 60 per cent of which were successful. The op-

pressed enjoyed at the same time the advantage of numbers and
the benefit of scarcity. And if the anarchists joined forces with
the employers in the sphere of contraceptive propaganda, it was
because they made Malthusianism a weapon in the class
struggle.

French capitalists were betrayed by their own capitalism:
this system, rooted in a sort of slavery, imposed on them the
exercise of a discretionary power over the mass; but it laid on
them at the same time the impossible task of continually increasing their needs for labour. Caught between the contradictory
demands of ruling and of gain, the employers tore out their hair:
how keep up profits without increasing production? How
sterilize the population without stimulating a rise in wages?
How make France a great industrial nation and at the same
time preserve in it the demographic appearance of an agricultural country?

The answers were in the questions, but our capitalists, caught
between fear and the profit motive, hesitated to look for them:
that is why two currents were to be found in France in 1914,
the one in favour of increasing the population, the other Malthusian, each of which corresponded with one of the terms of
the contradiction. Apparently, those in favour of increasing the
population would have ended by winning: the government made
this its official doctrine; but it was not much more than a practical joke. To fight in reality against the falling birth rate, it
would have been necessary to secure the lowering of the cost of
living; and since, on the contrary, everything was done to prevent that, the 'demographic policy' of our ministers was reduced
to a ranting uproar and to certain measures that were not carried.[52] However, everything indicated that the middle class had
secretly chosen the other solution. What was perhaps surprising
is that it had chosen this *for itself*: the abrupt proliferation of
the suburbs seemed to promote *within the city walls* a collapse
of the birth rate. As if, having failed to castrate the poor, the
rich had castrated themselves: middle-class sterility strongly
resembles a road to a dead-end;[53] capital became the tomb of
the race. At about the same time, the Comité des Forges, while
boasting of continuing 'the splendid progress of the preceding
years', made its first attempts at economic Malthusianism.
Everything was ready: in 1914 it only remained to construct the

infernal machine which would link reciprocally the abortionist activities of industry and those of the middle-class family. To persuade the employers nothing was less needed than the great shocks of the war and the post-war period. The élite were aware that civilizations were mortal: 'Poor France, it has been bled. What will the world do without it?' The world was indifferent, as was to be expected, but these academic lamentations hid a real terror: and neither the war nor coal was the cause; between 1917 and 1921 the employers had grown sure that final victory would be with the proletariat. It won't happen today nor, perhaps, even tomorrow, but slowly, surely. . . . It was an atrocious fact: but yes, YES! Those bastards were going to win. In seventy years the middle class had learned nothing and forgotten nothing, and all the perfumes of Araby could not wash the blood from its hands: suddenly it found itself once more the *same* as in 1848, the *same* as in 1871, with the same men facing it, those who had been butchered in the Commune whom it was going to be necessary to kill in vain for the third time. This time, they would end by winning; and no one would pity the middle class, since in its hour of glory it had had no pity. Our employers saw themselves lost, middle-class France began to talk of itself in terms touched with emotion. Of itself—that is to say, of the human race, which is one—predicting the end of the world, or the end of capital: since the worker is only a brute, the fate of mankind was at the mercy of these ants: when they seize power, these stupendous hymenoptera, we should lose our possessions, our lives, our position and all those refinements for which, even today, it would be worth dying; the new lords would give us to the worms to eat, the reign of man would take a plunge deep into the past. And it would be no good counting on history to do us justice, even after the event: the ants would re-write it. Our future is obstructed by this frightful catastrophe which will continue to destroy us after our death and which, in our own eyes, makes us already living dead or, better, explained and corrected mistakes.

At the same period, on the same continent, frenzy and fear generated forms of fascism everywhere: this was, if I may dare to speak so, the 'healthy' reaction. If the Italians and the Germans, a century late, started another Saint Bartholomew, it proved that they counted on winning and that they believed in capital. In the midst of these madmen, the old French middle class, loaded down by years and crimes, cut a defeatist figure. Napoleon III, Boulangism, carnage, camps of slow death: it had experienced everything and, in the end, could say that it led to nothing. Capitalism produced its own death; the proletariat resembled the Lernaean hydra: cut away one head, and ten sprang up in its place. Accordingly better not to cut these festering heads off: a better idea would be to seek a means of making all of them half dead. When the middle classes to the south and the east cried: 'To arms!', the French middle class answer was 'Temporize;' when the foreigner cried: 'Loot and kill! Slaughter!' ours answered: 'Underfeed!' Yes, it was about this time that we constructed the spiral machine: since the progress of capitalism led to its ruin, progress should be stopped; since the goods of this world must pass sooner or later into other hands, it should be arranged for only what was necessary to be produced and for all that was produced to be consumed; since the twilight of man had been foretold to us, we should prolong his decline by inventing a twilight economy. Since competition put pressure on producing more, we should throttle competition; since, when a riot was toward, the suburbs poured into the streets of Paris, we should apply the brake to technical concentration so as to slow down social concentration. It was, after all, only a question of holding up history. For a moment. Just a brief moment. Our employers wanted to hold back the cataclysm for some decades so that they would have time to die in peace. That presented no difficulty provided we were willing to ruin the country: for it is not a matter of gaining new strength, but of knowing how to use our weaknesses and reinforcing each one of them by all the others. The market tends to contract? Splendid: it can be strangled by raising prices. Prices tend to rise? The tendency will be emphasized by restricting production. There is a shortage of raw materials? Excellent reason for passing under foreign control. Children are uncommon? They will be made even more uncommon by reducing parents to despair; economic Malthusianism leans on social Malthusianism and accelerates it: a child costs money before it yields a return, it is a new undertaking which necessitates new investments; when the whole of France kicks at modernizing equipment, no one is going to renew human material for fun and without any necessity.

And then what? Often economic rebirth is accompanied by demographic upsets: people want sons because they are involved in a collective undertaking whose outcome those sons will see. But we are waiting only for the deluge: why produce children to be drowned? Let us rather persuade the worker that France is going to die, that the fate of the son will be worse than that of the father: it is the best way to open his eyes to his true interests. Thus, in the midst of the fascist uproar, our middle class organized a slow suicide which would perhaps spread out over half a century. Threatened, it fought back at once by obstructions; then it transformed obstruction into a defensive strategy. It was playing a losing game; it would therefore play so that the loser wins. Our revolving economy would turn more and more slowly and, one fine day, would cease to turn; but we should be dead; if the Russians took it into their heads to lay a hand on our beautiful France, they would find only carrion and would be deservedly caught. French Malthusianism was to its Italo-German brother fascism as the defensive to the offensive, passive to active resistance, feminine to masculine, pessimism to optimism—in one word negative to positive. In either alternative, the leaders had to re-establish absolute rule over the led: but the Nazis proposed to establish their power on the strength of repression; the French middle class drew its power from a depressive ultra-conservatism which reduced its class enemy to impotence.

We have noted the confusion of the employers in face of the numerical growth of the proletariat: 'If it goes on increasing, it will eat us up; if it begins to diminish, industry will be short of hands.' Malthusianism renders these fears vain: production stagnates when productivity tends to increase, conditions for technological unemployment are brought together, the containment of the working class seems desirable from every point of view. Malthusianism again provides the means of realizing this containment.

The proletariat increases unduly because the workers produce too many children, and because country people leave the soil in too great numbers. Economic ultra-conservatism makes it possible to regulate both factors.

To take births first: since 1935 the employers have won all along the line. Up to then, nothing had helped: those still uncouth peasants stubbornly maintained the fecundity of brutes. But a few years of economic depression were enough to produce a collapse in the working-class birthrate: this time, they had understood; they abstained, just like the middle class. Malthusian practices having been brought into play, an attempt was made to trace the cause to the internal evolution of the proletariat. That was not altogether false: the producing class had become more homogeneous, and working men's sons were more numerous than peasants'. But if each working man produced fewer children than each peasant, that was because the first had suffered longer the ordeal of the wretchedness of the towns and of despair. It must be conceded, of course, that every day they are more the product of that technical universe which they produce, and that little by little they learn the *techniques* of life and death: the fathers accepted the mischances of the body, the sons know how to control them. But regulation of births is only a means which can serve very different ends; that alone cannot explain the sudden and obstinate sterility of the new generations: it is not enough to know about Malthusian practices, it is also necessary to want to use them. Should we look to the inhuman exactions of mass production as the cause of this 'abstention'? If you like. But, in this form, the explanation remains insufficient since no similar lowering of the birth rate is recorded in countries with an advanced form of capitalism. The work of the conveyor-belt operative is always wearisome; for it to become altogether unendurable, the new standards must be applied within the framework of a depressed economy. Enquire in working-class households why they don't have more children; the answer is not in doubt: 'We're too well aware of our miseries to wish to inflict them on others.' Condemned to live in a repetitive universe, they cannot imagine for their sons any future other than their own past. From criminal, our middle class becomes abortionist; by its own methods it continues the work of its fathers: instead of perpetrating a massacre, it compels the adversary to its own decimation.

The rural exodus, then: it must be slowed down or counterbalanced or both. Nothing easier today: it is well known that the peasant is not attracted by the deadly fires of the towns but is pushed and headed towards them by excess of wretchedness; let us therefore assure him of wretchedness without excess. The great migrations of the nineteenth century are rich in lessons. The first, about 1860, was due to the concentration of lands and to the consequent transformation of tillage: industrialists invented the peasant market; ploughs and chemical fertilizers were manufactured and sold; the produce and the price of land increased, the demand for labour decreased, countless day labourers were thrown on to the roads; they were followed by others who were less wretched but had lost all hope of one day becoming owners. The lesson was learned: Malthusianism put a brake on the mechanization of agricultural techniques in order to maintain the parcelling out of holdings. Transport takes up more than half the time consecrated to farming. Splendid! Putting tractors beyond the reach of farmers and preserving for them 800,000 good kilometres of rutted roads will be evidence of a very special solicitude for them. If they go on foot, scratch the earth's crust with their old tools, sow with their bare hands: that's the best guarantee of social stability. It is true that social facts react in a circle; and certainly it is the parcelling out of properties that holds up mechanization: the small farms are too small for each one individually to get much advantage from motorization. Thus industrial Malthusianism finds its justification in scarcity of demand. And supposing the peasants were nevertheless to enter into partnership with one another? If they took it into their heads to buy tractors in common? 'In that domain,' say the specialists, 'nothing can be done without partnership.' But the real thing is to do nothing: the system has everything to fear from the social transformation machines would introduce into the countryside. Happily, there is red tape: our peasants are nowhere near agreement. Their particularism is deeply to be regretted—but behind the scenes it is protected. The State does all it can to safeguard the peasants' invaluable ignorance: in 1949 the Minister of Agriculture got 471 million francs for agricultural education while the Ministry of National Education got 14 milliards for technical training and craft apprenticeship. The result is that we are short of 10,000 teachers. Thanks to this carefully maintained deficit, two to three per cent of our agriculturists receive technical instruction; in Denmark, the figure is 95 per cent. We can be quite calm: those who are bamboozled will insist on the continuation of the system that bamboozles them. The machine rotates.

The other great exodus of last century—that of 1880—was the result of foreign competition. Our agricultural economy continued to be half shut down; development of communications put America at our doors and the New World poured its food products into our markets; prices collapsed: our farmers were on the roads again. Nearly a million men abandoned the soil; to keep the others at home, protectionist measures were hastily instituted. But afterwards? How prevent a repetition of the disaster? By increasing yield? Machinery would have to be introduced: progress, chased away on one hand, would have to be reintroduced on the other; to prevent a repetition of the exodus of 1880, preparations would be made against that of 1860. And then? Should we take advantage of the climate in order to specialize in the cultivation of luxuries, as Britain specialized in high quality industry? Impossible: to specialize cultivation meant teaching the cultivator. And that would certainly be followed by what we want to avoid: exodus. To be able to reach markets abroad, it would be necessary to mechanize, motorize, increase yields, reduce man-power—and the peasants would leave their villages. Damned peasants: with the least progress, they take to the road again! Happily Malthusianism offers the means of holding them fast: since progress drives them away, they must be protected from progress. Let them produce wheat, more wheat, always wheat, at the highest price, by the hardest work, the most out-of-date technique: the lower the output of each worker, the greater the call for man-power.[54] Against outside competition an Atlantic wall must be built, isolating France from world markets. As for internal competition, that was even simpler. All that is needed is destruction. Since the big producers of the north and the west could not put a brake on production as easily as industrialists can, the government must come to their rescue by buying their excess production for distillation. In short, France made a bonfire of its harvests, and each Frenchman, his stomach hollow, paid to see the smoke. The State swallowed milliards in the scheme, but the end was attained: among us, bread was dearest[55] and husbandry least well rewarded.[56] For that was the aim without doubt: in maintaining our prices above world level and our industrial prices above our agricultural prices, Malthusianism begets and preserves from moment to moment the French peasant, that absurd and pitiful monstrosity—represented by an interested propaganda as a wise man—who kills himself to earn nothing, believes he owns land of which he has not even a life tenure, defends the interest of the big landowners, and votes every five years for his own wretchedness through fear of becoming still more wretched. This man of nature does not realize that he is an artificial product and that his destiny, like that of working men, is manufactured in the towns: but he is set against the towns by reminders that his creditors live in them, and above all against the working class by having it pointed out to him that that class's claims lead to the rise in industrial prices. If the peasant set about producing more cheaply, if he demanded more tractors at lower prices, there would be a risk that one day he might notice that he has interests in common with the industrial workers. That must at all costs be prevented; stability insists that the working classes should be divided by barriers of misunderstanding and hatred. Convinced that to rule it is necessary to divide, top-level employers keep in the fields at our expense a swarm of splendid savages whose votes support their policy.

There was no need to ask too much: Malthusianism put a brake on the chronic exodus of people from the country, but did not stop it. In 1905, of 1,000 workers about 480 were agricultural workers; in 1930, not more than 370; in 1953, not more than 329; migration still goes on; but it changes in kind and is directed towards small administrative jobs. In debt up to the neck, dying of hunger on mortgaged soil, the peasant wants security for his son: he will make him an official. And then technical progress brings to birth or develops a new class whose rapid growth is going to balance, then restrain, stop, and exceed that of the proletariat: the wage-earning middle class. Colin Clarke has drawn up, for most industrial countries, a statistical correlation between the national income per head and the proportion of non-productive (or indirectly productive) wage-earners in the active population. To use his terminology, the secondary and tertiary groups[57] grew at the same time and in the same proportions up to the First World War; that was the period when capitalist industry settled at the same time its framework and its mass-man-power. After 1918, the growth of the tertiary group was accelerated while that of the secondary slowed down. The universal development of offices and of ad-

5

ministration corresponds with the effort made by undertakings to reorganize themselves in the light of technical progress and industrial concentration; services were centralized, the different sectors of exploitation were 'integrated', rapidity of communication was ensured, special groups were set to prepare tasks and to share them out, to interpret contingencies and gauge the fluctuations of the market, to regulate distribution: the aim being to increase productivity while ensuring control of production. Now, Clark's schema was to be found in France: save that, always, it was in the form of caricature. Among us production stagnated after 1929 and the numerical increase of the proletariat stopped about 1931, while the inflation of the tertiary has never stopped growing more marked.[88] This was the direct effect of Malthusianism: the manufacturer was not anxious to increase the number of his hands since he did not dream of producing more; he increased his administrative staff because he wanted to rationalize the undertaking in order to produce at a lower cost. Result: an excess of 800,000 active persons in the tertiary and genuine under-employment. If on the other hand it were desired today to satisfy the total needs of the nation, production would have to be increased by 46 per cent. It goes without saying that that is impossible, in the *first place* because of the shortage of labour. Where to find workers to build the millions of homes needed? And, given a delay of ten, twenty years, how to fill up the empty spaces in the secondary sector without first reducing man-power in the primary and tertiary sectors? But the employers do no such thing: they maintain semi-unemployment in the 'services' and keep France anaemic so as to put a brake on development of working-class strength. Malthusianism has not missed its aim: a backward agriculture, too many in the tertiary sector, and a shortage in the proletariat suffice to ensure social stability. And the employers, naturally, are covered; under-production promotes under-consumption, that is to say, contraction of the market, which in its turn justifies under-production. All is for the best on condition that part of the population is left to die of cold in the winter and of hunger all the year round.

A government which wished to increase the annual rate of productivity would, as we have seen, have to reduce the numbers in the tertiary group; but the employers are quite calm: that won't be done very soon, and this blood-letting, theoretically possible, is forbidden in practice because of the *social* resistances it would arouse. Nevertheless the tertiary group includes some whose wage is, at the most, equal to that of a manual worker: one would expect these borderline wage-earners to make no difficulty about passing in case of need, from one sector to the other. Well, in fact, no: his employment makes the employee as his habit makes the monk. By purchasing power the clerk is linked with the productive wage-earner; he is distinguished from him by the fact that he does not produce. The work of the typist is part and parcel of the activities of management: to that extent, she considers herself integrated in the management class. As a matter of fact, her functions do not remove her as far as she believes from the manual worker: certainly she does not *produce*; nevertheless, it is she who gives substance to the significant ideas worked out by the administration: so that, it seems to me, she is very close to the printer, who is a manual worker. The bureaucratic moment of thought is conceptualization: thought denies the reality of things and its own reality, language denies the existence of the object indicated: the bureaucrat is sustained on the level of statistics, of possibles and of clear ideas: ideas, that is to say, which do not admit of excess. Thought will rediscover its depth only in rediscovering materiality; as it never goes beyond anything except objects, it will go beyond itself only in receiving from outside the nature of the object. When she taps out a circular, the typist transforms an idea into a thing, she carries into effect the reciprocal going beyond of the significant idea through its materiality and of the matter by its signification. There is thus in her work, as in that of the forwarding agent, the carrier, etc., a certain character of productivity. But it is just this character which clerks seek to deny: they believe they take part in the drawing up of orders and tasks, and pass over in silence their true function which is to transform these into reality by writing them down. By their behaviour and their aspirations, the 'economically weak' of the tertiary group claim to show that they belong to the upper classes which oppress them. But they only ape their employers and their attitudes mask their obstinate refusal to be assimilated into the ranks of productive wage-earners. They have only a totally negative social reality, since they are not what they claim to be and reject all solidarity with those who most closely resemble them. In creating this white-collar proletariat which detests true proletarians because the working-class state fills it with horror, it has been enough to effect certain advance deductions on the primary and secondary sectors to set wretchedness against itself. In the framework of an expanding economy the evil would be smaller: even if, as a whole, the 'service' industries continued to grow, the working-class masses also would grow; the increase in the national income and the demand for man-power would contribute to increase the value of the productive sector and would work in favour of changes such as occur in the United States where vast floating forces are massed here and there along the frontier, always ready, according to circum-stances, to cross over and invade the tertiary or to flow back into the secondary. But economic ultra-conservatism promotes social ultra-conservatism: out of 100 sons of working men born a quarter of a century ago, 55 remained working men in heavy and medium industry; 10 went back to the land and worked as agricultural labourers; 35 crossed the line, 21 of whom increased the strength of the white-collar proletariat. In other words, a young man of the working class, round about 1930, had 65 out of 100 chances of remaining a working man, 86 chances out of 100 of remaining in the classes regarded with disfavour. If we add that the rural exodus had slowed down, that it was nearly impossible for lower grade clerks to rise into middle-class posi-tions, that small employers were protected and kept in their station by the State and the manufacturing industries, we must certainly conclude that our abortionist economy has partitioned off the social groups, and made of French society if not al-together a caste system, at least a society in the process of strati-fication. The advantage is obvious: Malthusianism is not content with reducing the proletariat, it ends by isolating it; people do still get into it, people still even get out of it: but, more and more, the working man is so born and so dies.

Nor is it enough to keep this dangerous class at a distance: it must be encircled. Last century, the middle class lived in a state of siege; today the middle class is arranging to besiege the work-ing class. Each is clamped to his place, to what he believes is his privilege: the peasant to his mortgaged soil, the small employer to his wretched business, the minor clerk to his starveling job.

The big men are in control of everything; by a gesture they can ruin the small folk, but they are careful not to do so; for these are their allies, their soldiers. These men who differ in everything from one another have a common hate: that of the proletariat. If he did not hate the proletariat, the small employer would notice that he is the victim and the accomplice of the captains of industry, the peasant that his land eludes him, flowing away like water, the clerk that he is exploited by his employer. But they see nothing: nothing except working-class claims which put up industrial prices, increase the peasants' debt, and lead the petty tradesmen to the verge of ruin: nothing except the dark pit which attracts and repels them. The body of French employers leans on these two-thirds of the nation to reduce the other third to impotence.

Intimidation no longer proceeds through massacres but by weakening working-class pugnacity from the inside; without hesitation, the proletariat is shut into a position with no exit, and so well contrived that, if it attempts to get out, it strangles itself or tears itself to pieces. The encirclement of which I have just spoken is still nothing but an external success. Another thing: since production produces the working man, and since Malthusianism is the dominant characteristic of our production, the French proletariat is both the victim and the product of it: we shall see how it is conditioned in its struggle even by the evil against which it must fight.

(i) Our fathers tell us that France had its shock proletariat between 1890 and 1911. And, in fact, it should be remembered that the working class took part in more than 18,000 strikes during those twenty-one years. Counting them year by year, we can distinguish maxima and minima. But both were continually increasing: the first moved from 261 to 1,025, the second from 267 to 1,525. Moreover, the percentage of successful strikes also rose: it was 53 per cent at the end of the century, 62 per cent in 1910. This blessed period came to an end with the First World War. On the average, the number of post-war strikes was higher. But, up to 1926, the yearly minima and maxima were constantly falling and, most important of all, the percentage of success fell from 70 per cent in the year 1919 to 35 per cent in the years 1930–35. After the tide of 1936, the number of strikes continued very high but the tendency to regression began again and became more pronounced: it still persists today, and the percentage of successes is below average. Must it be believed as a fact that the workers were more courageous during the time of revolutionary trade unionism, their leaders shrewder, more devoted? And, in that event, what can have caused the change? At this question, middle-class commentators wriggle: 'The cause, bless my soul, the cause?' There is only one: observe the triumphal rise of the proletariat until 1919, the blessed year in which the worker had only to take a vow for it to be fulfilled, and consider what happened afterwards: a multiplication of failures, renewed wretchedness, collapse. 1920 was the crucial year. And why 1920? Because *it was the year of the Congress of Tours* and of the split in the working class; henceforth the proletariat had its cancer.

The worker, losing courage because the Communist cancer consumed him, was all the same too stupid. Nevertheless it is *true* that a certain weakening of his actions was to be noted. Let us go back to facts and see what they say. We shall notice first of all that the annual number of strikes and their percentage of successes grows with industrialization up to 1912. We have noted elsewhere that this ascending curve was not without notches: at times, strikes were less frequent and each particular one had less chance of success. The general curve of prices presents the same appearance: the period of expansion does not proceed without minor crises. If the two curves are compared, it jumps to the eye that the *minima* of the one corresponds exactly with those of the other. From 1919 to 1935, the tendency is reversed, but the relationship does not change:[59] strikes increase with the rise of prices and diminish when they go down. The meaning is plain: in periods of expansion, the worker is differently *placed*, he is the object of demand; that means that the national income is growing to the full and that the demand for man-power is enough to bring about a rise in wages; if by social agitation the working class tries to accentuate this rise, it is because it demands a share in the collective enrichment. Put otherwise, the proletariat *passes to the offensive* and draws its aggressiveness from circumstances. For the rest, the competitive system allows the workers to consolidate their victories: the employer cannot take away the concessions snatched from him; if he tried to compensate for a rise in wages by raising prices, he would be lost: he must accept less profit or produce more: *praxis* is prefigured by the movement of the economy. Caught up by the currents which throw him right into battle, the worker finds himself once again acting without having decided to act and the efficacy of his actions is in direct proportion to the force of expansion in our industry. The proletariat cuts out for itself a future in the future of capitalism. We know now that this happy period had come to an end with the armistice of 1918. But *praxis* builds up its picture of itself by projecting to the infinite the immediate future which it begets: workers and employers, by simply going to the limit, had projected before them the myth of progress and the illusion of reform. It would be enough for the proletariat to pursue its conquests: that would compel capitalism to produce more steadily and would steadily bring the proletariat nearer to the seizure of power. This was expected by Jaurès about 1902 in terms which today seem to us shocking but which expressed the common hope:

'It is impossible for the trade unions to organize, to extend, to systematize themselves without soon intervening in the working of capitalist society.... And the day when working-class trade unions, even by inspection, even by regulation, intervene also in the setting up of mechanization, the day when they advise, when they impose such and such a machine, such and such a piece of technical apparatus on the employers, they are collaborating, whether they wish to or not, with the employers in the management of the capitalist machine. And I certainly am not against this collaboration by the proletariat: it is the beginning of taking possession.'

Thus the true but finite future of liberal capitalism was illusorily extended into the infinite, and the worker took it for his own future. This false perspective excited working-class pugnacity while, by the mirage of reformism, inclining the exploited to collaborate with their exploiter. The workers had not forgotten the Saint Bartholomews of the past, but in proportion as the middle-class world gave way to their activity, the watchword of revolutionary trade unionism became a dead letter; revolutionaries and reformers hardly opposed one another any longer except in speech: when the Revolution is revealed in terms of continual progress, what distinguishes it from simple evolution? The proletariat continued to be hostile to the poli-

ticians and to programmes, but was inclined to come out of its
voluntary exile, to infiltrate among the enemy, to 'enter an
appearance'. It had learned that, as Mauss said, the social fact is
a total fact. But the objective truth of its struggle was that every
day it was becoming more integrated into capitalist society and
that, in the end, it would have to subordinate trade-union organizations to the State.

During times of depression, on the other hand, the proletariat
fought with its back to the wall. Should it have been denuded of
its courage? Certainly not. But if its pugnacity is measured by
the number of battles joined, it must be confessed that it was
diminishing: that was because the strike had lost its efficacy: the
unemployed constituted reserves on which the employer did not
hesitate to draw; and, if a business was going badly, social conflicts could be made a pretext for closing it down. Yesterday the
worker had something to say about everything; today if he protests he is thrown on the street; he's lucky not to have been
sacked without saying a word. Yesterday he was an integral part
of the factory; today he seems simply to be there on sufferance.
It is not he, certainly, who submits to this devalorization: it is
his strength at work. That does not prevent his feeling that he is
attacked in his reality as a man. He thought himself indispensable; now he is told repeatedly that only chance, or the kindness of his employer, keeps him in work, and that there is, so to
speak, a kind of injustice in giving him work when it is being
refused to so many others; by force of hearing it repeated that
he is lucky not to be out of work, the worker tends to think of
himself as one of the unemployed who has been lucky: in short,
in times of crisis, it is unemployment that gives its meaning to
work. Now, the man out of work is a product of disintegration,
a passive citizen driven back to the confines of society and
meanly maintained in doing nothing so that it shall not be said
he has been left to die of hunger. Potentially unemployed,
actually unemployed, the worker feels there are *too many* of
him: crisis strips him at once of his powers and his responsibilities. He was under the illusion that he was 'collaborating' with
capitalism: he realizes his powerlessness. At present, it is no
longer enough to fulfil exactly the contract of work: if he wants
to keep his job he must deserve it, become what foremen and
employers call a 'good' worker. Moreover, employers take

advantage of the opportunity to choose their hands. The 'strong-minded', the trade unionists, the militants are dismissed, the others—those prevented by resignation, weariness, family burdens from protesting—are kept on; in this way a kind of shake-up of the working class is effected: the most militant disappear, exiles in that no-man's-land which is unemployment; they lose at the same time their means of action and their contact with the masses. Among those who, despite their relative powerlessness, continue to be capable of exercising pressures on the employers, the proportion who are resigned tends to increase. The worker has lost the illusion of collaborating with capital: yesterday by his activity in making claims he still contributed to the expansion of industry; today he suffers the effects of the depression without being able to check it. His progressive integration had led him to share his exploiters' responsibilities; the exile that frees him also isolates him, he loses all contact with the society which excludes him: that is what makes him particularly hostile to political demonstrations. 'The consciousness of the working class,' wrote Lenin, 'cannot be a real political consciousness unless the workers are accustomed to react against *all* abuses, all manifestations of tyranny *whatever the class* which is victimized and to react exactly from the social democratic point of view'. He is undoubtedly right, but it is very much easier to 'throw political revelations into the masses' at a time of industrial expansion than at a time of crisis: all links between the masses and the ruling classes have been loosened, including, above all, that of the social struggle; antagonism tends to give way to a relationship of uncompromising juxtaposition.[60] We must not come to the conclusion that the proletariat has lost the memory of its eternal task: the truth is that circumstances deprive it of any future by compelling it to set its mind on immediate interests: it fought to conquer, it fights to hold. Never, moreover, is the truth so plainly apparent: each class aims at the death of the other; if capitalism wants to safeguard its interests, it must keep the proletariat below the minimum living standard. Far from pushing industry to produce, the most modest claims may well drive it to ruin. And, as a matter of fact, if the crisis were to grow, it might lead to Revolution, that is to say to the break-up of an economy undermined by its internal contradictions. But this prospect itself often puts a brake on trade-union action: when circumstances are unfavourable to big movements, a local strike is likely either to be suppressed by force or to ruin the undertaking.

The lesson will not be lost: employers base themselves on the preceding observations to produce artificially the objective conditions of working-class discouragement. The number of strikes increases with production? Production is therefore prevented from increasing. If it falls below a certain level, insurrectionary troubles are to be feared? Things will be arranged so that it does not decrease either. It will be enough to maintain the national economy in a state of masked crisis. A paradoxical result of what Lassalle called the brazen law of wages is that each of the classes is reflected in the other: progressive employers—clashing proletariat; slothful employers—weary proletariat. In order to cloud working-class consciousness, our industrialists have chosen to reduce output to a minimum; they hoped that atrophy of production would be lived from the inside by the proletariat in the form of generalized anaemia. Thanks to their methods, in fact, there is at the same time both a shortage and a very slight excess in the numbers of the French proletariat. For an economy that proposed to fulfil all the needs of the nation by mass production, it is not numerous enough: Malthusianism thus keeps it in a state of underdevelopment. But for an economy which aimed at being depressive, for fear of a depression, the working class is always in danger of being too thick on the ground. In point of fact, crisis is our one prospect, and fear of a crisis conditions the whole set-up. By surrounding itself with small undertakings as a safety device, manufacturing industry hints that catastrophe is at our gates; by the extravagance of its precautions, the State succeeds in convincing us of this. There is no question of exorcizing this catastrophe, but of being able, by unremitting watchfulness, to defer it. Our one hope therefore would be the perpetuation of ultra-conservatism. Most certainly there is work for everybody, but the nation is imposing cruel sacrifices on itself in order to *prevent* unemployment. The worker would be the first victim of unfavourable circumstances; he is thus the first beneficiary of government concern. If a barrier were not put up against foreign products, he would find himself once more on the pavement; and if foodstuffs only were allowed to come in, that would mean the ruin of our farmers, the peasants would again take the road to the towns and would come to swell the proletariat at the very moment that industrial markets were suffering the consequences of the collapse of agricultural prices. Nor is that all: it is through the employer's kindness that his wage-earners keep their jobs; if he were to use foreign or colonial man-power recklessly, there would be a danger that dissension and competition would divide the working class; if he perfected his manufacturing processes without increasing production, the proletariat would be struck down by technological unemployment. By rights the French worker is unemployed; if he is not in fact, it is thanks to the protection of the public authorities and big Capital. He must be made to understand that our economy could crumble at the least breath of wind. Let him go on strike if he wishes: he will have been warned that he has everything to lose.

He still has to be convinced that he has nothing to gain by it. On this point, Malthusianism has done marvels; the method was brought into focus in 1936 and still works today. According to the Matignon agreement, 'real wages must be adjusted following a decreasing scale beginning at 15 per cent for the lowest wages and descending as far as 7 per cent for the highest wages'. As a matter of fact, it is not impossible that the total increase, under pressure by the masses, has risen to 20 per cent. To a suggestion by the government and the trade unions that the manufacturers could compensate for the rise in costs by increasing production, the employers turn a deaf ear. Supported by the petty tradesmen, who plead poverty, they deliberately raise prices. From May to November 1936, for industrial products alone, the wholesale price index showed a rise of 35 per cent. This rise continued during the whole Blum experiment; it always remained higher than the rise in wages. In February 1937 Léon Blum himself declared, in a speech to officials: 'The rise in the cost of living in the last eight months means for a wage-earning family costs higher than the benefits procured for them by all the measures taken on their behalf.'

From that moment, the loop had been looped and the famous 'infernal cycle of prices and wages' was organized. Needless to say, it was presented to us as an inexorable law of economics, but that is an absolute lie and there is here no law, no cycle, no hell. The truth is that the 'mass of consumable yield' cannot increase unless production also increases: inflationary paper money never enriched anyone. Readjusting wages produces only a shifting of income: it remains to be decided at whose expense this redistribution is to be made. In a liberal system, as we have seen, the employer must put up with new costs; in a monopolistic system, he passes them on to the consumer. The advantage is double: the middle classes are brought into conflict with the proletariat; to divide is to rule. And then the worker is fooled: whatever the nominal rise in wages, purchasing power does not vary. Everything and nothing changes; what one hand concedes in wages is extracted from his pocket by the other. After the people's victory of 1936, it took the employers less than two years to bring purchasing power per hour of work back to the level of 1929. Under the occupation, it fell still lower, and today, ten years after liberation, it has not yet reached the level of 1938: for a quarter of a century, in spite of various fluctuations and bitter social conflicts, the real wage of the worker has not budged: it ceased to grow at the same time as the national income and will begin to grow again only when the national income does. Here is the conjuring trick which takes the workers' breath away and I think it no insult to them to compare them with those bulls, full of courage, which charge the cape ten times and then stop suddenly, frustrated at encountering only a decoy. The worker does all he can, he accepts privations in order to win a strike, he attains victory exhausted, and all he has done is to help in a general rise in prices which will put the whole thing to rights. Every effort is made to convince him that he has wasted his trouble: certain manufacturers push impudence so far as hastily to raise prices in the canteen so that the new charges can be displayed on the same day the wage-earners receive their rise. A mere twinkling of an eye was all that was needed to restore the position. Without a crisis and without a massacre, the employers have worn down working-class pugnacity: the worker has lost all hope of winning; he may act, if he wishes, on wages, but unless he blocks prices he has accomplished nothing; and he knows very well that he will be able to block prices only if he seizes power and the other classes seem to have made up their minds against letting him do that. Must it be said that the proletariat, as in periods of crisis, is cut off from its future? No: but we have seen that, to begin with, that future is the future of capitalism.[61] Now among us a depressive ultra-conservatism gives to our contemporary state two contradictory characteristics: repetition and involution. Repetition is immediately obvious: days follow one another and are alike; during three centuries, the sons were better fed and better housed than their fathers but for the last twenty-five years nothing has changed and the quantity of goods to be divided has not increased; if some people live better, that is because others live much worse. The whole of Europe treats us as mean: a reproach that, to be sure, cannot be made against the proletariat since it simply has not the means to be miserly; nor does it affect the middle classes either. The meanness is in the system; it need not be seen as a national characteristic, but as the collective situation provided for us by our overlords. In countries with advanced capitalist systems, stinginess is a specific accident thrown up by the trend of the exchanges, but our Malthusianism discourages investment and among us money plays a decidedly conservative rôle: as it is diverted from new enterprises, it draws us in pursuit of the oldest; we grow afraid of risks because we are prevented from taking them, and we end by loathing whatever is new. We keep everything, it is true: but that is because the future being made for us is an exact reproduction of our past. The Americans throw things away before they are worn out: tomorrow's products will be better and cheaper. Among us, merchandise will not change in quality: it will simply be dearer. Why be surprised after that that a French home is like a thieving magpie's nest? Wedding dresses, worn suits, hats out of fashion, empty medicine bottles, soiled ribbons, battered cardboard boxes, string: in our cupboards there are enough relics and mementoes to recall half-a-century of history.[62] It would seem that we want at all costs to hold on to a decaying past.

This everlasting return to the past hides a continuous deterioration. Everything wears out; but replacement is niggardly: for preference, things are patched up. The country is mouldering away below the surface: old houses in old towns, out of date plant in old factories, old soil and old ways, an aging population, wizened children, old people's children.

Meanwhile, other countries, launched into great adventures, build up their high walls of steel round us.

They are ascending, of course: but everything happens as if we were going down. When everything is changing, it is necessary to change to remain the same: from its basic unwillingness to change, our economy begets its own death, and death becomes our future: every day we are told that our greatness is behind us, that every day we are getting further away from it. We have cracked up to us I don't know what comforts of living, known to our fathers when the equipment was new, but unknown to us. We live in a time of recrimination and regret; France is Joanna the Mad lying on her handsome rotting husband. Middle-class thought has fallen into prophesying; people like to speak of Europe in 'terms of destiny'; the deluge is forecast, but only as a way of covering up our longing to die in peace: the deluge, yes, but after us. We stop up the walls, sound the floors: they will hold well enough until the last flitting.

The working class works and fights in this debilitating climate. It is not in despair; and the workers are not infected with the infamous desire to die quietly since they are not allowed even to live in peace. But in this leaden future arranged for France, how can they help seeing their own future? The world of manual labour has always been more or less that of repetition. At least the worker in periods of expansion preserves the hope of improving his lot; at least wretchedness and rage push him, in times of sharp crisis, to throw down the burden crushing him and attempt a revolution. But today everything conspires to convince him that his lot will not change whatever he does. Kindness is pushed so far that the position is explained to him several times a day: what does he expect? Doesn't he know the national income is stagnating? Of course a juster distribution of riches would be desirable and, so far as the big employers are concerned, they are quite ready to concede him certain satisfactions: unhappily, this could not be done without ruining the small employers. And haven't they too the right to live? Conclusion: nothing will move, nothing can move. Why should the proletariat be revolutionary? It has something to lose. And why reformist? It has nothing to gain. The working man does not walk into these traps; but, all the same, he cannot do other than measure his powerlessness. As I have said before, he continues to believe in revolution: but he only believes in it. It is no longer his day-to-day task, he has lost the proud certainty of bringing it nearer by his efforts; in other times he saw in the ever-growing number of his local victories a proof of his power over the universe; but Malthusianism, by blunting his weapons, has stripped him of his grip on the world: he has proved that he had no fear of the employers—even the harshest—nor of the State nor of the CRS; but his chief enemy is a faceless, bodiless being which he is unable to lay hold on: *price*. In the course of the last twenty years, the trade unions have formulated little by little the notion of the 'minimum living wage', of the 'sliding scale': these new ideas are supposed to represent progress in the working-class movement. But, on the contrary, they are born of Malthusianism: the ultra-conservatism of our economy compels the worker to fight in order to hold on to the *status quo*. This makes it easier to understand his present aversion to political demonstrations. For the political and social aims of the proletariat are progressive by definition: when he is in sight of imposing his will in the economic sphere, political action comes to birth of itself: it is the meaning of the progress secured in the everyday struggle; but when trade-union action marks time, when the worker is reduced to the defensive, political aims, because they are linked with economic aims, are set back; they are likely to be left in the air. Because they are *advanced* positions, the worker thinks of them from afar as hopes or wishes, but he lives entirely cut off from them and can see no way by which he could get nearer to them again. Far into the distance, repetition of his work and his troubles is spread out before him; if he continues to regard revolution as his object, how could he imagine he is preparing for it? The world changes and France does not budge: the French proletariat wonders whether it has not fallen outside history. In China a new society is being formed; in the USSR the level of life is being raised: the worker among us learns these pieces of news with tempered feelings; they exalt his courage because they prove to him that social progress is possible, they depress it because they seem to indicate that he is standing still, separated from his Russian and Chinese comrades by a distance growing steadily greater, and that safety, if it ever comes, must reach him from outside. I shall return to this: but from now onward, if we want to understand him, let us remember what we went through under the occupation when we were waiting for the Allies to win for us a war we had not the means to win alongside them.[63] Thus the Malthusian strategy allows the employers to keep the initiative: the depressive economy controls working-class *praxis* from the outside, it sketches in depth the possible operations, it defines their characteristics, it delimits their bearing and significance; it decides aims and the chances of victory. As soon as the worker undertakes this prefabricated action, it closes in on him: he finds himself imprisoned in an unreal space which imposes on him its routes, its curvature, and its perspectives. The discouragement of the proletariat is a product of industrial under-production; it interprets subjectively the objective boundaries which the structure of the economy imposes on *praxis*.

(ii) Malthusianism, then, aims at keeping the worker in a state of dejection. But even that is not enough: to rule, it is necessary to divide.

Marchal has shown that the number of strikes between 1890 and 1936 increased and decreased at the same time as production. But he was the first to point out a remarkable exception: from 1920, the frequency of strikes and their percentage of success went down steadily; however, until 1929, our economy continued to expand. The fact is explained by working-class dissensions, and the explanation is not wrong. But where did these dissensions come from? Ah, you will tell me, from the war, from socialist treason, from the Russian Revolution, from everything except Malthusianism which was not yet being practised when they began to appear. It is true: trade-union pluralism dates from before industrial stagnation and our Malthusians found the proletariat cut in two. But who will say that they have not exploited this chance to the full and perpetuated a temporary state by putting a brake on production?

The proletariat, hierarchical in formation before the First World War, was the product of the steam engine. That had been substituted for muscle, but not yet for skill; it continued to be *dependent*: it had to be maintained, regulated, guided, controlled. The slide-lathe freed the worker from moving his tool and from putting it against the piece to be cut; there remained the preparation of the task, fixing the position of the piece, cutting angles, speeds, etc. By its very imperfections, the lathe determines the turner: there are some special outlines which the machine cannot give and which must be achieved by manual work, carried out with auxiliary tools; the operation preserves in part a craft character, and so, in consequence, does the operator. The man required by the machine is formed by society: it confers on him professional knowledge and technical experience by several years' apprenticeship. Competition then selects the best: those who give proof of a sense of touch, of 'flair', of physical ability, of initiative. But it is costly to make a qualified workman: in a liberal capitalist system, the parents have to assume the greater part of this expense. The peasants who have just left the soil and the sons of unskilled labourers have not, for the most part, either the means or the will to go through their apprenticeships.[64]

Thus the exacting demands of the machine came almost to prescribe the method of recruitment: skilled workers are the sons of skilled workers or craftsmen. This aristocracy includes a few intruders but the chief means of access to it is right of birth. The élite worker is, of course, exploited in the same way as his fellows: but he differs from them because his proficiency marks him alone out as controller of a machine. He is preeminently the producer. Chief agent and chief witness of the transformation of materials into manufactured goods, he becomes conscious of himself in the production of the inert thing. For him, apprenticeship represents much more than technical training: he sees in it revolutionary initiation and a rite of passage which gives him access to his caste and to the working-class world.

The machine, too, ensures the unity of the working group, or rather the complex and synthetic operation which the skilled man carries out by means of the machine and with the help of other workers. In a machine works, at the beginning of the century, in every hundred workers there were some twenty 'mechanics' who had been through their four years' apprenticeship and who devoted themselves to fitting up and assembly; some sixty punchers, tappers, mortisers and shapers, dexterous and competent workmen but far from having the training of the first; lastly, some twenty unskilled workers who lived away from the machines and took no part in the process of manufacture. The mechanic managed both his machine and his men: the semi-qualified workers who surrounded him he called his 'accessories' and made them 'do odd jobs' for him; the unskilled workers also worked under him: they freed him from the lower tasks. This technical hierarchy was underlined by the wage hierarchy: the skilled man earned seven francs while the labourer earned four. At that period, we were beginning to talk of the 'masses' to designate the working class, and we were wrong: the masses are amorphous and homogeneous, the proletariat of 1900 was profoundly differentiated, the hierarchy of work and of wages was repeated integrally on the social and political plane. A simple totting up of the unskilled workers would not have sufficed to constitute 'the masses': only in the abstract could they be separated from the other workers, and each of them was more closely linked with his workshop comrades than with other unskilled men in the factory and the town; the working class was formed of a multitude of solar systems, small structural wholes which revolved round a machine. These working teams communicated at the top: the form of trade union apparatus was determined by the composition of the working class: in 1912, France had more than 6 million manual workers and the CGT had only 400,000 members. Nevertheless strikes were conducted vigorously, briskly, with discipline, and, as we have seen, they were for the most part successful: that means that one militant was in general enough to draw in some fifteen who were members of no trade union; in the struggle to secure demands, the skilled workers retained the authority that they enjoyed at work. Not all of them, however, since they belonged to a trade union in the proportion of one to three: the best of them, those who had the courage to acquire some general education and in whom the will to revolution was joined to the clearest awareness of the state of the working class. A hierarchic proletariat belonged to the age of the steam engine, and in its turn produced a trade unionism in a framework based in the workshop, and having the undertaking as its battlefield, the élite workman as its militant force.

That seems to have been the good time: a quarter of a century after its end, our noble souls discovered revolutionary trade unionism and keep on presenting it to us as an example: in that golden age of the Congress of Amiens, bureaucracy did not exist; trade union apparatus sprang directly from the proletariat on which it rested as on a simple internal principle of organization. Defence of working-class interest was ensured by the workers themselves, who could be militant without leaving the workshop, and thus never lost touch with its concrete problems. As a matter of fact, the Bergsonian staff of the CGT came to champion spontaneity: on one occasion, Pelloutier evoked a 'mysterious link' uniting working-class organizations, on another, Greffuelhe praised the 'spontaneous and creative action' of French trade unionism. The trade union Self, in short, thrust its roots into the deep Self of the proletariat. Before the First World War, the class struggle had an indefinable something.

Of course, there was a certain amount of nonsense: the vital impulse of the working classes concealed dictatorship by the skilled élite. The 'active minority' despised what it already called 'the mass', and detested democracy. 'Before beginning the struggle,' said Lagardelle, 'it is not, as in democracy, the lumpish and backward mass which should decide. Numbers no longer make the law. An active élite should be formed which, by its quality, draws the mass on and directs it into the fighting paths.' Put another way: the 'superior' stratum of the proletariat took on the putting forward of both its own claims and those of the 'least favoured'; this élite alone claimed to assess what was good for all and sought less to understand popular opposition than to break it down. I shall not be so unjust as to suggest that these splendid fighters betrayed their class: if they distrusted their comrades, it was because they suspected them of being sheeplike rather than revolutionary; they were continually at pains to reconcile their own interests with those of the unskilled and, at least to begin with, in a prosperous country in process of industrialization, these adjustments were not too difficult. They became rarer and rarer in the last years before the war. The working-class struggle had two faces: for the active minority, it was a concrete experiment and an instrument of emancipation; for the majority who followed them, it was often simply an abstract imperative. And when the militants drew the unskilled workers into claim-making activity, it could be said, with our noble souls, that the working class was united in action and that its unity was immanent. As a matter of fact, more and more often it came to be fighting on two fronts: against comrades and against the heads of the under-taking. At the top, however, were to be found a handful of militants whose views were larger and who proudly called themselves 'active minority': against the particularism of the élite, they had taken as their aim the defence of the general interests of the class. But when they tried to convert the skilled workers to industrial trade unionism and to centralization, this minority went against the current. The working-class aristo-cracy continued to favour 'anarchic administration' and craft trade unionism. Without the abrupt alteration in industry, the Pelloutiers, Pougets, Merrheims, Monattes would have lost the game.

1884: the first practical transformers were introduced. Ten years later the electric motor was everywhere in competition with steam-driven machines and making increased mechaniza-tion possible. Little by little, technical improvement reduced the part played by the worker in the process of manufacture, and this meant that manual work progressively required less skill. The new lathe produced new turners: it needed only a flick of the finger to enable it of itself to transmit instructions to the executive machinery. Suddenly, between unskilled and semi-skilled workers an unknown figure appeared, the conveyor-belt operative who dealt with machines like a skilled worker, but, like an unskilled worker, did his job without apprentice-ship.[65] He was already there, but no one had noticed him: where had he come from? From everywhere: sometimes he was a countryman who had just reached town, more often he had been an unskilled worker in some other industry. From 1900, at Saint-Étienne, in certain workshops of the government small arms factory, 'there are 50 mechanics out of 250 workers; all the others are former miners or weavers;[66] they have in their hands perfected machines which make skilled knowledge use-less'.[67] These newcomers were still timorous: they had neither the time nor the will nor the strength to organize themselves by themselves; they called the skilled and militant élite to their aid. In 1912, Merrheim, at the federal Congress at Le Havre, reported these words by a mill-hand of the east: 'How could you expect us, poor mill-hands, who reach home weary in the evening, to attend to the trade union? Those who could attend to it, the technical workers, have created trade unions.'

As can be seen, their claims were modest: and if they laid claim to the right to join trade-union organizations, it was with the fixed intention of immediately delegating their powers to the élite. But the élite took no notice: it defended aristocratic trade unionism fiercely against the newcomers. Rather than merge the metalworkers and the moulders to form an industrial federation, in 1910 the Mechanics' federation preferred to leave the CGT. In 1900, there were 51 industrial compared with 34 craft unions; in 1911, there were 142 compared with 114: the proportion had not changed. During this time, without skill, without trade-union experience, without political education, the conveyor-belt operative was abandoned to propaganda and oppression by the employers. I call to mind the principal traits of this new proletariat, abruptly begotten by modern machines and the techniques of organization.[68]

Determined in the offices in relation to the different operations being carried out at the same moment in the works, the rhythm of his labour is imposed on him like an inimical force and rules him from the outside; his fatigue is the result less of the expenditure of muscular energy than of continual nervous tension and the constant effort to adapt himself to pre-established norms. At the end of the day, his weariness sticks to his skin; it stays with him during sleep and is still there when he wakes. This chronic lassitude becomes second nature, even the way in which he is aware of his body. It is written on his face, it limits his powers, and makes him, in the true sense of the term, *a diminished* man.

This degradation of work brings with it devalorization of knowledge; employers do not like the educated, above all the intelligent worker. Intelligence is prejudicial to output: the conveyor-belt operative and the machine formed so perfect a symbiosis that an idea in the one had the same effect as damage to the other. Still, total absence of mind won't do either: inattention and forgetfulness could occasion as many disasters as lucid thought; it is necessary *to be there*, a vigilance without content, a captive consciousness kept awake only the better to suppress itself. But if the worker rids himself of his own thought, it is to give place to that of others: since rationalization consecrated the divorce of conception from execution, he does not know the meaning of his actions; they are stolen from him, or conditioned from the outside, others instead of himself decide their target and their range. At the very moment he becomes the agent of production, he feels he is being acted on; in the depths of his subjectivity he feels himself an object. His employer's unwilling accomplice, he strives to forget the little he has learned because knowledge would make his condition intolerable; he takes refuge in passivity because he has been deprived of all initiative. Since he has been stripped of his own thought, how should he know that ideas are produced by man? He becomes accustomed to seeing, in the order established by technicians, an external fate of which he is the first victim. The social history of rationalization is contained in two formulae. At the end of last century, Taylor said *to* the workers: 'Don't try to think; others will do that for you.' Thirty years later, Ford said *of* the workers: 'They don't like thinking for themselves.'

The mechanization of work changes human relationships. Before 1914, the proletariat was a constellation: this aristocratic structure did not exclude solidarity or the linking of man to man in a manner vaguely resembling vassalage. Between the conveyor-belt operative and the 'élite', the solidarity due to their work was broken: the skilled worker used to decide the task of the unskilled; the man in the office decides the work of the conveyor-belt operative; he decides it from afar and for all of them, without ever seeing any one of them: today the conveyor-belt operative has no connexion except with his mates on the conveyor-belt. Still the machine interposes its rigidity between them: each one discerns the existence of his neighbours in the form of the collective rhythm to which he must adapt himself; the *other* appears through delays, faults, mistakes: in this mechanical universe, the person is an error leading to a loss of wages. The semi-automatic machine is pre-eminently the instrument of massification: it causes the internal structures of the proletariat to split asunder; homogeneous molecules are left separated one from the others by an inert and inelastic environment.

In isolating him from his comrades, work divided into small

portions throws the operative back on himself; but in himself
he finds only a general and formal essential being: everyone
can do what he is doing, therefore he is the same as everyone
else, and his *personal* reality is only a mirage. However,
imperious needs bring him back to the pure subjectivity of
desire and suffering: hunger, pain, fatigue push him to prefer
himself but do not justify this preference. Why you rather than
me? Because I am myself. —And who are you?—The same as
you. Unjustifiable subjectivity enters into conflict with objective interchangeability. On the individual plane, this results in
a profound sense of inferiority; on the collective plane, the
classic forms of protest have had their day: the advent of these
workers lacking the value of skill, *replaceable*, and obsessed by
fear of being out of work is in danger of rendering strikes ineffectual.

What is perceptible first of all, in fact, is not so much the
rise of an unknown worker as the liquidation of the old ones.
The mechanics thrown on the streets by the crisis of 1907 were
not reinstated; in 1913, during the strike at the Renault factories, the specialists held out longer than the others; they were
sure they were irreplaceable, the employer would have to give
way in the end. The employer did not give way: he replaced
them by machines and unskilled workers; it was clear to all
that the skilled worker had had his day. However, conveyor-
belt operatives multiplied, and trade unionism, demoralized,
bereft of its chief weapon, stagnated; to these new men, without traditions or past, the old militants no longer had anything
to say. And then suddenly, in August 1914, the war unsealed
the eyes of the trade unionists: they discovered the masses;
their surprise was harsh when they saw them issuing from the
ground as they shouted: 'To Berlin!' Twenty years of propaganda to end in this madness? 'What is left of our activity?' one
militant wondered, 'What is left of our anti-war meetings?' And
another: 'In a cattle truck, with other men bawling, "to Berlin,"
I felt the failure of the CGT, the failure of teachers, the intellectual failure of the country.' And Merrheim: 'The working class
has been roused by a tremendous wave of nationalism.' And
Monatte: 'The wave has passed, it has carried us away.' Ignored,
then abruptly discovered, the masses made necessary the
creation of mass trade unionism, a mass party, new propa-

ganda and a new ideology. Incapable of fulfilling these tasks, revolutionary trade unionism suddenly discovered that it had grown out of date! The old working-class apparatus fell outside the movement, the war surprised the leaders without the masses and the masses without protection; these young crowds, victims of the disaccord separating their activity as producers from the real content of their hopes, could no longer be to themselves what they were in themselves: their radicalism, their instability, their rage, followed swiftly by discouragement, expressed quite simply the fact that the new working-class state was unbearable; the fascinating myth of war was for some time to deceive their revolutionary aspirations and make them aware of the violence that was in them: but this violence remained captive, alienated.

It was from the war too that enlightenment was to come. From the war, and not from the circumstances of production; it was not trade-union leaders, it was the Somme, it was Verdun that were to tear up the illusory image they had of themselves. 'When I found them again at Verdun,' wrote Dumoulin, 'they bore a grudge against everyone; journalists, deputies, socialists, Parisians, policemen, those in the rear. The strongest, clearest impression among them was that of eye-wash, lies, exaggeration, mistakes.'

When in 1919 they poured back, drunk with anger and distrust, the masses were at anyone's disposal. To some extent, revolutions everywhere in Europe came to depend on the meeting of soldiers and workers. With us, two million demobilized men mixed with three or four million who had been working in factories. An unstable, explosive mixture: new militants swelled the ranks of the CGT. Revolution seemed possible and the middle class ready 'to agree to the heaviest sacrifices to the proletariat'. But the strike of June 1919 proved that the masses were not ready. How could they have been? Who had prepared them? On June 2, the metalworkers of Paris stopped work; the strike spread to three trade unions in Seine-et-Oise, there were 130,000 strikers, 80,000 trade union cards were issued. The strike was half political, half corporative: there were some claims but also 'a great distress . . . a general idea affecting the whole proletariat'. At first the strike was led by a consultative committee, a trade-union organization just created. But the immense crowd of new trade unionists—more than half of those on strike—distrusted all the delegates, invaded trade-union meeting places, treated its own representatives as traitors, and ended by electing a committee of action which claimed to take the place of the consultative committee. The consultative committee, overwhelmed, surrendered its authority into the hands of the metalworkers federation which took charge of the strike.

On June 22 the committee of action burst into the offices of the federation, insisted that it should be present at sittings, treated the leaders as dispensers of eye-wash. The federation wanted a general strike. It demanded a meeting of the inter-federal association. This refused to extend the conflict but advised the strikers against returning to work until they had secured guarantees. Now, from June 26, the committee of action itself, owing to the effects of a discouragement dating from long before the decision of the association, had ordered the strike to end. It was total defeat; people returned to their machines having gained nothing: the masses had found themselves at grips with a bureaucracy whose prudent methods and long distance forecasts disconcerted them, and they had elected a committee whose incompetence and unruliness had impaired resolution. The incident was valuable as an *indication*: recent product of the new mechanization, the masses needed leadership and discipline appropriate to their basic structure. They rejected the trade unionists who had rejected them before the war, they would have condescended to submit only to an authority of iron fighting implacably against the continual want of balance of mass formations. Where were they to find it in 1919? The leaders of the SFIO and the CGT accused themselves, justified themselves, confessed their sins; they agreed only in condemning the newcomers. The June strike supplied them with new 'reasons adduced' in support of their sentence. One spoke of 'committees of disobedience and indiscipline'. Another lamented that 'the instincts of the street crowd which howls and lynches have been brought into our meetings. . . .' For a third, it was the worst misfortune that a 'revolutionary situation without a revolutionary spirit in the masses had ever met in France'. Blum was to say in 1921: 'We know what the unorganized masses are. . . . We know they will follow one leader one day, and another on the morrow. . . . Those who would have marched behind you yesterday will, perhaps, be the first tomorrow to stick you against a wall. . . . No revolution will be made with these gangs who run behind all the horses.'

However, it was necessary either to give up the idea of making a revolution or to do it with 'those gangs'. Unorganized they certainly were but that simply proved that they needed an organization. Unhappily, with no awareness of their needs, they could not of themselves create an organization. Torn between a dying aristocracy and a multitude which exhausted its spirit of revolt in disorder, would the working class be reduced to impotence?

No: these disruptions seemed to be temporary; the situation could not but evolve. Organization, of course, was not going to emerge suddenly from the anarchic crowd, but already the youngest militants of the CGT and the SFIO were drawing near to those who met at Kienthal and the socialist opposition; their war experiences had led all of them to condemn the Third (*sic*) International; they had decided to serve the masses and to give them the apparatus they lacked.

And then, above all, it was assumed that the movement of concentration would go on, and would in the end liquidate the working-class aristocracy. A glance at statistics supplied about 1925 by the Ford works[69] is all that is necessary to be persuaded that ultimately conveyor-belt operatives would make up almost the whole of the proletariat:

Percentage of the Workers	43%	36%	6%	14%	1%
Length of training at Ford's	not more than one day	from one to eight days	from one to two weeks	from one month to a year	up to six years

In this undertaking, one worker in a hundred still deserved to be called skilled; out of ten workers, eight were conveyor-belt operatives. This pitiful degradation might well be horrifying: it swallowed up those fierce militants of revolutionary trade unionism of whom Marx speaks. But, on the other hand, it eliminated the unskilled worker. And above all it gave its strength to the working-class movement. Once this homogeneous 'neo-proletariat' found its framework and its battle formula, its cohesion would be stricter than ever, and working-class unity would cease to be just a term.

We have reckoned without our Malthusians. In stopping the movement towards concentration, they have postponed unification indefinitely. Manufacturing industries do not absorb more than 45 per cent of the workers; the rest are spread out among 500,000 undertakings. Naturally, the most important establishments are not always the best equipped: in the motor car industry, the construction sector is much more concentrated and much less automatized than that producing accessories. No matter: the medium-sized undertaking has not the means to push on with automation; the small works remains in the craft realm. In 1948, out of 3,677,000 workers in the processing industry, there were 1,306,000 skilled workers, 1,320,000 conveyor-belt operatives, and 1,051,000 unskilled workers. The first two are approximately equal (35·5 per cent and 35·9 per cent). The third is extremely broken up: in book production and building, where skilled workers are much more numerous, the archaic structure of the proletariat persists: the unskilled work under the orders of the skilled. In iron-smelting and the textile industry, the operative dominates; the skilled workers are detached from the process of manufacture; they form maintenance and tool making teams and no longer have any contact with the other workers,[70] while operatives and unskilled workers form a rather more homogeneous mass, the more so since a few hours or a few days suffice to change one into the other. It should not be assumed that this upheaval is of benefit to the proletariat by way of new experience: on the contrary, it provokes a break in experience and a splitting into two of the historical *subject*: the working class, to the great delight of the employers, is in danger of remaining cut into two almost equal pieces which have neither the same structure nor the same values nor the same interests nor the same techniques of organization and battle.

(α) *Duality of values*
The skilled worker has always based his demands on the skill of his work. He is the true producer, the sole source of all riches; he it is who transforms raw materials into social goods. The idea of the general strike, so popular before 1914, was born of this proud self-consciousness: to cause middle-class society to crumble, all the worker need do was cross his arms; if he laid

claim to the ownership of his tools, it was because he alone was capable of using them. For the rest, in small undertakings, his technical knowledge was rarely inferior to that of his employer; the trade union grouped proficiencies and thus judged itself entitled to control production: it would quite naturally be transformed, on the morrow of Revolution, into an organ of administration. Since its rights derived from its merits, this aristocracy was not far from considering itself as the sole victim of capitalism. At the federal congress of 1908, this intervention by a mechanic expressed the general feeling: 'To deny the value as a skilled man of the worker is more or less to provide capitalist exploitation with extenuating circumstances.' Whence a troubled spirit would conclude without too much difficulty that the exploitation of the unskilled is, after all, less criminal. The working-class élite would not go so far as that: but it does regard its auxiliaries as 'heavy weights'. Does it recognize their rights? That is doubtful. Let us say that it sees in them the permanent objects of its generosity. This humanism of work is ambiguous: it may willingly be agreed that it is an advance on the humanism of riches. Still, it is only a halting place: if things stop there, the multitude will continue to be excluded from humanity. It is necessary, you say, to deserve to be a man. That's fine so long as it is possible to *acquire* merit. But what would you do with those who have no means of doing so?

The new proletarian cannot lay claim to the least merit since every possible means has been taken to make him understand that he has none. However, weariness and wretchedness overwhelm him: he must either burst or get satisfaction. On what then is he going to base his claims? Well, on exactly nothing. Or, if you prefer, on his claims themselves: the need creates the right. With the advent of the masses, a reversal of values has taken place; automation has radically changed humanism. Don't take the conveyor-belt operative for a proud man aware of his rights: he is 'a sub-man aware of his sub-humanity' and claiming the right to be a man. The humanism of need is, in consequence, the only humanism which has as its object the whole of humanity: the liquidation of merit has blown up the last barrier which separated men. But this new humanism is itself a need: it has lived in a hollow like the very meaning of an inadmissible frustration. For skilled workers, man is made;

all he has to do is to re-organize society. For the conveyor-belt operative, man has to be made: it is what is lacking in man, what is in question for each of us at every moment, what, without having ever been, is continually in danger of being lost.

All would be for the best if the humanism of work were progressively obliterated before the humanism of need: and that is what would have taken place if Malthusianism had not stopped the industrial revolution. Today the two humanisms co-exist, and this co-existence throws everything into confusion: if the first solidifies and establishes a position for itself, it becomes the enemy of the second. On the other hand, the masses are secretly infected by the ideology of the working-class élite: in face of middle-class people, they have no shame, for the best among those, whatever they do, will never *deserve* the privileges they enjoy; but the skilled workers belong to the proletariat, they are exploited just like the operative, and if they live a little better than he, this difference appears negligible as soon as their level of life is compared with that of the middle class. And, above all, they claim that they owe these slight advantages to their merit. If that were true? I have said that they were, for the most part, sons of skilled workers: but after all, that is not written on their foreheads. The operative says to himself that his parents, if they had imposed some sacrifices on themselves, could have put him also through an apprenticeship. Or, perhaps, he blames himself for lack of will, of perseverance. The obvious inequality of conditions underlines, in his eyes, the inequality of values: if the skilled worker draws his value from his form of work, the conveyor-belt operative is worth nothing since he is, by definition, replaceable. In short, he is ashamed before those who ought to be his comrades in the fight; his pugnacity is in danger of being lessened. To free the masses from the sense of their inferiority, all pre-war socialist values would have to be cleared away: the masses would have to be made to understand that those values offered to every man the chance to look at man and society as they truly are, that is to say with the eyes of those treated the most unjustly. Since technical evolution has resulted in taking skill out of work, that final superiority of man over man, this young barbarism must be shown, against all morals and all élites, that the 'superiorities' are mutilations, that the only human relationship is that of the real, total man with total man, and that this relationship, disguised or passed over in silence, exists permanently in the heart of the masses and exists only there. But as the multitude becomes impregnated with this radical ideology, skilled workers, who see their *value* disputed, brace themselves in their positions. The aristocracy becomes aware of itself when attacked: since the last years before the first war, in reaction against the rise of the masses, well intentioned theorists baptized minority trade unionism as 'knighthood' and wanted to make a new Knight Templar of the militant: enlightened despot, the skilled worker agreed to devote himself to the masses but refused them the right to defend their interests for themselves. After the first war there was a new mixing, and revolutionary trade unionism vanished. But not its spirit: from 1921 to 1927, even inside the CGTU, advocates of the trade unionism of the élite were to resist the Communists fiercely. From 1919 to 1934, Jouhaux's CGT was forced to become bureaucratic 'on account of the growing complexity of trade-union tasks' but the trade union official represented only the working-class élite, and the masses remained outside the organization. In 1936 Sémard declared, at the Congress of Toulouse, 'Two principal ideologies continue to confront one another in the working-class movement and in the trade-union movement. They are the ideologies of Proudhon and of Marx.' Jouhaux was right when he answered, 'Since 1909, I have never before heard militants taking the floor to expound their points of view avail themselves of Marx or of Proudhon.' He was right *in form*, but in fact he was playing his fish. For the two tendencies of which Sémard spoke were not *to begin with* derived from Marx or Proudhon: they existed in the French proletariat outside all philosophical or political culture. Ask a militant Communist what he thinks of 'human *dignity*': he will shrug his shoulders. Was it chance that, during Jouhaux's reign, the federation of metalworkers and the CGT declared themselves in favour of the scientific organization of work, so long as it 'does not cast a slur on human dignity',[71] and that these same words are to be found again in 1945 in a declaration by the CFTC? The 'dignity' of the skilled worker is the superiority of his form of work. He is *already* a man, since he is proud of his work; *already* free, since the universal machine leaves a large place for initiative: in the name of liberty and of dignity, he lays claim to a juster society which will recognize his value and his rights. The masses are not *dignified*; they do not even imagine what liberty is: but their simple existence introduces, like a thorn in the flesh, the root demand of the human in an inhuman society.

(β)   Duality of interests

It has often been noted—and I will not insist on it—that the mass yields to a rhythm of work which is repugnant to the skilled worker. In the Citroën works, the strikes of 1926 and 1927 were against machinery and machine-working. The trade unionists—all skilled workers—would have liked to reduce norms of output; the conveyor-belt operatives wanted to accelerate the rhythm: since, anyhow, their work was a curse, however much it brought in, their piecework earnings could equal the hourly wage of the skilled worker: this was vengeance. At its birth, conveyor-belt production and semi-automatic machines had been condemned by the representatives of the proletariat: but, in the long run, it had produced new workers who lived by mechanization and, whether they liked it or not, must declare their solidarity with it. There is no doubt, in fact, that the 'neo-proletariat', by its very function, responds to the demands of mass production: this was apparent in the United States when the manufacturers, goaded by competition, wanted by increasing output, to lower costs, to enlarge their internal market and get the custom of the masses. That certainly did not mean that the masses were working for themselves: between conveyor-belt operative producer and conveyor-belt operative consumer, there lay the screen of profit and exploitation. But it is none the less true that a rise in the standard of living accompanied the increase in productivity. In 1949, an American worker produced four times as much in an hour as did a French worker. The same year, the national income per head of the population amounted in the United States to 1,453 dollars against 482 dollars in France. Among us, it was not in the interest of the conveyor-belt operative to intensify his effort or increase his hours of work: for the same effort and the same number of hours, he ought to demand a progressive increase in his productivity. But that implies nothing less than the surrender of Malthusian practices: it would have been necessary to renew equipment, push on concentration, rationalization and automation. Now, the fate of the skilled worker depends on the maintenance of archaic forms of production: he too, in a way, is tied to Malthusianism. Certainly the raising of the level of life could compensate for lowering the skill of the work and the breakdown of the wage hierarchy: but it is the privileges of the élite that are at stake, his pride, his 'joy in work', and his dignity: that is to say, his awareness of his superiorities. Thus the claims of the masses tend to smash the existing framework of our economy; the élite, on the contrary, moderates its claims so as not to provoke the transformation that would be fatal to it.

(γ) *Trade union pluralism*

Qualification as a skilled worker demands and develops in the worker judgment, initiative, and a feeling of responsibility; that is what makes him irreplaceable. The employer—at least in small undertakings where there is no automation—still remains close enough to his workers, the majority of whom are skilled. These, by the very finish of their form of work, are in a position to exercise a delicate and continuous effect on their employers; 'contact' and tension are maintained through the continual confrontation of working-class aristocracy and industrialists. On the scale of the undertaking, this élite, replaced as it is with difficulty, can secure a great deal by the simple threat of a strike, and in the end, since this threat is constantly implied, by negotiation. The skilled worker holds all the winning cards: he can discuss, bargain; he makes use of violence only in the last resort. He advances and draws back, threatens and becomes conciliatory again; he adapts himself to his employer's attitude, to the situation, to the always changing balance of forces of the moment, the whole proceeding *in words*: words which in reality are neither vocal whispers nor actions but *counters* which can be put down and equally can be withdrawn. Before passing to action, the skilled worker can draw back as many times as he likes. Reciprocal blackmail and threats, promises, breaking off and resuming of negotiations: these abstract and almost symbolic manoeuvres often make a trial of strength unnecessary, a compromise solution turns up just in the nick of time. The skill of the trade unionist allows the trade union freedom of manoeuvre.

Let us add that this élite is homogeneous: undoubtedly the movement towards centralization gave birth to bureaucracy. But the basic militant can regard himself as a potential leader, his experience and his theoretical knowledge are as great as those of his leaders; he exerts an effective and continuous control over them. Inversely, the leadership can make no mistake as to the feelings of those in the ranks: the members of the trade union speak, give their advice, currents of opinion are made clear; together and individually they contribute to setting the general lines of trade union activity. Continuing contact between leaders and led, constant pressure of the worker on the employers: the two conditions making for a trade union *policy* are brought together.

With the masses, the chances of negotiation decrease. Unskilled, their work ceases to be in itself a means of action. So long as the motors turn, the 'personal factor' seems to be negligible. By the same changes, the worker, deprived of the guarantee due to his value as a skilled man, and the leadership, every day further removed from him, are lost to one another in anonymity. Thus the new condition of the proletarian tends to break continuity of action: to bring any weight to bear on the employer's decisions, the workers' resistance must cross a certain threshold, on this side of which it is not noticed. In short, the strike—that is to say, violence— is their sole resource. But this 'specific weapon of the workers'[72] has changed in its nature: the skilled worker is indispensable; to stop production, he has only to stay at home. He is certainly making use of violence: but this violence is lawful and—in principle at least—tends to remain abstract and, as it were, passive. In this emergency, the employer's reaction has to be kept within certain limits; he can, if he wins, multiply penalties: but he would be hard put to it to cause blood to flow. But the conveyor-belt operative, being just anyone as a producer, can be replaced by just anyone; it is not enough, then, for him to stop work, he must prevent others from doing it. After twenty years of uncertainty and wavering, the masses discovered a new weapon, the only one adapted to their condition: a strike with occupation of the factories. This was to violate the most sacred middle-class rights, and to lay themselves open, in consequence, to the intervention of the CRS. Summonses, tear-gas bombs; if that were not enough, shots. Can we say that the masses are more stubborn, more 'ill-natured' than the élite? That would be simply absurd. The truth is that the evolution of technique has completely changed violence: to defend his wages, the conveyor-belt operative must risk his skin.

For the same reason, the masses have no other defence than massive action: the aim is, by general operations conducted on a national scale, to secure collective agreements valid for entire sections of industry. But these operations are possible only if the masses combine in a single movement with a single watchword. Now we have seen that it is wrong to suppose them distinguished by a kind of savage unity: they are a molecular scattering, a mechanical aggregate of solitudes, pure product of the automation of tasks. Undoubtedly the archipelago-like structure is a purely ideal limit of massification: in reality the disintegratory forces meet numerous obstacles. In particular, when social tension relaxes, the mere presence of the trade-union apparatus —this nervous system—preserves a 'residual tonus' in the proletariat. All the same, it is not easy to regard the working-class masses as an army on the alert. It is true that the class struggle does not stop for a moment: not for a moment does the violence done to the worker cease, and he, equally without cease, opposes to it his simple reality as a man. But individual activity is no proof that the masses themselves are active. It is wrong, as we have seen, to take them as a collective *subject* whose psychology it would be possible to expound. The behaviour of the mass is not at all psychological, and it would be the worst possible mistake to compare it to the conduct of persons. The man of the masses is anyone—you or me; and his personal attitudes have no importance. In himself, he is a conscious agent, but the forces of dispersion, in placing his neighbour opposite him like an *alter ego* who reflects back to him his powerlessness and doubles his loneliness, neutralize his activity and produce a collective whole which reacts as one, as a material environment in which excitations propagate themselves mechanically. The masses are the object of the story: they never act *by themselves* and all working-class action demands that they begin by suppressing themselves as masses in order to attain elementary

forms of collective life. We have no right to speak of the
'pressure' they should exercise on their employers; and their influence can be only negative: the employers know that exploitation, if it goes beyond a certain limit, works against the forces
of massification and is in danger of provoking a rapid crystallization of the working-class masses into a proletariat. But, so
far as the day-to-day activity of the militant is concerned, the
contradiction is obvious: his work acts on the object-masses in
such a way as to transform them into the subject-proletariat; he
endeavours, wherever he may be, to liquidate their granular
structure for the benefit of an organic unity. Now unity can be
realized only if in some way it has been given from the beginning: each man, seeing his loneliness in that of the next man,
can escape from it only if the other too escapes from it; in short,
wherever they may be, the beginning must be *elsewhere*. In the
great industrial concentrations, the method of mechanical propagation may, at first, take the place of unity. It is what is called
imitation: it cannot be taken as collective action, but this
anonymous movement makes action possible: it is for the militant to transform the contagious tide into an exact operation.
Only it must be added that the imitation itself presupposes a
certain previous unity. It is true that the 'laws of imitation'
govern solely the social sectors in a state of permanent disintegration:[73] what I imitate in my neighbour is not the Other,
it is myself become my own object; I do not repeat his action
because *he* has done it but because I myself, in him, have just
done it. In short, it is necessary that I should perceive his situation and his needs as *my* situation and *my* needs in such a way
that his conduct appears to me *from outside* to be a project
springing from my head; the one who imitates and the one who
is imitated are, at the same time, interchangeable and separate
and the imitative conduct is the result of a dialectic of identity
and of externality; the conveyor-belt operative being anyone,
the method of propagation of the claim-making movement
through the masses will be contagious because each one sees the
other coming towards him as anyone, that is to say, as himself.
To the extent that massification generates both isolation and
interchangeability, it gives birth to imitation as a mechanical
relationship between the molecules; and imitation is not a *trend*
or a psychical characteristic: it is the necessary result of certain

social situations. These purely mechanical connexions must still be based in a previous synthesis which allows at least that imitators and imitated should be brought *face to face*, whether through the purely material unity of habitat or of work place; at the very least there must be the unity of danger run or of hope experienced. Now the relative dispersion of French industry works in favour of the employers. Distance does not suppress contagious propagation: it raises the threshold of it; at a distance, the *same* becomes the *other*. For the unity of the situation to be noticed, the urgency of danger must increase: only exceptional circumstances will reveal to the scattered masses the concrete and actual unity of the proletariat. In 1936, to cite but one example, the political triumph of the *Front Populaire* released the contagious propagation of social movements: the masses learned of their unity when they perceived it outside themselves in the alliance of the three people's parties, and they reacted in their own way, almost mechanically, by the identity of their conduct; if there had been no brake on the movement, it would, sooner or later, have been transformed into revolutionary action.

The circumstances which bring about the crystallization of the masses into revolutionary crowds are rightly called 'historic': they are linked with the social, economic, and political transformations of the continent; it may be admitted that they are not encountered every day. Thus the passage from the state of mass to the primitive unity of the crowd is necessarily of an intermittent character. Masses are affected by an inertia which prevents them from reacting to subtle excitations: it is no good expecting from them rapid and rapidly stopped movements, demonstrations of power and detailed operations, feints and manoeuvres which allow of the exercise of continuous pressure on the enemy without starting an open struggle with him. Besides, the primary crystallizations have no equilibrium: mechanization of labour has stolen the future from the workers. If they budge, it is because their *present* condition is unacceptable, it is because they foresee the possibility of modifying it at once. They cannot be expected to wear themselves out in sustaining a long term venture: to the abruptness and discontinuity characteristic of mass movements must therefore be added a certain instability.

Above all, do not let us conclude that the 'neo-proletariat' is reformist rather than revolutionary: it is quite the contrary. It is true that the masses cannot be mobilized except in defence of immediate interests: but, when they do get under way, they want everything, immediately. Middle-class propaganda persuaded them that the least change made in their condition would produce catastrophe. Thus day-to-day reality became in their eyes a strict system of prohibitions. But what tears them from their mass state is a still more basic impossibility: that of putting up any longer with their needs. Before this major impossibility, all prohibitions break down and change becomes their most immediate possibility; desperation begets hope, crystallization of the masses into a crowd begets the belief that everything is possible. The skilled worker can limit himself to *some* claims; the masses want *everything* because they have nothing. Concerted action, based on years of experience, in full possession of techniques and traditions, with awareness that it is a long and exacting venture can be limited in a moment to a definite objective: but since the masses have no collective memory and since their 'awakenings' are intermittent, their action is always new, always starting afresh, without tradition or wisdom: nothing limits it, neither fear of failure nor historical reflexion; it poses in its pure essence as a sovereign efficacy and an absolute power able to change the world and life. By the same stroke, *all* needs will be revealed at the same time. The term 'minimum living wage' expresses well what they want to say: below that limit is death. For the man of the masses, to live is simply not to die on the spot. In a 'normal' period, the worker can satisfy only a very small part of his needs: those whose non-satisfaction would bring about his death; and since the forces of dispersion have impregnated him with the sense of his powerlessness, he must exercise a permanent censorship over all those needs which are not *vital*. Half forced back, half concealed, these needs are none the less always present: they are simply not recognized or named. But when an abrupt deterioration in his level of life suddenly places the worker in danger of death, a popular movement is born and the masses are transformed: at once, the connexion between the possible and the impossible is inverted and needs are unmasked because they can be satisfied by action. When everything is possible, it becomes intolerable to live on the minimum wage. From that point, the popular movement always goes further unless it is smashed against armed resistance from the employers: each success is an encouragement to exact more; always more radical without ceasing to be immediate, it necessarily questions the very essence of society. For half the French, wages oscillate about the minimum living wage: if from one day to the next their real purchasing power had to be increased by a third, middle-class France would blow up. It matters little, then, whether strikers or demonstrators have or have not the will to make a revolution: objectively every mass demonstration is revolutionary. Its initial cause is the wish not to die, and from that it goes on to the wish to live. And then, even if it were possible, within the framework of capitalism, to satisfy by a sustained policy, by ten, twenty years' labour, certain of their demands, the fact is they haven't the time to wait: a middle-class man badly housed can be patient: he is cramped for room, that is all; a workers' family huddles together in a hovel: it must burst or move house. But those promised houses do not yet exist: how move house unless to take up one of those which already exist? To obtain full satisfaction, the revolutionary crowd must seize power.[74] That would be perfect if wretchedness got it on the move only in a situation in which power could be seized. But how believe in this 'pre-established harmony'? It is true that every mass movement is a beginning of revolution; and, sometimes, the circumstances which determine popular action may at the same time weaken the resistance of the ruling classes. But the heroic and bloody history of the proletariat is enough to show that all the conditions necessary for a working-class victory are rarely present at the same time. Besides, the proletariat represents only a third of the nation, and the masses are only a fraction of that third. For them to be able to win one day, preparation for their triumph is necessary: alliances inside the working class and, at need, outside it, must be knotted, a plan decided on, strategy determined, tactics invented: those are the very things of which it is not capable. In consequence, the rôle of the militant is going to change entirely.

In the first place, he is an official. Collinet put it well: 'The mass cannot itself take part in trade-union life; it gives its confidence to responsible militants, judging them by the immediate results they bring to it.' But why does he go on to describe an

ideal militant who would serve as intermediary between leaders
and masses? Of course, it would be vain for this mediator, like
his comrades, to devote his day 'to purely technical and skilled
work', raising himself all the while by a succession of asceses
above his speciality so as to judge problems of skill, above the
skilled trades, so as to consider 'social problems in their
generality'. Unhappily this individual, both 'deep-rooted' and
'detached', has nothing in common with the contemporary
conveyor-belt operative; he is an old acquaintance and Collinet
quite simply presents us, under another name, with the skilled
trade-unionist worker of 1900. Do not let us be surprised if he
goes on to admit that the 'militant is uncommon and unreliable
among conveyor-belt operatives'. That certain men are at the
same time detached and in position is possible: it all depends on
their condition, their health, their leisure, their culture, in a
word on their kind of work. But it is not possible that those who
lie helplessly crushed under the weight of the World should
soar above it. At first sight, there is not the least difficulty in
principle in a conveyor-belt operative making a first-rate militant; the one serious obstacle would appear to be commonplace
and due to circumstances: it is fatigue. Only this fatigue is not
an accident; it piles up, like the eternal snows, without melting,
and it is that which *makes* the operative. Of course, it will pass:
when hours of work have been reduced or automation has been
pushed to the limit. But the operative will pass with it. And
then we are not dreaming of the possibilities of American or
Soviet industry or of the state of man in the year 2000: I am
speaking about 1954 and about Malthusian France; I am speaking about workers sapped *at the same time* by weariness and
wretchedness. Since 1912, the mill-hands cited by Merrheim
have complained that they are too tired to be interested in the
trade union and have wanted others to run it on their behalf.
Since then, things have grown only worse: to earn *as much as* in
1938, the working-man must work *more*. He gets up at four or
five o'clock, leaves at six, gets back home at eight o'clock in the
evening, eats a meal and goes to bed at nine. He complains bitterly that he is deprived of family life: where can he be expected
to find the time to go on the warpath? Work time-tables also
hinder trade-union meetings, unless they are held at work; often
it is necessary to provoke the workers to down tools if their

opinion on a question which concerns them is wanted. As for the 'uncommon' militants who would meet Collinet's demands, I understand that they are 'unreliable': they are obliged to impinge on their sleep and, sooner or later, they break down. *Unless* they give up manual work and are kept by the trade union: that is to say, by their comrades. It is certainly absolutely essential that the militant should emerge from the mass: but exactly— he *does emerge* from it. Will you still speak, after that, of 'Communist treason'? Nonsense! This 'bureaucratization' is a necessity of the era of *scientific management*; in the USA, where the CP has had virtually no influence on trade-union development, all the working-class delegates of the big factories— including the shop stewards—are permanent, paid by the local section or even by the employer. The division of work which takes place between the militants and the workers at the heart of corporative organizations simply reflects that which has taken place at the factory and has created the new proletariat; and trade-union 'bureaucracy' is only the exact counterpart of the empoyers' bureaucracy. Since 'others think for the conveyor-belt operative', since specialists, in the offices of the undertaking, are in charge of distributing his tasks to him, it is very necessary that other specialists, in other offices, should think against this thought and decide the modalities of claim-making action. The elimination of man by man[75] in the works must have its trade-union opposite, the 'tandem of the technician and the conveyor-belt operative' must be counterbalanced by that of the conveyor-belt operative and the professional militant. Is that a pity? Perhaps; but what is to be done about it? The form of the trade-union apparatus is determined by the structure of the proletariat. Into the bargain, these recriminations are irrelevant. Collinet shows the cloven hoof when he uses the word 'élite' to describe his teams of mediators: it is the name by which the 'active minorities' called themselves before the first war. Our author certainly knows the masses and shows a praiseworthy care for their interests; but when he wishes to judge them, he does not cast away aristocratic prejudices and, although he is not a proletarian, he provides the means of understanding working-class dissensions since he adopts the point of view of the other party about the proletarian party. Yes, it is in the name of the old élite that he criticizes the new bureaucracy, and his understanding of the masses is limited by the contempt he has for them.

But if we accept the perspectives of a humanism of need, everything changes and the new officials are justified by the need for them. They suit the masses better than any élite because they are not under the contradictory obligation of defending at the same time the general and a special interest. It might perhaps be said that they themselves also form an élite, but that is not true: the élite worker is he who carries out the same work as his comrades and is militant *into the bargain,* he is *primus inter pares*; his additional benevolent, gratuitous functions win for him merit, credit, the right to be listened to. The trade-union official is born, on the contrary, from the division of labour: he does what his comrades have no time to do and, for this very reason, he no longer does what they do. Since they pay for his services, he has no right to their gratitude or to other powers than those delegated to him. There are risks, to be sure: and the tendency of a bureaucratic organization to consider itself as an end in itself has often been pointed out but, contrary to what is said, this fault is least perceptible in mass trade unionism. The romantic and participatory idea of an élite thrusting its roots into the deep strata of the popular unconscious must certainly be given up for good: the masses, being a pure mechanical dispersion, have no unconscious any more than they have self-awareness: and it is certainly true, on the other hand, that they are incapable of exercising a permanent and detailed control over the apparatus. Must it be concluded that they can be led wherever their leaders wish? Quite the contrary: their dispersion in itself shields them from all influences. The old middle-class idea of the 'ringleader' is so difficult to eradicate that political writers today have not got rid of it. And Mr Burnham has given expression to a number of surprising stupidities on the subject. Collinet, much more prudent, all the same writes: 'The mass gives proof of explosive capabilities. . . . But, these extinguished, it resigns itself into the hands of the trained staff which sums up the totality of trade-union life.' Now, nothing is falser: of course, the masses have neither the will nor the means to change the trained staff; they prefer to keep the leaders they have. But this is less through habit than through indifference. Before 1914, a militant was raised to the office of trade-union secretary because he had deserved the confidence of his comrades; but afterwards he was obeyed because he was the secretary: in minority tradeunionism, the source of authority is in great part institutional. The masses of today jeer at institutions: to begin with because a very great number of conveyor-belt operatives remain on the fringe of working-class organizations, holding back to follow orders only when they have judged them to be consistent with their interests. The skilled trade-union worker obeyed because he recognized the authority of the leaders he had elected; when the conveyor-belt operative recognizes the authority of chiefs whom he has perhaps not even helped to elect, it is because circumstances have led him to obey them. Thus action is equivalent to a plebiscite: the masses never rebel or protest or exact replacement of the trained staffs, and it is not possible to speak of pressure by the base on the chiefs: they follow or they don't follow, that is all. This means that they organize themselves into an active collectivity or that they break down and give way to the forces of massification. And, according to the results achieved, trade-union membership swells or diminishes: the trained staff, of course, is not touched; only it sometimes happens that they themselves constitute the totality of the trade union. There is no doubt that this unreliability favours an oligarchy of officials; but it is false that it encourages routine: on the contrary, it obliges the leaders to adjust their policy continually. Of course, this ebb and flow cannot pass as *evidence* of satisfaction or dissatisfaction: it is a symptom and an unintentional indication. No matter: it constitutes in its way a strict though unconscious control; the masses control the militant as the sea controls the helmsman. He is a leader when they are on the move; when they scatter, he is nothing. Had he been more careful of the organization than of his comrades, he would have a general rather than a particular interest. He cannot realize his personal ambitions, if he has any, except by inspiring in the masses a confidence renewed from day to day; and he will inspire confidence in them only if he agrees to lead them where they are going. In a word, in order to be himself, he must be *all of them.*

No matter: he would have existed in vain but for them, he is no longer one of them; he did share his comrades' condition, but, since he became a militant, he has ceased to share it. How could it be otherwise? The masses are but a false unity of solitudes, disguising a perpetual scattering; if he had remained among them, he would have been vowed to isolation and to ineffectiveness like any of the others. In 1900, the differentiation of the proletariat made it possible for militants to remain within the class: differences in skill ensured the hierarchy; the basis of power was the bond which tied the skilled overlord to the unskilled vassal. The masses are as sand: if I am only one grain, how could I give orders to the other grains? The strange formal reality which is called 'anyone' is only an interchangeable solitude: I am anyone in the eyes of anyone; in my eyes, anyone is myself. Now this abstract character escapes me: he is always elsewhere; that would be of no importance if I could define myself by my particular activity; but since the conveyor-belt operative makes anything, he is reduced to this abstract essence which does not even belong to him. This perpetual flight from my reality explains the imitation we have noted: I imitate to recover my reality as a person who sees himself always as the Other and resting on the Other; but if anyone claims to give me orders, he is changed into *someone* and I ask him for his authority. When the masses stir, leaders certainly emerge from the ranks: but that is because they have ceased to be masses and have crystallized in some primary form of collectivity whose diffused sovereignty is concentrated and embodied in the improvised leader: when they revert to the scattered state, the leader disappears. The organization remains: it justifies its permanence by its character as an institution; but the authority of the militant is banished: if he gives orders to the masses in their own name, he does so by reference to their unity of yesterday or of tomorrow; that is, he has made himself the trustee of their sovereignty in eclipse. He bears witness of its metamorphoses to this multitude by reminding it that it was a terrible, violent, authoritative society which exercised infinite pressure on each one of its members. Now, the masses keep him at a distance: they do not dispute his authority since they cannot set up another against it and their scattered structure prevents them from being a legitimate source of power; nevertheless, they do not *recognize* his authority, which in fact comes from *elsewhere*, from that integrated group which they have ceased to be. The unity of the proletariat—permanently embodied in the trade-union organization—remains an abstract password or an un-realizable ideal rather than a living synthesis; there is even a kind of anti-trade-unionism of the masses: the workers always distrust a little these officials who, devoted as they may be, do not totally share the working-class condition. When the forces of massification carry it away, the presence of the apparatus pre-vents the total disintegration of the proletariat without ensuring the complete cohesion of the class; it keeps the working-class population in a state of imbalance which continues to swing be-tween a purely mechanical juxtaposition and an organic ar-rangement. Stirred by an imperious current, the masses will again become a collectivity; in the trade-union organization, they will again begin to see an emanation of themselves and the visible symbol of their unity; in recovering their diffused sovereignty, they will *recognize* the authority of the officials;[76] it matters little then whether the majority of the workers have a union card or not: orders are followed and are judged by the result. Speed binds the discreet particles, *praxis* integrates them by differentiating them, the apparatus is the connecting link be-tween one and all. But the origin of the current remains outside the trade union: it is hunger, anger, or terror which starts the swing, and sometimes, as in 1936, it is the lightning flash of hope. Without the trade-union organism, movement would per-haps be stopped: its presence maintains the semblance of unity which permits of contagious propagation; its journals and dele-gates suppress distance, put the worker of Strasbourg into immediate touch with him of Perpignan.[77] But it cannot of itself *produce* these movements; it sets them in motion because it has outstripped their real cause. On the other hand, it is—to a certain extent—responsible for their strength, their volume, their direction, their effectiveness: it enlightens the masses about their own aims, accelerates or decelerates local developments as a function of the general action. It must still know all about the economic situation, be acquainted with the social situation and the relative strength of the opposing parties. And above all it must be able to foresee working-class reactions: is the movement which is starting going to last? Must it necessarily be backed with all available trade-union resources and the worker be pushed to commit himself to it completely? Or is it not rather a flash in the pan which it would be better to allow to die down?

196 *The Communists and Peace*

How decide unless information has been collected, soundings taken, statistics consulted? The masses do not stop *giving indications*: it is for the militant to interpret them; it is no longer the moment to invoke some confused piece of knowledge brought to birth by digging or to prop up decisions on some creative intuition: being object by nature, the masses become the militant's own object[78] and there is a technique of the masses as there is of navigation. The following text from *Force Ouvrière* is characteristic:

> ... In our opinion, there is no doubt that they [the strike movements of 1947] were based on the material difficulties of life of the great mass of wage-earners in the low and medium groups. ... No accelerator is needed to start a vehicle stopped on an incline. It is enough to release the brakes. As for the special characteristics of this movement—because every strike process has its own—it would be well to recall what our nuclear technicians have taught us, that the origin of the atomic bomb lies in the releasing of a chain reaction by which the disintegration of matter is achieved and propagated.[79]

The frankly mechanistic character of these images is in striking contrast to the 'organicist' phraseology used before the first war. The rôle of contagious propaganda and the extra-trade-unionist character of the causes of the movement are explicitly recognized. But above all the terrorized trade unionists (soon they had to leave the CGT) candidly acknowledge their powerlessness: it is possible to put the brake on a movement, or to embank it, but if the brakes slip or the dykes burst, the motor coach rolls to the bottom of the incline or water breaks over the low plains. These pages contain an echo of the terror Blum and the old trade unionists experienced in face of the masses: the secession of the Force Ouvrière was a panic flight.

Centralization, bureaucracy, technique: these features of the new trade unionism are prescribed by the nature of the 'neo-proletariat'. And the same nature is going to upset trade-union tactics by introducing three new characteristics into them: the maintenance of social agitation, extension of strikes whenever possible, a striving for the 'radicalization' of conflicts.

Permanent Agitation

The masses are always later than or in advance of their leaders. But let us take care not to infer from this either their stupidity or the infamy of the bureaucrats: we should fall back into psychologism. In fact, this lag is only the *temporal* projection of the *spatial* distance which separates the militant from his object; it is to be explained by the conjectural character of the technique of the masses. Basically the militant is *opposite* the comrades whom he invites to action: he speaks *to them* and they listen; he can seldom speak *with* them. Guy Thorel, a trade unionist, expressed it thus: 'Go over the factories, go into the yards, chat in the offices, attend meetings with a large or a limited audience. Listen to the voice of the militants and observe the mass: you will be struck to observe that there is rarely any interchange between the militants and the mass. There is a monologue by the militants and great passivity in the mass. It often happens that the militants fail to penetrate this passivity. The mass listens but does nothing. And if you ask a direct question of someone in the mass, you will get no reaction which enlightens you.'[80]

This will not be surprising: these men are alone together. Separated by weariness and wretchedness, who among them would be bold enough to speak in the name of all? Brought together by a common awareness of isolation, who moreover would dare to speak in his own name? The militant remains a stranger to them: he does not yet reflect back to them their power and their unity. Nevertheless, it is for him to make guesses about their frame of mind, about the effect his speech has produced on them, about the objective possibilities of the situation. Assuming that his diagnosis be correct, it remains that transmitted messages alter in transmission: those at the centre receive information at second-hand, they rarely have direct contact, and when at last the summit assembles, all the reports in its possession, the synthesis which it effects is itself only a reconstruction whose probability, at best, cannot be more than a scientific hypothesis until it has been checked experimentally. Naturally, there is a counter-proof: but as it is the action itself which takes the place of experiment, a mistake is expensive and may lead to disaster. Very often, happily, there will be no need to await the end of a conflict before becoming aware that the struggle was a bad proposition from the beginning; the order

will soon be followed by a countermand. But, just because the
mass is *other* than the militants, the apparatus is in danger of
isolating itself by extracting from the troops what they cannot
instantly give, and, in order to correct their mistake, the leaders
are in danger of being taken in tow by the led. To be sure,
judgment, personal qualities come into play at all stages. But
'authoritarianism' and 'leading from behind' remain the Scylla
and Charybdis of trade-union action. The officials lead movements by successive approximations: steering now to the left,
now to the right. That is why the essential job of the militants
is to 'keep in touch with the masses'. These words would
have had little meaning in the days of élite trade unionism. Will
it be said that they have no more today? For in the long run the
attribute of molecular dispersion is to make contact impossible.
Contact with a group can be made through the mediation of its
representatives, but not with a summation of discrete particles.
If the militant wants to get into touch with the masses, he must,
to begin with, give them a semblance of organization. Is this a
vicious circle? No, because so far as he is concerned he must
have an unceasing effect on them in a kind of collective erethism
in order to keep them in the path of solidification. And, as
action alone can churn them to the point of making them
coalesce, watchwords will be multiplied to instigate without
ceasing the beginnings of action: even if these beginnings have
no follow-up, they bring individuals together, provoke
emotional currents, make it possible to test and control working-class pugnacity. The employers and the skilled élite will use
this as a pretext for reproaching the bureaucracy with preferring
disorder to true working-class interests: the 'good' trade
unionist, according to them, acts at the right moment, conducts
his activity correctly, and avowedly to obtain limited results,
and ends the struggle the moment these results have been
achieved. But this shrewd and exact struggle, which begins and
ends in orderly fashion, is possible only to trade unions of the
élite which are *nothing but activity*. The inertia of the masses,
on the contrary, means that movement reaches them from
outside; it involves therefore its opposite, agitation, whose
target is to hold together by constant stirring a rudiment of collective life where there is continual danger that death will super-
vene. Without agitation, great popular movements would be

more hesitant, would take longer to come to birth, and would
be brought to an end more easily.

Extension

The conveyor-belt operative is 'interchangeable', competition
has given place to monopoly: for this double reason: the strike
at the level of one undertaking can no longer succeed; it must
extend to a whole branch of industry or to the whole nation.
Now, in each particular factory, decision eludes the worker. Or
rather he still decides but under pressure. Before the first war,
he appraised a local situation, he balanced risks and chances, he
went into action for concrete interests; today he is asked to
take part in a movement that is beyond him and of whose significance he can perhaps catch only a glimpse. The militant acts as
intermediary between the whole and the parts. The apparatus is
identified with the movement which is starting: thus the local
official speaks *in the name of all*; each of his listeners is still
isolated in the mass but they are given to understand that
everywhere the proletariat is drawing together again: it is up to
them alone to give way to the general enthusiasm and so to
escape from solitude. Even before integration is achieved, they
feel the coercive power of a primary collectivity on the way to
recombining. That happens only through a profound change in
trade-union democracy, in the classic sense of the terms. As
soon as the collective subject appears,[81] it can be recognized by
the pressure it exerts on its members. Decisions are taken at
high temperature. There must, of course, be deliberation and
the masses mean to decide freely on the direction to be taken.
But they know that the efficacy of their activity will be proportionate to the strength of integration in the group. Each can
give his opinion; but for a proposition to be prudent it is not
enough that it should be *practical*. As the danger of collapse
continues to exist permanently at the heart of their unity, the
proposed movement must be sure of the *agreement of all of
them*. Should an opinion fail to reinforce collective unity, it slips
away and disappears leaving no trace, forgotten even by those
who first gave expression to it. It may be said that this resembles
what happens in parliamentary assemblies, since the minority
bows to the decisions of the majority. But that is not true: in such
an assembly, the minority bows to the majority, but it subsists,

side by side with the majority as its permanent temptation, and preserves its claims to becoming the majority one day. Or rather, there are minorities *in motion* which are outlined and disappear as soon as they have been counted; and unity is continually recovered by the liquidation of opponents: if they resist, violence may actually be used against them. In the eyes of the group, the dissident is a criminal who prefers his own feeling to the unanimous opinion, a traitor who, rather than recognize his mistake, accepts the danger of breaking working-class cohesion. Our government has turned this to account: it has imposed the use of the referendum and extended the right to vote to non-trade-unionists. It was, of course, a question of protecting the rights of man. As a matter of fact, the idea was to relax collective bonds. This fraud brought into the light of day the abyss which separates middle-class democracy from the democracy of the masses. It is true: to vote by raising a hand is to surrender in advance to collective pressures; but the vote by secret ballot plunges the masses back into their original dispersion. Each one, back in his own solitude, expresses only what he thinks when alone, for lack of knowledge of what he would think in a group; a few minutes ago, in the meeting or the workshop, he *saw* his thought take form, he heard it, he learned it from the lips of his comrades; at present his opinion, if he has one, is no more than his ignorance of the opinion of the others. In claiming to save the person, our ministers have made him fall back to the level of the individual. These expressions of opinion favour inertia: the decision to struggle is taken in common, at heat; enthusiasm is contagious. But in the polling-booth, doubt is reborn: each fears the failure of the others, becomes just anyone. One example among thousands: in November 1947, the workers at the Citroën factories decided to go on strike on the job. The police intervened and emptied the works. On that the public authorities organized a referendum; the target was obvious: the workers were made to vote on a half-failure. The CGT immediately advised them to abstain. The referendum was held: out of 10,000 registered voters, 3,821 abstained: these were the 'toughs', the men who refused to capitulate. And, quite naturally, they were also those most hostile to this form of popular consultation. Among those who voted, 1,201 declared in favour of the continuation of the strike: in agreement with the first on objectives and tactics, they had not followed the orders of the CGT; it was because they meant to use freely the right to vote, even if it was the government that guaranteed it to them.[82] In all, 5,021 supporters of the strike. In favour of a return to work, 4,978 votes. Now, the strike had started without a preliminary vote; but it is evident that no one would have dared to decide in favour of it by so feeble a majority. Put differently, the 5,000 'toughs' had dragged the others along with them; those who were hesitant had joined the tough group through fear of being left alone, those who were against had been silent, abandoning their resistance because they recognized it as without effect. Here, therefore, are two different classifications; the employers were free to claim that the second alone was valid: in fact, both were valid, but they correspond with two very different states of the group. It is true that the clearing of the works was a serious blow to the supporters of the strike. Nevertheless, without the referendum it would have continued: and those who were undecided declared for it for want of knowing any way of stopping it; the vote revived the hesitations of those who were 'weak', and encouraged those against it. Thus the strike gave expression to the sudden integration of the group and the referendum provoked its partial disintegration. The unity of battle is a primary formation established in passion and often maintained by constraint. The trade-union officials can *dictate* to the extent that the group has chosen them to exercise dictatorship in its name on each of its members.

Radicalization

The masses never *give a mandate*: they do not vote for programmes; they indicate the objective to be reached; it is up to the militant to show the shortest way. And their demands are so simple that their realization appears at first within easy reach: bread, homes, the repeal of a villainous law, the ending of a war. In fact, their most elementary desire is separated from its object by the whole world and can be fulfilled only by long and exacting labour. Bread, homes? We have seen that it would be necessary to produce more and, in consequence, totally to renounce Malthusian practices, and that means, *at the very least*, that another majority should be formed and a new government should impose its will on the big employers. The illusion of spontaneity inclines the well-meaning to believe that popular demand is a policy repressed: it should be enough to *open it out* to find in it the means of satisfying it. That is not so: need is only a lack; it can lay the foundation of humanism but not of strategy. In laying claim to bread, the masses lead their representatives to struggle against Malthusianism; but their demand does not *in itself* imply condemnation of Malthusian practices.[83] Thus, the militant takes over the permanent conflict, which is opposed to the revolutionary movement whose tasks are infinite, and the revolutionary impulse which propounds ends at a single blow so as to claim immediate realization. Since they cannot budge without shaking society, the masses are revolutionary through their objective situation: to serve them, those responsible must elaborate a revolutionary policy. But, even there, they are doubly opposed to the masses: the precise and limited objective which they propose to reach at such and such a moment of history is at the same time too distant and too particular for their troops. Too particular: in so far as the end proposed is only a means of reaching another means, they do not always recognize in it the absolute ends for which they have agreed to fight and die. Too distant: in so far as this end is only a tactical result, it draws away from the immediate satisfaction they demand. For to them it is all one to demand bread or the setting up of a humane order: but they will not conclude for themselves that it is necessary to be for or against the sliding scale. In brief, the very being of the masses prevents them from thinking and acting politically. And, without a doubt, the policy of the apparatus is the practical and temporal expression of their demand; and, as they represent the same forces which can realize the revolutionary undertaking, it can be said that they are the means of this policy in the same degree that they are its end. But, since strategy remains strange to them on principle, it is not possible properly speaking to maintain that they *make* this policy but rather that they are its instrument. Of course, the leaders set their face against *manoeuvring* their troops: they exhort without ceasing, ceaselessly they explain and seek to convince them. But the difficulty does not come from the chiefs nor from their relations with the soldiers: it reveals simply the fruitful contradiction which opposes the immediate to the deferred, the urgent to the lasting, the need to the venture, passion to activity. Convinced that it is altogether impossible to mobilize the masses for distant and abstract ends, the leaders make continual use of what is called the 'double objective'; this means that they support the more general and distant objective on one that is immediate and concrete, and that, conversely, they never neglect to show, behind the near objective, a distant objective which constitutes, so to speak, its political significance. Thus they will explain to wage-earners that the revalorization of wages is linked with the end of hostilities in Vietnam and with general disarmament. In a certain sense, this much decried use of the 'double objective' is only a way of *explaining* history: the distant effects of their active demands are revealed to the masses, they are taught in what general conditions their particular demands will be satisfied. And there is no doubt, in fact, that the proletariat, in present circumstances, must impose disarmament if it wants to raise its standard of living, and that, conversely, every day it puts a brake on the 'war effort' to the extent that it defends its wages against the employers. But the stumbling character of popular action, its 'getting out of step', its uncertainty, its abrupt stiffenings, its unforeseeable breakdowns have the effect of bringing out the political aspect of trade unionism. A strike won appears to be a complete fact; its political significance does not separate out. A strike lost is the opposite: the workers went back to work because the trade-union cash box was empty? It matters little: it always seems that they have repudiated their chiefs; and what have they disowned if not the political aspect of the strike? The apparatus remains in the air, an abstraction, its 'distance from the masses' becomes more marked; it assumes in everyone's eyes the aspect of a politician's bureaucracy. The leaders said to the masses: in struggling for your wages, do not forget that you are struggling *also* against the war. Defeated by hunger, the masses give up the struggle for the time being: from that it is assumed that they deride disarmament.

An explosion of the people's sovereignty corresponds to the splitting up of the proletariat. For the skilled élite, this sovereignty is based on merit, that is to say on competence, energy, and training: the unskilled worker, for his part, is 'sovereign' only to the exact extent to which he is enrolled, carried along, supervised. For the conveyor-belt operative, sovereignty proceeds directly from the masses, and from them alone; it is only one with the movement by which, under pressure of external circumstances, they gather together in a *body*. The working class is torn by a conflict of powers.

Trade-union pluralism is therefore an effect rather than a cause: certainly it contributes to an increase of working-class divisions, but in the first place it merely reflects them. Before 1936, Jouhaux's CGT was essentially a grouping of skilled workers, officials or workers in public service, and lesser black-coated workers; approximately the 'élite' of the secondary sector and some elements of the tertiary. After the amalgamation of 1936, which took place at heat and under the pressure of events, these militants became uneasy: they already talked of colonization; at the approach of war, they hastened to recover their freedom. After the Liberation, the membership of the CGT swelled anew; only the CFTC remained in face of it; organic unity was the order of the day. But almost at once the old militants of Jouhaux's CGT complained that they were no longer among their own kind. 'They were strangers in their own house,' wrote Bothereau in 1947. The phrase is revealing: the CGT of 1945, in spite of its venerable name, had all the characteristics of a new organization, of one still seeking its way; but the working-class 'élite' continued to think of it as a very old institution which belonged to them: it welcomed newcomers as if to its own house and lamented the poor education of the guests. Of course, these militants did not dream of indicting their comrades in rationalized manufacturing industries: it was the Communist leaders they accused; without them, working-class unity would have been maintained of itself. But their reproaches to the CP reached the masses *first of all*. The Communists, they said, prefer unorganized workers to experienced militants: the first are easier to handle. But isn't that to harbour resentment against them because they represent the masses rather than the élite? The new leaders resort too readily to violence, they keep up an aimless agitation in the works which is against the interest of the proletariat, they display an intransigence in negotiations that is in danger of resulting in failure? This barbarism may be expected to scandalize experienced militants. But violence, as I have already shown, is born of the very situation; agitation is only a perpetual struggle against the continuous action of massifying forces. As for intransigence, it has two principal causes: first of all, it is because the condition of the conveyor-belt operative is intolerable; secondly, it is because it has no possibility of *manoeuvre;* its only resource being violence, it is in the climate of violence that it makes the most of its claims: the works is occupied, the CRS perhaps are going to clear it; they will fire if there is resistance; the situation is not propitious for compromise: much courage and anger are needed to face the dangers. The masses therefore quite rightly deem the employer to be the enemy; they regard concessions, conciliation as treason: they demand everything as long as they hold on; if their strength fails them, they collapse. Communist leaders have choked trade-union democracy? So what? The only kind which has ever been practised was aristocratic. The 'élite' has forgotten that democracy can be authoritarian if the authority proceeds from the masses themselves. Trade-union 'dictatorship'—if there is dictatorship—is exerted on the minority in the name of the majority, but it would be absurd to believe that it could be exerted on the majority itself: it is not possible either to mobilize or to manoeuvre the masses, they resolve on action when they are changed into an active community as the result of external circumstances. The 'Communist' trade unions are politicized? That is because the existence of the masses as such is incompatible with the economic and social régime which produces them. Understand me: I do not claim that the actual structure of the CP, its objectives and its methods are entirely and exclusively determined by the objective demands of the conveyor-belt operative: this party has its history, its own dialectic; it is conditioned by the world. But I maintain that these charges are aimed essentially at the masses: it is they whom the militant of the élite condemns through third persons. He is afraid of them and they fascinate him: tomorrow automation of tasks may reduce him to the ranks of the conveyor-belt operative.

The representatives of the masses, in their turn, accuse FO and the CFTC of cunningly playing politics and they are not wrong. When all is linked together, Malthusianism and misery, rising prices, re-armament and Marshallization, to reject the policy of the CP is to accept that of the government; besides the CGT-FO leans on the socialist party and the CFTC on the MRP ministers. To keep working-class claims in the economic and skilled plane is to want to change effects without touching causes; it is, above all, to give a free hand to the parliamentary majority. The aim is to obtain the maximum in the framework of the régime; small favours are claimed and, to deserve them, Communism is condemned in 'apolitical' speeches and the emissaries of American trade unions are received 'apolitically'. Nevertheless the reproaches the CGT addresses to the leaders touch the militant basically: after all, until 1947 Force Ouvrière represented only a minority 'trend' of the CGT; neither Jouhaux nor his lieutenants wanted to take the initiative in breaking up unity, and it was militants in the provinces who forced the rupture by threatening not to renew their trade union cards. At the conference of the Amis de Force Ouvrière, hastily called together, the leaders proposed a compromise: 'democratization' of the CGT would be exacted from the 'majority'. In vain: the militants would have none of it, and the headquarters followed them unwillingly into secession.[84]

Shall we say that the entire masses have ranged themselves behind the CGT? That only skilled workers are enrolled in FO or the CFTC? That would be to simplify. Many skilled workers have remained in the CGT through class discipline.[85] Others have joined autonomous trade unions. And then the confessional character of the CFTC further complicates the problem in certain regions, the current of dechristianization has not yet penetrated the masses. Still, taking things as a whole, our division remains true: the CGT polarizes the revolutionary tendencies of the mechanized proletariat of the manufacturing industries; most of the other trade unions represent the reformist tendency of a skilled élite which struggles against absence of skill. In one sense, trade-union pluralism is legitimate since it is the reflexion of a profound split; in another, it is a catastrophe for the working class since plurality of organizations increases conflicts while giving an outline and limits to each of the tendencies and obliging each group to become distinct through its opposition to the others. But, anyhow, the split had a deeper cause: it is the handsomest present made by their employers' Malthusianism to the working class.[86]

AN ANSWER TO CLAUDE LEFORT

I have never denied the rootedness of the worker in society or the objective foundations of the class; I have never thought men among themselves to be like soldiers of lead on whom, in order to fuse them together, it was necessary to work from the outside. In my view, solitude and union are complementary relationships whose connexion is the measure of a society's integration. Certain restricted groups are obviously strongly integrated without any mediation. Why should not such a 'sociality' one day characterize the whole of society? Marx proclaimed that Communist society will resorb and dissolve all powers: the free blossoming of each will condition the blossoming of all. Notice, however, that this society must have liquidated its classes, that is to say, the principle of division. The class struggle: that is the rent in the social cloth: when this rent starts, where will it stop? Common sense suggests that to oppose one another, each of the classes must have a principle of unity within itself. But that is only a common sense argument: the nation is no more than a 'bastard dream'; it is made up of pieces; why shouldn't the class have this same illusory cohesion, why shouldn't division, beginning from a first opposition, go on to infinity? And doesn't this unity vary according to relative strength? In time of foreign war, the cohesion of the troops depends on action. Action brings them together, integrates them; suffering disintegrates them. In every collectivity, activity and inertia are to be found in variable proportion: the reciprocal externality of its members—that is to say, their tendency to disintegrate—depends on this inertia, that is to say, the forces which sway the group.

Have I said that inertia is the natural status of the masses? The masses are not natural: they resemble nature, but they are manufactured; the externality of the particles which compose them is produced; it is an historical status imposed on the proletariat at a certain stage in its evolution and in technical development. This mass state is never absolute, precisely because there exist (and have always existed) organs of centralization and inter-communication. Have I placed the Party outside the working class? But whence would it derive its transcendence? And if it were transcendent to the mass, how could it act on the mass? And transcendent to what? To the masses, when Communist cells are simply micro-organisms which form at their heart? To the class, when the masses are organized into a class by *means* of the Party? Where have I written that the Party is identical with the class? It is as if I were to call the thread which holds asparagus together the *bunch*. Still, the thread is *external*: but I could say—using your language— that the Party is 'what makes it possible for the workers to act and to think in collusion, and to think of themselves as a whole as different from society'. In short, it acts as a mediator between men. You think that this mediation would establish itself unaided among the workers; I myself think that it is, at certain moments of working-class history, both contact and *will*. Contact can come to life among the workers in so far as it is put forward to them, and can be desired in itself by the militant who tries to establish it: this ambiguity is the basis for the possibility of a dialectic which at one time puts the masses against the Party and at another unites them with it. Have I denied that the Party draws its strength from the proletariat? Shall I surprise you if I reveal to you that the Communists declare themselves, like you and me, persuaded of this? Its rôle is to break down the invisible partitions which tend to isolate the workers from one another; but that does not mean that it breathes life into corpses. It brings together passions, interests, it pools common hopes and ventures, it guarantees to some the solidarity of the rest; its orders demonstrate the will of all to each individual; to obey it is to become one of a group. Of course, its commands will have no effect if they go against social currents; but if it is to regulate itself by the true trends of the working-class movement, they must exist; and for them to exist, to become concrete, some degree of integration is essential. If the bond loosens, the masses spread and scatter, structures grow slack and soften, the whole collectivity slides towards molecular disorder; if it tightens, colours, structures, and guided movements reappear. And since you are pleased to quote Trotsky, consider these remarks as a simple commentary on what he wrote so judiciously in his history of the Russian Revolution: 'Parties and leaders are a non-autonomous but very important element in the process. Without a directing organization, the energy of the masses would volatilize like steam that is not contained in a piston cylinder. However, movement is due neither to movement nor to the cylinder, but to the steam.' After all, did you not yourself admit in your article, 'Political activity among the workers has remained dispersed so long as the most dynamic elements of the intelligentsia have not allowed it to crystallize in a single organization. But, left to themselves, these elements would have had no power.' So? Ought we to be in agreement? Not at all. For me, the class develops, falls apart, re-develops continuously—which is not at all the same thing as saying that it returns to the point of departure; in order to re-develop or to continue, I claim that, today more than ever before, it needs the mediation of a group which has been formed at its heart. That and nothing more; it seemed to me useless and dangerous, as well as presumptuous, to build a theory of the proletariat. I said: *today* the masses need the Party. You have had no such hesitation: we were entitled to your theory about the class and to a dialectic reconstruction of the working-class movement from its beginnings. The target: to show that the class writes its own history, that it progressively gets shipshape of its own volition and develops its experience *spontaneously*. Spontaneously: no. I must admit that the word is never spoken, but, as Saint-John Perse said of the sun, 'It is not named but it is present among us'. Or how will you name 'the effort of the class to behave like a unity and to affirm its total supremacy'? And to this 'natural but not unconscious process'? But you want to prove that the development of the class is autonomous, that parties are only the transitory *expression* of it. And you want to prove that *against* me. Let us see how you set about doing that.

The proletariat, said Marx, 'produces the material conditions of its advent...[which are] work in co-operation, the reasoned application of science to technique ... the transformation of particular means of work in motion being impossible to combine except in common, the management of all the means of production, of combined social work, the entry of peoples into the network of the world market, etc.' But while productive forces are being socialized, the profits of production remain individual. You conclude from this, then— and who would not agree with you?—that the most elementary behaviour of the worker at work is already revolutionary. On the one hand, in fact, the conditions of production—that is to say, the régime of property—become shackles for productive forces—since properly work is socialized. On the other hand, the proletariat, by its daily work, engenders little by little the 'material conditions' which, when the day comes, will allow it to seize power. In producing capital, the proletariat itself becomes the gravedigger of capitalism. It would be absurd to distinguish the workers' technical from his political activity. That would be to confound the purely abstract and negative task of the proletariat (to overthrow the middle class) with its positive and concrete task: which is to organize progressively the new contacts that will become established between men, to march little by little towards a 'modification of industrial data', etc. Besides, if it is true that the proletariat, in the depths of its misery, engenders its own course, inversely the material conditions of production from day to day form an impassable limit to its liberating *praxis*: today, 'They must ... begin,' said Marx, 'by producing of themselves the material conditions of a new society, and no effort of mind or of will can save them from this destiny. ...'

All is for the best: the proletariat makes its own history, it creates in pain and suffering that future moment when question and answer will be merged and when, as you politely put it, it can 'recast the facts of production'. And work, to be sure, has a value which I will call—and I feel sure you will agree— 'cultural'. In producing, the worker produces himself to the extent that technique socializes production objectively; subjectively, the worker determines his way of life, his behaviour, his system of values and his experience, as a *socialist*; the organization of the class for itself in its struggle against capitalism progressively outlines what post-revolutionary society will be.

This is what might be called 'the immanentism of class'. If I wanted to bring out the faults of the shameful finalism hidden under all dialectics, I should make you say that the working class is the most economical process for achieving a classless society. Such thankless labour would be required to produce the material conditions of this society that humanity, wishing to get beyond all oppression, could find but one means: to transform itself into an oppressed proletariat. How could a man wear himself out producing increment-value unless he were a dupe and a victim? Profit, in short, would be a trick of Reason. No, I am joking and you have said nothing of the kind;[87] but if I were a 'young employer', I should be a follower of Lefort: with your interpretation, you lay the bases of a Marxism for all. Exploitation, to be sure, exists. But what is it? Quite simply, the objective structure of the method of production. And, fundamentally, everyone turns it to account: while the workers prepare in the long run for the advent of a classless society, the employer takes his profit in the immediate future; the solidarity of labour and capital is re-discovered; convinced of the need and the inevitability of a classless society, the Lefortist employer sacrifices his honour to the revolution and defends the régime, at need, by force: he can help his working-class comrades only by constraining them to produce the conditions of their emancipation. Nothing to be surprised at: as we shall see, you want to prove that you will be of more service to the proletariat by anchoring yourself in the intellectual middle class. If the argument holds for you, it holds for others. And why not for the middle class?

I feel acutely that there is something lacking in your whole exposition. It would seem that Marx is no longer whispering in your ear; Engels has replaced him: Engels who draws dialectical materialism towards economism, Engels who describes exploitation as a physico-chemical process[88] and makes social conflicts spring not from the very structure of the system of production, but from the evolution of that régime,[89] Engels who shows us men produced by the system without making us see the system produced by men, and who reduces interhuman conflict to a mere symbolic expression of the contradictions of the economy. Hegel's panlogism is duplicated by pantragicism; and, in like manner, in Marxism, there is the process of capital and the drama of man: two inseparable aspects of the same dialectic. But when middle-class man is in question, you adopt the point of view of economism: he is not visible, he does not exist. Your quiet hatred is so radical that you have started by making a pure object of him, the passive product of capital and, in consequence, of the wage-earner. I am with you: what is missing is the class struggle. Since middle-class man is only one of the loudspeakers of capitalism, there is no means of knowing how to *struggle* against him, parry his blows, baffle his ruses, evade, feint, advance or break off; neither defeat nor victory is at risk. When you say the worker 'struggles' against the middle class, you want it to be understood that it is simply producing under the present form of production that is in question; this alleged age-long conflict, this civil war is reduced to the indefinitely growing pressure exerted by the forces of production, from day to day more numerous and more socialized, on the old formal framework containing them.

After that, you are free to give the proletariat all the human reality, all the kinetic energy, all the awareness which you refuse to the middle class; free to be a Hegelian in speaking of the workers and a disciple of Engels in speaking of the employers. You have thereby none the less suppressed conflict as the real drama between men; these two mortal enemies are unaware of one another. Even if, as though regretfully, you happen to recognize 'experience' by the ruling class as well as by the proletariat, you hasten to add that these experiences are parallel. Since they never meet, how could there be a confrontation between them? To be sure, the employer plays a part in the experience of the worker: but as a determinant without content; and in the system of the employer, the worker is hardly more determined: that is the *a priori* condition of the possibility of capital.

Do you, at bottom, believe in the class struggle? Yes and no: it overwhelms you. In a recent article, you allowed yourself to give expression to these very significant phrases: you reproached the CP for putting the accent 'on the necessity of struggling *against* capitalism, of overthrowing the middle class, of abolishing private property'. According to you, these concepts are 'abstract': their object is Revolution, which is a political episode, and not the organization of proletarian power.

The Party aims only at effectiveness in the immediate struggle, the working class shakes its hold and while contesting exploitation in all its forms, seeks to define 'the positive form of its power'. Which brings us back, of course, to your meditations. It could not be put better: the class struggle is not the real drama which continually confronts concrete men. It is an abstract structure of a much richer phenomenon: of *cumulative experience*. And, quite naturally, from that you go on to speak of the revolutionary movement as a 'work which the proletariat practises on society'. In every battle, it is true, there is expenditure of energy, action on nature, production, destruction, then work. Whence, nevertheless, comes reluctance to define the battle of Pavia as a work carried out by the Imperial army against the French army? It comes from the fact that this would be neglecting the properly agonistic element. If you reduce the struggle to work, you do so because behind the scenes you have done away with one of the combatants. After that, no one will be surprised at your coining this graceful euphemism to describe the Revolution: 'A modification of the data of industrial production.'

There stands the proletariat all alone. Alone it can 'write its own history'. Instead of being the pure inert effect of mechanical forces, it comes into being in producing its product and, whether it forces up output or goes on strike, it inevitably gets nearer the hour of its deliverance. 'The social experience of the class continues on all planes at once.' In short, the working class *has nothing outside it*. Besides, you have written, 'The proletariat is nothing objective. It becomes clear only as experience.' And 'the changes which affect the proletariat in number, structure, and mode of work make sense only in so far as the working class assimilates them subjectively and translates them into its opposition to exploitation. That is to say, there is no objective factor which guarantees progress to the proletariat.' A nice turn of phrase, and you learned early how to misuse language. You prove the unity of the proletariat by that of its experience, but unity of experience, when made progressively, assumes the unity of the proletariat. No, you will say, the one as it develops makes the other; experience is exactly in accordance with organization, and conversely. But that is exactly what doesn't happen: the proletariat is crushed by a perpetual present. The machine and its products are present, they are neither past nor future; the proletariat, 'produced from its own product', appeared without any tradition and after the destruction of all tradition; Marx called the workers 'new men', 'the invention of the modern age'. The endlessly unsettled environment is unfavourable to the formation of social memory: it is strange that you who quote Marx's text on agitation in the middle-class era have not bethought yourself of this. 'This continual upsetting of ways of production, this constant shaking of the whole social system, this agitation and this perpetual uncertainty mark the middle-class era. All traditional and rooted social links dissolve; those which replace them grow old before they have had time to harden', etc. As if that were not enough, disasters from outside shake the whole of society, change social structures. The profound changes affecting the proletariat in the first years of this century were enough to destroy their social memory: how can you conceive that those new workers who came into view towards 1910 would take up the aristocratic traditions of revolutionary trade unionism and of skilled workers? Change, yes; historical and cumulative change, surely not. But into the bargain, the war necessarily brought its disorder: two million wage-earners were mobilized, women workers increased tenfold, the young generation which went into the factories about 1917 knew nothing of trade unionism.

The same thing happened during the last war, and all observers have noted that young workers have almost no knowledge of the strikes of 1936. To them, they are legendary and rather incomprehensible. In brief, if you want the proletariat, in spite of so many hostile forces and so many reasons for forgetfulness, to preserve a common memory and a common experience, you cannot count on this experience itself to supply that minimum of unity entailed by memory. In a traditionalist society with slow changes, there would be no vicious circle; experience creates its own tools. A class in a perpetual state of upheaval, whose organization, as we shall see, is always *behind* that of the employers, needs frameworks, guide marks, sureties, experience. In so far as the past lives, whether by virtue of behaviour, of 'exis' or of a directing schema, it does so because it is preserved by specialized agencies; just as it needs

mediation between its members, the working class, far from
being unified by its memory, needs mediation between itself
and its past.

Let us leave that for a moment; let us suppose that the formal
conditions of this 'cumulative experience' are actual data. Here
is what I find more disquieting: you have talked to us of two
parallel experiences; that of the employers, that of the proletariat. I can also concede to you that there are others: that
of the peasant class, that of the middle class, etc. And I see also
that one middle-class man can express in his way the experience of the whole middle class, one peasant that of the peasantry. But *who* are you, Lefort? *Where* are you? And how can you
speak to us of the experience of this working class which has
'nothing objective' about it and which 'is concerned only with
its own activity'? I understand well enough: doubtless you
count yourself among those intellectuals 'who, by force of
work, have managed to acquire theoretical understanding of
the movement'. But to begin with, that is not so very clear and
you yourself tell us that Marx derided the social democratic
intellectuals who claimed to be the proletariat's masters of
thought. How distinguish the wheat from the tares? These
individuals, he said a little naïvely, must 'have a real value'
and must 'take up working-class concepts'. But he added—
and this seems indispensable, above all if your presuppositions
are to be admitted—that they must join forces with the proletariat in its struggle and must become 'constituent elements'.
He completed the picture elsewhere, in explaining that this new
contribution proceeds from a *real proletarization* of certain
strata of the intellectual middle class. Good: a proletarized
intellectual falls outside his class, rejoins the proletariat, adopts
all its concepts and, only then, is worthy to serve it by communicating to it the theoretical understanding of his own reactions. So far as I know, you are not proletarized—not more,
anyway, than a great number of young members of the teaching profession who quite simply consider themselves middle-
class. You have not fallen outside your class since you are on
visiting terms with other intellectuals and certain very well-read
workers, as were republicans under Louis-Philippe or radicals
in the time of MacMahon. You do not accept all the concepts
of the working class since the majority of the workers vote

Communist and you are hostile to 'Stalinists'. Finally, you cannot claim that you prove the practical value of your ideas by taking part with the workers in common action, since you do not act at all. How, then, can you describe and determine 'the subjective experience' of the working class? In a word, the truth about a dialectical movement can be established in only two ways: if a person is himself involved in the movement, *praxis* decides. Action and idea forming only one, the true idea is an effective action. If, like you, a person is outside and does not move, then it is necessary to know exactly the end of the story.

Do not answer that it would be possible to pose the same alternative in relation to any intellectual 'of the left': that is not true. Some of them, enrolled in such or such proletarian party, militate in the midst of the workers. Adherence to the Party is precisely what serves as mediation: through the medium of the Party, it is possible (with more or less success) to change class. But above all, God save me from refusing to anyone some knowledge, however slight, however incomplete it may be, of the working-class world. One man comes from it, another has parents who work in a factory, and even if the third has done nothing except read theoretical works on the proletariat, he has at least learned and understood a minimum of abstract ideas: for me, there is as much *communication* between groups and classes as between persons. Communication *and* struggle. Besides, struggle itself is communication. The other is there, immediately accessible—if not comprehensible—and his experience is there, it reaches completion in mine, or mine finds its end in him. All those imperfect, ill enclosed, interrupted meanings which make up our real knowledge are summed up in the other who perhaps knows the answers. There could be neither experience nor class struggle if man were not directly for man object and subject, and if I did not find the whole of the Other in myself.[90] But you assert that experiences are separate; like me, you live on interest on capital; and your activity remains unproductive. You have no right, therefore, to enlighten us on working-class subjectivity as if you were Hegel and it was Mind. Moreover, your reconstitution of the moments of this experience will be misunderstood for in fact, in *Phenomenology of Mind* it was after all his own consciousness which Hegel accompanies in his steps. But how is it possible to speak of the subjectivity of the Other if it has no outside? Still, studying it carefully, I see that in this subjectivity the internal is the pure interiorization of the external. The proletariat as subjective experience is the process of production unfolding in the pure medium of subjectivity. For example, the objective status of producer becomes subjectively 'familiarity with the method of individual production'—the continual change in techniques becomes adaptation to new tasks, transformation of the concept of instrumentality. If the automation of production makes individuals *objectively* interchangeable, the class acquires the feeling of universality. The subjectivity of the class is the method of production caught in the perspective of a past and a future whose parts are organized in the synthetic unity of an experience. Thus you pass from total subjectivity to complete objectivity. The thought and its object make one. Only: when a Communist makes known the interests or the feelings of the proletariat, rightly or wrongly he speaks *in the name* of the proletariat. But I am afraid that you, Lefort, spoke *on* the working class: your truth is not effective and it would be impossible to say that it embraces the totality of the real since history continues; if, however, you refuse to regard your ideas as opinions, surely this is because you hold the method as the progression of the thing itself. And no doubt you softly repeat that proud secret which Hegel expressed aloud: 'As the product of its activity, thought contains the universal which constitutes the very foundation, the intimate essence of the reality of the object.' The working class in producing produces the reason *for itself*, and you, like thought in act, produce the reason which produces the proletariat.

From this, it is to be understood that you are very prompt to grasp the relationships of agreement between the differing significances of working-class experience! As I understand it, the action of the mode of work on the proletariat seems to you so simple, so clear and, forgive me, so poor; and you deride the unhappy empiricists who believe in the opacity of that shallow stream, the world. Let us try to look at it more closely, this Absolute Knowledge which you mete out to us.

According to you, the origin of the proletariat as a class springs from its rôle as producer. Let us see how the class, in so far as it works, *develops* (experience-unity): that is to say, let us examine your system of transcription.

(1)   You tell us of the prime importance of concentration. A more concentrated class has more chance as a whole of opposing the middle class; the connexion which it achieves between its members increases its capacity for leadership. And you write with surprising assurance, 'The degree of concentration of a proletariat is synonymous with the degree of its social existence.' Why not? On condition, to be sure, that social existence is defined as degree of concentration. As for your remark about connexions, that is a self-evident truth if what you are trying to say is that contacts are more frequent; it is a mistake if you make the smallest possible claim to prejudge the nature and the meaning of these relationships. Must it be concluded that the proletariat of the USA, where concentration is more advanced than in France 'achieves a connexion . . . which increases its capacity for leadership'? And has its history, from the IWW up to the deplorable compromises of the CIO and the growing indifference of the working class, anything to do with density of population? Is the passive obedience of Lewis's 400,000 miners due to concentration and, if that should be so, is that what you call auto-organization? Connexions, yes: but between whom and whom? Will not the presence of workers who are outsiders—of a strong contingent of North Africans among us, of a black population in the USA—alter the effects of concentration? You claim that this need not be taken into account? Why, unless because you have arbitrarily over-estimated the rôle of formal factors? But when a fundamental structure of the proletariat is to be seen in the concentration, it would apply only in the direction of existing dispositions. At one time it will multiply images of anger and chances of disturbance, at another examples of resignation; in a period of equilibrium, it may be a simple factor of stability. It is a long time since Costes upheld his demographic thesis and, you see, I recognize that 'sociology has made some progress since'. He explained that 'the growth of a unified population . . . facilitates communication between different parts of society and makes possible a more and more exact representation of the unity of natural laws'. His sleeve has been plucked; it has been explained to him that quantity cannot produce social effects

except in the framework of an already constructed society and in terms of existing structures. Why then need you, convinced as you are of sociological progress, make the same mistake with the same formality fifty-three years later? Concentration acts only through environments and existing forms. Will you say that it is a question of a 'permanent relationship in the framework of a social structure which cannot be translated by an historical conditioning'? But I will not concede that to you. It is certain that concentration in a given region transforms a fundamental structure and is linked with the whole of production (industrialization, equipment, geographic distribution of resources, etc.). But the relationship of the proletariat to this concentration as a factor in its experience is conditioned in its turn by a series of secondary or historical factors which can transform it without any change in the number of factories and the extent of their labour force.[91] And it is true that Marx regarded Britain as the lever of Revolution. But it is also true that he did not credit it with the generalizing mind, the insurrectionary passion, and thought it probable that the initiative would come from France. Basically, what seemed revolutionary to him in Great Britain was not the proletariat: it was Capital.

(2) *Co-operation*: 'Co-operation [in work] renders their actions interdependent, organization makes the product the result of a concerted process.' Tell that to the marines! It is enough for this co-operation to exist objectively for you to be sure of finding a correspondence between method of organization and the subjective experience of the proletariat. But you, you alone, assert this parallelism. It *must* exist *because* your theory is true. You forget only one thing: exploitation. This co-operation—have you thought of it?—is not experienced by the worker as the happy sign of interdependence: he may well feel horror and rejection towards it as an interdependence of victims, or that he is under constraint to accept it since it depends on the rhythm of others and their work, or quite simply he may be unaware of it, as often happens in automation. The third situation is perhaps most frequent: weariness, the intensity of the rhythm imposed, *isolate*; and then the machine interposes between men; 'the non-human' rips apart human relationships. In the first and second situations, dependence is experienced. The worker is conditioned not only by the employer, but

also by his comrades; in this tense and external 'interdependence', a strange movement whose speed and frequency
have been fixed outside himself, cuts across him, shakes him,
makes him feel this horrible complicity in relation to the other
victims chained with the same chain. In every way, real co-
operation is on the other side, between the employer, the
manager, the higher employees: all those wage-earners who
live on the interest of capital, who share the ideology and
certain of the interests of the middle class, can co-operate,
make plans, organize labour. The co-operation of the workers
is precisely the opposite of that: they help to help the employer,
but they do not help themselves. Or rather, they help *nothing*,
they co-operate *in nothing*. And I am astonished that you, who
love to quote Marx, are not more troubled by the contradiction inflicted on you in advance: 'Their co-operation begins
only in the process of work; but then they have already ceased
to belong to themselves. As soon as they enter into the process
of work, they become one with capital. In so far as they co-
operate and are members of a productive organism, they no
longer represent anything except a special form of the existence
of capital.[92]. . . . The specific mechanism of the manufacturing
period is the collective worker himself, made up of many
assembly-line workers. The collective worker possesses . . .
every productive capacity . . . and uses them all—each applying all his means solely to specific functions individualized in
particular workers organized in groups of workers. The more
incomplete and even imperfect the assembly-line worker, the
more perfect he is as a part of the collective worker . . . .'[93]
And here is the passage where Marx shows that, contrary to
your revolutionism without class struggle, the *Other* is present
as real agent of the movement of production even in the
elementary act of production itself, even in that gesture by
which you would wish the worker to become already a revolutionary through simple apprehension of the objective characteristics of his task: 'Division of labour in manufacturing brings
them face to face with the intellectual powers of the material
process of production as with an extraneous ownership, a
power that rules them. This cleavage begins in the simple
co-operation by which the capitalist, in relation to each worker,
represents unity and the will of the corpus of social work. It

develops in the factory which makes of the working man a crippled assembly-line worker. It is achieved in manufacturing industries which use science as a productive power independent of labour and assigned to capital.'[94] Perhaps these texts may recall to you what you continually forget?—that working-class experience is at the same time experience of paid labour and experience of oppressors: 'Alienation appears... in that my means of subsistence is that of another, that the object of my desire is the inaccessible possession of another... that everything in itself is something other than itself...' Yes, from his first movement the worker is a revolutionary, but that is because he receives a total experience of the world and of the Other, because the other is present in his action and in the objects of his desire as the hostile power which robs him, and because he cannot wish to 'alter' his work without immediately claiming the wish to snatch the other's power.[95]

(3) 'The continuous upheaval of technique [compels] men to carry into effect new bodily conformations'....

There, candidly, you are odious. But you are to be excused since it is imagination rather than heart that you lack: you merely follow your opinion. You will judge Marx to be very romantic: see how he speaks of these bodily changes which you call so cheerily 'new conformations': 'The factory upsets the individual and attacks at its very root the individual power of work. It cripples the worker and makes of him a kind of monster by favouring, as in a greenhouse, development of his skill in detail by the suppression of a whole world of instincts and capacities.'[96]

Unhappily, biologists and cyberneticists would tend to declare that he, rather than you, is right. You have read them, of course. Read them again. But perhaps you are dreaming of the 'cultural' influence of assembly-line work: if so, I am sorry to tell you that Anglo-Saxon and German enquiries will puncture your beautiful dream: the cultural influence of assembly-line work is completely negative, it has liquidated the culture of skill, technical ability, and that intuitive understanding of materials of which the skilled worker was so proud; it has destroyed curiosity, interest, the desire to learn; it has produced various psychoses, it deadens those who do not lose their wits altogether: they repeat the same gesture, all day long, dream or count in

their minds or ruminate, brooding over the same phrase at each
new beginning. And then, as you say, there are those who 'adapt
themselves': they are done for. They accept things as they are:
'After all, we've no responsibility.' As for 'work on society', let
us talk of it: summer, winter: long tram journeys, additonal
hours. A man gets home, eats, yawns, goes to sleep. No matter, it
delights you to learn that, in discovering interchangeability of
workers, the proletariat has been elevated to an understanding
of universality. But I fear there is some mistake here: interchangeability means fear of losing the job, the alarming sense of
being replaceable. The worker who is out of work, or afraid of
being so, certainly has experience of a strange contradiction: his
immediate needs, his hunger, his weariness, his distress bring
home to him his singularity; but he no longer has the means of
thought, he is no longer a person; all that remains for him is the
idea of universal commutability (if he indeed has it in this form).
But I do not see that that contradiction can advance him much;
and if you had reflected on it, you would have seen that it
passed away as long ago as 1893. The worker has not waited for
you to conceive this universality of which you have so high an
opinion: it is quite simply the abstract universality of democracies. What, if you please, has it to do with the concrete universal of 'the individual as an integral development' and the
socialist community? Above all, how does this commutative
universality resemble the universal *reciprocity* which ought to
be the basis of human relationships? As to 'the influence of
social differentiation in the cumulative experience of the proletariat', I will add only a word. Some day there will, perhaps,
be a redistribution of rôles within the working class, but what
can be said today is that the 'second industrial revolution' has
acted rather as a leveller. The tendency (less marked in France
than in many other countries) can be noted towards the elimination of the extremes (unskilled and skilled workers) to the advantage of those in between (the conveyor-belt operatives).
There are, to be sure, still many undertakings of archaic structure (high number of unskilled workers), but, in so far as the
movement to rationalization must be followed, the proletariat
will come nearer, in its composition, to the American proletariat:
thin stratum of superior workers, highly qualified and very well
paid, having no links of skill with the conveyor-belt operatives,

a level mass, more and more homogeneous; interchangeability, moreover, leads to suppression of the frontiers between skills. More at ease than you on concrete ground, the Communists have been quick to see the ambiguity of *experience*: the mass is fluctuating, apprenticeship is no longer necessary; for these reasons, resistance to capital will be less strong. The worker feels his dependence more, he is no longer a cog-wheel: mass movements are possible. Less strong resistance, increased dependence: contradictory pressures; it is necessary to reinforce the one, weaken the other: a militant is needed to help his comrades define the sense of this ambiguous experience.

Besides, I haven't your cumulative experiences, and I think, in fact, that everything is of profit to the proletariat—provided that, by this word, the whole class with its internal links and its sentient organs is understood. But I wanted, as opposed to your schematism, your false severity, your weighty and over-simple conclusions (the product manufactured requires the co-operation of the workers, *therefore* the workers identify co-operation with their subjective experience) to show that an result of which each moment is presented to them as a confused whole of meanings and actions. To begin with, the facts are less experience is a living and active relationship for Everyman, as a segmented than you suggest: they must be reconstructed, then each one of them—even when general and essential facts such as concentration or internal differentiation are in question—is both obscure and significant. Obscure because it never gives an account of itself; over-significant because it contains a plurality of meanings each of which is revealed as an autonomous totality: one comes from weariness, hunger, bitterness; another, practical, is attached to the productive attitude or work; a third is given to everything else by the universal existence of the *Other*, the inversion of human relationships and alienation or illumination through past experience, etc. All the objective structures of the social world are surrendered in a first in-differentiation to working-class subjectivity. Nothing is made clear, there are no *guarantees*: resignation (crushing by the *Other*) and revolution (going beyond the Other towards the in-finite task) light up the situation simultaneously, but their connexion goes on changing. Is it a question of idealism, or of the irrational? Not at all: all *will be* plain, rational, all *is* real—

to begin with by this resistance to interpretation: it is simply necessary to take time. But if active experience begins in receptivity and uncertainty, it becomes possible, even necessary, to ask for help: intepretation *can* be made by a mediating agency. Not that one party can prescribe its keys: it *tries* them, that is all. But, with the intention of making all mediation useless, you have tried on us 'experience-which-allows-of-its-own-interpretation'. The difficulties we have met with lead us back to the common notion of experience: obscure whole of 'consequences without premises' interpreted in several ways.

That is just what you reject. Fundamentally, I understand you: the real is opaque and difficult of approach; and if that is so, it is because we are in a certain position. I imagine that the world is at first obscure to the workers in the degree that the world and the worker in the world are obscure to me. But you have no wish at all to be situated: you would lose Knowledge. Your *situation* would teach you what you are not (you are not Hegel; you are not Marx; nor a worker; nor Absolute Knowledge) and what you are (you are a young French intellectual, remarkably intelligent, who has ideas about Marx as people in 1890 had ideas about woman). You certainly accept it that the proletariat lives its relationship to production and its opposition to capitalism in the form of its behaviour, of its efforts towards unity, of the progressive discovery of its tasks, but *on condition* that you are there to make the transcription from one system to the other, to assign the objective its coefficient of subjectivity, to describe to us the living connexions of the workers among themselves, the ambiguity of their relationship to the working-class élite, and then to show us how much these connexions in the subjectivity of the class will lead to the reformist attitude. In making use of the 'reciprocity' of perspectives, you would be able to find in reformism *the meaning* of the inward links of the proletariat or in these links the *real* significance—in, that is to say, Absolute Knowledge —of this reformism. Rather than the militants, you resemble those psychiatrists who establish correspondences between objective behaviour and the talk of the sick without wishing to enter into their delirium. Everything becomes plain, no one is situated: neither you by a link with the classes nor the working class if not by connexion with production; you deny at the same time your individual position and that of the individuals who compose the class: 'Isn't it possible when speaking of the group to stop looking at the individual?' To be sure! Get off the line! The working class is only one universal experience of culture; therefore the subject and the object are homogeneous: forsaken thought and solitary class mutually supporting their solipsisms will make a common experience of the universal.

You have given your creation activity, strength, awareness, and life, all the gifts save one: inertia. Your proletariat has the right to advance continually: it has not the right to make a mistake, to be ignorant, to fail; in short to suffer. You have rejected pell-mell the fetters, the finiteness, the fatigue, the fear on the part of individuals, and then you have turned towards the impassive class. The bloody and sometimes obscure history of the working-class movement is merely epiphenomenon; you will never tell us of its risks, its disasters, and its renewals: situation, obscurity, anchorages, guide marks, passivity, all these qualities are linked; through them, man is the object of man, of the sun, of the dog; now it seems to you undesirable that an object-Lefort or an objectivity of the working class should exist. Naturally you are not so mad as to refuse to the workers a logical relationship with the real world; they may die of cholera, of famine. You yourself mentioned the depersonalization from which the conveyor-belt operative suffers and the deficiencies of proletarian culture. You would willingly admit that the massacres and deportations of 1871 upset the composition of the proletariat and deprived it of its leaders. No matter: in so far as it is *put up with* the change does not affect the class, it transforms individuals or, strictly speaking, limited groups. But the proletariat will share it only to the extent that it integrates it into its experience.

Here therefore is a proletariat complete and positive, like the God of Leibniz who does nothing but act and reflects his action in himself. But weakness, nothingness, passion have taken refuge in each of its members, in such a way that it is possible, without touching it, to decimate it from below and in the end to destroy it by acting on the individuals composing it. Could it not be said that the active history of the proletariat-subject and the fluctuating history of working-class movements develop on different planes? It would be possible to find that logically you

were a follower of Durkheim: does not your proletariat resemble
that collective awareness which 'in depending on the whole
without depending on the parts which compose it enjoys, thanks
to this diffusion, a ubiquity which frees it'? But no: you have
laid it down that 'the class is not a reality apart from the individuals'. To tell the truth, the formula, like all those of our
eclectic sociologists, is ambiguous, and Durkheim might also
lay claim to it. But let us take it for granted that 'Sociology
has made some progress' since the *Essai sur la Division du
travail social*. The class, according to you, would be 'what
makes it possible to act and to think in common', etc. A functional definition, in short; and one which aims at establishing a
connexion. The class is the sociality. But what is the sociality?
Well, it is exactly what allows individuals to belong to groups,
for example, to the class. We are back at the point of departure:
the class is a connexion, a continual process of auto-organization and integration, an experience: I am not much enlightened.
When you say: 'what makes possible . . .' the class is mediation, you make a 'neutral' of it and it is very well done. When
you make of it 'participation in a schema of action . . .' it is not
at all the same thing, for this participation is only an abstract
designation for the real fact of thinking and acting in common.
The two preceding definitions have at least not taken us away
from *neutral* ground. But when you write 'the class . . . trusts . . .
in a fraction of itself', I no longer understand what you mean,
and I wonder with disquiet if you are not speaking metaphoric-
ally. And when at last I read: 'the class is concerned only with
its own activity', I understand that it is not a matter of a metaphor and that you describe in these terms the subject of working-
class history—perhaps of history merely. Is there a gradation or
is it necessary to believe that these ideas are nearly synonymous? Is the fact of acting on itself in order to integrate
modifications of structure exactly similar to experience? Bah!
you will say, the class produces, and produces itself in producing, the class produces the man and the man produces the class
—it is translating into Marxist dialect the most famous formula
of our nineteenth century: to make in becoming made. But that
is not the real question: it matters little to me at this moment
whether it makes itself, or whether it is made. I should like to
know how this pure activity of integration can be distinguished

from individuals by the very direction and targets of its *praxis* while being nothing 'outside them'. Is it necessary to conceive of an activity, through and through social and collective, incapable of aiming at anything but the collective, that is to say homogeneous with the objects of its experience (capitalism, production, etc., class interests, in the framework of an infinite project)? But if that is what you ask of it, the class is no more than a verbal system, chosen to express collective *results*: you return to the 'as if'. As I conceived it, the class, unified by the CP, could doubtless have apprehended concrete totalities in its revolutionary movements, that is to say, syntheses of the singular and of the universal: *this* strike, *this* claim. For I see it, *in itself*, as a concrete universal: singular because it has been made with these men, in these circumstances—universal because it takes in a whole collection. In short, it is an undertaking whose actions and real thoughts are inserted in the real movement of history. But what does your class do? It organizes itself: which means that it integrates in its universality morphological transformations which are themselves universal. Changes of structure, of number, evolution in the method of work: these facts can be expressed by abstract, sometimes quantitative concepts; they are by no means *historical* in their essence; it would be necessary, to situate them, to add an external date to them. And the activity which will integrate these changes is itself abstract since it will make of it an *internal order* of its parts. In short, it will pass the time in defining and applying formulae of regrouping and redistribution. It will be seen, for example, that universality as the abstract significance of interchangeability will be interiorized, universality still more abstract, in universal connexion between the men. Do you understand that this is *one* of the aspects of working-class experience? That it also contains concrete, historical formulae of organization and concrete memories of great social events? But how can these different levels of experience exist together? And what are the connexions between them? Besides, most of your examples show us the transformation of empirical and practical contents which become general and schematized in moving from the objective to the subjectivity of the working class. That does not surprise me: when, to escape from the hard problems of the collective consciousness, the unity of a group is conceived as immanent, this unity is idealized in becoming interiorized and impoverished in becoming universalized.

After all, what is your class? What is its connexion with reality? If you wish it to be believed in, it must be shown to us, we must be made to see facts which would not be produced without it. And since it is active, its effective reality must be proved by the results of its action. You rightly place its originality in its connexion with production. If you are to be believed, we should meet it at the outset, in relation to the most elementary gesture of the man at work. At this level, it would already be the integration of his immediate reactions; and it would not even be difficult to distinguish the individual attitude from collective *praxis*: for the workers, taken singly, work as they can; that is to say, taking into account their needs, their weariness, their wages, the social conflicts in progress, etc. But, whatever their individual attitudes may be, the proletariat, their class, is made manifest in the unity of the collective movement which, through their labour, pushes capitalism towards its next crisis or which, as a result of their claims, exercises a harassing and harmful effect on the national economy. Thus, as Marx said in a passage you quote, it matters little what the worker believes he is doing; the important thing is that he cannot help doing it. There is the *original unity* of *praxis* and, in consequence, of the subject of *praxis*: the working class by a double converging and simultaneous action prepares material and social conditions for Revolution. You will say that the class is *this undertaking* in so far as men take part in it and lead the struggle against exploitation. Two workers, unknown to one another, are linked by something more than the simple identity of their condition: the very content of their acts is revolutionary *praxis*; their two converging activities create the closed world of the proletariat.

If that is your proof, I hold it of no account. The *objectivity* of production is what is revealed to the Marxist theorist or to the capitalist or to the worker who takes a reflexive view on working-class activity. Objectively, the worker prepares the next crisis. But *objectively* means in the world of economists and capitalists. As for him, he does what he has been ordered to do, he sells his working strength in order to live; it could equally well be said that the producer himself produces middle-class society and that the employer hurls himself with his competitors towards the ruin of the system by *taking* the proletariat *as gravedigger*. From this point of view, the path to profit is what will be the essential factor, it is what, through the agency of the employer and under threat, will oblige the proletarian to become the simple instrument of this suicide. It will never be decided whether it is capitalism which is destroying itself by its own contradictions or if it is the worker who 'carries out the sentence that middle-class society has pronounced against itself'. To tell the truth, these two interpretations are equally right, equally incomplete without any possibility of a summing up. This circle is in the image of the Other and of alienation.

In any event, you base the existence of your class *subject* on a half-truth. And if you answer me that this half-truth corresponds exactly to the *subjective experience* of the class, I should not consider myself satisfied. For the class may indifferently recognize itself as actively producing the ruin of capitalism or as working under constraint in order not to die of hunger.

In fact, this alleged unity as subject is a unity as object. Or, if it is preferred, the unity of the alleged *praxis* comes from the capitalist system itself. Hours of work unite outside the workers in order to augment productive capital; inversely, the structures of a middle-class democracy will give a special appearance to the economic crisis which strikes it and it is the very unity of the crisis and the interdependence of its reverberations in the different sectors of national life which will impose from outside and through the mediation of the Other a certain objective unity on the claims of the workers. The example of Britain is significant enough because the wages policy followed there is still, today, in extended order: it is known that the trade unions, unequal in development, unequal in strength, differentiated by origin, age, and structure, restrict themselves in general to defending each of them the interests of its own members, sometimes against those of other trade unions. One group which has secured a rise in wages has therefore acquired a 'differential' advantage, which is translated into a differential injury as regards other groups. Later on, other unions follow its example, always in extended order. The original advantage was differential and positive for the most favoured group; it tends to be rendered void, that is to say to be countered, by a rise in prices. This tendency always depends on different factors (the importance of the most favoured group, its situation in production, distance, concentration, etc.) which will govern the speed of the spread. Where the group is of restricted importance, the delay of spread may be considerable: the advantage gained is consolidated and the rise in prices remains weak. If it is very important, its example will be followed at once; at once the spiral of prices and wages begins again, and this will entail the intervention of the State. It is an example of what M. Lhomme[97] calls non-coherent policy; that is to say, 'without deliberate coherence where equilibrium is of a statistical nature'. The effects, nevertheless, have the structure of planned phenomena. The rise of wages can be considered as a working-class action in order to improve the pay of wage-earners. So that Lhomme himself will discover in the policy of the trade unions a *general* tendency ('improvement in the fate of the workers, major objective of *trade-union activity*, is most often sought by way of increases in the nominal wage') which varies under the action of a multiplicity of factors (particularism, individual structure of each group, corporate feeling, etc.). It is to this general tendency that their opponents will refer —for example the *Economist* when, in 1949, it accused all the trade unions *taken as one person* of playing the part of 'economic aggressor'. Now, it is true that each trade union—independently of the size of its membership—can be regarded as a 'decision-making unit'. (At this level we *really* meet the collective and the sociality.) But there are certain centres of decision, and they are very different: some conservative (in general the old trade unions), others more active (the mass trade unions recruited in new industries). The principle of imitation which has ruled the succession of claim-making acts supposes as a matter of fact the radical separation of groups.[98] Undoubtedly they serve as models one for another. But it is in the extent to which they are distinguished one from another and in which their interests are opposed. For the least favoured trade unions resent the differential advantage of the more favoured as a wrong done to them, and inversely the most favoured fear that their success may start a general movement: since a raising of *all* wages would cancel their gain. The action of one on the others is therefore separatist in the same way as individual antagonisms. If the results are *unified*, it is because actions in detail are integrated by the synthetic reaction of a semi-coherent system: the parts of the economic system are interdependent or, if you prefer, the *process* of capital is dialectical. Here also it could be said that changes in detail acquire their meaning only in relation to the whole: several similar excitations produced at different points of the 'production-wage-price, etc.' complex provide the opportunity for a single reaction. Besides, if the federal organisms do not manage to orchestrate their demands,[99] at least the policy of the opponent will unify them. Mortin does not think there is a threat of inflation from the raising of wages in the USA; the bank would refuse credits. In Great Britain, where it has not the same interests or the same function or the same connexion with the State and private persons, the danger would be more worrying.[100] If the unions become *one* aggressor, it is because *the* bank has decided to treat them as a single activity exerting an effect at several points. And if *it* has decided this, it is precisely because it is a social reality (in spite of the antagonisms and because of the effective union of its members) and because it can by a single reaction exorcise the scattered threats. At the higher level, the State will bring about the last unification by putting action and reaction, raising of wages and of prices, proletarians, employers, bankers, and trades-people back into the perspective of the national organism.[101] But in the very extent to which claims form an embarrassment for British industry and run the risk of precipitating a crisis or of compelling capitalism to change in order to remain the same (that is to say, to safeguard profit), economic aggression can, without too much misuse of words, be called *revolutionary*. That simply means that the worker cannot improve his condition without compromising the socio-economic balance of capitalism: everything happens *as if* a revolutionary group had formed itself and had really engaged in a struggle to the death against existing society and as if it made use of working-class wretchedness and anxieties to reach its ends. It is exactly the virtual existence of this group which is said to be revealed in the co-ordination of popular movements (when this co-ordination is simply the reflexion of the national unity of the economy); it is this ideal existence which gives a strange verisimilitude to the reproach so often made to the parties of using social movements for political ends.

The synthetic unity of effects is no proof of the unity of the undertaking. Quite the contrary. It is the synthetic reaction of the opponent (minister, organization of employers or of bankers) which gives to dispersed excitations an appearance of unity. Can it be said that this *objective* unification of different popular movements will have the result of bringing about their *real* reunion? That was obvious: in France the governmental repression of 1831, by mixing up the republicans with the first working-class associations, certainly hastened their agreement. But the workers submitted to this sham unity as to a class *ordinance*. Arrests, disbandments, lock-outs, etc., suddenly revealed to them their objective reality as an oppressed class. Let us leave your sheepfolds, your 'natural but not unconscious processes': these are words. The truth is that the workers go through—in the very prolongation of alienation—the experience of their *class in itself;* they come to know their class as something which is in the hands of the Other. They get to know it as having been first the object of the Other and they become aware of being first of all and in essence *objects*; their essence does not belong to them; and their first movement in order to claim class and awareness of class is not the peaceful development which you describe: it is a struggle to tear their objective reality from the Other, to re-interiorize their essence, and to oppose to the *class in itself* the class aware of itself and claiming its being. There is, in fact, as you have noticed, an experience of itself *as class* which develops with the evolution of the proletariat: but even this subjectivity is to tear from the enemy[102] the consciousness of the oppressed and is not the concomitant of a *natural* process: it *discovers itself.* By a double movement which leads it to reject being a thing and to assume again *for itself* in pride the objective characteristics imposed on it, the proletariat constitutes itself as consciousness. Its subjectivity is both the negation of the consciousness of the Other and of its own objectivity.

Not a word of all this in your article: it is no business of yours and you are concerned only to prove that the class produces itself. But what of these disconcerting coincidences, of the steadiness to be observed in social conflicts, of the totalization of industrial products? For what is taking up our attention, nothing: in looking for working-class unity on that side, we have found that of an oppressed class, and of a government obedient

to it. If you want to convince us of the *real* existence of an autonomous proletariat, *demonstrate it.*

You have understood that: that is why the brilliant dialecti-
cian has suddenly changed into the sociologist. You have *suggested* the proletariat, we had *foreshadowed* its ideal existence,
caught a glimpse of its evolution, natural and dialectical, reformist and revolutionary; that was all right. The only trouble was
that it remained invisible. What is seen every day, in fact, is a
sort of bastard proletariat, five million workers whose unity
evidently lies in their manner of work, of payment, of life, in
their claims, in 'their schemata of life and of action', etc., *but
also* and very markedly in their fashion of obeying (together
and *more* or *less* well) the orders of trade unions and parties.
They meet in Communist or paracommunist organizations;
often they learn from trade union journals about the attitude—
sometimes about the existence—of other groups. In short, observation alone is not decisive: it simply reveals an aggregate of
men with institutions, organizations, frameworks. *You* want to
show that the apparatus, the framework, the specialized organs
are simply the *expression* of spontaneous unity; the task is not
easy: your social genetics has led us to *class-autonomy*. It is this
autonomy which must be reached again through heteronomy
and bureaucratic exploitation. You assert that the class organizes itself by itself: it is thus necessary, in spite of appearances, to make us appreciate the ineffectiveness of all these
specialized organs of concord and intercommunication. The
class without the Communists, organizations without the class
at liberty: it is India without the English, Latin without weeping,
the Revolution without tears, Nature without Man.

Naturally you demonstrate nothing. You could not demonstrate anything since you would have had to suppress parties
and trade unions in order to ensure that their disappearance
led to no change.

What is more interesting is that you try all the same to appeal
to a positive experience. That's a necessity, to be sure. For you
have explained to me in vain that the brutal opposition of
activity and passivity, of unity and multiplicity, has long since
been overtaken by the eclectic concepts of 'hold-all' sociology,
you have in vain thrust aside the idea of synthesis which you
find in Durkheim, the idea of totality which you believe you

find in my article: as soon as you define the class as 'a different thing from the sum of individuals' the reason is plain. The class is *the connexion making itself the mediating agent*. And as in fact there are a great many connexions, it must at the very least be the connexion of all these connexions. Besides, that is not enough: consider a kaleidoscope: I can talk of the *connexion of the colours*. If I upset the kaleidoscopic panorama, the connexion changes. In this instance, the relationships are the pure passive products of induced changes. They do not *join up again*, it is the contents which holds them up, they are neutral. Your class connexion can be neither the result of a transcendent unification nor the active connexion of communication and interaction, nor therefore the connexion-epiphenomenon which passively exudes objective changes. You will answer that it is, and that it makes itself; it springs from a chance concord, but, scarcely risen, it reunites its terms to one another, etc. The patter is familiar: however, this 'metastable' idea—which mixes doing and being in such a way as to make inert externality pass for a *praxis* and the *praxis* for a way of being—is far from fulfilling all the tasks you impose on it. You want to show the sham, parasitic character of the activities of the Party; it is not the Party which unifies the class, it is the class which unifies the Party. Therefore we must be made to discover the class—that activity improperly claimed by the CP. Now, that is exactly what 'spontaneous' connexion would be unable to show. Unemployment, for example, is, without any doubt, for a given period a coherent and structured reality. But its unity, as we have seen, does not come from the workers who suffer it: it is the very unity of the capitalist process. You want to interiorize unemployment, to make it a subjective experience of the class? You are quite right: only, this re-interiorization supposes unity already, as activity of subjectivation. What is necessary therefore? That you will show us the whole of the workers at the same time as a multiplicity—that is to say, in one sense, as exterior from one another—and as a power of digesting externality. Unemployment can be a relationship between those out of work if they pass beyond the wretchedness which separates them, towards an experience of the proletariat. Experience *of whom*? Who is the subject? Experience *of what*? What is its class content? Shall we say that there is reciprocity of perspectives? That would be perfect if it were a question only of signifi-cances. For example, it is *true* that the suicide of a particular American of the Middle West is susceptible of assuming a double meaning in the eyes of the sociologist; it is *true* that the social significance is contained by the individual significance as the individual significance by the social significance. It is un-compromisingly a question of methodological precepts, aiming at the reconstruction of a fact. But in the matter which is oc-cupying us, the problem would remain whole if we restricted ourselves to saying that the individual worker is in the class (or that his consciousness is in the collective consciousness) as the class is in the worker: we should simply have shown the logical connexion of the extension of the concept with its connotation. In a structured social environment which possesses its own traditions, institutions, forms of publicity and culture, one can well imagine reciprocity of the individual will be forged from his birth by the social environment, from which he will receive customs and techniques, culture, etc. But social reality is in each one and in all, a cultural pattern which has no life except that which is given to it, which is *maintained* as tradition, and never evolves as an intentional movement. If the proletariat is subject, if it writes its history, there is another reality than this ideal unity: it is not a pattern, it is a real power of integration. Therefore you will not escape: we must return to the synthesis.

You try once again to obscure this necessary step: you appear one moment to content yourself with vaguely structured con-nexions, with a diffused presence of each to all, of a Bergsonian multiplicity of interpenetration which would be neither wholly total nor wholly synthesis but would be able, from instant to instant, to pass from one to the other. I recognized that our great urban centres are often enough in this colloidal state. And *massification* is never so pushed that the worker loses the feeling of belonging to an *environment*. But I see also that this 'partici-pation' is commonly given as a consequence of the social work of organization. And this work seems, at first sight, exercised on the masses by specialized organs. If the docker of Marseilles and the docker of Brest meet, it is because there exist parties, trade unions, newspapers, congresses which bring them together. It matters little that the majority of workers may be made up of people without party, outside trade unions: information is

passed on, watchwords circulate, collective sentiments spread
out from centres of activity, the action of the minorities agglom-
erates round it, draws on the masses. Good sense sees therefore
in all this jumbled unity, continually called in question, the resi-
duum of a constant effort of the working-class élite to organize
itself. *From there*, it works in the mass by deep reactions; currents are born which can flow back to parties, to trade union
offices, and even overflow them. If you mean to prove your
thesis, it is this activity of organization, of leadership, of induc-
tion which you must take away from the specialized groups and
give back to the totality. If not, how could you be justified in
writing: '... in order to organize itself, a class crushed by exploitation ... must clear up innumerable theoretical and practical tasks, and finds itself thus led to confide to a minority the
rôle of leadership while its revolutionary activity and its own
communist aspirations assume that it suppresses all relationship of domination in its heart and inaugurates a new method of
collective action'? Or again: 'The whole class ... perceives in
its privileged stratum an anticipation of its fate'? Or: 'The
movement of the class in order to organize itself leads it to confide the duties of representation to a fraction of itself ...'? Or,
in another article: 'The feeling that the class has ... of its low
cultural level ...'? And how speak of 'the *total* experience of
the class' if you have not previously given it the right of totalization?

In short, your thesis will hold only if you acknowledge your
secret *organicism*. And that in fact is what you are going to do.
Certainly you will not pronounce the word; but you will foist
the thing on us. The proletariat, you say, is concerned only with
its own activity; changes exist for it only in the extent to which
it integrates them. Well, isn't that exactly one of the great laws
of organicism? 'The effect of an excitation,' wrote Goldstein,
'depends in the first place on the significance which this excitation has for the total organism'. And if you object to Goldstein,
will you deny having read the *gestalt*ist Lewin, famous for having applied the same rule to social groups? Now he wrote, just
like you but without your precautions, that a 'social situation is
a dynamic whole' and that a modification of the parts existed
for this whole only through a synthetic modification of the
entirety. And, more explicitly than you have done, he applies

in sociology the principle of readjustment: a social group changes in order to repudiate change and re-establish equilibrium. Which leads him to declare the relative autonomy of each *Gestalt*: 'each of them creates its own movement.' Subjectivity therefore is indeed the internality of the group, defined as auto-determination. The trick is done.

But what becomes of your Marxism? And must I believe that it is really the *proletariat* you are describing as 'a participation in a schema of life and action, a *special understanding* of the environment', in short, as 'what allows them to act and think in collusion and to set themselves up together as different from the rest of society'.

The dialectic makes us imagine a proletariat-subject of history, substance and deep guarantee of the proletariat-object of sociology. Which at once implies the dialectical reversal of terms: the existence of the empirical proletariat, producing factual proof, becomes a guarantee in its turn. The 'participation', the 'understanding', etc., represent the proletariat for itself as cultural pattern reuniting individuals; as for the *praxis* whose meaning may escape the worker ('it matters little what he believes he is doing'), it is the proletariat in itself. And, as you distinguish between appearance and deep reality, it would even be possible to wonder if the proletariat-*praxis* is not, in your eyes, the intelligible characteristic of your proletariat-gelatin. But on the other hand, the subjectivity of the proletariat as participation lived according to the cultural patterns of the class becomes the *object* of sociology, while its deep objectivity as the historical reconstruction of the rational total opens into the proletariat-*subject of history*. The proletariat-noumenon is project, activity of auto-organization, unity in progress: but it does not appear. The proletariat-trembler appears but this variable mixture of viscosity and powderiness can after all produce separation, powerlessness, and solitude: all the mystical words used by eclectic sociology to express its feeling of the ineffable will not prevent men from being reunited by solitude, by common powerlessness, by resignation, and their manner of being each-for-the-other can be simply mutual aloofness, antagonism, repulsion. Look at Malthusianism: round about 1935 it reached working-class environments, the birth rate collapsed. It was a question of data so general and so plain that you are obliged by your principles to accept their social character. Or would you rather have us admit that there is between finished modes and their essential characteristic a collective inter-mediary, something like the infinite mode of Spinoza? Joking apart, what will you make of this growing tendency to sterility? Will you say that abortive practices are revolutionary? That they represent a spontaneous defence by the worker against the real fall in his wages[103] and that they would have as certain result the revalorization of human merchandise? I know that this is your system: from the beginning you have repeated that capitalism is unsteady and fragile; according to that, whatever the workers may do, they will end by smashing it; *therefore* the proletariat is in essence revolutionary. But this time you will not convince me so easily: fought against at the same time by the government, the middle class and the Party, Malthusianism (which anarchist trade unionism preached in the desert) today bears witness to a kind of lassitude, of despair, of resentment. Social duties no longer exist, whether towards comrades or future generations; this genocide is a rejection of the future whatever it may be, a distrust of all things. It is—like riot and savage strikes—a *radical* act which can rise only from the depths of a massified population—in that sense it is certainly a question of a *homogeneous* act in revolutionary channels, but inverted, negative, refusing what they assert and nearer to a revolt of slaves[104] than to revolutionary *praxis*. Now this asocial conduct is properly a factor of sociality: contagious reaction to a collective mode of life, it tends to spread; it reveals to each one that his life is intolerable and that it is a crime to 'give life', to feed the machine with other lives. In the middle class, abortive practices remain asocial because they are covered up. The paradox is that the Malthusianism of the workers makes no pretence of hiding itself: the women speak about it to one an-other, exchange advice, addresses and, above all, help one another. Abortion among the middle class remains, like suicide and eroticism, a fact of solitude and the persistence of these practices only shows the persistence of the forces of disassimila-tion which are exerted on the individual. On the contrary, work-ing-class abortion is a collective practice, a suicide in common; those men and women who practise it are united by a kind of pity. This refusal to give life, you see, is an answer to all your demands: it is certainly 'what reunites in apprehension of the same mode of life and action . . . a participation in schemata . . .', etc. Better still, it could be the direct reaction of certain working-class groups against the existing characteristics of mass production. Call to mind those nomadic Indians of Brazil who let themselves die quietly when the Portuguese wanted to attach them to the soil. I wonder sometimes if 'working-class sadness' has not exactly the same causes. The Indians were not liquidated by any formal characteristics of slavery but by changing their mode of work and their manner of life (bringing with it different food and the forced changeover from nomadism to sedentary life); would not the advent of 'automatism', assembly-line tasks, and mass production bring with it, to the workers of today, an analogous maladjustment? Interest in work decreases, weariness grows, the structures of the working-class world are broken down, depersonalization, physiological deformations, interchangeability end by taking away from the worker his reasons for working. Show us therefore from this example that the objective data of production are translated into the subjectivity of the proletariat by a revolutionary experience! No: there is no passing over from empirical sociality to the class writing its history.

The concept of *class* as pure similarity of condition and interest (peasant class) and that of *historical-subject* as subjectivity assigned by force of total history are equally empty. We have seen that it is not enough to bind them together in order to get away from verbalism. When you have reunited sociologism to history, water to fire and class as manner of life with historical subject as *praxis*, you will not, for all that, have begotten the proletariat. For it is still nothing to have 'rooted' it in society, in history, in the present situation, if you do not at the same time give it *passion*, that is the possibility of submission, of suffering, even of dying. In short, the proletariat is concerned not only with its own activity; it is concerned also with its inertia and—through that—with the activity of the Other class. For it is also through our passion that we achieve the painful and ambiguous experience of the real. Action—even triumphant—by its failures in detail, the rhythm which it imposes, the *prohibition* it exacts, the weariness it provokes—reveals our inertia to us; better, work implies it; if he were not sluggish, man would

neither construct tools nor make his own implement for himself;
Marx said this in so many words. And you who reproach
me with not seeing 'the work one does on oneself', how do you
not see that work is an affliction? And, if you do see it, why not
show that experience is also experience of passion; it is on this
one condition that it allows the painful and ambiguous 'apprehension' of the real. When Marx reproached Hegel with having
put the dialectic on its head, he did not merely oppose
materialism to idealism: he wanted to show that each moment
of the dialectic is a conquest by effort and work (if need be, by
combat) against chance and externality; he wanted to reintro-
duce into the most strictly planned undertaking delay, setback,
continual distortion of our operations. In short, the permanent
possibility of disorder which shows the continual risk that
humanity is coming to nothing. And when Hegel speaks of the
'moment which is set up for itself', Marx sees above all that
even the work of man, becoming thing again, shows in its turn
the inertia of the thing, its coefficient of misfortune and that the
human relationships which man has created fall back again into
inertia, introducing the inhuman as destructive power between
men. We rule the environment by dint of work, but in its turn
the environment rules us by the congealed growth of the
thoughts which we have inscribed on it. The Marxist dialectic is
not the spontaneous movement of Mind, it is the hard labour
of man to insert himself in a world which rejects him. Recently
a word of Brunschvicg reproaching Hegel with not having
known how to introduce a *resistance* in his system was brought
to mind. Without *delay*, that is to say without something which
puts on the brake, succession remains a formal idea, an order.
Concrete and real duration appears with effort, with waiting,
patience and impatience. Time is the need to be always in
advance or behindhand in the undertaking: here we are back
with the Bergsonian lump of sugar. But Hegel's time is neither
in advance nor behindhand and in his calm development things
occupy the only place they could occupy there. To be sure,
survivals, conflicts which may slow down the march of history
will be brought up: don't let us be caught by that; it is a question
only of auto-regulation: these fictitious applications of the
brake will allow the Idea to appear under all its aspects; these
are the tricks of Reason. Hegel's Dialectic is necessarily of time

past since it is not possible *to live* it, it is in past time that things are always in their place; and Marx brought us back to the true time of the dialectic. But you who accept in appearance the data of Marxism have taken away the resistance of things and of men, and are returning to the Idealism of Hegel. In reading you, it might be believed that the subjective experience of the class corresponds term by term with the contemporary régime or that a like reality translates itself simultaneously and without alteration in two different languages, the degree of subjective organization of the class expressing the nature and degree of socialization of the work. By this exact correspondence you destroy the real to the advantage of significance.

That working-class experience seeks continually to adjust itself to capitalist evolution; that it has sometimes been able to correspond exactly with the working-class condition taken in totality, and that this conformity of the subjective and the objective might be found again tomorrow—it is not for me to deny this. I say only that this reciprocity becomes idealistic if it is claimed that it comes about spontaneously. No, Lefort, adjustment is not automatic: trouble must be taken. I see in the working-class movement a conscious and constantly renewed effort of associations in order to catch up with delays, hasten developments that are too slow, and regain the level of the employers' organization, sometimes by overrunning a stopping place.

Enough: I only wanted to present to you the quickest and most superficial sketch of this confused history, full of delays and lost opportunities, in which the working class seems to become exhausted in catching up with the original delay, a history whose thread is often broken by external thunderbolts, wars, etc., and the subject of which changes completely and suddenly without anyone's having noticed the change. I note changes in the realm of production but also in political aspects of the situation; I see that it is impossible to have any understanding of it unless its aspect as *struggle* is accepted, I see that the leaders are nothing without the masses, but that the class has cohesion and power only to the extent that it has confidence in the leaders. Lastly, as to the authority of the chiefs, I see also that that is neither usurped nor illusory: but the leader interprets the situation, and by his plans illuminates it, its risks and dangers; and the class, in following orders, *recognizes* the authority of the leader. 'It is in *practice* that man must demonstrate the truth, that is to say the reality and the power, on this side of his thought.' And I don't know why you quote Rosa Luxembourg and Trotsky: for I say just what they say and it is they who say differently from you; it is not a question, in fact, of showing the Party dictating to the masses what they should think. The Party is to be distinguished from the masses only in the extent to which it is their union. It is by this very union that the masses produce their internal currents and it is from these currents that the Party interprets the *situation* of the class in society and its present position in the age-long struggle it leads. The Party forms the social frameworks of working-class memory, it is the sketch of their future, the organ of their action, the permanent link which struggles against their massification; it is the *perspective* from which the proletariat can put itself back into society and in its turn take as object those who make an object of it: it is the tradition and the institution. But the *content* of these empty forms will come to birth by the very linkage of the movement which the masses make in order to draw nearer to one another; it is by being brought into touch that particular interests are changed into general interests, it is through this that isolated individuals become *an undertaking*.

For proof of this all I want is the example of 'creativity' which you yourself quote. Experience of division presented itself as an evil: in 1903 it became clear that skilled workers were no longer irreplaceable, the strike lost part of its effectiveness; even more clearly the conveyor-belt operative appeared to be defenceless. Now, if you can count accurately, it has taken thirty-three years, in France,[105] to find a new solution, thirty-three years during which a slackening of social conflicts and an increase in the percentage of lost strikes were recorded, following the failure of revolutionary movements and the general retreat of proletariats despite their wretchedness, or rather because of it. Why, therefore, in 1936, when threats from abroad were becoming explicit and a weak business recovery started, why did the masses devise 'occupation of the factories'? No one had any doubt that this movement was 'spontaneous'. Must it therefore be seen as action by the class as a *totality*? Here we can determine the *true* meaning of this *spontaneity*: in fact, the masses are normally enclosed within a framework, they have newspapers, they are sub-

ject to the influence of parties and trade unions, there is a
nervous system in the crowd whose *tonus* spreads as it gets
weaker. Now, in this environment, already tolerably 'centralized', it is suddenly learned that under universal suffrage 146
socialists and 72 communists have been elected to the Chamber.
In 1935 (on July 14 for example) there had been *political* demonstrations which had at times brought together more than
half a million people, and the July 14 committee was 'carried
away by popular enthusiasm'. But it must be remembered that
the *Front Populaire* was a political union, and that this unison
had been effected at the top; the cantonal and municipal elections marked a slide to the left of the *electors,* that is to say of
those citizens within the framework of democratic institutions.
The access to power of the *Front Populaire,* after so many indications, was taken by the workers as a kind of promotion of the
proletariat: in the person of its leaders, the working class had
acceded to government; the solidarity of the two mass parties
and their unity of action reflected its own unity; to be in no
doubt about it, never since 1871 had the working class been so
vividly and completely aware of itself. Now, about the same
moment (May 11 at Le Havre, the 13th at Toulouse, the 14th at
Courbevoie), three strikes broke out accompanied by occupation of the factory. At first the press ignored this event. But on
May 24 *L'Humanité* drew attention to the fact that, in the three
conflicts, the workers had adopted new techniques of struggle;
that same day, at the Wall of the Federates, 600,000 demonstrators marched past. About the 26th the strike movement became
general in the Paris region. From the beginning of June it spread
all over France.

It is obvious that the working class felt its subjective unity in
the very extent to which it saw its objective victory in the elections; obvious also that it had translated into terms of movement the victory of its parties. In short, it had interiorized its
unity as object, and this unity as object was that of its leadership. Its victory through its leaders, within the framework of
middle-class institutions, had become actual in and through
occupation of factories. Pressure was slackening, something was
about to change, the worker was going to be able to talk to the
employer as an equal. The workers went on strike with delight
because it was easy. There is all that has long been said as to

the strength of this permanent repression, as to this continual presence of the armed enemy, which you seem to know nothing about, as to this active, deliberate, determined opposite side to exploitation, to oppression by the government with its 'coppers', if need be its army. These masses got on the move because their leaders were also leading France; and if they had *devised* occupation of the factories, it was because, for the first time, they had been daring enough. There is, to be sure, no doubt that they pushed the government further than it wanted to go: the masses, when they are united, have their rhythm, their manner of acting, their way of thinking. But if they had been able to go ahead with this activity from one frontier to the other, it was because they were constantly brought together by demonstrations in common, by speeches, by exciting newspapers, and saw their unity from the outside as a guarantee and a promise. In brief, it was *within the framework* of the taking of power by the elected members of the *Front Populaire* that the *already* assembled masses in their turn showed their bent and their true will. You will say, perhaps, that the SFIO and the CP in joining forces simply gave expression to the proletariat. A question of words: for if expression can determine this immense tidal wave, then expression is also action. That is what I tried to explain in my article: 'spontaneity' exists to the same extent that the already *united* class can go further than its chiefs, drag them further than they wish and translate on to the *social* plane a first decision which was perhaps only political.

But how could you even imagine what Trotsky called 'the dialectic of the party chiefs and of the masses', you who decide *a priori* never to interpret as *passions* the behaviour of the proletariat. How could you admit, for example, that the masses in 1936 gave the *social* interpretation of a *political* action: you are so afraid of crediting the 'apparatus' with some activity that you reduce political struggles to being merely an altogether secondary and intermittent aspect of proletarian experience: 'There are not two currents, one which moves forward by way of political demonstrations, the other by way of economic regrouping; there is an experience of opposition which is effected continually at the heart of and from the process of production, and which at long intervals crystallizes in explicit struggle on the scale of global society and confronts the power of the State.'

On one point we are in agreement: there are no two currents. But let us see what you deduce from that.

According to you, the proletariat has existed from the beginning: it lives its situation as exploitee in the active form of *opposition* to exploitation. Scarcely born, it questions the right of the middle class to govern. Nevertheless, do not let us go so far as to believe that it *rejects* its state: this rejection would lead us to believe that it *submitted* to its condition, that its status was imposed on it. Nonsense! 'Reject its state! When it is that state that provides the conditions of struggle and social revolution.' I know you well, and yet by this phrase you have succeeded in surprising me. It is true: the worker has the right to strike; and production which, in its existing form, 'empties the producer of his substance', in the long run produces the death of capitalism. But because this intolerable situation includes within itself the contradiction that (much later) will bring it to an end, is it necessary to conclude that the worker must accept it? As well say that the sick man wants his illness because it is the condition of his cure and the means of medical progress. The proletarian state is not defined only by manual work; it is defined also by the condition of the wage-earner; and when I said that the worker rejects his state, I believed I was repeating what Marx said a hundred times.[106] But you have allowed one of the principal theses of *Capital* to drop *because it inconveniences you:* it inconveniences you that wage-earning work progressively *destroys* the man who does it; this terrible progressive decline which Marx foresees on each page of his work inconveniences you. More than anyone else he insisted on the *degrading* character of wage-earning work; he showed it as physically undermining the worker, deforming him to the point of disability, stupefying him to the rôle of a *helot*, exposing him to every deception: he dared to write that Lassalle owed his success to the debasement of the German proletariat. I find scarcely an echo of all that in your article. Nevertheless, when Marx spoke of this debasement or when he called the worker a sub-man, he did not dream of insulting the worker: quite the contrary; it seemed to him that his only way of being a man today was to be 'a sub-man conscious of his sub-humanity'. He simply wanted to insist on the difficulty of the struggle, he wanted to show that from the beginning the worker is crushed, stupefied, enfeebled, weaponless, defeated in advance, thwarted, by capital: what is wonderful is that, little by little, he will tear himself from this state, exactly as man himself tore himself in the course of thousands of years from the condition of being a beast. Systematically, you have forgotten labour, the 'enemy force'. Marx wore himself out telling us of the dangers of industrial production; it is relevant that he—who chattered so little about the future—goes so far as to recommend to socialist régimes: 'Socialized man, joint-producers regulate rationally the metabolism between themselves and nature, subjecting it to their common control instead of being dominated by it as by a blind force',[107] and to lay down for them the substitution of 'the integrally developed individual for the assembly-line individual, simple executant of a social function. . . .' All that is very displeasing for you: you feel, I imagine, the difficulties that Marx met, you want to escape from the objection made to him from the time of Andler that he had two concepts of the proletariat, one of which is catastrophic while the other implies a kind of permanent revolution. Yes, it has been said a hundred times: if the worker falls into the last degree of degradation, how will he be capable of taking charge of man's destiny when the final crisis racks the capitalist machine to pieces? At bottom, that comes back to saying: if the worker is passive, how can he be suddenly transformed into an active power of history? But the two theses exist only in the analytical understanding of certain socialists: in fact, Marx admitted the necessity of a continual effort towards emancipation, the more sustained as the class saw its condition worsening. In brief, Marx's thesis has always been the reciprocal conditioning of progressive impoverishment[108] and permanent revolution. To transform wretchedness into a factor of revolution, it is necessary to know how to reveal to the worker his reason for existence and his demands. But that is exactly what inconveniences you: that, precisely, specialization is necessary. Yes: a part of the workers will unite first in order to summon the others to union; yes: the militants will bring the masses together and will teach them. Between the class, as activity and as historical undertaking, and the mass as passive product of production, a mediating agent is necessary. *Someone* is needed to transform into lifting power the weight which drags at it from below, to transform suffering into demand. That is where you lose your head: if the masses are affected by a certain passivity, then the Party can play an historic rôle; at all costs, that must be denied. And you replace the tough fight which breaks out, at the very heart of the working masses, between the forces of unification and the forces of dispersion, by a smooth evolution: from its birth, the proletariat was endowed; when quite small it already disputed the validity of middle-class power; this steady youth, with his happy disposition 'rooted in nature and history', vanished under the gentle influence of daily labour. Gentle and tough, to be sure; sometimes the position would be such as to make him lose courage; but he tells himself he has taken on this heavy task in order to free humanity; that restores all his energy, as also does this Latin tag which he often murmurs: *labor improbus vincit omnia*. However, he is getting on: soon he will be ripe for the re-shaping of the admitted facts of industrial production: then it will be Arcadia; primitive unity re-discovered in the heart of abundance. In short we revert precisely to the fallacies which I dismantled in my article: to put the party out it is necessary to suppress working-class passivity or, if you prefer, to get it digested by activity: we shall then have this 'natural but not at all unconscious development' which will lead us imperceptibly from proletariat-seed to proletariat-flower to proletariat-fruit.

That is all very well: to avoid recognizing the efficacy of communist action, you rapidly bring about a change of natures: you give the activity of the CP to the whole proletariat, you recognize in the CP only a passive existence: this inertia which you foist on it is the same as that found *also* in the proletariat; but have you taken into account that you are going to fall from Scylla into Charybdis? If the proletariat is autonomous, if it is never concerned except with its activity, if parties and association express only passively the degree of its organization, whence comes the *mistake*? If you reject the right to explain Lassalle's influence by the 'degradation' of the German working class, how will you explain it? For in the end, in the error, the political mistake, the hoax, there is non-existence. Where will you take this non-existence if the proletariat is pure activity?

You are so well aware that you have run against the old problem which ruins all dogmatisms, you are so conscious of the difficulties in which you are going to drown, that you begin by trying to destroy the very idea of a mistake. Let us take reformism: it seems to you impossible that it should be 'accepted', that it comes from a hoax or a betrayal. It is not and could not be an 'illusion' of the working class. Why? Because 'ideology expresses certain real social relationships and even the ambiguity [of reformism] expresses the double social characteristic of unity and diversity among the proletarians. . . . In its privileged stratum, the whole class discerns an anticipation of its destiny'.

Splendid. But why do you add: 'If reformism gave itself out for what it is, it would not be ambiguous'. . . .? It does not therefore give itself out for what it is? And what the mass perceives as the anticipation of its own destiny is not, according to you, the *reality*? The egoistic advantage acquired by the privileged stratum is not exactly what is called an illusion? You say no: the illusion would be a mistake not based on the real: where did you get that? If I take a tree for a man, this illusion is very well explained *by the real*. It implies first a certain organization of my senses, a certain structure of the field of perception, a global attitude, an instance of 'behaviourism' which puts me in the world exactly at this place; the fear which seizes me in front of this dark form is evidently the very meaning, the subjective expression of this whole. In that sense it is based completely in the real. That is to say, in so far as it expresses something which is. I recognize, on the contrary, that it is baffling in so far as it relates to *what does not exist* (this non-existent man who frightens me); but that is precisely what characterizes the working-class attitude in relation to reformism, at least as you describe it: its apprehension that the present fate of the privileged stratum represents its future destiny is in fact based in the real; in so far as it means *something*, it shows 'the distance within the unity' of the proletariat. But in so far as it seizes through this privileged fraction of itself an evolution which will lead it from reform and, *under the leadership of its chiefs*, to the ultimate upheaval, it expresses something which is not and which nothing real can give rise to. And when it realized in its heart the indissoluble union of reformism and revolution, it remains that this exteriorization, this alienation of its objective bent, this projection of itself, from the outside, this deflexion of the movement by a minority which exploits it, and this way of seizing as *necessary future* what is subjective will, with no guarantee in objectivity—all that leads us *precisely* to *reformism as illusion.*

From the mistake, we go on to the Evil: the class *is* always all that it can *do*, the political struggle is intermittent, subjective experience is translated by a continual progress of auto-organization; besides the proletariat is concerned only with its own activity and there is nothing in it which does not express and is not founded on real bases. Then why are you not a communist? Since the CP is not outside the class, since it is separated from the masses only by this 'distance' which the exercise of power creates, it must certainly *express* the class. And whence would come its influence on the class if it were not just what the class made it? Others have reproached it with representing the interests of a foreign nation but, as you have continuity in ideas, you do not hold on to this grievance and you realize this feat of strength by presenting us with 'stalinism without Stalin'. Opponents and friends of communism, all—and the communists themselves—without denying the extreme importance of national factors, refuse to study the developments of the Communist Parties of Europe independently of their links with the USSR; opinions differ when it is a question of *assessing* the rôle of the USSR and its influence on national policies. But you write quietly: 'Stalinism can be interpreted in this sense *even before* its connexion with the existing régime in the USSR has been stated precisely, but from all the evidence, the fact that it has been possible for it to be realized in one country ... has played a decisive rôle in the expansion and the coming to consciousness of Stalinian bureaucracy.' You cannot, in fact, admit that Soviet society's own evolution has had some repercussions on the internal structure of the French CP: it would be necessary to recognize that the CP receives its status in part *from outside*; the proletariat would be led by an ambiguous organism whose movement would be conditioned *at the same time* by the currents which cross the working-class masses and by the transformations of a foreign society, that is to say in the end by the Other and by the course of the world. But, in your monadology, the working class 'has neither door nor window through which something can enter or leave'. You will fall back then on pre-established harmony: each proletariat produces its own

Stalinism; if one of these bureaucracies lays hold of power in its country, a wonderful conformism makes an appropriate change appear inside each little national Stalinism; it is not a question, besides, of a change of structure: let us say that it will take less time to become what it is. The appearance *on the outside* of Stalinism-with-Stalin is felt *in the interior* by the Stalinisms-without-Stalin under the form of a link between the proletariat and its own activity. That is what the 'reciprocity of perspectives' leads to when it is used without discrimination: in the present composition of the French proletariat, you claim to find the USSR on a reduced scale; inversely, the whole of Soviet society seems to you an enlargement of regional proletariats. In each of these interiorities you can find repeated the dialectical movement of the others, you will be able to take each of them as the symbol of the others, but for each you must stand on the plane of auto-organization.

The result of this monadology? It is at least paradoxical: you who declare yourself hostile to 'Stalinism' have removed yourself from the means of condemning it, whereas I (in common with so many others who only use their 'good sense') do not hide my sympathies with many aspects of communist enterprise and yet maintain my right and option to appraise it. What you reject on principle, I accept without constraint. I admit that in the working-class memory there have been experiences partly or provisionally incomprehensible whose key is to be found in Cominform or in some other proletariat. Of all receptivities, those which you fight the hardest are the passions that come to us from the Other and that assume the intrusion of the Other among us: but as I meet the presence of the Other in myself, among all men, in all groups and even in all classes, not only as the foreigner to whom we are collusively opposed but as the objectifying power which impregnates us, divides us and possibly makes us traitors in the eyes of other members of the group, I understand very well the connexion of the French Party with the Cominform and with the USSR, and that each group feels the other within itself as its own inertia. Whatever the real dependence of the CP in relation to the Cominform, their relationship necessarily implies conflicts, opposition, concessions, compromises, arrangements; what is *yielded* to the Other is therefore presented in each one as inertia, as an opaque crystallization, as a stratum of *non-life* in the midst of life. Of course we are not debating fundamentals: I wish only to say that the French CP, subordinate, local agent, less informed on the world situation, permits the Other's activity to impregnate it and to become an unconditioned source for its own activity; and that, at the same time, the proletariat when it complies with the orders of the Party and of the CGT, engages in an activity which reflects its own tendencies, the political form which the Party gives them, and the most abstract, most distant imperative of the Cominform. In so far as the Party in the heart of the working class is the *subject* of its activity, there is in the subjective interiority of this subject a stratum of objectivity and exteriority and this subject cannot be subject of itself, that is to say 'be concerned with its own activity', except in so far as it is object for another subject. The 'distance' which is set up between the proletariat and the fraction of itself which represents it does not come only from the exercise of power; but from the very heart of the proletariat, the Other is introduced through the CP; the order given by the chiefs no longer aims at the workers in the immanence of class and, without altogether objectifying them, it also becomes the conducting medium for a transcendant activity which, at the greatest depth of the working class, seems like a certain level of its objectification (a much more intimate level that that of its objectivity for the body of employers). This purely formal description aims only at establishing the *existence of the Other* as objectifying activity in the deepest of subjectivities: it remains true in all hypotheses; that is to say, it makes no decision as to whether the relationship of the CP to the USSR is favourable or hurtful to the interests of the French proletariat. I claim simply that no reply can be found to this last question without accepting first of all the hypothesis of a continual interaction.

You reject that. Therefore you can only be silent. Those whom you call 'Stalinists' would concede to you without difficulty that the authoritarian Party cannot, any more than the Soviet State, be envisaged as the final form of proletarian organization. It is a question of provisional organs, adapted to existing conditions of the struggle, which the proletariat will resorb when conditions have changed. In return you concede that, for the most part, the workers preserve their liking for the CP. How would you wish it to be otherwise? It is 'the proper movement of the class for its self organization which stresses the process of social differentiation and the power of a working-class minority'. In Stalinism, as in yesterday's reformism, the working class recognizes its own reflexion, its work, the provisional trustee of its sovereignty.

Nevertheless, you judge that this minority wrongs the class. How can it do that? It draws all its power from the proletariat which cannot turn its own activity against itself. All-powerful to *express* it, the leading 'fraction' is only its very expression: to deny that, to put a brake on its development, it is necessary therefore that it should have a malignant strength which comes to it from nothingness. Since the proletariat is never concerned except with its own activity, since you have been able to write that 'the class *confides in* a fraction', etc., what sudden shame prevents you from adding that it has chosen by itself and for itself the authoritarian form of organization? You who see in the wage-earning class and in the inhuman harshness of work 'conditions and means' of 'recasting the fundamental ideas of production', why do you not present 'Stalinism' as the harsh but unique means of giving the unity of an army to the masses —or, according to your way of speaking, as the expression of inflexible discipline which the proletariat takes on itself in integrating its last social changes? Ah! you will say, there is something else: this bureaucracy exploits the workers. And there is your fairy-tale: (1) differentiation of a minority; (2) creation of *distance* by the very fact that, in the working class, political and economic functions are not autonomous. Bureaucratic authoritarianism. That goes as well for reformism as for the CP; (3) the minority 'becomes established in the system of exploitation'. It prepares a new organization which will transform the working class into an oblivious, militarized mass exploited by its own bureaucracy; (4) 'reformism' characterized a minority which wanted to establish itself in the system of capitalist exploitation. 'Stalinism' appears at the moment when capitalism has nothing more to offer the 'new men' of the working class. It will therefore lead the struggle to the death against the élite power. It struggles for the advent of a new form of exploitation characterized by the domination of working-class bureaucracy and the management of the economy under state control.

In reading you, I sometimes think I am deceiving myself, that I have inadvertently opened the *Contrat social*, so much you mix what is with what ought to be. For after all, there is nothing new about this description, *if it is applied to the USSR*; which is not to say that it is true. For a long time the Soviet government and administration have been presented linked with the Russian Communist Party as a minority (others say, a class—and you do not fear the word) which has instituted a kind of state capitalism and, in this new framework, continues the exploitation of the workers. The opponents of the régime, the Trotskys, the Serges (who, nevertheless, had helped to construct it) simply distinguished what it might have been from what it had become; they had recourse to *historical* circumstances to account for this 'degeneration'. The masses were tired, peasant resistance turned to civil war, etc. Besides Trotsky, while recognizing that circumstances prompted the bureaucratization of the Party, conceived all the same a certain range of possibilities inside this very bureaucracy: there was the *good* bureaucrat—who would have been Trotsky himself—and the *bad* bureaucrat—who was Stalin. In a trice you have swept all that out of the way: it was too much alive, it was inconvenient; and then, after all, you didn't make the 1917 Revolution. Thus all power comes from the Devil; all authority exerted by a working-class minority on the working class in the name of that class itself must *necessarily* transform itself into a bureaucracy of exploitation. Good: it is more decent like that, more dead. But it is a matter of course that historic circumstances do not justify your point of view: for example, you hamper yourself with your tales of 'distance' and you do not even dream that the present form of Russian experience could be dictated, at least in part, by the *vital* need of increasing production. This platonic description never takes account of the situation of the USSR about 1920, immense socialist country, therefore threatened by death, whose riches had been pillaged by the war and whose industry, although it had sprung into life in the early years of the century, had a hundred years' lag to make up. To push on industrialization, develop productive industry, create new frameworks, establish a technical organization: this resembles the 'tertiary' of capitalist societies: these duties do not seem fundamental to you? And you do not believe that Soviet society, in danger of death in the midst of middle-class democracies, had to impose an iron discipline on itself—or vanish?

Let us consider things another way: at this stage of production, industrial organization is dictatorial and division of labour militates against the *unity* of the workers; not for a second, however, have you asked yourself if the form of political power was not everywhere conditioned by the form of this economic organization (which has been incorrectly called *technocracy*). You show the bureaucratic fraction dreaming of basing itself on the capitalist bureaucracy within the framework of state-controlled management; but you do not even dream that this fraction of the proletariat could be on the way to constituting itself as an authoritarian bureaucracy *in order to struggle* against the bureaucratic authoritarianism of the middle-class democracies. In short, you do not even dream of showing that the fundamental needs of production, at the present level of technique, condition *above everything else* and for each of the opposing classes the present form of the class struggle. Your 'Stalinist' fractions are alone in the world; they have nothing to do either with exhausted masses, dispersed at the very heart of concentration and yet militarized, or with economic, social, and political needs, either with internal or with external enemies, or with a concrete combination of circumstances: that is to say, with a certain relationship of the powers among themselves, with the USA and the USSR. You have defined Stalinism without taking any of these data into account; your only explanation: the general morphology of the proletariat. At a certain stage of development, the working class produces an autotoxin, 'Stalinism' which can poison it if it does not succeed quickly enough in eliminating it. The rest does not count. And even, if you are to be believed, the *fact* of the Russian Revolution has not the importance often attached to it: auto-intoxication would have been produced without it, elimination will be carried out in spite of Soviet bureaucracy, everywhere and first of all among the Soviets. This episode has a meaning only for Russian and Czech workers who are suddenly discovering the truth.[109]

But this last remark all at once surprises me: how so? Is it essential to be *Russian* in order to discover the trick? 'Oh yes!' you tell me, 'as long as the leading fraction does not secure power, this exploitation will not be manifest.' And I note, in fact, that the French middle class does not share with the communists either its capital or its income; Stalinism can exploit nothing so long as it is 'an opposition deprived of all share of power'. Fine: *therefore* our communists are not exploiters, and it is with their authoritarianism that you reproach them. They 'form a passive element of the proletariat. . . . They involve it in fights and in alliances without paying attention to its conscious evolution. . . . Discussion, build-up, vindication of the concessions imposed on the proletariat never come out of the framework of a small minority of leaders'. But the proletariat cannot *be* passive unless it itself so determines: it can give meaning to the existence of the CP only by integrating it into the experience of the class. Besides, does it not seek a very precise end: the overthrow of the middle class and the seizure of power? It is, you say, the same target as that of Stalinism: struggle to the death with the middle class in the perspective of a conquest of the State. Well, agreement is reached. Certainly it is the CP which must lead the class to victory. But you protest: first of all, the radical opposition of Stalinism to the middle class 'does not translate *a priori* the revolutionary action of the masses' but the incapacity of the present middle class 'to open a perspective . . . of progress to the working-class aristocracy and bureaucracy'. What is 'working-class aristocracy' doing here? And when have you proved what you are advancing there? Let us admit that a distance is necessarily created between the fraction which leads and the rest of the class; let us admit that in the fraction a tendency is developed to establish a position for itself: it remains to be shown that this tendency inclines the 'bureaucracy' to 'establish itself in the system of exploitation', and, not finding there what it seeks, to try to substitute for it a new method of exploitation. After all, if you did not know in advance what conclusion must be drawn, you could conclude, on the contrary, that the failure of their attempt throws the leaders back towards the working class and reveals to them the impossibility of distinguishing their own destiny from the total advent of the proletariat. Is it not in this way that the workers discover the futility of their antagonisms and, in order to rise above their powerlessness, substitute the interest of the class for particular interests? On what ground do you write that they will exploit the workers? The example of the USSR? For this to be conclusive, it is

necessary to decide *a priori* to discard all historical circumstances; it is necessary to lay down in principle that the fate of
the revolution depends solely on the chiefs and that it is possible
to foresee its course strictly if only the nature of the directing
minorities is known; it is necessary to assert that every revolution led by the CP must result in a Soviet society. Or will you
rather base yourself on the present characteristics of the French
CP, on the nature of its authority? You are considering this, it
seems: you note that it is a similar thing 'to institute relationships of a military type into a group . . . and to set itself up
within the system of exploitation'. . . . But properly 'Stalinism'
does not set itself up 'within the system' since, according to
you, its only aim is to overturn it. And 'military' authority is
indissolubly tied to exploitation *only* in your mind: for if the
class defers to this authority, it is precisely because the actual
circumstances of the struggle, the power of the employers'
organizations, and the extent of the conflicts demand that it
submit itself to a dictatorial and centralizing power on a world
scale. But you have your idea ready: the class struggle does not
exist. Violence and hatred are to be found among the communists: the working class does not know that; to be sure, it does not
like the middle class much, but it has other fish to fry: and it is
not hatred which brings it closer to the 'Stalinists' but its simple
anxiety to re-organize industry on rational bases: in short, it
'shares certain aspirations of the bureaucracy'; to be brief, you
admit, not without embarrassment, that the liking of the masses
for the Communist Party is not the result of an 'illusion'.

This brings us back to our subject: whence comes Error?
whence comes Evil? How can the revolutionary masses *submit*
to the counter-revolutionary action of the Party? The exercise
of power creates distance. Very well: but if the CP were dis-
posed to treat the masses as a passive object, it could not do so
for a moment if the masses were not willing. You will not get
away from that: if the CP is counter-revolutionary, the class,
according to your principles, must likewise be so; if it is bureau-
cratized, the class must have produced bureaucracy as a
moment of its experience and of its auto-organization. Since
you are not a communist, you are passing judgment on the
Party. Do not believe that I, for my part, am going to oppose
you with another. And it is neither the place nor the moment

either to be on the defensive or to attack: what I am trying to make you understand is that, in replacing Trotskyite possibilism by Hegelian necessity, you have undermined your own positions.

You answer that you have not passed judgment: what turns you away from the CP is that the working class itself also turns away from it. This happens in the course of its going through the experience of opposition to all forms of exploitation, including Stalinist bureaucracy. In this way you save yourself from the task of enlightenment.

But how do you want to be believed, at least in sharing your Hegelianism? The proletariat undergoes, you say, a new experience. How do you recognize it? By certain indications. We know these indications as well as you do; the press of the right enumerates them each morning: the dull discontent of 1947, trade union division, growing apathy, strikes and repudiated demonstrations, the number of abstentions at the last by-elections in working-class neighbourhoods, the information which the CP itself gives us on the reduction in certain departments in the number of its members. It remains to interpret these indications. *Le Figaro* which aims, like you, although for different reasons, at separating the class from its apparatus, would like to see in all this the proof of *action* by the proletariat. Still, it does see it as an explosion of revolt after long patience. tired of *submitting* to an oppression which leads to destruction, the worker draws himself up and says: no. The CP prefers to explain it by *passion*: severance from the leadership has been produced; the masses have lost assurance; to be sure, it is rapidly added that 'for the most part, the workers have themselves put things to rights'. No matter: to excuse the masses, the mistake is thrown back on the central committee and the political bureau; but now at last there is a danger of concentrating all the activity of the class in them. In short, we are concerned with contrary interpretations; push them to the extreme and we shall have two gaudy pictures: the working class rebels against the bad shepherds who have led it astray—after a mistaken manoeuvre by the pilot, the proletarian ship seems disabled. Neither one nor the other is altogether false and the present situation cannot, I believe, be explained except by an inextricable mixture of action and passion where, provisionally,

passion rules. But that is not your way: the proletariat has
neither doors nor windows; it *submits* to nothing. From what we
naïvely took for deep but perhaps passing discouragement, you
make an active rejection and a new experience of itself. Some
months ago you were not so positive; you were still putting
questions to yourself: 'The aversion of the most conscious
workers in regard to a new party is evident. Is this repulsion
only a lesser aspect of working-class demoralization or has it a
deeper meaning?' But you were quick to find this deeper meaning and you served it up to us at once: the proletariat is in
process of drawing the conclusions of a new experience: 'The
class cannot become estranged from any form of stable and
structured representation unless that representation is autonomous.' Turning back on itself, the working class becomes more
deeply aware of its nature; it cannot *be divided*, it will exert
power totally and as a totality or not at all. So there we are:
the mainspring of your construction is revealed. It is a fact:
the workers seem discouraged but when sanctimonious knaves
suggest to them that they should join a new party, they are
sent about their business. The simplest way of understanding
their attitude is to ask them what they think of it: it is true that
we shall learn only their conscious reasons: no, they say, no
politics; we can do nothing, we shall change nothing. Or rather
they show a certain annoyance in regard to the CGT or the
Party, but they continue to put their confidence in them, as
trade-union elections prove; and if they distrust alleged revolutionary parties, it is not—if they are to be believed—that they
have tested the whole lot, but that they are very suspicious of
being sold. Are there other reasons for their behaviour? Deep
reasons? Perhaps: but there is no objective indication of them.
Whence, then, comes your absolute certainty? From a clearer
and richer understanding? from an exigence of the object?
from some new feeling which gives you access to unfathomable
depths? No: quite simply from your wish *a priori* to interpret
the common experience in depth. You have decided that depth
was possible: put otherwise, that the immediate data of sociological experience could always be translated in terms of *praxis*.
All goes, thus, as if you wondered on what condition these dis-
likes may express the proletariat as the subject of history. It
is a question, in short, of projecting the passive *into activity*

and of setting up a system of agreement between negative and positive realities, in such a way that those appear as the objective indications of these. And, in point of fact, when your system has become somewhat familiar, it raises no smile to read the phrase you wrote one day about the working-class vanguard: 'The reasons which prevent it from acting indicate its maturity.'

Only—the proof is lacking. Why should this agreement exist, since you have not succeeded in showing that the working class was *praxis* and subject. And if you had established that both an empirical and an intelligent proletariat exist, why should we believe that agreement, term by term, exists between them? Why shouldn't this discouragement be simply discouragement, and nothing else? Will you say that the workers' suspicion enlists them in a movement whose import is the abolition of all differentiated organization, of all particularized authority in the heart of the working class? Here we must be wary; when Marx wrote, 'It matters little what the worker believes he is doing, the important thing is that he is obliged to do it', he meant to intimate clearly that the objective results of action can be very different from those that were anticipated; and also that action, strictly defined by the situation itself and by objective structures, better expresses the reality of the actor, his powers, and his functions, than does the idea he has himself of his possibilities and his aims. It preserves, in a way, his practical organization, it relies always on an end as on the dialectical unity of the means, although it may be a long way from the first intentions of the actor. Thus the social world is peopled by actions which have lost their men. But the *intention* of these free acts, although they form one of their objective structures, has the peculiar characteristic that it re-echoes no consciousness. Intentions without consciousness, actions without subjects, human relationships without men, joining at the same time in material necessity and finality: such are, as a rule, our undertakings when they develop freely in the dimension of objectivity. Let us admit that the dispersed reactions of the workers, the subjective significance of which is discouragement, could be considered in their objective result as contributing to make all working-class parties impossible; how about that? That, certainly: that is what the workers *have done*. But the objective

result of working class action returns to a *virtual* intention as to
the ideal unity of moments of the undertaking; it cannot return
to a real consciousness—whether or not collective—nor to a
subjective experience. Quite the contrary, it could be said that
the objective reality of the action, precisely because it is objective, rejects all relationship with a real subjectivity. When therefore the result must be, later, the negation of all parties, this
negation cannot be put to the account of the class nor as subjective experience—since it has not yet been truly revealed—
nor as real intention—since properly it presents itself as *other*
than what the subject wanted. In short, *you cannot make a class
with that.* When you make the proletariat profit, as subjective
experience, from the objective implications of its behaviour,
you play a trick on us, you create a subject-phantom to resemble
virtual intentions which are, in principle, without subject; you
then pretend to discover this objective subjectivity outspread
through the consciousness of individuals and you alienate individual consciousness to this spectre in order to liberate them
from the CP. That is what you have done with regard to production: it has fatal consequences for capitalism since it
unceasingly increases the accumulation of capital. And as each
productive management is subjectively a whole organized for
ends and means, it keeps objectively certain petrified purposes:
among others, that of destroying the present system. But if you
form the very base of proletarian experience by the re-
interiorization of these purposes, called 'revolutionary opposition', you transform the real into unreality, the class into ideas
of class, and experience into the idea of experience. Your class,
Lefort, has never existed; that is why it has neither door nor
window. What is it? the objective structure of collective acts,
reconstructed according to their results and presented as the
subjective and deep content of *all* individual consciousnesses and
of each of them, that is to say as a presence of right *beyond* real
subjectivities. Thence comes the ambiguity of this spectre: by
its real objectivity, it is, in each one, *object* and you often speak
of it as of a cultural pattern; but by its unreal subjectivity it
draws nearer to the idea and a sort of ideal activity is to be
divined in it, that is to say precisely the activity of ideas. Your
proletariat does not exist: it therefore cannot have disapproved
of parties or had experience of itself. There is nothing to be

illuminated, Lefort, except, perhaps the obscure roots of your follies: but you haven't come to that.

Someone said about English philosophers: All empiricism is optimistic; he who refuses to the mind the power of laying down laws to Nature and of regulating its proper course, does so because he believes, without acknowledging it, in the existence of a natural order which imposes itself on the world and on the mind. In other words, passivity of contemplation necessitates the activity of the object contemplated. Thus the harmonious development which you lend to the working class has no other justification than that of justifying your inaction. You show that it organizes itself only in order to exempt yourself from all duty towards it and you wall it up in solitude so as not to be compelled to situate yourself in relation to it. You have put it out of play, you are out of range; passion could not change your judgments: you share neither its aims nor its way of life; pure object of knowledge for your pure mind, it develops with the inflexible rigidity of the idea; your only office is to mete out light to it: in you the idea of the proletariat is established for itself. A philosopher among my friends, after having condemned the madness of this century, said to me one day with a proud and bitter smile, 'We have nothing left except lucidity. . . .' He was to lose that some months later: today he has nothing. I am afraid you resemble him.

But, in fact, if your class encloses no passivity and if it is impossible to act on it, is it conceivable that it acts on others? Well, no: having to do only with its own activity, the proletariat can act only on its action. It organizes itself, in short; it does only that. 'The proletariat becomes clear only as experience . . . It is *nothing objective* . . . That is precisely what forms its revolutionary character, what indicates its extreme vulnerability.' This class does not stop preparing itself for the great 'reshaping' to which you destine it. It burnishes itself, cleans itself, prepares itself; it slowly transforms within itself the objective conditions of production in human relationships. When the ultimate crisis shall bring the great mechanism to a standstill, the proletariat will be just ready to welcome its inheritance. But, until then, this historical subject will have done nothing at all. You reproach me with seeing in its history only alternations of hope and of despair: and it is true that I do not cover up its defeats any more than its triumphs; but at least I know that it acts, that it struggles, that it compels history to change its course, that it intervened yesterday, that it will intervene tomorrow, that it exerts on institutions and on men a pressure which changes without ceasing. But what, *according to you*, is it doing? At what moment of its long adventure has it acted? In passing from 'reformist' exploitation to 'Stalinist' exploitation, it has changed only its master; to be sure, you show us how adversity educates it progressively: but I do not see that it has, in your concept, weighed very heavily on the destinies of the world. You seem to concede that it made the Russian Revolution: but only to add that that was stolen from it forthwith. In suppressing its action on the Other and the action of the Other on it, you have transformed bloody history shattered by the class struggle into a solipsist evolutionism. A certain Marxist tradition, as I have said above, presents world revolution as the effect of progressive breakdowns of capitalism. But these more and more serious crises bring pauperization and 'degradation' of the workers. Marx concluded from this the need for a 'class organization' to offset the destructive effects of these shocks by a gradual emancipation of the working class. But, in your anxiety to show the uselessness of the leaders, you have transported their function to the régime of production itself, and you maintain in short this strange theory that capitalism, sliding towards the final catastrophe, supplies the proletariat with increasingly numerous opportunities of enriching its experience and rounding off its organization. That is enough in my opinion to put you beside your reformist friends: according to whether, indeed, you refuse or admit the presence of the *other* in every moment of working-class life, and until, in the 'immediate data' of production, you are on one side or the other of the barricade, with the reformist socialists or with the revolutionaries. I would willingly compare your article with those long works which the Germans call *Erziehungsroman:* you relate, as did Marivaux in *Marianne* and Goethe in *Wilhelm Meister*, how adversity is going to make your hero worthy of the highest tasks.

Will he, at present, fulfil these tasks? Will the novel end well? At this question, you turn sharply: 'It is one thing to say that the proletariat must necessarily become aware of its

opposition to the middle class. It is another to know if the
future will allow it to translate this oppression positively into
frustrating its exploiters. It is enough for us to indicate that
class experience will go on *whatever may be its conclusion* . . .',
etc. Strange experience which seemed so harmonious and which
is in danger of bursting like a bubble. Perhaps the proletariat is
only a dream? What has happened to it, then? It is that, to
the very extent you make of it a pure experience which will bear
its fruits only on the day of the 'reshaping', you have left it
defenceless in the middle of the *real* world. You, who were not
situated and who have lost yourself in your dreamy lucidity,
come out of it suddenly and look at your hero from outside.
How frail he suddenly seems to you! From the time you were a
Trotskyite, you gave the decay of history a fifty per cent chance;
but, at least, it was only a question of possibles and you prepared yourself to struggle against them: the dies were not cast.
It was necessary to see how you took up Merleau-Ponty, suspicious of complaisance towards decay: 'The difference which
separates a revolutionary from Merleau-Ponty is that he has put
himself on the side of barbarism in describing it as a fact . . .
while a revolutionary draws from it the absolute need and
urgency of militant action.' If that is the difference which
separates Merleau-Ponty and a revolutionary, I ask you, Lefort,
what is the difference which separates you from Merleau-Ponty?
Where are they, then, the absolute urgency and the need of
militant action? Yes, I know: that was a youthful mistake:
today the very reasons which prevent you from acting indicate
your young maturity. Apart from that, to be sure, you are
always revolutionary. The day before yesterday the revolutionary used to act, today his activity is defined by militant inaction.
Who could be surprised at this since you are *the* revolutionary.
However, the pitiless experience of the proletariat unrolls
parallel to the history of the world but without reflecting it;
it resembles those recorded melodies which move inexorably
towards their apotheosis but stop for ever if the record is
broken.

At bottom, I wonder if all your speeches do not hide a more
secret and a more cynical idea: the dialectic is perverted from
the beginning; the middle class had to produce the proletariat,
its own gravedigger; the proletariat had to produce the

'Stalinist' apparatus as a moment of its auto-organization; but Stalinism was the gravedigger of the proletariat: history stops there; the last picture in your revolutionary pastorals represents the end of the World. This sudden reversal would be somewhat surprising if this terminal catastrophism were not with its initial optimism a necessary consequence of your quietism. It matters little to you whether the world is saved or lost, provided it is well established that you are not in on it. A phrase which you kept to define the working class could be applied to you with scarcely any modification: 'Lefort never has anything to do except with himself, with his own activity, with the problems which his position in the middle class impose on him.' That is the definition, isn't it, of the solipsist or of the perfect revolutionary?

AUTHOR'S NOTES

[1] The slimy rat has not turned traitor. But the Party is sure he might have done so if the occasion had presented itself. In short, it is a term which designates that category of individuals—very widespread, alas, in our society: the guilty against whom no charge can be made.

[2] Message to German and French workers (Lenin).

[3] He, in fact, was the only person severely condemned in Fajon's report.

[4] Aron: 'Les Deux Tentations de l'Européen'. *Preuves*, June 1952.

[5] I am thinking above all of the Persia business.

[6] Published in *Pravda*, No. 49, March 4, 1923. French version, *Oeuvres complètes*, II, 1041. (English version: V. I. Lenin, *Collected Works*, vol. 33, p. 498, Progress Publishers, Moscow, 1966.)

[7] In his June speech, under pretext of attacking De Gasperi, Togliatti scolded the French Communist Party sharply. 'We are not so stupid,' he said in substance, 'you massed your police and your troops in the streets of Rome, but we did not fall into the trap and have not responded to your provocations.' From that, it is not very difficult to deduce his opinion of the demonstration of May 28.

[8] Why shouldn't he know this since, as Duverger said, he had 'constructed a scientific method which allowed him ... to be at "the listening post of the masses" '? Local leaders were said to have kept higher leaders badly informed. That is possible: in which event the truth would be changed, but not totally hidden.

[9] Robert Mossé: *Les Salaires*, Rivière, 1952, 1952, p. 40.

[10] Marx: *Salaires, Prix et Profits*. (English reference: Marx: *Value, Price and Profit*, edited by Eleanor Marx Aveling, 1899, 6th imp. 1938, Allen and Unwin, pp. 84 and 92.)

[11] This is how family allowances are distributed:

Europeans, 1st child, 175 francs; 2nd, 550, etc.; 6th, 2,350.

Africans, 1st child, 93·72 francs; 2nd, 137·50, etc.; 6th, 597.

Frenchmen receive compensation for every kind of accident; blacks only where an accident has occurred as a result of an explosive or of a machine 'moved by some force other than that of men or animals'. To earn enough to pay for 1 kilogramme of white bread, the Dakar labourer must work 1 hour 27 minutes, the Paris worker 25 minutes; to earn enough to pay for one egg, the black of Dakar works 29 minutes, the Parisian 11 minutes.

[12] William Top: 'Valeur du travail des salariés africains', *Le Travail en Afrique noire*. *Présence Africaine*, No. 13, p. 252.

18 Mossé: *Les Salaires*, p. 128. (Sartre's italics.) (Translator's translation.)

14 It must be added that, if it is absurd, in a *liberal* economy, to limit trade union action to the defence of the skilled worker's interest, it is inherently stupid to want to keep up these limits to-day when the State has assumed new economic and social functions. How is it possible to distinguish politics from economics when the worker has to deal *with the State*?

15 Unhappily, illegality cannot be maintained unless decisions are taken clandestinely. And, anyway, in the instance we are considering, illegality did not depend on clandestinity: it was, on the contrary, proclaimed, sought after.

16 'The spontaneous development of the working-class movement soon ends in subordinating him to middle-class ideology.' (Lenin: 'Que faire?' *Oeuvres*, Édition de Moscou, 1948, I, p. 206; translator's translation.)

17 *Infant Mortality in 1939*:

	Deaths per 1,000 of children born alive, but under one year old
A) Upper middle class, higher officials, big business-men	26·8
B) farmers, office workers, medium rank officials, small tradesmen	34·4
C) craftsmen, skilled workers	44·4
D) conveyor-belt operatives	51·4
E) unskilled workers	60·1

18 Not as a means of attaining humanism. Not even a necessary condition. But this humanism itself, in so far as it asserts itself against 'Reification'.

19 *La Nouvelle Critique*, No. 39, September-October 1952, p. 38.

20 Written in 1952.

21 Speech made by Lecoeur on the XIX Congress of the Communist Party of the Soviet Union, October 29, 1952.

22 Written in 1952.

23 For example, those myriads of solar systems: operations revolving round one skilled worker.

24 L. Goldmann: *Sciences Humaines et Philosophie*.

25 What makes things even more suspect is that the sociology of primitive men *never* falls under these reproaches. There genuine *significant wholes* are studied.

26 In November-December 1947, at the time of the referendum about the general strike, there was some resistance. But it was effective only in undertakings where some other organization than the CGT existed (Christian trade unions, etc.).

27 Laurat: *Du Komintern au Kominform*.

28 *La Vérité des travailleurs*, October 1952.

29 A classic reproach: at the end of the first war, those of the minority reproached the majority in the CGT with having sacrificed the interests of the working class to those of the nation. Griffuelhes wrote: 'The middle class anticipated that it would be obliged to agree to heavy sacrifices to the proletariat . . . . But it soon collected its wits; it triumphed' (February

1920); and Monmousseau, in April 1920, wrote, 'The working class is there, trembling. But please! don't abandon corporatism: the Nation is in danger . . . '

[30] Speech at Nantiat, September 28.

[31] I am speaking of the Marxist historian, and not of the middle-class historian whose eclectic conceptions adjust themselves at the same time to the contingent and to the necessary, to liberty and to determinism.

[32] That is to say, a rigorous but circumstantial determination of a particular fact. It matters little that these particular facts are afterwards removed and that the course of history—imperceptibly retarded or deflected—takes up again its general direction. It remains true that the particular must be explained by the particular; you can put the fact back into universal history only if you have interpreted it in its particularity.

[33] I borrow this definition from an article by M. Frank.

[34] M. Germain does not claim—let us be fair—that it was *necessary* to seize power: 'It would have been adventurous.' He says that the working class had the necessary strength and impetus to take hold on it. But then, if he had been its leader, after having put it on the way, *in the name of what* would he have applied the brakes?

[35] *La Révolution permanente*, p. 317.

[36] The indescribable M. Monnerot has his own ready-made explanation: it is *selection* (by Russian bureaucracy, of course) that has created in France 'a type of man who derives from the discreet official, from the artful parliamentary politician, from the good-natured demagogue, and from the professional agitator of the masses'. He will, of course, be the leader of the CP. Isn't this delightful?

[37] The CP very rightly answers that powerful nationalist currents ran through the masses—currents raised up and directed by the myth of 'De Gaulle, leader of the Resistance', and that first of all a powerful work of demystification had to be undertaken.

[38] It is true: they want this change, but you under-estimate the havoc anti-Communism has worked in their ranks.

[39] Who, all the same, gave you the example, and reconstructed the Russian Revolution to show the spontaneous movement of the masses as an essential factor of history. But his conception remains much richer and more complex than yours.

[40] Recall, for instance, the strike of 1947 at the Renault works: those responsible in the CGT metal workers trade union were booed by the workers whose protesting action they wanted to restrain. The CP appreciated the lesson at once.

[41] Besides, what do these isolated examples signify? Has it been proved that the prosperity of 'advanced' countries is not based on the misery of the rest? Are these paradises the image of what we shall become, or the beneficiaries of existing inequality? You would like to have me agree with the first hypothesis, but you do not prove it; besides, even were it true, there would be no reason to rejoice in it: if American trade unions had understood their political duty, they would have tried to apply the brake to the course of the war instead of sending spies and propagandists to the French.

If history should one day apply to the American government the title of 'war criminal', which that government has hitherto been content to bestow on others and which it seems to wish to claim for itself, it is to be feared that the American workers, gulled by their 'advanced' trade unions, are its unintentional accomplices, as was the German proletariat—whether duped or crushed—of the Kaiser in 1914, of the Nazis in 1939.

But may I remind you—one courtesy deserves another—that the whole of humanity lives in a state of malnutrition? If, by chance, the Indian or European worker goes hungry so that American industry can maintain high wages, the *truth* of our present situation would not be the Ford or Kayser factories, but the famine which ravages the world. And in that case the truth of *praxis* is not the prudent reformism of well nourished workers but that of workers 'brutalized' by exhausting labour and continual propaganda: it would be revolutionary activity.

⁴² This industrialist, you say, is authoritarian. But what is authority? A trait of character? No or, at least, not directly. It is first of all a concrete right: he owns a factory, makes a hundred workers work, and *can*, in the name of the work contract, exact from them certain behaviour. The exercise of this right is an act: he orders, he 'runs' the undertaking. The act repeated becomes a sort of law: 'He's the man we need: he has an iron grip.' Ultimately everything is summed up in the oath he swears to himself: 'I will be a leader.' That all comes back to his taking it on himself to bring into existence *in action* the abstract link between Capital and Labour, that is to say, the exploitation of man by man. His authority is not lodged in a compartment of his brain; it is outside, in the way things are; he merely interiorizes it.

⁴³ Later, *integrated in the class*, he will claim these same liberties to lead his class action. But that is the very moment when the middle class wants to suppress them. And besides, if he claims them, it is for the militant he has become, for the member of the working-class Party, not for the isolated man he was.

⁴⁴ I say ideally. In fact there are the germs of division in the Party as there are everywhere else, and the exhausting struggle carried on unceasingly against 'fractionizing' activity is familiar. We shall return to all this.

⁴⁵ Will it be said that this discouragement is transitory? I willingly agree. Should it be added that the strikes of August 1953 mark an awakening of the working class? I am not so sure of that. These strikes of officials were surprising by their extent, and what gave them extreme importance was that they were the occasion of a *basic* coming together of the strikers. But they did not touch big private industry—or hardly so; and then the leaders of the CFTC and FO torpedoed them in the end because they would not be constrained to act in unison with the CGT. I ask the reader to be patient and not accuse me of pessimism or prevent me from drawing negative conclusions. I have no intention of making a damaging report of powerlessness: I undertake to prove that only by a *Populaire Front* can the working-class movement recover its strength.

⁴⁶ It is true that it develops its own limits: maximum production does not coincide with maximum profit; competition is obliterated in face of agree-

ments. But that Malthusianism, however harmful it may be, has nothing to do with ours.

[47] It may even happen that manufacturing industry agrees to pay wages a little higher than does home industry. A device to indicate its good will towards wage-earners, and to make its power clear to petty tradesmen.

[48] He may hate certain employers well known for their harshness, but this is the *accidental* and subjective aspect of the class struggle.

[49] Socialist deputies are middle-class though rooted in the people; in the middle-class State, they see an organ of oppression: yet nevertheless they take part in public affairs.

[50] There is no doubt that the prolatariat is the repository of human values: what it demands *for itself* it must claim *for all*. It could be said that it is the *only* repository of those values. But Sorel is to be upbraided for having confused the *fact* that the working class alone is faithful to human values with the *idea* that that class is the bearer of a *peculiar* and, on the whole, incommunicable message. That is to transform the radical humanism of the proletariat into a *particularism;* it is to bring the proletariat to a stop *at what it is* to-day, and to refuse to take into consideration its movement. This moment of Sorelian totalitarianism resembles the state of being a Negro among colonialized blacks.

[51] The sociological and idealogical causes of anarchism are well enough known; so far as France is concerned, an historic factor must be added: the bloody days of 1871. Anarchist terrorism draws its psychological justification from earlier massacres. An economic situation is enough to cause a strike; but murder is generated only by another murder or by unusual and epoch-making circumstances. That is why the Ravachols accept the honour and retributive punishment of the bandit: they kill those who have killed. It could be said that each one of them has generous and ideological motives ('Society' is this or that, Capital begets such and such a situation) and a very concrete driving power: to avenge the victims of the men of Versailles. It will be noted that Italian anarchism soon followed on the massacre of the Milanese workers and showed itself as a *vendetta* in condemning to death and executing Humbert I. This is a phenomenon which has no parallel in Germany and Britain because the class struggle there, pitiless as it may have been, has in general been restricted to the economic plane.

[52] Who, then, was in favour of an increase in population? The industrialists? Not at all: in economic Malthusianism they found the means of adjusting supply and demand in the sphere of man-power. No: it was the ground landlords, the military, the parish priests. These anachronistic persons believed themselves to be living still under the Ancien Régime, at the time when La Morandière advised rulers to 'multiply their subjects and their livestock'; they had not noticed that the middle class was losing all its powers one by one and had entered on its phase of *relative rule*. All the same, heavy industry gave them satisfaction: its clamorous demand for a rising population masked its underground workings in favour of depopulation.

[53] Strange situation. Middle-class households (except those belonging to religious circles) currently practise all forms of birth control and abortion.

But this same middle class votes for a government that punishes contraceptive practices with imprisonment (sometimes even with death). The contradiction would be astounding if it were not to be noticed that middle-class women are very rarely implicated in abortionist cases. Those brought to trial are nearly always low paid shop-girls or working women. It would seem that the ruling class is Malthusian on its own account and in favour of a rising population among the classes it dominates. *Now that is not true;* if it were, the middle class would be equally solicitous over infant mortality. But the children of the wombs of working-class mothers are later allowed to die like flies. The employers don't want *too many* workers; they simply want to deprive the proletariat of control over its births so that supply and demand in the sphere of man-power is automatic within the infernal machine they have raised up.

[54] In the United States, productivity per agricultural worker has grown in the last ten years by about 5.5% per annum. If, in the next twenty years, an annual increase of the same magnitude were realized in France, the income from agricultural production would rise from 2,500 to 3,500 milliards of francs, *but* the number of workers would diminish by about 30%.

[55] In 1951-1952, 2,880 calories cost 55,900 francs in Germany, 96,000 in France.

[56] Gross receipts from two-fifths of our farms did not exceed 300,000 francs a year.

[57] Clark divides the active population into three sectors: Primary (fishing, forestry, agriculture); Secondary (mining, power, processing); Tertiary (transport, commerce, banking, insurance, administration, personal services).

[58] In 1866, there were ten employees to 240 workers in the processing industry; in 1948, ten to 47.

[59] With one reservation, which we shall make later on.

[60] It is, of course, the *social* relationship that is in question: the economic link continues to be exploitation. As for this uncompromising contiguity, it need not be understood as a real and permanent connexion with the employers, but as a transitory form taken by the class struggle when working-class pugnacity tends to approach zero.

[61] Simply because the revolutionary undertaking, like the reformist undertaking, develops within the passing framework of capitalism.

[62] An appeal made by the Abbé Pierre brought to light astonishing flotsam-and-jetsam: coverings, heating apparatus, old apparel, etc.

[63] There were, to be sure, the members of the Resistance—and I do not under-estimate the importance of their activity. There was also the invisible, passive resistance of the masses: all that counts. To-day there are the Communist Party and the militant trade unionists; there is the enormous weight of the masses and the effect they produce from a distance, however inert they may be, on all social circles. But the Resistance was born of our military defeat; and the present organizations of the proletariat draw their principal characteristics from the great working-class ebb which began with Malthusianism.

[64] In *Travaux*, Georges Navel demonstrated the difficulties, as early as about 1919, met by the son of an unskilled worker in becoming a skilled

man. He and two of his brothers had to cheat in order to become fitter, boiler-smith or bench-hand without working their way up through apprenticeship.

⁶⁵ Or after a very short apprenticeship.

⁶⁶ Mechanization was already very advanced in the textile industry. The weavers were conveyor-belt operatives who had changed machines.

⁶⁷ Quoted by Collinet, *Esprit du syndicalisme*, p. 24.

⁶⁸ Naturally, there is no question here of making the process of semi-automation, which would be absurd, but of showing its effects *within the framework of capitalist production*.

⁶⁹ Table compiled by Julius Hirsch: *Das Amerikanische Wirtschaftswunder*. Reproduced by Friedmann in *Problèmes humaines du machinisme industriel*.

⁷⁰ Often the manufacturing sites are several kilometers away from those where the tools are made.

⁷¹ Confederate Congress of Metalworkers, 1927. Quoted by Collinet, ibid., pp. 60-61.

⁷² Léon Jouhaux. Conference at the Institut Supérieur Ouvrier, 1937.

⁷³ The members of an integrated community differ in function (and, consequently, in position) to the extent that they are linked by the law of the group: diverse in the heart of unity, why should they imitate one another? They co-operate.

⁷⁴ And when it has it, its leaders will *at the same time* have to satisfy it and to struggle against its impatience. A new dialectic is coming to birth: namely, that a long and exacting process is required to realize what the revolutionary crowd demands on the instant.

⁷⁵ The expression is Friedmann's (*Où va le travail humain?*).

⁷⁶ More or less. And in all the great movements of the people, latent or open conflicts between improvised leaders and responsible trade unionists are to be observed. As a rule, the 'permanent' leaders win in the end: they have more experience. Still, they must put their competence at the service of true working-class interests.

⁷⁷ The following facts indicate the importance of information, and the part it can play in checking or accelerating an allegedly spontaneous movement. In 1936, the first stay-in strike broke out at Le Havre on May 11; on the 13th workers at the Latécoère factories at Toulouse stopped work and stayed in the factories. But nothing was known of these two strikes in Paris; the trade union press did not mention them, and one middle-class paper only, *Le Temps*, gave them a few lines, with no details. On May 14, there was a new stay-in strike at Courbevoie. Silence in the press. At last, on the 20th, and at greater length on May 24, *L'Humanité* compared the three strikes and underlined the novelty and identity of their fighting methods. On the same day, 600,000 demonstrators, called together by the Committee of Socialist-Communist Understanding and the CGT, walked in procession past the Wall of the Federates. At the same time, the workers then learned of their new power and of new methods of struggle. From May 26 the strike movement extended to the whole Paris region, and from June 2 to the whole of France. The part played by *information* is clear from these dates: the almost total

silence of the press delayed the spread of the movement for twelve days. Toulouse and Le Havre were brought to the gates of Paris.

[78] Which, naturally, does not prejudge the *personal* relationships he may have with the workers.

[79] Issue of June 12, 1947. *Force Ouvriére* was still part of the CGT and Jouhaux's position was ambiguous: he did not want either to approve of the strikes or to condemn the strikers.

[80] Published in *Esprit*, July–August 1951, p. 170.

[81] I mean by 'collective subject' the *subject of praxis* and not some kind of 'collective consciousness'. The subject is the group *brought together* by the situation, constructed by its very action, *differentiated* by the objective ex- actions of *praxis* and by the division of labour, at first improvised, then systematized, which it introduces, a group *organized* by the leaders it chooses or throws up and finding in them its own unity. What has been called 'charismatic power' proves sufficiently that the concrete unity of the group is *projective*, that is to say it is necessarily external. The diffuse sovereignty comes together and is condensed in the person of the leader who subsequently reflects it back to each of the members, each of whom, accord- ing to the extent of his obedience, finds himself, in relation to the others and to outsiders, the depository of the total sovereignty. If there is a leader, each one is leader in the name of the leader. Thus the 'collective consciousness' is necessarily incarnate: for each one it is the collective dimension which he seizes in the individual consciousness of the other.

[82] It could be assumed—but details are lacking, and this is only a con- jecture—that skilled workers were in question: they are at the same time 'tough' and advocates of a suffrage guaranteeing individual rights.

[83] Or if preferred: *objectively* the satisfaction of these claims is incom- patible with the maintenance of a depressive economy. But they can be put *subjectively* without the workers' being fully aware of Malthusianism.

[84] The strikes of last summer, on the contrary, make possible the hope of a coming together imposed from the base.

[85] The Fédération du Livre, by 28,000 votes to 18,000, decided in 1947 to remain in the CGT despite a long reformist tradition.

[86] To-day (1964) this Malthusianism has been left behind. But it is bound to be a long time before the social structures which flowed from it can be replaced by new structures, and the trade-union struggle adapts itself to new needs.

[87] But I shall return later to this strange whim which has made you forbid him to 'reject his state'.

[88] 'Even granting that all individual ownership rests originally on the personal labour of the owner, and that, in the later course of events, he has exchanged nothing except equal values for equal values, we are nevertheless, by the progressive development of production and exchange, bound to arrive at the current method of capitalist production . . . . and this whole problem is explained by economic causes.'

This text is directed against Dühring's 'conception of violence' and, in that perspective, is admissible. Besides, Marx too sees two dupes in the free labour contract: the employer as well as the worker. Nevertheless the sound is quite different: capital is not a thing: it is a relationship between men, a perversion and an inversion of true human relationships. The whole difference lies there.

89 'The relationship in any given epoch between distribution and the material conditions of existence in the society of the same epoch is so much in the nature of things that it is unfailingly reflected in the instinct of the people. So long as a method of production is on the upgrade of its evolution, it is acclaimed by those very persons who are put at a disadvantage by the corresponding method of distribution. That is the history of English workers at the advent of manufacturing industry. So long as this method of production remains the normal social method, distribution gives satisfaction . . . and if a protest does rise, it is from the very heart of the ruling class . . . and in the exploited masses it finds no echo.' (A.D., II, 10.)

How understand, then, that the 'struggle of the proletariat against the middle class begins with its very existence'? In fact, there is never any struggle: there is an economic system whose real contradictions in the end lead to its collapse. The protests, the indignation, the hatred which are *only symptoms*' occur 'when the method of production is already definitely on the downgrade, when it only half survives, when the conditions which produced it have to a large extent disappeared'. And what do these warning reactions mean? That 'its successor is knocking at the door'.

90 This certainly does not mean that these experiences are *complementary* or that they may be founded in a harmonious whole which would, for example, be 'human experience', as idealists between the two wars believed. On the contrary, most of the time each of them is incompatible, contradictory, exclusive in relation to the others. But that does not mean you may not find them in the same field of your experience, or that you may not be reached directly by the hate of a native in a colony, or even that you could change your outlook and try to see yourself through other eyes, that is to say determine your objective reality in relation to other systems of reference. But in any event those values and points of view which are not yours although mixed up with yours, creeping in everywhere to confront you, offering themselves to you as systems of comprehensible relationships, will always retain their irreducibility: always other, always foreign; at once present and unassimilable. We shall soon see how, for want of sticking to this middle position, you fall from one extreme to the other. After talking to us of 'parallel experiences', you have no hesitation in totalizing the experience of the Mediterranean world.

91 For example, the appearance of machine tools and the 'nationalization' which threw the working class into confusion did not noticeably hasten the very slow movement towards concentration which characterizes French industry.

92 [Translated from the French of] Ed. Cortes, *Capital II*, p. 225.

93 Ibid., *Capital III*, pp. 247-8.

94 Ibid., *Capital II*, p. 244.

95 The only certain effect that can be attributed to co-operation is perhaps this 'military' discipline which, according to Lenin, has transformed factories into barracks. But quite rightly you do not want to hear this spoken of, and you will presently explain that the militarization of the masses is the very

sign of the bureaucratization of the leaders. You want to draw *spontaneous* solidarity from co-operation, like a rabbit from a top-hat.

⁹⁶ Ibid., *Capital* II, p. 263.

⁹⁷ Cf. Lhomme: *La Politique sociale de l'Angleterre contemporaine.*

⁹⁸ It is, of course, possible to deny the *real* importance of imitation. It goes without saying that need, the general situation, fear of being out of work, and other forms of opposition to capitalism are more important factors. People do not go on strike in a spirit of imitation; but we speak of imitation because it is a moving force, at once objective and subjective, mentioned by the unions themselves. The arbitrary demands of need are restrained by defeatism, by an over-estimate of the strength of the employers: 'We shall gain nothing!' On the other hand, success, by one group makes it plain that struggle is at least possible. Strictly speaking, there is no *imitation;* but the first trade-union action reveals to each trade union its own possibilities.

⁹⁹ The failure of all attempts to set up a 'national wages policy' is well known.

¹⁰⁰ W. A. Mortin: 'Trade Unionism, Full Employment and Inflation' (*Amer. Econ. Rev.*, 1930), quoted by Lhomme, ibid., p. 188.

¹⁰¹ This last remark does not in any way prejudge the nature of the State; the theory of the State has still to be set out. In any event, were it the organ of a class, it would be no less so because it sees further than the groups which form themselves within the class. It would manage the interests of the class in its capacity as that class, and would carry exploitation into effect on a national scale.

¹⁰² I mean by denial this struggle by which it 'works towards the death of the Other', and not the comedy of denial by which you reduce the middle class to nothing as an idea.

¹⁰³ After all, Marx said something of the kind in his day.

¹⁰⁴ Bastide has shown that the black slaves in Brazil used to practise Malthusianism through combined despair and revolt.

¹⁰⁵ Stay-in strikes started in Italy after 1918 and continued until fascism took over.

¹⁰⁶ 'The proletariat's necessary task is to revolutionize the conditions of its existence . . . . The proletariat sees its powerlessness and the reality of its inhuman existence . . . It is in deprivation, revolt against this deprivation, revolt to which of necessity it is pushed by the contradiction between its human *nature* and its way of life which is the obvious, total, and decisive negation of its nature', etc.

¹⁰⁷ *Capital, III*: trans. from the French of Eric Weil, *Critique*, Jan.-Feb., 1947.

¹⁰⁸ And relative, that is to say it represents the growing diminution of wages *in relation* to plus-value.

¹⁰⁹ Here my pen continues to hesitate, for fear of letting you down: *will* they discover it or *ought* they to discover it? Could you calmly assert that you have sufficient information at your disposal to undertake the study of the 'working class' in the USSR? And by valid information, I mean documents whose origin is indubitable, most of which are first-hand, documents

which have been subjected to criticism at home and abroad, which can be cross-checked against other documents, which present either a general view of a particular section of industry or a detailed study of a particular industrial concentration. And if you haven't such information, what can you say? That the worker *is* exploited in the USSR? In so doing, you are taking aim above all at the economic system. Discussion is open: but that is not what concerns us at the moment. That the working class in the USSR offers opposition to exploitation? Yes: *that* is our subject. But the only proof you have been able to adduce is that it offers opposition to exploitation because, if it does not do so, it puts you in the wrong.

TRANSLATOR'S NOTES

Allied Intervention in Russia, 1918: After the Bolshevik government signed the peace of Brest-Litovsk with Germany, March 3, 1918, some 60,000 White (anti-Bolshevik) Russians remained in the field against the Germans, and later the Bolsheviks. Allied units (British, French, and U.S.) already in Russia were attached to them, and some additional Allied troops, arms, and money were sent out. The last Allied forces were withdrawn from Russia in 1920.

Altman, Georges (1901–1960): editor-in-chief of *Franc-Tireur*, 1944–1957.

Andler, Charles (1866–1933): taught at the Sorbonne, 1901, at the Collège de France, 1926; published a thesis, 1987, *Les Origines du Socialisme d'Etat en Allemagne*; an edition of the Marx and Engels *Communist Manifesto*; a number of analyses of German Socialism; studies of Bismarck, Nietzsche, etc.

Annales, *Les*: monthly, founded in 1883; print, 1967, 40,000.

Antaeus: a giant in Greek mythology, son of Poseidon, god of the sea, and Gë, goddess of earth, who derived great strength from contact with the earth, his mother. He was overcome by Hercules who, lifting him high off the ground in his arms, squeezed him to death.

Arnauld, Antoine (1612–1694): the 'Great Arnauld', French theologian, a follower of Cornelius Jansen, Bishop of Ypres, and a supporter of the Jansenists in their unsuccessful struggle against the Jesuits.

Aron, Raymond Claude Ferdinand (1905–): journalist and sociologist; taught at the Sorbonne, 1957; author of *L'Homme contre les tyrans*, 1946; *La Sociologie allemande contemporaine*, 1949–1950; *l'Algérie et la République*, 1958, etc.; editor of *France Libre* in London during the Second World War; contributor to *Combat*, then to *Le Figaro*.

Artaud, Antonin (1896–1948): writer who published sur-realist poems, *Ombilic des Limbes*, 1925; *Pèse Nerfs*, 1927; was for a time, as an actor associated with Pitoëff, and in 1932 published *Le Manifeste du Théâtre de la Cruauté*. He visited Mexico 1936–1937 and was later, in Ireland, confined in a mental hospital until 1946. His unbalanced state of mind comes out in his books, e.g. *Héliogabale ou l'Anarchiste couronné*, 1934; *Le Théâtre et son Double*, 1938; *Van Gogh, le Suicidé de la Société*, 1947.

Aurore, *L'*: daily paper founded August 1944 in Paris under the direction of Robert Bony (*see* Lazurick, Maurice) and Paul Bastide (1892–). Print, 1967, 425,000.

Bastide, Roger Maruis César (1898–): professor at the University of São

Paulo, Brazil, 1938–1951; in the faculty of letters, Paris, 1959; published *Brésil, terre des contrastes*, 1957, etc.; did research for UNESCO on racial relations in Brazil, 1950.

Baylot, Jean Félix (1897–): police official (Préfet de Police, Paris, 1951–1954); later deputy (independent), 1958–1962.

Bidault, Georges (1899–): politician; captured by the Germans 1940: released after eighteen months as over age; organized in Paris the National Council of Resistance; foreign minister in General de Gaulle's first government; premier 1946; held various offices in subsequent governments. Opposed de Gaulle's policy in Algeria, joined the OAS (Organization de l'Armée Secrète); went into exile 1963, returned to France 1968.

Billoux, François (1903–): secretary general of the young Communists, 1928–1930; member of the central committee of the CP from 1926; of the political bureau from 1935; secretary of the CP from 1954; deputy 1936–1940, 1948, 1951, 1956; has held various ministerial posts.

Blanquists: followers of (Louis) Auguste Blanqui (1805–1881), violent left-wing leader, opponent of both monarchy and the parliamentary form of government; spent much of his life in prison as a result of his activities; a man of great sincerity, during his lifetime he achieved a prestige among French workers which did not survive him.

Blum, Léon (1872–1950): Socialist politician of Alsatian-Jewish extraction, contributor to *L'Humanité* from 1904; chairman of the French Socialist party, 1919; editor of *Le Populaire* from 1921 (after the breakaway in 1920 of the Communists from his party, taking *L'Humanité* with them). With Cachin (q.v.) inaugurated the *Front Populaire*, 1934; prime minister 1936–7 (when he introduced the forty-hour week and holidays with pay); and again in 1938. Arrested by the Vichy government, 1940, interned at Bourrasol, France, and Buchenwald, Germany; freed by Allied 5th Army, 1945; premier again, December 1946-January 1947, pending election of the first president of the Fourth Republic.

Bolsheviks (Russian *bolsheviki*, from *bol'she*, more): name used by the majority (25 to 23) of the Russian Social Democratic Party after the split in 1903 between those, led by Lenin, who followed Marx's teaching, and those (subsequently called Mensheviks) who believed in reform rather than revolution.

Bony, Robert: *see* Lazurick, Maurice.

Boulanger, Georges Ernest Jean Marie (1837–1891): soldier, protegé of Georges Clemenceau who had known him at the Nantes lycée, through whose influence he was made Minister of War in 1886. He had served in Italy, Algeria, and Cochin-China and distinguished himself in the siege of Paris, 1870. His red hair, blue eyes, and fighting record made him a popular hero among the Paris mob and, supported as he was by the Orléanists, he became an embarrassment to the government. He was returned in three departments at the election of 1889, and his enthusiastic supporters proposed to march on the Elysée. The government expected a *coup d'état*, but Boulanger himself did nothing. A warrant was issued for his arrest, and he fled to Brussels where two years later he shot himself on the grave of his mistress, Mme. Marguerite de Bonnemains.

Bourdet, Claude (1909–): journalist; member of the National Council of Resistance; arrested by the Germans and deported to Oranienburg, then Buchenwald; editor of *Combat*, 1947–1950; founder and until 1963 co-editor of *l'Observateur* (q.v.).

Boyer, Charles (1899–): French-born U.S. actor who went to Hollywood in 1934 and made a name in films there as a 'great lover'.

Briand, Aristide (1862–1932): lawyer and Socialist politician; ten times prime minister; completed separation of church and state in French education, 1906; a champion of the unification of Europe, in 1926 shared the Nobel Peace Prize with Gustav Stressemann (1878–1929). A great orator and a personally fascinating man, he was nicknamed the Sorcerer. With Jean Jaurès (q.v.) he founded *L'Humanité* (q.v.)

Brisson, Jean François (1918–): journalist; on the staff of *Le Figaro* from 1945; editor-in-chief from 1964.

Brunschvicg, Léon (1869–1944): philosopher; taught at the Sorbonne; published works on Spinoza and Pascal and philosophical studies.

Bukharin, Nikolai Ivanovich (1888–1938): Russian politician; he joined the CP in 1904; exiled to Siberia, 1910, escaped to Austria where with Lenin he founded *Pravda*. During the First World War he worked with revolutionary parties in USA, Scandinavia, and Switzerland until the October Revolution, 1917, when he returned to Russia. Editor of *Pravda*, then from 1934 of *Isvestia*. Suspected of being a follower of Trotsky, he was in 1937 tried and found guilty of betraying the Communist cause. He was executed March 15, 1938

Burnham, James (1905–): U.S. writer, professor of philosophy at New York University 1929–1953; author of *The Managerial Revolution*, 1941; *The Coming Defeat of Communism*, 1950; *Containment or Liberation?*, 1953; *Suicide of the West*, 1964, etc.

Cachin, Marcel (1869–1958): one of the founders of the French CP. He joined the Socialist Party in 1906, becoming editor of *L'Humanité* in 1918 and continuing to hold that post after the paper was taken over by the Communists, 1920. A deputy 1914–1932; supported the *Front Populaire*, 1934; first Communist Senator, 1935; re-elected deputy 1945. Suffered several terms of imprisonment in the 1920s for his paper's incitement of soldiers and sailors to desertion or acts of insubordination.

Carnegie Hall, New York: opened 1891 as The Music Hall, renamed 1898 in recognition of the large contribution made by Andrew Carnegie (1835–1919) to its construction. Carnegie was a great advocate of peace, among his chief contributions to that cause being the Carnegie Endowment for International Peace, New York, founded 1910.

Capital: English (and French) title of Karl Marx's principal work on Socialist economics, originally written in German under the title *Das Kapital*. Vol. I was published in 1867; vols. II and III, edited by Friedrich Engels (q.v.) from notes left by Marx, appeared 1885–1894.

Cavaignac, Louis Eugène (1802–1857): soldier who served in Algeria, becoming governor-general of that country in 1848, in which year he was recalled to Paris and made minister of war; crushed the workers' rising in June. He stood unsuccessfully for the presidency (against Louis Napoleon: *see* Napoleon III). When Louis Napoleon became Emperor in 1851, Cavaignac, who was republican in sympathy, retired to private life.

CFTC = Confédération Française des Travailleurs Chrétiens (q.v.)

CGT = Confédération Générale du Travail (q.v.)

CGTU = Confédération Générale du Travail Unitaire (q.v.)

Chambre des Mises: abbreviation for *Chambre des Mises en Accusation*, a special section of the Court of Appeal, with the duty of pronouncing judgment in criminal cases or of sending back the accused to appear before the Assize Court.

Chiang Kai-shek (1887–): Chinese soldier and politician, supported Sun Yat-sen in the revolution of 1911; fought subsequently against various war lords, the Communists, and the Japanese; leader of the Kuomintang from 1925; president of China 1943-1949, receiving the surrender of the Japanese 1945. As a result of Communist victories in China, he flew to Formosa in 1949 and assumed the title of president of (nationalist) China. His régime continued to be recognized by the USA and the United Nations as the lawful government of China.

CIO = Congress of Industrial Organizations (q.v.)

Citroën Works: one of the great motor vehicle manufacturing companies of France, founded in Paris in 1915 by the inventor André Citroën (1878–1935), taken over by its principal creditor, the Michelin Company, when it was in difficulties in 1934. It was turning out 300 cars a day in 1939; badly bombed during the Second World War, it recovered and in 1951 for the first time passed the 100,000 car mark in the year.

Clark, Colin Grant (1905–): British economist; lecturer Cambridge University 1931–1937; Australian appointments 1937–1952; Director of the Institute for Research in Agricultural Economics, Oxford, 1953. Numerous publications.

Clark, Mark Wayne (1896–): US soldier; fought on the western front in the First Great War and was wounded in 1918. Subsequently with US occupation forces in Germany. Chief of Staff, US ground forces in Europe, 1942; fought in Italy; commanded US occupation forces in Austria 1945–1947; UN commander in Korea, 1952; retired 1953.

Claudel, Paul Louis Charles Marie(1868–1955): diplomat, poet, playwright; ambassador to Tokyo 1921–1926, Washington 1927–1933, Brussels 1933–1935. A fervent Catholic. Elected to the Académie Française 1946.

Cominform: abbreviation of Communist Information Bureau, set up in 1947 in Warsaw at a secret meeting of the CPs of USSR, Bulgaria, Czechoslovakia, France, Hungary, Italy, Poland, Rumania, and Yugoslavia (the last expelled in 1948). It was dissolved 1956. Its activites varied little from those of the Comintern (*see* International, The).

Comintern: abbreviation for the Third (Communist) International, organization founded by Lenin in Moscow in 1919; dissolved 1943.

Comité des Forges: Organization of French ironmasters formed in 1864 to co-ordinate research and marketing. It was dissolved in 1940 by the Vichy government.

Commune, The Paris, 1871: insurrectionary government set up in Paris March 18, 1871, following the withdrawal of the Prussians, in opposition to the government of Adolphe Thiers (q.v.) at Versailles, as a result of the rejection by the Parisians of the humiliating peace terms. The insurgents shot hostages, burned down the Tuileries and other buildings. They were defeated by troops from Versailles and the Commune overthrown May 27; 877 of the Versailles troops, 20,000 *fédérés* (among them women and children) were killed.

Compagnies Républicaines de Sécurité: mobile police units, about 60 in number, created in 1948 and placed under the authority of the ministry of the interior (unlike the mobile formations of the gendarmerie, which is under the ministry of war).

Confédération Française des Travailleurs Chrétiens: trade union organization formed in 1919 to co-ordinate the Christian trade unions (the oldest of which was formed in 1887).

Confédération Générale du Travail: trade union organization, formed in 1895 (roughly the equivalent of the British Trades Union Congress); one of the most powerful labour bodies in the world. In the early days, it was without political affiliations. Dissolved by the Germans in 1940, it was revived in 1944 and came under the domination of the CP, as a result of which a Socialist group, calling itself Confédération Générale du Travail—Force Ouvrière (*see* Force Ouvrière) broke away in 1948.

Confédération Générale du Travail Unitaire: trade union group with anarchist tendencies which broke away from the CGT in 1921; it rejoined the parent body in 1936.

Congress of Industrial Organizations: US trade union body, originally the Committee of Industrial Organizations, formed in 1935 under the leadership of John L. Lewis (1880–) to promote industrial rather than craft unions among mass production workers. The CIO unions were expelled from the American Federation of Labour in 1937; but the two bodies merged in 1955 as the AF of L-CIO.

Contrat Social, *Du, ou Principes du droit politique*: famous book, published 1762, by Jean-Jacques Rousseau (1712–1778) which had a great influence on Robespierre (1758–1794) and his followers.

CP = Communist Party, in this work usually the French Communist Party (PC, Parti Communiste).

CRS = Compagnies Républicaines de Sécurité (q.v.).

Decazeville, Aveyron: industrial town established as a result of the setting up of forges on the site by the Duc de Decazes in 1826. There was a great strike in 1886, in the course of which an engineer named Antrin was lynched by the strikers.

Draveil-Vigneuz (Seine-et-Oise, now part of the district of Paris): Industrial area making electrical cables, optical glass, etc. There were serious clashes here between strikers and troops in 1908.

Duclos, Jacques (1896–): Communist leader, member of the French CP from its foundation in 1920; helped to organize the Resistance during the Second World War; deputy 1926–1932, 1936–1940; Senator 1959. Harold Nicolson, *Diaries and Letters, 1945–62*, p. 77, remarks: 'I am introduced to Duclos, the Communist leader. He is an unbelievably repulsive man. Tiny, grinning with gold teeth, shiny with cleverness.'

Durkheim, Emile (1858–1917): philosopher, teacher of sociology in Paris, 1892. He held that religion and morality originated in the collective mind of society, and that human progress is mechanically maintained.

Duverger, Maurice (1917–): teacher of polical sociology in Paris; leader writer of *Le Monde*, contributor to *L'Express*; numerous publications dealing with the French constitution, political science, etc.

Economist, The: London weekly journal dealing with political economy and allied subjects; founded 1843 by James Wilson. Subsequent editors have included Herbert Spencer, 1848–1853; Walter Bagehot, 1859–1877; Sir Geoffrey Crowther, 1938–1956.

Eisenhower, Dwight David (1890–): 34th President of the USA, 1953–1961; 5-star general; supreme commander of British and US expeditionary forces in Europe 1944–1945 during the Second World War; C.-in-C. US occupation forces in Germany 1945–1947; Commander in Europe of the North Atlantic Treaty Organization 1951–1952.

Engels, Friedrich (1820–1895): German Socialist writer who came to live in England in 1850, at first in Manchester and from 1870 in London; friend of and collaborator with Karl Marx.

February Revolution, 1848: overthrew Louis-Philippe (q.v.)

Fajon, Etienne (1906–): teacher; member of the central committee of the CP since 1932, of the political bureau since 1945; deputy 1936–1940, 1946–1958, 1962; director of *L'Humanité* from 1958.

Federates (*Fédérés*): name given to the national guards of Paris formed during the Paris Commune, 1871; effectives never numbered more than 40,000, though in theory there were 80,000 active members, 115,000 sedentary; 26,000 were arrested and thousands killed May 21–28; 20,000 were executed in the course of the following week, shot against the Wall of the Federates (*Mur des Fédérés*) in Père-Lachaise cemetery, Paris.

Figaro, *Le*: Paris newspaper, weekly 1854–1866, daily 1866–1942 and from 1944. Print, 1967, 485,000.

FO = Force Ouvière (q.v.).

Force Ouvière: In full CGT-FO. Working-class body formed in 1948 by a Socialist group which broke away from the CGT owing to the Communist domination of that body.

Ford, Henry (1863–1947): US industrialist, founder 1903 of what became the largest motor vehicle manufacturing concern in the world, based on the Model T, a car popularly called the 'tin-Lizzie' and the subject of many jokes; 15,000,000 were turned out 1908–1928. It was simply designed, produced on the assembly-line basis, cheap to make and cheap to run, and, as Ford is reputed to have said, 'Of any colour, provided it is black'.

Fourmies, Nord: manufacturing commune where on May 1, 1891, the 1,500-strong labour force of Le Fourneau factory, who were on strike, tried to bring out the workers of La Sans-Pareille factory in a demonstration which was fired on by troops; nine were killed, among them two children, and some sixty were wounded.

Four Sergeants of La Rochelle, The: four non-commissioned officers of the garrison who were members of the Carbonari and were involved in one of a series of incompetent conspiracies against the Restoration government in 1822. The chief of the incompetent conspirators was the Marquis de Lafayette: he managed to escape all responsibility, and in 1824 paid a visit to the United States where he was received with enthusiasm. The four sergeants were executed.

Fourth Republic: proclaimed August 25, 1944, in liberated Paris. Its first president, 1947–1954, was Vincent Auriol (1884–1966). It lasted until the Fifth Republic, under General de Gaulle's leadership, came into being on October 6, 1958.

France-Soir: daily evening paper. It was founded in 1941 as a monthly of the Resistance (called *Défense de la France*) on the initiative of a group of students of the Sorbonne, and was financed by the industrialist Marcel Lebon. The name *France-Soir* was adopted in 1945, and it came under the control of the Hachette and Salmon-Lazareff groups. In 1953 its circulation passed the million mark. Print, 1967, 1,270,000.

Franc-Tireur: newspaper started in Lyons towards the end of 1941 as the journal of the Resistance movement.

French West Africa: former group of French colonies, under a governor-general, capital Dakar. They were Senegal (independent republic, 1960); (French) Sudan (independent republic of Mali, 1960); Mauritania (independent Islamic republic, 1960); (French) Guinea (independent republic, 1958); Ivory Coast (independent republic, 1960); Upper Volta (independent republic, 1960).

Front Populaire: term meaning people's front, often translated popular front which has not quite the same meaning. It was used in France to describe the alliance formed in 1934 by the Socialists, Communists, and Radicals under the leadership of Léon Blum (Socialist) and Maurice Cachin (Communist). *Front Populaire* governments (with Blum as premier 1936–1937 and again in 1938) held office 1936–1938.

Gabriel-Robinet, Louis (1909–): journalist and lawyer; attached to *L'Echo de Paris*, 1934; *La Revue des Deux Mondes*; editor-in-chief, then assistant director, 1965, of *Le Figaro*. Publications include *Bras de Fer*, *Histoire de la Presse, Je suis Journaliste*.

Gallifret, Gaston Alexandre Auguste, Marquis de (1830–1909): soldier. As a cavalry officer, fought in the Crimea, Africa, Italy, Mexico. Responsible for the massacre of the Communards in 1871; opposed Boulanger; minister of war under Waldeck-Rousseau 1899–1900.

Gasperi, Alcide de (1881–1954): leader of the Italian Social Democrats; prime minister of Italy 1945–1953.

Gaulle, Charles André Joseph Marie de (1890–): soldier and statesman. Three times wounded in the First World War; a prisoner-of-war 1916–1918 (five attempts to escape). Author of *Vers l'Armée de Métier*, 1934, advocating formation of armoured divisions, ignored by France and Britain, studied in Germany. Escaped to London in June 1940 when

Pétain asked the Germans for an armistice; led the Free French (later Fighting French) until the end of the war. Landed in Normandy, June 14, 1944, formed a government in Paris as soon as it was liberated, August 25. Resigned January 1946, and in 1951 retired from politics until called on by President Coty in 1958 to form a government in face of possible civil war. Chosen president of the Fifth Republic under the new constitution after six months as prime minister.

Goldman, Lucien (1913–): teacher and writer. Studied at Bucharest, Vienna, Zürich, Paris; author of *Sciences humaines et philosophie*, 1952; *Le Dieu Caché*, 1956; *Recherches dialectiques*, 1958; etc.

Griffuelhes, Victor (1874–1923): syndicalist; working shoemaker at Nérac, Bordeaux, then Paris; joined the Socialist Revolutionary Party; a follower of Blanqui; secretary-general of the CGT 1902. Arrested by Clemenceau's order 1906, 1908. Resigned from the CGT 1909. His chief publications were *Le Syndicalisme français et l'internationale syndicale*, 1907; *L'Action syndicaliste*, 1908.

Grouès, Henri (1912–): an ecclesiastic who entered a Capuchin monastery in 1930; curate at the basilica of Saint Joseph, Grenoble; worked in the Resistance from 1942 under the name the Abbé Pierre deputy 1945–1951. In the early 1950s, using his Resistance name, launched a movement to clothe, house, and feed the down-and-outs of Paris.

Gurevich (or Gurvitch), Georges (1894–1966): Russian-born teacher of sociology at the Sorbonne. His books include *L'Idée du droit social*, 1935; *Essais de Sociologie*. 1939; *Karl Marx et la sociologie du xxe siècle*, 1948.

Haiti: republic occupying the western third of the West Indian island, the whole of which is also called Haiti or Santo Domingo or Hispaniola (the old French name was Saint Domingue). Discovered in 1492, settled by Spaniards from 1496. The native inhabitants were wiped out and thousands of Negroes were brought in as slaves. French settlement in the seventeenth century led to the cession of the western part of the island to France, 1697. In 1791 the Negroes rose in successful revolt, and under Toussaint l'Ouverture expelled the Europeans from the island, proclaimed independent in 1804; it was divided into two republics (Haiti and the Dominican Republic) in 1844.

Halbwachs, Maurice (1877–1945): French mathematician and sociologist, a pupil of Durkheim; taught at Caen, 1918, Strasbourg, 1919, Paris from 1935. Made a special study of standards of living and the development of needs. Works included *Le Cause du suicide*, 1930; *L'Evolution des besoins dans les classes ouvrières*, 1933; *Psychologie collective*, 1942. He died in Buchenwald.

Hegel, Georg Wilhelm Friedrich (1770–1831); German philosopher.

Hitler, Adolf (1889–1945): Austrian-born German leader. He took over leadership of the German Workers' Party, founded by Anton Drexler, in 1921; changed its name to the National Socialist German Workers' Party, and led it to the control of Germany in 1933. Proclaimed himself *Führer* and Reich chancellor in 1934. Overran in turn Austria, Czechoslovakia, western Poland; war declared on him by France and Britain

1939; invaded Rusia, June 1941; declared war on USA, December 1941. Died (probably by suicide) in an underground bunker in besieged Berlin.

Humanité, *L'*: daily paper founded by Jean Jaurès in 1904 as a Socialist journal; passed under Communist control when the Communists split off from the Socialists at the Congress of Tours, 1920. Suppressed by the French government in August 1939, it was published clandestinely from the following October until August 1944 when it reappeared openly. Edited by Marcel Cachin from 1920 till his death, then by Fajon. Print, 1967, 185,000.

Industrial Workers of the World: an international revolutionary industrial association formed in Chicago in 1905. It was against orthodox trade unionism and favoured 'direct action' by labour organized in one great union. The rise of the Communist movement (with which it did not agree) in the 'twenties robbed it of its earlier effectiveness. Branches were established in the UK (especially in the docks), in Australia, and in New Zealand. Members acquired the nickname 'wobblies'. At its strongest had some 100,000 members; by 1930, less than 10,000.

International, The: The First International developed from the International Working Men's Association, founded by Marx and Engels in 1864. Following the collapse of the Paris Commune of 1871, dissensions developed between the evolutionary Socialists and the revolutioary Communists, and the First International came to an end. The Paris World Exhibition of 1889 gave the stimulus for the formation of the Second International in that year. It too was affected by internal dissensions, and the outbreak of war in 1914, and the voting of war credits by German, French, and Belgian Socialists (the organization having ruled that workers everywhere should demonstrate against the war) destroyed it. The Third International was the Communist International (Comintern) founded by Lenin in 1919 which admitted only revolutionary Communists. The Comintern dissolved itself in 1943, but a new body with similar aims, Communist Information (Cominform), existed 1947–1956.

iron curtain: term in common use after the Second World War for the political and economic barrier cutting off the USSR and the countries of eastern Europe under Russian domination from the countries of the West. As long ago as 1920, Ethel Snowden said in her book *Through Bolshevik Russia* of her arrival with other Labour delegates at Petrograd [Leningrad], 'We were behind the "iron curtain" at last'; but it did not become popular until Winston Churchill used it in a speech he made at Fulton, Missouri, March 5, 1945. (Churchill himself had used it in a private telegram to President Truman, May 12, 1945: 'An iron curtain is drawn down upon their [the Russian] front and we do not know what is going on behind', but this was not made public till some time after the Fulton speech.)

IWW = Industrial Workers of the World (q.v.).

Jaurès, Jean Léon (1859–1914): philosopher and politician. Elected a deputy in 1885, joined the Socialist Party 1893, becoming its parliamentary leader. Founded *L'Humanité* 1904, and was its first editor. An active Dreyfusard; apostle of international peace. Murdered July 31, 1914, by Raoul Villain (who was acquitted 1919 as irresponsible).

Joanna the Mad (1479–1555): daughter of Ferdinand of Aragon and Isabella of Castile, and heiress of both; married Philip of Hapsburg (1478–1506), called the Handsome, son of the Emperor Maximilian I and Mary of Burgundy. The son of Joanna and Philip was the Emperor Charles V (King Charles I of Spain) (1500–1558). Joanna's madness became apparent after her husband's death.

Jouhaux, Léon (1879–1954): Socialist leader, secretary of the CGT 1909–1940; arrested by the Vichy government; a prisoner in Germany until 1945. Awarded Nobel Peace Prize 1951.

July Monarchy: Charles X (1757–1836) succeeded his brother Louis XVIII in 1824, but was overthrown by the July Revolution of 1830 and replaced by Louis-Philippe (1773–1850), 'the citizen king,' himself overthrown by the February Revolution, 1848. Louis-Philippe's reign is called the July Monarchy.

June Days of 1848: insurrection of Paris workers, dissatisfied with the results of the February Revolution (which had overthrown Louis-Philippe); ruthlessly put down in four days by the army under General Cavaignac (q.v.).

Kienthal: small village in Bern, Switzerland, site of an international congress in 1916 called together by those Socialists who remained pacificists in spite of the outbreak of the First World War and the desertion to the war ranks of so many of their comrades.

Koestler, Arthur (1905–): Hungarian-born British writer; joined the CP in 1931, but soon left it, disillusioned; newspaper correspondent during the Spanish Civil War, when he was condemned to death by Franco. Imprisoned in Vichy France 1940, he escaped to England and became a British subject. Author of *Spanish Testament*, 1938; *Darkness at Noon*, 1940; *The Yogi and the Commissar*, 1945; etc.

Korean War, 1950–1953: after the Japanese surrender in August 1945, the Japanese were expelled from Korea and the country was arbitrarily divided along the 38th parallel of N. latitude, the north being held by Russian, the south by US forces. Russian troops left at the end of 1948, the last US forces in June 1949. A year later, June 1950, the North (Communist) Koreans invaded South Korea; an emergency meeting of the Security Council of the UN (which was being boycotted by the Russian delegate at the time), declared the invasion a breach of the peace, and UN (chiefly US) forces went to the help of South Korea. Hostilities continued till 1953, when the North Koreans withdrew from the South.

Lagardelle, Hubert (1874–1958): economist and politician, theorist of revolutionary trade unionism. Mussolini took the basis of fascism from a speech Lagardelle made at a Socialist congress in 1908; he became a personal friend of Mussolini.

Lassalle, Ferdinand (1825–1864): German Socialist of Jewish extraction; friend of Heine; imprisoned in the revolution of 1848. Associated with Marx in the formation of the General Association of German Workers (later the Social Democratic Party); died as the result of a duel at Geneva with Count Racowitz, his successful rival for the love of Helene von Dönniges.

Lazurick, Maurice (called Robert) (1895–): lawyer and, under the pseudonym Robert Bony, journalist. Socialist deputy 1936–1940; mayor of Saint-Amand-Montrond 1935–1940; contributor to *L'Ere Nouvelle, La Volanté*; secretary of *Le Soir*, 1925; director of *L'Aurore*, 1951, 1951.

League of Nations: international body set up, with headquarters at Geneva, in 1920. The setting up of such a body had been the fourteenth of President Wilson's Fourteen Points, 1918. Its charter was incorporated in the peace treaties of 1919, but the USA did not sign these and never became a member of the League. It remained in existence, with diminishing effect, until replaced by the United Nations in 1946.

Le Chapelier's Law: law introduced in 1791 by Isaac René Guy (1754–1794) which forbade the formation of any kind of association among people of the same calling, in accordance with the revolutionary suppression of corporations. It was applied up to 1864 against combines, 1884 against trade unions, and 1901 against groups.

Léger, Alexis Saint-Léger (1887–): diplomat, at one time Briand's aide in the French foreign office. Under the pseudonym Saint-John Perse, he published volumes of poetry, highly esteemed in France, e.g. *Éloges*, 1911; *Anabase*, 1924 (translated into English by T. S. Eliot, 1930); *Exil*, 1944; *Amers*, 1957; *Oiseaux*, 1962.

Leibniz, Gottfried Wilhelm (1646–1716): German philosopher and mathematician for whom Frederick I of Prussia founded the Prussian Academy of Sciences, 1700. Louis XIV tried to persuade him to settle in France. Invented the differential and the integral calculus, 1674; involved in a bitter controversy with Isaac Newton.

Lenin, Vladimir Ilyich (1870–1924): Russian revolutionary, son of a school inspector named Ulyanov and his Volga-German wife; his elder brother was hanged for taking part in a students' plot against the life of the tsar; he himself was expelled from his university (Kazan) for taking part in a students' demonstration. Practised law in Samara (Kuibishev); exiled to Siberia; escaped and went to Munich, 1900; adopted name Lenin in 1901. Spent the First World War in Switzerland until the March revolution, 1917; with German help returned to Russia; overthrew the existing revolutionary government and introduced 'the dictatorship of the proletariat'. Made peace with Germany and consolidated the rule of the Soviets.

Leroy-Beaulieu, Michel Pierre Paul (1904–): diplomat; has held posts with UN; ambassador to Costa Rica, 1951–1955; published *Le Prix de Munich*, 1938.

Lewis, John Llewellyn (1880–): US miners' leader; worked in the pits; agent for the United Mine Workers of Illinois, 1908–1911; organizer of the American Federation of Labour, 1911–1917; president of the United Mine Workers Union, of which he was the virtual dictator, 1920–1960.

Lhomme, Jean (1901–): teacher (philosophy) and writer. His works include *le Problème des classes*: *doctrines et faits*; *la Politique sociale de l'* *Angleterre contemporaine*; *la Grande Bourgeoisie au pouvoir*.

Louis-Philippe (1773–1850): King of the French. Son of Philippe Egalité, Duc d'Orléans, he supported the Revolution in its early stages; fled the country 1793; returned in 1814; became the 'citizen king' after the July Revolution, 1830; abdicated after the February Revolution, 1848, and went to England where he died. His reign, during which Algeria was conquered, is called the July Monarchy

Lussy, Charles (1883–): journalist, politician, and official of the Postes, Télégraphes, et Téléphones. Contributor to *L'Humanité, le Quotidien, Paris-soir*; deputy 1936 and 1945–1958; mayor of Pertuis, Vaucluse, 1938–1953.

Lyautey, Louis Hubert Gonsalve (1854–1934): served as a soldier in Algeria, Tongking, and Madagascar, then Algeria again. Able administrator as Commissary General in Morocco, 1912–1925 (except 1916–1917, when he was minister of war). Made Marshal of France 1921.

Machiavelli, Niccolo di Bernardo dei (1469–1527): Florentine author and diplomat. Wrote *Il Principe* (the prince), the first objective analysis of how political power is gained and kept, and other works of what to-day would be called political science. An advocate of a united Italy.

MacMahon, Marie Edmé Patrice Maurice (1808–1893): President of the French Republic, 1873–1879. Served as a soldier in Algeria, the Crimea, Italy. Made a Marshal of France after his victory over the Austrians at Magenta 1859; governor-general of Algeria, 1864–1870. Taken prisoner at Sedan; released at the peace; crushed the Commune, 1871. A Royalist, he hoped to restore the Bourbons.

Malthus, Thomas Robert (1766–1834): British economist best remembered for *An Essay on the Principle of Population*, 1798, revised edition 1803, in which he contended that poverty is inevitable because populations increase by geometrical ratio and the means of subsistence by arithmetical ratio; but he advocated only 'moral restraint' as a check on the birth rate. He has given his name to Malthusianism, a term extended from his original thesis to cover checks on any form of production or reproduction.

Mao Tse-tung (1893–): Chinese leader who fought in the revolution of 1911–1912; becoming interested in the writings of Marx, he joined the Chinese CP in 1921; worked until 1927 with Chiang Kai-shek who then turned against the Communists. Mao led his followers on 'the long march' of 6,000 miles to Yenan in Shensi province where he set up a Communist government. After the defeat of the Japanese in 1945, he secured control of all the Chinese mainland, 1949, and in that year became chairman of the central government council and virtual dictator of Communist China.

Marivaux, Pierre Carlet de Chamblain de (1688–1763): dramatist and novelist; wrote forty pieces for the Comédie-Française and the Théâtre-Italien; fell on evil days; went bankrupt; later published a journal in imitation of Addison's *Spectator*. *La Vie de Marianne ou les Aventures de la comtesse de*. . . appeared 1731–1741.

Marshall Plan: name popularly given to the proposals put forward by General George Catlett Marshall (1880–1959), US Secretary of State, in a speech at Harvard University, June 5, 1947, for economic co-operation among European countries in their own post-war recovery, with assistance from the USA. It resulted in the creation of the European Recovery Programme, 1948, which contributed much to the post-war recovery of Europe.

Martin, Henri (1927–): sailor who in 1950 was sentenced to five years imprisonment for distributing among fellow sailors at Toulon leaflets against the (French) war in Vietnam.

Martinet, Gilles Henri (1916–): journalist, attached to Agence Havas 1937–1939; editor-in-chief, Agence France-Presse, 1944–1948; director of the weekly *France-Observateur*, 1963. published *Le Marxisme de notre temps*, 1962.

Martinique: volcanic island in the Windward Islands, West Indies; discovered by Columbus 1502; settled by the French 1635; overseas department of France 1946.

Marx, (Heinrich) Karl (1818–1883): German economist, founder of international revolutionary socialism. Met, and formed a lifelong friendship with, Engels in Paris where he lived 1843–1845. In Brussels in 1847 drew up with Engels the Communist Manifesto. Moved to London 1849 where he lived for the rest of his life. *Das Kapital* was his chief work (*see* Capital). His theories form the basis of Russian Communism, and so of all orthodox CPs.

Mauriac, François Charles (1885–): noted novelist and poet, preoccupied with the struggle between material and spiritual values. His works include *La Chair et le Sang*, 1913; *Le Noeud des Vipères*, 1932; *La Fleuve de Feu*, 1933. Elected to the Académie Française 1933; awarded the Nobel Prize for Literature, 1952.

Maurras, Charles (1868–1952): writer and journalist. He joined the staff of *L'Action Française* which he made a monarchist journal; in 1908, with Léon Daudet, turned it into a daily. Imprisoned in 1937 for incitement to murder the premier, Léon Blum. During the Second World War, he collaborated with the German occupying forces; arrested 1944, and in 1945 condemned to solitary imprisonment for life. Released seven months before his death.

Merleau-Ponty, Maurice (1906–1961): philosopher, teacher, and writer whose writings were at first in sympathy with Sartre's existentialism; with Sartre he founded the review *Les Temps Modernes* in 1945; parted company with Sartre and with the review in 1953.

Millerand, (Etienne) Alexandre (1859–1943): President of the French Republic, 1920–1924. Elected deputy as a Radical Socialist in 1885, he became the leader of the socialists in the Chamber; held office under Waldeck-Rousseau, 1899–1902; Briand, 1909; Poincaré, 1912. Premier and foreign secretary 1920, in which year he was elected President. Resigned 1924 and retired into private life.

Molotov, Vyacheslav Mikhailovich (1890–): Russian politician whose original name was Scriabin. Secretary of the central committee of the Russian CP, 1921; foreign commissar (later minister) 1939–1949;

signed the Russo-German pact, 1939; led the Russian delegation to San Francisco, 1945; Sent as ambassador to Outer Mongolia, 1957–1960: expelled from the CP 1964.

Monatte, Pierre (1881–1960): a printer's reader, he became a member of the Fédération du Livre; of anarchist sympathies, he refused all participation in the defence of his country in 1914; joined the Communists 1920, expelled 1924; founded the *Révolution prolétarienne* 1925 to defend revolutionary syndicalism.

Monde, Le : daily paper, founded 1944; publisher, Hubert Beuve-Méry; editors, André Chênebenoît and Jacques Fauvet; print, 1967, 290,000.

Mossé, Robert (1906–): teacher of political economy; has taught at the University of Washington, Illinois; New School of Social Research, New York; Lisbon University; Grenoble, etc. Has served on UNESCO. Author of *Assurance contre le chômage*; *L'Economie collectiviste*; *les Salaires*, etc.

Mouvement Républicain Populaire (people's republican movement): political party formed in 1944 under the leadership of Georges Bidault (q.v.) from the Roman Catholic democratic section of the Resistance. It put up candidates for the first time at the first municipal elections held after the liberation of France, April 1945, gaining control in 447 (out of 35,307) communes; secured 150 (out of 586) seats in the constituent assembly 1945, 167 in June 1946. In the Council of the Republic, elected 1946, it had 70 (out of 315) seats; in 1948, only 18, after which it faded out.

MRP = Mouvement Républicain Populaire (q.v.)

Munich Agreement: signed (without the agreement of Czechoslavakia) September 30, 1938, by Germany, Great Britain, France, and Italy. It confirmed the cession to Germany of the Sudeten-German area of Czechoslovakia. Germany occupied the rest of Czechoslovakia, March 15, 1939.

Napoleon III (1808–1873): nephew of Napoleon I. Organized a mutiny which failed at Strasbourg, 1836; fled to New York; returned to Switzerland, then 1838 to London. Landed at Boulogne 1840, but was arrested and imprisoned in the fortress of Ham. Escaped 1846 and went again to London. Following the February Revolution of 1848, he returned to France, was elected to the republican assembly in June, and in December was elected President by a majority of five to one. In December 1851, a plebiscite conferred on him ten years' presidency, and a year later still he ascended the throne as Emperor of the French. He declared war against Germany in 1870, was defeated at Sedan and captured. Released when peace was signed, he spent the last two years of his life in England.

Nenni, Pietro (1891–): Italian politician, editor, then director of *Avanti*; joined the Socialist party 1921; emigrated to France where he became secretary-general of the Italian Socialist party; fought in Spain, 1936; arrested by the Germans at Vichy, 1943; Italian minister of foreign affairs, 1946; protested against the peace treaty, 1947; gave up his party post, 1958.

North Atlantic Pact: twenty year defensive alliance formed in 1949 at

Washington, D.C., by Belgium, Canada, Denmark, France, Iceland, Italy, Luxembourg, the Netherlands, Norway, Portugal, the UK, and the USA under which the North Atlantic Treaty Organization (NATO) was set up. An integrated defence force was organized in 1950 with General Eisenhower as its first supreme commander; he was replaced by General Matthew Ridgway (1895–) in 1952. Greece and Turkey were admitted to membership in 1952, the Federal Republic of (West) Germany in 1955. Its headquarters, at first in Paris, was moved to Belgium 1966–7.

Observateur, *L'*: weekly left-wing, non-Communist paper, founded 1950 by Claude Bourdet, Roger Stéphan, and Gilles Martinet. Name changed to *France-Observateur* in 1954, to *Nouvel-Observateur* in 1964. Print, 1967, 150,000.

Paris-Presse: daily paper founded in 1944; published under the direction of Pierre Lazareff, H. Massot, and R. Salmon. Print, 1967, 99,000.

Pavia, Battle of: victory, February 24, 1525, of the Emperor Charles V over the French who were besieging Pavia. French losses were some 10,000, and Francis I of France was taken prisoner.

Pelloutier, Fernand (1897–1901): syndicalist. Entered into relations with Aristide Briand, then took up anarchist revolutionary syndicalism. In 1894 he became joint secretary of the Fédération des Bourses du Travail, of which he edited a history.

Perse, Saint-John: see Léger, Alexis Saint-Léger.

Pierre, The Abbé: *see* Groués, Henri

Pinay, Antoine (1891–): industrialist and politician, mayor of Saint-Chamond from 1929; deputy 1936–1938; senator 1938–1940; again deputy 1946–1958. Held office in a succession of governments.

Pleven, René (1901–): company director and politician. Joined de Gaulle in 1940, became minister for the colonies 1944; deputy from 1945; held various offices; premier 1950–1951.

Politburo: contraction for the political bureau of the Communist Party of the USSR which formulated the 'party line' until 1952, when it was replaced by the Presidium of the Party.

Pravda (Russian, truth): the official daily paper of the Russian Communist Party. Started in 1912 by Lenin (then in exile), it was suppressed by the tsarist government in 1914; revived after the March Revolution of 1917.

Preuves: monthly founded in 1951; published under the direction of François Bondy; editor-in-chief, Jacques Carat.

Proudhon, Pierre Joseph (1809–1865); political philosopher, forerunner of Marx. His *Qu'est-ce que la Propriété?*, 1840 (English translation, *What is Property?*, 1876) declared private property to be theft. Elected to the Assembly, 1848; imprisoned 1850–1853; prosecuted for publishing *De la Justice dans la Révolution and dans l'Eglise*, 1858; lived in Belgium 1858–1863. He believed in individual moral responsibility rather than imposed authority.

Rassemblement du Peuple Français: movement founded in April 1947 by General de Gaulle; among its most acitve members were Jacques

Soustelle, André Malraux, and René Capitant. At the municipal elections of 1946, it won 38 per cent of the votes; at the general election of
1951, 22 per cent of the votes, with 121 deputies elected: 32 of them left
the group in 1952, and it ceased to play a serious part in politics.

Ravachol, François Claudius (Koenigstein, called) (1958–1892): Anarchist
leader who in 1892 committed bomb outrages against MM. Benoît
and Bulot, legal officials who had taken part in the trial of the Paris
Anarchists the year before. He had previously murdered an old man and
robbed graves for the good of the cause. Guillotined 1892.

Renan, Joseph Ernest (1823–1892): great prose writer, philosopher, and
philologist; wrote on Arabian philosophy, the Semitic languages,
religious history. His best known work is *Vie de Jésus,* 1893. Elected to the
Académie Française 1878.

Renault Works: one of the first large scale motor vehicle factories in France,
founded in 1900 by Louis Renault (1877–1944), a skilled inventor, e.g.
in 1907 he designed and built the first efficient air-cooled aero engine;
the 70-ton Renault was the heaviest vehicle of its type in service with
any army at the outbreak of the Second World War. The Renault plant
was nationalized in 1945.

Republic, The French; the First French Republic, set up 1793, lasted until
1804 when Napoleon I became Emperor; the Second, 1848–1852,
followed the abdication of Louis-Philippe; the Third, founded 1870
after the defeat by the Prussians of Napoleon III, ended with the setting
up of the Vichy government, 1940, following the surrender of France to
the Germans; the Fourth, established 1946, was followed in 1958 by
the Fifth.

Resistance, The: name given to the secretly organized groups actively
opposing the occupying forces in France (and other countries) overrun
by the Germans in the Second World War. These groups produced and
distributed clandestine news sheets; sheltered and passed on to safety
Allied air personnel escaped from aeroplanes brought down, and
escaped prisoners-of-war; sabotaged industry, railways, bridges, etc.
Hundreds were captured, tortured, and shot or hanged.

Revue des Deux Mondes: Twice monthly periodical dealing with politics,
history, literature, and art, founded 1829; published at Royat 1940–
1944.

Rhee, Syngman (1875–1965): Korean politician, a rebel against Chinese
rule; imprisoned 1897–1904 (during which time he was converted to
Christianity). Went to USA, returning home in 1910 to agitate against
the country's new Japanese rulers; was expelled. Returned again in 1945,
and became President of (South)Korea 1948 until forced to resign by
riots against his rule in 1960, when he again left his country.

Ribbentrop, Joachim von (1893–1946): Nazi leader. He saw service in the
First World War, after which he became a champagne salesman.
Joined the Nazi Party in 1932; became Hitler's adviser on foreign
affairs; ambassador to the UK 1936 until made foreign minister, 1938–
1945; negotiated the Russo-German pact of 1939. He was largely responsible for the aggressive policy of Hitler's Germany. Captured at

Hamburg June 14, 1945, by British troops; tried at Nuremberg and hanged as a war criminal October 16, 1946.

Ridgway, Matthew Bunker (1895–): US soldier; served with distinction in the Second World War; succeeded MacArthur as commander of UN and US forces in the Far East, including Korea. Succeeded Eisenhower as Supreme Allied Commander in Europe of NATO forces, 1952–1953.

Robinet: *see* Gabriel-Robinet, Louis.

Rousseau, Jean-Jacques (1712–1778): writer and philosopher who maintained that man, in nature good, is corrupted by civilization. He published a number of works and contributed to the *Encyclopédie*. Apart from his *Confessions*, published after his death (and not regarded as entirely truthful), his best known work was *Du Contrat Social* (q.v.), 1762.

RPF = Rassemblement du Peuple Français (q.v.).

Russian Revolution of 1917: revolutionary activities in February led to the abdication in March of Tsar Nicholas II and the setting up of a weak provisional government, ousted in November (October O.S.) by a strong Bolshevik government led by Lenin.

Russo-German Pact: pact of friendship between the USSR and Nazi Germany concluded August 23, 1939. It enabled Hitler to start war in the west, in the assurance that there was no threat to his eastern frontier. It did not save Russia from invasion by the Germans, June 22, 1941.

Sauvy, Alfred (1898–): economist and statistician; full professor of social demography in the Collège de France, 1959; member of the UN commission on population, etc. Publications include *Richesse et Population*, 1943; *La Prévision Economique*, 1944–6; *l'Europe et sa Population*, 1953.

Schneider: name of a family of French industrialists of whom Henri (1840–1898) greatly developed the firm's output of armaments, etc. at Le Creusot by introducing new methods of forging; Charles (1898–1960) reconstructed and modernized the works after the devastation they suffered during the Second World War.

Second Empire, The: the reign of Napoleon III (q.v.) as Emperor of the French; it lasted from December 1852 to September 1870.

Second Republic: *see* Republic, The French.

SFIO = Section Française de l'Internationale Ouvrière: name habitually given to the French Socialist Party.

Sorel, Georges (1847–1922): philosopher and writer who glorified violence and advocated syndicalism (i.e. control of each industry by the workers in it organized in the appropriate trade union; it rejected parliamentary methods). His ideas had a considerable influence on fascism. His chief published work was *Réflexions sur la Violence*, 1908.

Sorokin, Pitirim Alexandrovich (1889–): Russian-born historian and sociologist, banished by the Bolsheviks, settled in USA 1923, naturalized 1930. Works include *Social and Cultural Dynamics*, 4 vols., 1937–1941; *Russia and the United States*, 1944.

Stakhanovism: Communist term of praise for exceptional feats of industrial output, derived from the name of Alexei Grigoryevich Stakhanov

(1905–), a miner in the Donbas who in 1935 hewed 102 tons of coal (some sixteen times the normal output) in one shift

Stalin (from Russian *stal*, steel): name adopted by Joseph Vissarionovich Djugashvili (1877–1953), a native of (Russian) Georgia. Educated for the priesthood, he joined the Social Democratic Party in 1898 and was expelled from his seminary 1899 for carrying on Marxist propaganda. Exiled to Siberia five times during 1903–1912, he escaped on each occasion and continued his revolutionary propaganda. Probably during the 1917 Revolution he attracted Lenin's attention; became a member of the Politburo, 1917; distinguished himself during the civil war by his defence of Tsaritsyn on the Volga (renamed Stalingrad, 1925; Volgograd, 1961). General Secretary of the CP, 1922; secured sole leadership of the Party, and of the USSR, 1927, and held it until his death. The mention of his nose (page 5) is a reference to Blaise Pascal's remark: 'Le nez de Cléopâtre: s'il eût été plus court, toute la face de la terre aurait changé' (if Cleopatra's nose had been shorter, the whole face of the earth would have been different).

Stil, André (1921–): writer and journalist, at one time a teacher. He was secretary-general of the Lille journal *Liberté* 1944–1949; editor of *Ce Soir*, 1949, of *l'Humanité* 1950–1959. His books included *Le Premier Choc*, 1952 (awarded the Stalin prize); *Nous nous aimerons demain*, 1957; *Le Foudroyage*, 1960; *Viens danser, Violine*, 1964.

sugar block loader: *metteuse en plaques*, the expression used in the original text, proved difficult to identify, and therefore to translate. It does not appear in any of a number of French-English dictionaries, general and technical, which were consulted, and was unknown to various French people, and English persons knowledgeable in French, whose help was sought. However, after considerable trouble, a Paris friend, M. Raymond Landy, Docteur en Droit, discovered that the process set out in the text was described in a book, long out of print, *Une Société Anonyme*, by a militant woman trade unionist which related the conditions of work at the Raffineries Say at Nantes: the process seems to have been unique to this firm. At this point, Mr J. W. L. Graham, of the firm of Tate and Lyle, took up the trail: he found that the Raffineries Say certainly did at one time use the process described, but the machines in question were scrapped in 1947. Work as a block loader was voluntary, and as extra wages were paid, there was never any lack of volunteers. The weights handled were as stated in the text; the work consisted of taking cube slabs (uncut), turning them through 90°, and putting them into a slot where they were stoved. The actual physical effort was not, in fact, very great except when the worker had to bend down to place the slab in one of the lower slots.

Taine, Hippolyte Adolphe (1828–1893): critic and historian; publications included *Les Philosophes du XIXe siècle 1856*; *Histoire de la Littérature Anglaise*, 1863–4; *Les Origines de la France Contemporaine*, a series of works (the last unfinished), 1875–1894, studies of the process and evils of centralization in France. Elected to the Académie Française in 1878.

Taylor, Frederick Winslow (1856–1915): US engineer, promoter of the scientific organization of work which he put into effect in the Bethlehem Steel Company. He published *The Principles of Scientific Management*, 1911.

Temps, *Le*: evening daily newspaper founded 1861; it ceased to appear in 1942 when Paris was under German occupation.

Temps Modernes, *Les*: quarterly review started in 1945 by Jean-Paul Sartre in association with Maurice Merleau-Ponty; Merleau-Ponty broke with Sartre and the review in 1953.

Thiers, Louis Adolphe (1797–1877): lawyer, historian, politician. Opposed Charles X and proposed Louis-Philippe as his successor, 1830. Minister of the interior 1832–1834; premier 1836 and 1840; leader of right-wing liberals under Second Republic and Second Empire; voted against declaration of war on Prussia, 1870; as head of the provisional government on Napoleon III's fall, he negotiated peace with Prussia and suppressed the Commune. Chosen first President of the Third Republic, 1871; forced to resign, 1873, by a Monarchist-Radical coalition.

Third Republic: *see* Republic, The French.

Thorez, Maurice (1900–1964): coalminer who became a political leader. A member of the Socialist Party, he joined the Communist group which split off in 1920. Secretary-general of the French CP 1930–1964; went into hiding in 1939 to avoid military service, finding his way to Moscow; returned 1944; elected to the consultative assembly; member of successive cabinets until 1947. He suffered severe cerebral haemorrhage in 1950, went to Russia to recuperate, returning 1953. Though a semi-invalid, he retained his Party post.

Titoism: form of Communism adopted by President Tito (name adopted by Josip Broz, 1890–) in Yugoslavia, a deviation from Russian Communism successfully maintained by him from 1948 despite Russian pressure.

Togliatti, Palmiro (1893–1964): Italian journalist and politician, secretary general of the Italian Communist Party from 1927, retaining that post while in Moscow 1929–1944. He held cabinet office after the war until June 1946.

Tours, Indre-et-Loirs, Congress of: congress of the SFIO held in December 1920 at which there was a split between those who wished to adhere to the new Third (Communist) International and those, led by Blum and Longuet, who wanted to continue adherence to the Second International. The Communist group took with them *L'Humanité*, and a new paper, *Le Populaire*, was founded by the Socialist group.

Trotsky, Leon: name assumed by Lev Davidovich Bronstein (1879–1940). Of Jewish parentage, he was educated in Odessa, arrested 1899 as a member of the South Russian Workmen's League and exiled to Siberia; escaped in 1902 to join Lenin in London. President of the Saint Petersburg workers' soviet in the abortive 1905 revolution, he was arrested and exiled to Siberia for life, but escaped within six months and lived in Austria, France, and Switzerland until he joined Lenin in the Bolshevik Revolution, 1917; he organized the Red Army in the civil war of 1918–1920. After Lenin's death, he lost influence; expelled from the CP, 1927; left Russia in 1929; settled in 1937 in Mexico where he was murdered.

Turgot, Anne Robert Jacques (1727–1781): economic theorist and reformer who, after success in reforming the finances of the province of Limousin, was called on by Louis XVI in 1774 to reform the financial administration of France. He instituted the abolition of internal barriers to trade, sought to establish a system of local government, and attacked the exemption from taxation of the privilaged classes whose hostility led Louis to dismiss him, 1776.

United Nations: organization of states set up at a conference held in San Francisco April-June 1945 by representatives of the 50 nations which had at that time accepted the programme set out in the Atlantic Charter, drawn up by Winston Churchill and President Roosevelt and issued August 14, 1941, which envisaged a permanent system of general security. The UN General Assembly held its first meeting in London January 10–February 13, 1946; its headquarters is in New York. Membership reached 125 during 1968.

Vailland, Roger François (1907–): journalist, novelist, playwright; took part in the Resistance; of Communist sympathies. Works include *Les Mauvais Coups,* 1948; *Un jeune homme seul,* 1952; *325,000 Francs,* 1955.

Vallon, Louis (1901–): economist, follower of General de Gaulle; deputy 1951–1955, 1962. His publications include *Socialisme Experimental,* 1936; *Le Dilemme français,* 1951; *la France fair ses comptes,* 1958.

Vietnam: country of South-East Asia, covering the former French colony of Cochin-China and the former French protectorates of Tongking and Annam. The Vietnam war referred to in this work is the French struggle 1946–1954, against the Viet-minh, the Annamese independence movement set up under the leadership of Ho Chi-minh (1892–) (trained in Moscow, 1925–1927), during Japanese occupation of Indo-China in the Second World War.

Weil, Simone (1909–1943): teacher, later student of working-class life whose works, which advocate political quietism, were published after she had died in an English sanatorium.

A
BOMB
IN THE
BRAIN

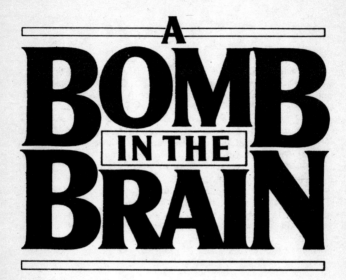

A
BOMB
IN THE
BRAIN

STEVE FISHMAN

AVON BOOKS ◢ NEW YORK

Grateful acknowledgment is made to the following: Oxford University Press, for excerpts from *The Death of Ivan Ilych and Other Stories* by Leo Tolstoy and translated by Alymer Maude, copyright 1935 Oxford University Press, used by permission; Temple University Press, for excerpts from *Having Epilepsy* by Joseph W. Schneider and Peter Conrad, copyright © 1983 Temple University Press, used by permission; Alfred A. Knopf, Inc., for excerpts from *The Magic Mountain* by Thomas Mann, translated by H. T. Lowe-Porter, copyright 1929 Alfred A. Knopf, Inc., used by permission; Doubleday, a division of Bantam, Doubleday, Dell Publishing Group, Inc., for excerpts from "Academic" by Theodore Roethke, in *The Collected Poems of Theodore Roethke*, copyright 1941 by Theodore Roethke, used by permission; Year Book Medical Publishers, for excerpts from *Pictorial Manual of Neurologic Tests*, 2d ed., by Maurice W. Van Allen and Robert L. Rodnitzky, copyright © 1969, 1981 by Year Book Medical Publishers, Inc., used by permission; Farrar Straus Giroux, Inc., for excerpts from *The Counterlife* by Philip Roth, copyright © 1986 by Philip Roth, used by permission; Tobias Wolff, for excerpt from "The Other Miller," used by permission of the author; E. P. Dutton, Inc., for excerpts from *Awakenings* by Oliver Sacks, copyright © 1973, 1976, 1982, 1983 by Oliver Sacks, used by permission.

AVON BOOKS
A division of
The Hearst Corporation
105 Madison Avenue
New York, New York 10016

First Avon Books Trade Printing: April 1990

This is dedicated to my mother and father and to Julie

You're making a career out of this.
Dr. Irvin Kricheff

Contents

Preface
My Career in Neurosurgery

In our rush to control disease we have neglected the detailed contours of illness as a lived, personal and social experience.
Joseph Schneider and Peter Conrad, *Having Epilepsy*

THIS IS A PATIENT'S BOOK, its engine not wonder but fear. Other authors have written about brain surgery as a challenge to the skills and the nerves of highly trained doctors. They point out that the brain will tolerate almost no surgical error and that neurosurgeons are asked to perform, as one book explained, "not quite miracles."

My perspective on brain surgery is different. One muggy fall morning I had a brain hemorrhage. Inside my head a vein popped. My vision swirled. I had the worst headache of my life. On the right side of my brain in the back, I was for a few seconds bleeding to death.

The first time I met a brain surgeon, it was as his patient. Within a week of our meeting he and his assistants had drilled three holes in my head, sucked out of my brain a clot of blood, and excised the cause of the hemorrhage. Only later would I learn the change that had been effected in my health. I would never hemorrhage again; in return, I have epilepsy and will be subject to seizures for the rest of my life.

Initially I had every hope of putting this experience behind me. I had just returned from six months in Central America—the hemorrhage inconveniently occurred while I was in Nicaragua—and planned to write about my time there. But while still in the hospital, I had a telephone conversation with the editor of *Science Digest*, a magazine for which I'd written in the past. He was very concerned with what I was about to undergo, which he immediately let me know. "What an opportunity!" exuded Scott DeGarmo. He insisted that even as my head was being shaved and the consent forms were being signed, I take notes. Would it be possible, he asked, to get a photographer to the hospital before my bed was rolled into the operating room? I was a little dismayed. I thought of the people whose personal tragedies I, as a reporter, had tried to exploit—and on deadline. Now, in my hour of crisis, someone—and maybe that someone was me—was proposing to exploit my need. The photographer couldn't make it, but DeGarmo kept after me to put the notes, which I found myself unavoidably taking, into an account of my experience.

That was only the first step in what became a years-long obsession. I continued to read medical texts, attend conferences, and interview doctors. I trailed residents—the best peephole into the day-to-day workings of neurosurgery—took call, and attended operations. With the permission of the chief of neurosurgery at New York University, the residents accepted me as someone who belonged there and asked me, as they ask anyone who is around the OR for any length of time, to hold this or pass that. One resident I was friendly with said the others had wondered if they should talk so loosely in front of a guy who toted around a notepad and pen. Some did and some didn't. But over a period of more than a year I watched them engage in the routine aspects of care and then, gradually, the heroic aspects.

I also watched the attending surgeons, including the one who had operated on me, at work. In the end, my own brain surgeon became for me a symbol of the climactic nature of brain surgery. He was ferociously enmeshed in the theater of surgery, a person who rose to its challenge almost psychotically, with fits and shouts, suffering visibly his role of man fighting evil, and yet never backed down. It was as exciting as anything I'd ever seen. And a life was on the line! And then, though gripped by the surgeon's feats, I thought of myself. Finally, brain surgery for me is a process a patient undergoes; the book is structured to reflect that view.

Chapters proceed chronologically from illness to diagnosis to treatment, and to recovery and its consequences. This narrative is told in the present tense, first person, just as it unfolded to a person unaware. Since this is my story, it begins with an account of what it is like to suffer a life-threatening illness in a Third World country. To this medical thriller is added another tale. Illness has a profound effect on those who experience it with the ill, in my case, my family and girlfriend. By attempting to give my relatives and girlfriend their own viewpoint, the book explores some of the ways in which illness infiltrates healthy relationships, and in some cases, erodes them. To this very personal and in some ways idiosyncratic account is added another aspect. What every patient suffers, as he suffers his illness, is a lack of knowledge about the illness and also the cure. Why the pain? What is the giant machinery that he puts his head into? Why is hospital life organized the way it is? Who are those men in white coats, what do they do, and what do they think about what they do? Also, anyone who delves into the history of medicine is struck by the progress that has been made. Had I suffered the same illness fifty years ago, I no doubt would have been dead. Even twenty-five years ago my chances of coming through at all would have been greatly reduced. Brain surgery is still probably the riskiest surgical field, but something has changed. What? Where the answers to these and other questions are either necessary or enriching, the plot stops. The issue is taken up directly. At each stage that a branch of medicine is discussed, the doctor presented is my doctor. Names of the major characters are real.

If it had been possible, I probably would have covered my own operation. Since it wasn't, I relate in detail other similar procedures. After one particularly harrying time in the OR, one resident said to me, "How does seeing that your surgeon is a wild man make you feel?" Had there been wildness at my surgery? I gathered the evidence on film, in reports, and through the testimony of people who were there. Over the course of many weeks, I reconstructed the event, and what I remember most is being afraid of the answer.

The conclusion to this book changed several times. I had spent a period of months on the neurosurgery service tagging along with residents and their bosses, the attending surgeons, assuming that I would conclude by writing about the drama of becoming a brain surgeon. Their world is extremely enticing, its reality heightened beyond anything I've known. I had hoped to quickly forget my own experience of illness; I wanted it to be no more than an example of medical prowess. Only after beginning to write did I realize that I'd had another motive all along. By looking through the eyes of the surgeons, I wanted to come to grips with my own medical adventure, to find a way to integrate this real and disturbing interlude into the rest of my life. It didn't work.

I think that some of the subjects of this book will be disappointed that I couldn't always move beyond my own fears and see the glory of their work. I tried. There were times when I assumed the mock-bully air of the residents. Cause of death? "Bad protoplasm," related the resident who had lost his last fifteen patients. We all laughed.

I was never immune, though, the way the doctors were. I viewed the enterprise as an outsider, a part of me reacted emotionally. Each time a doctor blandly asked, "How are you doing?" I had to backstep. The patient in me wanted to mention these new epileptic seizures. I decided not to, believing that would disqualify me as an intimate of neurosurgeons.

At times, I felt like a patient who had slipped behind the lines and was given, under false pretenses, special access to the meticulousness and mayhem that is high-powered medicine. People tend to see illness as deviancy and recovery as normalization, as if the surgeon's view is really true: Cut out the fault and all will be well. Being unexpectedly stricken and then, I believed, just as abruptly cured was an experience that seemed for a long time separate from my life, something that was clamped on it like a lid and then, like a lid, flipped off. When I realized that was not true, that the effects were lasting, I was overwhelmed. Eventually I came to see myself as very different from the young neurosurgeons. For eventually I came to understand, as I don't think they always did, that illness was not a matter of growths or defects but of identity. And mine, far from being restored, had been changed. In the conclusion, I use some of my experiences with the neurosurgical residents to try to understand the differences in our worlds, which I think speak to the differences in how doctors and patients experience illness. In the end, I used their stories to tell my own, picking from the hundreds of hours I spent with neurosurgeons the anecdotes that illuminated my experience, not theirs. If this is a story of a career in neurosurgery, it is mine.

Acknowledgments

I WANT MOST OF ALL to acknowledge the help of the professionals and patients who shared their lives with me. Dr. Joseph Ransohoff, chief of neurosurgery, gave me permission to roam the neurosurgery service and the operating room at New York University Medical Center and didn't monitor my activities or worry about what I was going to write. For that freedom—as well as for sharing his insights—I am very grateful. I have many social workers, nurses, residents, and attending doctors to thank, but I am especially indebted to Drs. David Chalif, Eugene S. Flamm, and especially Irvin I. Kricheff. I found their candor as remarkable as their medical skills. Linda Michaels and Laverne Cummings were other staff members who provided invaluable assistance by cutting through the hospital bureaucracies. Among the patients who helped shape my experience and whom I can mention by name, I want to thank in particular John Corallo, David Lubarsky, Kimberly Dorcy, and Barry Milione. Milione has formed a support group for people with arteriovenous malformations (AVMs) and can be contacted at (415)334-8012.

Many people commented on versions of the manuscript, listened to me talk about it, and generally put up with the obsession that this research became, and I thank them for that kindness. Some of them were Jennifer Bartlett, Catherine Breslin, Mathieu Carriere, Ken Cummins, Lenore Davis, Denise Doherty, Cal Fussman, Julie Losch, Melissa Malkovitch, Jim Mintz, Russ Nockels, Sallie Sanborn, Joe Starita, Leslie Stein, Bob Strozier, Larry Wieder, Karen Wolny, and especially Buddy Garfinkle, Debbie Bookchin, and Mindy Levine, who, when I was most obsessed, agreed to *listen* to parts of the manuscript. Scott DeGarmo abetted me, and I am grateful for that. I want to offer special thanks to Dolly Holmes and to the Bleecker Street Pastry Shop.

A
BOMB
IN THE
BRAIN

Prologue

1983

I work as an editor on the international desk at United Press International (UPI), a great job that I have hated for almost the entire six months of my employment. Every day copy bangs over the wire from Managua, San Salvador, Nairobi, Kathmandu, Tokyo, places I long to visit, and I grow unhappy. "Good morning, sir. New Delhi now manned" comes a cheery message, and I am sullen. Last year I worked as a free-lance reporter in Africa. That the excitement I'd known covering coup d'états should have won me a desk job in New York seems unjust. The whole world is out there! And I am squinting in front of a video-display terminal, thwarted and unrecognized.

Is it any wonder that I am drawn to Sandinista Nicaragua, a country in revolt? I don't have the gumption to simply walk away from my great job, but, it turns out, a foundation exists whose principal purpose is to educate young North American journalists about South America. It accomplishes this admirable task by paying gringos to live in Latin America. A few weeks ago I applied. A friend translated my essay into Spanish, the language required on all applications. (If selected, I'll tune up my college Spanish.) The Associated Press (AP), *Newsweek*, the *Christian Science Monitor*—which I wrote for from Africa—sent recommendations. Just in case, I asked a friend, a newspaper correspondent in Washington, to write another one. "Happy birthday!" was penciled at the top of the copy he mailed me.

For weeks and then for days I tried not to think about the grant, to accustom myself to my life as it is. I can work harder on my own projects, sleep less. I know, though, that the winners will get the news by telegram. Yesterday I walked a mile just to check the mailbox, only to find three postcards from Amsterdam put in my box by mistake. Today, Sunday, I can't keep it from my mind. Through the mailbox slot protrudes a folded yellow paper, which I assume is another of those Chinese menus delivered more often than the newspaper. Then I realize it is a Western Union telegram and can't be anything else, and before opening it, I think, I'll have a smoke. My heart is beating very quickly. I pace the narrow, gutted hallway of my apartment building, where I meet a neighbor. He says that if I am a journalist, I must be a very fast typist. I say yes, I am very fast, and then, when I can wait no longer, I run up the four flights of stairs and realize: I am frightened to go to Central America. Too late. The Inter-American Press Association is funding six months in Central America. What I experience then is not happiness, really, but relief, like a stomach upset that finally goes away. I am stepping off this treadmill of indecently mundane work. From UPI, titillating as a travel agency, I am being sent to Nicaragua, a place of real adventure.

My father is proud and annoyed. "Congratulations, I guess," says Dad, who with Mom worries that I am not putting down roots. I tell my girlfriend Julie that I won't go if she is against it, though I think she knows that isn't true. Others said she must resent me for taking off, but Julie had scouted her emotions, and uncovered no bitterness. She didn't think it would harm our year-old relationship. Later, she told me, "I just thought it seemed like a great opportunity, and you made such a big deal about it."

After two months of language training in peaceful, neighboring Costa Rica—where, by strange circumstance, I have cousins—I arrive in Managua, the capital of Nicaragua, and find the country on a war footing. The counterrevolutionaries, Contras for short, ten thousand strong, are attacking in both the north and the south. Warnings of an imminent Yanqui invasion are broadcast daily. In the poor *barrios*, boys and girls troop onto baseball fields in spanking new army uniforms—perhaps the only new merchandise in the country. They shout as one: "*De la frontera! No pasaran! The border! They will not cross!*" To be caught up in this is all I can ask. With another journalist I drive to Ciudad Sandino on the northern border. On the door of his navy Volvo we fashion a T and a V with white adhesive tape, which is supposed to protect us from attack on the unsecured roads. When we dip into the streams that interrupt the pavement, temporarily stalling the engine and stranding the car, we get out and push. I hike a dozen miles with a Sandinista patrol, scanning the beautiful rolling hills for bands of Contras and watching the sweat stain enlarge on the back of the soldier in front of me. Only later is it pointed out that a single sniper could have picked off the entire bunched-up line of us. The bulletproof vest that a photographer lent me and that I wore like a hot white diaper under my shirt would have meant nothing against the enemy's assault rifles.

In Africa, all said and done, I'd written about political unrest and strange cultural habits—coups and caste systems—reinforcing the stereotypes of the place. In Nicaragua, I promised myself, I was going to write something more insightful. My intent is to avoid the capital, where the major media lurk, and cover the revolution from the towns, where entire populations are now armed. Two months after my arrival in Nicaragua there is talk that rebel incursions will reach as far south as Matagalpa, a midsize city 100 kilometers from the border. Fighting that far inside the country will challenge the civilian-defense network. I board a bus to Matagalpa.

At 11:00 A.M. on Saturday, September 24, 1983, as I walk from the bus stop toward the hotel, a single line of slow-moving soldiers shuttles through the center of Matagalpa. These are the local volunteers, the men who store a single-shot American M-1 or, if they are lucky, a Soviet bloc assault rifle under the bed during the week and participate in military drills on weekends. Most wear algae-green fatigues; some carry rifles, slinging them over a shoulder as casually as book bags. They jostle and joke, testimony, it seems to me, of the banalization of war. So much is fighting a part of lives that, like any get-together, it is an opportunity to have some fun.

I trail alongside the line of weekend soldiers as it pushes past the city's most magnificent building, Matagalpa's Catholic cathedral, where another body of faithful is assembled. In their best lemon-yellow dresses and powder-blue pants, loyal Catholics are gathered in Matagalpa's principal church, vaulted, majestic, and cool as a cave. The Catholic archbishops are outspoken opponents of the Sandinistas, and their masses are swollen with opponents of the government. Today is a feast day. A choir of teenage boys, who appear to be wearing their older brothers' cinched-in pants, leads a song. I recognize the tune: "Those Were the Days My Friend."

On the church's stone steps, I buy a creamy orange ice cream pop from a street vendor and stop to watch. Here it is, the entire spectrum of political thought in full-dress regalia, a picture postcard of Sandinista Nicaragua.

Then I head to the hotel and to excruciating pain.

Part I

EXPLOSION IN MY HEAD

Disease is life under changed circumstances.
Rudolf Virchow, founder of cellular pathology

1 When the pain starts in my head, I am in a hotel lobby in Matagalpa, Nicaragua. The lobby is constructed of egg-yolk-yellow cinder blocks, like somebody's rec room, and is crowded with soldiers in green fatigues. Their rifles bang clumsily against the floor. Soon one of them points, and they lift their weapons like bags of groceries and scurry up the wooden stairs, disappearing out of sight. They are here for a luncheon, someone explains to me, "*Un almuerzo.*" I nod, and as I nod, the pain begins. "Begins" is not the best word. The pain explodes. So sudden and enormous is the sensation that for an instant I believe I have been hit. Have my protests to the desk clerk been rewarded with a sucker punch? Has one of the soldiers landed the metal butt of his rifle over my ear?

Pain is an announcement and a call to action. Do something, implores the pain. Find the danger and dispatch it. Your pinkie is scalded. The sensation draws your attention, and you discover that the unlucky finger is hanging like kindling out over the burner. You may delay—long enough to even imagine the blister rising—but within a few seconds the urgency registers. A patch of central nervous cells snaps to attention, and your endangered digit is snatched to safety. What happens, though, if the source of danger is nowhere to be found after pain sounds its warning?

When the pain hits my head, my senses fan out on reconnaissance. And promptly return with nothing, or almost. My hands clamp my head like ear muffs but detect no lump, no evidence that I have been walloped by a gun butt; my nose, sniffling, brings back only the rancid scent of sweat and dirt; my ears capture nothing but the accelerated thump-thumping of my heart. I take mental inventory of my person, waiting for the blow, the shot, the thing, to announce itself. Where is the blood? I see no blood. Indeed, I see very little. Here is a clue. My vision is not only out of focus; it undulates, as if I'm looking up from the bottom of a very deep, very rough swimming pool. It is 11:30 in the morning on the fourth day of a blistering autumn. I am twenty-eight years old, in excellent health, and something is wildly out of whack, something without mark or wound, just this strange blindness and this pelting inside my head.

9

In times of trouble knees really do shake. Mine rattle, then bend, as if beginning a curtsy. I smack one hand on the front desk for support. It seems to me that if I can only put a finger on the fiery nerve endings, I might snuff out the pain. I run a hand through my stringy, moist hair. I press my eyes closed, then spring them open, trying to blink my vision into focus, as if this might really be just a piece of dust tucked under an eyelid. Nothing helps.

Should I scream before I pass out? Silently I move across the room to the spot where a second ago I spied a single high-backed chair. My neck seems too thin, too frail for the task of supporting my heavy head. I struggle to keep it erect. Sitting, though, is luxurious, almost like being in control. I summon reassuring thoughts. This will pass, like bad weather. Soon, I tell myself, a courteous and efficient hotel manager will arrive, eager to hear me out, just as I had demanded moments ago.

When the clerk behind the chest-high counter had replied, "No rooms available," I had explained, indulgently, as if she had misheard me, that I had a reservation. I had folded my hands on the counter, as if preparing to shuffle cards. She hadn't budged. My voice had gone high, pinched with anger, and I had said something like If the revolution did not respect reservations, then where would it ever end? This also had moved her very little, which had left me no recourse. "The manager, I want to see the manager," I had said, unironically, as if I were sorry that it had to come to this.

When the manager appears in front of me, my hands are dug into the armrests, as if I am weightless and in danger of floating away. He is a tall man whose features, in my imperfect vision, swirl. His manner is abrupt. What is the problem here, he wants to know, in a tone that communicates he has many other things to do. What *is* the problem? If only I could say. My breathing is fine. I can walk and talk. I'm not nauseated.

With the manager before me I have no tirade. The pain has cowed me. All I know is that I will do better inside a hotel room than roaming the streets in search of one. "I telephoned," I say plaintively, like a tourist whose luggage has been lost. And then, because it is all I can think of, I appeal to his pride as a hotelier, "That's not good business."

For an instant he is silent. What does he think? I raise a flattened palm to my brow, as if to block out the sun. Why, he wants to know, is this gringo pushing through the backlands of Nicaragua?

Admittedly, in this moment of need, far from a pay phone and a 911 operator, my presence seems stupid. What should I say? Writer in search of assignment, political tourist? Shall I tell him that I am here because I hated my job and my prospects? "I am a journalist who wants to better understand the Sandinista revolution," I say, shamelessly copying the tone of the young revolutionaries. I fish out of my wallet an ID card issued by the Sandinista Press Office.

He is silent again, a big brooding silence. Does he believe that this *periodista Norte Americano* with the badge and bright, unfocusing eyes is worth going out of his way for? Or does he, seeing better than I, know that I am sick and decide to help? He calls to the girl at the front desk. "Take him to the room downstairs," he tells her. "Next to the Cubans," he says to me. Then he turns and goes.

My room is so white it shimmers. It smells of new paint. There are twin beds. I pull off my shirt, patched with sweaty circles, and spread out on a mattress, so stuffed that it seems inflated. With each heartbeat, pain arcs from the forward edge of my hairline to the back of my ear. My vision eddies. Even when I close my eyes, I see movement: oranges and reds. The danger was supposed to be *out there* in the Nicaraguan jungles, where the Contras ambush in the night and where I, who desired to be so close to danger, elbowed my way to the front lines. I am trying to stay with the present and not a thousand dire outcomes. Just ride this out. But my brain has latched on to future details, none of them promising. My cash supply is low. (How far will I get in Nicaragua with an American Express card?) What's more, I've carelessly let my visa lapse. I'll need permission just to get out of the country. I've written about the attacks, financed, it's now admitted, by the United States. Who cares if an unknown American can't see, suffers a headache? This is more than I can bear. I want to switch off the pain, somehow undo it. Like a character in a novel I once read, I envision a triangle in my mind and try to force the pain inside of it, secure the hurt behind a geometric cage. No dice. "Go away, go away," I chant. I ball the bed sheets, as if a solid enough grasp might stop my fall through the bottomlessness of these sensations. My vision is seething. The room begins to reel and bear in on me. My breathing is lead heavy. Fear rises, rises. One by one my senses will fail, I am sure of that now. I am skidding off, losing control. Panic is a breath away. I bolt to my feet, my arms whipping the heavy air like a pinwheel.

Then I hear myself say, "No." And I tell myself, If only I stay calm, the pain will pass, my sight will return. There is nothing in my experience to support the hypothesis that my vision should be permanently impaired, this thudding pain irreversible. I reason, as any reasoning person would, that I am suffering from the water or the sun or the food. Could it be that ice cream I ate on the steps of the church?

"Focus on the immediate future," I mutter, my voice a low hum. What to do next and next and next. I will put on a new shirt, fingering the buttons I can't see; comb my hair with a comb that for an instant seems to be alive, its spindly legs folding and unfolding like a spider's; and find the house of Magdalena,* a woman I've met a single time, who is expecting me and who I imagine, in this moment of peril, is the friend I need.

2 Hemorrhage, derived from the Greek words *aima* for blood and *regnunai* to burst forth, is a general term that might be applied to bloody occurrences as benign as the scrape of a knee. Most hemorrhages are no big deal. A spot on a pant leg and that's the end of it. Inside one of the body's cavities a hemorrhage has potentially graver consequences, especially if it is inside the cranial cavity, which is the one containing the puddinglike brain. To paraphrase one neurosurgeon, Think of the damage that would be done by a fire hose aimed at a child's sand castle.

Each year fifty thousand Americans suffer a hemorrhage inside the cranial cavity. Hemorrhage is the third leading cause of stroke, which is the third leading killer in the United States, behind heart attacks and cancer.

Several factors contribute to the great danger of an intracranial hemorrhage. The softness of the tissue is one, but perhaps the most important is that the tissue is so densely packed with cells. The brain's gray matter is more crowded with cells than any other tissue in the body. These three pounds of tissue are crammed with billions of nerve cells—as many stars as there are in our galaxy. Each one of them has intertwining connections with as many as a thousand others. And then there are supporting glial cells, which are said to outnumber nerve cells by a factor of ten. In the liver, at least 20 percent of the total tissue volume is outside the cells—occupied principally by a bloodlike fluid. In the brain, there is perhaps half that amount of extracellular space. The myriad branches of nerve cells are separated by a film of fluid .00002 millimeters thick—thousands of times thinner than a sheet of paper. An advantage of this density is that it is more difficult for poisons to penetrate the brain than the liver. Yet this configuration also means that when a hemorrhage occurs inside the brain it is almost impossible to avoid damaging nerve cells.

Swedish photographer Lennart Nilsson—famous for his photographs

*Identity changed.

of a living human embryo for *Life* magazine—has squeezed a camera device through an animal's artery and photographed a hemorrhage in action. In a documentary film, *Portrait of a Killer*, his footage was replayed in slow motion. Erupting through a tiny hole in the vessel, the hemorrhage looks like a vascular geyser. Blood pounds the surface of nearby brain, battering tissue and severing long neural connections. Brain tissue has some give. Sometimes blood bursts forth against brain tissue, displaces it, and the brain bounces back, like a sponge poked by a finger. At other times, though, the blood cuts along the pathways of nerve fibers, compresses tissue, and tears tiny blood vessels, which add their store of blood and feed the process.

Though I did not know it then, as I stood near the registration desk, trying to secure a room for the night, a vein had just popped in my brain, on the right side toward the back. I had hemorrhaged, was perhaps hemorrhaging still. A jet of blood could hit any center in the brain, knocking out, for instance, speech or hearing or an aspect of muscle control. Inside my head the tip of the bleed targeted the brain's visual center. Several ounces—a little less than half a cup—shot into my brain. Nerve cells were bruised, some destroyed. My sight went.

One way to distinguish the different kinds of intracranial hemorrhage is by where they occur inside the skull. Two types are subarachnoid hemorrhage and intracerebral hemorrhage. A subarachnoid hemorrhage bleeds into the space between the brain and the arachnoid, the filmy covering around the brain. An intracerebral hemorrhage occurs inside the substance of the brain or cerebrum.

"Subarachnoid hemorrhage is probably the only intracranial lesion capable of producing almost instantaneous death in an otherwise healthy individual," writes James Toole in his textbook *Cerebrovascular Disorders*. Intracerebral hemorrhage, he notes, can kill in a couple of hours. In a subarachnoid hemorrhage caused by an aneurysm—a bubble on a blood vessel—two or three of ten victims might not survive the "bleed." In an intracerebral hemorrhage associated with an arteriovenous malformation (AVM)—a patch of malformed vessels—closer to one in ten can die of the hemorrhage.

The longer bleeding continues, the greater are the chances of coma and death. Within the skull—an evolutionary strategy that protects the noodle-soft brain—there is little room to accommodate a growing mass. Hemorrhaging blood, pumped steadily by the ignorant heart, searches for a place to go where there is none. Pressure builds. The brain herniates. Cerebral tissue shifts, pushing on the brain stem, bearing down not only on the areas that control vision, speech, and movement, functions a person could live without, but on the centers in the brain where breathing and consciousness are regulated. One script that follows cerebral herniation is this: The medulla and the cerebellar tonsils are forced into the narrow confines of the foramen magnum, which is the opening at the base of the skull where the spinal cord becomes the brain. Then in a perversion of nature the hemorrhaging brain, once the body's command post, starts shutting down the body's major systems: respiration, heartbeat, consciousness. The heart rate drops, becomes unsteady, and arrests. The death certificate, always penned in black ink, lists cardiovascular failure as the first cause of death.

In my head, pressure mounted; even the vessels behind my eyes would show the changes. Tissue sought a place to go, pressed on the vital centers, and threatened to close down the body's life-sustaining apparatus, until, tamped by the very pressure it introduced, the bleeding slowed. Blood has a clotting quality; after just a minute or two without movement it will harden. While I tried to imagine what was happening inside my head, in the back on the right a wonderful little clot formed.

What should a person stranded far from a medical center do while bleeding in the head? Or immediately after having bled, when the consequences and the cause are not established and another bleed may be likely?

Any knowledgeable doctor would make several specific suggestions. Keep fluid intake down. That will help keep the already swollen brain as slack as possible. Avoid aspirin, an anticoagulant, which counteracts the clotting power of blood, the last thing a hemorrhager wants. And of course avoid rugged exercise. Doctors say that what initially pushes a debilitated vessel past the breaking point may be activities as mundane as bending, heavy lifting, defecating, or even making love. "In many instances sexual intercourse precipitates the rupture of an aneurysm," says one neurology text. A weak blood vessel, having shown a propensity to bleed, doesn't need further provocation. Toole suggests treating the patient with extreme caution until the cause of the hemorrhage is known: "[After his condition appears stabilized], he should be transported by ambulance or airplane to a center where complete facilities for surgery are available. The patient should be accompanied by trained personnel. There are no hard and fast rules regarding [timing of the trip], leading one to suspect that survival through the trauma of this transportation amounts to a Darwinian test of survival of the fittest. Those who arrive intact at the medical center are a select group."

3 The brain is a story-making device. Its instincts are narrative. No matter how incomplete the input, it churns out logical scenarios, plausible fictions. Like this one: I am experiencing an extended flashback; a reprise of the half-dozen tabs of LSD I swallowed as a younger man, when I stared at the sunny walls of the bathroom and discerned, there on the dappled plaster, Egyptian soldiers sweeping into battle. This idea lulls me. All I need do is wait.

Unable to read the street signs, I count the corners and track toward the house where Magdalena lives with her parents. When I finally arrive, I walk past her. She is leaning against the open doorway of the brick house, and I don't recognize her. I can make out the parts of a person, but I have no idea *who* it is. "Hey, gringo," she must call, retrieving me from drifting.

Sooner or later, a North American who spends any time here comes to believe that he fits in. Me, too. The first time that Magdalena called, "Hey, gringo," I imagined coyly that someone else was being addressed. Not for long. This was two months ago on a bus that was taking me on my first visit to Matagalpa. "What do you think of what your president is doing?" came the pointed interrogation, and then Magdalena shifted in the seat beside me. I'd heard varieties of her question many times since arriving in Nicaragua. Most of the time it was the way a Sandinista introduced an attack on Tio Sam. Nicaraguans don't blame individuals for the sins of their government; their own history of dictatorship argued amply for forgiveness. Yet they collared Americans and held them in conversation as if indeed each traveler had some hand in shaping U.S. foreign policy. The problem, the Nicaraguans invariably explained, was that they simply couldn't understand what was going on. It seemed to them an unambiguous case: A disadvantaged people finally inch out from under the boot. Why would a country as powerful as the United States make trouble for such a little one? Indeed, it was impossible to explain to some of the poorest people in the hemisphere how their battle to survive affected the future of Texas and New Jersey. It was crazy, I would muster, and nod penitently as they dressed a list of their good intentions. Magdalena, though, wanted none of that. She was everything that a peasant was not. Her long amber hair had a silky sheen. She was shapely, not the ironic fat of privation— of beans and fried beans and refried beans—but the fleshiness of a woman coming into her own. The nose was perfect, a plumb line, the eyebrows

15

carefully arched, the lips meaty and full of expression. Two spit curls guarded either side of her face—What American magazine had they come from? They bounced like mini-Slinkys. She was at the university in Managua, a political science student, and bold. "Reagan should keep it up," Magdalena popped. In Sandinista Nicaragua, that sentiment was treason. Magdalena looked me in the eye, which made me wonder this, Why did I only attract Contra women?

Magdalena had once been a Sandinista. "We all used to be Sandinistas," she said. In 1979, Nicaragua was united by one of the most popular revolutions in history and then quickly divided by its aftermath. From my air-conditioned office in New York, I had been drawn to this torrid country by the real chance of change. The Sandinistas, I thought, were remaking the world, and making it better. The revolution drew me; I was not so interested in the complications of the settling up. Yet every so often I had been called aside, taken for what I represented, not what I thought, by the ones who said, "Hey, gringo, keep it up," or, "Hey, gringo, you live in a paradise," and then gave me an embarrassing look of solidarity.

That night Magdalena and I had gone to dinner. She mentioned her cousin, whose car had been stopped for no reason by the Sandinista police, and her uncle, whose supply of American periodicals had been interrupted by the unavailabilty of hard currency. Warming to her, I wondered if I, too, would have fallen to the side of the discontent, with the rest of those of means. On the walk home I took her hand and ushered her toward the romantic route by the river, which, at this time of year, was a stream between mudbanks. Magdalena, faithful Reaganite, would have none of it. She preferred to strut her ribboned curls and her heeling gringo past the Sandinista boys who showed up on the main street with torn dungarees and Russian-made rifles.

When Magdalena yells to me from the doorway, her "Hey, gringo" is welcoming, like a call to come in for dinner. This is someone I know, who knows me. In a voice void of alarm she asks, *Cómo estás*, and I have an impulse to throw myself at her well-bred ankles and call out the truth: I need help. I believe that if this were an English-language version, I would put forward that plea. I would describe the hammerlock of pain, and I would do so without blathering, without seeming the idiot. Admittedly, it's a weird time to be preoccupied with my self-image. Yet there it is; pained and blind I can handle; pained and blind and dithering is too much.

Más o menos, I say, tilting my hand like a seesaw.

Magdalena procures two aspirin for me, bringing them nurselike with a Coca-Cola and a message from a back room that her mother is worried. Worried? Imagining that some maternal force, able and sure, is about to be brought to bear, I almost yelp with joy. The mother will cup her hand to my forehead. "Oh, my," she'll say, and hastily summon the family doctor. That is not the case. I get nothing but the polite assertion of her concern. She remains out of sight, giving me, I imagine, a little action on her rosary. I know that this is a time to be vigilant, to hunt symptoms for clues to what is going on. But to me the evidence, plain as a car crash, is unfathomable. So I fall back on my own spare medical education, which dictates this: For a headache, take two aspirin; for everything else, eat a little something. The aspirin downed, I announce, "Let's go to lunch." I tell Magdalena to give me her arm. This is not an advance. I don't want to take a tumble on the uneven sidewalk.

The restaurant owner, an entrepreneur with an enviable corner lot, is solicitous. He asks for my order and says he hopes I like the *new* Nicaragua. His door, I note, opens on to a steep staircase without a banister. "That is next on the list," he says, and takes my order of steak, french fries, and Coca-Cola, his arms waving, it seems to me, spasmodically. Magdalena's face swims, broken and distorted, a Humpty Dumpty after the fall. I cover one eye, then the other. The distortion is the same. I couldn't pick her out in a crowd. And then there is the pain! I gobble my meal and two Coca-Colas. Magdalena watches in silence. Is she concerned? "You don't seem sick," she says. This is not encouragement; it is fussy, an assessment of the facts that implies that I am making more of this than I ought to, that I am being a bad sport.

"I do feel a little better," I offer.

"Good," she says. "My brother wants to go to the carnival tonight, and you can come, too."

She hasn't taken in a thing! My lips twitch the way weird people's do, I answer her shyly. "I hope so."

Is pain always personal? It is true that pain exists without an object. This is fabulous in a way. Like some extraordinary thing outside the agreed-to rules, pain is self-referential, and thus language, which builds on common references, falters. How do you describe a hurt? We can each of us agree that a leaf is green, a ball of cotton soft, but what is a rasping pain, a stinging pain, a gnawing pain? Is yours the same as mine? To have pain is to know certainty; to be told of someone else's pain is to know doubt. My pain is private, and that, in others' minds, suggests that maybe it is my own creation. So I, despairing not only of the pain but of communicating it, wrap more tightly into silence the real misery of pain and suffer its humiliation like any other fraud. What's more, I will have to find someone else to save me.

Because it is Saturday and a religious holiday, doctors' offices are closed. I resort to a rickety referral network that includes anyone I've ever met. On my one previous trip to Matagalpa I had been introduced to an American woman married to a Nicaraguan doctor. This is just the couple for me. I stick to the sidewalk as if it's a trail through the woods, asking passersby to point in the direction, then following their arms until I can ask someone else. When I arrive, feeling like a pioneer, the housekeeper says that *la señora* is napping. I will wait. Once my vision pushed my existence beyond the confines of my body; now I am conscious of sight, but only of its dreadful limitations. Imagine being inside the fishbowl, unable to see out. This is oppressive, and when, after a few minutes, *la señora* descends, I jump up so quickly that she is startled. Oh, yes, I expect her to say, these symptoms are quite common, no need to worry, it is a parasite or an amoeba, and it frightens the bejeezus out of foreigners all the time. I once knew someone who contracted amoebae. What were the symptoms? Stomach problems, I think. Cramps, diarrhea. That doesn't fit. I remember a friend who'd been infested by parasites, and that's right, he had a sharp pain in his head!

La señora, the best I can tell, is a woman past her prime, perhaps always was, who does indeed offer counsel. "It sounds to me like a stroke," she says blandly, the way the man at the grocery counter says, "Is that everything?" Her doctor-husband is out. She walks me to the door. The new hospital, which the Cubans are constructing on the hill, is not yet complete, she says. "If I were you," she says, knowing that she isn't, "I would go to the old brick hospital at the bottom of the hill."

In the center of my visual field is a tunnel of clarity, narrow like a flashlight beam. I focus it on my feet and tell myself to walk until I am no longer walking downhill.

A short, hefty attendant stationed on a stool behind a metal-grille gate instructs me to take a place on a wooden bench with the tea-colored peasant women and their sick, crying babies. The women stare; their babies rear up in anger. I fix the beam of my gaze on my hands, which seem unreal, jittery and blue with veins, like a Rand McNally map. In my life I have walked into dozens of doctors' offices, my throat sore or my head aching. How many times has it happened? As soon as I crossed the waiting-room threshold and scooped up from atop the lighted tropical fish tank a magazine I'd never read before—*Yachting* or *Stereo Review*—panic struck.

The pain that had kept me up all night had disappeared with a swallow. That was worse than being sick. I was going to disappoint the doctor and embarrass myself. Sitting now on a hard, narrow bench with squalling kids, I admit, I take irrational pleasure in the persistence of this lode of pain.

After a few minutes, perhaps uncomfortable that an unknown gringo is in his waiting room, the attendant swings open the gate. The women stay, and I go. My country is financing the war against his government, yet the white coat of the young Sandinista doctor soothes me. His stethoscope, cold on my back, is a comfort. Not friendly but efficient, he checks my pulse and slips a blood-pressure cuff over my arm. He shines a light in my eyes, tests my strength and my reflexes. My knee bounces under his hammer. What does he think? I ask hopefully, squeezing my still-buttoned shirt over my arms. My vital signs are normal. He can find nothing wrong. The young physician thinks I should return at the beginning of the week when an eye specialist will be at the hospital. In the meantime, he prescribes some sky-blue pain pills. Nicaragua, suffering under a U.S. economic boycott, has shortages of many products, including medication. But the doctor doles out ten pills in a clear plastic baggie. He gives them *gratis* because, as he points out, "In my country medical care is free." I shake my head, sharing his political meaning, and think, At least these pretty blue pills will take away the stabbing pain. "*Gracias, Doctor*," I say, making sure to roll my "r's."

The blue pills don't do a thing.

Down the hall from my hotel room is a group of Cuban doctors, imported to work in the Sandinista rural health centers. It is in fact their arrival that preempted my reservation. I have wanted to meet some of the Cuban "advisers" that the U.S. government says are helping the Nicaraguans in every aspect of running their country. They have not been so easy for me to find. Here, at last, is a chance. I am using the sink, which is in the hall, when a tall young man walks by. He pauses, as curious about this foreigner, I suppose, as I am about him. I ask if he likes Nicaragua. The tall man speaks emphatically. It is an honor for them to be here. Also, he says, it is fun to be abroad. For a Cuban, Nicaragua is "abroad," a place where he can escape from it all. He is very nice, almost eager to please. Then, proud of how well I am negotiating this difficult interaction in Spanish, I ask if he doesn't mind if I pose a question about a specific medical problem, my problem.

The man, who is big and burly, pauses thoughtfully, then says, "We have troubles with the water, too."

He goes to the closet in his room and hauls down from the shelf a battered brown suitcase that is as big as a coffee table. A woman, who I take to be his wife, zealously picks out handfuls of clothes, rummages in side compartments, undoing zippers and unsnapping buttons, as if on some kind of raid, until she finds what she's after. Then, holding a pudgy arm in front of her, she offers several yellow pills and says, "These will help the pain." I have no idea what these pills are, but for a moment I believe that she has searched through her doctor's bag and uncovered something that, by merely popping it in my mouth a couple of times a day, will return me to health. "Gringo Cured by *Dos Médicos Cubanos*." It would be a nice enough story.

The yellow pills don't help, either.

The carnival is out of the question. When I tell Magdalena, I get in response a perfunctory "Oh, that's too bad," which hardly masks her relief. At least I'm not going to tag along and ruin the evening. "Get some rest," she says, and placing a hand on my weary forearm, promises to check in on me later.

Blocks of my vision float. Though I can pick out visual details, my picture of the whole is scrambled. I can't *understand* the relationship of one visual element to another. I can, for instance, zero in on my shoelaces, but I can't comprehend how to tie them. The visual part of my brain is simply not up to the work of coordinating the maneuvers of my fingers. However, if I close my eyes or look away, my fingers can easily accomplish the task of making a bow.

I have a similar experience when I look at the clock in my room. I can pick out the stubby hour hand and the slender minute hand, but somehow my witless eyes can't grasp them in relation to one another. It is only when I verbalize, saying aloud, "The big hand is on the six, and the little hand is on the eight," that I can figure out it is probably eight-thirty at night.

I spend the evening taking showers; they cool me and also pass the time. I swallow a cocktail of sky-blue pills and daisy-yellow pills, no longer counting on results, and trudge the narrow hall, my fingertips spotting me along the wall, to the communal bathroom. With the bolt shut and the light flipped out I fold my legs on the tiled floor, twist open the stream of water, and think of the metronomic pain. It is awful to be in pain, but it is also awful when there is none; then I gird myself, waiting for the next beat of pain.

Pain is no warning at all. It arrives too late and stays too long. With my eyes closed, I see a bonfire of colors as close as my eyelids.

What am I, a college grad reared for a corner office, doing in the new Nicaragua with my head between my legs? Maybe I should give up. Crawl into the park, where the shoeshine boys slap on polish with their fingers, and wait for what mercy comes my way. Helplessness *is* inviting.

I would like to say that though belittled and overcome, I resist panic because of an inner fortitude, a fundamental nerviness. That's not true. Rather, part of me is completely and perversely exhilarated. This seems a great adventure, the best so far. The water on my back feels like the tips of pencils, a dull pain that is unexpectedly pleasing.

By the time Magdalena raps on the door to the hotel room, I have been in and out of the wet gloaming half a dozen times. In all likelihood I have been hallucinating. The body, I believed, was a vessel occupied by two masses, one of them pain and the other fatigue. When the mass of fatigue grows larger than that of pain, I will tumble into sleep. If only I could sleep! And awaken eight hours down the chute of time to a new, anesthetized day! I can't sleep a wink. Magdalena sweeps into the shadeless room, her heels drumming like thimbles on trash cans. A night breeze accompanies her, and with it the aroma of charcoal dinner fires. She starts to shove open a window. It is stifling in here, I know, but even the idle sounds of Nicaraguans calling to one another reverberate in my head like a blown muffler. *"Por favor,"* I say, and she desists. At the edge of one of the beds she hugs her knees. I imagine her sharply boned face, smooth as marble, a smile working her lips like a gay bug. Oh, how I hate to be a slug! How I prefer to be entertaining! Just when I know that I must ruthlessly face my condition, my heart goes plunk, plunk, and I want to look my best.

"Hey, gringo, *cómo estás*?" she asks.

Collapsed on my back like a drunk, I wriggle my hand in the air and rely on the voweled vocabulary of pain: *"Aiiii."* This must be the wrong response. Her lips droop, gravity suddenly overtakes her curls, and she, in her designer jeans and button-down Oxford, is gloomy.

"La carnaval?" I ask with pep.

"Maravillosa," she says enthusiastically.

I drag my ringing skull from the pillow. Heroically, I sit upright. Part of me wants to lop off my head. And part wants to give it a go with a girl I can't see.

What is so enticing about Magdalena, anyway? Her selfishness? Her complaints? Or is it that desire is my ailment's invention; in it my health is affirmed?

It is Saturday night, and a woman who, by my best recollection, is pretty as hell has just walked into my hotel room. I touch the bed for her to join me. But when I reach for her face, it is cool and uninterested. She takes my hand in hers. She plants a gooey kiss on my cheek and, patting me the way an older person pats a child, says to get some rest. She has to leave for Managua tomorrow. "We will go together," she says. "There you will find a doctor." Then, mercifully, she departs. "*Vaya con Dios*," I call bluffly.

4 We are at the bus station by 9:00 A.M. I am exhausted, a victim of pain *and* fatigue. The depot is an unlevel dirt yard. Toward the bottom of the grade, water has settled into stinky puddles. At the top, heat has baked the ground into a hard crust, which kicks free and gets in my clothes and my mouth. At the crest, people shuffle into a wood shack for coffee. When one customer finishes, his plastic cup is rinsed off in a barrel of rainwater and passed to the next in line.

The bus to Managua is an old school bus, one of a herd of buses that seems to be grazing every which way in the yard. Though my eyes still cannot focus, I am aware that the number of people who wait for a seat is much greater than the number of seats. Lining up is just a drill, anyhow. When the driver climbs abroad, people rush the doors. Magdalena lurches, and I hold tight first to her arm, then to the bottom of her shirt, which is no mean feat. She cuts against the grain like a halfback, ducking under one outstretched arm, nearly stepping over a mother's tag-along child and landing us not only on the bus but in two seats.

Through the window a boy sells clear plastic bags of water. Another hawks *La Barricada*, the Sandinista newspaper printed in red and black, the national colors. Already the day is a steamer. I buy a water bag, nibble a hole in one corner, and let it drain into my mouth. I wrap both damp hands around the metal bar on the back of the seat in front of me. It's cool and also substantial, orienting me in space in a way my eyes can't. A woman with a peasant's wide body and an aquamarine dress that shines as though it's wet drops in as the third in our two-person seat, her butt nudging mine for room. The plastic seats are already sticky. Hours in these overcrowded conditions is more than I can bear. Soon, I know, the stiff bounce of this bus on the potted road will cramp my stomach. I don't budge.

The scenery is a series of blotches, like the watercolors I painted with sponges as a kid in grade school. I count six shades of green, from a pea-soup green to an ominous forest green. I am incapable of conversation, and thankfully, Magdalena isn't much interested, either. I pass the time by playing a game. It is like a domestic squabble in which I play both sides. First, I adumbrate complaints. This brimming, wheezing vehicle is over-heated. The air, too heavy, too close, is almost palpable. Then, when I am nearly convinced that the conditions are intolerable, I take the counterpart. What is a little heat but a few degrees, a little sweat but a few beads of moisture! And magically the oppression backs off like the bully it is.

In Managua I climb into a taxi. Magdalena has to slam the creaking door with both hands. She urges me to stay in touch; I agree, knowing we will never see each other again.

My hotel is on a back street lined with cyclone fences, landscaped shrubs, and the tombstones of kids fallen in the war against the Contras. Once in my room, I flip the air conditioner on and turn off the overhead light. I lay in the afternoon's half-light for I don't know how long, listening to the humming of the machine, which is to me the sound of coolness. That evening I ask the hotel owner what she thinks I might have. She is a stout cow-faced German woman who stands sentry at the refrigerator during blackouts, making sure no drinks are consumed for free. She also changes money at above the legal rate. Most of the hotel's clients are foreigners who can't afford the luxury InterContinental Hotel, where re-porters from the TV networks stay and where the Sandinista press office is located. Most are supporters of the revolution. But their dollars go to the hawk-eyed proprietress, who, like the entire middle class, it seems, is stockpiling American currency for the day when she can get the money and herself out of the country. Miserly though she is, she is not unsym-pathetic to my condition. "The sun is responsible. It affects me, too," she says as I write her my last traveler's check.

Early the next morning I walk the three miles to the American embassy—a trek that occupies several restless hours. The lobby is air-conditioned, institutional. A framed letter hanging over the water fountain actually thanks the U.S. government for its help to the Sandinista regime. (When I'd noticed it on my first visit to the embassy, I thought it was a joke.) Marines with near hairless heads keep guard from inside a glass cage, watching TV screens and flicking levers that unlock distant doors. I hear a bolt slide. Someone has let me into the corridor to the medical section.

The embassy nurse is a tall, pleasant middle-aged woman who wears a pressed white uniform, white shoes, and white stockings that give her legs the dull gleam of ice cream. When she looks me over, claps her hands together, and says, "Oh, you remind me of my son," I really believe that I am saved. She says she will take care of me, and I think my odyssey, which I still insist is part adventure, will come to a happy and harmless conclusion among the English speakers and the bulletproof glass.

I tell her about the pain. "It feels like . . . ," I begin. But how do you describe pain? I imagine causes. "It feels like the jolt from an electric socket," I say finally.

"I know, I know," she says, and directs me to a bed with tight hospital corners while she makes some calls. It's a protocol that seems entirely reassuring. I hear her nasal voice on the phone in the next room, and suddenly the apocalyptic explosion in my head seems irrelevant. In a minute she is standing near me, a list in her hand, like an appointments secretary. She has scheduled a visit to an eye doctor and then to her husband, who happens to be a Nicaraguan internist in the private sector. She even worries over how I will get there! No problem, I'm quite a walker, I assure her.

The ophthalmologist, a sour, serious young woman whose stationery boasts that she is a graduate of the University of Puerto Rico, looks into my eyes and sees an inflamed optic nerve. Neuritis, she says, but won't tell me the implications. It doesn't matter. The internist reveals to me the best news of all. He depresses my tongue with a wide popsicle stick, gazes down my throat, and sights, lo and behold, a virus. "Why didn't you tell me that your throat was sore?" he chides. It isn't, I almost reveal, but then I swallow and think, Well, maybe it is, a little. He prescribes a mild antibiotic, erythromycin, and tells me the headache, like the blurred vision, will soon disappear. For the immediate pain he offers a migraine medication. I shouldn't worry, he says, touching me on the shoulder as every doctor should. My aplomb, such as it is, has been based on the assumption of such a prognosis. It was just a matter of finding the expert. I love this man for confirming that notion! As much as I love the idea that what I have is a flu, a bug, a late-summer cold.

As if the news alone has made me better, I force myself to do another interview with a leader of the political opposition. Sunglasses on, I march to his office in the thick heat. As he points out pictures on the walls, claiming that his side, too, has martyrs, I admire his hand, which is as far as I can clearly see. I put the tape recorder on, and ask my questions. I can't concentrate on the answers but plan to listen to the tape later. It turns out, though, that the cassette is faulty and my valiant effort will be rewarded with screeches and noise.

My cash, which has been precariously low for some time, runs out. To the snout-nosed hotel proprietor I am now a drifter. She asks when I will be leaving. Who can I turn to? This is how I now measure the success of my stay in the new Nicaragua. I'd twice met a woman who works in the consulate section of the American embassy and seemed nice, the understanding type, a better Magdalena. I don't know what else to do. In sickness, someone said, we seek our mothers. When she's not around, well, then others will have to do. Linda* is the best one yet. Before I know it, she is driving up in her Mustang and carting my two brown shoulder bags to her place. She is in her twenties, not long out of school, and though she is single, she has been assigned, as all embassy staff are, a large house in a wealthy suburb. She has hired a gardener and a housekeeper—and a watchman, whose job in part is to keep an eye on them. Though she doesn't enjoy it much, her duties include entertaining every month or so, and once, she says, she even managed to serve baked potatoes, a real treat in shortage-ridden Nicaragua. Her place is sunny and big and packed with appliances: washer, dryer, refrigerator (with ice maker), stereo—each one imported from the United States. My suburban psyche eases. If I just take the antibiotics and wait a little, I am sure the hurt in my head will go away here. Soon I will be back on the job.

5 What explains the pain I experience?

Psychologists who spend their lives researching pain find the phenomenon so complicated they can't agree on its definition. Yet everyday life, it might be said, serves up a simple definition. Pain is what happens when a burning, crushing, pinching, or cutting stimulus impinges on the body. As far back as the seventeenth century the philosopher René Descartes suggested pain's mechanism of action. He postulated that there is a "delicate thread," like the cord attached to a church bell, that connects the pained spot on the body to an alarm in the brain. That a pinch felt on the hand or the foot might in fact be a signal coming from the brain is still a key concept in understanding pain. Physiological research has confirmed that though there is no "thread," even the most distant parts of the body are linked to the brain by a chain of chemical and electrical messages.

A question that Descartes could not accurately answer, however, was

*Name changed.

this: How does the skin detect pain? By the end of the nineteenth century anatomists had developed staining and dissection techniques that permitted an examination of the minute structures below the skin. What they found were nerve endings, the final points of the nerve networks that travel from the brain, track through the spine, and cover almost every inch of the body. And the nerve endings were different—you could tell just by the shapes. Of the million nerves that terminate under the skin, some end in little bulb shapes, some in tiny dish shapes, and some in elaborate branchings.

At the end of the nineteenth century a physician named Max von Frey fashioned a few simple tools out of ordinary objects: One was a pin attached to a spring, another a strand of horsehair. With them he set out to map the skin, looking for those spots that were sensitive to the pain of the pin and those that responded to the caress of the hair. What he found was that the skin was not equally sensitive to pain and touch—and some sections were not sensitive at all. Then he did a straightforward bit of reasoning. The anatomists had discovered nerve endings of various shapes; von Frey knew there were different categories of cutaneous sensation: touch, cold, warmth, and pain, he said. Maybe a nerve ending specialized; perhaps each shape corresponded to a specific sensitivity. Free nerve endings—those that branched like minitrees—are the most abundant type. Since pain spots are almost everywhere on the body, he reasoned that the free nerve endings must be pain receptors. Von Frey was correct. It seems bizarre, but buried under the skin are separate nerve endings for touch, temperature, and pain. Pain, physiologically speaking, is not simply too much heat or too heavy a touch. No matter how intensely they are stimulated, the nerve endings that register the sensation of touch will not cause pain. Pain exists only where receptors of pain are found. What's more, there are specialized receptors for cutting pain, burning pain, or crushing pain. Consider, for example, the case of a man, identified in the medical literature as Tom, who in the 1930s drank a searing liquid that destroyed his esophagus. A hole was pushed into Tom's stomach that allowed him to be fed liquids and also permitted H. G. Wolff, one of the early pain researchers, to experiment. To his amazement, Wolff learned that fire didn't cause a twinge in Tom's stomach. Neither did cutting. Pain is what the pain nerves are programmed to feel, and in the gut that is mainly the pain of stretching.

Descartes conceived of pain as a straight-through system—peripheral nerves gathering information and communicating it to central nerves. Von Frey, by simple, inelegant cogitation, extended this notion, suggesting that the basic unit of information gathering was a highly skilled, very specialized pain receptor. Pain theory for a long time has been based on these two insights. Most medical students are still taught something along these lines: Crush a toe and pain is sent from the toe's pain receptors along pain pathways through the spine to the brain. Pain, it is suggested, is due to tissue damage; the more damage, the greater the pain. It is as if the nerve endings of pain evaluate the pain sensation and then report it faithfully to the brain.

Clearly, though, that doesn't explain everything about how pain is experienced. Doctors, for instance, have found that as many as 10 percent of amputees suffer "phantom limb pain." With an amputated arm, it's common to feel that the nonexistent fingers are digging into the nonexistent hand. This is not explainable by von Frey's heirs, who insist that the pain starts when the painful stimulus starts and ceases when the stimulus ends.

There are other, more mundane examples of the seemingly weird ways in which pain behaves. With a prolonged backache or headache, it's easy at first to locate the pain in the back or head, but if the hurt continues, it builds. Pain triggers what amounts to a state of pain. Soon it hurts everywhere. Then even previously pleasurable stimuli can make the entire body uncomfortable. Think of migraine sufferers—40 million Americans suffer recurrent headaches, the worst of which are migraines. According to neurologist Oliver Sacks, a migraine sufferer, three hundred years ago Thomas Willis, a forefather of modern neurology, reported the case of a noblewoman who suffered nearly constant headaches for over twenty years. During the worst stretches, which lasted days at a time, "she was impatient of light, speaking, noise, or of any motion, sitting upright in her Bed, the Chamber made dark, she would talk to nobody, nor take any sleep or sustenance."

It's also clear that athletes in the heat of a contest won't feel pain. Soldiers in battle—and after—can be immune from pain, too. In a well-known report, H. K. Beecher, an anesthesiologist, found that World War II patients carried out of battle with gaping wounds suffered comparatively little pain. In fact, he found that despite similar wounds, postsurgery patients required four times as much morphine, nature's most powerful analgesic. If two people receive the same wound, how is it possible that they don't feel the same pain? If we believe that the sole cause of pain is damage to tissue, this difference in sensation is difficult to understand. The only logical explanation is to label one group complainers, which is often the tendency of doctors as well as relatives.

Another explanation, though, is that a theory that labels pain nothing more than a communication of pain signals from skin to brain is inadequate. "Pain is not merely a sensory experience," explains Ronald Melzack, professor of psychology at McGill University, but "a perceptual experience." If that is the case, then perhaps the meaning of the experience influenced what the soldiers and the postsurgical patients felt. The soldiers no doubt were happy to be out of battle and heading home. For them the wound was a happy occasion. For the surgery patient, perhaps it portended disease and early death.

Melzack is, with Patrick Wall, anatomy professor at University College, London, author of the gate-control theory of pain. This theory suggests that somewhere between the nerve endings that detect pain and the brain that registers it is a structure that serves as a gate. If the gate is open, more pain messages will get through to the brain; if closed, fewer. The key to the theory is that it is the areas of the brain that control emotions, memory, and attention that help determine whether the gate swings open or shut. Pain is an "experience whose quality and intensity are influenced by the unique past history of the individual, by the meaning he gives to the pain-producing situation and by his 'state of mind' at the moment," writes Melzack. The key physiological tenet of this proposition is that the brain is not merely a receptor passively collecting signals of pain. The brain can also inhibit pain through the signals it sends out, acting on the pattern of pain messages *before* they turn into what we know as pain. (Perhaps it is not such a leap to suggest that the brain can also register pain where there are no pain signals, as in the case of phantom limb pain.)

The argument that proponents of this theory have put forward, and which physiologists have found to be essentially correct, is that pain is relative, not absolute. It is an event, like other stressful events, that must be viewed in an environmental and emotional context, *because that is how the brain views it*. Once pain is thought of as a processed perception and not just the recording of a sensory data, some bizarre cases become understandable.

For instance, in 1927, Ivan Pavlov, the renowned Russian psychologist, zapped dogs with an extremely painful electrical stimulus. Zapped after dinner, dogs understood their meal as a prelude to excruciating pain. They chose to starve rather than subject themselves to the pain. But if the dogs were zapped before dinner, they failed to show "even the tiniest and most subtle" signs of pain. Instead, they salivated in anticipation of a meal. Living things, it seems, can experience the same pain in almost totally opposite ways, as a warning of extreme danger or as a dinner bell. Pavlov's argument is that the context in which pain is presented affects not only the meaning the pain is assigned—its value as a message—but in fact how much suffering is actually felt.

"As a rule [the patient with a subarachnoid hemorrhage] is seized by excruciating headache, more severe than he has ever experienced before," writes Toole. How I experience this pain and, perhaps, the *amount* of pain I feel depend in large part on the intensity of the painful stimulus or, in other words, on what is going on in my head. The brain, monitor of the body's pain, does not itself have free nerve endings. The brain is unfeeling, but the "cerebrovascular accident" that occurred in my head might affect the dura, which is one of the brain's coverings, or blood vessels at the base of the brain, both of which are rich in free nerve endings. The intensity of the pain I feel, though, won't depend solely on the amount of blood creating pressure in my head. Other factors intervene, including what I think will go on in the future and what else is going on in the present. Pain is a psychic battle as well as a physical one.

"Our cognitive capacities to think, to believe, and to hope enable us, probably all of us under the appropriate conditions, to find and employ our pain inhibitory resources," wrote psychologists J. C. Liebeskind and L. A. Paul. Perhaps, physiologically, ignorance really is bliss—if it permits hope. Because I have never undergone anything like this, I sometimes tell myself I have no basis on which to conclude that it is serious. At times, I exhibit an almost pathological naïveté. I circumambulate the city, even conduct interviews as if still in pursuit of my big story. Does anyone's past prepare him or her to expect a brain hemorrhage? When a doctor avers that I am suffering from a virus, nothing out of the ordinary, perhaps this news aids in closing the gate like any placebo, which, reports show, helps relieve pain in about 35 percent of patients.

Perhaps also the stresses of my daily existence mitigate the felt pain. One of the therapeutic ideas that has come out of the gate-control theory is that if inhibitory messages can be triggered and the gate closed—no matter by what means—then *all* pain will be shut out. This has led to this seemingly nonsensical idea: One way to diminish one stress is to create another. Perhaps the need to cope with my meager financial and medical resources is a psychic stress that has called forth my pain-resisting energy. Or perhaps it is something more tangible, like the pain I administer to myself, the pain of the ice packs. Consider the case of TENS, or transcutaneous electric nerve stimulation. TENS is an electrical device for stimulating pain nerves that, according to von Frey's approach and common sense, as well, ought to produce more pain. That's not what happens.

Perhaps the new pain stimulates production of endorphins, a pain suppressor more powerful than morphine that is produced by the brain itself. Whatever the mechanism, the frequent result of induced pain has been pain relief, often for hours after the stimulation stops. This may be the reason why hour after hour of ice compresses is the only measure that budges my headache. Ice causes an aching or burning of its own. So numb that it hurts is how I think of it. Is the pain gate closed by this auxiliary stress? A group of patients suffering acute toothaches were given ice massages—not on their painful jaws but on the back of one hand. According to the researchers, the ice decreased the intensity of the dental pain by 50 percent or more in a majority of patients.

Perhaps the dull grinding of my ice packs, my childish optimism, and the competing stresses of my daily life keep the gate partially closed, inhibit an even greater pain.

If the internist is correct and the pain recedes, these few days will be little but a bad memory. And since we tend to have little capacity to remember physical pain, perhaps the memory won't even be so bad. The other prospect, of course, is that whatever now palliates the pain will lose its power. The disappointing aspect of "stress-related analgesia" is that its effectiveness tends to diminish once the novelty of the competing stress has faded. Then pain might become crippling pain, the pain that brings panic, that becomes a disease in itself. "Ordinarily strong persons can be reduced to a whimpering, pitiable state [by continuous pain]," say Raymond Adams and Maurice Victor in *Principles of Neurology*, a textbook not given to the hyperbolic.

6 I spend the days on Linda's flowery couch, counting my blessings: first, that I am no longer on that shock absorberless school bus, and second, that what I am suffering is only a passing virus. I fumble Bruce Springsteen onto the stereo and cock the arm so that the needle falls automatically to "Born to Run." The ice maker spills out cubes like loose change. I fold them into a towel and arrange it on my flat forehead as if it were a place mat. I am wronged! I think, I am not the one who deserves this punishment! Yet the worst, I know, would be to hope that the pain might stop. Then, I am certain, despair would quickly follow. Instead, I try to dissect the pain into parts, the sum of which is something less than the whole. Pain is just a form devoid of meaning, a regular prick that marks time, an arc tracing a shape on my skull. I no longer understand this experience as pain. It is like the way someone entering a darkroom for the first time can't comprehend that a photograph is a piece of paper run through pans of clear liquid. When this willed ignorance works, when my concentration deconstructs the experience and holds the parts up for examination, and when the ice makes my brow tingle until it is hot, comfort comes, and I roll in and out of sleep.

The rest of the time, I set simple goals, promise myself small rewards. If I feel a little better, I will get up off this couch and take some air, walk to the corner. I look forward to this outing; plan for it. I will take a shower. Oh, yes, and shave. I will find my disposable razor, packed in my suitcase on the floor of the guest room. This is what it must be like to be old: the ecstasy of small dreams. No pain, I think, almost no pain. Get up and go, and breathe. Then I unbend my legs, stand, and am brought to my knees, as on the first day. The pain is back, pitchfork sharp. Worse, this thought hits me: Danger is at hand, and I am resting on a chintz couch! I have no peripheral vision, can see almost nothing to the left. My head kicks all the time. The internist's rosy forecast is silly. He is a fool. And, it strikes me with a thudding certainty, so am I. I was ready for adventure, and now I am ready for the adventure to end. I need new medical input. With that admission the pain seems to grow, as if my openmouthed optimism had been all there was between me and catastrophe. Retreat! I think.

I am calling to myself, "I've got to get out of here," when this sane, comical voice intercedes.

"Don't you have time for dinner?"

Linda, returned from work, has been listening. She is concerned about my affliction but finds me, I think, a little dramatic. Caught in her pragmatic gaze, I am embarrassed, which is a tranquilizer. What if this does turn out to be nothing? Is it fitting to end my Central American adventure fleeing a headache? I will take a halfway measure. I think of San José, the capital of neighboring Costa Rica, with its pay phones, copy shops, parking lots, cable TV, and dozens of American-trained doctors, and where I have family. Costa Rica is one of the places to which a branch of my Polish ancestors fled earlier in the century. In Costa Rica rice is not rationed, and I am related to every Fishman in the phone book, where they now number in the dozens. I love the excitement of Nicaragua, where the true revolutionaries are idealistic, dedicated people, but I suddenly long for Costa Rica, where teenagers worry about the cut of their Calvin Klein jeans and don't carry assault rifles. Costa Rica is a land of peace and familial welcome, and I associate that with health. I'll head for San José, recuperate, then return. This seems reasoned.

I rise, wince. "What's for dinner?" I say, my appetite the only aspect of my health still intact.

The next day Linda lends me twenty-five dollars and finds out that AirNica, the Nicaraguan national airline, will accept my American Express card. Plane ticket in hand, I go to the government office to reinstate my expired visa. I surrender my passport in the morning, then spend the day pacing alongside the frantic mothers of the middle class. They have come to plead for exit visas for sons now subject to a mandatory draft. Every Nicaraguan must be prepared to defend his country, not just the poor, say the Sandinistas. Together we smoke Nicaraguan cigarettes, which have a brown filter painted on, though they are really filterless. I buy a cherry popsicle, leave it in its paper wrapper, and press it against my forehead. Periodically, I push my way to the counter. "*Compa*," I call, using the shortened form of *compañero*, which is how Sandinistas address one another. A motion is made toward the offices in the back. They are checking. It is a mystery to them, too. Toward 6:00 P.M., two hours before takeoff, a man in a khaki uniform hands my passport across the counter. An exit visa is stamped inside, valid for twenty-four hours.

At Nicaragua's Augusto Cesar Sandino airport no one does any leisurely reading. Whenever more than two people move together, everyone grips his own luggage, ready to follow. The previous night's flight was canceled because of fighting at the border. Nobody wants to be left off this one. Fear bubbles up in me, too. I can't imagine returning to that bureaucrat's office. I make sure that when boarding is announced, I am near the front of the line.

From the airport in Costa Rica, I call a third cousin and bluntly ask if I can stay with her and her husband. I'd only met them a couple of months before, but, I figure, the ties of blood ought to be worth a few nights. Raquel and Gabriel, both retired, settle me in their son's bedroom. He is off in Colombia studying to be an eye doctor, which seems unfortunate timing. I sneak cubes of ice from the refrigerator, telling the housekeeper that I am preparing a drink. In the afternoons I close the door and hold the ice to my temples with my fingers. Too soon the cubes are gone, turned to wet clouds on the bedspread. There are moments when my head doesn't hurt. Then I lie motionless, contemplating the luxurious absence of pain. In the middle of the night, when the hurt pushes too hard and awakens me, I climb into a bathtub of warm water and repeat the story of the two masses, one of fatigue, the other of pain, hoping that the mass of fatigue will grow swiftly larger.

I pass the rest of the time in doctors' waiting rooms and offices. Taut and wiry Gabriel, who started life as a salesman on horseback, graciously chauffeurs me, while implacable Raquel, seated next to him, makes sure he keeps his eye on the road.

"You know," Gabriel says to me seriously, "I think it must be something the Communists did to you."

"Ach," says Raquel, "Watch on your left."

"I see, I see."

Settled in the backseat of the immaculate Buick, I feel silly. Among these healthy senior citizens it seems dumb to be sick. Out of politeness people invent culprits. It has to be somebody's fault. Gabriel blames the Communists, but I feel like a bumbler. Pain comes from the Latin word for punishment; for pain, like all disease, was once a judgment on the ill. Has that changed? I think that everybody secretly blames me, for malingering or for just being unlucky. And perhaps I, too, feel blameworthy, a feeling that is not allayed when a Costa Rican internist finds no virus, an ophthalmologist detects no neuritis, and a neurologist, uncovering no neurological damage, decides that my throbbing pains should be treated as a headache. Each of their walls is bedecked with diplomas from American schools, and none can tell me that anything is wrong. Raquel, whose husband travels to Dallas every year for a physical, takes me aside. She thinks I should return to the United States.

Ten days after this all began, my vision is gradually returning. *Something* continues to be wrong, though I can't say exactly what. Then one day I read a sign on a cash register: "*Se aceptan cheques.*" A strange policy to advertise. But I have not seen the entire message, "*No se aceptan cheques.*" It is as if I have blind spots, islands where my sight does not go.

Another eye specialist confirms that there are gaps in my vision. They are on the left side. On the Bausch & Lomb chart of the visual field, the technician pens in a tongue-shaped area of darkness, about 65 degrees of the 360-degree circle, where my vision drops off. On the back the doctor writes "CT scan." He suggests a computed tomography scan of the brain. I have visited seven doctors in two countries—a survey of a sector of Central American medicine. I've become a medicine chest. I collected Phenaphen with 15 milligrams of codeine, Avamigran, Sandomigran, Ponstan—added to the cache from Nicaragua, the erythromycin, the yellow pills and the blue pills, whose names I don't know. The only agreeable aspect is the price. Medication included, the cost of my medical care is ninety-five dollars. It is time to go. I am disheartened, and yet, also, as I decide to alert my parents in New Jersey that I am on my way home, there is a measure of relief, as I imagine there always is in surrender.

What do I say over the phone? This is not as straightforward as it might seem. One lesson of my upbringing was that the way to get something was not to ask for it. An outright expression of need might bring a gruff and unpleasant response. "I don't know what to tell you," my father would say, suddenly inept. In my house, complaining was often seen as whining, and the whiner got little but instructions to clear the table. The trick was to *seem* to be in abject need while demanding nothing.

Thus, two weeks after my vision blurred and my head exploded and the vengeance of the Lord or the lordless Communists or the water or the food or the sun had come down with both knees on my chest, I called my father long distance to ask him a question. Did he think, I began from Raquel and Gabriel's television room, it would be less expensive to get a CT scan in Costa Rica or in New York?

Part II

PEERING INTO THE BRAIN

And Hans Castorp saw . . . what it is hardly permitted man to see, and what he had never thought it would be vouchsafed him to see: he looked into his own grave. The process of decay was forestalled by the powers of the light ray, the flesh in which he walked disintegrated, annihilated, dissolved in vacant mist and there within it was the finely turned skeleton . . .

Thomas Mann, *The Magic Mountain*

7 The call from Costa Rica panics Ruth even before she gets on the line.

When she'd heard the ring, Ruth, fifty-three, had been in the bedroom, propped on two elbows, reading. She wasn't a book fanatic, but she'd gone to college late in life and had taken up the habit of study. During one period she'd read *Newsweek* with a Hi-liter in hand. Erv, her husband of thirty years, was in the next room in front of the television. After the office, Erv, fifty-four, liked to plunk into his swivel chair, remote control in one hand, cable controls on his lap, and flip between two, sometimes three, programs. This habit drove Ruth "a little nutsy," but Erv vowed never again to endure a commercial.

Erv picks up the phone first. Steve telephoned occasionally to share a choice story, and in Erv's voice there is a catch of excitement as he calls, "Honey, it's Steve." Then Ruth is watching her husband pace. Erv is broad, bald, average height, powerfully built. "What the hell are you getting a CT scan for?" she hears him say. The conversation exasperates Erv, which sends Ruth's alarm signals out. Erv's free hand shoots in the air like the start of a karate chop. If only Steve would help. But no, Ruth thinks, when he had something on his mind, he schmoozed and brought it up in an "Oh, by the way" fashion. He begrudged you his emotions, then sulked if you didn't respond. You ended up having to pull things from him, which frustrated Erv.

"What is the matter?" Erv is shouting, except that his mouth is shut, trying to contain himself. Ruth listens to him repeat an improbable checklist: "blurred vision," "headache," "not sleeping," "not working." In the family, really bad news was always introduced with the phrase "Everything's all right, but . . ." Now Erv, agitated, is saying, "Everything's not all right."

"Let me talk," says Ruth, stepping into the fray. But when she pulls the receiver from Erv's hand, the voice on the other end is *sotto voce*, calm to the point of sleep. "Fine, fine, fine," she hears. The conversation is over, though the receiver remains in her hand, pointed like a fly swatter.

Ruth and Erv's apartment in New Jersey is smaller than the house where they brought up three kids, yet they got rid of hardly any furniture. A rug covers the carpet, and end tables, coffee tables, and lamp tables are lined up like pawns. Ruth bangs the receiver into place on the end table and fiddles with the cord.

She says to Erv, "I don't want to start acting like a hysterical mother, but what the hell"—she pronounces it "hail" for emphasis—"kind of Nicaraguan bug could blur somebody's vision?"

As Erv stews, worried and put out, Ruth snaps to action, just as I knew she would. When they are sick, every mother wants her kids! When I was already twenty-two years old and suffering from a stubborn sore throat, my mother had insisted on carting me off to the doctor's office, which, of course, was the pediatrician's office. I was old enough to be the father of the other patients, I complained. That didn't matter. "Lionel is an excellent physician," she said, calling the doctor by his first name. Make friends with doctors, my mother had counseled me. That had been her lifelong policy. She and my father had socialized with—and become true friends with—a pediatrician, a dentist, and a neuroradiologist. It was as if, unable to defeat disease once and for all, she worked it like a stern lobbyist lining up allies for the crucial votes.

She grabs the receiver again and squeezes it between her shoulder and ear. Ruth, frail, wispy, a person who said about food, "I like it, it doesn't like me," feels she's got to do something. She dials the dentist's wife and says she needs advice. Should she bother the neuroradiologist? If the opinion is that she is crazy and shouldn't get alarmed, Ruth figures she will call Lionel, the pediatrician. "Don't be ridiculous," says the dentist's wife. "Call the neuroradiologist."

IRVIN KRICHEFF, director of neuroradiology at New York University Medical Center, answers the phone in the kitchen, hears Ruthie's voice, and figures it is one of her hysterical-mother calls. He's grown accustomed and doesn't mind them. He is her irascible medical maven. And he plays the role. He calls her Ruthie—"because she is so thin and vulnerable, if I have to make up a reason." Usually he tells Ruthie, sometimes in raised tones, to stop getting upset and to take some over-the-counter medication or the like or refers her to someone else who will say the same. Nothing touches his narrow area of specialty, disease of the central nervous system. He deals with brain tumors, defective blood vessels in the head, esoteric stuff—"the luxury diseases"—that most of the population doesn't often encounter.

Except this time. The symptoms Ruthie is describing are those he deals with every day. Swift impairment of a function; sudden, excruciating, and now enduring headaches are textbook clues. For a Nicaraguan doctor concerned primarily with poor hygiene, malnutrition, and their associated diseases, disturbed vision might seem to be a problem of the eyes. Misdiagnosis of brain disease is a problem all by itself, even in the United States. One study at the University of Iowa Medical Center found nearly one-fourth of one type of brain hemorrhage was initially labeled infectious disease, migraine, hypertensive crisis, or neck strain. Kricheff had been around long enough to know that in a young, healthy person experiencing "flashing lights" and a headache so bad it woke him in the middle of the night—which is what Ruthie said—those weren't likely causes. Nor was the sun or the food or the water. As every doctor since Hippocrates knew, pain could be an extremely useful diagnostic tool. Most headaches tend to be dull, aching, and passing. This one was sharp and persistent. "The [head] pain which awakens the patient from sleep is likely to have a demonstrable organic basis," report Adams and Victor. That organic basis, Kricheff is almost certain from the start, is an intracranial hemorrhage whose pain can last for weeks.

"Is his neck stiff?" says Kricheff. The neck can become sore after blood leaks into the subarachnoid space, which surrounds the brain and connects to the spinal canal. A stiff neck indicates a sterile meningitis, not dangerous in and of itself but an important indication of a hemorrhage.

Ruthie isn't sure.

"Call him back and ask him," Kricheff says.

Either way, Kricheff has enough information to be convinced that the condition necessitates further attention. Sure, Kricheff knows the Costa Ricans have a CT scan. That's all that's needed: to have some hero from the developing world muck around with a brain hemorrhage. Kricheff doesn't take on many cases as primary physician. That had been part of radiology's attraction. "You get this guy who is in a diabetic coma and you bust your ass to get him right and three weeks later he's back in the hospital because he's drinking all the time. Who wants to deal with this? It's going to be more interesting dealing with other doctors than dealing with patients, more interesting intellectually, more of an exchange." A radiologist consults with doctors, not patients. But here is a family friend. And Kricheff feels he is the only person in a position to see that this friend gets seen by the best people and receives a definitive diagnosis.

Now the dilemma. It is one thing to tell someone to rush home because a blood vessel in his brain may have broken. It is another to tell him *how* to get home. Kricheff considers that the pressure in an airplane cabin might spur another hemorrhage. Kricheff knew a guy who went blind every time he flew. A cyst swelled up and pushed against the optic nerve. He also considers that time might be of the essence. What is the alternative? Taking a boat? There is another factor to consider, Kricheff thinks. If Steve waits too long—and survives—this episode might resolve without treatment. Steve'll say the hell with it and not get it checked. He'll think those damned Third World doctors were right with their stories of migraine and virus. And then the thing will blow up on him again.

Kricheff tells Ruthie, "Tell him to get his ass on a plane and get back here." He says he'll arrange for a CT scan in New York.

Kricheff's voice is serious and firm. There is no harangue this time. Which scares the hell out of Ruthie. She wants to know what it is.

Kricheff is all for telling the truth, unless the truth doesn't do any good. He explains his view this way: What if a patient has a delicate condition that anxiety might exacerbate? Should a doctor describe the worst-case scenario, creating anxiety and possibly contributing to the deterioration of the condition? Kricheff's answer in his own mind is no. His purpose is to tell Ruthie enough, without throwing her into an acute something or the other, to ensure that she insists that her son come home.

"It sounds," he says to Ruthie, "like something not to screw around with."

WHEN THE PHONE RINGS, I am still in the TV room with Raquel and Gabriel. They, too, have cable, which in the Republic of Costa Rica means, in addition to Mexican soap operas, access to American television. "The Dating Game," "Kojak," MTV, and baseball, though for reasons I don't understand, they mostly receive Chicago Cub games. We are watching "Let's Make a Deal," one of their favorite shows. The curtains are drawn. Gabriel and Raquel sit side by side on the square-pillowed couch. They don't speak much English, but they adore American television. It seems to me that they appreciate most the display of merchandise—the rest of the program providing pleasant background, the way ferns do for roses. Together, we ooh at the washer-dryer, the new Mustang. They are very concerned about me and very solicitous. As we watch TV, Raquel asks if I would like some candy. "Of course he would," says Gabriel, and hands Raquel his key chain, which contains the key to the shuttered cabinet.

She unlocks the doors and slides out a giant apothecary jar jammed with gum balls. I take one, not daring to ask why they are under lock and key.

"No," she says, almost indignant, "take another one."

Gabriel grabs the phone and says it is for me, which is a surprise. Who knows I'm here?

Mom does. She says she has spoken to the doctor. She has on her "Dragnet" voice, just the facts. She wants to know if my neck is sore. "Yes, yes, it is," I say, almost with excitement. This is the first time anybody has asked me an on-target question. What does that signify? She says she doesn't know, but our friend the neuroradiologist says to get the hell home. "I told you," I say, "I'll be home within the week."

I'm on my second gum ball when the phone rings again. A woman dressed like a vampire has just won the washer-dryer. Gabriel, miffed, I think, at the interruptions, says it's for me. Again? Again it's Mom. She has been reflecting on my situation and wants to know something: If I'm not able to travel, she will come pick me up. Like after school, I think. "Come on," I say grandly, "I can handle Air Florida."

The CT technician at New York University Hospital wears white shoes and white pants and seems so cheerful, as if he wouldn't rather be anywhere else. He answers my questions with an indulgent bend of the head, as if he is hard of hearing. He finishes each response with a congenial "hmm?" which sounds like someone humming through a comb, and which seems to say, Is that all right? Each time, his eyebrows, thick like iron filings, float up on his forehead.

The mouth of the CT scan looks to me like the opening of a cream-colored cannon. He says not to worry. "The CT scan is a doughnut-shaped X-ray machine, hmm?"

My past two weeks have left me hyperalert to pain. Will it hurt?

"You won't feel a thing, hmm?"

Will it take long?

"Not long at all, hmm?" He is pleasant but vague, volunteering nothing but a wacky grin.

The Q & A over, he instructs me to lie on my back on the narrow plank that slides into the center of the doughnut. Then he ties me down. "Standard procedure, hmm?" he says, his eyebrows inclined like the sides of a funnel. He fastens me to the planks with two straps, one around the legs, one around the chest. He lifts my head and drops it onto a foam pad. Then, as if my skull might roll away, he winds a strip of white tape under the plank and across my forehead. I feel as though in a wild moment I have agreed to let a kindly barber shave my beard, only to realize, once it's much too late, that a total stranger now has a straight-edged razor to my throat.

"Think nice thoughts, hmm?" says the technician, walking out.

The CT scan seems huge. In part, I am aware that this is the effect of the room around it being so small. The paneled walls are close; the tile ceiling is dropped low. There's a single rectangular window, large, like a picture window, on one wall, the only break in a decor whose theme might be easy assembly. The glare, however, prevents me from seeing through the window. Nice thoughts are beyond me. I imagine that I have been forgotten. I close my eyes and count backward from 100, as I sometimes did when I was younger and couldn't fall asleep. Without warning there is the grinding noise of a motor. The plank that I am on advances; I advance with it. My head slides into the doughnut's hole. I open my eyes. All I can see, a few inches above where my nose stops, is the smooth plastic surface of the doughnut's interior. All I can hear is the whoosh of air through nearby vents. It sounds as if the tiny room is breathing.

WHAT WAS GOING ON inside his patient's head? Kricheff didn't need a million-dollar computed tomography scanner to take a pretty good guess. Kricheff had been in the field almost as long as the field had existed. But even a beginner should recognize the clinical symptoms of an intracranial hemorrhage. Kricheff wasn't a neurologist, but based on the information he possessed, the neurological background he did have allowed him to form an idea of the location of the hemorrhage he was dealing with; he could even take a guess at what had caused it. Doctors reason by assembling clues culled from the patient and comparing them to what they know about how the body works. A lot of it is probability: This symptom is most often typical of this ailment; this ailment is most often caused by this change in the anatomy.

What clues did Kricheff have? The subarachnoid space is the space between the surface of the brain and one of its membranes, called the arachnoid. The abrupt onset of extreme pain was a classic symptom of a hemorrhage into the subarachnoid space.

What argued against the subarachnoid hemorrhage was the brain damage, which is what the loss of vision signaled. A person's visual center is located in the occipital lobe of the brain, which is the back part of the brain. The swift loss of vision strongly suggested that the hemorrhage had occurred inside the occipital lobe, inside the brain itself. Thus, the call had to be, at least in part, an intracerebral hemorrhage, a hemorrhage inside the cerebrum. The cerebrum is the main part of the brain; the occipital lobe, one area of it. The problem with saying that the hemorrhage was intracerebral was the pain. The cerebrum is sensationless. You could drive a nail through the main section of the brain and not provoke even a thin "ouch" from the victim.

How, then, to account for an intense headache suggestive of a hemorrhage outside the brain and visual loss indicative of a hemorrhage in the substance of the brain?

Blood must have leaked. It wasn't uncommon. Blood was propelled out of the brain and into the subarachnoid space. Most likely it was an intracerebral hemorrhage first and then, almost immediately after, perhaps, but nonetheless secondarily, a subarachnoid hemorrhage. (That the visual symptoms and the pain had appeared to the patient to occur simultaneously was probably testimony to the force of the hemorrhaging blood, which quickly bored its way out of the brain.)

Kricheff was looking for a disease process whose primary feature was a pressurized bleed inside the substance of the brain. What could that be?

The three leading causes of hemorrhage inside the skull are hypertension, an aneurysm, and an AVM, in that order. Bleeding due to hypertension usually occurs inside the brain, but Kricheff knew that he wasn't dealing with a person who had high blood pressure. Aneurysms, thin-walled blisters on a blood vessel, usually occur outside the brain. An aneurysm sitting on the brain's surface might rupture into brain tissue. That happened, but not often. This patient was maybe on the young side for the typical aneurysm, but over the course of more than twenty years as a neuroradiologist, Kricheff had seen them in kids much younger. An arteriovenous malformation (AVM) is, as it sounds, a defect in the way the arteries and veins are joined. Usually it extends inside the brain. The typical AVM patient is between twenty and forty years old. The patient was just the right age for an AVM, so it had to be considered a strong possibility.

There were other alternatives, of course. The medical literature is filled with exceptions and rare cases. Diagnosing is a process of ruling out possibilities. But if Kricheff had learned anything over the years, it was not to rule anything out until he'd seen the pictures. And even then, he knew, a definitive diagnosis might require other tests. Given these symptoms, you couldn't entirely rule out, for instance, that a highly vascular, malignant tumor growing rapidly in the brain had snapped a blood vessel. That happened. The way to make mistakes in this business was to lock your mind onto one or two possibilities and overlook what the scan or the symptoms might really be trying to say.

Kricheff had gone into radiology because he liked problems just like this one. Take the elements of a puzzle, pick out the significant ones, and fit them together in a meaningful way. Then test your cleverness against the great seeing power of the X ray. "The game of diagnosis," that's what Kricheff called it. This was the challenge of the job. This was where you might have an impact on somebody's life. A radiologist at Mt. Sinai Hospital in New York once said, "So much of medicine is repetitive. Sometimes you have a chance to put your finger in a hole in the dike." Usually Kricheff worked in conjunction with a neurologist, submitting his judgment to another doctor's, but there were times when he had made snap decisions that directly affected the patient. Ask him what his best call was and Kricheff would remember the X-ray films of a four-month-old baby girl. The mother had rushed her to the emergency room after the infant stopped moving her legs. The admitting doctor said the clinical picture was suggestive of polio. Kricheff saw a front view of the baby's spine. He thought he noticed a slight deviation in the alignment of the vertebrae. He asked that a side-view X ray be taken. There it was plain to see. A vertebra was out of line. It was pinching the spinal cord. Kricheff got on the phone to the surgeons. Once traumatized, a cord won't recover. If intervention had been delayed, the infant probably would have been paralyzed. The surgeons operated to adjust the vertebrae, relieving the pressure on the cord. A few years later mother and daughter stopped by the office. The mother told her child to walk over and say hello to the man who had saved her legs. In a lot of work in neuroradiology a doctor could stare at the floppy black-and-white negative, make a brilliant diagnosis, and it wouldn't mean a thing for the patient. This one had been difficult, and had helped.

On the other side of the big picture window, in the control room, the technician operating the CT's panel of dials wants to know what's up today. Kricheff isn't always polite. He shoots from the hip sometimes, and it can come out smart-alecky and rude. It is a habit he has attempted to curb. He tries to catch himself, and instead of saying what he was going to say, he thinks of the most diplomatic guy he knows and asks himself, Now how would he say it? Kricheff tells the technician, "This patient is my nephew." It's a lie, but it's also easier than going through the tedious explanation of knowing his parents and watching him grow up and "almost like a relative" and probably losing patience somewhere in the middle.

In the small control room there is a panel from which the entire process can be regulated. It has the look of an air traffic controller's console. There are switches to advance the plank or bring it back, dials to set the distance between cross sections, and a typewriter keyboard that enters information into the system. With a light pen—a slender flashlight—the technician draws on the computer screen about a seventy-degree angle. That marks the angle of the cross section the CT would make an image of. The images roll up on a computer screen, from top to bottom, thirteen slices of the brain 10 millimeters apart, one every 11.6 seconds; it's a tour of the brain, layer by layer. The beauty of the CT scan is that like no previous X-ray device, it can actually see into the brain. If there is a hemorrhage, the CT will detect it 95 percent of the time, showing a clear polka dot in the forlornly gray brain. In a healthy brain the two hemispheres are mirror images. In those coming up on the screen now, in the rear, on the right, a cloud hangs. Kricheff turns a knob, which brings out the contrast in the black-and-white image. There it is in the right occipital lobe. Not thrilling but not unexpected. The cloud is blood, both intracerebral and subarachnoid. It's better to find the blood than to set off on a wild-goose chase that might never yield an answer, thinks Kricheff.

The radiologist's report would later state: "There is evidence of a triangular-shaped entity located in the right occipital region surrounded by irregular lucencies that is felt to represent edema." Edema is an abnormal accumulation of fluid.

"Your nephew walked in with that?" says the technician, emphasizing the word walked. Even two weeks later, after some of the blood has been absorbed by surrounding tissue, the size of the clot is striking. In the brain it's probably bigger than a quarter, which is unusual to see in an outpatient. The CT localized the bleed in the brain. In some cases it might also reveal the cause. So far, though, the cause isn't visible.

Kricheff orders a second set of scans. This time he asks that contrast fluid be injected into the blood. Contrast has an iodine base that, because of its high density, is picked up by the CT's X rays better than blood. The contrast scan often shows features in bolder outline, especially blood vessels, giving the radiologist more information. Kricheff knows it's a hemorrhage. Hell, Ruthie and Erv could see that on the scan. With contrast, he may be able to discern the source. An aneurysm filled with contrast would show up as a dot; an AVM's tangled vessels might look, as one text put it, like "a bag of worms." Contrast adds danger to the procedure, but not much. The mortality rate is perhaps 1 in 20,000. Kricheff tells the technician that he'll start the intravenous line himself.

Kricheff is edgy, maybe more so than the patient. He knows, after all, what a morbid corner of the medical world he labors in. People show up expecting the worst, and often enough their fears are confirmed. So much is still untreatable. In a hundred years of attacking malignant brain tumors, the only real accomplishment has been to get a better handle on how fast a person will die, usually within two years of diagnosis. Perhaps some doctors get accustomed to delivering an ominous opinion. Kricheff doesn't think he ever will, especially when the recipient is somebody he is close to. Occasionally he can't get out of it. A neurosurgeon will stalk into his office, trailed by the patient's son or daughter. He'll slap the patient's films up on the light box and say, ''Well what do you think this is?'' even though the surgeon can see, as readily as Kricheff, that the lesion is a wildly malignant tumor. It would be nice to be able to tell Ruthie that she doesn't have to worry, that they know what it is and can take care of it. Kricheff is a realist, though. That's one reason he arranged for an appointment with a neurologist immediately after the test.

9 When Kricheff saunters into the room, I am tied in place, an adhesive headband tight on my forehead, not in a position to shake hands, which is my first thought. Kricheff is short and handsome, with fierce brown eyes and thick, curly hair that, I realize, has recently gone gray. Kricheff's feet are squat, injured, the result of polio he suffered as a child, and when he walks, he rolls stiffly off his heels. He has been handicapped as long as I've known him and always fearless about it, unapologetic. If a ball rolled by, he'd take a kick at it, though it risked his balance. He wears a white doctor's coat, an overlong one that hangs to his knees. As he crosses the room, it trails behind him like a cape, which makes me think for a second of a pint-sized Superman in rep tie.

''Hey, there he is,'' I say genially, ''How are you doing?''

''The question,'' snaps Kricheff, ''is how are *you* doing?''

I grew up in the same suburb as Dr. Kricheff, had known him, his wife, and three sons as long as I could remember. Kricheff had always been a talker. He never kept his mouth shut. But when I say, ''I'm fine,'' still sunny, my tone seems to bring down a curtain of silence.

Dr. Kricheff is bright, but his is not a calm, reflective intelligence. He could be disputatious. He probably meant argument as a compliment, a form of attention, though when he told me that journalists were full of crap, as he liked to do, he could seem loud or just argumentative. He was, however, capable of real kindness. For my brother and me he served at times as kind of an auxiliary adult, close to but outside the family circle. We had the impression that he cared about us and called on him for advice. For all his talking, he was not the type to use confidences as something he had over you. I'd always known that he was a medical doctor—before we could pronounce Kricheff we called him Dr. K. But I had no idea that he was a neuroradiologist. Until today I didn't really have any idea what a neuroradiologist did.

"Hey, Dr. K., am I in quarantine?" I say, which, like a cue, perks him up. He asks about Central America, but halfheartedly, not listening to the answer. It doesn't matter. Irritable as he might be with others, here in the room with this sleek white contraption that doesn't move and doesn't speak, that doesn't do anything but breathe heavy, inelegant breaths, I count Kricheff a friendly presence. He is an assurance that I am just a visitor, not like the patients I saw parked in the hallway, in wheelchairs or on stretchers, an arm or a breast having worked its way out from under the covers and no one interested in stuffing it back in. This will be over soon enough. If you've grown up healthy and athletic, then I think you come to believe that when you are sore it's because muscles are stretched and when you ache it's just a matter of laying off for a few days. Let's get this test over with, I think.

Dr. K., though, is having trouble getting the needle to sink into a vein. "You do this a thousand times without a problem," he says. "You do it once to someone you know, and it doesn't go." A bag of clear liquid hangs from a straight metal pole, ready to flow into my arm. Kricheff scratches around the inside of my elbow. Holstered into the machine, I can't see my arm, but I can feel it. It feels as if he's trying to remove a splinter with a sewing needle.

"Hmm?" I say when the needle jabs me, feeling a little like the mood-elevated attendant.

"Just a minute," says Kricheff. He has it; he's speared a vein. "See you later," he says, and bounces out, leaving me alone with the CT, alone *in* the CT.

IN THE CONTROL ROOM, Kricheff is back at a computer monitor, a featureless screen in the midst of a swarm of controls. One of the first prototypes of a CT scan took more than a week to yield one image. Kricheff will only have to pause a few seconds. Still, it's like the moment of truth approaching and can seem like a long time. On how many occasions had he waited for somebody's future to appear on the screen? A person who innocently checked in with a doctor because of a sudden weakness or a sharp pain, only to be informed that he had a malignant tumor eating away at his brain or that he needed an immediate operation that would put his vision and maybe his life on the line?

The first cut of the second set of scans is uninteresting, as is the second, third, fourth, and fifth. On the sixth cut, right on the edge of the clot, Kricheff sees something. He thinks he can make out a shiny ring around the circle of the clot. He experiences a sudden gastric spasm. "Oh, shit, no, no," he says aloud. A ring in a CT scan makes interpretation tricky. When contrast is used, some extremely malignant gliomas, a category of tumor, are characterized by a whitish spot surrounded by a lucent ring, like a lethal Saturn. The tumors may have lots of little blood vessels feeding them, and the ring is produced when contrast is taken into this new vascularity. A blood clot in the process of being absorbed into surrounding tissue could also produce a ring in which contrast has seeped past leaky cell membranes.

Misinterpretation is frequent. Kricheff's impression is that there is no question; he is looking at a malignant tumor. Steve has no future, Kricheff thinks. He's dead. Then, like any doctor taught to move from theory to practice, from idea to implementation, he has a second thought. The appointment with the neurologist will be no buffer. How, he thinks, am I going to tell Ruthie that it's a malignant brain tumor?

Kricheff's mind is momentarily flooded with awful outcomes. Then he tells himself to wait. Make sure it's on the next cross section before writing the death certificate.

10

Kricheff had not gotten into medicine for the suspense. His motivation for becoming a doctor was simple: polio.

Irvin Kricheff was born Isador Gandler, a boy who was supposed to have every advantage that a solid home and hardworking parents could provide. Those advantages began to disappear the day he was born. His birthday was just a few months after the stock market crash of 1929. Four years later, his father died, and he was legally adopted by his grandparents, the Kricheffs. (Another Isador had already convinced his parents that the name would make him the butt of jokes. So his parents had undone their choice. He would be called Irving. The final "g" was dropped because as a kid he couldn't write "g".) At age five, he contracted polio. Kricheff emerged from childhood with a new name, and a new lot in life.

Months of Kricheff's youth were spent on the sidelines on crutches or in a knee-high cast. By age twelve he'd had five transplant operations to link muscles that still had strength to areas where muscles weren't working at all. He'd miss six weeks of school or spend the summer vacation laid up, watching his buddies play from the window. "When I had my operations, the big worry of my grandmother was my hair would get too long," Kricheff remembers. "It was expensive to have the barber come to the house." Every couple of weeks a guy from the local car dealer—"He was like the biggest guy I ever saw in my life," says Kricheff—would carry Kricheff off to the barber.

And yet, for all the limitations it imposed, polio gave him an unshakable direction. Kricheff was going to be an orthopedic surgeon, just like the distinguished orthopedic surgeon who treated his polio, Dr. Custus Lee Hall, a president of the U.S. chapter of the International College of Surgeons. Kricheff could remember Hall walking around with buckets of plaster at the Crippled Children's Clinic, which the Kiwanis Club helped support in Washington, D.C. "He said to me: 'Go to medical school, I'll take you into my practice.' I have no reason to believe he wasn't serious." Kricheff held to that plan through his senior year in college. "We knew what we wanted back then, and we went after it," he says.

Two events intervened to keep Kricheff from orthopedics. Hall died on November 10, 1951, when Kricheff was a freshman in medical school. And Kricheff realized that he wasn't interested in operating on limbs and shaping casts in diagnosis. That realization led to another, for the art of diagnosis, so central to medicine throughout history, had changed. For centuries no disease had presented itself for inspection. Diagnoses had to be deduced from observation and the untrained testimony of a patient who, like me, was so traumatized by the experience that he could hardly be expected to accurately describe its details.

Radiology proposed an alternative. It didn't counsel bypassing the close clinical study of the patient—at least not out loud—but, by taking a single photograph, it could make the careful examination unnecessary. Kricheff says, "I had two acquaintances who were radiology residents at Philadelphia General, a few years ahead me. I remember them calling me in and showing me an X ray and saying, 'See, that's what's wrong with the patient.' That was neat." Here was the disease and the diagnosis, visible as a black and blue mark. Suddenly, says Kricheff, "it was the radiologists who were coming up with most of the diagnoses, especially the difficult ones."

After four years at George Washington School of Medicine, during which his radiology career was highlighted by missing an obvious case of pneumonia on a chest X ray, and a one-year internship in general medicine, Kricheff signed up in 1958 for a three-year residency in radiology at Philadelphia General. Kricheff knew that radiology—younger than brain surgery—was the product of a single technology: the application of X rays to medicine. Perhaps it was clear to him even then that as this technology advanced, specialities like neuroradiology would move forward, too. Not that Kricheff, or anyone else for that matter, could have predicted the revolutionary changes that were to come.

11 That it was Wilhelm Conrad Roentgen, a secretive, at times paranoiac physicist at the University of Wurzburg, who stumbled onto a ray so mysterious he called it an X ray was a most improbable circumstance. All radiology, which grew from an accident in Roentgen's lab, was not only created by chance but, it would seem, by the wrong man. On that fateful Friday afternoon in 1895—which Roentgen kept secret from his closest assistants for weeks —shaggy-bearded Roentgen was working with a Crookes tube, a pear-shaped vacuum tube that had been the delight of scientists for nearly two decades. At one end the tube had a source of electric energy; toward the other, a metal terminal. When sufficient voltage was applied, a stream of energy flowed through the tube. How had William Crookes—after whom this tube was named—been sure that something was going on inside? Anyone could see that the tube glowed a ghostly greenish-yellow. Crookes, a tailor's son who taught himself chemistry, studied every aspect of the eerie glow and even posited that it might comprise a new state of matter. He noted that the luminous matter cast shadows of objects placed inside the tube and that it could turn a delicate paddle wheel. The energy inside the tube he identified as cathode rays—which, though he didn't know it, are composed of moving electrons. What Crookes failed to realize was that X rays were pouring out of his tube. Alas!

"As we turn the pages of Crookes' lectures and read the exhaustive investigation of every possible phenomenon within the tube, we can hardly believe that the next page will not describe what is taking place in the space outside," wrote historian A. W. Crane. Crookes committed this oversight despite the physical evidence that was literally laid out around his lab. New, unopened photographic plates were found fogged and damaged. What had ruined them? Crookes returned them to the manufacturer, alleging shoddy workmanship, though it must certainly have been X rays emanating from his glowing tube. Hapless Crookes. What, after all, did it matter that a paddle wheel spun amusingly when the tailor's son overlooked the *great discovery*, the one that would change the course of mankind?

Initially, Roentgen hadn't competed with Crookes, whose tubes or cathode rays didn't hold his interest. What kept Roentgen reading late into the night was subjects like the compressibility of water and the electrical properties of quartz, both areas in which he published papers. Then, in 1895, when Roentgen delved into cathode rays, it was as if he'd gotten the bug. He dropped all other lines of investigation.

Still, on the afternoon of Friday November 8, 1895, Roentgen had no suspicion that X rays existed. He was a man of habit, and in the afternoons his habit was to work alone. He devised an experiment to determine whether cathode rays would penetrate the walls of a Crookes tube. First, he covered the glass tube so he wouldn't be distracted by the glow. He glued black paper together and covered the Crookes tube with an improvised jacket. To test his paste job, he darkened the lab and energized the tube. No light escaped from the tube, and Roentgen was about to cut the current when, on a bench several feet from the tube, he noticed an object glimmering. Not daring to turn on the lights, he lit a match. By chance, a sheet of cardboard coated with a fluorescent material—it was to be part of his experiment—was lying on a workbench a yard from the tube. Across that fateful paper "a faint flickering greenish illumination" appeared, as the first president of the British Roentgen Society would later describe it.

Where was it coming from? Roentgen turned down the power in the Crookes tube. The glow dimmed. He turned it up, and the illumination grew more intense. Clearly the cause was inside the Crookes tube. Yet Roentgen realized that three feet was way beyond the known range of the cathode ray. This was something new, something unknown—which is why he dubbed it an X ray.

This accidental observation plunged Roentgen into a frenzy of activity. His lab, on a broad tree-lined boulevard, became a fortress from which he could not be moved. He slept in the lab; had meals brought to him. He would tell no one what he was doing, not even his assistants. Badgered by a friend, he confessed only, "I have discovered something interesting, but I do not know whether my observations are correct." Roentgen had just made one of physics' great discoveries, yet the explanation he at first favored was that maybe he was bugging out! Perhaps it was his nature or perhaps he knew that in the physics lab things are not always the way they seem. "I . . . believed," said Roentgen, "I was the victim of deception." As if X rays were a little sleight of hand!

To prove the existence of this new ray Roentgen turned to experiments "to extract secrets from nature." His papers on the X ray—there are just three—are concise reports of simple, clever experiments. Roentgen would never figure out that when an electron propelled at high speed is suddenly stopped or slowed, the energy lost can appear as an X-ray photon, a unit of energy with no mass. But in a few short months he outlined most of the X ray's known characteristics. If X rays could penetrate air, Roentgen hypothesized, maybe they would penetrate other substances. He placed a book of a thousand pages between the tube and the fluorescent screen. The screen still glowed, though somewhat less strongly. A single sheet of tinfoil held between screen and tube seemed to disappear. Roentgen tried blocks of wood more than an inch thich and chunks of rubber, glass, and aluminum. The rays penetrated each to some degree. The only substance it wouldn't penetrate was a lead coin, though when he held up the coin, he noticed that his fingers didn't cast shadows but the bones of his fingers did. Then Roentgen substituted photographic paper for the fluorescent screen. Finally he had lasting proof of what he thought for a time was a private delusion.

Everything, he concluded, was transparent to the X ray, in differing degrees. The denser an object, the less transparent it was or, put another way, the darker the shadow it cast. Bone, for instance, absorbed a lot of X rays, skin comparatively few. To demonstrate his point, Roentgen placed his wife's hand between a Crookes tube and photographic film for fifteen minutes. On the film, Bertha Roentgen's hand was light where X rays were absorbed by the dense bone as well as what appears to be a large wedding ring and dark or almost invisible where they encountered less dense skin. Her reaction? Show me no more, she said. Gazing at the outline of the bones in her hands, bones where hand should be, she had the premonition of Hans Castorp, of flesh disintegrated. Bertha Roentgen shuddered, but the public seemed almost giddy with the idea of a beam that could peer through objects. Mail-order houses offered an X-ray kit for fifteen dollars, "with full guarantee"—whatever that meant. A London firm advertised X-ray-proof underwear. The Bloomingdale brothers used the X ray as an attention grabber in their store. (Unfortunately, the demonstrator's skin began to burn and his hair to fall out.) And for the next seventy-five years interpreting shadows cast by body structures would be the principle behind all X-ray exams. It would transform diagnostic technique from asking questions and deducing information to *seeing*. "The application of the Roentgen rays to medical science has already given to surgery a method of diagnosis the precision of which makes it of the greatest value," said Dr. Charles Leonard of the University of Pennsylvania in 1897. There were still some kinks to be ironed out. The early tubes, for instance, were often powered by a static machine—a device with a hand crank that yielded static electricity—and required twenty minutes to produce one image. The system was frightfully inefficient. Most of the energy generated inside a Crookes tube—some 99 percent—was transferred into heat. The heat and the need to keep them going for long periods meant that the early tubes didn't last long—perhaps a dozen sessions. Reported one pioneer radiologist: "You might melt the glass wall so that it gave way and exploded inwards." He added thoughtfully, "Patients, especially children, disliked this."

AS PROFESSOR ROENTGEN KNEW, X rays were of limited use in many parts of the body, and that included the brain. X rays were a great help in distinguishing between objects of dramatically different densities, like bone and skin. They could peer underneath swollen, bruised tissue and reveal bone fractures beautifully. They showed the cracked bone as a jagged line on what should be an unbroken surface. They could also silhouette bone position, as Kricheff had demonstrated when he noticed a vertebra out of alignment in that infant girl. Yet, unaided, X rays weren't sensitive enough to distinguish a brain tumor, a blood clot, or normal brain tissue from the water in a cup of tea. There was another problem. On an X-ray image three-dimensional objects were flattened. X-ray images did not reveal whether the rays passed through one very dense layer or three moderately dense layers. One shadow was superimposed on top of another, and the same image resulted. That didn't hinder interpretation if one structure was much denser than the others, as was the case with bone and skin. But in a nonbony structure like the brain, overlapping shadows could turn the X-ray images into a hopeless blur.

For most of neurological history the drawbacks of X rays stymied anyone who wanted to peek into the brain. So surgeons sometimes opened the skull for a look-see. Hard to imagine, but brain surgeons once routinely went into the brain uncertain of what they were going to find. Other doctors circumvented the problems of X-raying the brain by devising methods to visualize the cavities that lay inside it or the blood vessels that crisscrossed it. In ventriculography, an idea first tried in 1918, cerebrospinal fluid was removed from a cavity of the brain, called a ventricle, and, using a long syringe, was replaced with air. Then the brain was X-rayed. In angiography, first tried in 1927, a contrast fluid was introduced into the bloodstream of the brain through an artery in the neck. Then the brain was X-rayed. Air is considerably less dense than brain, the contrast considerably more. When the brain was X-rayed, air showed the ventricles as dark blobs on photographic film; contrast revealed the vessels as white squiggly lines. By comparing the shape of the ventricles or the position of the vessels to those in a normal brain, doctors located distortions. Where distortions occurred, doctors deduced that something was wrong. For instance, if arteries appeared pushed to one side, doctors assumed that a "space-occupying lesion," usually a tumor, was doing the pushing.

Each of these methods was in turn praised as the revolution for which neurodoctors had been waiting. They did provide more information about the brain than had ever been available. They were also, said neurologist W. H. Oldendorf, "arduous, tedious tests which provided only limited and indirect information about the brain." The patient, immobilized for long periods with needles dangling from his body, at times had to endure them like torture. The worst aspect, of course, was that they could give the *wrong* information. In the 1950s a textbook of X-ray diagnosis by British authors concluded: "In recent years there have been more negative operative explorations for intracranial tumor resulting from faulty radiological diagnosis than from any other cause." At a medical conference in the fifties, just mentioning the term "neuroradiology" provoked laughter.

In 1961, the year Kricheff finished his radiology residency, neuroradiology was still in its infancy, especially in the United States. The American Society of Neuroradiologists (ASNR) wasn't organized until the following year. And its grand total of fourteen original members, who first met at Keen's Chophouse in New York, relied on techniques developed before Kricheff was born.

At age thirty-two, Kricheff was at a crossroads. He had just received an offer to join a private radiology practice in Washington, D.C. The economic implications of that proposition weren't difficult for the financial-aid kid to appreciate. As a boy, Kricheff had attended a clinic for handicapped children sponsored by the Kiwanis Club. "Rich ladies in Buicks drove you there and gave you Tchaikovsky records for Christmas," he remembered. He attended Pennsylvania State University on a scholarship from the state department of rehabilitation, and the ladies in Buicks took up a collection to help with spending money. Medical school was financed in part by a foundation that sought out the handicapped. (Polio had not only shaped his career but had also financed it.) Kricheff, who could recall selling pints of his blood to finance dates, knew private practice would, as he put it, "make me rich." He was one of the bright, ambitious poor who saw in doctoring a way to bootstrap himself out of poverty. But Kricheff saw another aspect to the offer to go private, too. "I would've been rich and bored," he said, "unless maybe I'd taken up other activities like golf."

Neuroradiology was where the challenge was, Kricheff thought. Angiograms, ventriculograms, and pneumoencephalograms (like the ventriculogram except that air was injected into the spinal canal instead of directly into the brain), limited though they were, were way beyond what had been available. And for the first time they were entering everyday use. Once the radiologist was the guy in the darkened back room, gazing at a lit-up wall of negatives and dictating into a microphone. Angiography was a semisurgical procedure. The angiographer put the patient at risk. Gradually, neuroradiologists were winning the right—and it was a battle—to dress for surgery and do the procedures themselves. By the 1960s the field started to attract an aggressive breed of radiologist eager to ditch the Dictaphone and work in an OR-type situation. There was new excitement about the job of the radiologist in the neurosciences. Kricheff got caught up in it. If you could do an angiogram precisely, there was even a chance it might, in some cases, provide an exact diagnosis of brain disease. What's more, as Kricheff quickly learned, the blobs and squiggly lines were inscrutable to someone not trained to interpret shapes and lines that didn't correspond to anybody's idea of what a brain looked like. "The neurodoctors desperately needed you," Kricheff said, the neurologists to inform diagnoses, the neurosurgeons to guide surgery. Perhaps to fatherless Kricheff it was important to be wanted as well as to be rich.

There was another consideration. Kricheff said: "I had just had surgery, my ankle fused, the left one. Normally I should have been in the hospital for ten days, then in a walking cast and out of it in two months. But I had a lot of complications. So there was a lot of anxiety about what was going to happen when I came out of the cast." Kricheff wasn't about to hit the golf course. Rather, he wondered if he would be able to walk.

The National Institutes of Health (NIH) had moved to fund the first neuroradiological training program in the United States—previously, academic training was only available in Europe. In 1961, Kricheff was awarded an NIH fellowship. For Kricheff, the field that recently drew laughter looked like the safe bet. "In an academic institution, if I'm not carrying my load, it's not money out of somebody's pocket," he said. He was also clearheaded about his future. Being a member of the first generation of American-trained neuroradiologists could only open career opportunities. "If I don't like neuroradiology, at the end of the year I'm even more sellable because I'm a radiology resident who has extra training in neuroradiology and I'll go look for a job then."

Instead of wealth, Kricheff opted for the NIH's $8,300-per-year stipend. By then he had a wife—he'd married the girl in whom he'd invested his blood—and two kids to support. But Kricheff and his wife had always lived frugally. As a first-year resident in 1958, he'd earned $1,200 a year, a salary that climbed to $3,600 by his third year. His wife said: "Our needs have never been so great that we have to own the best, buy the best, or do the best."

"In fact," said Kricheff, "we tend to buy the worst."

Kricheff remembers calling Dr. Juan Taveras, founder of the ASNR and his prospective boss at Columbia.

"Congratulations. Getting selected is such a great honor," Kricheff remembers being told by Taveras, probably the father of neuroradiology in this country. Taveras was developing his knowledge of neuroradiology by reading and experimenting and was achieving real breakthroughs in how to locate tumors angiographically. He told Kricheff that he was so happy he'd be with the program, which couldn't be more exciting.

That was the capper. How was I going to turn down such a great honor? thought Kricheff.

Kricheff's training at the Neurological Institute of New York, at Columbia-Presbyterian Medical Center, prepared him to be an angiographer, an X rayer of the blood vessels of the brain. His earliest contributions were in finding better ways to locate brain tumors. "The Angiographic Localization of Suprasylvian Space-Occupying Lesions" was one of his first papers.

When Kricheff finished the program in 1963, he had job offers in Boston, Philadelphia, and New York. At NYU, the new chief of neurosurgery had vowed to create a top-notch neuroradiology section. He'd already raided Columbia's radiology department and hired NYU's first neuroradiologist, who'd been allotted two rooms in the psych department at Bellevue, the city hospital affiliated with NYU. Traditionally neurosurgical residents were responsible for performing angiograms, which meant that every six months somebody new was trying to figure out how to do and interpret the examination. At NYU, Joseph Ransohoff, the chief of neurosurgery, believed the neuroradiologist should take over the job. So provocative was this stand at the time that the government sent a team to evaluate it. Why are neuroradiologists doing these semi-surgical tests? the team wanted to know. "Because they do them better," said Ransohoff, taking a stand that later got him elected as one of the few honorary members of the ASNR.

For Kricheff, going into an unestablished field had advantages. His entry-level job was codirector of neuroradiology at NYU with the only other neuroradiologist in the section. Kricheff joined in 1963 for $24,000. Two years later, he was director. "Things were working out just as I'd planned," he said. Except for one thing. No matter how hard he worked, how excellent an angiographer he became, he still wasn't looking at the brain, but at its blood vessels, and that meant the margin for error was great. On one of the first angiograms he did, Kricheff remembered blowing an obvious call: a large blood clot. Kricheff had accepted the role of supporting player. He had envisioned being a trusted adviser to neurosurgeons and neurologists. In reality, his word was sometimes good and sometimes not. In 1972, NYU did 600 angiograms on which nothing out of the ordinary was found, even though the patients' symptoms—like impairment of function or headache, for instance—offered convincing evidence of a mass in the brain.

12 The irony of the CT scan* is that the people most responsible for it, and thus for the medical revolution it launched, had no real experience in medicine and, in fact, little interest in it. The inventor of the ventriculogram and the pneumoencephalogram was a neurosurgeon; the inventor of the angiogram, a neurologist. These doctors strove to solve problems they faced every day. Allan Cormack is a nuclear physicist who worked out the mathematics of the CT as a hobby. Godfrey Hounsfield, who created the first workable CT, is an electrical engineer at EMI Ltd. in England who was initially more interested in techniques for revealing the contents of a closed box than those of a bloody cerebrum. (EMI had never before undertaken medically oriented research!) When Cormack and Hounsfield shared the 1979 Nobel Prize in medicine and physiology, it marked the first time in the seventy-eight-year history of the prize that two recipients had started out so indifferent to the field in which they were honored.

Yet no one could doubt that the day in 1972 that EMI introduced the

*The machine has gone by different names and still does, including the popular "CAT scan," though CAT has been said, in different publications, to stand for computerized axial tomography and computer-assisted tomography. CT, for Computed Tomography, is the generic name and the one its creator settled on.

CT was the biggest moment in radiology since Roentgen's fateful afternoon in his lab in Wurzburg. The CT was the X-ray machine that finally allowed the doctor to peer into the brain itself, not just its cavities or its blood vessels. (Later, the CT would be adapted to scan any part of the body, but it was introduced as a door into the unassailable brain.) In one fell swoop, an era of diagnostic medicine came to an end; a previous generation of technology was junked. Suddenly, diagnosis of neurological disease, a painstaking, painful, sometimes harmful, and not always dependable procedure, was quick, painless, almost always harmless to the patient, and simple for the doctor to decipher: Push a button and presto! the CT proferred a diagnosis, plain as a stain on a white shirt.

What in retrospect seems most odd about the history of the CT is how widely and exaggeratedly this machine's importance to medicine was underestimated. When Cormack first published the mathematics that would permit CT scanning, he got back, instead of a cheer of delight, "virtually no response," as he said. It wasn't that nobody believed him; it was that nobody cared. When he published his papers in 1963 and 1964 no one could envision the kind of computerized medicine that the CT would inaugurate. In 1963 one X-ray manufacturer, responding to an inquiry from someone else—it was Oldendorf, the dissatisfied neurologist—said: "We cannot imagine a significant market for such an expensive apparatus, which would do nothing but make a radiographic cross section of a head."

Cormack himself had not always seen the significance of "a radiographic cross section of a head." Born in South Africa, educated in nuclear physics at Cambridge University, Cormack was a member of the physics department at the University of Capetown in 1955 when the medical physicist at Groote Schuur Hospital resigned. South African law required that a physicist oversee radiation treatments. Since Cormack was the sole nuclear physicist in Capetown, he was asked to spend a day and a half each week for a few months at the hospital. He quickly became aware of two things. First, he recognized that in order to calculate the correct dose of radiation for a patient it would be important to take into account where the soft tissue was and where bone was; and second, that nobody knew how to figure that out. "I was dissatisfied with treatment planning," Cormack said. "How can you give a correct dose of radiation if you assume the body is homogeneous?"

Cormack perceived this, as Hounsfield would, as a mathematical problem. He also saw it as fun. In 1956, while on sabbatical at Harvard University to work with nuclear physics, Cormack spent his spare time figuring out a mathematical solution. In 1957 he joined the physics department at

Tufts University—he is still the only member of that department without a Ph.D. For about two hundred dollars of machine-shop time and two days in the lab, he built a crude model that looked like two large juice cans facing each other across the top of a turntable. Cormack was delighted with the results, which eventually did stimulate at least one response. A Swiss avalanche center wondered if his method might be useful in measuring snowfall in remote regions. (If there was a way to sink a detector under the snow, it would.)

Hounsfield was able to push beyond Cormack—whose work he didn't know about—for a couple of reasons. First, he found support inside his company as well as outside of it. Second, taking up the problem a few years after Cormack, he could harness a faster computer to his project. Computed tomography was possible without a computer—Cormack had done some of his first calculations by hand!—but was extremely laborious and, as a result, not commercially feasible.

Hounsfield grew up on a farm, a place he found dull. "To prevent myself from being bored," he said, "I started to reason why things might work." At thirteen he built a record player from a collection of spare parts. In his mid-teens he built his own radios. "I'm not the sort of person to build model planes," Hounsfield has said. "I've always searched for original ideas." At EMI Ltd.'s Central Laboratories in England, where he has been employed since 1951, Hounsfield designed radar systems and led the design team that created the first large solid-state computer built in Britain. "Ninety-nine of (his ideas) are rubbish," a colleague has said. "But the hundredth is ten times better than anything anyone ever thought of before."

In 1967, Hounsfield was trying to figure out how machines could recognize patterns. He wanted to know how a machine could tell what was inside a closed box, for instance. An X-ray picture gave a confused image of the contents because, as even Roentgen knew, the shadows it cast were superimposed on one another. Yet Hounsfield postulated this: If X-ray images were taken from all possible directions, he'd have collected all the information he needed, albeit as part of a hodgepodge. The problem was not collecting data but deciphering it. "It became clear that there were many areas where large amounts of information could be made available, but the techniques used for retrieving it were so inefficient that a large proportion of the available data was completely wasted," wrote Hounsfield. "[It] would require only a mathematical solution, and this could be performed on a computer."

Only later did it occur to Hounsfield that the closed box could be considered a skull; its contents, the brain.

At EMI, Hounsfield enjoyed the special freedoms of those singled out as "creative." One day in 1967, Hounsfield was told by his bosses: "Go away and think of something new." Hounsfield loved to walk in the mountains in the lake district near his home. It is said that he was on one of his rambles when he started thinking about what would become the CT scan. "I had several projects on the boil at the time, but gradually this one bubbled to the top."

Hounsfield decided that the best way to present the mathematically derived data about the three-dimensional brain was as a tomogram, a term taken from the Greek word *tomos* for a slice. It is sometimes said that the CT scan offers a three-dimensional image of the brain. Not exactly. Hounsfield, like all his successors, provided a dozen two-dimensional slices of the brain—from the crown of the head to the base of the neck—that, taken collectively, allow a doctor to visualize the brain in three dimensions.

Unlike Cormack, Hounsfield was able to interest some farsighted radiologists at the British Department of Health and Social Security in his project. With their encouragement, he set to work building models, the first one on a lathe bed. The image was impressive, though it required an astounding nine days to produce one tomogram of the brain of a freshly killed steer, which, during that period, started to rot.

In EMI's first commercial CT scan, introduced in England in 1972, the brain was positioned inside what Hounsfield described as "a circular orifice"—the doughnut. On one side of the orifice he placed X-ray sources. Opposite the X-ray sources Hounsfield put detectors, which were much more sensitive measurers of how much X-ray energy made it through the head than photographic film. One source was aligned with one detector.

After a first view was taken of the head, both X-ray sources and detectors rotated, and again columns of radiation were passed through the brain, this time from a slightly different angle (though still in the same plane).

The second set of X rays intersected the first. At each point of intersection, Hounsfield could mathematically calculate the density. Although Hounsfield's idea was ingenious his mathematics were a little clunky. ("I find I've got other tools of thinking than math," Hounsfield has been quoted as saying.) Hounsfield used an iterative formula, which meant that the solution was arrived at by a series of estimates and corrections. Later technology—including nuclear magnetic resonance and ultrasonic scanners—would employ different mathematical schemes, but "reconstructive imaging" was introduced in Hounsfield's CT scan as a series of trials and errors.

The CT scan made diagnostic medicine what we think of today: technology intense, authoritative, and extremely expensive. Yet news of the CT caught Kricheff off guard. His first reaction to the CT was "There's no way you can X-ray the brain." In 1973, when EMI's Mark I became available in the United States, Kricheff wasn't even sure he wanted one. He had just successfully argued for $4 million to buy equipment; he had the best facilities in the radiology department. He was embarrassed to ask for more funds. Some money existed in a budget controlled by the city of New York, but government health administrators were cautious. They felt the CT scan was unproven. Certainly they weren't alone. As late as 1976, the *Journal of the Canadian Association of Radiologists* was expressing a not uncommon sentiment: "We have not adequately weighed the tremendous cost of the equipment against the possible benefit. . . ."

It was only after the Mayo Clinic got the first EMI scanner in the United States and reports of its capabilities filtered back that NYU's top doctors decided they needed one. Once convinced, they "ran roughshod over the hospital administrator" to get the money to pay for it, according to one observer. In 1974, NYU received the sixth CT scan in the country.

Overnight the CT scan made many of the painful studies obsolete. The great debate of the first textbooks on neuroradiology had been when to use "air studies." The answer was finally in: never. Kricheff tossed out his pneumoencephalography equipment to make room for the CT.

Kricheff also had to retool. The first clinical textbook on interpreting CT images wouldn't appear until 1975. So Kricheff flew to the Mayo Clinic in Rochester, Minnesota. He bundled a hundred of their CT images under his arm and took them back to his hotel room. He set up a tripod, mounted a 35-millimeter camera atop it, and began making his own textbook. Organized in a looseleaf noteback, the photographs were for a time Kricheff's only reference book.

Hounsfield calculated that his method of "image reconstruction"—it was no longer a process of casting shadows on photographic paper—would be 100 times more accurate than conventional X rays and also use less radiation. Practically, that meant that the CT could distinguish the different densities of the various components of blood. The CT quickly went through four generations of improvements; each model had a life expectancy of three to five years. By the 1980s a CT would detect 95 percent of brain tumors and about the same percentage of blood clots inside the skull.

Initially, it had been suggested that the CT should *replace* the neuro-radiologist. Now that the X rays were so easy to read, who needed another doctor just to interpret them? went the argument. Once that idea died and neuroradiologists claimed the CT scan as their own, the term neuroradiology no longer provoked chuckles. Suddenly a field that had been working with fifty-year-old technology was at the leading edge of medical development. Instead of debating "what certain symptomatology was suggestive of," doctors shipped the patient to the CT, and in a few minutes the question was definitively settled. Now it was the neurologist who felt threatened. A neurology journal related (in a tone of scandal) the tale of two young doctors, trained as neurologists, who had taken up the more lucrative endeavor of selling CT machines. "The neurologist can closely examine a patient and suggest a brilliant diagnosis," said Kricheff. "Then we can scan him and in a few minutes find out if the diagnosis is right."

From a bureaucratic point of view, perhaps the most important impact of the CT was economic. Unlike the angiogram, the CT was a quick test. Instead of a few angiograms per day, dozens of CT scans could be administered. Prior to the CT scan, neuroradiological services cost the radiology department considerably more than they brought in. Their expansion or even continued existence depended on the goodwill of other specialties, which had to lobby for the neuroradiologists on clinical grounds. "The CT scan has dramatically changed this," said Kricheff. "Neuroradiology has become a major, if not the major moneymaker in many large radiology departments." In 1972, the year the CT was introduced, the ASNR had 200 members. By the mid-1980s, a decade after the CT came to town, there were 1,000 members.

By the time I was strapped onto the table, NYU Medical Center had acquired seven CT machines and employed seven neuroradiologists. Kricheff was a leader in a field that had become an essential part of the neurosciences. He knew all the important players. They weren't names in books he studied. They were his buddies, which gave him a certain freedom in the group. At one meeting of the ASNR, members dressed up the major players in costumes befitting their roles. They clad Kricheff in the robes of Cardinal Richelieu, the onetime prime minister of France, and gave him a ring that people could kiss and a goblet of holy water—really white wine—to sprinkle on the faithful. (After drinking a little of his own holy water, Kricheff got into the fun, anointing a colleague by pouring the wine over his head.)

Kricheff could be bullheaded, iconoclastic, and opinionated. About one neurosurgeon he said, "[His results are] not as good as someone else could do." Just as some people, through timidity or smugness, like to hold their peace, Kricheff liked to butt in, almost recklessly. Provocation was a thought-out style. In a difficult case, with scans that no one could figure out, Kricheff would propose some off-the-wall diagnosis. "Probably it would turn out to be incorrect," a colleague remembered, "but Kricheff's attitude was, Why not think of something outrageous? Then if it actually turns out to be right, everyone will always say, 'Remember when Kricheff made that great diagnosis.' "

Still, in NYU departments characterized by stormy personalities, Kricheff had the grace to get along with all. One of the other radiologists said that if somebody hasn't kicked Kricheff in the ass in the past six months, he likes him. He had friends all over the hospital. Early on he learned to do favors for others; if he needed a favor, others would in turn accommodate him. When his wife's father had a heart attack, the internist couldn't get a bed on the medical floor and suggested putting him with indigents at Bellevue, the city hospital. Kricheff made a few calls, and a bed was found in the neurosurgical intensive care unit (ICU). "When we went upstairs, a surgeon and several residents happened to be looking out the window. I asked what was going on. The surgeon said they were all looking at the patient they had to throw out the window to make room for my father-in-law."

Some in Kricheff's position would have wanted to be chairman of a radiology department. Kricheff had received inquiries but never pursued them. As another radiologist explained: "Why should he? He's got the best of both worlds. He is like a chairman but doesn't have any of the hassles." Kricheff didn't want the extra prestige or the money. "Money just isn't worth that much," he said. He had a house in the suburbs and a house in a shore community, though it was modest and wasn't on the shore. "We could have bought a fancier place, but that's really not our style. I've always preferred to have time with my wife, the kids, when there were kids around, than go out and moonlight. Or maybe I'm just too lazy. I've always claimed one of the secrets of my sucess is that I'm lazy. I try to get really bright guys and train them to do the work, and then they get famous and they're doing all the work." He enjoyed supervising. He prided himself on having turned out excellent neuroradiologists, a Kricheff school of neuroradiology. "I'm the number-two expert in everything in the department," he said.

EMI, a company better known for its sponsorship of the Beatles than its diagnostic equipment, first underestimated the CT market at less than ten machines and then went out of the business. But other companies

quickly moved in—at one point it may have been one of the more competitive businesses in the country: Twenty manufacturers offered CT scans.
One of the leaders, General Electric, had installed 2,000 CT scans—average
price about $1 million. My head is inside a GE 9800.

13   In the control room, Kricheff, a forearm flat on the table,
supports himself on the desk in front of the monitor. The
light is dim, his eyes the brown of dead leaves. Stuck on the
wall behind him is a TV monitor, which flashes images from
other CTs around the medical center. Kricheff doesn't give them a glance.
He is waiting the few seconds for the detectors and simultaneous equations
to offer up another slice of brain, which will determine my future—whether
I have a future. The GE 9800 has a single X-ray source and, opposite it,
742 extremely sensitive detectors, 1.2 millimeters apart. Between air and
bone, the detectors can distinguish a million gradations of X-ray atten-
uation, as if between black and white the CT has introduced a million
shades of gray. To reconstruct one image, the CT takes 1,968 views from
slightly different angles in two seconds. The GE 9800 then solves 406
million computations.

Then there it is. The image of a slice of brain, 10 millimeters higher
than the previous slice, rolls on to the screen, top first. "There was no
possibility in my mind that nothing had happened. I knew there was a
hemorrhage. From there on everything could only get worse. I was going
on the premise of what I thought was there, thinking it was a malignant
tumor. So I couldn't think of anything better than what I saw."

Kricheff does not believe he sees the fateful ring of a malignant tumor.
The previous scans hadn't revealed a huge inoperable AVM or a giant
aneurysm. Now, Kricheff thinks, there is no evidence of an invading glioma
that was turning the brain to goo. To his trained eye, the scan shows a
hemorrhage, plain and simple, an old hemorrhage gradually being absorbed by surrounding tissue. "That's one of the best hemorrhages I've
ever seen," Kricheff says. He puts both fists over his head and lets out a
cheer, "Yeahhhh." The scan does not reveal the cause of the bleed. "Unknown etiology" is the official verdict. For the time being Kricheff feels
that is just fine. He is elated to have ducked death. Of course, nothing is
absolutely certain yet, as the formal radiological report, written by another
radiologist, will indicate. "The possibility of hemorrhage into a tumor cannot be completely ruled out," it said, and recommended further studies.

I WAIT FOR THE RESULTS in a cubicle with windows across one wall and X-ray viewing screens across another. I spin in my chair, a mud-colored stitched chair with balding leather and a single pivot, like a barbershop chair, and gaze through the window. It seems to me a factory setting. There are curved gray machines in near darkness and men in white coats huddled and talking. I've arrived home a couple of weeks short of six months in Central America. One suitcase was almost entirely stuffed with notes and papers, enough material, I'm sure, for the story, which, as I trail my feet on the ground, I begin to contemplate. Then, before I can say hello, Dr. K. drops into a chair. A plastic copy of the CT images flaps in his hand, making a cracking sound, as if it is alive. Usually Dr. K. slouches comfortably when he sits, belly up. He is at a crisp right angle today. He pushes off a wall, and like a torpedo, his chair wheels toward me.

Kricheff would later tell me that he felt the best thing to do was just to say what it was, partly because his patient was being a little too casual. Kricheff didn't want me to say, "I'll go home and come back in a couple of weeks," which he thought I was fully capable of doing with my laid-back, low-key image. "And second, what else is there to say? 'Well, there's this little drop of something in there,' when there's this big white ball on the CT scan?" Kricheff realized that the person hearing the news might not initially understand it because he wasn't ready to accept that it happened, but eventually I would come around. "It was hard for me to conceive that you really didn't know that SOMETHING had happened," Kricheff said.

PEOPLE DIGEST BAD NEWS differently. Some register relief. They toss their hands in the air like worshipers and make a remark like "At least I know now." Others admit they are in over their heads. "I'm not accustomed to this," a woman in one account said after learning she had a brain tumor. "And I don't know how to handle it." Still others experience anger, a retaliatory emotion. "It just wasn't *fair* for me to be having a heart attack," wrote a middle-aged man.

I go blank, as outwardly reactive as a rock.

Having negotiated the jolly, unskilled doctors and the aimless bureaucrats and the entire landscape of terror, I had assumed I would be rewarded. Dr. K. was going to boot me out of this dark cubbyhole into the blinking daylight with a prescription or a word of caution. I think this must be why when, in that room lit only by the harsh light of X-ray reading lamps, Dr. K. begins to talk, I hear almost nothing after the words "brain hemorrhage." I had abdicated authority to the incredible CT scan, and it had betrayed me, telling me in a few minutes that I was much sicker than weeks of consultations had even intimated.

My mouth hangs open, and my respiration comes in percussive bursts, like a cap gun. Each breath pokes the fingertip of this new danger into my ribs, and hurts. My eyes work the shadows, I can't meet Dr. K.'s gaze. He says in befuddlement, "Steve, Steve, are you still there?" But his voice is trimmed back and far away. It's not thoughts of death, of flesh deserting bone, that grip me. I have an incredibly mundane thought. I imagine a navy-blue baseball jacket with a gold team patch, the one I wore as a clumsy teen to make me feel pride. This isn't like me to be so sick, I think, which is also a reaction of awkward pride. Then the pride goes. And after weeks without flinching, I am tired and teary and ashamed.

Part III

ASSESSING THE EVIL

The doctor said that so-and-so indicated that there was so-and-so inside the patient, but if the investigation of so-and-so did not confirm this, then he must assume that and that. If he assumed that and that, then . . . and so on. To Ivan Ilych only one question was important: was his case serious or not?
Leo Tolstoy, *The Death of Ivan Ilych*

14 The neurologist's waiting room features a row of hard-backed seats, one of which is occupied by an older woman whose hair is the shade of gray that looks blue. She is doubled over, her spine curved like a wave, and is thumbing through a booklet. Something entered my life today, and now everything I think about is in relation to it. I wonder, Is everyone in the world ill? What disease has *her* in its grip? I hook at the waist, as subtly as someone wrapped around a pole, trying to make out the name of her reading material. Perhaps in this room everything passes as a symptom and thus merits nothing but polite tolerance. The woman merely ruffles the paperback toward her bosom, protecting herself, though, in the process, revealing the book's title. In bold sans serif is written *Parkinson's Disease Handbook,* three words that right me as quickly as her quivering gaze. I bounce my own mustard-colored envelope on my lap, my fingers playing at the edges as if I am doing scales. I grin. We are none of us very happy today, I want to say. Then a funny thing happens. An older man with sparse hair and a shuffling step, as if his shoes are too big, exits the doctor's office. The woman in the waiting room hustles briskly over to meet the man, who is obviously her husband.

Dr. Kricheff, my medical chaperone, has arranged for me to go directly from the CT scan to neurologist Dr. Albert Goodgold, whom Kricheff sometimes calls Big Al. "You want to see Goodgold, who will take a thorough approach, get all the details which I didn't get, some of which may be very significant," Kricheff later explained. "There's no law against somebody having two things going on." Kricheff knew that other tests would probably be needed. He also wanted an outsider who would manage the case appropriately, regardless of what the tests showed.

Goodgold's office is long and narrow, the proportions of a railroad car. It is carpeted and has a bookshelf along one wall and a sturdy but unimposing desk that supports a small statue of a horse. It looks like any study except that at one end there is a slick leather bench covered with thick white paper that unrolls like toilet paper. Goodgold is wearing a handsome plaid suit, no white coat. He stands politely when I enter and extends a hand, but not in greeting. He wants the folder. I turn it over, as if consigning him my secret. He flattens it on the desk, out of the way, with the precise motions of someone folding paper. Then he uncaps a pen and pivots his rectangular face and wide forehead my way.

I feel as if a big arrow of pain is digging in behind my eyes.

"You seem a little punchy?" he says.

"Punched is more like it," I say.

He chuckles. Goodgold, middle-aged, bespectacled, is jovial. And I am personable, a guy who makes jokes. Doctors underestimate the power of their attention. A moment ago my past had leapfrogged into the present and claimed it. Goodgold's voice, alert and jolly, has brought me back. What would he like me to do? Name it. I have a story but no complaints. He is casual, as if beginning a chat, as if the trauma is psychological, not physiological. First, he wants to take a history. Tell me what happened, he says.

I am rehearsed at relating my tale, bilingually. In Spanish, it helped me build vocabulary. I learned words like *nubilado*, which means clouded, to describe my vision. In Spanish my metaphors tended to the meteorologic; in English, the marine. Suddenly, I say, my vision swam. I was seeing underwater. Goodgold likes that. "That's a good description," he says, as if he's heard the phenomenon described many times before but never so well. He writes:

"Was in Nicauraga—Writing

   9/24/83—11:30 A.M.—Standing in a hotel lobby—

   severe R sided headache—vision revolving (?) around the fringes. HA lasted—severe—ca 10 days—left with sporadic aches but also always feels on the verge of the headache. In general feels much, much better. Blurred vision lasted for ca 4 days—Gradually has cleared—but still will not see the first of something at time

   Never before   No antecedent events

Goodgold's eyebrows bunch in concentration, as if we are really making progress. Anything else remarkable before the headache? I have searched for telltale signs. "Well, I was nauseous," I say, aiming to please, though the rice-and-bean menu had my stomach upset most of the time, anyway. Trying to settle it, I had downed Coca-Colas like water.

He makes a note: "One week before headache, nauseated."

"When it happened, what was there besides the headache and the visual deficit?" he wants to know.

Deficit? The word sticks. By his deficits, it is said, does a neurologist know the man.

I, too, had recognized that something was wrong. It didn't register as a deficit, a deficiency, a lack, a want, an absence, a shortfall, an omission, though. After all, *Something* was there. I knew a woman who suffered constant visual interference, as some people get with migraines, except hers never went away. She always had flashing lights or vertical lines or a wall of static in the lower left part of her vision. When I asked what it was like, she said, "Oh, it's so *neat*." Given the right state of mind and the absence of insistent pain, I might have experienced my own hallucinations as something very interesting. This is hardly a deficit. What am I doing in the office of this jovial ham-fisted man, anyhow? I've already visited three eye doctors. Why am I not visiting another? A neurologist works on the nervous system. It was my eyes that had gone blooey. What did that have to do with my brain?

15 The first two thousand years of neurology might be viewed as an attempt to answer the question: How could vision be impaired when the eyes worked impeccably? To come up with the answer, a neurologist had to possess a sophisticated understanding of the brain's function and its method of operation, an expertise unavailable for most of human history.

Consider what cause would have been cited if a patient were stricken with a sudden, ferocious headache and equally spontaneous visual distortions in the age of Aristotle. Nature created nothing without purpose, Aristotle believed. The purpose of the eyes was evidently to see. But what did the gelatinous brain do?

Aristotle had noticed that he could poke the brain of someone wounded and yet not provoke pain. Thus, he concluded, the brain had nothing to do with pain perception nor, by extension, with any kind of perception. The brain, he decided, cooled the heart, which he called the organ of intelligence. Aristotle maintained that visual perception occurred in the eyes. Thus, clouded, undulating vision, he no doubt would have concluded, was due to a problem of the eyeballs.

"Aristotle! What a thing for you to say!" huffed the Greek physician Galen four centuries later. Meeting Aristotle's teleology with his own, Galen said, "In that case [that the brain cooled the heart], Nature would not have placed the brain so far from the heart." Galen did more than argue logic. He was perhaps the first experimental neurophysiologist. He did some novel work. For instance, he cut the medulla, a part of the brain stem, and observed that respiration stopped. Clearly, Galen concluded, the brain had something to do with regulating breathing. Galen gathered other evidence of brain function. He knew that when a person suffered a stroke his "sense instruments are all uninjured." His eyes, for example, could be functioning perfectly. And yet, he also knew that the patient "receives no benefit from them in distinguishing sensations." The patient, in some cases, could hardly see. How could this be? unless there was something more to sensation than what the "sense instrument," in this case, the eye, was doing; "unless," deduced Galen, "the alteration of each sense instrument comes from the encephalon." (Encephalon is the Greek word for brain.)

In Dr. Galen's time, my problem would probably have been correctly understood as a dysfunction of my encephalon, not my eyes. From there, though, medical understanding would have gone downhill. For though Galen had established the paramount importance of the brain, his idea of how it worked was a fairy tale. Without doubt, Galen's worst contribution to medicine was the doctrine that "*spiritus animalis*" from the brain supplied motion and sensation. As ridiculous as it seems, no theory in modern science has endured longer. At the end of the eighteenth century, after the positing of the laws of gravity and the calculation of the speed of light, some physicians still preached that mental processes were governed by spirits that, produced in the ventricles of the brain, raced in and out of the body's organs. According to Galen, the injured brain supposedly lost its sensory, motor, and psychic functions due to escape of the animal spirit. What could have hampered a spirit so that vision faltered? The flow of the spirit was stopped up, probably because of an accumulation of heavy phlegm, one of the four "humors" that had to be balanced to ensure health, according to Galen. (The others were black bile, yellow bile, and blood.)

By the beginning of the nineteenth century, the brain's central role in human activity was an accepted fact. The form, size, color, protuberances, fissures, and cavities of the skull's contents had been elaborately described. But its functioning was a complete mystery. In 1820, Dr. John Cooke, author of the first history of neurology, despaired: "We are utterly at a loss to form any rational conception concerning the manner in which the mind acts, and is acted upon in sensation and motion." In the first part of the nineteenth century, the astute physician could only say for sure that the brain behaved strangely, defying in many respects common sense. For instance, it was known that small tumors could cause more damage than large ones; or, illogical as it seemed, that if the brain were crushed, the effects might be dramatic, but if compressed slowly, a person could remain relatively symptomless for years. As long ago as the sixteenth century, the renowned anatomist Andreas Vesalius had, on autopsy, retrieved nine pounds of liquid from the head of a two-year-old girl. (The average adult male brain weighs only three pounds!) Her senses had been normal, and she hadn't suffered paralysis, though her head was as large as any man's Vesalius had ever seen. "I marvelled at nothing more than that such an amount of water had for so long collected in the ventricles of the brain without greater symptoms," he said.

Doctors diagnosed neurological ailments, of course. (The wealthy considered it a prerogative of money to have a doctor in attendance.) However, without an understanding of how the brain worked, their judgments had little explanatory power. Cooke separated neurological disease into three categories: apoplexy, palsy, and epilepsy. What I had, no doubt, would have been called apoplexy. Cooke's two-volume work listed everything from wearing a tie too tightly to coughing as a cause of apoplexy. Nowhere, though, did he suggest that blood-vessel disease might lead a blood vessel to rupture. Certainly autopsies of the brain had revealed hemorrhages. But doctors did not yet understand the most basic building block of modern clinical medicine: that symptoms (as reported by the patient), signs (as observed by the physician), and pathology could be correlated. Doctors didn't do a physical exam. They didn't listen to heartbeat or check respiration. They didn't shine small lights in the eye to look for reactive pupils. They didn't even notice what signs were staring them in the face. Beautifully detailed woodcuts from the sixteenth century show semistuporous patients with one dramatically dilated pupil. The artist had rendered this clear neurological sign. Yet all indications are that its importance escaped the doctor on the case. "The artist was more of a neurologist than the doctor," reported Eugene S. Flamm, a neurosurgeon who has also written about the history of medicine. Indeed, through the mid-nineteenth century no one knew that a sign as glaring as a dilated pupil meant that the patient was in imminent danger of an intracranial hemorrhage. (It wouldn't be until 1867 that Jonathan Hutchinson discovered that a dilated, unreactive pupil signified that pressure was building dangerously inside the brain and pressing against the third nerve.) One happy result of medicine's collective ignorance was that at least patients didn't have to travel long distances for treatment. Since doctors didn't need to examine a patient before issuing a verdict on his health, diagnoses could be made by mail.

Perhaps nobody was too troubled about accurate diagnosis because no matter what the illness, treatment was almost always ineffectual. The neurologist possessed pages and pages of supposed remedies, but as one historian concluded, the quantity was more indicative of a "zeal to treat" than therapeutic capability. Whether a person suffered from apoplexy, palsy, or epilepsy, the treatment was a variation on a single theme, which might be quickly summarized: Get the poisons out. One poetic doctor put it this way: "For in ten words the whole art is comprised; Piss, spew and spit, Perspiration and sweat, Purge, Bleed, Blister, Issues and Civster." (Issues are discharges from the skin; clysters are enemas.) Chemotherapy, in the form of potions of roots, herbs, and even fecal matter, was prescribed to increase the flow of menstrual blood, unstop the nose, discharge the bowels, and induce salivation, urination, or sweating. To give some idea of the proportions of these treatments: In 1833, France alone imported 42 million leeches. This worm, which women gathered by wading in ponds and then peeling it off their legs, was used in bloodletting. When William Morton, one of the discoverers of anesthesia, fell ill, he was barely able to stand; his hands trembled so that he couldn't hold anything. His doctors prescribed leeches for his temples, cups for his spine, and ice for his head. (Cups were used to raise blood blisters.) This was in 1868. A more invasive approach to bleeding employed the lancet. With the help of this little knife, patients were bled to the point of unconsciousness. Since doctors before Pasteur didn't understand how infection spread and thus did not sterilize the lancet, the germ-ridden knife may have caused as much disease as it cured. A physician of Cooke's day, noting my symptoms and diligently pronouncing me apoplectic, would have asked himself but one question. *How much* to purge, bleed, cup, or blister.

The breakthrough in neurology that led to a comprehension of brain organization—and also an understanding that my visual loss was a symptom and not a disease—transpired in the latter part of the nineteenth century. That's when medicine first grasped the fundamental organization of the human brain. What is probably most curious is that the concept that would revolutionize the approach to nervous disease was first popularized not by a neurologist but by a figure now in disrepute, the phrenologist. History's most famous phrenologist was an obsessed Viennese physician named Franz Gall, who, it turns out, drew inspiration from an experience he had in 1767, when he was a nine-year-old.

Gall remembered:

> Out of thirty classmates, when it came to reciting by heart, I had always to fear those who, in composition, achieved only the seventh or even the tenth place. As they all had prominent eyes we nicknamed them Cow's Eyes. Later I said to myself, if memory shows itself by physical characteristics, why not other faculties?

Gall, an otherwise respected neuroanatomist, set off on a study of hundreds of human heads. He perused portraits and busts and preserved skulls. A head with an odd bump attracted him as a magnet drew metal. Not only did Gall manage to find territories in the brain corresponding to imitativeness, hope (for both the present and future), love of children, love of animals, wit, and thrift; he came to the position that they could be identified by "cranioscopy," or simple inspection of the shape of the skull, as had been the case with cow's eyes.

Gall's theories were so widely accepted by the general public at the beginning of the nineteenth century—as well as by many doctors—that people literally began to shape their lives around them, or at least the lives of their children. In fashionable circles the ancient Egyptian practice of "head shaping" returned. The Egyptians had applied pressure to the pliable cranium of babies to elongate and flatten them into what was considered a more beautiful shape. In the nineteenth century, the French, equipped with the maps of the phrenologist, intended to sculpt the skull for the development of bravery, moral uprightness, sincere feelings, and intelligence.

This was a wacky start for what would be a cornerstone to modern neurology. Yet Gall, as much as anyone, helped promote the idea that the brain divides its work. Gall's arguments, however, were not founded on accepted experimental evidence.

That was first presented in 1861, the year Paul Broca, a French surgeon, brought before the Paris Anthropological Society the brain of a patient who had suffered a stroke twenty-one years earlier. Since the stroke, he had been unable to speak except for one syllable, tan, which is the name he is given in the medical literature. Six days after he was admitted to Broca's surgical service—with nothing more than an infected leg, it's worth noting—Tan died. An autopsy revealed damage in the posterior half of the second and third left frontal convolutions in the left hemisphere—in the very region, by the way, that one of Gall's colleagues had previously identified as the speech center. Gall had gone overboard, searching out specific brain areas—and corresponding skull bumps—for such clearly social constructs as love of parents, courage, and attraction to wine. But perhaps the abilities that every human was born with, the abilities to speak or to move or to hear that man associated with his throat or his legs or his ears, were indeed mapped onto the brain. Perhaps vision, too, had its spot in the brain. Then perhaps a sudden disruption of vision was a symptom of damage to the brain.

A few years later, German investigators tested this theory of brain localization. With electric current, they stimulated circumscribed areas of the brain of a dog. One time a leg would move, the next time an arm. As

Scottish neurologist David Ferrier said, "A scientific phrenology appears to be possible."

The issue, however, was hardly settled. In fact, the debate was still raging as late as 1881 when the Seventh International Medical Congress in London brought together the world's top medicine men to consider, among many other things, the validity of the claims of localization. It was an extremely productive era for modern medicine. Three thousand doctors, including the hemiplegic Louis Pasteur (founder of microbiology), Joseph Lister (founder of antiseptic surgery), and Rudolf Virchow (founder of cellular pathology), attended what was not only a medical conference but also a Victorian gala. The guest list included 120,000 people, among them the crowned heads of Europe. Soirees and garden parties were part of the schedule; one night, 1,200 people dined at the Crystal Palace. The medical journals of the time read like society pages. Commented one, "Guests have probably found pleasure a harder taskmaster than so-called work."

Amid the gaiety, a bitter battle was fought. Rarely have two sides of a medical controversy been so clearly staked out—and the confrontation so decisive. Friedrich Leopold von Goltz, who had been so eager to start his career that he initially worked at home on frogs he caught himself, believed the theory of localization was a fantasy. Goltz, a physiology professor at the University of Strasbourg, maintained the brain was as homogeneous as the liver. Every area of the brain, he contended, could accomplish every human function. Goltz set out to disprove localization by using a circular drill with cutting edge. "By means of such an instrument it is comparatively easy to remove portions of the brain of any desired size," he said. He planned to take the localizationists at their word. He would systematically excise from the brains of dogs the areas said to govern muscle and sensory control. If the localizationists were correct the animals should be paralyzed and unable to feel any touch.

Before a crowd in the Hall of the Royal Institute, Goltz opened a suitcase and lifted from it the damaged skull of a dog. Goltz was known to be brusque and blustery. But it was with a certain warmth that he seemed to cradle a tiny preserved remnant of the dog's brain. In a normal dog the brain weighs 90 grams. This one weighed just 14 grams. "This dog, whose skull and brain I have here, survived four major operations and was not killed until a full year had passed after the last operation," he explained. The living dog had made no response to men or animals; it was effectively an idiot. But, and this was the crux of the matter, Goltz claimed that nothing remained in this brain fragment of the areas said to control motor and sensory functions, and yet the dog could move and feel.

"Not a muscle of his body was paralyzed, not a spot on his hide robbed of sensation," reported Goltz.

As further proof that the brain did not divide its labors, Goltz had transported to London one of his experimental animals, this one alive. That afternoon at the physiological laboratory of King's College, Goltz paraded the pride of his damaged collection before a gathering of doctors. Goltz boasted of the extensive destruction of the animal's brain. "You can easily thrust several fingers into the huge gaps in the bony structure [its skull]," he explained. The dog, though a little clumsy and a little stupid, wasn't paralyzed. It could taste, smell, see, hear, feel. This "proves beyond a shadow of a doubt that Ferrier's theory is . . . completely wrong," said Goltz.

David Ferrier, a slight man with great energy, had also performed some animal experiments within the past year. Ten months before, Ferrier, in collaboration with a surgeon, had damaged with an electrical cautery a 1-centimenter plot of the middle and ascending frontal and parietal convolutions, believed to be part of the motor-control area, in the brain of a monkey. Six weeks before the same team had cauterized the superior temporal convolution in both hemispheres, the areas said to correspond to hearing, in another monkey.

In the lab, Ferrier invited the doctors to wait as he paraded in the subjects of his experiments. "It's a patient," cried a doctor when he first glimpsed one of the big monkeys dramatically limping before the audience. The other was stone deaf and didn't blink when a percussion gun was set off next to its ear.

Later, Goltz's dog and Ferrier's two monkeys were sacrificed, and a committee of doctors examined their brains. The lesions in the monkeys' brains corresponded exactly to the areas that Ferrier said had been mutilated. But, and this was important, the destruction of the dog's brain was not nearly as extensive as Goltz had believed. It was a clear victory for Ferrier and for localization. (Ferrier soon had another battle. When the congress finished, he was summoned to appear at the Bow Street Police Court under the Cruelty to Animals Act of 1876. He was acquitted.)

Medical journals at the end of the nineteenth century were inundated with reports connecting specific brain areas to particular human functions. There was the area that corresponded to the wiggle of the thumb and the one that governed the lapping of the tongue. Some claimed the brain could have several hundred separate areas, ten times more than the phrenologists had claimed. (Modern estimates put the number at between 50 and 100.) Even personality could be located inside the brain, in the frontal lobes. It could be touched or altered by touch, which was why operating on the frontal lobes—a procedure first tried in 1935—made angry, agitated patients docile. This fabulous idea, that the brain had homes for each of its jobs, would continue to enchant researchers in the neurosciences. In the 1940s, for instance, Wilder Penfield, a Canadian neurosurgeon, placed an electrical probe in patients' brains. He reported that touching an electrode with a three-volt charge to the occipital lobe led to "reanimation of visual images" that a patient had formed in the past. It was as if that memory— a girl from a high school dance, a summer cottage, a particular embrace —was stored there ready to be called up. Each time the probe jolted the spot, the same image floated back. More recently, researchers have located specialized neural systems on the underside of both occipital lobes that are concerned with such specific tasks as recognizing faces.

Localization is the idea that underpins modern neurology, and neurosurgery, as well. Says Charles Ballance, the early twentieth-century surgeon, in his history of neurosurgery, "Till the doctrine of localization of the functions of the brain was accepted no progress in diagnosis was possible." Only after localization was established could the abrupt loss of visual acuity—which was one of my symptoms—be understood as a failure of the brain. And not of the entire brain but of a carefully delimited area.

Which area? In the course of his experiments Ferrier had damaged both occipital lobes in a monkey. He found no loss of smell, taste, or motion, but complete blindness.

The occipital lobe is the area of the brain that specializes in processing visual signals picked up by the eyes and transmitted along the optic nerve. Visual images are first processed in the lobe's outer layer or cortex, whose 150 million nerve cells cover the area of a book of matches. As the result of the work of two young neurophysiologists, the occipital cortex may be the best understood of any of the brain's specialized centers. In the 1950s, David Hubel and Torsten Wiesel of Harvard pushed a microelectrode—a probe small enough to fit into a single nerve cell—into the occipital cortex of a macaque monkey, one of the great apes, the closest relation to man. They then presented the ape with a variety of visual images. With their minisensor they monitored electrical activity. To their astonishment—and the world's—some nerve cells showed increased electrical activity when a tilted object moved into view. In fact, some cells only responded to an angle of 10 degrees, or 20 degrees, or 30 degrees, covering a total of 180 degrees. For some cells, the shape that triggered a reaction was a corner; for others, a tongue shape. (Another researcher discovered that frogs have nerve cells that respond exclusively to an object shaped like—guess what?—a bug.)

Ferrier, the nineteenth-century localizer, could not have scripted a more dramatic illustration of his claims that the brain parceled its labors among specialized units. Still, Hubel and Wiesel warned that more complicated processing of visual data had to go on somewhere else in the brain. Breaking down an image into lines and slants didn't go far toward recreating the complex visual world. "This cannot by any stretch of the imagination be the place where actual perception is enshrined," said Hubel and Wiesel, recipients of the 1981 Nobel Prize in medicine. "It must be a local analysis of the sensory world." Hubel and Wiesel's point is well taken. Those enthusiastic about localization could sometimes get carried away. Yet the important point for the clinician was that localization provided a rational basis for the diagnosis of brain disease. Localization made some of my own symptoms understandable. My occipital lobe had to be a chief suspect. "One fact stands out clearly . . . ," writes A. R. Luria, the Russian neuropsychologist, in his discussion of occipital lobe lesions. "The structure of the visual act is incomplete." Luria suggests one possible scenario: "The patient identifies a particular sign from a complex object or picture or sometimes may manage to pick out a second sign, but he cannot synthesize these signs visually and cannot convert them into the components of an integral whole."

I had gone through a similar experience. In the hotel in Nicaragua I could make out details of objects, could even describe them, but wasn't able to put my detailed knowledge to work. For instance, I was able to see my shoelaces but couldn't understand how to tie them. Indeed, the idea of having to tie my shoes while looking at them was almost unbearably confusing. Here was localization at work! The damaged seeing part of my brain—having been knocked out—was no longer able to send adequate information to the part that controlled fine hand movements. It wasn't that I'd lost the ability to tie my shoes. For when I bypassed the visual center of the brain—by closing my eyes—and gave control of this project to the center where tactile memory lodged, then I was fine. The fingers got the right instructions; my laces got tied. It was the same with telling time, another task I found impossibly frustrating under visual guidance alone. Whatever part of my brain told time couldn't get the data it needed from the visual center. But if I said aloud—circumventing the damaged visual center—that the big hand was on the six and the little hand on the eight, then information got to the time-telling section by way of the hearing system. I could figure out that it was 8:30 at night. Had I only considered more carefully this startling evidence of brain organization at work, I might have puzzled my way through to the root of the problem a long time ago! I might have understood why the problem wasn't lodged in my healthy eyes—and thus why an eye doctor would be (indeed, had been) of little use—but in my compartmentalized brain, which was properly the neurologist's domain. What more than two thousand years of neurology had imparted was a conceptual basis for linking a specific deficit with a malfunctioning part of the brain or, as in my case, a sudden blindness with something gone bonkers in the occipital lobe.

16

Goodgold's arms lay on his desk. A thumb plays with a forefinger, as if he is shelling peanuts. It is the distracted gesture of a loan officer about to reject an application. The history taking done, he wants to see me in action. His is a humorous face, not pudgy, but what is often called "expressive." His cheeks blow out sometimes, and one lip folds over the other. He instructs me to get (almost) naked. My dungarees, frayed at the cuffs, loose at the waist, tumble into a heap. I unbutton my shirt; I can do that now without feeling for the buttonholes. My chest is meatless, my ribs like the keys of a xylophone. I can see my heart beat. Another once-difficult project, unlacing my shoes, comes off without event. The rubber soles drop, clunk-clunk, to the carpet, and I get set for the humiliations of the patient who must cavort around an office in his underpants. I am buffing a foot with a sock when a little sound from Goodgold, a tap from his pen, I think, brings me to attention. Goodgold fixes me with a sidelong glance. He is waiting.

He wants me to walk from one end of the room to the other, turn quickly, and walk back, which I do. I walk a straight line heel to toe, heel to toe, as in a sobriety test. I stand still, heels together. Can I put my arms out? asks Goodgold. I hold both arms in front of me like a diver concentrating before going off the board. Goodgold instructs me to sweep my forefinger around to the tip of my nose as I close my eyes and hold my arms out to the sides. Hard to believe that this digital missile will find its way in the dark. But it does. Goodgold keeps saying, "Good, good," as if I am doing something very difficult and keeps studying me as if I'm a Rodin. It is my nature to respond to encouragement; my inhibitions go. "Hop," he says, putting me through my paces. Enthusiastically, I hop, first on my right foot, then my left, as high as I can, performing. "Good," he says again. He is leaning forward now to get a better view, almost toppling the cute bust of the horse from his desk. To a person who has just exited Kricheff's state-of-the-art setup, it is an incredible idea that this nice man in a plaid suit can test my brain by watching me jump in place. Suddenly, this atechnological routine seems a little silly.

It gets sillier. Goodgold sits me on the edge of the examining table, my legs dangling as though they are cooling in a pool. He taps my knee with a rubber hammer. A rubber hammer! He scrapes the bottom of my sole with a key. It tickles. My foot curls in. What does he make of all this? I have no idea. Machine-free Goodgold is inscrutable. He has me dress, then ushers me back into the chair across the desk. "Smile," he says, and smiles, showing me how. "Stick out your tongue," he says, his own fat tongue drooping from his mouth, as if this were a kid's game of Simon Says. Tongue out, he is the picture of concentration.

Goodgold tells me to stare at his nose. He holds his arms out to the sides, as if spreading wings. He flutters two fingers on each hand. "Tell me when you see my hands," he says, and glides them toward his motionless nose. I cover one eye, then the other. In each case I see the hand to my right before the one to my left. Goodgold has me open my eyes, then close them tight.

There's nothing unpleasant, nothing imposing or scary, and after the menacing report from the CT scan, it's easy enough to to get lost watching a grown man wag his fingers at me like the tail of a happy pup. In the neuroradiology suite a patient senses the imposition of the modern medical apparatus, the one he reads about in the newspapers; in the neurologist's office a patient feels he's reverted to an afternoon of hijinx led by a fellow named Big Al.

Goodgold is not a high-pressure guy. He seems to have an awareness of his own limitations, which maybe the neurological exam gives you. Four years of med school plus a year of internship plus three years of residency and you end up watching people stick their tongues in your face. Later he would explain that at medical school in Switzerland—he hadn't been accepted to a school in the United States—he didn't choose neurology. He studied internal medicine and thought about surgery. "You watch surgeons, they're like kids on a playground; you can pick out the naturals right away." Goodgold, though, wasn't a natural. "It was just like when I was a kid, I had trouble with Erector sets, while my friends were building machines. I couldn't draw a straight line. I had no surgical ability." He excelled at neurology but was a surgical clod. Perhaps, it occurs to me, making a patient toe dance in his skivvies on the office carpet is Big Al's revenge.

17 The neurological exam, ridiculous as it appears to the patient, is no joke. "The nervous system is almost entirely inaccessible to direct examination; the exceptions to this are trifling," said nineteenth-century neurologist W. R. Gowers. What the neurological exam proved was that the nervous system is accessible to indirect examination. Long before the radiologist found a way to prowl around inside the skull with X rays, the neurologist developed a method to track the culprit lesion with circumstantial evidence. That method assumed— just as the localizationists had demonstrated—that the body's movements represented the brain in action. "The good neurologist," says Melvin Yahr, chairman of neurology at Mt. Sinai Hospital in New York, "is able to home in on where a problem is from the moment the individual walks in the door, sits down, starts talking, moves his face."

The person first responsible for transforming this insight into a carefully administered diagnostic tool was probably the nineteenth-century Scottish neurologist John Hughlings Jackson. Jackson was neurology's Plato, said one admirer; he marked "the beginning of that systematic orderliness that now characterizes neurology." But he might just as easily have been thought of as its Sherlock Holmes,* the man who believed intense observation was the key to knowledge. In Jackson's hands, the neurological exam, crude and laughable to the hopping, smiling, winking patient, became a thing of revelation to the doctor.

Unlike his contemporaries, Jackson never did an animal experiment, hardly ever looked under a microscope. Instead, he watched patients. This break with the methods of other neurologists—think, for instance, of neurologist Henry Head, who servered the nerves near his own elbow to learn the effects—was perhaps less a result of methodological calculation than temperament. Head, a leading neurologist of the early twentieth century, carried out his observations over years. Jackson didn't have the patience to tolerate an evening of theater in one sitting; he had to return on two

*It was no coincidence that Sherlock Holmes manifested the diagnostician's ability to draw conclusions from small details. Author Arthur Conan Doyle was a physician, and his character, born in 1887, "was partly suggested by his memories of Dr. Joseph Bell of the Edinburgh Infirmary, whose diagnostic intuition used to startle his patients and pupils," according to the preface of the *Complete Sherlock Holmes*.

different nights. Jackson, in fact, had almost dropped medicine, fearing it would bore him. In 1859, he had decided, as a friend put it, that medicine did not "afford attractive scope for his mental powers." Fortunately, Jonathan Hutchinson—the same physician who had discovered the significance of the dilated pupil—talked him out of quitting. (Later, Hutchinson called *this* the most important contribution of his career.) The upper limit on Jackson's mental endurance, it would seem, was the time it took to examine a single patient. However, with that patient, Jackson was all attentive. He recorded exactly what a patient said and did, every delay, hesitancy, faulty response. The examination was a drama that gripped him, for Jackson believed he was watching, as he put it, "the outward phenomena of an inwardly suffering nervous system."

Never before had it been possible to treat based on the neurological status of the patient. Jackson and other localizationists changed that. One of their boldest claims was that the knowledge gleaned from intense study of symptoms would make possible not only the precise diagnosis but also the treatment of brain lesions. In other words, if you could figure out where in the brain a problem was, you might be able to get at it. In 1884, neurological symptoms (including epileptic seizures and lancinating head pains) led to the diagnosis and localization of a tumor in the brain of a twenty-five-year-old farmer. A neurologist then lobbied a surgeon to operate. (It was more difficult to convince the surgeon than the patient!) "Is there any reason why a surgeon should shrink from opening the cranial cavity, who fearlessly exposes the abdominal viscera?" Ferrier asked. On November 25, 1884, with both Jackson and Ferrier in the audience, surgeon Rickman Godlee opened the skull with a drill and a chisel and began a two-hour operation under the direction of neurologist Hughes Bennett. On the frontal convolution Godlee saw a slight swelling and cut a one-inch-long slice on the surface above it. One-quarter inch below he found a glioma the size of a walnut. Godlee poked in a finger and tried to pop it out. Half broke off. With a sharp-edged spoon he scooped out as much as he could. Later, this operation would be signaled as the birth of surgical neurology. But everyone at the time understood it for it was: the triumph of diagnostic neurology. (One indication that it was diagnosis and not treatment that prevailed that day is the often overlooked fact that the subject of what would be recorded as the first "successful" tumor removal died twenty-eight days after the operation—of an infection related to surgery.)

Led by the doctors at London's National Hospital, Queens Square— where Jackson served for forty-five years—neurology, which probably was dull when Jackson pondered dropping out, moved into an "age of diagnosis." As one historian put it, by the end of the nineteenth century, "inspection became scrutiny." And the neurological exam, refined, expanded, and honed, was the principal tool of the new scrutinizers.

The exam itself was a loose format into which new information could be continually incorporated. Most of the hops, skips, and jumps that a patient is put through are the expression of some neurologist's understanding of how a part of the brain works. For instance, when Goodgold instructed me to put my feet together and balance, he was drawing on Moritz Romberg's insight into the cerebellum. It was Romberg who, in the middle of the nineteenth century, discovered what a revealing test standing still really is. Holding your own ground on a narrow base—without losing balance—requires strength, sensory information about the rate and direction of position change over time, and an ability to make quick adjustments. Most often, if a patient with feet together can't hold himself erect, something is going on in his cerebellum. The Romberg test becomes more difficult when the patient closes his eyes, as Goodgold had instructed me to do. With the eyes shut, the visual guide to posture is lost. The patient may even fall. What then? The neurologist notes to which side the patient plunges! Generally, Romberg had discovered, that is the side of the brain in which the lesion is lodged. (Compared to the Romberg test, hopping in place is a much more sensitive indicator of neurological functioning! If a patient doesn't collapse on the floor or bounce around the room while trying to jump up and down, then the long motor and sensory tracts, the cerebellum, the basal ganglia, the peripheral nerves, the muscles of the hip and lower extremity—in short, much of the nervous system—are functioning.) By 1875, examination of the reflexes had become part of the exam. That was the year the famous knee jerk, which Goodgold went after with his rubber hammer (a tool originally borrowed from chest doctors), made its appearance. For the knee to jerk, the tap of the hammer has to be sensed, that sensation transmitted along the peripheral nerves to the spinal cord and a message returned that sends the quadriceps muscle into action. Diminution or disappearance of the knee-jerk reflex is one sign of polio, a virus that can attack the central nervous system and which had attacked Kricheff as a child. In 1896, the neurologist Joseph Babinski reported that the plantar reflex, a reflex that had been noted for decades, could be employed to test the long motor pathways through the spinal cord and to the brain. If a simple scratch on the sole of the foot causes the patient's toes to extend and spread it is said that

"Babinski is present," which means damage has been done to the long motor pathways. Fortunately, my toes curled healthily inward; Babinski was absent.

Neurologists readily acknowledge the simplicity of their methods but are quick to add: Everybody looks; not everybody sees. The more elementary the tests, the more sophisticated must be the evaluation, goes the argument. "You can teach anybody to do the exam, but how to observe, interpret, put it together into a meaningful business, that's the artistry," said neurologist Yahr. One of the great examples from neurological history comes from Dr. Gordon Holmes, one of Jackson's students at Queens Square. In Holmes's hands, the exam was insightful and dramatic, a bit of medical wizardry as well as medical theater. Once a week, physicians from all over London crowded into an examining room at Queens Square.

One afternoon in 1920, Holmes was caught in action—working with nothing more than a broken stick—by Wilder Penfield, who, as part of his neurosurgical training, studied neurology in England. At the stroke of two, the door burst open, and Holmes entered. For a moment, Holmes, tall, erect, with black eyes and dark curly hair, inspected his audience. When the resident wheeled the patient into the room, he abruptly took the single seat reserved for him in the front row. Wrote Penfield:

> The patient, in a dressing gown . . . was an appealing young Cockney woman. "Notice the smile," Holmes remarked in a clearly audible undertone. "Notice too that the angle of the mouth moves less actively on the left than on the right when she laughs. You remember that she told me she has lost consciousness on several occasions. She told me too that each time she did so, it was preceded by difficulty in finding her words."

From just these few tests Holmes had already elicited an enormous amount of valuable information. He knew that one side of the brain controlled the opposite side of the body. Thus, the faulty smile on the left side suggested a problem with the right side of the brain. The loss of consciousness was not as important as what immediately preceded it: the patient's inability to find her words. This pinpointed the region of the problem in the speech area. What is confusing is that the speech area, as Broca had learned with Tan, was usually located on the left side of the brain, whereas the imbalanced smile suggests a problem on the right side of the brain.

Holmes drew the dressing gown aside and asked her to lean back against the chair. He broke a thin wooden spatula and used the tapering end as a wand to stroke the abdomen.

"When I stroke the skin," he said to us, "here on the right side of the abdomen, the umbilicus moves to the right quite briskly. Not so on the left. There is only a flicker there in the upper quadrant. In the left lower quadrant, the abdominal reflex is absent."

He scratched the soles of her feet with the spatula; glanced back at us, then turned and stroked them, once more, with great attention.

"I think Babinski's sign is present on the left," he said. "The great toe makes a small abnormal movement upward there, but not on the right."

In someone who is healthy, the abdominal reflex is seldom absent. Absence suggests, among other things, a lesion of the spinal cord or disease of the brain on the side opposite the faulty reflex. The presence of the Babinski sign on the sole of the left foot again suggests that something bad is happening on the right side of her brain. Still the puzzle remained: Why should all clues point to a right-sided lesion except one? The loss of speech suggested the lesion was in Broca's area, which is on the left side of the brain. Then Holmes asked a key question.

"Are you left-handed?" he asked the woman.

"Yes," she replied.

This was a crucial response, and after the patient was escorted out of the auditorium, Holmes explained why.

" 'So much to live for, with a husband and two little children! The attacks are epileptic. The cause is a lesion in the cerebral cortex of the right cerebral hemisphere." The cortex, a coating on the folds of the brain, is as thick as two pennies and, flattened out, the size of a doormat, and much of human function is initially processed there. Holmes continued: " 'Like [some] left-handed people, the speech area is in the cortex of the right instead of in the left hemisphere.' "

Then, says Penfield, Holmes drew on the board what he believed to be the limits of the speech area and the pathway of the motor tracts. Even slight interference would cause the left-sided reflex abnormalities he had elicited by scratching the abdomen and the sole of the foot and asking the patient to smile. Unfortunately, he said, there was no treatment; the woman would die.

THIS IS JUST THE KIND of exercise, minus perhaps the showmanship, that all subsequent neurologists would put their patients through, including

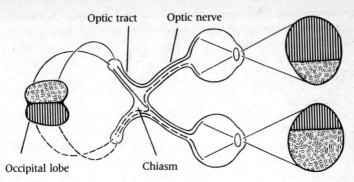

Optic tract   Optic nerve

Occipital lobe   Chiasm

Adapted by Dorothy Holmes from *Pictorial Manual of Neurologic Tests*, 2d ed., by Maurice W. Van Allen and Robert L. Rodnitzky, New York: Year Book Medical Publishers, 1981.

Goodgold. In addition to the Romberg, the knee jerk, and the Babinski tests, a neurologist employs other simple tests to zoom in on other areas of the brain. For instance, Goodgold, like all neurologists, was interested in the health of the twelve pairs of cranial nerves. The seventh controls the muscles of the face. That's why Goodgold ordered the smile. The two sides should move together. If not, as in the case of Holmes's patient, trouble is at hand. The twelfth has dominion over the movement of the tongue, among other things. Thus, Goodgold wanted to watch me stick out my tongue. The second cranial nerve, and one that might particularly interest the neurologist in my case, is the optic nerve, which is actually a grouping of a million nerve fibers. A person can usually see 120 degrees side to side and 130 degrees up and down. Visual acuity through this entire range depends on the optic nerves doing their job, which is to initiate transmission of visual signals from the eye toward the occipital lobe in the back of the brain. One symptom of a malignant tumor of the optic nerve is dimness of vision; another is blind spots. There is a chance that the visual problems I'd reported are not in the brain itself but in the optic nerve. The neurological exam includes a simple way to test this. It's a good example of how a doctor can examine function in order to find where in the brain a problem is located.

Consider first the anatomy of the optic nerve or, really, the optic nerves, since there are two, one for each eye. (See diagram.)

One starts at the left eye, one at the right eye, but as they travel toward the back of the brain they split in half and the inside halves cross one another. From the top, the configuration looks like an "X," or the Greek letter chi. The chiasm (derived from chi) is the centerpoint of the X. In front of the chiasm the fibers are called the optic nerves; behind the chiasm they are known as the optic tracts. Take as an example the left eye. The optic nerve travels from the left eye to the chiasm, where it splits. There the fibers that attach to the outer half of the eye, the left half, continue toward the left part of the brain. But the fibers that attach to the inside half of the eye, the right half, don't. They cross and steer toward the right side of the brain. The same setup occurs in the right eye; the fibers on the inside of the optic nerve cross to the opposite side of the brain. Add one more bizarre neurological fact, that the eye's lens reverses images from the outside world—left is right and right is left—and it becomes anatomically understandable how the right side of the brain is responsible for seeing what is on the left half of each eye.

This anatomy is extremely useful to the neurologist, who wants to know where a lesion is located, or at least where it is *not* located. Think of the two forward legs of the X. On the left, from the chiasm forward, is the optic nerve transmitting signals from the entire left eye; on the right, from the chiasm forward, the optic nerve is connected to the entire right eye. What is now clear is that if disease is located in the optic nerves, that is, in front of the chiasm, then the visual loss will strike only one eye, the one on the side of the disease.

Because the anatomy is different behind the chiasm, so will be the manifestations of the disease. Consider the two rear legs of the X. On the right, behind the chiasm, is the optic tract that sends signals from the left visual fields in both eyes toward the right occipital lobe. On the left behind the chiasm is the optic tract that shuttles signals from the right visual fields of both eyes to the left occipital lobe. Thus, if the neurological problem is behind the chiasm (in the optic tracts or in the occipital lobe), the visual loss will hit part of both eyes—either both right halves or both left halves. This condition is called homonymous hemianopsia.

Goodgold held his arms out to his sides, birdlike, twitched his index and forefinger, and then moved them toward his nose. With my left eye covered, then with my right, I stare at his nose and tell him which set of twitching fingers I see first.

In Nicaragua, my visual symptoms had initially shown impaired sight in both halves of both eyes. It's possible that the rise in pressure inside my head, due to the sudden infusion of almost half a cup of hemorrhagic blood, had widespread effects on both my optic nerves. The Nicaraguan ophthalmologist had gazed into my pupils and diagnosed optic neuritis

—one sign of multiple sclerosis. It's easy to mistake the effects of intracranial hemorrhage for neuritis; in both, the tissue where the optic nerve joins the retina can look swollen and congested. In both, my vision would have been affected. But as my hemorrhage was reabsorbed, it was clear that the damage was localized on one side. Which one? That's what Goodgold was testing by gliding his fingers toward his nose. Which fingers do I see first? In Nicaragua, one doctor had discovered a large blind spot on the left side of my vision—in both eyes. Still I have trouble picking up Goodgold's fingers to the left. In both eyes there is some visual loss to the left. On his initial report Goodgold writes: mild left homonymous hemianopsia. The lesion in my brain, he can conclude, is behind the optic chiasm and on the right, which is consistent with a problem in the right occipital lobe.

Furthermore, the exam revealed that the lesion didn't appear to be part of a degenerative problem or encroaching from the neighboring parietal lobe. Injuries on their border could cause complicated spatial relation deficits. The brain has a position sense; some call it a sixth sense. At any given moment the brain knows where the limbs are and their relation to one another. It is this sense that keeps a person from constantly tripping over himself. If a person could close his eyes and guide his forefinger around to touch the tip of his nose, a lot of his nervous guidance system had to be in order. And that meant the parietal lobe was probably all right. Mine appeared to be fine. The lesion appeared well contained.

Mostly the news was good, given the situation. It was clear to Goodgold that most of my nervous system was working. Some visual loss but no other deficits.

"You're intact," he says to me, as if it is something I don't already know.

Then he unsheathes the CT scans, hangs the negatives on his light screen, and turns his attention from all this hopping and smiling to the Rorschach-like blobs on the clear plastic.

18 Goodgold posts the CT scans on the light box next to his desk. Overriding an hour's examination, his lips make a little motoring sound, and he blurts out, "Oh, boy," a dire phrase that charms me. His tone, in which I hear my prognosis, is not extraordinarily gloomy. It is surprised, which seems so undoctorly. I had been, I realized, preparing myself for the conference that was to come. Be cool, be smart, be reasoned, I was thinking. Perhaps doctors use their jargon and their hurry to shield themselves, too. Goodgold's exclamation, unwieldy and close, something I'd hear during a pickup game or a quarrel, disarms me, I think, because it suggests emotion, which is already what I understand illness to be about.

"That's quite a hemorrhage." Goodgold's history and examination had ruled out quite a few diagnoses, suggested others. The CT scan showed what was there: a clear triangular white wedge in the occipital lobe, in the back on the right.

Lately, the diagnostic game, once so spare in tools, has changed. "Traditionally [diagnosis and localization] has been held in esteem as representing a high order of knowledge and capacity for observation, analysis and synthesis," said the original foreword to *Pictorial Manual of Neurologic Tests*, a neurology textbook published in 1969, not long before the introduction of the CT scan. Yet after a hundred years of sharpening his diagnostic skills, the neurologist finds they are no longer so important. Diagnoses that previously had to be pieced together from obscure symptoms are now available to anyone who can order a CT scan. In an age of computer-reconstructed images, the neurological journals, like ornery Luddites, have turned to talking about fake issues like the overuse of the CT scan. As a group, neurologists demean the technologists, suggesting that technology can be a crutch. A younger generation of doctors, they say, may skip over neuroanatomy because the CT scan is supposedly easy to read. But then, the argument goes, they have no check on the machinery. It's only been in the past thirty years that neurology has become a way to earn a good living. In 1949, the country had only 100 full-time neurologists; others were neuropsychiatrists. By 1984, a hundred years after a neurologist had first talked a surgeon into entering the cranial cavity, there were some six thousand neurologists in the United States. But they were worried. "Is the neurological examination becoming obsolete?" That was the pointed question posed in the April 1985 edition of *Neurology*. Maybe not. But the art of diagnosis had become less artful. Said Goodgold, "It calls for less diagnostic talent today."

The CT scan changes Goodgold's mood. His knuckles dent his chin. Goodgold is impressed with the evidence in a way he has not been while watching my acrobatics. He is not grave. Are doctors ever? Then it's as if in the fraction of a second after their hopes crumble and the good news blows away like confetti and all they can say is "Oh, boy," something else rushes in, a mood strengthener, a distancer. Goodgold turns to me decidedly, exaggeratedly and impersonally upbeat. His hand smacks his desktop. I hear the sound and think of a team breaking huddle. The location is fortunate. It hadn't hit speech or disrupted motor skills, which might have been the result had the blood spewed forth a few inches one way or the other. It is my turn to discover localization. Like most patients, I am stunned that this catalog of abilities associated with mouth or hands is something that could be spoken of as a few inches of brain.

"A little more over here, you could have been paralyzed. Over there, you would have lost speech," Goodgold explains.

We turn over the problem, tweezing out the good news.

"Would it have been permanent?"

"Who knows?" says Goodgold, his shoulders lifting as if he's trying to squeeze through a narrow passage. Medicine, it seems, had taught him caution. "Everything in this domain is probability."

Then he says, "Okay." It's a simple word, another one, but it cuts the air, as if demarcating something. Goodgold has a firm fix on what he can and can't do, and faced with the latter, he is the kind of doctor who shrugs as if to say, "What can I do?"

Neurology is still largely a descriptive branch of medicine. In *A Leg to Stand On*, neurologist Oliver Sacks writes, "It is commonly said: 'You neurologists, you examine but what do you do?' Neurology has no answer to this—it charts impairment of mechanism and function, and hopes that time and nature may effect some sort of cure. But it is essentially a passive science." The neurologist, even at the top of his diagnostic game, can't cure. He assesses the evils and chooses the lesser.

The bright spot for the neurologist is the neurosurgeon, without doubt the most exciting therapeutic development in the neurosciences in this century.

In 1920, Gordon Holmes brilliantly diagnosed the woman's tumor, then consigned her to the mortuary. Holmes hadn't thought the surgeon capable of doing anything but harm—and this to a patient who would surely die. Holmes was probably just being realistic. In his experience, neurologists had urged hundreds of surgeons to undertake surgery on the brain. Examining the results was anything but encouraging. A search of medical journals in 1906 turned up 828 brain-tumor operations, with a mortality rate of 32 percent. Perhaps a one-out-of-three chance of dying made the risk reasonable. But further analysis showed that even in the cases of successful operations, most patients lingered on for a time "paralytic, epileptic, or blind," then succumbed. The general opinion was that real recovery was rare—perhaps 5–10 percent of the time. In 1920, Penfield, commenting on Holmes's performance, had said, "Diagnosis would make it possible to label, and then, at least, to comfort and guide these patients—even if no physician anywhere had, as yet, learned to cure the ailment." Not exactly a medical triumph.

Neurologists, as a rule, still don't rush their patients into surgery. Most neurological disease isn't amenable to surgical intervention. What's more, Goodgold believed, "a surgeon is a plumber." Yet Goodgold also knew that those patients whose disease could be attacked by a surgeon are the fortunate ones. They have a chance at actually putting the illness behind them. And, Goodgold had found, "there are some very good plumbers." In my case, Goodgold was already thinking of which plumber to call.

Much of my visual disturbance had already settled. Would the missing part of vision return? The occipital lobe had taken a blow. A kind of blindness had resulted. Luria, the Russian neuropsychologist, had pointed out that a hemorrhage in the occipital region was the rare instance when "mind blindness" might lift and vision, after passing through "indistinct intermediate stages," might return to normal, or almost normal. The deficit would likely be loss of part of a visual field. How much? It would depend on how much damage had been done and how adaptable the visual brain still was.

Time would tell. So would the course of treatment. Goodgold doesn't share with me his thoughts on treatment. What he mentions is that more tests are necessary. We've got to learn what has caused the spot on the CT film. Then he pushes back from the desk, a gesture that seems to me filled with meaning. The future is what he is pushing back from, leaving it there on the desk. He invites me to do the same. It is as if this disease, this hemorrhage that has invaded my brain and my life, is something I should consider a medical problem for medical specialists. Let's leave it to them. Let's not jump the gun. Let's not personalize it. Session over.

Goodgold will make the arrangements for me to check into the hospital for an angiogram.

Goodgold is another adherent to the theory that I have been lucky. The funny thing is, I feel lucky, weepy and lucky. What would it have been like to lose motor control or speech in that hotel lobby in northern Nicaragua? It is easy to indulge in the terror of what might have been. "Go home and wait," Goodgold says. "The hospital will call when a room is available."

Once they make a full report, doctors grow restless with patients who dawdle. Under the influence, perhaps, of witnessing so much trouble—of participating in it—they forget that to be sick is to be alone. A doctor who has just done the most intimate thing, confirmed to a patient how really sick he is, is no longer *a* doctor, but *his* doctor. I say, "I understand," and nod in tremulous agreement, like a Parkinsonian. But I don't budge. Goodgold has been conversational, not ominous or stern. He put me through my paces, which felt anodyne, and proved to me that I was in control of my body. He has a sense of humor, is easy to get along with, realistic. Yet, by some paralysis of will, I am fixed to this spot. I just don't want to leave his office. I can't imagine waiting at home for the hospital to call—turning home into a waiting room. I can think of nothing more to ask, yet as long as I am seated across from my doctor, discussing symptoms as if they were ball scores, I feel protected, within the reach of expertise. As long as I have my doctor's attention, everything will be all right, as if the whole matter is nothing but an emotional upset, a misunderstanding that he can talk me through.

The doctor, though, has other things he must get on to. "Let's take it one step at a time," he says, and stands. "Let's not rush ahead of ourselves."

I am so changed since the start of the day. Not physically—that had apparently happened weeks ago—but in how I regard myself and my future. How am I going to bring this up in conversation? Goodgold has nothing to add. I rise and with extravagant gesturing pull on my coat. I am dazed; my eyes, again unfocusing, look on the world as if it were a wall. Then, out of nowhere, that nice, goofy man breaks the silence. He begins to sing. He rewords the song "Edelweiss" from *The Sound of Music*. Instead of, "I'm so happy to meet you," he croons, "You're not so happy to meet me."

BY THE TIME I leave the doctor's office, it is evening, my third evening back in America. It is the time of day when the sky is a leathery blue; the streetlights look like holes. There's the city sound, which is a hum and scrape. When I was in college, I sincerely believed that dying would add significance to my life, bring it to a boil. Is that because dying seemed so difficult then? How common it is to die!

Do I take a cab? I must, though I don't remember. It's not like amnesia, just a lapse of concentration. Focus! I shake my head, like a wet poodle's. I plan to hook up with Julie at her apartment on the Upper West Side. I swing by the Grand Union, cruise the wide aisles, load a shopping cart on whim, then abandon it. I don't even feel much. My stomach isn't tight. My voice is flat. Maybe it's just disappointment. I pick out a package of chicken in cellophane, because red meat is bad for you, and a carton of fried frozen potato balls, because Julie once told me that her mother served them for dinner three nights a week. They will make Julie laugh, I think.

When I arrive, having trudged up the four flights of stairs, I put my brown shopping bag on the table only to discover that Julie has already bought chicken. My hand, too long in one position, is cramped. I don't know how to begin, so I don't. I go to the bathroom to wash my face. When Julie asks how the test went, I call out, "Okay."

"What did it show?" she says.

"I had a hemorrhage," I call banally.

I'd forgotten to take off my windbreaker. When I turn from the sink, Julie is in the doorway. Her face is blank, without affect. Her hands are at her shoulders, as if someone has announced a stick up.

"What do you mean, a hemorrhage?"

"That's what the test showed," I say, and push past her. If I can have another second or two, I can control myself. But Julie catches me. Her long arms, the first thing about her I'd loved, are around me, inside my jacket.

Then the phone rings. It is my mom. Always Mom on the phone. She's spoken to the doctor. My parents want to drive in from New Jersey. I tell Julie to tell them no, definitely not.

In the bedroom Julie changes shirts, one after the other, indecisive, the way she is before going out, and cries.

"Why are you so upset?"

"I always cry when I see men cry," says Julie, whose eye makeup is in splotches on her cheeks. Then I squeeze her hand and tell her that I love her, and she lurches like a cat getting out of the way of a car. Is this the truth of this charged moment, or is it more? "And you carried those damned groceries up four flights of stairs," Julie says, tossing away my hand, "that was really smart."

My parents arrive in twenty minutes. The brown paper bag of food remains on the counter, stranded. We go to a Japanese restaurant, take a table by the window, and discuss how lucky I've been. "His mom gave that speech to perk us up," Julie remembered. "She'd found out all the info about it. She said that it was really in the least bad spot. He was really lucky, and everything was going to be okay, and I just cried. It was awful. I was just shocked; it didn't matter what she said."

Part IV

LIFE AND DEATH ON 11 EAST

I would rather die than go to the hospital. Why? Because I hate to be in the hands of strangers. They don't let you take the pills that you know work, then if you need one of their pills, even if you buzz, they don't come. The nurse and three interns are making out in the information booth. I've seen it.

Grace Paley, *Enormous Changes at the Last Minute*

19 Toward one end of the quaint Greenwich Village street on which I live is a food shop that sells chocolate mousse tort with mocha, by the slice; a store that is part suntan salon, part flower mart; and a café that serves plates of charcuterie with lentils vinaigrette. Some of the buildings have been renovated and feature brick facades and gilt-edged porch lamps. One even has a doorman. My building, toward the other end of the street, is in the old style, which is shabby. It has the allure of a shelter for the homeless, who sometimes, in fact, have to be chased out of the entryway.

On the day after the CT scan revealed that a hole had been punched in my brain, I return to this street, walk the fifty-seven bare, cracked stairs, arrive at my apartment, and am distraught. Not over the state of my health but over my living conditions! In Costa Rica I'd rented an apartment twice the size of my New York dwelling, which is, I think, not much larger than the room housing the CT scan. What's more, my Costa Rican abode featured parquet floors and grand, high ceilings. Here the floorboards are unfinished; my imposing ceilings are waffled like the bottoms of cheap shoes. Worse, junk is everywhere!

Perched on a round wooden cable holder—which I've long employed as an end table—I come to a realization, sudden, like a shove: Everything must change. Thus, while waiting for the hospital to call with news that I am a welcome guest, I begin to gut my apartment. The pink-brick and plain-board shelves; the woven straw settee that drops twigs whenever sat upon; the varnished raft of circular wood that serves as tabletop—I drag them all, the inventory of my life, to the center of the tiny living room. My respiration comes in hearty puffs as I add the dresser, whose knobs have long since gone, and the stereo speakers that pick up CB messages from passing truckers. I heap them under the bare light bulb, a ziggurat of secondhand stuff ready to be carted back to the street. I don't stop there. I rip squares of mirrors off the walls; sweep the mantel clear of books, bottles, and samples of my rock collection, leaving only the photograph of Julie, the one with the bow in her hair, which makes her look like Jeannie from "I Dream of Jeannie."

The only furniture to remain is the couch/bed of stacked single baby-blue mattresses, for, I reason pragmatically, I need a place to sleep; and my desk. It is seated behind the grainy desk top that I intend to begin work on my Nicaragua story.

Grandly I lick a finger and turn the pages of a notebook. Lots of action, little purpose. In fact, I do nothing but count. The steam heat ratchets like a carpenter's tool. My eyes circle the plundered apartment as if on patrol. There is in serious illness the sense of helplessness, but from the very start this thing also imposes itself on my schedule, and dominates my attention, like a kind of hypnotism.

It is the ring of the phone, shiny like patent leather, that breaks the spell. Although I have been expecting nothing else, the sound transfixes me. For a moment I watch the phone ring.

Julie's voice is dry, twiggy, and a great relief. She sounds distant, like an overseas transmission, as if I'm still in Nicaragua, checking in. Our phone bills to and from Central America were outrageous, but she wanted to hear the details of my exploits, and I wanted to tell her. "I want to know," she says, her voice itchy, careful, "if I should bring Chinese over for lunch?"

I am saturnalian, pumped up. Merrily, I decline, as if to say, Why the special treatment? "I'm organizing the place a bit," I announce, which elicits a complacent chuckle, since that is what Julie had goaded me to do since the first time I'd led her, after persistent entreaties, up the four flights to what I'd long billed as my pied-à-terre. I remember she had swallowed dyspeptically and, gathering her coat with both hands, fallen onto the three mattresses, stacked during the day as a couch. Her wrist had tilted toward the half-sized tub perched next to the kitchen sink. "Is that," she had said, "where you shower?"

"Bathe," I corrected, impish.

Julie had been scandalized, I know, but then her droop perked, like a pup tent when the stakes are set. "A fix-'er-upper," she had pronounced kindly.

"Don't overdo it," she tells me over the phone, fake huffy, then laughs at herself and her stern posturing. Julie, I think, laughs easily, which brings out her cheekbones.

"Of course not," I assure her, enacting the self-sufficient, a form of the imperviousness I would like to achieve.

Mom phones next. Neither she nor Dad had wanted me to leave the United States in the first place. Two years ago, when I'd departed for Africa for a year, they hadn't been crazy about that trip, either. But they, who in their lives had gotten right to work, also envied me. Dad saved my letters in a manila folder and circulated them to relatives. Central America, however, didn't arouse envy. Enough already. What was so bad with marriage, with raising kids? Hadn't we done okay? They wanted to see me with mortgage bills, no longer a renter. This turn in my health seems like an argument for their side. "If you ever leave again," Mom had said when I returned, "I'm going to kill myself."

I take the offensive and ask how she is doing.

"Keeping busy," she says, fighting the dirge. We all have a piece of one another now. I am not marching to doctor's orders but to everyone's. That's what illness does to a family that is close. Everything anyone says from now on is measured for its effect on the general mood. Our conversations are bowdlerized, monitored for tone and content. Sickness's tyranny begins, and we fall in lockstep, divvying up the work of worrying, all the while exchanging lusty "goooods" and "fiiines" as though we are cheering from the bleachers.

"Change any lives today?" I say. My mother and father own and run a school that helps kids in need of remediation.

"Damn straight," she says, and launches into a tale of a kid she's taught to read, a tale that I don't follow.

My mother called from the second floor of the school. My father calls from the first floor. My brother Dave, a computer programmer, calls from his job. Lenore, my sister, is the only one not to check in. She is away in Europe, and purposely kept in the dark.

I return to my desk and stare at the brick wall off of which someone did a mediocre job removing the Sheetrock. We are all of us negotiating in narrow emotional straits. My public voice, salutary and strong, is a fake. Doesn't anyone notice? My former life is warehoused behind me, and I am listless, overtaken. Over the sink in the kitchen is a medicine chest. The workman cracked the mirror the day they installed it. On either side of the crack the glass forms a right-angled triangle. My face, in the left triangle, looks the same as always: narrow, weak chinned, anchored by a nose the shape of a hitchhiker's thumb. "You look like you just got out of a concentration camp," Mom had greeted me, her palm rubbing the side of my face, her tone full of bonhomie. She possessed exaggerated ideas about weight, though perhaps the cheeks are a bit sunken. The color is a little sallow, olivey. And my glasses—always there now—the tortoiseshell frames, broken like an ice chip and then taped together, are too big. Like loupes they distort the face, give prominence to the brushed-blue eyes, turning them a little comic, and make the effect on the whole, I have always feared, a bit feminine. But not sick, not harboring some bloody misdeed. Cancer turns up one day as a lump or a brown splotch. A hemorrhage hides in a headache. How paltry is experience! Why, it takes a doctor to explain the meaning of what you feel.

I prop a mattress against the wall, throw punches at it as if it is a heavy bag, and feel awful. It bucks with my blows. The stuffing is coming out one end in wads, like cotton candy, but it is not my doing. It is the mildewy age of the thing. Something cataclysmic has happened, but the lesson here seems to be the slightness of my impact.

When five o'clock arrives, I believe that my chances of hearing from the hospital today have passed. That is why when the phone rings, my tone is full, let out, and why, when the voice, identifying itself by its function, says, "This is admitting," I am confused. I have thought that this would go away, if not by direct action, then by inattention. But hospitals, it seems, are like casinos: they are open around the clock. "This is admitting from University Hospital," continues the voice. A room is available, but it is a private room. Private hospitals, like NYU's University Hospital, make their money by catering not only to the medical but also to the social needs of patients. Someone who prefers to bunk by himself must pay $100 more than the fee that standard health insurance covers. I ask for a few minutes to think about it. After all, this isn't an emergency. "Don't wait too long," says the voice.

I call Kricheff at his office. I don't want to spoil our relationship, which is that of adult to adult, so I preface my question with an inquiry about *his* family. Then I suggest that I think I'll just stick it out until a less expensive room comes available. Kricheff is not so tactful. "You have an irritation in your brain," he says. "You shouldn't be walking around the streets." The redecorating will have to wait.

SINCE I HAVEN'T BEEN in a hospital in a long time, I ask admitting what I should bring. "A toothbrush," says the voice. "We supply the rest." In my brown bag, one of those with which I'd toured Central America, I pack a toothbrush and half a dozen books, imagining that the hospital will be a quiet place in which to get some reading done.

The admitting offices are in a section of the lobby of this 878-bed hospital. By the time I arrive, the lobby is peopleless. The overhead lights have been turned off, and the day's rush is over. This isn't a bad time to check in. There is no line. In fact, I am the only person sitting in the Naugahyde chairs, which are a shade of licorice-red I have never seen in furniture. Behind me is a hedge of leafy plants set in wood chips. The only signs of life are the signs posted on the walls. "Institute of Reconstructive Plastic Surgery." "Varsity Club Center for Craniofacial Rehabilitation." "Lila Motley Radiation Pavilion," and in stylish forest green, "Do something useful. Take a break. Give blood." Each heralds a medical triumph, no doubt, but as I wait in the half-light, my imagination sticks on the catastrophes that must necessarily precede something as wonderful as craniofacial reconstruction. One sign does stand out from the others as unalarming. Is it a joke? "Balloons," it reads, "are not permitted on patient floors. Thank you."

There are half a dozen cubicles, each featuring a computer, floor-to-ceiling blinds, and portable walls, a layout synonymous with grinding paperwork. The officer who beckons me into the end cubicle is polite and even nice. It seems to me, though, that he is overdoing it a bit in his dark blue dress-for-success suit. Is this the starting gate for a man on the way up? Maybe not. He asks me how to spell journalist. Then he clamps a plastic ID bracelet on my wrists. "Just in case," he says, breaking the mood. In case of what? In case I lose consciousness or am delirious or decide to lie about my name. ("No, give *him* that operation!") Does the hospital believe it is accommodating the ill by letting them know that, like children, they aren't held responsible for remembering their own names?

Julie arrives, flowers cradled in her slender arms, her eyes shining. I don't see fear there or an eagerness to escape. "Flowers for the hospital room," Julie says, and I think, Julie thinks of everything. She isn't generous, but extravagant. Without fail she'd fight for the check even if it meant borrowing cash the next day. I let out a sigh and realize I'd been holding my breath for some time. The flowers are long-stemmed red roses, and they are beautiful. Yet the idea of adorning a hospital room, which is a way of claiming it as my own, makes me sick to my stomach. We need balloons. "Yeah," says Julie, "I saw that sign, too. Isn't it weird?"

Because it is after 5:00 P.M., the clerk can't contact the insurance carrier to verify the extent of my coverage, which will turn out to be a big break for me. (I know my coverage is limited, *very* limited.) He marks my admission slip "emergency" and hands me a square booklet printed in violet and white, NYU's colors and about the size of a 45 rpm record. It is called "Getting SET" and is "designed to help patients make the most of their stay." There are sections on bedside barber services, the gift shop (for "anything you may feel 'caught without' "), and Pap smears for women over twenty-one.

When I enter 11 East, which is the neurosurgical floor, it is early evening. "Getting SET" is no preparation for this. Nurses, working in groups, lift the bedridden into wheelchairs and roll them into the corridor, where they can take in the sights while being fed dinner. Passing one of these patients is like coming across a skull and crossbones that warns against entry. One man can't hold his neck upright or catch the food that flops out of his mouth. Another pokes a finger at his plate, while some kind person, his wife, maybe, bends at his side and asks, "More?" The ambulatory patients aren't much cheerier. A man in a bathrobe moves ahead at half pace, pushing a metal walker conscientiously in front of him, a foot at a time, as if measuring out distance. A woman, a round, bloody drain hanging from her bandaged head like an extra ear, marches down the hall, concerned, it seems, to just keep moving. Some patients wear thick gauze head dressings; the evening strollers favor oatmeal-colored stockinettes, the neurosurgical headgear that I realize is supposed to hide the hook-shaped scars but which in fact only advertises them. Facing the slack legged, the weak, the unresponsive, I consider for an instant calling the whole thing off. I am terrified, not of my disease but of the cure.

At the nurse's station, a young nurse says to me, "Oh, hi, we've been expecting you," and to her colleagues, "The admission is here. I'll take care of him." The nurse's face is doll pretty, and her voice is squeaky, also like a doll's. She is buxom and exudes friendliness as well as busyness. She says, "New patients always want to know, 'Am I going to look like them?' " I don't want to hear the answer. Just don't let any of them come near me. She leads me to a room with an empty bed, points out a locker, urges me not to keep any valuables there, and then says, "Okay, I guess you might as well get changed." Have I brought pajamas? I haven't. The nurse fetches a pair of the hospital-issue nightclothes. The blue pants hang off me like clown's pants. The smock top has only one button in the back. She locates a thick insulated wire that dangles from the wall and attaches it to the bed rail. If I want anything, I should push the button at its tip, she says. Then she leaves.

I know by now that my headaches and blurred vision were caused by a brain hemorrhage that occurred two weeks ago. That seems to me a well-defined problem. Some tests will be done, a faulty part found, and the necessary repairs done. My metaphors are automechanical. I know that I am lucky to be in a top medical center. One thousand patients come to this floor's thirty-four beds every year. The popular wisdom is that this is the place where miracles happen, this is where lives are saved. But I don't need a miracle. I am counting on a short visit. My admission form specifies seven days. I am here for a tune-up.

I am not the type to fret about patients' rights; I don't feel that I'm being mistreated. Yet, during my first fifteen minutes in the hospital, my status has slipped. I've stored my clothes, given up my valuables, and traded my independence for a call button. My room, aseptic yellow, offers a spectacular view of the East River, but I notice the latches have been removed from the windows; it's impossible to open them. I don't know what to do with myself. And so, though it is much too early to go to sleep, like all the others, I climb into the narrow bed with the metal gates. I wait for Julie, who has gone off to find us some dinner.

20 My first morning in the hospital I awake at seven. Rather, I am awakened. A short man with either an olive complexion or a great tan is fiddling with my arm. He is not embarrassed when I jerk away my limb and hug it prudishly to my ribs. He needs blood, he says, as if that should ease my alert. He is impatient, but I am still drowsy, not oriented in space or time, merrily dreaming I am somewhere else. "You could have asked?" I say. Turning to me, he snaps on my bedside TV—the news. He adjusts *its* arm—a mechanical one—to his liking. "I hope you don't mind," he says blandly and prepares to wait me out. But I do, I do. What to the hospital staff is daily routine calls for a leap of faith on my part.

Every few minutes he floats his hand under my nose, palm open, close enough for me to sniff, until finally I swing my arm slowly across the bed and drop it, like a cigarette ash, into his hand. He ties a rubber hose around the bicep. He taps the inside of my elbow with his finger as if flattening a lump. He works silently over the spot where my arm is the widest and the veins the bluest, until a news report is broadcast from Lebanon. "You know what they should do with the whole fucking country?" he says without looking up from my arm. "With the whole fucking region?" He selects a vein and slides in a needle. "Murder them. Murder every living one of them." My blood, which is cordovan, like penny loafers, fills the tube at the end of the syringe. He presses a cotton ball to the wound and withdraws the needle. "That wasn't so bad, was it, now?" he asks.

To the hospital this is a facet of monitoring, the bedrock of good care. To the patient it is part of a scheme to invade his privacy and his person. Nurses constantly remind me to "void" into the yellow plastic container whose handle fits over the rail at the end of the bed. They pass by like searchlights, rattle the jug, point into its mouth, and say, "Don't forget, now." They measure the quantity of liquids I put out and, gazing arithmetically at the leftovers on my food tray, calculate the quantity of liquids that I take in—one Jell-O is 100 cc, one ice cream, 120 cc. They examine my urine, my feces. They test my blood ten times for, among other things, its type, its red blood cell count, white blood cell count, coagulation ability, sedimentation rate, oxygen level, even its syphilis content.

A little after 7:30 A.M. the residents show up in a group of six. These early risers are the surgeons in training, doctors who work for the attending surgeons. They are responsible for the hour-to-hour medical care. They dress as if they are still in college, corduroy pants and knitted navy-blue ties under white coats; a couple show up ready for action in blue surgical scrubs. Out of one shirt pocket a card is visible: Glasgow Coma Scale, a guide for determining just *how* comatose a person is. Even death is something that has to be translated by someone else. The brain might be dead, after all, while the chest thumps with vigor. ·

My first reaction to the young doctors is delight. Bunched around my bed in a medical scrum, they make me feel important. They appear very concerned, very competent, even friendly. I think that because they are my age, we will have a conversation. I am not hostile, demanding, or litigious, I want to say. Talk to me. And what if they responded, Okay, what is it you want to know? Would I grab a white sleeve and ask, as one patient asked, "Tell me the truth, Doc, how long do I have?" Or, angrily, would I say, as I heard another patient say, "I just want to know if I should invest in having my clothes altered?" My questions would be pointless, a rehearsal of private fears. And yet I feel that they know more than I do and more than they are telling. I am in an alien culture, one in which, it dawns on me, I don't even feel comfortable asking for help.

The chief resident, with a boyish face, asks how I'm doing. One resident taps a pen on my bed; another holds a clipboard. None sit. One nods, tells me I'm doing fine. This is bedside manner: pleasantries, a suggestion of taking time out from a hectic schedule. It occurs to me that they really believe they are competent listeners, open-minded. I want sincerity but get manner, which is a subject matter to be learned, like any other on the curriculum. These residents are task oriented, disease oriented, skill oriented. Right now they are exercising empathy. It's true, says a study of doctors, that overwhelmed by facts and scientific explanations—seemingly the real guts of medicine—physicians probably unconsciously draw a line beween the sick and themselves. "In fact, most medical students are not as interested in the humanistic aspect of medicine as in the purely biological, the implication being that [the humanistic] cannot cure, and the human bedside manner and all the rest of the psychological elements can be acquired when needed at a later stage in real medical practice."

The chief asks me to follow his finger with my eyes and asks when my last headache was. Then they turn to each other and talk about me in the third person. I am like a Kremlin watcher trying to shake loose the *real* story from what they don't say, the inclination of their heads, the hush of their tones. The chief resident points out what needs to get done; the resident with the clipboard—whose nameplate says Dr. David Chalif—jots it down. Chalif is a junior resident, and the one who must see that the chief's orders are executed. At the foot of my bed, the chief says, "Let's get his IV started. He's scheduled for an angio as soon as they have room for him." It is a kind of nonexistence that they bestow. Don't worry, we'll take care of it, they seem to say. A patient has two choices: to trust or to go to pieces. The huddle breaks, and they follow their chief toward the next bed. I call to him, the one in charge. When does he think the angiogram will take place. "You're Kricheff's nephew?" he says. "You probably have more influence than I do."

It is fair to say that despite the uncertainties of diagnosis or prognosis that loom over time in the hospital, all is not dreary. When I manage to settle back in my movable bed, which folds at the knees and raises behind my back, when I am able to accept that things are proceeding just as they should, then there is an element of comfort in the hospital's routines. The staff marches in and out on dutiful missions. All these people ministering to my needs; bringing me food, taking away my urine. I am relieved of all responsibility. Sickness isn't only estrangement and pain. At its core is an invitation to respite. I experience this aspect of my condition as the most seductive pleasure. I had trudged around with that pain in my head for how long? It might have been my whole life. Then a doctor said, "You're sick," and it was, for me, as if the whole imploring world, pacing at my door, had been told to cool its heels. I feel unburdened. All my inabilities—whether to see clearly or to get ahead—are forgiven. "Leave him alone," says the doctor, echoing my secret thoughts. "It's best to keep the pressure off." I think every sick person must discover a portion of happiness in his disease.

Over any length of time, though, the pleasure fades. A patient who imagines he is being catered to soon realizes he is subject to the order, not master of it. Patienthood becomes a torment. My day is circumscribed by a series of inconveniences, of limitations that I have never before felt. It's not just the prick of the syringe but the fact that I can't do what I want.

It's a question of life-style. At the outset I am not worried about my chances of leading a normal life. What concerns me is that no one knocks on the door before entering my room and that they want me to live like those grim, shuffling figures with socks on their heads.

One day in the hall a nurse tells me to get back to bed. I tell her my doctor says it is all right to walk around. She turns to another nurse, "Is he allowed out of bed?" For someone accustomed to being treated like an adult, being a patient is difficult. To be a patient is to be helpless, not because of physical inability but because of how the system has been calculated. For those employed there, the hospital is a very busy place. If you are a patient, no initiatives are expected; none tolerated. Are you confined to bed? Do you have "bathroom permission"? The nurse doesn't ask you; she refers to your chart.

21 Someone who visits even the most sophisticated medical institutions today expects a kind of low-grade mistreatment. Is this due to bad faith on the part of the care providers? Or budget cuts? Or is it something that inheres to the status of patienthood? Why are capable, commanding people, once they become patients, promptly intimidated by hospital surroundings? Is there a patienthood that is different from personhood?

In the 1950s, Talcott Parsons, a sociologist and shrewd observer, proposed the "sick role," one of the cornerstones on which all subsequent medical sociology has been built. Parsons looked at sickness not as a set of pathological syndromes but as a way of getting on in the world. He considered that, like the role of parent or spouse, being sick is a role with established parameters of behavior. It carried privileges—primarily that a patient could legitimately opt out of activity and responsibility—and duties, in particular that the sick person endeavor to get well.

Outside the hospital a person has some leeway in deciding how he will assume the sick role. For instance, someone with a cold or a headache might decide to forgo it entirely. Only one in three people who reported illnesses in a household interview actually sought a doctor's advice. Estimates from the same kinds of surveys indicate that only 9 of 750 of those who reported illness ended up in hospitals. Even if a person believes himself sick, he has other priorities for which, outside the hospital, he may reject the sick role. One respondent to a study said: "Sometimes I've felt so bad I could curl up and die, but I had to go on because the kids had to be taken care of, and besides, we didn't have the money to spend for the doctor—how could I be sick . . . ?''

Once inside the hospital, though, the person loses the freedom to decide when or to what degree he will assume the sick role. Inside the hospital, roles are strictly enforced. They are color coded. The nurse is in pastel or white, housekeeping in yellow or brown. Those in the blue uniforms bring in the food trays. Doctors, of course, wear white, as do the technicians who draw blood. And those in pajamas, cut off from the gay sociability of the doctors and nurses, are the patients. If it is true, as Parsons says, that the sick person has no responsibility, it is also true that in the hospital this is not necessarily the result of a choice he has made. The patient may in fact want to take on some responsibility. That is not within his power. He decides neither when to rise in the morning nor when to eat nor, in some cases, when to go to the bathroom. It might, on first consideration, seem that the sick person naturally seeks the sick role and the hospital only accommodates the patient's desires; however, on closer inspection it is clear that the hospital, having created the sick role, then enforces it. The nurses and doctors and the larger health apparatus of the institution allow the patient no choice but the sick role.

In an investigation at a well-run 850-bed hospital, sociologists Daisy Tagliacozzo and Hans Mauksch set out to examine patients' sick-role experiences. In Parsons's formulation the role doesn't sound all that bad. A patient doesn't have to do anything except try to get better. The reality of the sick role in the hospital, the two sociologists found, is much harsher. At every turn they discovered fear, insecurity, and isolation. Nurses were seen as too busy and doctors as much too busy by patients who feared they would be, from one moment to the next, in urgent need of care. As a result, patients were afraid to even claim the privileges that the sick role is supposed to grant. "You dare not ask a question; you know, they're too busy. And they come around, 'Fine, that's it, we'll see you next time,' " said one patient. A patient experiences his condition as a loss of control, since everyone else in the hospital is too busy to accept the responsibility he might like to give up. The sick role is not part of a melodrama the complaining patient concocts; it is something he suffers, like his disease.

One thing that their research led Tagliacozzo and Mauksch to question was why the patient is so accepting. Why doesn't a patient demand the rights of a paying consumer? Why, for instance, doesn't a patient who is paying an astronomical sum of money—enough to pay for a stay at the Plaza Hotel—to share a room with a stranger consider that he can *demand* a nurse's attention when he presses the call button?

Parsons didn't entertain that question. In part, perhaps, because as an observer he didn't see patients raising it. In part because the model Parsons used for understanding the sick role did not lead him to such an interrogation. He did not look at the issue of being sick from the point of view of the individual patient but from society's. Illness, in this view, is a type of deviation from the norm, a deviation that in large numbers could have grave implications for the very survival of the society. If half the population calls in sick, the other half will be doing little more than working to support them. The doctor's role is to cure disease, sure, but it is also to reintegrate the temporarily incompetent back into society; to reduce the millions of dollars that sickness costs America in lost workdays. "The individual who is incapacitated from performing his role-functions would be a disturbing element in the system if he still attempted to perform them," writes Parsons. "Hence we may say that it is important to have some way of preventing him from attempting to do so, both in his own interest and in that of the system itself." Medicine, reasoned Parsons, is a form of social control. "The practicing legal professions may be said to carry out functions of social control . . . which are in some ways parallel to those of the medical profession in the field of health," says Parsons.

If this sounds less like the goal of a luxury hotel and more like the goal of a maximum security prison, it's no coincidence. Certainly the sick aren't condemned for the same reprehensible acts that criminals have committed. But moral judgments aside, it's clear that our activist society believes that both these sets of citizens hamper the machinery of progress. Rehabilitation is a term we apply to both groups. Criminals are to be rehabilitated in institutions called prisons, patients in institutions called hospitals. The institutionalization of illness, like the institutionalization of crime, is a fact of life, as a patient is aware from the moment the ID bracelet is clamped on his wrist. "You're no more . . . no more a patient but just a number . . . ," says one of Tagliacozzo's patients. Perhaps not a number, quite like the inmate who wears it on his back, but something less than a customer who can call the front desk for service. Something like a case, perhaps, as one resident referred to a patient, "that big meningioma that just came in." In either institution, patient or inmate is at the bottom of the hierarchies of responsibility, trustworthiness, and competence. "The role of illness tends to place him in a position of *dependency on* persons who are *not sick*," observes Parsons (his emphasis). By virtue of past acts or current afflictions (a history of murder or a clot in his occipital lobe), it is considered that he doesn't know what is best for himself. He is disqualified from making decisions about his future, long-term as well as immediate. An expert, doctor or warden, must intervene if he is to be rehabilitated and returned to society. He, patient or inmate, is valued most for his cooperation, which means he simply doesn't cause problems.

The dilemma of the modern medical establishment, it is repeatedly stated, is that at a time in history when medicine can do more for a sick person than ever before, patients are less appreciative. Opinion polls and malpractice suits show patients distrust those who treat them. It has been argued that the technologization of medicine, with its unparalleled advances in diagnosis and cure, has sadly taken the human touch out of medicine. The kindness of the GP went out with the CT.

Is it the million-dollar diagnostic machines that have crowded out the kindness? Or is it rather that medicine, and hospitals in particular, are stuck in antiquated behaviorial models that conceptualize care the same way as any large institution for managing deviance?

Are there alternatives? Yes.

A host of hospitals, most of them smaller and private, have attempted changes. They have upgraded the quality of the food and dressed up the staff that serves it. Some are building new facilities, heavy on private rooms and outfitted with real furniture. Clearly this is an attempt to change the role of the sick in the hospital. Rather than treat the patient as a "control problem"—how many times are patients labeled "complainers" or "difficult"?—why not assume the patient is someone to be pleased, for instance, a consumer in a facility that sells itself on its personal touch? In one hospital in California the adminstrator has a policy of greeting new patients in person. He invites them to call him with any complaints. It is an admitted bit of salesmanship, distasteful to some in the medical community but consistent with an attempt to cast the patient in a new role: someone who can demand service. Perhaps this is not the way that all institutions should go, but it does affirm the possibility of establishing new roles.

There is nothing to do! The usual rhythms of work and relaxation no longer hold. It seems that all I do is wait. I wait to take the tests, to learn the results, to be treated, not understanding why I should be stricken or by what scheme of things I am to get better. My plight is not the toughest one.

The more care the patient requires, the greater the subjugation he experiences. One of my roommates for a couple of days is Leonard,* an immigrant from Russia who owns an auto-parts store in upstate Connecticut. He is a big man in his sixties with a flat chest and skinny legs who has had a brain tumor removed. The stitching on his shaved head makes me think of the seam on a football.

The swollen postsurgical brain can leave a person temporarily impaired. There is a special excitement in looking on as a faculty returns over a period of days, though sometimes, of course, it never does. Immediately after his operation, Leonard cannot talk, and so he cries. Perhaps he doesn't understand that he will be able to speak again. His son says that with all his hair cut off, Leonard looks like a marine. He also tells his father, ''The doctor said the operation went very, very successful. So just relax. Stop crying. Mom, can you clean his nose a little bit?''

The wife says, ''Leonard, you'll be yelling at me in a few days.''

Leonard's more pressing concern is with his bowels. Though he is unproductive in the bathroom, he constantly feels the need to go. During the day, when his family is not there and Leonard wants to make a trip to the bathroom, he presses the call button for a nurse. The nurses assure him that someone is on the way, but it takes so long. In the hospital a patient must constantly fall back on his own resources. Most of the hospital staff have other things to do besides tend to what they deem a patient's noncrucial call. University Hospital has hired social workers to whom patients can talk about their disease and their treatment. But these professionals can't undo what hospital life does. Decades of routine, designed to make things easier for the staff—restricted visiting hours, no privacy, pajamas—serve primarily organizational, not therapeutic, ends. With control over his life, and also his body, preempted, the patient may have to assert himself to get what he wants, which is what Leonard does.

He simply can't wait for the nurses. He reaches around and unlatches the railing, climbs out of bed, and starts out, another difficult migration. He leans on a tabletop, which, like most hospital furniture, is on wheels and skids away. He props himself against the wall and pushes off. From my side of the room, from behind the curtain that passes for privacy, I hear banging as the railing falls, then furtive animal sounds. I spot Leonard leaning on the wall, making his way hand over hand toward the bathroom. What a fierce old man! I rush to take his arm, to lead him like a dance partner the dozen feet to the bathroom. They have already threatened him: If he doesn't stay put, they will put him on a bedpan, a humiliating portable

*Leonard's name and details of his identity have been changed.

potty. Leonard wants the dignity of the toilet, even if it doesn't yet work
for him.

He accepts my hand without expression. I wonder if he even knows
I'm there. Or does he think I am a hospital employee? I tell him to signal
me and I will help whenever he wants. He is as responsive as a tree. Or
is it that he knows but is unable to respond? Or is this his pride's silence?
How does it feel to be sixty and incontinent? I huff down the hall and
locate a nurse, Jacqueline Mawby, who is one of the head nurses. I am
upset; my hands work the air as if I'm slapping water onto my face. In
truth, this man with the railroad tracks up his scalp grosses me out. He
smells. What's more, I am afraid of him. "I don't want the responsibility,"
I tell her. "Someone has to get there to help him. What if he falls!" Mawby
is pretty without affectations, a clean, unmade-up look. She wears one of
the 11 East nursing buttons, "Neurosurgical Nurses: It takes nerve and
brains." She understands. Nobody wants that to happen, she says. "Can
you imagine what it's like to not be able to speak?" she says as if to herself.
She is tall, perhaps six feet, and bends her head toward me, which suggests
candor. She'll look into it, she promises. I return to bed.

Nothing changes. Though they call him "Love" and "Honey" and are
afraid he'll spill onto the tile floor, the nurses don't seem to be able to get
to Leonard in time. And Leonard, whatever his reason, does not turn to
me. His ring unanswered, his bowels moving, he makes his own unsteady
way once, twice, more. Finally, two exasperated nurses—"Honey, you are
going to hurt yourself," they implore him—put him in a restraint, a strait-
jacket, so that poor, speechless Leonard, now safe from falling, is tied to
a chair in the corner of the room, where he cries. And for all my
concern—and how much is it really?—I feel like a coconspirator, abetting
in this abuse.

23 How could this happen—a patient straitjacketed because no
one can walk him four yards to the bathroom? How could
a nurse let it happen? Head Nurse Mawby, thirty-seven, knows
exactly.

Mawby had decided on nursing because of a childhood experience:
the helplessness she had felt when her grandmother had been sick. As a
nurse she would be taught how to make people better. "I chose nursing
because I care for people," Mawby says. "I like helping them and teaching
them." Yet that wasn't always how it worked out on 11 East. "Day in and

day out you see a lot of very sick patients, a lot of emotional trauma, and on this floor a lot of times you know what is waiting at the end," says Mawby. What was waiting was deterioration and death, no matter what you did. Joseph Ransohoff, chief of neurosurgery, a tyrant who nonetheless had Mawby's respect, once told the American Association of Neurosurgical Nurses:

> Are there special problems which we who treat diseases of the nervous system must face with our patients? The answer to this question is an obvious yes. . . . Progressive loss of brain function leads obviously to personality changes, deterioration in judgment, the ability to conceptualize, and often prior to the development of frank speech and cognitive disturbances a host of more subtle phenomena as well as plegias and eventual coma.

What's more, nurses' duties on 11 East challenged their physical resources. It took two nurses to move one 150-pound patient who was paralyzed on one side of the body. To shift a heavier patient into a wheelchair, three or four nurses might be needed. A nurse didn't get into the field to lift heavy objects. What compounded these pressures was what Mawby discreetly calls the hospital's emphasis on "the business" of medicine. Mawby is extremely, almost sentimentally, sincere. And though she endeavors to be diplomatic, to hold to lines of authority, her politeness can break down when it challenges what she really feels. "I'm more comfortable speaking from the heart than the head," she says, folding her hands tightly, pinching the knuckles. The floor was understaffed—a chronic problem on many nursing services. As a head nurse responsible for personnel scheduling, she witnessed the effects. In 1984 she had twenty-five nurses to provide twenty-four-hour-a-day care 365 days a year. Every nurse got six weeks off—a month's vacation and two weeks of holidays —plus two free days a week. That worked out to an average of five people available for each shift. The ICU, which housed the sickest patients, could require as many as four nurses for just seven beds. And there were twenty-seven other beds on the floor! The pressure got passed along. Lots of nurses were asked to work double shifts. Support staff took on added responsibilities. Mindy Rothenstreich could remember being the only RN on the floor one night. She'd pulled double shifts, back to back, and once a triple, though she promised herself not to do that again. Mawby says, "This floor is emotionally and physically devastating." That was true for patients and also for nurses.

Most nurses, because they worked so hard, were surprised and then angered when patients complained. Perhaps there was even an overlay of guilt. Maybe a nurse had done something wrong. Maybe a family had made that accusation. Mawby, who came up through the ranks at NYU —staff nurse, assistant head nurse, head nurse—over fourteen years, understood how, emotionally stressed, physically pressed, and hearing complaints to boot, a nurse could grow insensitive to the niggling details of a patient's day. A nurse didn't come in one day with a different attitude. It was just that she just didn't have time to dally with a patient. There were beds to change, medicines to distribute, reports to write. A patient had to fit into a nurse's schedule.

When Mawby has something important to say, she sometimes gropes for a word or trips over one she's said a thousand times, as if language really fails to convey her emotion. She repeats the name of her listener, encouraging an effort of comprehension. And when she still gets back a bewildered look that this talk, which is, after all, about things like bedpans, should stir such emotion, she blurts out, "It sounds so stupid." Then, exasperated, she takes a last fling at explanation. "Who wants to use the damned bedpan?" she says, using a word she seldom uses, damn.

Consider an example: "Every morning at home, a patient gets up and pees; it's something he takes for granted. Then he's told, 'You do not get out of bed until you ring the bell.' Or he has to be told, 'Now you have to use a bedpan because I don't have time to take you to the bathroom because you take twenty minutes to get in there.' Or the patient says, 'I always brush my teeth before I eat breakfast.' But the nurse says, 'Tough, I can't do it now. You do not brush your teeth until after breakfast.' " On the neurosurgery floor, such problems could multiply. Patients with aphasia are unable to express themselves clearly. "They can't say, 'I need a straw to drink,' or, 'I need a glass of water.' " A nurse has to stand there for twenty minutes saying, "Do you need tissues?" "Are you in pain?" "Do you have a headache?" When there were a dozen patients to tend to, a nurse didn't always feel she had time to be understanding. Clearly this was what happened to a patient like Leonard. Nobody disliked him; everyone was trying to be conscientious. But when he had to go to the bathroom three times in a morning—and it took a long time to get him there, and a nurse didn't have the time—well, he'd just have to wait, even if he had to be restrained.

In the scheme of things, especially if those things are brain surgery, perhaps it is unfair to demand that the presence or absence of a bedpan or other detail of comfort should command attention. Mawby doesn't think so. Normally she is mild mannered, but episodes like these make her simmer with anger. She turns haughty, which is not her nature. "I have my own standards of care," she says. Her voice gets shaky with distress. From where does this depth of feeling spring? Different nurses, if they are good nurses, get compassion from various sources. Maybe some are born with a capacity for caring; perhaps others develop it through years of experience. For Mawby, it came from the "most dramatic" experience that she had as a nurse. "I felt the anguish and helplessness of a family member," she says, referring to the time in 1980 when her father was her patient on 11 East.

"I heard Dad discussed in morning report as a confused, incontinent patient, too flat to realize he was even wet," she remembers. When he stood up from a chair, he lost his balance. Worse, Mawby couldn't believe the foul things that were coming out of her gentlemanly father's mouth. He was totally "disinhibited," as they say on 11 East. At University Hospital doctors discovered what appeared to be hydrocephalus. Too much of the fluid that normally circulated in the brain had accumulated in the ventricles, putting pressure on the soft cerebral tissue. Surgeons proposed to run a tube from one of the ventricles though a hole in the skull, under the scalp and into the pleural cavity in the chest—to drain off fluid in a setup called a shunt. "It was a minor procedure, but I wrung myself out," she says. "I knew he was in the best of hands, but I had seen too many tragedies; I knew all the things that could go wrong."

The day following the operation, the surgeons had to return the patient to the OR to adjust the tube. It was badly placed, and they were afraid it would block. "I had truly reached my saturation point and become the hysterical family member. I couldn't help it. I said something to them about what the hell were they doing."

When her father returned, he was better than ever. Bladder control was back, and he was rising from the lowest chair. Mawby worked as his private nurse at night, feeding him juice and Jell-O, rubbing his back. Quietly, hoping he wouldn't notice, she put him in a harness so that while he slept he wouldn't disturb the tube that came out of his brain. "I know you are tying me in this bed," he said. Mawby was mortified. She felt a guilt that perhaps few nurses permit themselves; she knew suddenly what doing her job could mean doing to a patient. How could you lovingly tie someone into a bed?

The best nurses are those who learn that the patient and not the nurse bears the burden of the bedpan or the call button or physical restraints. The snare was that if a nurse was too compassionate, she got caught up in her frustrations. Each lapse in care piqued her anger; every inability to meet a patient's demands—a patient who might be her father—encouraged a sense of helplessness. "I find that I can't keep to my standards," Mawby began to feel. The procedures gave her father three more good years. He died in 1983 at seventy-six. After his death, something snapped. "I was more sensitized than ever," Mawby said. Burnout is real. "There is not enough staffing, too many patients," said Mawby. "You get angry at the checks-and-balances systems. You go out of there knowing you haven't accomplished one bit of what you wanted to do." Within two years Mawby would drop out of nursing and return to school, trying to figure out if she wanted to stick with the profession.

24 Against the grimness of life on the floor, I hatch my own strategies. Neurologically I am intact. Every day a nurse, a resident, another nurse, another resident, verifies that. I can follow their fluttering fingers with my eyes, touch my own fingers surely to my nose. I faultlessly answer the oft-repeated questions. I know the president's name—how many times must I repeat Ronald Reagan, Ronald Reagan?—and that I am not in my apartment. Much of my energy is expended just trying to act normal. I am put out when a new battery begins, as if to say, Do you take me for an idiot? Nobody notices. They care about my neurological status, not my mood. I answer before they ask. Ronald Reagan, University Hospital, October, Steve, and no, I don't know why I am here. I'm waiting for the tests. I tell the nurse I have a question for her now. What is your telephone number? She is not amused. She has a Brooklyn accent as thick as putty—she says "fuh" instead of "for." And now she looks at me, lips sucked in as if suppressing a cough, as if she is sorry for me. I can't even bug her. She *understands* what I'm going through and offers a doleful look, as if gazing at the poor furry animal whose rear legs have been taken out while crossing the road. "That's fuh later," she says. Her report will read: "No complaints voiced. No motor deficits noted. Patient out of bed *ad lib*. Gait steady."

I try to act as if I am not the hospitalized one, which is to say, not the needy, the helpless one. I heard the story about the patient who packed her bags and headed for the elevator. They had to bend her over in the hall and smack a syringe of Haldol into her butt in order to get her down for the night. Not me. If a disabled patient needs a drink of water, I run to get one, even as my pajama top flies open in the back. I am, I believe, still partly convinced that a mistake has been made, that any moment someone will realize the error and I will be sent home with muttered apologies. I pad through the cold tiled halls in bare feet, looking not for help but for peers. I engage everyone in conversation, doctors, nurses, even Maria, a housekeeper in a yellow dress who speaks only Spanish and who complains that her grandchild speaks only English. I enjoy speaking Spanish; it reminds me of my talents, of what I can do, and not of the many restrictions I face.

I am urgent to get on with my own agenda, so urgent that at one point I dispatch my brother with $2,500, my life savings, to buy a personal computer, which I am convinced is essential for the lengthy writing project that awaits me.

It is, of course, not always easy to maintain my nonchalance. In the hall I meet a young man with a crew cut. He wears blue jeans and a blue sweatshirt. I am eager to talk with him. Because his hair is cropped, I think he may be a former patient who looks to be doing well. In fact, he is the husband of a young woman in the ICU. He is twenty-six; she, twenty-four. In a way, he says, it is fortunate that the blood vessel in her head has ruptured. The tumors made her sick enough to be hospitalized, but because one of the tumors encircled an artery, doctors had been divided on whether to risk an operation. This way, the decision was made for them. They took her to the OR toward midnight and removed two tumors, one from each side of her head, though because she has a very malignant form of cancer, it is nearly certain they will soon be back. This is her second batch of tumors in two years. Her husband says he clipped his hair to imitate his wife's haircut. He says he thought it would cheer her up. In the ICU she was still groggy, but when she saw what he'd done, she had giggled and told him, "You're crazy." He says he has taken a leave from his job. They are going to go on a macrobiotic diet. He doesn't know if that will help; he kind of doubts it. But her tumors are bound to recur if they do nothing. "After a while," he says, "you just get numb." Then he catches me by surprise. "How do you feel?" he says. "Don't you have cancer?"

I want to say, Oh, no, I'm not *that* sick, but in the hall, stepping on the cuffs of my pajamas, I am suddenly self-conscious and can only agree, "Yeah, of course, you do get numb."

AFTER DINNER, 11 East is transformed, for that is when the visitors troop in. Men arriving from the office loosen their ties, drop leather cases and folded, thumbed-through newspapers to the floor. The scent of perfume is everywhere. Relatives who haven't seen each other in years invade the lounges and the bathrooms like robust conquerors. Dutifully they look on as one of their clan dies. For the healthy, it can be a moment to catch up on family news, not all of it happy, of course. I heard one man tell another a story about a third: "With his wife of fourteen years it was never a question of if they'd get divorced but when." At times, visitors can get engrossed in their own conversations and forget the patient. Once feeble, impacted Leonard slipped through the net of his momentarily inattentive family and beat a path towards the bathroom, where he tumbled to the floor.

"Ma, I thought you were watching him," said the son, his father sprawled on the ground.

"I was on the phone," she responded, clutching her pocketbook, as if to add to all the other worries, there are also thieves among us.

Most of the time, visiting hours are tough on the visitors, one of whose chores is to prop up patients' illusions, which may also be their own. It is their job to stroll stick-pole relatives by an arm and say, "You're doing much better," as if the measly improvements were really noticeable. Life is doled out here in small portions and each evening the visitors come to measure their relative's share. "She seems a little more responsive today," I heard one daughter say about her unresponsive mother, though further questioning revealed that her judgment was based on a flickering of eyelids, probably involuntary.

The proximity of so much disease is frightening. Illness is arbitrary and maybe final, and perhaps the average person can't resist imagining himself the victim. To the visitors who come night after night, 11 East can begin to seem like the anteroom to a funeral home; and they are properly funereal, which means they see themselves as the real sufferers. One woman visitor extracted an emory board from her pocketbook. "I get up at dawn," she said to another visitor, a man with hair and pants the color of snow.

"Why?" he asked.

"To pray," she said, working the board like a power tool. "Only God could have gotten me through this last year."

My brother Dave, three years younger than I am, is often the first of my visitors to arrive. He is edgy and a little aloof. Perhaps for Dave the flaws in his brother implicate his own genetic make-up. It's difficult to catch his gaze. His girlfriend says that he wakes up in the middle of the night and is tearful for no reason. He is a computer whiz and generally a fun guy, but in the hospital he hardly ever removes his brown leather motorcycle jacket, in the pockets of which he has hidden a couple of tall beers. I'm not that communicative on personal matters, and Dave is even less so. For years he locked his diary in a safe. When his girlfriend of four years actually broke into the safe, desperate with curiosity, what did she find? Poems. The moment seems to call for some closeness between brothers. But there's been so little training. And I've got an intravenous hookup, a hose coming out of my arm. I guess the timing just isn't right.

My sister is in Europe for a month, but every evening Mom, Dad, and Julie catch up with Dave at my bedside. Not since my grandfather died a decade ago have I seen my family so often. We are not always in the best of shape, not many families around here are. People shuttle around excessively well mannered, afraid to bump into anything, to touch anything, lest they upset it. Our visits lapse into forced chitchat, everybody trying to avoid the topic at hand. It's a unanimous decision, never stated, that we don't talk about brain hemorrhages. We talk about the World Series, which is just beginning, and the Middle East, which is perhaps about to end. We play card games and argue over the rules. My notebook is interspersed with diary entries, letters I start again and again but never finish ("Dear Linda, Well you're probably wondering what became of me after I lost my Nicaraguan tan. A bizarre thing . . ." begins one), columns of scores from gin rummy, and Julie's list of things to do: lengthen pants, fix red sweater.

Each night my mother lays out a plate of sliced corned beef ("very lean," she says), salami ("which your father loves but isn't allowed to have" because it gives him indigestion), bagels, Gulden's golden brown mustard, oranges, apples, and her own silverware. I add my square of Jell-O, saved from dinner. My raisable, rollable tray, designed to wheel over the bed, functions as serving table. The place smells like a deli.

Mom smokes constantly. Julie isn't hungry, but is cheerful, if a little subdued. Dad is doing his best but isn't chatty as usual, or voluble, or difficult. He slaps some corned beef onto rye bread, sneezes a chain of sneezes, then plunges his nose into his wrinkled handkerchief and blows, producing a loud sound, like a trumpeting. My sister once identified the sound as an E flat, the only note that unmusical Dad is able to consistently hit. Leonard's family looks over when he trumpets. Dad holds his hand up, palm out, as if to acknowledge the attention, and to say, I'm all right.

Most visitors are respectful before the sick, even if not out of respect. Disease gives the lie to the lies we tell ourselves. My mother and father work together in their own business, six days a week, sometimes twelve hours at a stretch. Once a year they take an eleven-day vacation to Italy. They are putting away for their retirement, which is supposed to begin within five years. They plan to travel in Europe. "You know me, I hate when I can't make plans," Dad says. A jolt like this is portentous. You work so hard, plan and save.

"What protection do you really have?" says Mom glumly.

The truth is I don't want to think about protection. I heard the story of a patient who did not want to know the results of his biopsy. I am a kindred spirit. I hate the carefulness, the good behavior, the fearfulness, that no one will talk about. The hospital environment challenges my family's coping resources. We've been ambushed. As a unit we are supportive, but not especially close. We lack the skills to meet this head-on. We throw blankets over the little fires, everybody trying to protect everybody else, to protect the collective self. My preference is for hijinx. I want it to be gay. If this is denial, fine, I am denying in high gear. It makes me feel better. Most of the time we take my cues. Once, at my instigation, we phoned in an order of pizza, as if it was a party.

In fifteen minutes a guy in a red and white stripped shirt appeared in the doorway, balancing a square cardboard box on his hand. "Who gets the pizza?" he said, skittish as a cat near fire.

"That's for the brain hemorrhage, over here." I said. Dad harrumphed, a swift, whale-like spouting. Dave smiled, but didn't take his jacket off. Julie poked me in the ribs. Mom, caught between two emotions, stamped the floor with one foot. "Oh, Stevie, I'm busting, you didn't really say that?" She pinched her side and laughed, sprinkling her ashes on the floor like fairy dust. Then, she bent to wipe the ashes.

25

"At first we thought we had simply overreacted." Ruth says, "Steve's first weekend home, he was fine. He was regaling everybody with anecdotes. It was like a mirage. I thought I had pulled this whole hysterical mother thing. It was like when your kid has a 104-degree temperature in the middle of the night and is lying there like a lox, so you call the doctor. And the doctor comes in an hour. But by then you've given him two aspirin and he is up out of bed shooting his toy guns at the wall.

"I kept asking Steve if he wanted me to come with him for the test, but he kept saying, 'No, no, no need, what for?' So Erv called the hospital twice but couldn't get through. Then Dr. Kricheff called and was very upbeat. Dr. K. said that things were better than he'd thought. He painted a rosy picture. I heard him talk about a blood-vessel thing, like varicose veins. And it was all very easy to take care of. Maybe I only understood what I wanted to, but to me it was as if right from the X ray it was going to be exorcised. I didn't realize that Dr. K. was referring to a brain hemorrhage. I can't remember hearing the word hemorrhage.''

The cheery mood lasted until they set foot on University Hospital's 11 East. One glimpse of the floor and the idyll is over. To be placed among that crowd seems irrefutable evidence that something is very wrong.

Erv, a bull in most areas of his life, suffered most—or at least showed it most. At age forty he had walked away from a vice-presidency at a giant ad agency to open his own small tutoring center. And yet he has to talk himself into entering 11 East. "I know that woman walking around with the drain coming out of her head is there; I just can't emotionally cope with seeing those things," he says. The only way to move ahead, to literally put one foot in front of the other, is to avoid eyeing anybody. "I look at my feet or else straight ahead. I just pull a curtain down over what I don't want to see. I don't even want to look at Steve's roommates."

In his son's room, Erv, usually gregarious, must make an effort to converse, to be mentally *there* at all. His gaze settles on a spot on the floor. He nearly shuts down, except for his new allergy, which he thinks of as his anxiety. His eyes water. He sneezes. His nose reddens. He is never without a white leafy handkerchief in his hand. No doubt he is, in his way, trying valiantly. Kricheff says: "Through the thirty years I've known Erv, he gets queasy at the slightest sign of blood. And he realized he's the father, he can't go throwing up out in the bathroom, he can't faint on the floor if he sees a drain, he's got to support Ruth. For some people it's easy; for Erv it must take a tremendous effort to act the way he does, to go out to dinner, to put up a front."

Ruth feels near hysteria or catatonia or some extreme of emotion. She works with her husband at the tutoring center, where she is in charge of the teachers. This is her first real job and with it has come a new appreciation of her own talents. But now she feels helpless. They both do. Yet the less in control Erv seems, the more Ruth tells herself she has to stay the course. She enters a hyperfunctional state. Ruth lugs in rations, her shopping bag scraping the floor. She doesn't want Steve subjected to the hospital fare. And everyone else needs to eat, too. Moreover, she likes having a project, being goal oriented. If someone asks for something, she responds, "How many do you need?" And she is on her way to the store. Ruth, in her anxiety, has become almost compulsively generous, a person who can't be complimented for fear she will turn the flattery around. "You like it, here, honey, take it." Erv says that Ruth would like to be at bedside all the time, but he won't permit it. She'd drive herself and Steve crazy.

So Erv imposes business on her just to keep her occupied. And Erv, too, counts on her support, her presence.

They have decided that the most important service they can render the patient is to not let on that they are in the least bit nervous. Erv says: "Steve seems okay. The only thing is a kind of control that has crept into his voice. Maybe he talks slower, tends to be much more interested in small talk." Their strategy is to seize any bit of happy news and dwell on it. Erv makes a big deal about the computer purchase. He is aware that by cold, rational standards a patient on the brain-surgery floor is ill advised to put down $2,500 in cash for the purchase of anything. To Erv, such an investment seems an outrageous statement of optimism, and just what's needed. "What kind of computer are you getting?" he wants to know.

THE FAMILY, the basic economic unit, is also the fundamental unit of health care. After all, as sociologists have long pointed out, more illnesses get treated at home than in the hospital—one estimate put the ratio at seven to one. Yet serious illness tends to overburden the modern family. That is when, already loaded with heavy financial responsibilities, families turn to the technologized medicine of the hospital.

This is the right thing to do, of course. Brain hemorrhages will not submit to loving care alone. And yet the choice to let the hospital and not the home be the center of healing has a price.

In an influential article, Theodor J. Litman, of the University of Minnesota, pointed out that the family's greatest influence on serious illness —maybe its only influence—is exerted in choosing the first doctor. From then on doctors make almost all the decisions. When and in which institution hospitalization occurs, for instance, is a matter that the doctor dictates. The patient, welcomed into a protective medical environment, may find in the sick role an element of pleasure. He is relieved of normal responsibilities; the hospital staff takes up the load. The family, once the focus of care, is left out of this transaction, and virtually all others. It is disenfranchised, left to spectate.

Family members can experience a profound inadequacy. The family members must be at bedside—they even say they want to be—but they have no expertise to bring to bear. They command no respect from the hospital staff; indeed, they are treated as people who should try to stay out of the way. In most things, a parent—whose fantasy is omnipotence over a child—believes that he or she shared responsibility for an offspring's problems. Ruth, who clings to that fantasy, says, "The pain you feel for each other is different. It's such a vulnerable situation when it's one of

your kids and you have always been in control of your child's well-being.''
Johanna Shapiro, of the University of California at Irvine Medical Center,
reports that even minor inpatient procedures on a child can lead the parents
to exhibit symptoms of helplessness, including guilt, blame, denial, and
depression.

NYU is a big medical center, and Kricheff's a big shot there. Beyond
that, Erv doesn't know how to begin to evaluate a doctor's qualifications.
He thinks: How the hell am I going to figure out who the right doctor is?
Erv makes an analogy to his own situation. "At the tutoring center, parents
ask me what my qualifications are to teach their sons or daughters sixth-
grade math. Does it matter that I don't have an education degree, that I
come out of the advertising world? Or that I've been doing this for ten
years, that I've taught over a thousand kids? Either they believe you or
they don't, are soothed or not. It probably doesn't matter what you say.
There are standard questions you feel you should ask a doctor. But you
can never judge the answer, anyhow, so why bother asking? You just cross
your fingers and have faith. As a lay person dealing with a professional,
you can say all you want about established credentials, you really end up
tongue-tied. You feel impotent.''

Illness raises issues of vulnerability. And not just for the ill. The parent,
shorn of power, is at the mercy of a process he or she helped initiate but
can't control. The parent, too, must find ways to cope. One way, say the
psychology texts, is to gain a sense of mastery. It need not be over the
threat itself, which is out of the question. Just over something, anything.
Which is clearly what Erv attempts to do in his relationship with Lenore,
his daughter.

The conversation takes place on Route 3 as they pass the Meadowlands
and the Brendan Byrne Arena on their drive to the hospital. Each afternoon
Erv and Ruth depart their blue shingled schoolhouse in New Jersey and
head to the medical complex that stretches ten blocks along First Avenue
in New York, from the Veterans Administration Hospital at Twenty-fourth
Street to the Howard A. Rusk Institute of Rehabilitation Medicine at Thirty-
fourth Street. Their economical Ford Escort is black, the only color that
was in stock the day Erv told the salesman he wanted a model he could
drive off the lot. Unlike Erv, Ruth has never quit smoking. As Erv drives,
she assumes her smoker's pose. One arm is folded across her stomach; the
other, braced on top of it, holds a Merit. In the backseat is a shopping bag
of food in plastic containers.

One day Ruth interrupts the lightheartedness, which is a rehearsal of
the patter to be effected at the hospital. Ruth says that they ought to

telephone Lenore, twenty-two, their last child, and tell her to return home
from Europe. Lenore is a pianist who is giving several concerts in Germany.
Ruth, having had an uncaring mother, is especially sensitive about the
forms of caring. Ruth thinks the whole family should be together at a time
like this. "I think we're making a mistake," she says. The ashtray overflows,
each butt hooped with Ruth's lipstick, a shade of pink. She cracks the car
window and pushes the cigarette out. "Lenore will be hurt that we kept
it from her."

Erv categorically refuses.

"Bringing her home would be like calling her to a death bed," he says.
His voice is airy, coming from way back in his throat; his bald head rotates
a quarter turn, as if he is squirming out of something. Instead, each day
Erv phones Germany from the pay phone in the hospital's visitors lounge.
He asks Lenore how she is and what is new. If she wants to know, he tells
her he is at home watching TV.

Adversity tries marriages, busts them, but Ruth and Erv had been
sweethearts since age fourteen. Taped to the refrigerator door in the kitchen
was a single square of paper, a poem clipped from a newspaper. It reads
in part:

Two hearts beating as one can weather any strife
Together we'll find treasured things that make a happy life . . .

"Ervy," says Ruth, her voice sharper, higher. She puts a hand on his
shoulder, on his unshaved neck. She thinks, Erv has to be in control, and
this is how he is maintaining a sense of control. Then she thinks that part
of her job is to take care of her Ervy.

26 Visiting hours end at 9:00 P.M., and the visitors invariably
rush out as if an alarm has sounded, bending just long enough
for a peck on a bandaged forehead. My roommate's eyes are
like paper in water, washed out and enlarged. "You're looking better and better," he's told. The covers are smoothed, and the family
hustles to the elevators. Abruptly, the floor is still as a deserted house,
though this one is chock full of bodies, dismal ones with eroded faces,
punctured cheeks, and absent, catarrhal expressions. My family departs,
too, scooping up shopping bags and serving plates, promising a resupply
effort tomorrow, probably as relieved as any of them to get into the quench-
ing night breeze.

From my windows I can watch visitors spill into the parking lot, past the canary-colored maples. Neither the scrape of the leaves nor the birds' autumn song penetrate the locked panels of glass. In here there is no sound but the rush of vented air, like white noise, and occasionally the twitter of nurses as they joke at their station down the hall. The lights go off, and the specters fall quickly to sleep, mostly a deep chemical sleep. I don't know if Julie has on her mind to leave, too, but every night when I say, "Are you leaving?" she stays.

"That Julie, she is something wonderful," I remember my mother saying, and then snapping her thin finger against my ribs until I thought they would break.

At night 11 East is sepulchral, eerie, and a good place to be in love. Is it the closeness of death that deepens emotions? I don't know. But in this time between hemorrhage and treatment Julie and I are at our best. Maybe we really feel more, or maybe just focus better. For a time our relationship doesn't seem so difficult.

Julie was the first woman I'd met after returning from a year in Africa. In the beginning we'd spend entire weekends together, ordering in food and making love, excited by the suddenness of each urge and never refusing it. Sometimes, I remember, Julie would be washing dishes, and the fact that she wasn't paying me complete attention would drive me crazy. I couldn't stand that she was talking to me over the running water. So I would sneak up behind her and say, "I'll dry," but I wouldn't. I'd press against her, close like a staticky ball, talk over her shoulder until, protesting, "Let me dry my hands at least," she'd trail me with suds dripping from her fingers. I told her that above all I didn't want to get involved. She was against that, as well. Indeed, though kind, she kept me at a distance, maintaining a host of friends I wasn't allowed to meet, which made me cling all the more fiercely. I wanted her opinion on everything. Moreover, I sought her approval and believed that when I had it I could do no wrong. After a while, though, Julie wasn't amused by my myriad demands. She found me hypersensitive, overly exigent. "Childish," she said once. Empathy was often more than she could drum up. But here in the hospital, amid the lugubrious and the dying, she *feels* for me, she says, her hand balling into a fist and clapping her heart, as if she is pledging. And I am joyous.

I escort Julie to the visitors' lounge, walking behind her in my synthetic blue uniform, watching the pleats on her skirt open and close. I am barefoot. Julie's concern with my grooming, I note, is excused for the present. We sit on the vinyl couches, whose cushions, as they collapse under us, yield clouds of cigarette smoke, the day's worries. We play cards—gin rummy—at a round white table. Julie keeps score. When I win, she tosses the cards dejectedly out of her small masculine hands. People tell her she looks like the actress Elizabeth McGovern, though McGovern has green eyes and Julie's are forest brown, and, when she is angry, peer obstinately past you. "Hey, big girl, what's wrong?" I bait her.

"Just deal," she says. Julie is there, not just the husk of her, and it's as if what I worked so hard to persuade myself of is true. I *am* different; not really a patient but someone apart. In these moments the tragedies I see in this hall are events that happen to someone else.

Sometimes when Julie stays late, we remain in my room, draw the curtain, stretch out on the hospital bed. We crank it up like a chaise longue and watch my TV. Lying arm in arm one night in the climate-controlled air—nothing but a thin blanket ever needed—a thought occurs to me: How close to naked am I. "Don't," says Julie, her lips pressed together like the lips of a vice. "I mean it." Cross that line and it might take hours to make up. Better to humor her. I step to the edge of the cloth curtain, the boundary of my world. On the other side, my roommate's snores sound like somebody moving furniture. When she doesn't halt me, I go ahead. I wave my hand behind my back for her to follow. Who cares about an irritation in the brain? I've only been back in the United States a few days. I cough weakly. "C'mon," I say, my voice sputtering.

WHEN JULIE REACHES HOME from the hospital every night, she gets on the phone to her best friend Marianne and recounts the events of the evening at the hospital.

"I'm trapped," Julie says. "All of a sudden I'm thrown into this situation and I'm enveloped by the family and I don't ever have a chance to be distant. Before I felt very independent. Now his family really depends on me to be with him, to support him, to be there for him, make him feel comfortable."

It would have been different if she were in love. But she'd met Steve less than two years ago, and he'd been away for the last six months. Her idea was that he'd return and they would date. She would have a chance to see how she felt about him. A brain hemorrhage did not make her feel in love.

"I feel like a victim," she tells Marianne. "Not *the* victim but a victim. I feel like this isn't something I can control, so it is happening to him and me. . . . We just go along with what everyone tells us to do." Julie was honest with herself. "If he needs a mother, I'm not it, because

I'm too needy," Julie once said. "I'm pretty realistic about myself. I'm the kid type."

Marianne tells Julie, "You're in a really difficult situation." Which is true.

Another difficult aspect is that Julie hates hospitals. "I've spent too much time with people that are dear to me in the hospital." When her father was diagnosed as having leukemia, Julie was the only child at home with her mother. He died in six weeks. "I went to see him every day, and he got worse and worse, and it was really terrible. We had to wear gowns and masks—in isolation. I didn't have any idea he was going to die. I never even thought he had something that wasn't going to go away. Even the last time I saw him, I didn't understand. If anybody told you he had leukemia, you'd know, but I was really stupid. He went from weighing 200 pounds to weighing less than 100. He could barely lift his arm off the sheet. I looked through the window when I was saying good-bye the last time I saw him. Oh, God it was really awful. I can't think about it." Julie was twenty-five when her father died, and for a long time she thought to herself, I know he knew me that last time.

Julie complains to Marianne that she can't do this because she just doesn't want to go through another round of medical care, but she really feels like "You complain about it, but emotionally you don't have any choice." Julie reconciles herself to the idea that now isn't the time to work out their relationship. "Whatever I feel, I can't ever leave right now. Something like this brings out the Florence Nightingale in me. Go down with the ship and all that stuff. I have to kick in, do my bit." Julie comes to the hospital with white cardboard cartons of Chinese food in her hand and roses. She plays the concerned, constant, the bearer of gifts.

And at least he isn't a complainer. "It was real fun to visit in the hospital. Everybody was yucking it up, sort of like a party. Actually, he was very different than anyone I'd known who'd been sick. He was always doing the entertaining. The way he was dealing with it was like a comedian. I think he just didn't accept that he was sick. And it was going to be over with, and he was making jokes. He treated it very lightly. I don't think he really did underneath, but he certainly didn't let on that he had any serious concerns. It seemed a little like he had a hangnail. I was really glad. That really helped me. It made it easier. I think that's what kept me around, the fact that he was really good about it. This is probably the worst thing that would ever happen in his life. If this is the worst thing and if he's lived through it and it wasn't so horrible . . ."

Sex in the hospital strikes Julie at first as a very bad idea. It's immature.

She is against it. Then she brightens. "There has to be something fun about this hospital stay." She purses her lips, as though she's mad. But where? Certainly not in this bed with the door unlocked and Steve's roommate barely snoring on the other side of the curtain. Steve suggests the bathroom. "You've thought about this," she says in a tone of scandal. Oh, well. Julie goes along. She rolls off the bed and steals up to the curtain. A patient's bathroom, in the corner of the room, is just a little larger than an airplane bathroom. Oh, no, Julie thinks, the door doesn't lock. Of course, patients aren't allowed to lock themselves in the bathroom. Steve says he'll keep one hand on it.

"Don't pull that string!" Steve stage-whispers irritably, and almost with pleasure. "That calls a nurse."

"Don't yell," Julie says in a normal voice.

27

Each evening the residents slide chairs around an old metal table whose surface is decorated with beautiful illustrations of the brain. The ostensible purpose of the meeting, in the room behind the nurses' station, is to bring up-to-date the resident who will be staying in the hospital that night. But really it's a social hour. With an elbow pushed against a glossy parietal lobe or smack on top of the optic chiasm, people swap stories about what they do, one story calling forth an even better one. This isn't just entertainment, not just war stories, though there's plenty of that. It's in a forum like this— or crammed into the residents' cubicle or walking the steps because the elevator is too slow—that residents convince themselves that they are the doctors best qualified to handle life-and-death situations. It's here that the brutal day, with its phenomenal pressures to perform, is framed for the resident as a positive value, a source of pride. Any resident who fails to pick up the principles passed along in these casual chats will fail altogether.

For instance, on any given night, the chief resident, straddling a chair at the head of the table, might offhandedly say (as I once heard him remark), "They tried to assassinate that patient on the neurology floor." The prematurely balding one, who broke into tears when the chief last chewed him out, might tell the prematurely gray one about the unbelievable temper tantrum an attending threw in the OR that morning. And the newest resident, no doubt, would talk about the vast pressure he's under, while the rest of the crew, so unimpressed they are capping their yawning mouths with the backs of their hands, would moan in mock sympathy.

You think that's bad, one will goad another, tell him about *your* first week. Then the stories really begin. The one whose face has the greenish tint of wet cement—because he hasn't slept in thirty-six hours—will launch into a tale about the time he was called to the Bellevue emergency room during his first week as a resident.

First week? The new resident will go, his jaws dropping as if he's suffered a stroke.

That's right, first week. "A victim of a car accident is rushed in unconscious, with multiple trauma. The chest surgeons carry him off to the OR, but it's obvious a head injury has to be ruled out. So I call up the chief resident at home, who says, 'Well, it sounds like he needs a ventriculogram. Put a burr hole in the skull, pass a catheter in, shoot in some dye, then take an X ray. Call me when you find out what it says.' It sounds like he's saying, 'Run upstairs and get me a sandwich,' but he's talking about half an hour's worth of invasive work on somebody's brain. *And I'd never put a burr hole in before.*"

The new resident, his eyes by now fixed and dilated, can't believe it. He's been there six months and still can't imagine crossing the threshold into someone's brain.

"I had to go into the OR while they were opening the chest and, trying to be as polite as I could, say to anesthesia, 'Excuse me.' Nobody even listened to me. Finally, I pushed anesthesia out of the way and guess what?"

The new resident shakes his head.

"The ventriculogram was normal," goes the tale, as if it's a real disappointment.

"But what happened to the patient?" the new resident persists.

And then comes the line that, when I heard the story, carried a hint of a swagger.

"Oh, the patient? He died of chest wounds."

What is most phenomenal about residents' bull sessions is that no one complains. Arguments are periodically raised against the exceedingly long hours a resident works, but that is by others. It's true that experiments dating back to the 1930s have demonstrated that people sleepless for forty-eight hours can't write coherently and after sixty sleepless hours they get irascible and irrational. Residents, though, brag about the abuse.

"I love the pain," Chalif told me when as a third-year resident his take-home pay was $420 a week. It's a brand of neurosurgical macho.

"We've all been awake forty, fifty, sixty hours without sleep," one resident says.

Then, like it's a game of chicken, they one-up each other with tales of how long they've gone without even a nap; it's a game in which an attending passing by readily joins in. "Yeah, but it's nothing like the old days when we used to take call every other night instead of every third night like you wimps," I remember one attending saying.

To the resident this braggadocio has a subtext, a crucial one. Overworking, in the end, supports one of the key tenets of the neurosurgeon's training: Only by my vigilance do patients survive. For what the resident's six years of training is supposed to teach finally is that it is not his skills but his attitude that makes the difference. And that attitude, communicated in gossipy conclaves behind the nurses' station, is: total responsibility. "We don't consult," says Neurosurgery Chief Joseph Ransohoff almost meanly. "If we look at a case, it is ours."

As a first-year resident taking call, Chalif had once acted nonchalantly, like a consultant, he told me. He had been phoned in the middle of the night to check a patient at the Veterans Administration hospital, which is affiliated with NYU. That entailed going outside, walking the few blocks to the VA in the miserable cold, and probably for nothing—rarely was there something that couldn't wait. It was the first sleep he'd gotten in he couldn't remember how long. Chalif said over the phone to keep the patient under observation and went back to sleep. In a half hour he was called again, and again he decided it didn't sound serious. Another half hour later the message was emphatic: You better get over here. When he finally arrived, the patient was crapping out, neurosurgical vernacular for dying. "It was the one time I fucked up," said Chalif. "I made a mistake. If I had gone quicker, there would have been less pressure on the brain stem. It was a big thing then; my judgment, my prestige on the service, was called into question." The guy died three months later.

Chalif swore that laziness would never overcome him again. "You can teach yourself to be compulsive," he said. I know Chalif believed that, almost cultlike. The marginals, the shirkers, he had no use for. "He's a clock-watcher" was the worst that Chalif could say about someone, as a doctor or as a person. The point is: It isn't merely us against disease. On the neurosurgery floor, it is us against *them*. Every night around that beat-up table, what really goes on is a fearsome bonding; the band of those who will take responsibility solidifying their forces against those who won't. Who won't? How vast are their ranks! They include the incompetents, the blunderers, the fearful, the hesitant, which, until proved otherwise, is everybody in the medical community; certainly anybody from "another institution," as the rest of the medical world is anonymously and disparagingly called; most any "private" doctor, who, low blow of low blows, works, it is suggested, *only* for the money. Even neurologists, one floor below, are dismissed as "consultants," the kind of doctors who pen their impression on a patient's chart and then tool off for a weekend house in the Hamptons. "As a brain surgeon, you've got to assume that every other doctor doesn't know what the fuck he is doing," Chalif once said. Clearly this was a grandiose formulation, since no resident really knew what the fuck *he* was doing, but it was the perfect expression of the neurosurgical creed.

Tonight is Chalif's turn to take call, his turn to keep vigil against the muddlers. A lot of residents don't like to take call—"to suck down some call" the residents said—since they usually get just a few hours sleep, if that. Chalif saw a night on call as an opportunity. Sometimes Chalif would say, "I want some big action," or just, "How about some BA?" which meant he wanted some hemorrhaging lesion that would send him to the OR or put him in some other direct face-off with death. Hadn't Dr. Eugene S. Flamm, the vascular specialist, called brain surgery "an emotional roller coaster"? On call, you were there for the ride. One night Chalif had lived the perfect resident's moment, frightful and thrilling. A woman in the ICU had suddenly become comatose. "Probably the most difficult part of the residency is that you have to convince yourself that you have the confidence and ability to invade someone else's head," explained resident Al Cohen. Chalif, convinced, drilled a hole above her wrinkleless forehead and plunged a tube into her ventricle, swollen with hemorrhagic blood. She awoke, batting her eyelashes as if shaking off sleep. The next day, Chalif, groggy but in his glory, said: "A woman tried to die on us last, but we wouldn't let her."

Of course, you couldn't tell what would develop overnight. And some nights call proved to be nothing but scut, which stood for "some clinically useful training" but which, in fact, meant shit. Scut was the shit work, poking intravenous lines into veins, changing bandages, checking blood samples, stool samples, urine samples. Talking about scut, Cohen had mused, "To be a neurosurgeon, you don't have to be smart, but you do have to be compulsive."

Chalif referred to doing scut as scutology, the science of doing scut efficiently. "I'm great at scut," he'd say, though it also "bummed him a little" to contemplate a night of nothing but scut. I imagine that it must be in a mood like this, energized and a little bummed, that Chalif figures he will stop by my room to visit. Chalif had definite favorites among the patients. Usually they were people he identified with, people his age, with his interests. I was one of them. "You were personable, with a nice girl-friend," he later told me. He was by nature exuberant, in love with what he did, and naively—though this was part of his charm—assumed that everyone else must be, too. He would often say that neurosurgery is "soooo interesting," dragging out the "o" like a stutter. I'm sure, in contemplating our visit, he is sure I will say the same.

SWINGING OPEN THE bathroom door, Julie and I are straight-faced, al-most melodramatically serious. I reach back to flush the toilet (a nice touch) as we file out and almost collide with Dr. Chalif, who is entering my room. Everyone is blinking and flustered, as when a bright light is unexpectedly switched on in a dark room.

"What's going on here," Chalif says. He looks like a person whose car has just backed into a pole. Is he going to yell at us?

Mischief is fun in the hospital. Rules are omnipresent—is any activity unregulated?—and yet the consequences so slight. After all, few fellow patients notice. I could climb over their bodies, fuck under their beds, and not a call button would light. Julie and I are young, mobile, able to speak out against the censorship that illness imposes; so we do. And maybe that is what it is about us that appeals to Chalif, too.

"Nothing," I say, contrite, and realize my pajama pants are on backward.

Then there is one of those silences during which people become aware of the physical space between them. Chalif breaks it. If he had an intention to scold, it is gone. "Okay," he says. Maybe this isn't the moment to chat. He'll stop by another time, he says and leaves.

28 By the 1980s there were ninety-five neurosurgical training programs in the United States and Canada. NYU, a top res-idency program, annually offers two entry-level positions in its five-year program—a resident also needs at least one year of general surgery. A hundred inquiries are pared down to about thirty applicants, based on their credentials: grades, test scores, recommenda-tions, experience. Those thirty are invited for interviews, ten on each of three successive weekends. Each candidate gets fifteen minutes with each of the eight attending neurosurgeons. NYU, like every other program, comes up with a list of its top choices. Each candidate does the same. Since 1983 the choices have been fed into a computer, and on a prescribed day the machine matches selections and spits out the destinies of future neurosurgeons. In 1985, 242 people competed for the 121 first-year neurosurgical residencies in the United States and Canada.

Is this the best way to select the human beings who will open our heads and root around in our brains? It's hard to find anyone who will argue in its favor. "The selection process is flawed," says Richard Rovit, chairman of neurosurgery at St. Vincent's Hospital, an NYU affiliate. A statement from Rovit carries particular weight, since he is also chairman of the Congress of Neurological Surgeons' committee on graduate education, which is charged with investigating such matters as resident selection. To read what Rovit has written about the selection process is to become truly dismayed at the way young brain surgeons are chosen. First, Rovit says everyone who has examined the subject has come to the same conclusion. "Previous studies have demonstrated that [standardized tests] provide either limited or absolutely no predictive value to future clinical performance." Not that you don't have to be fairly intelligent to be a brain surgeon, but that is a minimum. "We know how to pick the brightest," says Rovit, "but it's not clear those will become the best neurosurgeons."

What a selection committee would really like to find out, because the data indicate that this may be what makes a good neurosurgeon, is something that a candidate has probably already learned, or never will. The current thinkers call it "moral reasoning." Rovit reports that a study of several hospitals demonstrated that "a high level of moral reasoning virtually excluded the possibility of being a low performer." What is moral reasoning? It bears on questions like these: Is the candidate honest even when he makes mistakes? Does he push on even though he's tired? Is he intrepid even in the face of inexperience?

To the layman, neurosurgery is the application of meticulous technique. Not so, say surgeons. NYU has never let anyone go because he couldn't do the surgical maneuvers. The most serious error—and the only unforgivable error—a resident can commit is dishonesty, which is a judgment on intent rather than consequences. How, says the attending, can I entrust my patients to a resident whose word I can't rely on? "My claim is that postgraduate training of surgeons is above all things an ethical training," wrote sociologist Charles Bosk in his study of general surgical residents. The same holds for neurosurgeons.

The dilemma that attendings choosing residents face is this: How is it possible to determine the level of a candidate's moral reasoning in a brief interview? With great difficulty, says anyone who has participated in selecting future brain surgeons. "They've all done well in medical school; they've all got recommendations saying they are terrific," says Flamm, vice-chairman of neurosurgery at NYU. What does he go on, then?

"I'd say that right or wrong, it's more a personality cult or assessment. I pay attention to the interview to try to get some kind of feel for the person, whether he's got some depth of understanding of how the world is, as best I can tell in fifteen minutes. Do I like him as a person? You might argue that that can't be determined in a few minutes. I think personal relationships are established very quickly. You say hello to somebody, and you decide if you want to pursue conversing with this fellow or if you never want to see him again."

Chairman Ransohoff agrees. "We want guys who are bright, have done research, and guys we like. It's a pain in the ass to train someone you don't like."

What might seem amazing to a layman is that the manual dexterity of future surgeons isn't evaluated. Ransohoff asked a neuropsychologist to look into how such an evaluation might be done. His research uncovered some coordination tests that might be administered, tests that were given to factory workers in the 1930s. Examinations like these might be useful in ruling out the real clods, but not much more. As it stands now, though, nobody ascertains how nimble a resident's fingers are until probably the second year of the program, when he is first called on to perform tasks in the OR.

Once interviews with candidates for the residency are complete, each attending takes his notes to a roundtable discussion. Flamm describes it this way: "We sit around like a bunch of pompous assess and say, 'Oh I think this guy is going to be just terrific.' We finished somebody a couple of years ago, and we were afraid to release this guy. We thought he was not going to be a good neurosurgeon. And we pulled out his folder and found we all had these glowing comments, things like 'This is the greatest guy I've ever interviewed.' 'Let's hire him.' "

Some residents do live up to expectations. Chalif had good recommendations, went to an excellent medical school at the University of Chicago, and was extremely likable. Flamm and Ransohoff feuded, but they both liked Chalif. Ransohoff called Chalif cocky, a quality he admired. "When I call him a son of a bitch, he knows I don't mean it," Ransohoff said. Flamm would later say that Chalif was the best resident he'd seen in ten years, and a delightful person. Such success was not to crown every resident's endeavors.

According to Rovit, "The current selection process is almost a crap shoot.'' His frightening estimate is that one in five residents will end up a mediocre neurosurgeon.

29

In this place, more costly than a good hotel, I do not sleep well. I fiddle with the controls on the bed, hump it up under my knees, and try to read. My concentration is shot. I flip through pages, retain nothing, and slam the book shut as if I'm after a fly. Nurses arrive at all hours of the night, their rubber soles squeaky on the tile floor. They rattle paper dishes of pills under my nose. I stare at the neon-blue numbers of the clock radio Julie has brought me and calculate the hours until light. Or, I reflect on the events of the day.

One afternoon a resident had turned one of my roommates on his side and administered a spinal tap. He wanted to extract cerebrospinal fluid, probably to test it for the bacteria that could signal meningitis. It's a simple procedure, though of course disastrous sequels are always a threat. The spinal cord and brain are suspended in fluid. If, for instance, a large tumor has raised pressure in the head and a lot of fluid is suddenly withdrawn, the brain can herniate. Normally, the resident slides the six-inch-long needle between vertebrae, below where the spinal cord ends. Cerebrospinal fluid flows from the syringe as if the resident has hammered a spigot into the patient's back. I think that it must have been when that giant needle was already inserted and the fluid was already pouring out of it that my hefty roommate began to toss and the resident must have started to feel a little out of control. "Don't move, don't move, don't move," I heard through the drawn curtain, the resident's voice pumping the words, the way a driver pumps bad brakes. Hearing the urgency in the command, I, too, had pleaded—though my plea was silent—that he remain still.

In this place both the natural world and the one pitted against it are filled with threats. People end up here because they drive their cars over bumps in the road and land paralyzed, bang their heads on a chandelier, get beaned by an overthrown baseball, do a line of cocaine, hemorrhage, and end up hemiplegic, or get poked in the eye by an umbrella point that finds its way into the brain. It can seem as if all the mundane objects of the world—its baseballs and light fixtures and bumps—have turned evil. And so have the cures. A simple diagnostic test that could cause the brain to cave in on itself! "Don't move, don't move," I hear in my mind all night long, in a voice like an inquisitioner's.

The company is not reassuring, either. When I talk to other patients, it is always initially about illness. We swap stories on the location of the hemorrhage and the nature of the symptoms. All the while, I attempt to gauge how sick they are in relation to me and how much better—or worse—I will get. I have been oversensitized and live vicariously the fates of everyone I see. I count myself lucky or doomed depending on whose bed I've most recently walked past and what I imagine their future to hold. On this floor there are all kinds of fates to imagine. Every capability the brain possessed could be turned against a person. There is, for instance, alexia, a condition in which a patient can write but can't read; or para-praxis, in which a patient constantly loses his way. A victim of brain disease might neglect part of his visual field, so that he shaves only half of his face, eats from only one side of his plate; or he might execute appropriate actions but to inappropriate objects, for example, buttering his sugar rather than his bread. He might have prosopagnosia, which is an inability to recognize a person by face, though he can recognize people by voice. Dick Howser, the manager of the Kansas City Royals' baseball team, said that one of the early symptoms of his malignant brain tumor was confusion. He would go to substitute pitchers, but instead of signaling for the right-hander— the one he really wanted—he'd call in the lefty. Sometimes only short-term memory is affected, so that a person, though he recalled perfectly the old days, could hold on to something new for just, say, a minute. It was like straddling a persistent present and a long-gone past. At the other extreme, there has been reported the case of a man who could forget nothing, whether the information was from the morning's paper or a passage from a book read to him a decade ago in a language he didn't understand. The malfunctioning brain deprives some of all sensation, or taste or smell or hearing. In some brains the entire cerebral cortex atrophies, as Alois Alzheimer first reported in 1906, causing premature senility. It is probably fitting that Harvey Cushing, the founder of modern neurosurgery, loved the circus, and in particular the freak shows. He wandered the scene with notebook in tow, befriending the giants and dwarfs, marking down their case histories as if he were at a neurology clinic, which indeed he was. He was a pioneer in understanding that giants and dwarfs were not the result of maledictions of nature but of aberrations of the pituitary gland inside the head.

What bothered me most, though, wasn't the weird, who, if they were frightful, were also marvelous, their maladies suggesting our prodigious capabilities. What got to me were the incoherents. There the brain was not trumpeting its powers but folding and departing. People who looked like people, could eat, ambulate, knew the syntax and the grammar but were fundamentally dotty, those were the ones that upset me most. This floor made you guard with precious fury what you had, what you were, and it unleashed in me a real cruelty toward the doddering.

For example, there was one of my new roommates, Sam.* Sam was a gentle, incoherent old man who responded to care as if being mugged. When the nurses turned him—which they had to do twice a day to prevent bed sores—he hollered and kicked. They addressed him as Mister. Calm down, Mister Sam, they shouted as he writhed. Though doctors could do nothing more for him, the nursing home for which he was destined had a long waiting list. He had been at the hospital for eleven weeks. This would have concerned me a lot less if the nurses hadn't decided that Mister Sam should be turned each morning at two and at four. A nurse's aide and the biggest person on the staff did the job with a helper.

The first night, I stayed in bed during the brawl.

However, the next night the fighting was too much. At 4:00 A.M., when all was quiet save for struggling, screaming Sam, I could take it no longer. I stormed down the hall toward the nurses' station, rolling my IV pole along with me. It was not a generous feeling that motivated me, not a protest against patient conditions or the dread outcome of disease. I was pissed off at the racket. "If I have to be awake, then everyone else should get up," I yelled, and felt like an inmate rattling his cup against the jailhouse bars. In the calm that blanketed the floor at night I was like a car alarm. Nurse Mindy Rothenstreich was there. She confided that I was right, which helped, but counseled me to protest in the morning. Chalif later said that though Sam had to be turned twice in twenty-four hours, it did not have to be in the middle of the night. That was Nursing's decision.

The next day, I called everyone I could think of, including doctors I'd met only once, the social worker, the hospital's patient advocate, even the hospital administrator's office—I'm taking this all the way to the top— protesting that I had to be moved. I had a sense that I was being "inappropriate," as the saying goes around here. A patient, though, can't always find an appropriate target for his anger. At whom should he shout? His family, who wishes him well? His doctor, the person who is going to treat him? I heard the story of a patient who, on his way down to the OR, told his surgeon, "I don't want to do any more fucking waiting around." I wasn't about to insult the doctors I depended on. With Sam and the late shift, I'd discovered the perfect objects for abuse. I wasn't counting on them. Nobody even seemed very disturbed. Like the bad kid in class, I was

*Name changed.

permitted to act out. Well, fine. I enjoyed my anger, wallowed in it. I made elaborate plans for the moment, which I was sure was not far in the future, when hospital security would have to be called in. I would lock myself in my room, taking Mister Sam as hostage. I had already measured my bed —to make sure it could serve as barricade against my hospital-room door—when, sadly, my plea was answered and I was given a new room-mate, a patient who had been instructed to stay quiet and inactive after suffering an intracranial hemorrhage in an Atlantic City hotel.

On a folder taped to the door of my new room someone had scrawled in big letters "aneurysm alert." Neither of us knew what that meant. All John Corallo, forty-two, knew was that he had been confined to bed and told to remain quiet. That was not easy. John was loquacious by nature, and he was frightened. He had been demanding to use the phone!

"What are you going to do when you leave here?" he wanted to know.

"The same as before," I said.

John had a full head of jet black hair and nice white teeth, which popped out at one point, showing two filed-down stubs where his incisors were. He didn't wear a shirt, and on his chest a circle of hair had been shaved away so that a detector could be fastened on. His voice was a deep, loose smoker's voice, and he talked fast.

"I'm going to go to Florida and relax, for a long time," he said. "I'm going to stop living the way I've been living. Money. That's what I've cared about. My wife and me, we get up early, go to bed late. Trying to get ahead. I've been successful enough. From now on, take it easy. Who needs it? If I get out of here alive, I'm a changed man." John hadn't gone to college. He'd gone to work. He owned a couple of garden centers and was doing pretty well. He was married for the second time, to a beautiful woman fourteen years younger than he.

John had suffered a hemorrhage at a hotel and had been rushed to "another institution," which had discharged him with a diagnosis of possible meningitis. At NYU it would be discovered that he had an aneurysm of the anterior communicating artery. Sometimes it did seem true that the rest of the world was incompetent. Didn't the other institution have a CT scan? Was it being saved? Aneurysms can be cured surgically. But usually surgeons won't risk an operation until a patient like John has survived the risk of vasospasm. In vasospasm, an artery in the brain contracts for un-known reasons. On an X ray of the brain's blood vessels, vasospasm looks dramatic. The curved cerebral arteries fill with blood until the point where one vessel is constricted, as if it had been pinched. In the most severe cases, hardly any blood can pass the pinch, and the branching arteries are barely visible. A patient with a ruptured aneurysm will develop symptoms of vasospasm perhaps 30 percent of the time; 7 percent of the time he will die from it. The timing of aneurysm surgery is a delicate balancing act. If a surgeon operates right away, surgical complications are much more likely. If he waits too long uncontrollable organic processes—like vasospasm—might kill the patient. After statistical comparisons, it's been decided that patients like John must survive a week before going to surgery. In any case, no matter the treatment course, studies show that as many as 42 percent of anerysm patients will die or suffer serious disability.

John didn't understand what he had at this point, but he knew he'd come very close to dying, and still might. John talked as if he'd had some hand in blowing the blood vessel in his head, as if our diseases were a ruling on the kind of lives he and I had been leading. I didn't see it that way. I might be mischievious with Julie or overly chipper with my family or gloomy at night alone, but none of that would last. For me, and this is what I told John, the hospital was a pit stop and shouldn't have any real effect on me one way or the other. That is what I believed.

Part V

FANTASTIC VOYAGE

The stethoscope tells what everyone fears.
Theodore Roethke, "Academic"

<table>
<tr><td>

30

</td><td>

By the time Dr. Alejandro Berenstein, a neuroradiologist, enters my room, it is dark outside. Do doctors kill time until evening visiting hours to assure themselves an audience? Julie and my family are there. So is Kricheff, who, seated on

</td></tr>
</table>

the end of the bed in his overlong white coat, interprets events like a guide. When a doctor enters, we come to attention. My brother Dave slips his beer inside his bomber's jacket. Mom says into the phone, "The doctor's here," and hangs up. Berenstein announces that he is here to talk about the angiogram.

"Alex was one of my students; let's see if he remembers anything I taught him," says Kricheff. Though I know Kricheff's affection often has an aggressive edge—as when he calls Berenstein *maricón* (faggot)—this sounds like badgering. Berenstein reacts with a little noise, like a cough or a snort, hardly acknowledging the taunt. But to me it's as if the congenial ambience, which is the ambience of good health, has been broken by an exchange of head butts. Guys, guys, guys, I want to say. Let's focus on the problem at hand, which is this gob of blood in my brain. Berenstein takes a position against the wall next to van Gogh's ecstatic *Sunflowers*, courtesy, indicates the "Getting SET" booklet, of the art cart, which is courtesy of the Hospital Auxiliary. His hands folded behind his back, a thick black looseleaf braced in the crook of his arm, he rests one sneaker on the other. It's the awkward posture of an undergrad addressing his class for the first time, except that instead of a pullover he is dressed in wrinkled OR scrubs and instead of talking about his semester's project he is discoursing about an invasive diagnostic test, informing me about the chance that it might precipitate pain, injury, or death.

The hemorrhage I suffered was probably caused by a ruptured brain aneurysm or AVM, though a fast-growing tumor might also have caused a blood vessel to burst. The angiogram will tell. From my viewpoint the angiogram cannot bring good news unless nothing turns up, unless my brain is boringly regular and whatever I once had destroyed itself when it shot its bloody wad, a phenomenon that Kricheff let me know occurs occasionally. Berenstein is short, with a yellow beard and clipped bangs that make him look elfin. He is a hybrid: a Polish Jew born in Mexico, which gives his English a Hispanic accent, except for the Yiddish words. His sentences rush out and are filled with images. "Let's not go after a fly with a hammer," he says at one point. The overall effect is of fluid high-speed conversation, though there are few entirely grammatical sentences. "We don't use none of those," he might say. Or, "You didn't put it there, I don't put it there." In another environment I think this Polish Jewish Hispanic Puck on a mid-autumn night's excursion might be hilarious. But when he says he plans to thread a slim plastic tube from my groin up my neck and almost into my brain, no one chuckles. Through the tube he will inject a contrast fluid into the arteries of the brain. Think of the contrast as a dye. An X ray will take a series of pictures that, like the frames of a film, will show step-by-step how the dye, and thus the blood, circulates in the brain, which Berenstein refers to as "your brain."

The angiogram will hurt; some patients report more pain than others, Berenstein mentions.

This may be the most bizarre thing I have ever heard. I've been anx-iously awaiting the angiogram, the test that will determine my immediate future, but this? A doctor says he's going to wend a tube through half my body, as if the body were a kitchen sink and the doctor a plumber who intended to crouch underneath and play with the pipes. A moment like this is so out of sync with the rest of my life; in a jam, I always believed I could thumb through the manual and repair the thing myself. "You can really do that?" I peep, like a kid just coming into a man's voice. Berenstein nods, but I turn to Kricheff to see if I have misunderstood. Kricheff nods, too. "I guess we have to," I say, pushing the words manfully out, so manfully, in fact, that it sounds as if I'm sneezing. This is an intimate moment. And yet the doctor is no confidant. Doctors addressing patients are pitchmen who refine a spiel until it works. "The chances of something bad happening are very small, but if some *meshugena* thing happens to *you*, that's one hundred percent," says Berenstein.

What are the chances? Complications, including death, are possible but unlikely. One in 1,000 is a national average, though Berenstein says his rate is closer to 1 in 10,000. "Not bad, not bad," says Kricheff, which seems like a commentary on Berenstein's low complication rate but is in fact an appreciation of his smooth presentation. "See, he did learn some-thing."

What's so amazing about 11 East is that a person walks in, his mind preoccupied with his lousy job and his next unpleasant assignment and the rush of his own day, and the doctor starts talking about how frequently he kills people while trying to save them. Isn't that what a complication statistic explains?

I think that patients probably find Berenstein warm and approachable. Since that is often the basis for patients' medical judgments, they probably also believe him to be a good doctor. I like him, too. He doesn't respond to Kricheff's baiting. He invites me to trust in this sure technology—at least 9,999 times in 10,000. He downplays the chances of pain and death, which is what I also want to do. Berenstein propels himself off the wall, black looseleaf in tow. He wets a finger, turns to the release. I sign on the dotted line.

Later that evening, after everyone departs, a slim, tall middle-aged man comes to my room. He has a black kit with him and looks at me sideways. "I'm here to do some shaving," he says, his eyebrows lifted conspiratorily. He breaks open the kit and out comes the shaving cream and the disposable razor. He is as uncomfortable as I am with the task. The World Series is on television, and it looks as if Philadelphia might win one from Baltimore. We follow the contest intently, chatting like fans, as he shaves one side, then the other, of my groin. With the ball game on, it's as if we're at the neighborhood barbershop, which both puts me momentarily at ease, then raises a new concern. When Philadelphia's star Mike Schmidt steps up to bat, my barber, lost in the game, whoops excitedly, unconcerned, it seems to me, where his razor is momentarily circling.

31 The angiogram room is brightly lit. It is lined with green tiles, which give it the look, I think, of a bathroom. People in azure uniforms move around. They talk. They arrange syringes and shuffle paper packets with plastic windows as if they are organizing playing cards. There is a sense of something in preparation, but not anything so serious that the atmosphere can't be casual. Berenstein has a Spanish name for the assistants, Joe is José. Or he adds an -ela suffix to the end of a name. Once I heard him call Mindy Rothenstreich Mindela. Berenstein is intense, and also familiar, a hyper Tevye. "Sweetheart," he calls to a nurse, asking for a piece of tubing. At one point he growls, pivoting his neck 180 degrees. "I've got a headache the size of a truck," he says. I am wide awake and feel at first like a participant doing my part in mounting this production. My job, I think, is to stay out of people's way, not to add to the headache. Even as Berenstein palpates the two sides of my groin, hairless and weird as a turtle's head, and covers them with a stick-on plastic sheet, I feel like a member of the crew, an illusion I merrily maintain until Berenstein punctures the artery in my right thigh. We aren't working together; they are working on me. I am the patient, etherized on the table, except I am not etherized but fixed to the sheets by straps. I feel as if I am gone or lapsed or am really invisible, the uncomfortable invisibility of the houseboy in front of whom the mistress of the house unthinkingly undresses.

Before I really know it, the procedure begins; Berenstein is feeding a plastic tube into my new wound. My system, for all I really know, is being Roto-Rootered as I lie serene as a sponge. I am fearful as a child, and yet my actions are formal, self-possessed. I don't want to meddle. I can hear my mother saying to the handyman, come to fix a leaky faucet, "You're the expert, so I'll just get out of your way." I adopt a similar attitude, according to whose rules it would be not only intrusive but impolite for me to stop the proceedings and, for instance, demand an explanation of what the hell is being done to me *now*. This abdication may sound dumb, but at this instant it is warm and wonderful, a brand of protectiveness. After all, what could I say that wouldn't come out, paced by my thrumming heart, adolescent?

Above me a black-and-white TV is suspended on a mobile metal arm. Berenstein stares at the screen as he feeds tubing into my body. I expect to chafe or itch or receive some signal that everything is going horribly wrong, that the plastic rope has knotted and hangs like a noose around my heart, which I, too, through the magic of TV, can watch on the overhead monitor. This is like a video game, it occurs to me. The doctor is the race-car driver, and my blood vessels are the roadways. A line, which is obviously the catheter, steams forward against a gray background, cruising onward, from my gashed thigh to my beleaguered brain. Then Berenstein announces: "There it is," meaning, I surmise, that the tip of this catheter has nearly snaked its way into *my* brain. He connects the end of the catheter that protrudes out of my groin to an injector, a Day-Glo-orange machine about the size and shape of a jackhammer. That's not difficult, but it has to be done carefully. Let an air bubble in and he'd be shooting a stroke into my brain. Once I'm hooked up, everyone files out of the room.

I am the benefactor of vast medical expertise, I tell myself, but that suddenly sounds as falsely hopeful as a medical release, which, while promising to save your life, ticks off all the things that might go wrong. Lying there alone, threaded through like a piece of stitchwork, I feel like the object of a joke.

* * *

THE CONTROL ROOM, behind a big picture window, is the heart of this $2.5 million setup—one X-ray bulb costs $40,000. There gauges are adjusted, and the number of frames to be shot per second is set. This is synchronized with the injector. A console, the centerpiece of which is a digital imaging machine, stores up to 300 images. Once the images are stored, the doctor can flip through them at different speeds. He can watch the arteries, then the veins, fill with the contrast that courses through the cerebrovascular network at normal speed, the speed of blood, about two miles per hour. Or he can slow it down and, in effect, take the movie frame by frame. He can also move forward or backward, stop frame, adjust the intensity and the brightness. Later he can transfer the images to a plastic sheet as a permanent, visible record.

Over the speaker, I hear Berenstein's voice, loud and unfunny: "Don't move, don't move, don't move," which obviously means that this medical marvel is about to deliver an unbelievable wallop. I hear the injector go wham and the X-ray device go bang, bang, bang, bang. The injector shoots contrast through the catheter and into my internal carotid artery, which fills my anterior and middle cerebral arteries. The pain begins. It is a searing pain, and it originates at a point source and then fans out to the nose and ears. It mounts continuously for perhaps ten seconds, and the way I get through it is to tell myself that each moment of pain is an instant less in a fixed total of pain.

32

Oddly, angiography wasn't conceived of as a way to uncover defects in the brain's circulatory system. It was devised by a fearless neurologist as a method to hunt for hidden lumps of tumor. The reason was simple enough. In 1927, when angiography debuted, no surgeon had successfully operated on a cerebrovascular defect. Even the possibility seemed remote. Tumors were different. For the first time in history, a feisty band of neurosurgeons was proving that not only were neoplasms removable from the brain, but some patients might even be returned to health. Tumor localization became extremely important, for the more accurately a tumor could be pinpointed, the less brain matter a surgeon plowed up, and the better were the patient's chances of a full recovery. Neurologists, with their few simple tools, had gotten better at deducing the site of disease, but at least half the brain tumors discovered at autopsy escaped the neurologist's detection during a patient's life. Clearly the neurologist needed help. What if there were a way to confirm the neurologist's best guess, or even to advance his knowledge, with visual evidence?

A decade before angiography, neurosurgeon Walter Dandy rose to this challenge. As a thirty-two-year-old resident at Johns Hopkins, Dandy, who had refused a Rhodes scholarship because it would postpone his medical studies, cleverly combined two long-noticed phenomena. First, that air sometimes seeped into the brain during a skull fracture. Second, that air, so much lower in density than the skull or the brain, showed up black on X rays. Why not use air to outline parts of the brain? In 1918, Dandy drilled holes in the skulls of twenty hydrocephalic children and pushed a needle into one of the four swollen ventricles of their shrunken brains. He extracted up to 300 cc of clear cerebrospinal fluid, the liquid in which the central nervous system bathes, and replaced it with the same amount of air. Then he took an X ray. The air outlined the ventricle. If the ventricle was misshapen, then he concluded that a bulky tumor was distorting it. In 1919, Dandy introduced a variation on ventriculography called pneumoencephalography. It was a similar procedure except that instead of drilling open the skull and pushing air into a ventricle, air was injected into the cerebrospinal fluid in the spinal canal and allowed to float up into the subarachnoid space. This space around the brain also communicates with the ventricles. Special chairs were designed that enabled a doctor to maneuver a patient—even turn him in a somersault!—so that the physician could, in effect, guide the air's trajectory until it rose up against the surface the doctor wanted to examine.

Dandy was among those who felt sure he had revolutionized the diagnosis of neurological problems. "It is difficult to see how intracranial tumors can escape localization," exclaimed the young neurosurgeon, who, two decades later, would be operating six days a week—as many as five times a day. Indeed, discovering a method to inspect visually even a portion of the inside of the head was a daring break with the past.

In practice, though, it was a painful, sometimes dangerous, and often inaccurate procedure. For the patient, the procedure could cause a week of nausea, vomiting, perspiration, headache, low blood pressure, and faintness as the injected air was gradually reabsorbed. At times, the consequences of the test were as fearful as the disease. In 100 cases, Dandy recorded 3 deaths, but others reported death rates of more than 13 percent. Furthermore, despite Dandy's enthusiasm, ventriculography wasn't always a dependable way to find a tumor. A survey of the literature in 1925 showed 392 ventriculograms had produced correct diagnoses in 124 cases, less than one-third of the time.

In 1927, Antonio Caetano de Abreu Freire Egas Moniz, a Portuguese neurologist, reviewed this bleak state of affairs. "If the cerebral vascular network could be visualized," Moniz said, "this would also contribute to the localization of tumors." Fill the blood vessels with contrast, then take an X ray. Any mass in the brain would tug at the countless branchings and shift them. A careful eye could use that information to discern the spot where a space-occupying lesion hid, Moniz believed.

Moniz's idea wasn't new. Outlining the blood vessels with a radio-paque substance was an idea that had been kicked around as long as X rays existed. The problem had always been that contrast materials either did not stand out against the X-ray image of the bony skull or they showed up but killed the patient. In 1922, two researchers had tried injecting Lipiodol, a mix of iodine and poppyseed oil, into the cerebral arteries of lab animals. A beautiful image could be obtained, but the animals didn't survive the diagnosis. Air, of course, would also be deadly in the arteries. The outcome of work with the early opaques—including at one point cobra venom—was a resounding failure. Writes one author, the early contrasts were like "strong vascular poisons."

The solution to this dilemma didn't call for a clever theoretical turn; it required someone stubborn enough to assume the risks of dangerous testing. Moniz was just such a person. Perhaps it was a life spent in politics that inured him to failure, even when it jeopardized human life. A neurologist who had studied with the famous neurologist Joseph Babinksi in Paris, Moniz had also served his country as a member of Parliament, minister of foreign affairs, and ambassador to Spain. In 1926, a dictator was installed in Portugal, and Moniz gave up politics, returning to neurology full-time. In 1949—after having been shot and almost killed by a schizophrenic—he would win the Nobel Prize in physiology and medicine for the introduction of prefrontal lobotomy.

Moniz did not set out to discover a new, less toxic contrast. He understood the issue as a problem of dosing. How much of a contrast would show up under X ray and yet not poison the subject? Moniz did some lab work on animals, but it was the human experiments that he knew would substantiate his work. Moniz was a staff doctor at an asylum for the insane and terminally ill, the clientele of which conveniently served as test subjects. Whether he should have been trying out his ideas on human subjects was apparently not something that greatly troubled Moniz. "If we are able to determine the site of the tumor, we would then try to obtain a definitive cure," he wrote. "To accomplish this, we feel that all can be risked." The prospect of risking all—not his all but his patients'—would be unthinkable today. Erik Lindgren, one of the pivotal figures in European neuroradiology, later commented, "Ethical demands prevalent in most countries today regarding human experimentation were disregarded entirely."

Moniz's 1927 paper introducing angiography is clear, honest, and horrifying. Moniz first tried strontium bromide, a compound used to treat some forms of arthritis. He injected it into the carotid artery in the neck and let the blood take the contrast up into the brain. Once it was there, Moniz X-rayed it. Most of the patients who submitted to the test appear to have had some neurological problem. As a result of the angiogram, his first five patients suffered transient fevers and pain; in each case the procedure failed. When the sixth patient died eight hours after the angiogram, Moniz turned to a different contrast material. This time he used an iodine-based substance. It, too, was a poison, as the users of iodine-based Lipiodol had learned years earlier. Yet it was also known that at certain doses some iodides had been used to treat neurosyphilis without terrible side effects (or much effect on the syphilis, either). On his ninth patient, a twenty-year-old with a suspected pituitary tumor who was blind, vomiting, and stricken with a terrible headache, "for the first time, we employed a good technique." On June 28, 1927, Moniz obtained the first image of the cerebral vessels, the first cerebral angiogram. The blood vessels stood out, said one observer, like steely wires.

Moniz compared this image to X rays of the normal vascular anatomy he had already obtained from cadavers, an exercise that had presented other problems. Because his lab didn't have adequate X-ray facilities, after injecting a cadaver with contrast, Moniz loaded the dead body into his car and drove across Lisbon to a radiology service, worrying all the while that he might have a car accident. (And then how would he explain to an impatient policeman why one of his passengers was a corpse?) His industriousness paid off. In the case of the twenty-year-old he found that the carotid, middle cerebral, and anterior cerebral arteries were bent out of shape, proof, he concluded, that a tumor was indeed hidden nearby.

Moniz demonstrated that angiography was possible, but most of the world was hesitant to use it until the dangers could be diminished. Early users noted side effects of epilepsy, paresis, and aphasia, most temporary, though some permanent. In 1928, Moniz became enthusiastic about a new contrast substance, Thorotrast, a trade name for colloidal thorium dioxide, which is radioactive. His first results were even less promising. The initial six attempts brought six deaths. Moniz pressed on, assuming, as he always did, that his errors were a matter of adjusting his technique, not rethinking his theory. "Of what steel [Moniz] had to be forged to dare to persevere under such conditions and with such results," said J. Lepoire, former president of the Society of Neurosurgery of the French Language. Moniz eventually gained better control of the procedure with Thorotrast, though when it was shown to be a carcinogen, it, too, was rejected. Moniz had demonstrated angiography's capabilities, and yet, for want of a suitable contrast, the procedure was not accepted as the primary neuroradiological exam until Kricheff's generation. It was then that a new contrast—triiodinated water-soluble contrast—finally made the exam safe.

For Kricheff's peers, neuroradiologists of the 1960s, angiography changed the way the craft was practiced. All of a sudden a radiologist could hurt the patient. And did. Just twenty-five years ago, complication rates were reported as high as 12 percent, which means one of eight angiography patients was injured or killed. As recently as the 1960s, a neurologist, who had the patient's and not the radiologist's interests in mind, pondered long and hard before subjecting his charge to the procedure. By the 1970s, permanent complications, including death following cerebral angiography, occurred in about 1 percent of patients, still high for what was, after all, just a diagnostic procedure, but acceptable.

The advent of the CT scan finished off the ventriculogram and the pneumocephalogram. Almost as soon as a hospital got a CT scan, it stopped shooting air into patients' heads and spinning them in movable chairs. Angiography survived but was repositioned. Moniz had billed the angiogram as a technique for detecting tumors, and Kricheff's generation had subscribed to this goal. The CT scan, though, was better at that task. Probably as often as not, angiograms missed tumors.

Yet by the 1970s vascular abnormalities of the brain were being successfully attacked by neurosurgeons. The angiogram, which once provided indirect evidence of mass lesions, could now offer the cerebrovascular surgeon just what he needed: a map of the cerebrovascular system in action. The angiogram became the definitive test for suspected blood-vessel disease, in particular AVMs and aneurysms. In the OR, the brain surgeon pinned the angiograms on the light board next to the scans from the CT, which was used to screen candidates for angiograms.

Since Moniz, angiographers searching for the best route to the head had punctured vessels in the neck, in the chest, and under the arm. In the 1950s, doctors in Stockholm tried a new point of entry: the leg. They threaded plastic tubes through the femoral artery in the groin, controlling them like kite strings with a push, pull, and spin. At the forward tip, the tubes or catheters were manufactured with a hook to the right or the left or an S-shaped curve—and given names like Sidewinder and Head-hunter—to facilitate entry into the desired vascular path. The advantages of this technique are enormous. From one hole at the top of the thigh an angiographer has access to either side of the head. He also has a choice of routes. From the femoral artery, a catheter tracks to the aortic arch atop the heart. There a catheter could duck into the common carotid artery or pick up, by way of the innominate artery, the subclavian artery that leads into the vertebral artery or, as in my case, do both, one after the other.

Instead of dumping contrast into the carotid in the neck and letting it float, as had once been common practice, a doctor could selectively guide the catheter into subdivisions of the main vessels, actually guiding the tube deep into the small arteries of the brain, and then, by delicately squeezing a syringe at the groin, shoot in contrast.

33 The first time Berenstein saw an angiogram, it was a femoral catheterization. "Did you ever see the movie *Fantastic Voyage* where the submarine shrinks down and travels through the blood stream?" he said. "That was like a dream, but it is true now. We're navigating through the blood vessels." The body's vascular network is a system of roadways. And Berenstein had become, as he said, "a maniac driver." He could guide a catheter inserted at the groin to the feet or the arms or the tip of the nose. Berenstein could get within striking distance of the capillaries, 1/25,000th of an inch in diameter.

Berenstein had attended medical school at the University of Mexico, then trained at Mt. Sinai in Hartford, Connectict, and Mt. Sinai in New York. Berenstein fit the personality profile of the new angiographer. He had good hands and an aggressive mind. On April 27, 1976, while he was chief radiology resident at Mt. Sinai in New York, Berenstein was per-forming an emergency angiogram on a patient who had just returned from spleen surgery—and who was dying. On the film he could see the cause of the impending death: Blood was squirting from a leaky blood vessel into the stomach. No surgeon could get to the bleed faster than the ra-diologists. Berenstein's attending that day was Dr. Harold Mitty. Mitty, who would later become an interventional radiologist, had never before intervened to treat a patient. In radiology circles treatment was still some-thing that most people only talked about; only a few actually tried. Mitty and Berenstein looked at each other. The case in front of them seemed a perfect therapeutic opportunity. They attempted an artifical embolization. They floated tiny bits of gelatin sponge through a catheter that had been positioned in the leaky vessel. The bits were sucked to the hole. The bleed was plugged; the patient survived. Berenstein says he retains a picture of the case for sentimental reasons, meaning he kept a copy of the angiogram and not a photo of the thankful patient.

Mitty had expected Berenstein to depart the competitive world of New York medicine to be a big shot in Mexico. But in Mexico, Berenstein decided, he would have none of the facilities he needed. "I only wanted to go to a place where they did angiographic embolization," he said.

At NYU, Kricheff had started a program in artificial embolization. Under angiographic guidance, he floated rubber pellets into people's brains, trying to stop up AVMs that were too big for surgeons to operate on—much the way Berenstein had done in the stomach. In 1977, Kricheff was looking to step out of that position. Ransohoff, the chief of neurosurgery, agreed that the techniques represented a potentially better way to attack some brain disease. The job needed someone full-time. Other people in the department had tried embolization but didn't enjoy it. You could help patients, but you could also kill them, right there on the table. "I didn't have the stomach for it," said one neuroradiologist, and returned to the light box. "Every day I learn something new reading films."

Kricheff hired Berenstein. He once called that the best personnel choice he ever made, though he wished sometimes that Berenstein, a self-starter if ever there was one, would inform him of what he was doing. After all, Kricheff groused, he had started the program. Kricheff later explained to me: "I'm exceedingly proud of Alex. I pat myself on the back for having selected him for this role, for having supported him and guided him and given him a lot of advice. In the early days he would come to me constantly, 'Should I do this? Should I do any more?' That became less and less and less. And you say, 'Geez, for ten years I was the guy doing it, that kind of thing.' Maybe that's why I'm always giving Alex a little twist. Maybe it's guilt: me feeling inadequate that I am not doing your angiogram myself because I haven't done them for many years. It's hard to analyze."

Berenstein is hyper, in an adorable way. Outside the angiographic suite he often bums a cigarette. "I thought you quit smoking," someone says.

"I did," says Berenstein, taking a drag, reaching for the can of soda in someone else's hand, and offering, in return, a bite from his bagel. Before he had his own office, he would be talking about the day's events with a secretary, when because he was in a rush, in mid-sentence he'd take off his street clothes and change into his scrubs. Says Berenstein, "You've got to be pushy. Dr. K. says calm down. If I calm down, I won't get nowhere. He says to get organized. If I get organized, I'll be dangerous."

Says one radiologist, "We forgive him his excesses because he's in the vanguard."

Berenstein's attitude toward Kricheff has evolved. (Maybe that's why he alternately called him Irv, Dr. K., and Kricheff.) Berenstein felt as if Kricheff was at first a father figure, then a teacher, then a competitor. "Now he lets me do what I want," says Berenstein. Berenstein still seeks out his opinion on a tough case, but he sometimes bristles at Kricheff's way of taking his junior under his wing, which seems like putting Berenstein second. Like any influential figure, he both liked Kricheff and could find him difficult to like. Once, he remembered that as a joke Kricheff tossed a glass of wine in Berenstein's face. "Dr. Kricheff always tells me I should tell him what I'm doing," says Berenstein, "but I get too busy."

First in the lab and then in the angiographic suite, Berenstein moved past the crude technique of floating pellets into the brain. He learned to tie a tiny balloon to the leading end of the catheter. When the balloon was inflated inside a vessel, blood carried it—as it would carry any object—deep into the brain. In 1975, a neuroradiologist named Charles Kerber figured out that a tiny hole made in the forward end of the balloon could be used as a delivery system for contrast or medicines or even a medical grade of Krazy Glue. When the balloon is in position, the doctor fills a syringe with glue, attaches it to the tube coming out of the patient's groin, then squeezes glue into the brain. Berenstein is one of an elite group of neuroradiologists who has begun to do delicate cerebral repair work intraluminally, that is, from inside the blood vessels. By injecting glue through a catheter, for instance, he plugs leaky or useless vessels and, in effect, removes an AVM from the brain's circulation. The pellets and now the glue can stay in the brain forever without, so far, any side effects. Most of Berenstein's work is done on AVMs. One report says that 27 percent of all AVMs are located beyond where the surgeon's knife can safely reach.

By comparison with angiographic embolization, diagnostic angiography—which I was undergoing—posed few risks, though an unlucky doctor could knot one of the thin, flexible catheters in the heart cavity. When that had happened to Berenstein, he had snaked a catheter up the other femoral artery on the other side of the groin, hooked the knot, and shaken it until it came loose. If that didn't work, surgery might be necessary. In interventional procedures the types of dangers were multiplied. Once one of Berenstein's balloons had floated off the end of a catheter and blocked a blood vessel in the brain. The patient was rushed to the OR, where the head was entered, the vessel sliced open, the balloon extracted, and the vessel closed with microsutures two and one half hours later—without, luckily, any damage to the patient.

Diagnostic angiography, which Berenstein still did part-time, was something that he could live without. It just wasn't that challenging. There were two reasons he'd be called in. First, in cases where embolization was being considered as a therapeutic possibility, the angiogram was usually done by the embolizer. That way he could make sure the study answered all the questions he needed answered. Second, as a favor to Kricheff. A doctor taking extra specialization after his residency might normally do the angio, but not when the patient was the friend of a doctor.

34

At first, Kricheff waits in the corridor, but then he joins Berenstein at the monitor. Maybe Berenstein would rather have done the exam himself and brought the results to Kricheff later. But Kricheff isn't the type to keep put. "That's not the way I am," he says. Besides, he isn't there as an angiographer. He is a concerned citizen and defers to Berenstein as the doctor in charge.

The injection done, the computer reproduces the winding cerebral vessels on the screen, making the head look for an instant like a mesh helmet.

In a healthy brain blood flows first into the arteries, which feed into the capillaries that feed brain tissue. Used blood then drains out through the veins on its way back to the heart. On a normal angiogram the arteries should fill with contrast first. Then the veins.

Kricheff hangs back but can watch what's going on as easily as Berenstein. The right-carotid angiogram comes on the screen. Fine, so far. Then something is wrong. There it is; Berenstein sees it, and Kricheff can see it, too. The arteries are filling properly when on the side a vein fills, too, like a wayward squib. It's too early for a vein to fill. Yet the temporal-occipital branch of the middle cerebral artery is filling what looks like a vein. An abnormal connection exists between the arterial and the venous systems.

Berenstein wants another view. Any vessel that by the wildest stretch of the imagination could be feeding the abnormality has to be injected with contrast and filmed. This abnormality is near the surface of the brain. He wants to make sure that there is no supply from the arteries in the dura, the brain's outer covering.

Berenstein returns to my side. Working again at my groin, his porthole into the brain, he gives the catheter a pull. Under TV guidance, he directs the tip of the tube into another vessel. From the internal carotid he heads it to the other half of the fork, the external carotid, then into the occipital branch. Then he leaves.

Over the loudspeaker Berenstein chants again, "Don't move, don't move, don't move." More contrast is injected. "It's almost over," says Berenstein.

Somewhere along the process Kricheff wonders if Berenstein isn't being a little too thorough. The final report will say: "Via transfemoral catheter the right internal carotid, right vertebral, right occipital, right ascending pharangeal, and right middle meningeal arteries were catheterized." Fine, thinks Kricheff, I asked him to do the study, it's up to him how he does the study. He knows more about it now than I do.

The results make the diagnosis apparent. "A one-centimenter abnormal collection of vessels is seen in the right occipital lobe." The history is now complete. A tumor is out; an aneurysm is out. One sunny day, at a very precise moment, in a very specific place, but for no apparent reason, a vessel in my head had given way to arterial pressure. One of the branches of the posterior cerebral artery is definitely feeding an AVM, a 1-centimeter tangle of vessels. The only other supply is a small branch of the occipital artery that gives a very tiny dural supply.

The angiogram showed the vessel that broke. The veins were emptying except for where a vein held on to its dye, meaning it was partially clotted. That had to be the vein that hemorrhaged. It's resting on the inferior surface of the occipital lobe, on the bottom of it. "This collection appears to . . . drain into a partially thrombosed vein running laterally along the superior surface of the tentorium."

The hemorrhage itself shows up as a tumor would, as a displacement of the vessels. On one side, some vessels are curved compared to the other side. An area is a little elevated. A couple of the vessels are a little straighter than the other side. The clot probably squeezed some of the area that controls vision, but the mass of it came just to the tip of a thin strip of occipital lobe. If it had crossed onto the strip, it would have destroyed rather than squeezed the strip. Had that happened, there would have been much denser visual loss—the central part of my vision would have gone —without chance of recovery.

* * *

I SHOULD HAVE WORRIED about the results and their consequences, but I think only of the pain, of how intensely it burns and how long it endures. It has wearied me. So that when Dr. K., swashbuckling on his small feet, hurries out of the control room, I am too fatigued for suspense. "We're not dealing with probabilities anymore," he says with excitement. "It's an AVM."

In the strange new environment I am in, I had even found myself hoping for this. Now I'd won. Why, then, am I crushed? Because really what I'd held out for was something entirely different. Kricheff had made the mistake of mentioning to me that sometimes—he put his hand up like a traffic cop's on that word—sometimes these things destroy themselves. The hemorrhage obliterates the malformation. "I've seen a malformation the size of the whole hemisphere, which five years later was gone, it was just gone," he said. I really had imagined that what would happen to me was this: Someone would stop by my stretcher and announce, Everything's cleared up. I am tired and tired of being brave. Kricheff, as always, points out the merits of my case. "The malformation's in a good position, near the surface of the brain," he says. A good position for what? He rattles the plastic sheet of films in my face, like something I should be proud of. He has already selected a surgeon who, he says, is an "absolutely sensational surgeon." I have no more test results to wait for. I think this is the moment that I understand I am about to undergo brain surgery.

Part VI

PERILOUS BATTLE

You could be going along just fine and then one day, through no fault of your own, something could get loose in your bloodstream and knock out part of your brain. Leave you like that. And if it didn't happen now, all at once, it was sure to happen slowly later on.

Tobias Wolff, *The Other Miller*

35

When Eugene Somer Flamm, one of 3,427 neurosurgeons certified by the American Board of Neurological Surgery, lumbers into the crowd of my parents, Julie, and me, Mom jumps up. The surgeon waves her off with a gesture, as if he is wiping a windshield. But she is insistent. The surgeon must have a seat. The two white-coated residents who walk at his sides must sit, as well. Mom's eyebrows are performing some kind of high-wire act; first flat with surprise, then hooked with dismay. "Sit, sit," she says with vigor, and guides the surgeon like an elderly guest into the corner chair. I know that when she'd first caught a glimpse of Flamm near the nurses' station, something had been going on. He was standing in his blue uniform. There was an obvious sense of his collecting himself. Her immediate reaction was that she hoped he wasn't our doctor. That was then. Once he became our doctor, she made sure he had the place of honor and got the right kind of attention. Her supposition is what? If you're nice to the surgeon, he'll give you a good operation. Suddenly the dignity of my hospital room gives way to a frivolous game of musical chairs. Everybody but bedridden me stands; the doctors sit.

Flamm is wearing a green sports coat the color of cooked peas and a tie with maroon ribbing, Brooks Brothers casual. He stretches an arm along the windowsill, assuming the let-your-fingers-do-the-walking pose. His fingers are broad and square—surgeon's fingers! He is glad to see me, he says, though hardly excited. He doesn't seem the excitable type. He is friendly but collected, businesslike, nothing like the doctors of my childhood, the pediatricians and GPs who were as sorry as anyone that you were sick even if they couldn't always do much about it. Flamm is here to take care of the mess. All week I've been waiting for that announcement. All week! I could shout.

Mom leans against the window ledge, velvety darkness behind her. Her role in life, as she sees it, has been to "make nice." At dinners when I was growing up, she was like a short-order cook, preparing individual portions of lamb chops for one kid and grilled cheese for another and hamburger for a third, just so everybody should be happy. In the hospital, though, so much is beyond even her cagiest attempts to make nice. There's her kid sitting on the bed in front of her, and there's nothing to do. Dr. Kricheff told her that the problem could be taken care of. "It could have destroyed itself," he'd told her. "Then the angiogram wouldn't have shown anything and we'd always be nervous." Taken care of, she thought, was a far cry from brain surgery, which is what she now understood to be in store. She assumes her bad-news stance: bolt upright, her thin ankles almost knocking together. As Flamm speaks in an unwavering voice, the corners of her mouth widen in a weighted smile; her darkened front tooth shows. Then she backs off a small step, as if the words have force. It is as if she is really fearful, and watching her, I feel as if I'm the one doing it, making her afraid, which I could have easily avoided.

This gathering is so congenial, I want to say, What can go wrong? We are concerned, sure. But our attitude is a pinched-in-cheek concern, like at tax time, nothing more.

"You've already come through the most dangerous part," says Flamm by way of introduction. See, I think and arrange my arms like chicken wings. The hemorrhage is history. I am recovering from that; my brain, wondrous thing, is absorbing the spilled blood. The danger, Flamm says, not giving the word "danger" greater emphasis than any other, is that this AVM nestled in my brain has "demonstrated a predisposition to bleed." It sounds promiscuous.

Flamm has a big head with a small mouth, a nickel where a quarter should be, and eyebrows that are bushy and narrow, like minihedges. His hair is brown with silver streaks, which makes it look metallic, and is not quite combed but put into place, patch by patch. In the front, he has a Flash Gordon widow's peak, a triangle that comes to a sharp point. His eyes, behind gold wire-rimmed glasses, are a piercing blue. Flamm's laugh is inviting, but he's not jolly, and he has a way of laughing with you and then stopping short. He is no kibitzer. His natural expression is a non-expression, which suggests almost ennui, as if what is at hand is the most mundane thing. His job, he says, is to go over the facts and lay them out so I can make a decision, which seems reasonable.

"The danger is that the AVM could bleed again," he says, the drama of that statement lost on him.

When?

"We have statistics. In the next year there's a six-to-nine-percent chance; in every year after that the chance is two to three percent," says Flamm.

I like statistics. They seem precise. Give me pencil and paper and I will calculate my chance of going batty eyed with another hemorrhage. A little applied mathematics and I will come up with a formula for my health. Unfortunately, I don't remember how probabilities are calculated. Do I add each year's percentage? But then if I live to be seventy-eight, which is another fifty years, at 2 percent a year, I'll have a 100 percent chance of hemorrhaging. That's alarming indeed. Maybe I multiply? Maybe it's a combination? I look to Dad, who is so good with numbers, who I have watched calculate problems in his head, his blank eyes focusing on a spot in the air, his teeth chewing his gums. Without a grin, but as if it were routine, he'd offer the solution, and Mom would pinch his arm. "How do you do that, Ervy?" she'd say, as if it were the neatest magic trick.

The father of my boyhood *was* a magician. He built a patio of cinder blocks and cement behind our house; he terraced our yard with fat railroad ties and planted azaleas, rhododendrons, and a garden of red and yellow roses. He even tried to drill his own water well. From the roof of the kitchen he swung a sledgehammer onto the head of a steel pipe, beating it into the ground. To me the effort seemed magnificent. Not the cataclysmic strokes, just the idea! My father would move the earth and pump water from our square of suburban yard. The world he showed us was completely manageable, its threats tameable, convictions I continued to hold even after the steel shaft foundered on rock, to remain ever after adrift in its trench, an unused flagpole.

In the hospital room I wonder this: Where is the father I grew up with? As he listens to the surgeon, his mouth flutters as if there is a bee inside. It is the tic of a senior citizen, like his signature, which, I noticed recently, has grown loose and wiry. He blows on his hands as if to keep them warm. His two strips of hair are combed straight back, the bald spot between them the color of a fresh potato. Where is his mathematical assuredness, his stern, unbearable will? How quiet he is! I am dying, threatened by a fetal miscue, and he dallies, craning his neck for an improved view. We are all spectators waiting for a hero or the beginning of a new day. Who, I want to know, will protect me from the surgeon's gleeful knife?

My capacity for contemplation is gone. The probabilities seem part of a game; and the play has gone out of me.

"We just don't know which ones will go, or when," says Flamm, unperturbed.

All, so far, is prologue.

In some cases, I learn, the risk of treating a problem in the brain appears greater than the dangers associated with living with the lesion. Then a patient, as all patients once did, does nothing. Monitored by a doctor, he waits out the odds, hoping for the best. However, today three major therapies are available for most brain problems, mine included. In certain AVMs, particularly when they are buried deep in the brain, surgeons cede to neuroradiologists like Berenstein, who weave their catheters from the groin into the brain and then fill the malformation with glue. In Sweden specialists have also reported good results with gamma rays—they call it a "gamma knife"; in California, with helium ions from a 184-inch cyclotron. In both techniques radiation is directed through the scalp and skull and, with great precision, targets the AVM's feeding arteries. Radiation causes the arterial walls to grow thicker until over the course of a year the vessels close off. Because they are new techniques, neither embolization nor radiation therapy can point to results over a long period of time.

My AVM has apparently caused little hand wringing among the doctors. Flamm has spoken to Berenstein about embolization. It is possible, they think, but so is surgery, and that, he explains, is the proven therapy. If a surgeon cuts out an AVM, clips off the feeding and draining vessels, then the patient is cured. That is established. Flamm says my AVM is well located for surgery. What does that mean? It isn't on the dominant side of the brain, near the really expensive real estate, like speech or memory. It isn't deep in the interior. He won't have to go through much brain to get there.

How much?

He holds up his thumb and forefinger, the distance between them the height of a quarter. Flamm is never ruffled. This is what he does for a living, cuts into heads. He is telling me he can cut into mine, grab the AVM, and not damage my vision any more than the hemorrhage already has. Of course, surgery can always go bad; visual loss is the primary risk, though obviously any botched brain surgery carries the threat of death. He doesn't have to dwell on that. Nobody at the time mentions the chance that I could develop epilepsy, a possible consequence of any invasive procedure in the brain.

Flamm leans forward, his wide furrowed forehead aimed to the floor, his shining blue eyes angled up at me. I hit one of the control buttons and slowly, noisily, bring the head of the bed upright. Some people don't make it past the hemorrhage. The question I have to face now, Flamm says, is will I be lucky if that thing in my head goes off again.

It is possible to survive additional hemorrhages. On the other hand, there is no guarantee that future damage won't be more serious, and lasting, or fatal. "I'm not going to operate just because an AVM is there. Once they've bled, it's a different issue. Most of us think we can do a better job than just letting nature take its course." Flamm sees it this way: "Is a neurosurgeon going into the brain safer than the explosion of an unguided missile inside the skull, that is, the possibility of a random rupture?" Flamm's offer is to prevent the problem. He is suggesting preventive brain surgery.

36

Before Flamm cruised up to 11 East to see me, he had stopped by Kricheff's office. It is windowless, ornamentless except for a few of his wife's homemade clay pots. It is like a place designed for nothing but viewing scans, which is fine, because Flamm wasn't paying a social call. Flamm had taken the elevator down from the recovery room, a postop scan from a woman he had operated on secured between thumb and forefinger like an admission ticket. The bending plastic sheet produced a liquid *thwump*. Kricheff spun in his chair, screwing himself a half turn into the floor. He was always glad to see Flamm, whom he'd known since Flamm's residency twenty years ago. The glow from the light box over Kricheff's desk was like light seen through ice. Kricheff slipped the scan onto the box. His eye was immediately drawn to the area of interest. Flamm's head shook from side to side like a dust brush. In the penumbral cast his skin was the color of flour. Kricheff saw what Flamm saw. For no good reason that Flamm could discover, his morning operation had suffered a stroke. Flamm was hoping that Kricheff, the CT expert, might scrutinize the scan and pick out something he had missed. It was worth a try, Flamm said almost embarrassedly.

W. JOST MICHELSEN, a neurosurgeon at Columbia-Presbyterian Medical Center, who may operate on as many AVMs as anyone in the country, once said: "I think what's happened in the last five years is that though I can probably do the operations better now than before, I've never been so scared in all my life as when I'm in the OR, no matter what I do. Because I know everything that can go wrong. Other surgeons say you have to take your lumps. So the patient's half-paralyzed. You have to live with that. I don't want to live with that. I hate it."

Living with that was the hardest part. But sometimes you just were unlucky. That was the business, Flamm had said many times, which did not grant absolution. Guilt stuck. Maybe every surgeon didn't go through self-recrimination, but as Flamm reviewed the videotapes of his mishaps, he told himself there must have been some detail that could have been done differently.

Flamm kept a computerized record of each of his cases—each surgeon keeps his own records. His rate of surgical mortality and morbidity depended to a great extent on the type of case. (Mortality referred to deaths; morbidity to nonlethal complications of surgery, including serious ones like paralysis and less serious ones like a slight loss of vision.) With ophthalmic aneurysms, most of which were at least 2 centimeters wide, complications ran as high as 16 percent, half in morbidity, half in mortality. Overall, though, he put his morbidity and mortality rate at 2–4 percent for aneurysms and 6 percent for AVMs, which compared favorably with the best in the profession.

Yet, viewed another way, those numbers decreed that four or six or perhaps sixteen times in a hundred, despite whatever talent Flamm brought to bear, the breaks would go the other way. Failure was as certain an element of neurosurgery as was success. ''The excruciating part,'' Flamm once said, ''is that you may do a perfect operation, as far as you can tell, and the patient might wake up dead.''

Other specialists get annoyed that the neurosurgeon is consistently singled out by the public and the press for admiration. Eye surgeons work on smaller structures. Even the watchmaker's craft demands finer eye-hand coordination. Perhaps what brain surgeons possess is not such a rare talent. ''Anyone with enough experience, if he has a decent brain and he's not a left-footed batter, can, from diligent training, become a very good journeyman neurosurgeon,'' said Edward Schlesinger, who directed the neurosurgery service at Columbia-Presbyterian Medical Center in New York City. Flamm didn't necessarily disagree. The hand movements needed to play a stringed instrument well were more difficult than surgical maneuvers, a realization he came to after years of frustrating attempts to master the cello.

Why, then, isn't ophthalmologic surgery the glamour job? The reason is this: The admiration that accrues to the brain surgeon doesn't result solely, or even primarily, from the technical difficulties of the endeavor. The eye surgeon deftly removes cataracts off the clouded eye. A difficult undertaking. Somebody has to do it. ''Among ourselves we say, For God's sakes the ophthalmologists have it easy. Everyone has two eyes. The worst situation in ophthalmology is that you lose one eye. It's terrible. I don't mean to make light of it,'' Flamm said, his voice popping an octave. ''On the other hand, you lose one brain and you don't have another you can rely on." It is a strange argument. Returning to a family with news of a stroked-out relative is about as bad as it gets for a neurosurgeon. And yet the very occurrence of neurosurgical failure affirms what a heroic undertaking it is in the first place.

"It doesn't take very much to take someone who was a thinking, creative individual into the slag heap where he can carry out nothing but a manual chore," said Flamm. "Take someone who writes poetry who has an anterior communicating artery aneurysm. He can move, talk, everything. His poetry may be nonsense. Take a person who ends up aphasic. He may be able to walk, carry on activities, but he can't speak or understand what is said to him. These are the kinds of things that are worse than death. An exquisite part of the brain has been damaged irrevocably." Really, are you going to enlist watchmakers to fight the advancing armies of tumor, aneurym, AVM!

Not all brain surgeons shoulder the same burden. Within the neurosurgical community there are many recognized levels of skill. A neurosurgeon in a county hospital who does a couple of dozen major operations a year is somewhere near the bottom of the ladder. He would be useful in skull fractures, concussions, clots on the surface of the brain, accessible tumors, malignant tumors, peripheral nerve surgery. A surgeon who toils in the emergency room is also considered less skillful, something like a medic in the field who provides immediate attention to disasters—the car-accident victim with multiple trauma. In the neurosurgical hierarchy, operating on the spine is not a glorious feat, either. After all, no matter how difficult the job—and the spinal cord is extremely delicate—if you operate on the spine, you aren't a brain surgeon; you are a back surgeon. You risk paralyzing a person, not killing him. And though tumors can be tough, the accessible ones usually don't get you into trouble, and the worst ones are incurable no matter what you do. The elite of the neurosurgical world is "the bomb squad," as one young neurosurgeon dubbed it, the surgeons who go after vascular malformations, lesions that blow up at the bottom of a narrow hole three inches into the head, one outing in ten.

Flamm, a scholar as well as a surgeon, knew as well as anyone that vascular neurosurgery was a recent development—even within the young field of brain surgery. Long after surgeons had begun to operate on tumors of the brain, no one dared to operate on an AVM or an aneurysm. "The diagnosis [of an aneurysm] is, as a rule, impossible," wrote William Osler, one of the world's preeminent physicians, in his *Principles and Practice of Medicine* in 1920. If, while looking for a compact, self-contained tumor,

an unlucky surgeon came across an AVM's tangle of pulsating vessels—
like aneurysms, AVMs, too, were only discovered by mistake—he hastily
closed the head. At a time when Harvey Cushing had already encountered
1,437 intracranial tumors, more than anyone alive, he believed that to
attack an AVM surgically was "unthinkable." Cushing could not see how
to cut into this knot of vessels without provoking a massive hemorrhage.

> Elsewhere in the body where tourniquets could be applied or pressure be
> temporarily exerted against resistant tissues, bleeding [from an AVM] can
> be controlled but this is not true of the brain. There is little to be said from
> our own experience in any way encouraging in regard to the surgical attack
> on one of these formidable lesions. The mere exposure may be attended with
> great risks.

It was not always easy to keep away from AVMs. Prior to the angiogram, the principal distinguishing characteristic of AVMs was believed to
be that they sometimes produced a *bruit*, which is the French word for
noise. In 1641 the French barber-surgeon Ambroïse Paré reported hearing
"a noise or blowing sound . . . in consequence of the impetuosity with
which the spirit passes in and out of the small opening of the artery." Later
doctors doubted a spirit's presence but confirmed that in some AVMs the
velocity of blood traveling through the AVM did indeed create a noise.
Sometimes a doctor could hear a bruit over the AVM by putting his stethoscope to the patient's head. Sometimes it was loud enough to be heard
by the unaided ear. Cushing believed that the key to diagnosing an AVM
was the presence of a bruit, but that probably indicated how many AVMs
Cushing missed. Later research showed that a bruit existed in less than 10
percent of AVMs.

For a time it was hoped that by tying off big arteries and thus reducing
blood flow through the AVM—as well as through much of the brain—
the malformation could be successfully managed. It was a vain hope. If
its principal blood supply was cut off, the AVM recruited other sources.
Tiny feeding vessels swelled until they were dangerously bloated, which
led early researchers to believe mistakenly that an AVM was a cancer
that grew.

Cushing concluded: "Prognosis is unquestionably most uncertain if
not actually bad."

Yet even as Cushing's grim forecast was going into print, Walter Dandy,
the radical student of the conservative Cushing, began to attack AVMs
surgically. In his first publication, he reported on eight cases, including
two "heroic" efforts to remove all of an AVM. None succeeded. On Feb-

ruary 11, 1922, Dandy had operated on a fifteen-year-old with a mild case of epilepsy, probably caused by an AVM. Dandy's strategy was to tie off the vessels on the surface of the brain, then take out the tangle of the AVM as part of a mass removal of brain tissue. "As this was our first experience with this type of lesion, we little realized its extreme difficulties and dangers," said Dandy. He quickly learned. Unfortunately, the surface vessels Dandy had tied off were veins that drained the blood. With nowhere to go, the blood swelled inside the remaining vessels until finally they burst. "Blood flooded the operative field," said Dandy. "The bleeding became profuse. Pressure with cotton and gauze accomplished little more than to check the bleeding temporarily. A rapid extirpation of the mass was attempted but the bleeding vessels multiplied." The boy died in a few hours.

Three and a half years later, Dandy tried again, this time first carefully tying off the arteries *feeding* the AVM. He was able to remove the AVM and close the scalp without observing any bleeding. The patient died from hemorrhage six days later, though in the early days of AVM surgery this was considered a victory.

In 1927, the Swedish surgeon Herbert Olivecrona reported on a sixteen-year-old boy with a history of headache and vomiting who had sought his help. The patient showed signs of a cerebellar tumor, but when the tumor was exposed in the OR, it turned out to be an AVM. It was inoperable, a determination made after two operations and the death by hemorrhage of the young patient. Five years later, in 1932, Olivecrona proved an AVM was operable with the first total excision from which the patient recovered.

Vascular neurosurgery, though an outgrowth of neurosurgery, was in many ways a new field. It drew into its sweep new problems, once as unsolvable as tumors. Among them were aneurysms and AVMs. To attack these lesions was to face, once again, colossal morbidity and mortality rates. Killing one in three patients who went under the knife was not uncommon.

By 1965, J. Lawrence Pool and D. Gordon Potts of Columbia-Presbyterian Medical Center, in their book *Aneurysms and Arteriovenous Anomalies of the Brain*, searched the medical literature and found 187 surgical excisions of AVMs. The morbidity and mortality rate of surgery was 26 percent; nearly 11 percent died.

To Pool, then chief of neurosurgery at Columbia, the risk of surgery seemed worth it. "Excision of lesions in the occipital lobe may, for example, lead to permanent homonymous hemianopsia [loss of half the visual field], but this seems a small price to pay for relief from the threat of progressive brain damage or fatal hemorrhage."

Two decades later, the operation was hardly routine, but Flamm's morbidity and mortality of 6 percent, according to his count, was one-quarter of that reported by Pool. Such an improvement was testimony, no doubt, to the progress of the field. Yet neurosurgeons, like athletes, personalize. Statistics are one's own, not the field's in general; the result of individual skill and judgment, not simply technological advance. Which may be true. "It is a sad fact that not all series [of AVM operations] show such a low operative mortality," said neurologist Henry Troupp of Helsinki University Central Hospital. "As there is a trend toward subspecialization within neurosurgery, perhaps operations upon AVMs should be channeled into a few skilled hands."

By the 1980s, Flamm was being invited to lecture at vascular-neurosurgery conferences around the world, on panels with people he had grown up admiring. Cases that other surgeons declined began to come to him. For instance, Flamm had built a referral base among Jehovah's Witnesses, adherents to a Christianity that understood the Bible to permit brain surgery but prohibit blood transfusions. "I can still do the surgery," Flamm said. "It's just like having one hand tied behind my back."

Vascular neurosurgery, the elite of the elite, with one hand tied behind your back! It was crazy, unless, of course, you pumped up your ego and conjured up the conviction, as Flamm did, that you were one of the best vascular neurosurgeons in the world. Hell, he was the best. "You bet," that's the expression Flamm used. He'd look down thoughtfully, wait a beat. Then, the seriousness sunk in, he'd break into a spoon-shaped grin. "You bet," he'd say. Flamm was giving the patient a better ride with one hand than some county-hospital hacker who treated neurosurgery like pulling teeth with two, or four or five. You bet.

The pride that Flamm took in these difficult accomplishments didn't mean that he wanted to operate with one hand tied behind his back all the time. He didn't need to get his jollies off by watching a patient try to bleed to death on the operating table every day. He did a hundred major operations a year. And there were times when he really did wish for a respite, perhaps especially after bad news. Maybe he didn't want a run of spine cases or a series of shunts. That's when the comparisons between brain surgery and carpentry or brain surgery and plumbing probably had some accuracy. But he didn't want nothing. A surgeon without OR cases might tell himself he was fortunate to finally have time to catch up on grant applications or on an article he'd been intending to write. He could take more time with his convalescing patients, personally supervise their blood tests, urine sampling, menu selection. Flamm was totally dependent on referrals. Every lull, if it lasted a little too long, could seem like the end of the line, leaving the surgeon to read or write, consult, teach, tidy up, but not to operate. And when he didn't operate, he was like a person bereft. One colleague whose practice was slow wasn't even planning to attend the weekly conference of neurosurgeons. "That's like *watching* pornography," he said. "You'd rather be doing it."

Flamm understood. "If thy right brain offend thee, take it out! We're neurosurgeons, we operate," he said.

"I haven't done an interesting case in six months," moaned one junior attending.

"Join the club," said Flamm. Flamm's vacation had lasted only one week when he said that, but there was real grief in his voice.

No, Flamm didn't want nothing. Something nice and accessible, something that wasn't white knuckle all the way down, as Flamm put it. He wouldn't mind loosening his grip for a while. A lesion that wasn't malignant and gooey, a patient that wasn't going to stroke out or wake up dead. Something on which he could show hours of sparkling technique, wave a thank you to the OR crew, and, lighting his pipe, return to the waiting relatives with an enthusiastic report. In this profession you had to bounce back. You had to strive to do better, and that meant shaking off the failures. Let them reaffirm, not undermine, you. Once when Flamm was gloomy over a monstrous case that didn't do well, another surgeon said, "If you play with bombs, sometimes they go off." After, if something went wrong, Flamm thought of that comment, and it cheered him.

The patient waiting for him on 11 East was somebody Flamm could give a life back to. He was healthy. His heart and his kidneys weren't shutting down. He wasn't a junky. He'd return to society, and he'd be thankful for it. The clot was contained, the AVM not too far from the surface of the brain. The bleed wasn't so recent that with one prod the whole thing would come undone. The family was apparently nice; they'd understand what the surgeon was talking about and the risks of the work. This wouldn't be one of those that broke the wrong way. Of course, Flamm never thought that any operation would be one that broke the wrong way.

When Flamm left Kricheff's office, the scan of his damaged patient in hand, he had been really depressed. But he'd taken a deep breath, thrown back his shoulders, and headed off to talk to his newest patient. Sitting in the corner chair, a resident at each side, Flamm wasn't bored; he wasn't nonchalant. He was cooling out. He was coming back.

37

The diagnosis is a certainty. Now the cure is dumped in my lap. I think of the patients I identified as skulls and crossbones when I first walked onto 11 East, convinced of my invulnerability. A tumor is awful, a silent bud growing in the brain. But this is a device set to explode every once in a while. Am I going to awake each morning and say, "Is today the day that the statistics play themselves out and I experience another 'cerebrovascular accident'?"

There is a special charm to being ill in front of one's family. The length and breadth of the universe is stretched between silent, pecking Mum, sneezing Pop, closedmouth Dave, and constant Julie, ebullient and, I think, in the throes of some willed oblivion. These are in their way rich moments, close, tender. But now I must break from this dreamlike gathering of those I know and care about; must move past the statistics, the X rays, and the consultations to the unblinking violence of surgery. I eye the doctors. As if someone in a hospital bed might really enjoy free will, might really be able to say no. The suspense, which was killing me, killing everyone except Flamm, is over.

At some point in the medical decision-making process, a patient gives up responsibility for his health. The choice I make is not what to do but whom to trust. How is that decision made? Do I attempt to evaluate the surgeon's past performance? Check references? Get another opinion? Things I might do if I were, say, hiring a babysitter. Who is this surgeon, anyway? He might be a wigged-out fanatic, the Ayatollah himself, or another ordinary being under too much pressure. Kricheff says he is a great vascular neurosurgeon. My decision, finally, rests on that recommendation, some limited eye contact, and a desire to unburden myself. Flamm, relaxed, square fingered, reasonable, promises to take away the threat once and for all. That's what I want. Take this problem, which is too big for me. Let's get it over with. That's what I want to say. Instead, I smile. We are in this together, I'm told. Why don't I feel that way? Why do I feel as though the physicians, dressed in protective white, are perpetrators, greedy for more disease, more calamity, more people to help? If I could only manage to utter a curt "fuck you"? But no, with everyone crowded in together, huddled and listening for the next pronouncement, it would be so out of place to show irritation, which is a form of ungratefulness. Instead, I think, Which one of you will open my head like a flip-top can?

My silence is taken as assent. "Okay, then I'll get you on the schedule," says Flamm, tapping the radiator with his index finger and pushing himself up, the same implacable arrangement on his face as when he entered. Business concluded, they leave as they came, in an entourage, though this time they are tailed by my mother, the worrier, who no doubt wants answers to the questions she was afraid to ask in front of me. She, I know, ignored the percentages. Perhaps she really suspected that something was being hidden. Or perhaps it was that she needed some personal relationship to the caregiver, beyond the numbers. She had judged Flamm harshly; now she wanted to be assured. Her mission was to put her arm on his arm, get some sense of the guy. Was there anything else? Anything that maybe he didn't want to say in front of the patient? she asked. Flamm, I learned later, always said no, very plainly and directly, there wasn't anything.

38 When Dr. Goodgold, the neurologist, saunters into my room, I don't at first have any idea who he is. He takes short, prim steps, a dancer's march. He has no white coat, but is dressed in a suit and carries a soft leather briefcase, which he places by his feet, like a businessman at a commuter bar. "Well?" he says, "how are you?" He is here to consult. About what? I wonder for a moment, but then, of course, I realize: the singer whom I wasn't so happy to see. I am still not ecstatic to see him, though he is still as chipper as a game-show host. I am partially his patient, however. He admitted me, and in the way responsibility, medical as well as legal, is divvied up in the hospital, that makes me someone for him to check on. He apparently doesn't know that my ballot has already been cast in favor of the operation; his opinion either ignored or, what seems more likely, incorporated without my knowing about it.

My habit is to ask bunches of questions—usually the same ones—and then let the answers sail past me like rays of sunlight. Once, Kricheff, who visits once a day, got annoyed with me. He said: "How come you are asking all these questions, like what is an AVM or what does the surgery entail. These are things that I've explained to you, and I've heard Goodgold explain them to you, and I've heard Flamm explain them to you. Since the first day in my office you haven't heard a thing. Talk about putting up a defense!" It's true; my relation to information is ambivalent. Journalist by trade, I am, to put it directly, afraid of the news. With some difficulty, I have plotted my course. I don't want to be swayed. I don't want to factor in more advice. My resources, such as they are, are devoted not to listening but to coping, which in my case means blotting out. My impulse is to wave off the parley that Goodgold's presence announces. And yet the temptation is there. In my imagination there is even the chance that Goodgold has been feverishly at work on my case and has come to relate an unexpected development, medical clemency.

"Ten years ago I would have hesitated," he begins, which confirms my initial intuition: I don't want to hear any part of this. Doctors love to scare the hell out of you as a way of illustrating how lucky you've been. I want to believe in the surety of medical treatment, a solidness born of long experience, not recent enterprise. That, however, is not the case. Goodgold puts his briefcase across his knees, as if it is a keyboard he will now play. Until recently, I learn, the debate has been whether to treat me at all. And until recently neurologists came down on the side of forgoing surgery.

As late as 1963 neurologist Russell Brain—Head and Brain were two of England's leading twentieth-century neurologists!—wrote that a patient who had suffered a subarachnoid hemorrhage such as I had "must be advised to lead as quiet a life as possible and avoid any activity likely to raise blood pressure." In 1977, Dwight Parkinson, neurosurgeon from the University of Manitoba, Winnipeg, Canada, had accumulated perhaps as much experience with AVM surgery as anyone. Over a twenty-year period he'd operated on ninety AVMs; 11 percent died surgical deaths; another 20 percent had neurological deficits following surgery. Does almost one in three patients dead or impaired constitute an acceptable alternative to leading "as quiet a life as possible"? The neurosurgeons might say yes, but in the early seventies many neurologists said no. Some of the most convincing arguments came from Henry Troupp, neurologist at Helsinki University Central Hospital. In 1970 he reported on 137 AVM patients he had followed for an average of five and a half years. None had received treatment. Troupp didn't argue against surgery altogether. He was, however, against what he saw as a rush to operate. His statistics showed why. While morbidity was somewhat higher—24 percent were disabled—only 10 percent of his patients died of their malformations.

By the 1980s the situation had changed.

Surgical experience had been gained with new techniques. The sub-subspecialty of *vascular* neurosurgery had emerged. The result was a vast improvement in surgical results. In the 1980s, M. Jomin, of the neurosurgery service of the Centre Hospitalier Regional in Lille, France, reported that his mortality rate was 2 percent when the patient was conscious before operating; 17 percent of his patients were left with deficits.

Furthermore, as Troupp's own data demonstrated, it was learned that if nothing was done, the untreated AVM eventually killed and disabled in alarming numbers. In 1976, Troupp returned to his caseload to update his report. His sample group, initially followed for 5.5 years, had now been tracked for an additional 6 years, 11.5 years all told, which was longer than any other large group of AVM patients. What a difference half a dozen years made! In 1970, 34 percent of the untreated were dead or disabled from their AVMs. In 1976, 58 percent were dead or disabled. The combination of improved surgical techniques and the dismal survival rates without treatment had brought neurologists, Goodgold included, around. They favored intervention.

"The operation is scheduled for Monday," says Goodgold, smacking the armrest with the flat of his hand as if it is a conga. "Now you know what I think."

Goodgold had dropped out of my life and then returned almost after the fact. He urges no last-minute change of heart. The neurologist's historical perspective is nonetheless sobering. A person takes the present for the ever present. My fate, it seems clear to me, is decided because I have had a brain hemorrhage as a twenty-eight-year-old and not as an eighteen-year-old.

39 Once I decide on surgery, I want it right away. Unfortunately, hospitals do only emergency operations on weekends. As Goodgold informed me, my case is scheduled for Monday, at noon. I spend the weekend waiting around, intending to think about the future and instead picking up information about the present. One resident, explaining the excitement of his chosen field, says: "One slip and there goes speech." I feel as though I'm driving too fast around a sharp curve.

Another I hear talking across the room. "He opened her up on the other side, and she got better right on the table in front of us," he says. "There's no substitute for experience."

Kricheff, usually a reassuring presence, offers encouragement. "Don't worry, if worse comes to worse and they have to lop off a portion of your brain, all you'll lose is peripheral vision," he says, "so you won't be able to play center field anymore."

What I look forward to most is the time each evening when *my* surgeon will arrive at bedside and report in, as if he'd been at work on my case all day long. It's a silly vanity, but ongoing. All day I make mental notes of things to cover, subjects that seem of the utmost importance and that I forget as soon as he appears. On Friday evening, Flamm wanders in. He has a funny, stiff walk, as if falling on one foot, then on the other. He takes his corner seat. I am buoyant with expectation. Flamm is gentle, even toned. "Everything is fine," Flamm begins and ends. That is the extent of his initiative. He is not a talker. He is prepared to tell me whatever I want to know, but he has nothing to add.

Once I overheard Flamm telling a man that his wife—resting in the ICU—had two vascular malformations, one on each side of her head, and required two operations. Flamm was quiet, attentive, and still as a stone. The man fidgeted, shifted in his chair. Flamm sat for twenty minutes as the man fired off uninformed question after question. In different ways he asked whether an operation was really necessary. Then whether two were necessary. The man's wife had collapsed with a hemorrhage at their son's Little League baseball game. Flamm told the man there shouldn't be any problems. This was straightforward. He did this type of thing twice a week. First they would do one side of her head; then, a few weeks later, after she'd recovered from surgery, they would bring her back to do the second. The man played with his hands as if rubbing the brim of an imaginary hat. He seemed resigned but not satisfied. Then, as Flamm got up to go, the man flung another question at him. It was as if as long as Flamm was around he might really be able to puzzle out why this thing had happened and what should be done about it. "Should I get another opinion?" the man asked.

Flamm sat back down. "We always encourage a second opinion," Flamm explained, "if a patient wants one." That set the man off, talking rapidly, fearing that he'd insulted the person who was going to poke around in his wife's head.

"If I got a second opinion, you would just be the person I would go to," he said. "So that's ridiculous."

I felt like that man, boldly posing a question, then fearful of the answer. I would like to know: What *is* this thing in my head? What is an AVM? Flamm is helpful, willing, a storehouse of information. He takes out a nail clipper, gives a nail a turn, pockets the clipper. I know almost immediately that I don't want to hear the answer.

Flamm operates primarily on AVMs and aneurysms, which are paired in the category of vascular anomalies. What causes a vascular anomaly? Both AVMs and aneurysms are usually the result of a developmental mishap that occurs in the womb, though vascular defects aren't considered hereditary. Blood vessels begin life as simple tubes that, at the directions of a still undeciphered genetic code, gradually turn into either arteries or veins. Arteries, the stronger of the two, develop muscular, elastic walls that can withstand the pressure of new blood pumped from the heart. Tiny capillaries form between the arteries and veins. Capillaries have two purposes. First, they take nutrients from the arterial blood, deliver them to tissue, and return the depleted blood to the veins. Second, they depressurize the blood, turning it over to the weaker veins at one-half or one-third the pressure.

What a wonder, it is sometimes said, that so many miles of delicate vascular tubing are so finely crafted. Not in an AVM. In an AVM the fetal blood vessels don't differentiate. They become neither veins nor arteries, but half-breeds that conglomerate like a skein of yarn. In an AVM the arterial side is connected directly to the venous side without the interuption of capillaries. An AVM is thus a kind of shunt through which fresh arterial blood pours directly into the veins. It is as if all of the brain's circulatory highways divide into smaller and smaller roadways except in the AVM, where the highways persist. The danger? Blood in an AVM isn't depressurized before being turned over to the weak-walled veins.

AVMs can occur in any part of the body; it's only in the brain that they have life-or-death consequences. Normally, pressure in the brain's circulatory system is self-regulating. When blood pressure suddenly shoots up—for instance, if a person jumps in icy water—muscles in the wall of the artery contract, reducing the amount of blood that can enter. But the AVM, composed of misbegotten vessels, has no such control. Arterial force is present on the arterial side and also on the weaker venous side. A jump into freezing water or the cumulative effect of too much pressure for too long may be enough to blow the AVM, causing a hemorrhage. In my brain, it appeared from all the tests that a portion of blood vessels about 1 centimeter in diameter had not differentiated.

How many people have vascular malformations? Short of having everyone submit to an angiogram, it's impossible to know the exact number of vascular malformations. But through autopsy and diagnostic studies researchers have estimated that as much .5–1 percent of the population or 1.25–2.5 million people harbor an aneurysm. A 1966 report, still cited as authoritative, says that aneurysms in the United States are about seven times more common than AVMs. By these numbers* there may be between 178,500 and 357,000 people with AVMs. Most will never be symptomatic. If a person makes it past forty without finding out about his AVM, through either hemorrhage or seizures or some other clinical sign, he will probably never know about it. It is as if AVMs mature for two decades, become symptomatic in the next two decades, and then reach a state of homeostasis, the host ultimately adjusting to the parasite AVM, says one authority. Interestingly, William McCormick, who as chief of neuropathology at the University of Texas microscopically examined more than a thousand mal-formations, says most, if not all, have, at some point, bled. The size of the hemorrhage may be so small, and thus its effects on the person so limited, that in most cases they won't be detected by a doctor, if a person even thinks it worth getting examined.

I WANT TO KNOW, I say, what exactly it is that Flamm is going to do to my AVM. My voice isn't strained. I know I am in the right in posing this question. Flamm isn't the least bit taken aback. In 1984 there were sixty-seven aneurysms operated on at University Hospital and Bellevue and twenty-one AVMs. Flamm did the lion's share.

"You start sucking out the clot; then, when you see a big piece of it, you pick it up with the forceps and tease it out, scoop it out," he says.

Doctors aren't about to provide a course in medicine. Instead, they do whatever the patient likes, responding to the letter, if not the spirit, of his re-quest. If the patient wants detail they pour it on; if he wants an outline, that's all right, too. In neither case is there real communication. Maybe physicians really do want to help a patient understand and just can't make the connec-tion. Maybe patients, either by lack of training or by emotional condition-ing, are unable to take in what doctors say. Normund Wong, a psychiatrist, wrote about his own critical illness: "One wonders whether sick people are truly capable of understanding the complexities of their infirmity. . . . [They] cannot stop thinking about their illness [but] they lack knowledge that is es-sential to fully appreciate their circumstances." Nurses tell you to write down your questions. It doesn't matter. A doctor takes the list of questions, reads

*In that 1966 paper, the ratio of 1 AVM to 7 aneurysms is an aggregate figure. It combines the ratio in the United States, which is reported to be 1/5.3, with the ratio in the United Kingdom, which is 1/13.8. Since it's safe to assume that there are not more AVMs per capita in the United States than in Britain, perhaps they are being underreported in the United Kingdom and the overall ratio is closer to the one in the United States.

them one by one, and reels off the answers. What occurs is a sophisticated brush-off, which can seem like a subtle ploy not to cooperate. Flamm says he will be glad to continue the description as long as I want. He could continue until he's blue in the face. This talk of a blood clot in my brain grosses me out. I raise my hand; what difference does it make how he is going to do it? What I really want to get are not the details of my surgery but some assurance that it will turn out just fine. And that, of course, I've already gotten. Thanks, I've had enough for tonight.

The anesthesiology resident, Kenneth Schmidt, comes to see me on Saturday night, two days before surgery, while my brother is visiting. He wears green surgical scrubs and a loose-fitting green hat that, though it is part of the OR uniform, resembles a green shower cap. He is young and seems approachable. My stomach has settled, my nerve consolidated. I start in again with questions about what is actually going to happen to me. He heeds me, telling me things I really can't bear to hear. He explains that a large hemispheric incision will be made in the scalp and the loose skin lifted back like the flap on a winter hat. What will it feel like? Will it hurt? is what I want to know. The brain doesn't register pain, but the scalp is filled with nerve endings. The pain would be on the order of getting hit over the head with a bat, he made me understand. He smiles, a bright, doughy, what-me-worry smile. He says that I shouldn't be concerned; fifteen seconds of drug administered into a blood vessel in my arm will have already put me out. He'll keep me there, pain-free, for as long as necessary. I don't have to be concerned about pain. Then, as if to end this sketch on the right note, he turns to my brother and asks if they haven't met somewhere before. My brother shrugs. The anesthesiologist asks if Dave has been under anesthesia lately. We laugh. "See you Monday," he says. "I'll be the one wearing the mask."

40

It may be difficult for some doctors and nurses, so long habituated, to sense the horror that accompanies the experience of illness for the patient. That the hospital, a center of healing, could also be a source of distress seems contradictory. Yet research by behavioral scientists suggests that almost every aspect of the hospital experience—admission, special testing, surgery, even discharge—represents a time of heightened fear for the patient.

So what? Soon, it might be argued, the experience will be over. Fear, like the hospital stay itself, will have been no more than a temporary inconvenience in a person's life-style. Not really. Recent research has implicated persistent stress as a factor in delayed recovery, increased pain, suppression of the immunologic system, even, say some researchers, in creating disease. "To consider the impact of the hospital environment on patients is not mere compassion, but a medical necessity," says Donald Kornfeld in *Advances in Psychosomatic Medicine*.

That emotions have an impact on the body's other systems is no great secret. Everyone knows that even a brief scare can make a pulse race, palms sweat, breathing accelerate, attention focus, and fatigue vanish. Not bad for simply hearing "boo." Feelings, and perhaps especially negative feelings, have systemic repercussions. "It is quite another thing to demonstrate that these feelings produce bodily dysfunctions or increase susceptibility to a variety of diseases," writes sociologist David Mechanic. In other words, is it possible to link the way somebody feels with the way his cells act?

In 1973 researchers reported just such a connection in a publication of the American Association for the Advancement of Science. The death of one family member, they said, raises the statistical likelihood that other family members will get sick. It's a phenomenon many people have noticed. First the grandmother dies; within months, the previously healthy grandfather is gone, too. A possible explanation for this correlation was proposed by a group in Australia led by R. W. Bartrop. Bartrop's methodology was straightforward. Find very sad people and check their immune systems. The sample group? Twenty-six recent widows. In 1977, Bartrop's group reported that after the death of a spouse, the widow had significantly lower activity levels of T cells, a type of white blood cell whose job it is to protect the body against intruding disease. This was only the first of many studies to suggest, as Hans Selye, the father of stress research, says, that "the . . . adaptability of a living being is always finite." Stress works by degrees. At some point, Selye, an M.D., suggests, a too intense stimulus—like the blow from the death of a loved one—saps our capacity to adapt, wreaking havoc on our mental and also physical well-being. One extreme example involves wild rabbits, which, Selye reports, can literally be stressed to death by the fear they will be chased by a dog. Much lower levels of stress also have a negative impact. Selye discovered that "relatively brief stints of stress, below the intensity that most people ordinarily experience at some time in their lives can provoke pathologic changes in our body." Many common diseases—high blood pressure and some rheumatic, allergic, cardiovascular, and renal diseases—are due largely to an inability to adapt to stress, Selye concluded. In his own life, Selye beat the odds and survived a usually fatal cancer. The price he paid? He developed a stress ulcer.

What all stress has in common—whether death of a wife or being chased by a dog—is loss of control. Stress results when the individual can't stop something unpleasant. That, of course, is the essence of the patient experience. The loss of control wrought by illness is stress; and so is the loss of control imposed by care. Medical procedures, including those as innocuous as drawing blood, are frightening to the patient. So is living a routine over which he can exercise no decision-making power—and being called "honey" to boot. (According to something called the Hospital Stress Rating Scale, even the rigid mealtime enforced by the hospital is stressful.)

Given the bad news about the effects of stress on health, perhaps something should be done to reduce it in the hospital. Unfortunately, that's easier said than done. Some institutions have tried. They have, for example, attempted to lessen the traumatization that accompanies treatment by providing patients with more pretreatment information. Anesthesiology has taken the lead in this area. One study showed that if patients received an informational preoperative visit from an anesthetist, they required fewer painkillers during recovery and left the hospital sooner. The problem, it turns out, is that people are different, and so are their reactions to stress. Optimistic researchers had once hoped to pinpoint the key causes of hospital stress and then abolish them. It's not that simple. Stress is not an absolute but a perception interpreted by each individual. Thus, depending on how it is viewed, the same phenomenon might produce a lot of tension or none at all. For example, researcher R. S. Lazarus screened a film of a gory male circumcision rite for three groups. However, he gave the film three soundtracks: one emphasized the mutilation; a second denied that any pain was experienced; and a third presented the view of a detached, scientific observer. Lazarus found that those most disturbed—as measured by readings of heart rate and skin conductance—were those told about the mutilation. Those who could deny that the sharpened stone implements caused pain, who were led to believe that the whole affair was nothing but a happy occasion for adolescents to pass into manhood, actually experienced much less stress. In a similar way, it turned out that different patients interpreted preoperative visits differently. Frustratingly, while some studies discovered that information contributed to patient relief, other studies showed that patients didn't react well to information. One group of patients simply didn't want to amass new knowledge, on the intuition, perhaps, that the more information they had, the more they had to worry about. Add to this group's data bank and the stress increased.

How does all this bear on my case? Certainly the primary source of stress for me is that I am ill with a potentially lethal illness. The secondary source, though, is that this floor and its attendants keep telling me I am ill. I am one of those patients who reacts to the calamities around me by attempting to ignore them. I deny. "Almost everyone I've known is afraid that he or she will end up a vegetable," says Mary Leong, a social worker responsible for patients on 11 East. "I still think that until a patient goes through it and sees himself talking and walking, some of that fear remains." Not I. I ignore the prospect that I might emerge from surgery as animated as a tomato. For a time the hierarchy of information, even my loss of power, had permitted me a mental detachment that abetted this strategy. I had wanted everything to be fine, and everyone to act as if it were. People put down denial; it suggests dishonesty. And yet, as Donald Bakal writes in *Psychology & Medicine*, "Psychological processes involving denial and detachment are capable of changing the basic emotion itself." Like Lazarus's merriest movie watchers, I am sure that it is my ability to intellectualize, my knack for denial, that, at least at the start, helps me make my way through an experience worsened by having to face it on 11 East.

As surgery closed in on me, denial, sadly, became more difficult. Try as I might, evidence that nothing was really wrong grew dispiritingly slim. Even the anesthesiologist, whose information was supposed to head off my fears, accomplished just the opposite. It was as if the film's soundtrack had changed. The mutilation that awaited me appeared so horrible that I couldn't bear to think about it. Have I squandered my "coping capital," as Selye called it? As a result, will my recovery be more difficult, my pain greater, my ego less solid? It's not possible to say. But with my denial strategy shot, the vast stresses of a place like 11 East are likely to find an easier target in me, and that, given the evidence about stress, is not good news.

41 On Sunday morning, the residents, who make rounds every day of the week, say aloud, "He's pre-op for tomorrow. What needs to be done?" They check my "loading dose" of steroids, antibiotics, tranquilizers, diuretics, and anticonvulsant, Dilantin. I need a haircut. David Chalif, my friend, volunteers. "I'll come by late tonight," he says, poking a finger in the air as though *I* shouldn't forget.

At one point a social worker visits. She has black curly hair and wears diamonds on her finger. Nice enough, though you can resent anybody on this floor who acts carefree, as if the firing squad isn't really being mustered. Is there anything I would like to talk about? she asks. She has nothing but time. Leonard's voice has returned, a croaky revelation, but he is stubbornly uncommunicative, refusing to speak anything but his native Russian. I would certainly like to talk to him and ask what secrets he has learned on the other side. But her? What would I like to ask her? My week on 11 East has hammered away at the supposition that I am a vigorous person here for an adjustment, a repair. It is difficult at times to maintain the idea that I am a person at all. To the hospital staff I am my illness. Certainly it has been made clear to me; its fate is mine. And yet I am unable to express my fears over this fate—perhaps unable to really recognize them. So what I choose to talk about with the pretty woman with the diamond ring is my hair. "I really don't like the idea of having my head shaved," I say. "You know, baldness runs in my family, and I'm not really sure it will grow back." I look at the tip of my nose as I talk, which makes me look cross-eyed. She looks perplexed, as though she hears a fly in her ear. My palms have begun to sweat lightly, creating a pair of pancake-sized stains where they touch my pajamas. I insist, taking up the same theme. "It's true that I think of being bald and can't stop thinking about it," I tell her. "It seems to me that the operation will begin when Dr. Chalif comes with a razor to clip my hair." She shoots back a blank moon face and makes this note, which I later saw: "He displaced much of his anxiety onto having his head shaved."

In the afternoon I'm told to practice breathing. Seated in a fake-leather chair next to my hospital bed, I exhale into a blue corrugated hose, forcing a rubber stop up a plastic cylinder. Rothenstreich, the nurse, explains in a sweet, chirpy voice that this breathing exercise is one I will do after surgery to keep my lungs free of fluid. She is one of those energetic young nurses who, she told me, has never been sick a day in her life, never been in the hospital except to work. What else will surgery bring? I ask. I should expect lack of coordination, nausea, dizziness, weakness, fatigue. And oh, yes, I will have a Jackson-Pratt drain. Blood will run from under the scalp into a plastic grenade. It will hang from my head dressing, like the one I'd spotted on the woman the day I arrived.

Through the locked hospital window I can see a construction site. Workmen in white hard hats march wheelbarrows across the fourth floor of a building-in-progress. The men's puny bodies are outlined against the sky, which is blue enough to have been poured from a paint can. The workmen transport copper pipe, which glints in the sunlight, on green metal carts that resemble golf carts. At the base of the scaffolding is a cement mixer decorated with dots the colors of party balloons. A red crane, tall as a skyscraper, hoists a tub of concrete way up in the air, then leaves it dangling at the end of a long wire. Apartments will soon be there. Already a giant sign announces that they are for sale. This scene brings forth in me a great wave of emotion, and because I feel a need to call this emotion something, I call it love. I love this scene, its industry, the human progress that it represents, and then I think how these preparations depress me. The air in my room is heavy, dead. The smell is the smell of nothing at all. My good humor goes. My lips press against the plastic breathing machine, and it occurs to me how quickly you are alone, in Africa or Nicaragua or in a gummy leatherette chair waiting for the start of surgery.

THE BLACK LOOSELEAF BINDER arrives, and with it another consent form. "I recognize that the practice of medicine and surgery is not an exact science, and I acknowledge that no guarantees or assurances have been made to me concerning the results of such procedures." Often the head can heal itself, as everyone who has endured a passing headache knows. Sometimes, though, a person is told that the only way to help himself is by having his skull drilled open and his brain attacked with knives. Legally I can argue over treatment, even refuse it. How else will I battle this biologic evil? I've already signed consent forms to receive a CT scan, to be admitted, to have an angiogram. I sign again.

At 11:00 P.M. I tell myself that I hope Chalif has forgotten. Do I still expect that this might be overlooked, that I really might go home, unscathed, untouched? Chalif is there at 11:10 P.M., peppy and bright. He is twenty-nine, thin, almost six feet tall, and has dark hair, which he keeps long and bushy. One front tooth overlaps another, which makes his lips pucker when they close. This gives his face a boyish turn so that patient after patient asks him, "Are you a doctor?"

"It's awful late to be working," I say.

"Neurosurgery is like a drug," he says. "The more you get, the more you want."

I mention that I've read the dire warnings of the consent.

"I guarantee you're going to be all right," he says.

"The wording of the consent," I say, "is probably required by the lawyers in case somebody makes a mistake."

"We don't make mistakes," Chalif says.

He runs a hand-held razor from the back to the front of my head, four, five times, dropping my hair into my lap and leaving a quarter-inch stubble. I know the department's glib, unofficial motto is Better Lucky Than Smart. Just now I don't want to contemplate mistakes or the possible outcome of brain surgery or the role that luck might play in determining them, and so I ask Chalif about his work, and Chalif, who loves to talk about what he does, straddles a chair at the end of the bed and seriously and scientifically tells me about his paper on inducing strokes in laboratory rats, which recently won a prize.

42 It is Monday, a beautiful fall day. My admitting slip indicates I should be going home tomorrow. Instead, at 6:00 A.M. an orderly spreads hair depilatory on my head. She smooths it on like fluffy shaving cream, though after a few minutes it turns gritty and hard. With a tongue depressor, she scrapes off the crust and the remaining stubble of my hair. My head is so light and cool. I pad to the bathroom, a bag of serum dangling from a pole and running into my arm, going wherever I go. The mirror's flat-eyed gaze is too much. I duck, hang out at sink level. Don't be ridiculous, I think, and inch up from a squat, like giving up a hiding place. This is not like aging, which gradually ushers in the suety belly, the blanched hair, the bulging eye pouches. This disfiguration is as quick as a guillotine. My head weaves. It is the unconscious motion with which I once tossed back bangs and which is now an ironic tic. I am two people; one of us has a white bulb of a head, an onion head, and one of us, still unconvinced, shadowboxes with the mirror and thinks a sequence of thoughts like Ugly . . . ugly . . . ugly . . .

Fellow patients (what a fraternity we are!) see me bald and know that I am next. They stop by to wish me the best of luck. Maria, the Spanish speaker from Housekeeping, enters my room, lightly drying her hands on her yellow crenellated dress. She explains that she is a Pentecostal, announces she will pray for me, and with one wizened hand palms my head, as if it is a crystal ball. Her eyelids drop. She moans, and as I look on, real teardrops squeeze from the corners of her eyes.

Nurse Rothenstreich gives me a dose of phenobarbital, which is a barbiturate, and Dilantin, an anticonvulsant. Two medical students who are following my case as part of their third-year curriculum stop by to wish me well. "I looked right at you and looked away," says one excitedly. "I didn't make the connection that you had your head shaved." It is his first time, too. He says that I seem "cool" about the whole thing. They will attend the operation and, in a moment of politeness, say they are looking forward to it. "Oh, good, see you there." "See you there."

John Corallo, my friend, talks about his own operation. He says he has psyched himself. Can't wait. He has been given a single room, the aneurysm alert room, where he is supposed to remain still and quiet, two very difficult activities for John. With his head shaved and his false teeth out, John shows his grizzled nubs when he smiles. "I couldn't be more ready," he says, and shoots his fist in the air. It is a pregame gesture. John looks like a tough man except that he is scared witless and talks like a guy on speed. "Before, everything was work and getting ahead," John is saying. As soon as this is over, he still claims he is headed to Florida to relax and forget about money. John puts stock in prayers. "My whole town is praying for me," he says, and adds that he will pray for me.

Hold your prayers, I almost say. This is a cinch. I'll be back soon, as if I have anything to do with it. I am unwary, trying not to play the patient. Or maybe it is that I am trying to be a better patient, the one who doesn't complain, who is thankful for the care, fun to be with, even in pajamas, and who, in recompense, is given good care. At moments I even think this: Isn't it lucky this happened to me? I can handle it.

IT IS MID-MORNING. We are in the solarium, a grand name for a dingy lobby with a commanding view of the elevators. The room has the aroma of old tobacco. There are no visitors at this time of day. The place is ours. We balance on the window ledge, flop onto the couch and cut up, nervous pranksters. Have we ever been so playful together? My camera is passed around. Julie and Mom take snapshots of the three men in the family: my brother balding, my father almost bald, and I completely bald. "It makes you feel better to laugh," says Dad.

Then the nurse in a skirt the color of chalk pokes her head in the door, like the end of recess. "So there you are," she says, "They're ready for you downstairs." The time has snuck up. What had I been hoping? That as in a dream the appointment would be forgotten or overlooked? That in a lovely transgression of roles my family and I would play together all day?

Returned to my bed, I think cruelly, Someone else should be in my place. I am supposed to feel momentarily put out, then spin through the hospital's revolving door into the October breeze, my head filled with career plans or what I will eat for lunch. Instead, drugs administered, two nurses wheel me and my nomadic bed to the elevator. I prop up on an elbow and wave a little. There is a confusion of kisses, squeezed hands, tears. It is a farewell scene. Julie's strong, narrow fingers are like stripes on my forearm. My brother Dave hangs back, a nervous wrinkle on his top lip, like a vandal's. Mom, tiny and arch, waves with one hand, as if I'm leaving on a trip. "See you soon, lovey," she says, and grips her brown leather pocketbook to her chest. Dear flappable Dad rocks forward on the balls of his feet.

Then the elevator doors slide shut on my girlfriend and my family, and my last opportunity to escape. There is the mechanical burbling of the elevator in flight. I am alone with an attendant whose job it is to escort sick bodies from floor to floor eight hours a day. My family and I have been full of mirth and yet this whole thing, the hospital and the close attention it foists on us, has been dreadful. I have set the tone, insisted on the generic charm, the pumped-up gaiety, the stage whispers and the shopping lists, the "Oh, Stevies" in the voice for strangers. The healthy, I think, must feel guilty about their health. How unsociable it would be for me to iterate fears! It is, I have believed, my rigorously cheerful demeanor that has kept the crowds visiting. Now, for the first time in my week in the hospital, all is quiet, and it is disturbing. My urge is to engage the attendant in small talk, which I think is a desire to have this invasive procedure be a simple subject of conversation. How do people act on their way down to brain surgery? I could ask. Do they ever demand to turn back? And then there is a feeling. In this isolated chamber, racing to what end, it is as if for an instant my hold on the future unhitches and I wonder what things might have been like if what happened had not happened.

The doors open on the sixth floor, and I am towed down a hallway and deposited in a line of patients in beds. We are a traffic jam of people waiting to be operated on. I look at the other patients. They are old, their hair not gray but white, their skin flaky, their bodies inanimate, and I think the same demented thought that has sustained me all along: How lucky I am to be healthy! And then my hand touches my gravelly head, and I know this cannot possibly be true. Where has my health gone, and how will I ever get it back? I wonder.

43

Saying good-bye at the elevator, Julie thought about fare-wells and felt herself getting upset.

Julie had already withstood a week of doctors' reports that, while good news—at least everyone kept pounding that into her head—had taken them along the path to brain surgery. Others had been nervous—Steve's mom was smoking one long cigarette, his dad was doing nothing but sneezing—but she really hadn't been. She realized she'd come up with a way to handle this whole affair: "Take it day by day and then forget it day by day." A couple of times she'd followed Flamm out of the hospital room. She never would have left, but Steve's mom had jumped up. Even then, and then later, with his mom's arm around her as though *she* were supposed to do something, Julie maintained her equanimity. At one point, she'd suspected that the numbers were a fiction. What did "a two percent chance of hemorrhage" really mean? she'd thought. It was just a way of handling the conversation. But then, she'd told herself, she trusted Flamm. He gave her kind of a warm, confident feeling, even though he wasn't particularly warm and friendly and open. The fate she imagined for her boyfriend was not to be blind or paralyzed or dead. Julie felt really confident.

Why, then, when the elevator doors whisk shut, does she experience a surge of emotion?

Maybe good-byes were never great for her. It was true that when-ever she waved good-bye, she had this premonition that, as she once said, "it was the last time she was going to see someone." It was probably also true that every good-bye dredged up *the* good-bye, which was the wave to her father through the hospital window on the day he died. She knew she had a capacity to carry on while people were dying, as if nothing were going to happen. That worried her. Maybe a good-bye really carried this message: She was fooling herself. Maybe that's why, standing at the elevator after the doors shut, with a silence that made each person feel alone for a second, Julie wondered this: Did everyone else know, while she, bouncy and light, shuttled through the days unaware? Was this like when she didn't realize her dad was going to die?

ERV HAD A GIFT for optimism. He believed what he wanted to; he could be strong willed in that way. Ruth said that if Erv tossed a ball in the air three times, tried to hit it three times with a bat, and three times missed, he would, undisturbed, conclude: Wow, what a pitcher. "I *want* to believe that the surgeon walks on water," he said. "I want to believe all the positive things; it's my only defense against the impotence of not being able to do the surgery myself, to make sure it's going to be okay." He grew up in an era in which the popular idea was that something as exotic as brain surgery was a last-ditch effort with little chance of success. A person who packed his bags for the neurosurgery floor was, for all intents and purposes, packing them for the last time. Diligently, he excluded this background from his mind. He said, "Flamm almost without saying it said, 'I can guarantee this surgery is a piece of cake.' There was almost a sense this was a pleasant kind of thing." Hell, it had seemed to Erv, why hadn't they thought to have this done before? That's the way it sounded.

Nevertheless, Erv understood that hanging around the hospital would be unpleasant. The night before he had decided, "I did not want to sit and wait having nothing to do and all the time having these terrible feelings." As soon as the elevator doors closed, Erv headed out, too. He jumped in the Escort and hustled back to the Tutoring Center to put in a few hours with kids he could help learn to read.

ERV BOLTED, Ruth thought, and decided she had to stay. I have to hold Julie together. (Dave, too, made his way back to his job.)

Julie figured her job was to help Ruth. "I know that his mom is a nervous wreck. Just because she is, I'm not. I am more stoic." Because they couldn't think of what else to do, they went to lunch. Julie had a spinach pie and ate the whole thing. And dessert. "I just feel he is going to go through this; it is going to be over, he is going to be fine," she told Ruth. And also, though she didn't say this, she thought, Flamm didn't really give us an option. Ruth chain smoked and thought what Julie said was wonderful, though she didn't really listen. They were very conscious of the time and didn't want to stay away too long. Then they were back in the solarium, with the figures in bathrobes and seamed heads drifting in and out. That place was pretty depressing, because they watched surgeons deliver bad news to other families.

44 I hadn't imagined that I would be pushed into the OR awake. What a crowd of people, chatting or taping down tubing. It is almost social. Everyone is in blue and sports head coverings like shower caps and tie-on masks, except me. I feel silly, as in one of those dreams in which you go out in public without putting on your pants. A nurse smiles at me, which I know because her pleated mask ruffles and her cheeks ball up. She tells me to urinate and hands me a yellow plastic carton, like those that had been hung off the end of my bed. Discreetly, I slip it under my gown. This will help reduce pressure in the brain, the nurse cheerily explains. This is all so *interesting*, to use the resident's favorite word, but suddenly my spirit sags, and I don't want to be here. The nurse says that everything will be fine. I simper and can't even pee. My hand touches my head, rough as a grater, and I'm frightened. I know that some people want to be conscious for their surgery, monitor their surgeons. Not me. I tell myself, as a single-minded goal, that soon the anesthesiologist, just as he promised, will put fifteen seconds of narcotic into my arm and say, Now you are going to sleep. Then my part will be over.

Part VII

THE EXCITEMENT OF BRAIN SURGERY

The confidence gradually acquired from masterfulness in controlling hemorrhage gives to the surgeon the calm which is so essential for clear thinking and orderly procedure at the operating table.

William Stewart Halsted, surgeon

45 Flamm, at my insistence, has invited me to observe surgery. I will see many operations, but this is the first, and that no doubt is one reason that my impression of it endures. Another reason is what happened.

The operation today is similar to mine, vascular neurosurgery. This vascular defect, an aneurysm, has ballooned off the middle cerebral artery in a businessman who, like me, has already been lucky once. One morning three months ago he had been awakened by a splitting headache and nausea, symptoms, he would find out later, of the hemorrhage that had ripped through his brain. Over five years the significant morbidity and mortality of aneurysm patients who don't undergo surgery and who survive an initial hemorrhage is as high as 65 percent—not higher, but about twice as fast as the morbidity and mortality associated with an untreated AVM. "With aneurysms, we have 007 status," Flamm once claimed. Whenever an angiogram divulges one, whether it has bled or not, he strongly recommends surgery. In this case, as in mine, the patient had escaped the hemorrhage's devastation and entered the hospital in good health and without deficit. This is the kind of case a surgeon likes: no heart collapse to worry about, no shrunken arteries to make a stroke more likely. (This is also the kind of case that a surgeon dreads to hurt. If someone walks into the hospital and can't walk out, a surgeon feels awful.) In today's operation the aneurysmal bubble, initially deflated by the hemorrhage, is under pressure again. The dome is at least 1.5 centimeters in diameter, as wide as an index finger, according to the angiogram; stretched so tight that one more bit of pressure might prove to be one too many.

Flamm turns to me. "Don't feel you have to be a hero," he says. "You can leave whenever you like." I nod an exaggerated nod because my mask, which covers half my face, forces breath up my cheeks and fogs my glasses, making me feel as if I can barely communicate. Flamm's gesture is thoughtful, though I feel unduly singled out. The subtext, it seems to me, is, Can you take it? I can, I want to assure him. Though I make certain that no one is between me and the exit, it is not, I know, as if this corpse breathing on the table is me. It *is* possible to dissociate myself from the procedure at hand. I am standing over here in a blue scrub suit, a blue shower cap, and blue booties, my back against the grooves on the green tiled wall. If I have a personal intent, it is merely to reassure myself of the orderliness of this science, the exactitude. Later I will track down a videotape of my own surgery. But for now my attitude is that of the interested observer. I am fascinated. Notebook in hand, I poke around the OR like a tourist nosing up to the glass at an aquarium.

 Once the anesthesiologist puts the patient to sleep—too deep even to dream—relaxes his muscles, interrupts his pain, the residents and nurses who have been holding to the sidelines, impatiently snapping the rubber of their gloved fingers, move in.

The first act is to strip the patient of his gown. His modesty, so steadfastly preserved while awake, is removed as soon as he nods off. Thus, the OR is a place of great activity in the middle of which, as if perversely, a naked body has been placed. Bald, almost lifeless, the patient has no beauty; he seems sexless, hardly human. Can this thing with tubes taped to its mouth, its arms, its chest, be the one who has a favorite blazer, jingles change in a pocket? The patient, once a personality, becomes a work site.

"We gotta do this one quick," one resident says to the other.

"Why?"

"Else we'll miss the food cart."

"Right."

Residents might want lunch, but they would never miss the OR. Chalif said that no matter how little sleep he got, he was never tired in the OR. The OR is exciting. I once heard him scold another resident for "being nice," doing some scut, and passing up opportunities to go to the OR. Caring for patients on the floor is an important group of skills. In the OR, though, is where the trade is learned, where the surgeon, if he trusts a resident, lets him do a little, then a little more. To the outsider it is a little scary to think that neurosurgery is a skill learned in the doing, but by the time he graduates, Chalif will list over five hundred cases on which he has been either first assistant or principal surgeon.

"Can you give me a hand?" one resident asks the anesthesiologist. He is trying to roll the patient into position without dropping him. ("Only once I dropped a patient," says one resident. "That was at Bellevue.")

"Which side up?"

"We want to flip him on his left and put in a spinal drain."

"Which side up?"

"Right."

This is the spinal-tap position. The residents perform a tap by slipping a long needle between two vertebrae into the spinal canal and draining off one-third of the cerebrospinal fluid, further reducing pressure in the brain.

A patient doesn't urinate for himself. A lubricated tube is pushed up the urethra into the bladder so that urine drains into a clear plastic bag, where it can be measured.

On the operating table, a patient can be placed in any of a number of positions: prone, supine, park bench (on his side with his knees toward his chest), slouch, knee-chest (prone and with his knees to his chest). The position is determined by which area the surgeon wants to get to. When the patient is on his stomach, as I was, the body is slid up on the table so that the head extends over the edge. It is suspended there—as if on display—between three sharp steel pins, a deadly-looking contraption but a real innovation. The patient's head was once supported by a malleable doughnut of foam rubber and liable to shift during an operation, which made microsurgery impossible. The head holder is like a vice, except that instead of two flat pads to squeeze an object, it bears down on its prey with a trio of pointed prods. One resident cradles the patient's head in both hands, the way a bowler holds the big black ball in two hands before his approach. The head is too awkward and heavy to be balanced in one hand. What's more, if it slipped, the patient could die. Anesthesia has taken away his muscle tone, and so the head would fall easily, snapping the neck. The other resident twists the head holder tight. The pins puncture the scalp, which bleeds in slim rivulets down the cheeks and onto the floor, and then anchor in the skull. The head is now solid as an end table, and sometimes a resident casually leans an elbow on it, as if it really were a piece of furniture. A razor is used on the last stubble. The head is bathed in Betadine, a disinfectant, the skin being a haven for staphyloccus germs. The floating head is now orange, the color of a pumpkin.

There is a breezy nonchalance about the work. The naked patient lies at the center of all this industry, unperturbed, though some reports suggest that at some level of consciousness patients are aware of what is going on. Hearing is the most difficult sense to put to sleep in humans. (Certainly this was a survival advantage in a time when man slept out in the open.) Even when adequately anesthetized, hypnotized patients have later offered verbatim accounts of OR scenes. One resident tells of a doctor who sang during surgery and of a patient who, upon waking, said, "Doctor, what a lovely voice you have."

The first order of surgical business is to determine the shape, extent, and position of the opening in the head. At home at night, I know that Chalif studies this aspect of the procedure. He takes out his skull, a real skull ordered through a medical catalog, and his purple felt-tipped marker. He arranges himself at his desk with a glass of wine and sketches flaps for the next day's operations. In the OR, the clam-shell shape of today's flap is outlined with a long pin on the orange scalp. Blood drips in fangs from the scrape made by the pin. If the cut is in the wrong place, a surgeon might not have the exposure he wants, which could really be a problem if he gets into trouble. Then he may need to find a vessel and discover the hard skull bone in his way.

When the surgeon arrives, the mood changes. It tightens. People in scrub suits, masks, and head cover still come and go through the swinging door, marked boldly "No Entry," but there is less talk, more directed activity, as if the teacher has just walked in.

Flamm tries on his headgear. It looks more like the headdress of a cave explorer than a neurosurgeon's. Attached to a gray plastic headband is a spotlight, right in the middle of the forehead, like a third eye. The light is produced by a separate generator, and the surgeon steps up to the bright orange box and plugs in his headgear's fiberoptic hose. Flamm will work under this light until the microscope—which has its own light source—is rolled in. He places his thumbs together at the level of his chest and adjusts the beam on his headband so that it focuses just right, though it looks for an instant as if he is lost in prayer. The box that generates the light for the headgear carries a warning sign, put there by the engineering department. "Not approved for use with explosives," it reads.

"Then what's it doing in a neurosurgical operating room," says Flamm, his mask pumping in and out with laughter.

In his operating blues, Flamm looks muscular. He plays squash, runs his barrel-chested Labrador to Central Park occasionally, but mainly it is the OR that keeps him in shape nowadays. Flamm wears open-heeled clogs. The wooden soles make a heavy clump that sounds like a tree being chopped.

It takes an hour to get ready for neurosurgery. Flamm is there not to participate but to supervise, as actively as the situation requires. With the preparations well along, he leaves for the washroom where he will scrub in, a lengthy procedure in and of itself. With a disposable brush he raises a head of lather on one hand, then the other, as if polishing them. Each hand gets five minutes, making sure to get the nails. Everything is designed to keep the cleaned hands uncontaminated. For instance, the long steel wash basin is built so that water flow can be regulated with the knees.

The OR probably features, foot for foot, more practical know-how than any other medical forum. Waves of technological breakthroughs, procedural discoveries, Eurekas, and dumb luck coincide here, like nodal points, over the body of the sleeping patient. And yet the entire edifice of modern surgery might be ruined if the surgeon forgot to wash his hands, a detail that took hundreds of years to figure out.

Before Louis Pasteur proved that infections didn't materialize out of thin air, surgeons, like Johnny Appleseeds of germs, probably spread more disease than they cured. Richard von Volkmann, a leading surgeon of nineteenth-century Germany, then the world capital of surgical technique, reported that 80 percent of wounds or sores became gangrenous. In his hospital, 40 percent of all patients treated for compound fracture of the leg—a broken leg!—died. Throughout history doctors had tried to avoid wound complications by freezing wounds with ice, cauterizing them with a red-hot iron, bathing them in alcohol, and searing them in oil. The prevailing theory at one point was that the suppurating wound, scummy with pus, was a necessary step on the road to recovery. If only it had occurred to them to wash their hands! Or to listen to those who did! Ignaz Semmelweiss, a Hungarian obstetrician, had required doctors in his clinic to wash their hands with a chlorine solution before examining pregnant women, a lone act that dramatically dropped the mortality rate. His fate? He was dismissed from the University of Vienna. His colleagues believed him nuts, and bellowing that he wasn't, he died in 1865 at age forty-seven in an insane asylum due, of all things, to sepsis.

Two years later, applying the principles that Pasteur discovered and that Semmelweis had intuited, Joseph Lister developed antiseptic surgery, ending once and for all the era of "laudable pus." A surgeon bathed both his hands and the instruments and sprayed the air and the wound in carbolic acid, a germ killer. In some ORs, mists of vapor blew across the patient, ran off into special gunwales built into the operating table, and drained into buckets on the floor. Surgeons wore rubber aprons and boots.

Eventually—because the carbolic acid was so irritating to the hand!—someone thought to wear rubber gloves.

The methods must have made the OR seem like a ship going through a storm, but they worked. Immediately after adopting antiseptic techniques, Volkmann treated 135 patients, and not one succumbed to wound disease. "Never do I feel more solemnly and gratefully inclined to Providence, who has permitted me to live to see this blessed change, than when I make this comparison," Volkmann said in 1881. By the early twentieth century antiseptic method had given way to aseptic method, the intent no longer to kill germs but to exclude them from the operative field. ORs once had windows that opened on to the outdoors. Neighborhood kids are reported to have climbed trees to watch one famous neurosurgeon at work. (At one point he had to admonish them to be quiet.) The modern OR, lit by artificial light, is breezeless and scrubbed. Masks have been added to the surgeon's garb. Tools, sheets, clothing—anything that comes in contact with the wound—are sterilized in advance. The hospital, founded as a place where the poor could die, has turned into a place the patient has a chance of leaving alive.

WHEN FLAMM RETURNS to the OR, pushing the door open with his back, the room smells of soap. Flamm's cleansed hands are held high, as if he is about to conduct an orchestra. A nurse hurries to bring him a gown. Flamm punches his arms through the sleeves. The nurse holds a paper tab on a string belt, which detaches so as not to compromise the sterile surface, and Flamm spins, wrapping himself in. Rubber gloves come in individual packets. The rubber is thin, the surgeon sacrifices little sensation, but they are impermeable, and some report that they make the confined hands hot. Flamm asks that the thermostat be turned down. "Brrrrr" goes a nurse, who fetches something to put over her arms.

The rules are that Flamm can only touch what is sterilized, which excludes such important objects as the rims of his eyeglasses. When his glasses slip down on the bridge of his nose, he calls to one of the nurses and bends his head. She pokes them back up with a finger. Some OR personnel wear a cap with an elastic band; Flamm wears a hood to cover his hair, like the hood of a sweatshirt.

When I explain to the anesthesiologist that this is my first time observing an operation, he is happy to explain what he is doing. As soon as the patient was put to sleep, he says, he opened the mouth, sluiced a breathing tube down the throat into the lungs—tracheotomies were once the rule—and hooked it to a ventilator, giving the patient the appearance of a snorkeler. A barbiturate relaxed the muscles, to ensure the patient didn't jerk. Anesthetic gases produced a deep sleep. The patient could slumber dreamlessly for ten, twelve, or twenty-four hours while the anesthesiologist manned the controls from his own portable workshop, two closet-sized stacks of monitors that could be wheeled around the OR. For a long time the administration of anesthetic agents was considered the lowliest job in the OR. Residents or, if they could get out of it, medical students were handed the equipment. Neither blood pressure nor respiration was monitored. Just make sure the patient doesn't stir! That was the order of the surgeon. The fumbling student obeyed as best he could, which sometimes wasn't very well. E. A. Codman, a student at Harvard Medical School in the 1890s, remembered he was distracted one day when the anesthetizing fell to him. His patient meanwhile inhaled his own vomit and died. In the modern OR, leads went into the patient's blood vessels—one into an artery, two into veins—so that the anesthesiologist could get constant blood-pressure readings. A tube was passed into the food pipe and positioned behind the heart. This allowed the doctor to double-check the electronic sensors through an ear piece, which each anesthesiologist has molded to fit his own ear. Body temperature and carbon dioxide and oxygen levels were scrutinized. The patient, crossed with hoses and wires, gave up his carbon-based will to the silicon-based machines at the anesthesiologist's disposal. To the anesthesiologist this seemed the ideal state. "Take a guy whose heart is in bad shape. His heart is probably working better than it has in the past five years. You're regulating everything that comes in and everything that comes out," anesthesiologist Kenneth Schmidt, who worked on my case, once explained to me. Even danger was signaled automatically. When I ask about the alarms, the anesthesiologist eagerly unhooks the air hose from the patient's mouth. "You'll see," he says, and looks off into the distance. The patient's chest, which a second ago had been heaving rhythmically, goes flat as a skillet.

"I see, I see," I say, feeling like the real victim of this showiness. But the anesthesiologist lets the test run its unnerving course until in a few seconds the respiratory monitor mercifully whistles and the doctor snaps the air hose back into place.

NOT ONLY ARE anesthesiologists relatively new figures in the OR, so too is anesthesia.

Certainly painkillers would have been useful to previous generations of surgeons. Not many people, no matter how sick, could tolerate the pain of being sliced open while awake. Indeed, the few operations attempted were not manned by efficient nurses, but by muscle-bound guards who held the shrieking patient in place. Of necessity surgeons had turned into sprinters. One rapid British surgeon, William Cheselden, could incise the gall bladder and remove a stone in 54 seconds! A good time for amputating a leg, which involved scalpel *and* saw, was under three minutes. Few surgeons imagined that surgery could be any different.

That is, not until William Morton, a lowly dentist, proved otherwise. In the 1840s Morton owned a false tooth factory which earned him the important yearly sum of $20,000. Yet he feared expansion was limited. Before new dentures could be installed, rotted old teeth had to be pulled. That was torture. And torture, Morton had learned, was bad for business. Morton knew that ether could dull sensation. Could the effects of ether be generalized? he wondered. He experimented on the only subject available. "I shut myself up in a room," he wrote, ". . . I then saturated my handkerchief and inhaled. I . . . soon lost consciousness. As I recovered, I felt a numbness in my limbs, with a sensation like a nightmare, and would have given the world for someone to come and arouse me. I thought for a moment I should die in that state, and the world would only pity or ridicule my folly." The year was 1846. Morton was twenty-seven. Eight minutes later, his strength crept back, and Morton ran to his co-workers, shouting, "Eureka."

Within just three weeks Morton had arranged for a test on a patient at Massachusetts General Hospital. After the test, surgeon John Collins Warren wrote: "A new era has opened on the operating surgeon."*

---

*What turned out to be perhaps the greatest aid to surgery since the fabrication of the knife soon became entangled in some of the pettiest, unhappiest accusations and counteraccusations in medical history. Ether was for sale at every drugstore in the country so Morton disguised it, probably adding a little oil of orange, a little opium, perhaps. He called it Letheon gas, though anyone who smelled it immediately recognized the sweet odor of ether. Horace Wells, another dentist and Morton's former boss, had previously worked with nitrous oxide (laughing gas), which could also be used as a general anesthetic. A third figure, Charles Jackson, a respected scientist, helped and supported Wells and Morton up until the time that success struck. Then, like the shadowy "bad guy" waiting to strike during the happiest moment, he claimed to have been the real pioneer, an argument his legitimate credentials helped advance. These battles drained much of the material and, it would seem, almost all the mental resources of these three inventive men.

Wells was the first to go. He left dentistry altogether and became the huckster he had been taken for. He traveled through Connecticut with a troupe of singing canaries. In 1848, just thirty-three, Wells was arrested for tossing deadly acid on prostitutes. In jail, he inhaled chloroform and, before losing consciousness, slashed his femoral artery. He bled rapidly and, thanks to his own work, painlessly, to death. In 1868, at age forty-eight, Morton collapsed

In today's case, the era of painless surgery had opened with a blast of pentathol, which in 15 seconds traveled to the heart and then to the brain where it induced sleep.

THE SCRUB NURSE ARRANGES the tools on a table, which, like most OR furniture, is on wheels. There are a welter of instruments, neatly aligned so that the nurse knows where they are when she needs them. There are scalpels, big ones to slice the scalp, middle-size ones to work on the dura, microscalpels to lace open the arachnoid; curved needles, each threaded with a length of black silk thread, good for one stitch; retractors, tabs of flexible metal five or six inches long, which can be attached to a flexible metal arm; a flap elevator, a nerve hook, scissors for different purposes, a dural scissor with a guard to keep from cutting the brain, a microscissor, whose scissor is about the size of a drop of water; squeezable bulbs with eye-dropper ends, which the nurse fills from a tureen of saline solution; strips of cotton; a Bovie or cautery, a pencillike tool that uses diffuse electric current to cauterize a patch of tissue, a bipolar coagulator that passes current between the tips of a large tweezer and cauterizes only what is between them; and many more.

The tools for microsurgery are long-handled tools—called bayonet style—permitting the surgeon to work without getting his hands in the sights of the microscope. An instrument doesn't have to be particularly strong to work in the brain, but it must have excellent balance so that the bladed tip does not tug down. A surgeon, like any craftsman, often brings his own tools with him. In the early seventies Flamm had paid Swiss watchmakers $1,200 to manufacture a set of seven stainless-steel tools to his specifications. Sometimes he will try out a new scalpel in the OR. If he doesn't like it, he calls over the salesman, who with blue stretchable boots over his wing tips has been allowed in the room, says, "Sorry," and hands it back to him.

The preparations and even the operation itself consist largely of grinding, boring routines. And yet, every resident is taught, very small deviations

---

in the midst of preparing yet another response to Jackson's claims. His doctors had restricted him to bed. But Morton sped off in his buggy and raced through New York's Central Park. Complaining of the heat, he was said to have plunged his head into a lake. Poor and persecuted, he collapsed in the park and never recovered. Jackson, the illegitimate heir, outlived them both. He passed the last seven years of his life in the McLean Asylum, attached to Massachusetts General Hospital, where both Wells and Morton had made their demonstrations, writing dastardly letters from the calm of the mental ward, where he died in 1880 at age seventy-five.

can make a big difference. Explained one resident: "You have to pay supreme attention to detail: how to tie a knot, how to cut the drain that goes under skin, everything. Everything has a reason. And maybe one in a hundred times it will make a difference." This resident carries with him a deck of index cards, noting everything he has to do for each patient, for each doctor, even for his girlfriend.

Two giant saucer-shaped light fixtures are hooked to the ceiling. They slide on tracks almost the entire width of the room. The scrub nurse focuses their beams on the tool table. The kettle-drum exterior isn't sterile, but, cleverly, each light has a snap-on handle that is.

The tool table is rolled over the patient, and blue sterile drapes are hung from it, creating a tent over the patient. Drapes are sewn or clipped into the scalp, leaving nothing of the patient but a slim triangle of skin on his hoary head. No longer is it possible to identify, even in the imagination, a person. The problem is now a matter of a patch of scalp, an area of skull, a cylinder of brain.

"Scalpel, please," says a resident. The scalp is cut first. His first few times, a resident is timid with a scalpel, almost delicate, and has to be encouraged to put some force behind the blade. To penetrate the scalp, with its layers of skin, dense tissue, muscle, and fibrous membrane, takes some effort. Once cut, it spreads as if it had been pulled tight. The scalp, the body's thickest skin, is rich in arteries, and the blood has to be stanched with an electric cautery. The odor of burning meat fills the room. For a few minutes it seems to me the OR has the aroma of a barbecue.

"Is the cautery connected?"

"Yes."

"It's not working."

"Is it working now?"

"That's better."

There is nothing gentle about brain surgery yet. The disturbing sound of metal scraping wood is heard as the surgeon's tool rips the scalp off the skull, a smooth, pale, bloodless curve. A wide tongue of scalp is tied back to a sheet. From underneath it looks like a slab of raw meat.

The skull is body armor, an evolutionary strategy to protect the brain. At its strongest section, the skull can withstand 1,500 pounds of pressure per square inch, 100 times more than the pressure normally exerted on it by the atmosphere. Man has surgically poked holes in the skull of his fellow man for at least ten thousand years, or about as long as he's had flint and obsidian tools with which to do it. Some ancient patients even survived. In one collection of 400 prehistoric crania with openings in the dome, 250 had advanced cicatrices, indicating an astonishing survival rate of 62 percent. By the Renaissance, European barber-surgeons had refined the entering technique. Ambroïse Paré, barber-surgeon, had discovered it best, for instance, to "stop the patient's ears with Cotten-wool." Paré and his colleagues used carpenter's tools: brace, chisel, mallet, the same basic tools still employed in every OR in the world. The residents call this aspect of the procedure "bone work" and still employ the principles their ancestors had initiated—with one chief exception.

Instead of drilling bone out of the skull, and leaving a hole, at the end of the nineteenth century a German surgeon realized that a "cap" could be cut out of the skull and then, some hours later, replaced. Bone would regrow at the margins of the scar and make this "flap" solid again. The replaceable flap allowed the surgeon to uncover larger areas of the skull, since he wasn't going to leave the patient with a giant unprotected section of head. This procedure was called a craniotomy. Sometimes, in a procedure called a craniectomy, bone was still entirely removed and then replaced with a wire mesh screen. But at least a modern surgeon had a choice. In 1985, 34,000 craniectomies or craniotomies were performed in the United States. I had three holes drilled in my head, then connected to form a removable plate of bone the circumference of a softball.

In the NYU OR, the initial holes are made with a hand-held brace and drill bit. As the brace spins, twists of skull climb into the bit. Shavings sprinkle over the surgical gloves and look to me like grated cheese. This is muscle work; the resident is told to put his shoulder into it, to drive the drill toward the brain. The patient's head shudders in its clamp. I'm told that the drill is designed to lock when its forward edge meets no resistance, though I can't help but imagine the steel projectile of the bit crashing through the doughy brain. In fact, one resident, when he was at another institution, put his weight behind a drill that jammed, forcing the equipment into the brain and killing the patient, a young boy. A burr attachment is used to enlarge the hole until it is the size of a quarter. A power drill, called a craniotome, has a bone-cutting attachment that is employed to connect the holes. Neither the burr nor bone-cutting attachment locks automatically.

The resident calls for a flap elevator, which is a tool with angled end. The resident slips it under the trapdoor of skull and eases the bone up, making sure not to pull too quickly and tear the membrane covering the brain. The resident hands it to a nurse, who wraps the oval flap of skull in a towel soaked in Betadine and plunks it in a bowl of antibiotic solution, safekeeping it for later.

Now it is the surgeon's turn. If he's not there yet, he is called by intercom, and the residents throw a towel over the open head and stand at ease, chitchatting about whatever is on their minds.

When the surgeon arrives, for just a moment he holds the scalpel aloft, like a man with an umbrella. "I'm opening now," he says, giving the signal to the rest of the OR that the exercise of preparation is over, the real thing is at hand. Bone surgery has ended. Brain surgery is about to begin.

47 The surgeon's passage from the skull to the brain is not only the crucial moment in any single neurosurgical procedure; it also represents the turning point in the history of the field of neurosurgery. Craniotomy may be the oldest major surgical procedure; it was once used to treat epilepsy, unbearable headache, and probably melancholy. However, it provided the brain surgeon with little encouragement and even less instruction. After all, it was bone surgery, not brain surgery. Not much more than a hundred years ago the great German surgeon Volkmann spoke for his peers when he warned that brain surgery was hopeless except in a few limited areas. Indeed, well into the twentieth century it was contended that only simple skull surgery was of benefit to the patient. General surgeons should simply leave the brain alone. As late as 1904, according to John Fulton, Harvard Medical School's E. A. Codman reviewed the twenty-eight brain-tumor operations attempted over the previous decade at Massachusetts General Hospital—not quite three per year—and came to this conclusion:

> The chance of any success by radical operation was so small that in any given case diagnosed as brain tumor, even if the symptoms gave evidence of a more or less exact localization, it would be wiser to do an operation simply for the relief of intracranial pressure, rather than to explore with the idea of removing the tumor.

Codman recommended simple decompression, which involved removing an oval of skull to give the brain more room. In other words, stick to skull surgery; drop the brain surgery.

What changed? Certainly the advent of neurosurgery is due to a con-fluence of events: improvements in anesthesia, general surgery, and neu-rology. Yet it is also true that the contributions of a few individuals totally recast the medical possibilities of the field. Neurosurgery became the most important therapeutic innovation in the history of the neurosciences, and how that happened is a tale of sheer bullying persistence by a few pioneers.

One of the biggest bullies was Victor Horsley. When he was called to the National Hospital at Queens Square, Horsley was twenty-nine and had already proved himself an able surgeon and keen neurophysiologist. In one experiment he surgically inserted a balloon into the brain of an animal. By gradually inflating the balloon, Horsley demonstrated that an expanding tumor could impair brain function. More importantly, deflating the balloon showed that function could be restored if the tumor was removed. As a by-product of his experiments, Horsley had, by 1886, operated on over one hundred animal brains, many of them monkeys. By the standards of the time, that gave him greater practical neurosurgical background than almost anyone in the world.

Queens Square, primarily a hospital for neurologists, was not equipped for a surgeon, and so Horsley revamped the far end of the general medical ward, turning a day room into an OR. His start was auspicious. His first year at Queens Square, 1886, Horsley performed ten brain operations. Not many, perhaps, but enough to send a message to the world: The forbidden brain was accessible. Between 1886 and 1896 the medical literature bulged with accounts from more than five hundred surgeons who breached the frontier of the skull and performed operations on the brain, according to R. H. Wilkins's *Neurosurgery*.

The world followed Horsley's lead, yet at home his neurological col-leagues had mixed feelings, at best. For instance, the man leading the charge into the brain was not given the right to admit patients to the hospital. The surgeon had a predetermined role, clearly conceived by the neuro-logical hierarchy. He was their scalpel. He operated only when they invited him. And that was usually only after they considered a case beyond hope and any measure, including surgery, worth the risk. Horsley fumed when, in 1905, he was asked to operate on a tumor that had been diagnosed thirteen years earlier. The neurologist's fear, of course, was self-justifying. Caught early, a tumor was easier to remove and the patient's symptoms more likely to be reversed. The desperate patients that Horsley was being sent, their tumors so big that they were blind or paralyzed, were the types of subjects least likely to yield success.

And yet the neurologist's instincts weren't without justification. Tes-timony of physicians who observed Horsley suggest he was a dexterous operator. Certainly it was also true, as Paul Bucy, editor of *Surgical Neurology*, commented: "Almost nothing that [Horsley] did could be classified as within the accepted standards of surgical practice today." Consider that Horsley would take his horse-drawn cab to the homes of his private patients and perform brain surgery in their parlors! One eyewitness account from 1900, when Horsley was forty-three, gives some idea of how crude this brain surgery was. Horsley sterilized his instruments at home—which probably meant boiling them in water—then packed them in a towel and set off in a buggy to a well-appointed West End mansion in London. Horsley dashed upstairs, had the patient under ether in five minutes, and was operating ten minutes later. He made a great hole in the woman's skull and pushed up the temporal lobe. Horsley was performing a gasserectomy, a now outdated procedure to alleviate excruciating facial pain. Blood was everywhere. Horsley packed gauze into the middle fossa, cut the gasserian ganglion, stopping nerve signals from face to brain, then closed the wound. He was finished in less than an hour.

Horsley's surgical mortality rate at one point was estimated at 38 percent for brain tumors. The sad fact was that brain surgery, as practiced at the turn of the century, was a discouraging field, as many newcomers quickly learned. In the decade after 1896, Wilkins went back and counted the number of reports from surgeons operating on the brain. This time he found only eighty—almost 85 percent fewer than in the ten previous years.

Horsley may have been the only person not discouraged by these dreary statistics. Mortality could be reduced, Horsley believed, but not by shrinking from surgery. "There must always be high mortality with or without operation," Horsley said in 1913. "This period of surgical activity has been a necessary stage in the development of cerebral surgery." To put such arguments across to his colleagues, Horsley, the lone neurosurgeon in a hospital of neurologists, would have needed more than a deft hand. He would have required a winning way. But Horsley, vocal teetotaler, strident, almost completely antisocial ("Evenings are for work," he once said), could not manage that. He might be generous and kind, particularly with a junior colleague. But in public, where he might have been politic, he was blustery and vehement. His superiors, he let it be known, were not just liars, but archliars and, he added, scoundrels, as well. Eventually he so alienated neurologists that they refused to refer patients to him. In the years before World War I, Horsley, the world's first full-time brain surgeon, watched his private practice dwindle to almost nothing. Groundbreaker was the role Horsley played, and perhaps it was the one that best suited him. His aggressiveness, his temerity, qualities that ostracized him from his community, must also have put him beyond self-doubt. After a string of ten operations on pituitary tumors—with little success—Horsley, undeterred, prepared to operate on an eleventh.

"Victor, if you operate on that man, he will die," a neurologist told Horsley.

"Of course he will die," riposted Horsley, "but if I do not persist, those who come after me will do no better."

AFTER VICTOR HORSLEY came Harvey Cushing. Unlike poor Sir Victor, knighted by his queen but unloved by his colleagues, Cushing would develop his neurosurgery in an environment not of neurologists but of surgeons.

At first, it hadn't been clear that Cushing would even become a neurosurgeon. Cushing's boss for thirteen years was William Stewart Halsted, who beat a cocaine addiction to become the major figure in American surgery in the nineteenth century. Halsted, chief of surgery at Johns Hopkins, had discovered that surgical care and not surgical speed was what produced good results. He dissected layer by layer and would have worked cell by cell if possible. No tissue should be unnecessarily bruised, no bleeding unchecked, he said. At Massachusetts General Hospital, where Cushing had been a medical student, patients returned from the OR deathly ill after procedures of just minutes. Cushing had been accustomed to shocking patients into recovery with strychnine, a poison that in small doses stimulates the heart. Halsted's patients awoke unaided, healthy and sound. Halsted wanted Cushing to apply these techniques to orthopedic surgery. Hopkins needed a specialist, and Cushing, Halsted argued, would be good at it.

Cushing demurred. He favored brain surgery, though even in retrospect it's difficult to understand why. In 1887, W. W. Keen was the first American to extract a brain tumor. (It's still preserved in a medical museum in Philadelphia.) But that was an isolated episode in his career as a general surgeon. In fact, when Cushing was considering brain surgery, no American earned a living as a brain surgeon. Looking at statistics like Horsley's, Cushing himself wondered whether brain surgery was worthwhile. "I can hardly imagine an optimism sufficient to carry a surgeon into a class of work in which one out of every two or three patients dies obviously from one's intervention," Cushing said.

At first, Cushing chose his cases very carefully, which meant choosing very few. In 1905, Cushing found eight tumors on which he dared to operate; in 1906, it was ten, and in 1907, ten more. In his career, Cushing had operated on barely thirty tumors, yet in 1907 he published the first text explaining not only how to enter the cranial chamber but what to do once inside; how to pass, in effect, from skull surgery to brain surgery.

The turning point for Cushing, and perhaps for neurosurgery, as well, was the case of Maj. Gen. Leonard Wood, a rugged national hero who, just for fun, would square off against pal Teddy Roosevelt with broadswords. Wood was set to be chief of staff of the U.S. Army until paralysis started to creep down his left leg and seizures began to run up it. In 1909, the year Cushing saw Wood, neurosurgery barely had a foothold: Four American doctors identified themselves as neurosurgeons. Cushing knew that the fallout from failure might be serious indeed, and not just for the patient. But Cushing certainly also understood that for a young surgeon in a new field Wood represented the chance of a lifetime.

Wood's problem was a big bloody but benign tumor for which Cushing would coin the name meningioma, though not until thirteen years later. Meningiomas didn't grow out of brain tissue but out of the meninges, the coverings of the brain. They could be removed without damaging the central nervous system, and the patient cured. That was the theory. In practice, they were usually fed by minuscule vessels that bled uncontrollably at surgery. Cushing, one of the first to realize that some kinds of tumor were more amenable to surgery than others, had been studying meningiomas since 1895. But he had not successfully excised a single one that, like Wood's, pushed into the brain. The year Cushing examined Wood was the year he lamented: "Glad that [the patient's] operation has been postponed; for everyone dies that I touch." Without surgery, Wood's tumor was a death sentence. Surgery, Cushing feared, was an execution. In January 1909, Cushing bought some time. He told the general there was no need to rush to the OR.

But in February 1910, General Wood, unable to climb a ladder in front of his men, phoned Cushing. He was arriving the next day. The general lied to the press—he was quoted as saying the operation was to remove an old scar—while demanding that Cushing operate on the tumor. Cushing still hadn't successfully removed a meningioma like Wood's! To add to the pressure, an official from Harvard University, which would soon be looking for a new chief of surgery, planned to be in the amphitheater.

To someone accustomed to the speedy surgery of Horsley, the procedures—there were two parts—would have seemed unbelievably tedious. "Having been brought up to believe that convalescence is shortened by attention to the technical details while the patient is on the operating table, I have no dread of a long session," said Cushing.

Three days after the final operation, Cushing entered the general's room. "My god, General, what are you doing?" said Cushing in amazement.

"I wanted to see if I could get my left hand into my trousers pocket once more," replied Wood, "and I can." His lameness was going; his left hand was coming back, too. He was walking eleven days after brain surgery. Following his inauguration as army chief of staff, Wood wrote Cushing, "I owe everything to you." Cushing also had cause for thanks. As late as 1915, Cushing said: "What is recovery from a tumor operation? If it is extirpation and cure, then we probably none of us see more than a possible five percent." Yet, three years after his success with Wood, Harvard appointed Cushing, forty-one—the only brain surgeon in Boston!—chief of its department of surgery. With the chief physician, Harvard charged Cushing with organizing the new Peter Bent Brigham Hospital. Unlike poor Sir Victor, condemned to play out his career among neurologists, Cushing, vehement but also politic, would have a hospital at his disposal.

In the first eighteen months at Peter Bent Brigham, Cushing did 149 cranial operations—as many as Horsley had performed in ten years—with a mortality rate that was an almost unbelievably low 7.3 percent.

The dramatic improvement was testimony in part to Cushing's surgical skills. "No one has ever excelled Cushing in fastidious care and devotion to detail," wrote neurosurgeon Wilder Penfield, director of the Montreal Neurological Institute, in 1977. "Frequently when debating any change in routine operative surgery we have referred back to the complete notes which I have of Cushing's every move." Those notes dated from 1918, when Penfield interned with Cushing. His successes were due also to, as Horsley had put it, "modification of the procedure." Cushing was a fearless innovator. In 1906 he hired his own anesthesiologist, the first full-time anesthesiologist in the United States; he footed the bill himself if the patient couldn't. He insisted on constant blood-pressure monitoring in the OR. He also ushered into neurosurgery the "electric knife" to cut tissue and cauterize bleeding.

Cushing was a prodigiously talented figure who seemed to do whatever he attempted better than anyone else. Added to that, he was almost inhumanly driven. (He went on with an operation even after learning his son was killed in a car accident.) On top of this, he was nearly inexhaustible. He skipped lunch, refreshed himself with catnaps, and during one period wrote 10,000 words a day, most of them standing. When he wasn't operating or writing, he was frequently drawing. Some of his detailed sketches, made while still in the OR—before removing his surgical gloves—illustrate his books. He was an excellent student of medical history; his book col-

lection, particularly of Vesalius, was second to none. He was a good organizer and became, in 1920, the first president of the Society of Neurological
Surgeons, each of whose eleven charter members was trained as a general
surgeon. If that wasn't enough, in 1926, the year he introduced the electric
knife to neurosurgery, he won the Pulitzer Prize for a biography of Hopkins's first chief of medicine and his mentor, William Osler.

Cushing so dramatically advanced neurosurgery, his personality so
dominated its formative years, that he is often said to have created it. Two
biographies have been written about him (one of which he took care to
help finance himself), and anecdotes recollected by his students are published in the *Journal of Neurosurgery*. Returning from the 1931 International
Neurological Congress in Berne, one doctor reported: "Cushing is undoubtedly the outstanding medical figure of the world." (It didn't hurt his
renown that his son married the daughter of Franklin D. Roosevelt.) By
the time Cushing gave up his chair at Harvard at age sixty-three, his own
legs hobbled from disease, he had excised 2,000 tumors, far more than all
the tumors taken out before he entered the field. His rate of operative
mortality was 6.8 percent, an enormous decrease over anything that could
reasonably have been expected when he entered brain surgery. Born into
an era when brain surgery was unthinkable, he proved that it was practicable on a daily basis, without killing one of every two or three patients.
Every American neurosurgeon draws parentage from him. Flamm, it might
be said, is a third-generation Cushingite, his chief having trained under
one of Cushing's residents.

And yet no one was more aware of the limitations of the field than
Cushing, as General Wood's second operation would underscore. When
Wood, his leg, arm, and this time his vision failing, returned for treatment
seventeen years after his first operation, Cushing was the world's expert
on meningiomas. He had learned, among other things, where he had erred
during Wood's first operation. Cushing should not have replaced the membrane or bone that had been infiltrated by tumor. Tumor might *appear* to
be completely extracted, but a few tumor cells almost always remain. Over
time they grow, reconstituting a tumor that, in Wood's case, was as large
and dangerous as the first. (In two cases of meningioma, a phenomenal
twenty-five reoperations had been recorded.)

Wood's second operation started at 8:30 A.M. August 6, 1927. Cushing
had the electric knife. A confident Wood had drafted no will, left no final
instructions. During the day-long procedure, blood loss required transfusions from two medical students—bags of transfusable blood didn't exist
—but the procedure appeared to go well. "It was so near to success,"

Cushing later wrote. An autopsy would show an unsuspected hemorrhage had spilled into one of the ventricles. Four hours after the operation, Cushing's most celebrated patient died. For days Cushing couldn't sleep, complaining that he repeated the operation every night in his head. For nearly two weeks he refused to operate.

Almost single-handedly, Cushing had overcome many of the barriers to brain surgery. After Cushing, skull surgery would be a preliminary to brain surgery. Yet one of the neurosurgical lessons Cushing had to learn repeatedly was that just when success was supposed to come easily, failure could intervene. Then, like the very first time, the surgeon would be miserable.

48

Flamm snips open the dura, the tough outer membrane, with dural scissors, and there is the brain. It looks glossy, as if wet, occupies the space of three pints of liquid, and it is where the being lives. Intracranial pressure rises and falls with the arterial pulse, which, with the membrane cut and sewn back with black stitches, makes the brain shimmer in the light. Some describe the color as oyster-gray, some pink. To me it looks more like the hue of skinned, uncooked chicken. The gyri (bulges) and sulci (indentations) look like opaque bubbles packed tight, revealing luscious, neat curves. Thick veins weave along the surface, a dark, wiry girding. One of them, the sagittal sinus, is thick and purple.

Each step of the surgeon's way is marked with danger. For instance, nick the sagittal sinus, as Chalif once did, and trouble starts. Chalif was opening. He had been talking to someone, the brain exposed, a scalpel in his hand, when plum-colored blood began to spurt. The sagittal drains into the jugular. The patient faced the immediate threat of bleeding out. No attending surgeon was in the room. Chalif tried to control the bleeding with direct pressure, the electric cautery. Nothing worked. "I knew that an attending [surgeon] was in the room next door," Chalif said. "I told the other resident to run and get him." Already scrubbed for his own case, the attending moved in. He ligated the sagittal on each side of the nick, at the same time removing the tumor. The patient was lucky. The remainder of his venous system compensated for the lost sagittal.

During an operation an observer can stand behind the surgeon and look over his shoulder. As long as I am careful not to brush against the surgeon's gown, which would contaminate it, I can get close enough to whisper in his ear. But if the surgeon is working deep inside the head, the better view is on the color video monitor that is stationed about six feet away. It is hooked into the microscope and shows, magnified, on the screen what the surgeon sees through his binocular eyepiece. A dime-sized bit of brain fills the twenty-one-inch screen. A vessel that is no wider than a swizzle stick has the width of a thumb. I take up post behind Flamm, watching his hunched shoulders and following the action on the TV screen.

Brain surgeons have a vast lexicon to describe brains they don't like: congested, bulging, tight, edematous, full. If a brain is under too much pressure, each small incision can produce hard-to-control bleeding. In the most dramatic cases, one snip of the dura and the brain can herniate, rising right out of the skull. Flamm is pleased with the brain on the table. He compliments it. It, he says, is relaxed and slack, a result in part of the mannitol, a drug which works like tiny sponges, absorbing fluid and eliminating it through the kidneys. Also the anesthesiologist, with his potions, has dropped blood pressure from the patient's normal of 130 mm Hg to between 90 and 100 mm Hg.

All neurosurgeons know the same basic techniques but evolve different styles. One of the neurosurgeons on staff is known to work extremely meticulously. Residents knew that a case they started with him in the afternoon could go well into the night. Joseph Ransohoff, the chief, is speedy and efficient. Get in, get out. Flamm is probably between the two.

For a moment Flamm turns on his wooden heels, his blue-robed back to the brain. His attention is drawn to the light box on the wall, where he studies the angiogram and CT scans. They are his road maps. If he reads those right, the aneurysm will be dead ahead. Get them wrong and he could churn up good brain until he comes out the other side. He wouldn't be the first. Walter Dandy, one of Cushing's star pupils, once opened a patient's head on the wrong side. (He did no harm—paid for the operation—and went back in six weeks later.) It could still happen. At least once during Chalif's residency a flap had been carved out of the skull in the perfect spot but on the wrong side of the head. Flamm's arms are folded Indian style across his chest, his hands pressed into his armpits. It's the position that surgeons assume to keep from accidentally bumping some unsterilized thing with their gesturing hands. In this arena every detail is purposive, reasoned, clever, though to the unacquainted, the OR's hundreds of careful rituals can seem strange, even funny. For a moment I think Flamm looks ridiculous, a giant blue insect tangled awkwardly in his own webbing.

Flamm is silent except for a noncommittal "Hunh," which sounds like a door slamming shut. It is impossible to tell what he thinks about what he sees; whether he has in mind a particularly difficult passage or a Sunday drive with the top down. Of course, no matter what he anticipates, Flamm counsels, "Out of left field could come something that goes against everything that is planned and everything that is logical." Then the blood-filled pod would hemorrhage, and a life would teeter. Bleeding is the disaster. That's when a neurosurgeon has to marshal his concentration and his courage and *do something*. To prime himself for such an occasion, Flamm explained, he puts himself through a mental drill. Every few minutes, like a tune he can't get out of his head, he asks himself, What do I do if it blows *now*? Soundlessly, he rehearses the maneuvers that he could try. Is there a major artery across which he could slide a temporary clip to stop the bleeding (and should he thus work to clear a way to it), could he get a sucker on the bleed itself and then dissect further, should a right-angled clip be ready or a fenestrated one? Though it might not work, there is always *something* to be done. "It doesn't matter how bad it is, I'm not going to sit there with my thumb up my ass," says Flamm. People think that brilliant surgery depends on the fine manipulation of slender needle-nosed tools. They are wrong. It is a thinking man's game. If he doesn't exercise good judgment, all his technical finesse will only help to bury him more quickly. If he doesn't plan, then sometime later the surgeon will review the films of the case and say something horrible to himself like "Geez, I should have thought of that. It was so obvious."

A circulating nurse, whose job includes squatting on hands and knees to pick up the bloody bandages the surgeon lets drop to the floor, has spread out a sheet, like a picnic cloth, on the floor. That's where she lines up the discarded bandages. Nothing gets thrown away. If, at the final tally, a single strip of gauze is missing, the patient will be X-rayed to ensure the bandage hasn't accidentally been left inside him. (Bandages come with a center strip of radiodense material.) It seems impossible to forget a sponge inside the brain, but with the blood flowing and the surgeon focusing on something else and excitement generalized throughout the room, the nurse knew how things could get confused. Cushing himself had once stitched up a person's scalp with a strip of gauze still inside.

Poised in front of the scans, cross-armed Flamm ends his latest rehearsal with the same reassuring thought he always arrives at: This one isn't one of the 10 percent that is going to blow; this case, the one on the table, will be one of those that passes without event.

One neurosurgeon has a handwritten sign in his office: It's a lot easier to stay out of trouble than to get out of trouble. "The point," Flamm says aloud, as if in prologue, "is to avoid excitement."

Nurses, bringing the doctors what they need, talk among themselves, sometimes about the surgeon. Earlier I'd overheard them in this exchange.

"He's so obnoxious."

"He's nice till he gets his hand on a patient."

Now one nurse says, not quite to herself, "Count on Flamm to keep it exciting."

Flamm calls for the microscope, which has been sheathed in a sterile plastic gown. It is as big as a person, and two people must wheel it across the room. Its size is deceptive, though, since actually it does not magnify much. An electron microscope could enlarge an object a million times. The operating microscope that Flamm raises and lowers with foot pedals has a magnification of from six to forty times, less than what a child with a chemistry kit can manage. And yet that modest capacity has been enough to give surgeons a huge advantage. After years of cursing clumsy hands, they were not the problem at all. A human hand is amazingly dexterous —one report say that a person can move a finger in increments of 1 micron, a distance smaller than the point of a pin. The problem is that at such fineness, the eyes fail. Structures are too small to see. Microscopes had been around for centuries. Ear, nose, and throat surgeons had even been hauling them out of the lab and into the OR since the 1920s. In 1953 a manufacturer finally decided that an OR microscope was a commercially feasible product. Carl Zeiss, a German lens maker, designed a microscope with two eyepieces, a hookup for a camera and a video monitor, and its own light source. Moreover, it was a piece of standardized equipment that could be ordered through a catalog. The impact of the microscope on a range of surgical fields was astounding. "The first experience using the microscope for a vascular anastomosis [sewing blood vessels together] can be compared to the first time the moon was seen through a powerful telescope; a welter of previously unrecognized detail could be seen," wrote Julius Jacobson, chairman of vascular surgery at Mount Sinai Hospital in New York City. Under the microscope surgeons could sew together blood vessels the thickness of a penny. Some pioneers used the scope in neurosurgery as early as the 1960s, but it was incorporated into routine OR procedure just fifteen years ago.

Flamm wants the overhead lights off. All is a soothing dark in the room except for the spots of light on the tool tray, the scope's bright beam, and the pink-and-blue glow of the TV screen.

One resident serves as first assistant and watches through the microscope's second eyepiece. He holds a squeeze tube of salt water that he spritzes into the head when the surgeon calls "irrigation." That keeps the brain from drying out. The other resident, the second assistant, watches on the TV screen with the other observers. (If the TV isn't working, the second assistant, shut out of the action, can drift and sometimes fall asleep, only to be awakened when he is yelled at or when his knees bang the table.) He works the foot pedal on the cautery, which the surgeon uses to cut through tissue or cook small bleeders. For a peaceful few minutes the only sounds in the room are "On . . . bzzzt . . . off." A puff of cloud rises from where the tissue is charred. Again the room smells of grilled meat.

FLAMM CAN DO a straightforward aneurysm, if everything is really humming, if the drill doesn't malfunction and the scalp doesn't bleed a little extra, in two to two and a half hours, skin to skin, perhaps as smooth a procedure as anybody in the world. If it is complicated and he gets into bleeding, it will take longer, five hours, perhaps, though he's gone twelve hours on an AVM and, fourteen hours on big tumors at the base of the brain. Physically, the body gets tired, and the shoulders ache from holding the arms up—in the position of someone cutting meat over a plate—though Flamm says he isn't aware of it until the next day. His mood depends on why the case is taking so long. If he gets bogged down in preliminaries, if the chair isn't there or the microscope isn't covered correctly, he gets frustrated. "This place is a fucking zoo," he's shouted. "Doesn't anybody remember how I operate?" On the other hand, he explained, "If it's just taking long because I am working slowly and carefully but everything is going slick, I'll be on a high, excited by it and not even thinking of the time." He said, "Time flies when you're having fun."

Indeed, brain surgery is fun. More than fun. Completing a case successfully, especially a difficult one in which the technique is extremely demanding, is deeply satisfying, beyond even the rewards to the patient or the family. Ransohoff, the chief, has a line about the satisfaction. A lot of neurosurgeons were a little disgusted at the comment when it was published, but it was unforgettable. "There aren't many times I leave the operating room without at least a quarter of an erection," Ransohoff had told a writer. "You're dealing with danger, blood, power, conquering the man or woman on the table. No wonder wives of patients fall in love with surgeons. Aren't we the male who conquers her male? I tell you, the man who says he isn't turned on by surgery is either a liar or a eunuch or both."

Ransohoff played the part of the not-to-be-messed-with saver of lives as well as anyone. He had been consultant to the TV series that brought brain surgery to the public, "Ben Casey." The boss cursed, scratched his crotch in public, chain-smoked everywhere but in the OR, didn't hesitate to call a colleague a liar, and generally behaved like a street brawler, though he was really the third generation of distinguished Cincinatti doctors, raised with a maid and a nanny. Flamm had trained under him for five years as a resident and, like every other resident, had loved him from the first interview, a moment Flamm still remembers with affection. Flamm, who tended to the formal, had dressed in one of his three-piece suits. When he couldn't find the elevator, he hiked six long flights, arriving at the neurosurgery office puffing and overheated. Ransohoff's first words were "For Christ's sake, take your jacket off. Sit down." Ransohoff kicked his feet up on the desk and rolled up his sleeves. For his moxie, his brazenness, his honesty, for generally cavorting as if the whole world were his stage, fatherless Flamm found Ransohoff, twenty-three years his senior, irresistible.

By the 1980s, Flamm would say there was nothing he disagreed with more than that his neurosurgical technique was equivalent to that of Ransohoff, who hadn't been trained under the microscope. Yet it was also true that Flamm had worked for Ransohoff for more than two decades and the influence of all those years was there. Flamm was a student in the Ransohoff school. Like the teacher, he was aggressive, self-confident, and temperamentally, at times, as much of a cowboy as the chief. "What was that absurd, outrageous, off-the-wall comment Ransohoff said about leaving the operating room with an erection?" Flamm said, "In a sense, I mean, I do know what he was saying." Flamm elaborated: "What distinguishes a surgeon is someone who does enjoy going through the exercise of an operation, the manual aspect of it, the appreciation of anatomy, in visualizing something in three dimensions. If you don't really get excited about the technical aspect of what you're doing, then you're wasting a great deal of your effort and time being a surgeon." For Ransohoff surgery was a hard-on, a triumph of one person's power over that of others. He made it sound like a primal conquest, not merely over disease but over the patient, who, as in a caveman's dream, had been dragged into the OR and beaten over the head until it parted and revealed his brain. Flamm experienced surgery as a sense of mastery, divorced from the patient; as if he had thought up an extremely difficult task and then accomplished it. Either way, there was hardly a satisfaction that rivaled it.

* * *

UNDER THE SCOPE, Flamm uses a microknife, with a nine-inch-long handle and a quarter-inch-long blade, to open the arachnoid, a filmy membrane around the brain. To get to someplace inside the brain, Flamm can cut through the cerebral tissue or even suck it up a tube. (Brain matter has the consistency of soft, moist cheese.) As a rule, a surgeon likes to avoid ruining brain tissue whenever possible. He prefers, as often as possible, to work along the brain's natural seams, spreading the tissue rather than cutting it.

Flamm searches the neurolandscape for a moment, checking the features he sees through the microscope against those he remembers from the X-ray maps on the wall. There is the right Sylvian fissure, the crevasse between the temporal lobe and the frontal lobe. Splitting the fissure is sometimes straightforward. For instance, when there has not been a hemorrhage and the brain is virginal, the fissure splits very cleanly. Then a surgeon will be staring at the middle cerebral artery. Sometimes the frontal and temporal lobes are stuck together and the fissure can only be split by working meticulously to separate the tissue millimeter by millimeter. Flamm calls that "a sticky fissure."

Once it is split, Flamm slides in metal retractors, one flat against the frontal lobe, one against the temporal lobe. The retractors are attached to a flexible metal arm, an OR innovation inspired by a toy the inventor's daughter was playing with. Flamm slides the retractors in firmly, but not roughly, expanding the cleavage. The object is to wedge the brain apart, which seems an incredible idea—it looks to me like prying the thing apart—but is a fundamental bit of brain surgery. The brain is plastic, though only to a point. Surpass that point and the patient won't be able to remember his name. The trick is to get the job done but be gentle. Always gentle. Still, a surgeon has no illusions: At the cellular level—which is where a neurophysiologist claims life is lived—the surgeon's finest stroke is brutish. A certain amount of beat-up brain is a casualty of any neurosurgery.

Flamm is still in the prepatory stage; the site of the aneurysm has not yet been uncovered. One peril in placing the retractor is that it can disturb the taut, pressurized aneurysm and, in some cases, cause a rupture long before the surgeon is in position to handle it. This is one of the worst possible complications. Ten visiting surgeons—Flamm called them "visiting firemen"—once came to the OR to observe Flamm's technique in clipping what was supposed to be a routine aneurysm. Just as Flamm was adjusting the retractors, long before he was able to see the aneurysm, the blister broke. It was white-knuckle time. Flamm maneuvered furiously to find the bleed and clip it as the doctors watched on TV. "Bastards, that's what they wanted to see, anyhow; they wanted to see me get into trouble," fumed Flamm after he had managed to find the source of the bleed and clip it.

An operation is a drama with a beginning, middle, and end. The plot is always the same: Prepare the brain, get to the lesion, then excise it or clip it or drain it. It is not altogether different from the narrative line of an adventure movie. Instead of bandits or slippery jungle passages or armed enemies that lie in ambush, the neurosurgeon must surmount adherent tissue, abnormal anatomy, unforeseen bleeds. In both cases, routine is constantly threatened by crisis.

For an outsider like me, I admit, it is the possibility of trouble that makes brain surgery exciting. My interest is plot driven. I can discern some anatomy, which I watch on the TV or, when invited, through the binocular lens of the microscope. But the reason I am glued to the wide screen is that I want to know what will happen to the patient on the table. I am an action junky, riveted like a resident, and am filled with anticipation. There are moments when, in the midst of what can look like a big pajama party, I believe that what I would like to see is not the calm, measured progress toward the goal, which in truth is difficult to follow, but just like the firemen, grace in the midst of danger.

Once the lobes are pulled apart, Flamm can look down the barrel of the Sylvian fissure and easily pick out a large branch of the middle cerebral artery, a continuation of the carotid artery. Follow this and the pictures on the wall say that it will lead to the aneurysm. What would he do if it ruptured *now*? With the middle cerebral accessible, he could always push a clip across this feeder while he dissected toward the aneurysm. That strategy won't be necessary.

There it is, the aneurysm. That is the good news. The bad news is that it is bigger than expected; almost a 2-centimeter dome, which qualifies it as a giant aneurysm and signifies that the abnormal balloon is under even more pressure than at first assumed. What Flamm must do is find out where it originates. Like most balloons, most aneurysms have a thin neck. Get a clip over that and circulation to the dome will be shut off. Aneurysms generally come from weak spots on the wall of a vessel, and most weak spots are found where vessels join, as if the welding had been imperfect.

The view through the microscope isn't going to make this aspect of the job easy. Flamm is looking straight down on top of the dome; the neck is hidden somewhere under the stretched hide, the most fragile part, which can only be touched with severe risk.

For decades it was this risk that held surgeons at bay. Rather than prod the pressurized ball, they ligated distant arteries, attempting to reduce blood flow through the aneurysm and thus, theoretically, diminish the risk of a hemorrhage. They tried to "trap" the aneurysm, tying off the artery on both sides of the malformation, which also sacrificed what might be an important vessel in the brain's circulatory system. It wasn't until 1938 that Walter Dandy, perhaps history's most fearless brain surgeon, actually slipped a silver clip across the neck of an aneurysm, eliminating it while also preserving the artery from which it originated. To accomplish this, Dandy lost his first sixteen aneurysm patients. His classic work on aneurysms, published in 1944, reported on his series of thirty cases, about five per year. He experienced a 30 percent mortality rate! But he proved that it was at least possible to manipulate the sac of the aneurysm itself, which is the dangerous mission that all future vascular neurosurgeons would undertake.

In one hand Flamm holds a suction device, a pencillike attachment on the end of a plastic tube. It sucks up liquid from the work site. In the other, he balances a bipolar coagulator. Flamm prods the aneurysm with the forceps, which amounts to actually handling the trigger device of the bomb. He calls for the microblade and cuts thin membrane off the aneurysm, almost shaving the bulbous growth. Chalif once explained: "Not many brain surgeons can do that." It can look at moments as if he is daring the thin globe to break. What do I do if it breaks *now*? Is he ready to go? He'd rather not find out. Still, by one means or another, he has to clear a path to the neck; otherwise, there is no way to slip on a clip. He pushes the bloated aneurysm aside with a forcep, trying to get a look underneath. On the screen, the aneurysm is as big as a grape. The neck originates between two branches of the middle cerebral artery, right in the crotch.

Some surgeons play music in the OR. Some sing. Some curse the entire way through, merrily, as if they are in a schoolyard pickup game. Perhaps Flamm is never low-key; in the OR he is wired. He would like the OR to be as still as a library. When he doesn't get silence, he stops. He raises his hooded head from the microscope and growls, "Quiet."

"Irrigation," he says, and a resident splashes on water. Flamm pokes in his sucker to clear the area.

"I have no suction," says Flamm suddenly.

"Checking" comes a voice from across the room.

"What good does that do, goddamned son of a bitch?" replies Flamm.

49 Why had Flamm chosen medicine? Growing up, Flamm didn't put the question that way. His father and his stepfather had been doctors. A cousin he was close to was a psychiatrist. The father of his teenage girlfriend—who would later be his wife—was a GP. "It seemed like everybody I knew in the world was a doctor," he said. The question Flamm asked himself was What else was there to do? He never found an answer. One person in 70,000 is a board-certified neurosurgeon. Flamm set out on that difficult trail almost from the start.

He was raised in middle-class Brooklyn, a precocious kid, with lots of IQ points and plenty of interests. He attended private school—his was the hundredth class to graduate from the Polytechnical Preparatory Day School, located on twenty-five acres near Fort Hamilton—and summer camp. He collected stamps—his collection is still stored away in a closet, because he can't part with it—and one year sat down and read an entire encyclopedia A to Z.

Yet it's fair to say that one of the early lessons of his life was that many things wouldn't come easily. Flamm's father died when he was two. A stepfather died soon after. If that wasn't enough, in the day-to-day world of playgrounds and playmates, Flamm, a pudgy only child, was not a natural athlete. Halsted had been captain of the Yale football team, Cushing, captain of the Yale baseball team, experiences that gave them an early sense of their own skills. As a ten-year-old, Flamm was the last pick when teams were chosen for baseball. "I couldn't catch a fly ball worth shit. I was stuck out in right field. That has a certain stigma," Flamm said.

Other kids who face similar experiences become meek or bitter, or they turn their back on sports altogether. "By the time I was twelve years old, I decided if I couldn't catch a fly ball, I would learn how to pitch," says Flamm. Lonely but determined, he went off by himself to practice tossing a ball. "When I started, I was terrible," Flamm says, "I worked at it." Every day? "You bet," he says, his bottom lip curled in a grin. By age fourteen he had become pitcher on the Camp Adventure baseball team and one of the more valued players. That was the summer he met Susan Levine, a Brooklynite he would take to his junior and senior proms and, seven years later, would marry. By the time he graduated high school, he had learned some new games, gotten some instruction, and was captain of the lacrosse team.

At Princeton, Flamm majored in an interdepartmental program in humanities. "It was a great exposure to interesting literature, art," he says. "I got a great deal out of it." One thing he didn't get out of it was good grades. "I wasn't goal driven," he says. To put it mildly. At the last minute he realized that if he wanted to attend medical school, he'd better do something to demonstrate it. He searched for a thesis adviser who could still take on another student. The only guy he could scare up was a botanist. Flamm's senior thesis was on snapdragons.

Of the dozen medical schools to which he applied, only one would have him: Buffalo Medical School, a pretty dumpy one in his estimation. The lesson of his early athletic career was that when he bore down, he succeeded. At medical school, Flamm became goal oriented. You bet.

He graduated near the top of his class and was appointed to a prestigious surgical internship at Cornell Medical Center. After a couple of years at Cornell, Flamm spent two years at the NIH, where he performed his first neurosurgery on humans. He then studied neurosurgery as a resident at NYU for five years, a requirement as stiff as that of any specialty. (No wonder neurosurgeons represent less than 1 percent of all doctors!) It was a long, careful preparation, yet Flamm remembers that his reaction after finally performing brain surgery alone was surprise. "I can do it; I can really do it," he said.

Unlike most of his colleagues, Flamm's interests extended beyond the techniques of surgery. He had an intellectual bent. He must have seemed a little weird for it, especially under a master as rough and ready as Ransohoff. Ransohoff wasn't close minded—just the opposite—but his favorite pastime was going off on his boat. As a young man, Flamm adored Ransohoff, and yet he had other role models. Perhaps he wanted to be more like Cushing, whose 1,371-page biography of Osler he had read as a teen. Flamm took up collecting ancient medical texts, especially those of Vesalius, the fifteenth-century anatomist who was Cushing's favorite. Flamm once traded a secondhand Porsche—"the family car," his wife groaned—for a Vesalius! (He promised her that would be the most expensive book purchase he'd ever make. It wasn't.) Flamm also got interested in the typesetting process, in bookbinding. He even *read* the books, penciling notes in the fifteenth-century margins. To his loaded schedule Flamm added the study of Latin, attending a weekly class while still a resident. He may have been the only person there who really wanted to learn the language. Flamm took up the history of medicine—later he'd work with Erwin Ackerknecht, one of the world's authorities—covering a daunting list of primary sources in a variety of languages. While still a resident, he published "Historical Observations on the Cranial Nerves" in the *Journal of Neurosurgery*.

When, at forty, he took up the cello, he awoke at 5:30 A.M. to practice. He had collected Bach's unaccompanied cello suites played by eight different cellists and recorded them one after the other on a single tape. After deciding which was best, one imagines, he tried to emulate that musician's technique as he stroked away at sunrise.

No doubt Flamm could come off a little stiff. Casually wish him "Bon voyage" and he returned an overcorrect "Merci." A resident remembers that during a medical convention most of the surgeons were at poolside, Ransohoff sporting a T-shirt that showed off his tattoo, while Flamm, buttoned up in a suit and sunglasses, skirted the crowd and headed off to a rare bookshop. He may have loved Bob Dylan—and owned every one of his records, of course—but he also said "the beach is so boring!"

As a resident, Flamm knew, from his study of medical history as well as from his OR experience, that vascular neurosurgery was an area in need of improvement. Decades after Cushing boasted a surgical mortality rate under 7 percent, mainly for tumors, the surgical morbidity and mortality rates were as high as 43 percent for aneurysms and 31 percent for AVMs, a throwback to the brain surgery of Horsley. To an outside observer, this is the kind of risk that makes brain surgery seem daring. To a young resident who had entered the field to save lives, this state of affairs was depressing as hell. When, as an intern in general surgery, he had gone after a gallbladder, Flamm had been able to distinguish the structures of the abdomen just as they were diagramed in the textbook. He could see when he had snared the irritating stones. But, alas, when it came to the brain, the body's capitol, which Flamm had been studying for nearly a decade, frankly it was impossible to differentiate deep anatomic features in the OR. A brain surgeon was winging it. Clipping an aneurysm was like wriggling a half-inch-long bobby pin down a shaft three inches into the brain and then placing it over a bubble so thin you could have watched—if you could have gotten close enough—the blood swirling through the overstretched walls. As a resident, Flamm had assisted Ransohoff in the clipping of aneurysms. Although Ransohoff was as good as any vascular neurosurgeon of the pre-microscope era, whenever he had to go after one, he was so hyper he was up on the ceiling. "It was terrifying," said Flamm. The first thing that looked like an aneurysm, you stuck a clip on and then you closed.

"It was like playing Russian roulette trying to dissect that aneurysm without rupturing it," said Dr. Ransohoff. "You'd clip it and then you just ran."

On the postop angiogram, you'd not uncommonly find the clip was on everything but the aneurysm.

To Flamm it was clear that vascular neurosurgery needed new techniques, microsurgical techniques. NYU had purchased a microscope, but nobody knew how to use it, Flamm included, though he tried. It was awkward, but he bulled ahead, teaching himself what he could. Brain surgery under the microscope wasn't possible with bulky forceps and knives of the kind surgeons had used for a hundred years. Regular surgical tools are held in the flat of the hand and depend on the movement of the wrist. Tools designed for use with the microscope have long, narrow handles. A surgeon manipulates them like chopsticks with his fingertips, gripping them at one end and working with the microblade or microscissors at the other. It was clear, even from Flamm's first clumsy efforts, that the microscope was going to advance neurosurgery. Flamm resolved that he would be in the forefront of that advance. Why don't I go off somewhere where the microscope is being widely used to learn nuances of it? Flamm thought.

A few American neurosurgeons—like Pool in New York and R. M. Peardon Donaghy in Vermont—had already begun to work microsurgically. But it was in Switzerland that the newest techniques were being worked out. Mahmut Gazi Yasargil, a brilliant, driven, sometimes unpleasant Turkish-born microneurosurgeon, worked in the department of Hugo Krayenbuhl, one of the dominant figures in European neurosurgery for the past thirty years and, as chance would have it, the father of a man Flamm had bumped into a decade earlier at a New York art gallery.

When Flamm had said he'd get in touch, Thomas Krayenbuhl assumed that was a quaint American way of saying good-bye, since so many other Americans had said the same and never called. Flamm, true to his word, phoned, and the two couples became fast friends. "I knew Thomas for a couple of years before it occurred to me that the name was so darned unusual perhaps he knew the man in Switzerland who was a neurosurgeon," Flamm says.

"Oh, sure, he's my father," said Thomas, who was working in the United States.

Hugo Krayenbuhl was a feared and respected figure at the Kantonsspital Zurich. Nurses ran down the halls—their wooden clogs clomp-clomping on the tiles—to fetch him a piece of equipment or deliver his messages. But the Flamms were like members of the family, and to them the imposing

Dr. Krayenbuhl was simply Poppie. (In fact, one of Dr. Krayenbuhl's grand-children is Flamm's godson.) When the time came to leave NYU, Flamm wrote to Poppie that he would like to spend some time with Yasargil. Typically, Flamm also began German lessons.

Flamm was already a neurosurgeon when he traveled to Switzerland. He knew how to do all the major operations, and he thought he could do them pretty well. Yasargil was doing two, sometimes three, cases a day. Flamm scrubbed in with him every morning. Yasargil had no illusions about why visitors came to his OR. "The whole world comes to see if I make a mistake," he said. He wasn't much interested in teaching. Indeed, he had developed a neurosurgery in which he could do everything himself. Almost. "Push the pedal, *mein lieber*," said Yasargil, and Flamm stepped on the pedal that activated the videotaping of the operation. Still, Flamm got to watch.

What he saw in Yasargil's OR was like nothing he'd witnessed before. It was as if this "bloody wizard," as Flamm called him, had reinvented neurosurgery and all that Flamm had already learned was merely back-ground. "It was like a different disease and a different operation," said Flamm, "It was just so exciting."

Yasargil, a square-shouldered, powerfully built figure, patiently, fas-tidiously dissected down to and around the abnormality. "Under the mi-croscope, you could plan the operation and have a strategy based on the anatomy. You could visualize it and know where you were," said Flamm. Yasaragil's approach emphasized control every step of the way. Instead of the dead panic in which Flamm had been accustomed to clipping aneu-rysms, Yasargil eyeballed the thing, manipulated it, and made sure no vessels would be trapped by the clip. "All of a sudden all these things that you'd see in textbooks but never see in the operating room were there in front of you," he said. Under the microscope, the finest arteries, some as narrow as a hair, could be seen. "Those were the ones that made the difference between what looked like a good case and came out great and what looked like a good case and left the patient paralyzed or worse," said Flamm.

When Yasargil had first studied microneurosurgey in the lab in 1966, he had nearly quit in despair. He had pulled on a suture and irreparably damaged a vessel. Microsurgery was not practical, and he wouldn't waste any more time upon it, he announced to the director. Half a dozen years later, in 1972, Flamm wrote a paper reporting on 250 of Yasargil's oper-ations for aneurysm. Aneurysm surgery no longer laid a patient to waste 43 percent of the time. The surgical mortality and morbidity was an astounding 5 percent. "If he weren't such a difficult personality, the world would be lauding him like Cushing," Flamm said.

Flamm had enjoyed Zurich, a quiet, sleepy town, where he'd had an opportunity to work with Ackerknecht at the University of Zurich on a paper on Jean Cruveilhier, the nineteenth-century French neurologist; it would be published in the journal *Medical History*. He'd begun lab work on the cause of deadly blood-vessel spasm. He also kept in touch with Ransohoff. "When I left, he said he didn't really see how I could fit in," said Flamm. "When I told him what I was learning, he got all excited and said, 'You've got to come.' " In 1972, Flamm returned to NYU as a member of the first generation of microsurgically trained neurosurgeons, at a salary of $25,000. He worked in the lab, wrote papers, and introduced new operating techniques he'd learned in Switzerland. "I was an idealist, I wanted to spend time in the lab," he said. Five years later, when he was forty, Flamm was earning $50,000, steep enough, but not by the standards of neurosurgery, whose practitioners are generally among the leading earners in medicine, with an average of $142,500 per year after expenses in 1982 in the United States. Flamm would eventually be made director of the lab and vice-chairman of the department, but he saw himself getting left behind. He wanted to operate more. "I was getting a little bit antsy to do the kinds of cases I thought I should be doing or getting a chance to learn how to do them; you don't read about a case and learn how to do it," he said. And he wanted the rewards that operating brings, one of which is money. "People I had done my residency with were moving into their second co-op by then, and I was waiting for the monthly paycheck." Perhaps his idealism had faded. Flamm remembered that Ransohoff yelled at him, "If the only thing you want to do is make $100,000 a year . . ." Flamm screamed back that that was just *one* of the things he wanted to do. Ransohoff called him at home. He saw Flamm's side. In 1979, with Ransohoff's encouragement, Flamm opened a private practice within the setting of the medical center, which is one of the benefits that NYU doctors enjoy. It has only been within the last few years that his private practice has become more than a part-time job.

Flamm has looked at other jobs but decided they couldn't rival what he has at NYU. Except for one thing: He would have liked to be chairman, to succeed Ransohoff. The boss has declined to step down, though he is well into his seventies. Ransohoff, who got into neurosurgery during World War II, passes on the vascular cases. But, with an important reputation, he maintains the busiest schedule of anybody on staff, working mainly on tumors, many of which are meningiomas. Bad feelings have set in where once there seemed to be mutual admiration. "It should all be so different," wrote Dandy after Cushing in a fit of anger refused to take him along to Harvard. Maybe it should be different at NYU, too. Certainly part of it is a question of stifled ambition; Ransohoff is clogging up the chairman's job, a post he once promised would be Flamm's. In 1984, at age forty-seven, Flamm was trying to make peace with himself. "Is it so important to leave NYU just to be called chairman of a department—and take a major cut in salary and in prestige?" says Flamm. "I said to myself I was going to be the top vascular neurosurgeon, and I think I am. A lot of people point to Yasargil or a couple of others; I don't have any doubt I could operate as well as they can. I'm not trying to brag about it, but it's a source of great personal satisfaction."

Unlike the title of chairman, that satisfaction has to be re-earned each time a surgeon enters the skull.

 At the patient's feet, nurses fiddle with the suction, trying to resuscitate it. A couple of times they call out, "Working on it," amid some hectic chattering, which doesn't ease Flamm's displeasure.

At the head of the patient, draped like a sofa in storage, Flamm paces. His wooden clogs make a sound on the tile floor like rain on a metal roof. "I don't think I make it look easy," Flamm once said. "I think I'm working damned hard, even when it is a straightforward case, if there is such a thing." Flamm wants everybody to keep up, including the equipment.

I crouch. I'm not sure why. Is it a self-protective reflex? I don't have any sense of proportion, of how bad this breakdown is. But Flamm is acting as if he has just received news that ruins his day. Then, without explanation, a rosy voice shouts, "Working." The hollow plastic stiletto, held between thumb and forefinger, slurps into action. Suction returns.

Flamm clears fluid—cerebrospinal fluid and the water he's added—out of the head so that he can get a better fix on what he is working on. A key skill of the microsurgeon is to mentally translate the two-dimensional image that appears on the scans into three dimensions. This helps a surgeon know where to put the clip. Flamm estimates the diameter of the neck at 10-millimeters (or 1 centimeter). To be safe, he calls for a 12-millimeter clip. It is loaded on a long-handled, long-nosed clip applier, a pliers that pulls open the stainless-steel arms. Once Flamm has nudged the clip around the neck of the aneurysm, he will ease his grip on the handle and let the clip squeeze the deformity's neck.

This is the most sensitive moment of the operation. An indelicate touch can rip the overinflated aneurysm just at the moment it is being removed from circulation. A rent in the wrong place might make it unclippable.

"Stop taping every two minutes," Flamm yells at the junior resident, who has been turning the video recorder on and off, trying to catch the clipping on film. "It drives me crazy."

In the OR, neurosurgery seems to me like sport. Three men in uniform, surgical scrubs, and blue paper hoods standing over a hole, crowding for position. Under the bright lights, every morning and every afternoon, hacking away at the brain. They alone, united by their aseptic gowns, can touch each other and the exposed brain. A bloody brotherhood with fingers in the works!

To my untrained eye the brain at this depth is a savage landscape, a thicket of tissue and vessels filled with colors and shapes without distinct borders. The 12-millimeter clip is easily recognizable. Its two arms are like twin silver skewers. On the screen I can watch Flamm slide them across the neck, then let them clamp shut. So far so good. Flamm scuds a second clip into that strange terrain, just to make sure. This might be one of those two-and-a-half-hour cases. Everybody might make the meal cart. In truth, I am relieved and a little disappointed. It is a special kind of peccancy, that of the spectator who hopes for both drama and success. Flamm invites me to take a look through the microscope, where the focus is better, the colors lusher, the surroundings prettier. Most of all, I don't want to touch anything, jeopardize anything. I have a sense that this is so fragile. My arms are behind my back like a penguin's, and I can see little, though I mutter an interested "Un-huh" and am glad to retake my place against the wall.

To be certain that an aneurysm is securely clipped, Flamm's policy is to puncture the sac. He watched Yasargil do it. It is common sense. If you want to know if a seal leaks, test it. This assertion, simple as it seems, had been the basis for heated controversy among neurosurgeons. For a surgeon who'd been trained to clip aneurysms before the microscope, puncturing the bloody, pressurized balloon was out of the question. Respected brain surgeons had told Flamm to his face, "That's an unnecessary risk." What if it starts squirting blood over your shoulder. Then where will you be? The message was If it isn't bleeding, don't mess with it. The older, conservative faction maintained that with experience a surgeon should be able to determine by visual examination how effectively the clip is placed.

"Bullshit," retorted Flamm. "So many times an aneurysm looks like it is clipped but isn't." If it is going to bleed, let it bleed while the brain is open on the operating table and not one day while the patient is walking to work. With all due respect, said Flamm, the upstart in this argument, if you couldn't handle the bleeding, what the hell were you touching the aneurysm for in the first place?

Flamm saw a moral issue here. This was not an argument over technique but over honesty. If you honestly wanted to demonstrate that you'd done the job, you had to pop the aneurysmal balloon.

The history of neurosurgery might be understood as a history of attempts to control bleeding, the nemesis of every neurosurgeon since Horsley. Consider that the brain represents just 2 percent of the body's weight but that fully 20 percent of the body's blood is passing through it at any given time, three cups per minute. In general surgery, a little blood might ooze into the abdomen after an operation. It will clot and soon stop. A little seepage of blood in the head could cause a patient not to wake up.

Flamm compared brain surgery to general surgery. "With all the other major body cavities that one works in, you can look around for a bleed. If you make a big slit in the abdomen, you stick your head in there and look. You don't see the bleed, so you shove the guts over to the other side and take a look. Same thing in the chest. You move the lung around and you take a look to see where the hell it is. In the head you can't do that. You're damaging the brain if you start looking around."

Horsley introduced bone wax—mostly beeswax—to stop bleeding from the skull and relied on speed and direct pressure to limit the hemorrhaging of tissue. When Cushing learned that general anesthesia increased blood flow to the head, he dropped it. For two decades he and other brain surgeons used local anesthesia, cutting away at the patient's brain while the patient received visitors, drank coffee, even chatted with the surgeon. (General Wood was awake during his ill-fated second operation. In fact, Cushing had wanted to halt the day-long procedure and resume later; it was the bold, talkative army general who implored Cushing to get it over with.) But it was really the discovery of chemical and electrical methods of blood control that permitted neurosurgery to advance. Cushing had packed the head with muscle cut from the patient's leg. Thromboplastin, which promotes blood clotting, was released from the muscle. In 1926, Cushing recruited physicist W. T. Bovie, and they ushered electrosurgery into neurosurgery. High-frequency electricity, capable of generating hundreds of degrees in heat, had been used in other ORs, but it was assumed that an electrical prod in the brain would cause convulsions. Bovie, however, discovered that currents of high-frequency alternation don't stimulate the nerves. The Bovie, as the electric knife came to be called, had two high-frequency circuits, one to cut tissue, the other to coagulate bleeding. Anesthesiologists later tried to reduce blood pressure—and thus bleeding—by a straightforward procedure called an arteriotomy, which simply meant extracting blood for reinfusion later.

When, after World War II, drugs were introduced that could constrict arteries, the era of chemically induced hypotension began; and brain surgeons gladly took up general anesthesia again. At least ten different agents shrink the blood vessels by affecting muscles in the arterial wall. The anesthesiologist, with his new potions, could drop blood pressure to 40 mm Hg, one-third normal, though that was not usually safe.

Hypotension was one aid to controlling violent aneurysmal hemorrhages. Another was microsurgery.

Under a microscope a surgeon could visualize the source of bleeding. If he could see it, he could control it. Microsurgerons brought to brain surgery a new level of command and with it an unprecedented boldness. They were hotshots. In 1981, Flamm went so far as to publish a paper suggesting that a good way to clip a giant aneurysm—which was 2 centimeters or bigger in diameter—was to punch a hole in it intentionally. To induce a bleed! If ever there was a statement to make an older neurosurgeon go for his pacemaker! In reality, puncturing the aneurysm made the balloon slack, easier to manipulate, and simpler to clip. Though of course the surgeon had to go ahead and clip it right then, no hesitations, before the patient bled to death through the sucker.

51 With two clips already across the neck, Flamm announces he will puncture the sac. As soon as he jabs a hole in the bloody ball, it seems proof positive that the conservative neurosurgeons were right about leaving well enough alone. Two inches below the surface of the skull, a pool of red blood accumulates. The neck of the aneurysm is clipped. *Two* clips have it strangled in their steely tines. Yet blood pushes from somewhere, drowning the structures. When Flamm inserts the suction to drain the blood, the trouble really begins.

There is no suction. None at all. The TV screen, all twenty-one inches, turns a sanguinary red.

Throughout the operation people have casually walked in and out the swinging door—marked with the "No Entry" sign—which is about ten feet from the surgeon's stool. They are changing shifts or checking things or just poking a head in to see if anything interesting is going on. Suddenly Flamm brings the room to attention.

"*Where's the suction*?" he demands, shouting across the tented body. "Get the sucker on! Of all times for this to happen!" Flamm stomps his wooden heel on the floor; his butt pounds the seat of the hard plastic stool.

The outcome of brain surgery depends not only on making the right moves but on avoiding the wrong ones, which isn't always easy. The mechanism of Yasargil's microscrope once broke in mid-operation. Somehow he got a police cruiser to race across Zurich to fetch a technician. At a New York University Hospital OR, a hand-held laser, normally used to burn away tumor, once ignited the drapes covering a patient. The woman survived but suffered second-degree burns on her head, neck, and shoulders. "Mishaps sometimes occur in the operating room just because there's equipment failure, human error," one of the anesthesiologists explained. "There's probably no other field where you rely so much on the ability to avoid human error." Flamm is in the midst of a grave error. And the timing is bad; it couldn't be worse. As the patient hemorrhages, Flamm is obliged to stand by, watching. During at least one other operation suction had also cut out. Then a despondent Flamm had uttered something the residents had always remembered: "At least give me a straw."

From the foot of the patient a nurse calls, "We're checking," an item of nonnews that seems as infuriating as the error itself. "Goddamnit," mutters Flamm.

I know that it is no longer possible for one person to keep abreast of every development in medicine. Isn't that the underlying message of medical reporting: the hectic pace of progress? Lasers are being used for cutting and ultrasound for intraoperative imaging; embolization and therapeutic radiation are among the more recent alternatives to surgery. Yet now, it seems to me, development grinds to a halt, medical advance itself stalls, for want of a five-dollar length of plastic tubing.

The rubber accordion opens and closes to mark breathing. White pollywogs float across a green oscilloscopic screen, measuring heart activity.

Here is excitement, I think, and then, like someone who has overcome his fears and inched to the cliff's edge, the look down frightens me. My own heart races. My cues aren't medical. I react to tones of voice, gestures. And Flamm's gestures are like a mugger's, irrepressible,

almost violent. Is Flamm performing? Everyone else looks around skit-
tishly, barely making eye contact, which seems to say, We are in it now.
I want to be meek and unheard. My twin urges, those of the journalist
and of ex-patient, are not in harmony. As a reporter on the beat, I want
things to be as dangerous, as scary, as threatening, as can be. In the
service of the narrative, I even hope things will go wrong. As Chalif said,
"I was thinking, if I stuck my hands into somebody's brain, that would
be good for your story, wouldn't it?" It would. And yet the real mishaps
frighten me. I catch myself hoping for a climactic turn and realize that
secretly I am afraid that the next detail or the sheer weight of detail will
bring down the thing my research is really supposed to substantiate: that
I am just fine. My research is carried out in a slurry of fascination and
fear. I marvel at my previous self. Not only had I been overtaken by the
disease. How ignorant I am of the cure. My experience, like that of all
patients, is that of the innocent.

Then, as mysteriously as it vanished, suction returns. Flamm is under
the gun, but at least he can get to work. He empties the pool of blood and
begins a search for its origin.

Brain surgery demands a team effort. When the bleed began, the patient's blood pressure dropped ten points to 80 mm Hg. The anesthesiologist, an unplanned arteriotomy on his hands, no longer worried about
hypotension. Just the opposite. The patient's blood pressure was in free-
fall. If it gets lifethreatening, he has several options. He could, for instance,
administer chemicals to constrict the vessels going to the voluntary muscles
in the arms and legs while dilating those going to the kidney, the heart,
and the brain in an attempt to preserve vital organs. For the time being,
the anesthesiologist transfuses blood.

I know that the anesthesiologist can buy the surgeon some time. But
in the hush that falls over the room—yes, Flamm finally has the quiet he
liked!—all eyes watch the video screen. Neurosurgery seems a test of one
person's abilities.

"When bleeding starts, that's when you meet your maker," Chalif
once explained with some emotion. Residents tell each other stories about
these moments of courage—that's what they are called—until they become
a kind of folklore. Perhaps Ransohoff isn't an intellectual. But, explains
one of his residents, "he has a very agile mind; he can very rapidly assimilate all of the basic information needed to make a surgical decision." With
a vessel gushing blood, one resident related, Ransohoff once reached a
gloved hand into the brain and pulled out a tumor the size of an orange,
a move that exposed the source of bleeding. "Flamm showed me that if

you panic you're dead and so is the patient," said resident Larry McCleary. McCleary remembered when a sixty-five-year-old woman with an aneurysm was on the table. The operation was going smoothly until the aneurysm ruptured. McCleary, who was acting as chief surgeon, could not locate the origin of bleeding. In one and a half minutes the patient's blood pressure dropped from 100 to near 30. The anesthesiologist started shouting, She's going to arrest. McCleary recalled: "Flamm said, 'Well, you want me to give it a try?' He took one sucker and put it on the aneurysm, letting it bleed through the sucker. With the other sucker he finished the dissection. He put a clip across the aneurysm in about thirty seconds. At the end of that, he looked at me and I looked at him, and he said, 'Well, that speeded up the operation.' That was the only time I think if I had been there without Flamm the patient would have died."

"Clip remover!" Flamm whomps his heel to the ground. "Put it in my hand, damnit." The nurse does seem slow or distracted. Can she even see the TV? Is she aware of what is going on?

"What do you think?" Flamm says to no one in particular.

No one responds.

Flamm takes hold of one of the clips crossing the aneurysm and reorients it. With the clip applier, he wedges on a third clip. Still the blood comes.

"What is the matter here?" he says, hopelessness in his voice. He places one clip, then another, over the sac of the aneurysm, which, punctured, flaps like extra skin off the vessel. The blood won't stop. It jumps from the head, like ocean spray, I think, and hits the sterile plastic sheet that covers the microscope. "I'm doing something wrong," shouts Flamm, providing his own grim play-by-play. "Usually you look around, you look around, and you see what the problem is, but I'm absolutely stymied here."

In a sense, it is this very situation that Flamm has prepared for his entire professional life. He had enjoyed at various stages in his career the research, the lab work, the paper writing, all aspects of academic neurosurgery. He never considered working in a private office, which would have cut him off from conferences, teaching, and the pool of basic scientists that populate a place like NYU. In a bad mood, Flamm said that a large medical center shouldn't waste its resources training private neurosurgeons, who, the stereotype goes, see their skills as a path to personal gain. Flamm wasn't against the profit motive. Yet a surgeon had to get ego gratification in ways besides money—or in addition to money. A brain surgeon also had to operate for the challenge, the pure athletic thrill of it.

This, then, became his proving ground, the bloody arena of the brain when a vessel blew and a patient started to die. Every vascular brain surgeon, at some point, told himself that he lived for that moment. ''If that's an overwhelming situation for you, then you should not be in neurosurgery,'' Flamm explained.

According to one survey of medical specialists, a neurosurgeon spends an average of two hours a day in the OR, more than any other surgeon. Added up over the course of a year, that amounts to nearly a springtime of eight-hour days in the OR.

I once asked Flamm, ''How do you live with that kind of pressure?''

''I don't know. How do you live without it,'' he said. ''I've always done it. I don't know what to compare it to.''

''The risk is an exciting element?''

''That's right. I think that enters into being a neurosurgeon.''

When Flamm called those visiting firemen-neurosurgeons ''bastards'' for delighting in his frantic efforts to clip that aneurysm, he was grinning. For, of course, that was what Flamm, without ever wishing it, most wanted to be able to show them: command under fire.

52 Flamm watches the blood come. He has inspected the clips, has readjusted them, has added another. He has closed off blood flow to the aneurysmal sac every way he knows, to no avail. Now is when mental rehearsal counts. ''Temporary clip,'' he says to the scrub nurse. The anesthesiologist notes the time. Flamm is shutting down the middle cerebral artery, turning off the major source of blood to a portion of the brain. This maneuver allows him to work on a depressurized aneurysm; it also puts him up against severe time limits. The cerebral environment is forebodingly fragile. The brain has high demands, consuming 20 percent of the body's oxygen and glucose; yet, unlike other tissue, it has no reserves. Deprived of oxygen or glucose for more than a few seconds, brain tissue may temporarily cease to function; after a few minutes it will die. Injury to tissue alimented by the middle cerebral artery would affect sensory and motor control on one side of the body, more in the arm than in the leg. Some circulation may filter in from other vessels, but not much. Flamm is allotting himself five, maybe ten minutes before the lack of blood triggers a stroke. Every patient's tolerance is somewhat different.

He calls for another clip. There are more than forty kinds of clips, right angled, straight, fenestrated (which has a loop through which a normal vessel can pass). The basic one, a sample of which Flamm carries on his key chain, is two 10-millimeter prongs of straight stainless steel with a coiled end that provides the spring action. Flamm slides different kinds of clips on the aneurysm, settles them, arranges them, decides he doesn't like them, and calls for another. When the one Flamm desires isn't ready, he gripes, he curses. "You've been playing catch with me all day," he yells. "Now damnit get it into my hand."

The heart and respiration are normal. The patient, so far, is okay. Not Flamm.

"This is a fucking travesty," Flamm says.

"Three minutes," says the anesthesiologist.

Flamm's anger is omnidirectional. Residents who have only known him in the hospital can't fathom that he is a gentle family man with an adoring wife and two sons he calls "darling." A resident wants an operation to go well. He also wants action, big action, to be there when the craft is flat out. What every resident wondered was whether, when it was his turn, he would be able to meet his maker, and return. To be at the surgeon's side when all hell breaks loose is like practice for that time, though it is also, without doubt, the most trying moment to be an assistant. The decibel level soars. Manners go by the board. Emotions are raw.

"There are days when I am afraid to go into the OR," admitted one resident. Perhaps it is another aspect of the training, a kind of pyschological boot camp whose purpose, it seems to me, is not to help the resident along but to disqualify him, make him buckle.

"It was once explained to me that if you're a soldier on the front line, you have to expect to get shot at," said one resident. Some residents don't thrive under combat conditions.

"One thing I hope to quickly forget is that the way to get something done is to scream the loudest," said Larry Lehman, the first assistant. Lehman hates the yelling. It doesn't help him perform; just the opposite. He remembers that one time he moved too slowly and Flamm punched him in the arm. After, it was a joke between them. If Flamm made a sudden movement, Lehman flinched.

A resident believes, and it may well be true, that at moments of crisis he can't do anything right. McCleary remembers, "Flamm would say: 'Look, you haven't said anything all case long. Your job here is to help me.' So I'd make a suggestion and Flamm would say, 'Shut the fuck up; when I want to hear that, I'll ask you.' "

Sometimes after leaving another surgeon's OR, Chalif would say, "Did you see all the brain he beat up? I'd work methodically, like Flamm." But after one particularly tough day in Flamm's OR, Chalif said, "Neurosurgery should be like art, thoughtful, relaxed, not like this, this is Vietnam." How, I wonder, would Flamm have gotten along during the two decades when brain surgery was performed with the patient awake?

To some extent, Flamm uses his anger. He pumps himself up, brings into play his resolve. There is a theory about the "gentleman surgeon" who not only remains cool and collected in a crisis but also polite. Flamm thinks the idea ridiculous. "I don't think that if I said, 'Hey, guys, if we get this going, you know, please, we could save this guy's life,' it would have much of an effect." Shouting is his way of taking control in an emergency, of gathering and focusing attention on the problem at hand.

It is also true, though, that Flamm isn't in full control of his anger. Tales of Flamm's angry deeds are legion and a source of some amusement around the hospital, though it is whispered that added up, they amount to a tragic flaw: He is the person who gives himself entirely to his work and in return is consumed by it. The drama can seem to overtake him. At a moment like this his responsibility balloons up and is enormous, like the aneurysm itself. The bleeding continues, the clock runs, and suddenly it does not seem a matter of manipulating some tissue a little to the right, a little to the left. Flamm is in the grips of a primordial struggle. Fighting what? Imperfection itself. Worst of all, the whole world is, through wantonness or lack of will, lined up against him.

The oddest part is that much of the emotion is self-directed, which produces the strange spectacle of a man furiously screaming and also standing up to the abuse. It is like the bizarre neurological deficit produced when the corpus callosum has been severed to combat some cases of epilepsy. When this happens, the two hemispheres of the brain can't communicate, and a patient has been known to try to strangle his wife with one hand and, Strangelove-like, attempt to rescue her with the other. Such is the pattern of Flamm's behavior at this moment.

"What the hell am I missing here?" he rants. Flamm exhorts himself, eggs himself on. "Control that bleeding." The room is absolutely silent but for his cries, his stomping, the dialogue of his inabilities. He is either gripped by despair or having an adolescent fit. "What the hell am I missing?" he shouts. "Is there another branch someplace?"

Flamm might have preferred to go at things differently. "If I could find some way that I didn't have to go through what I go through, it would be okay, too," he said once. The sense of emergency that hounded him in the OR could extend to other aspects of his life. This wise, cultured man, who collected fine wines and medieval medical instruments, once raced after a bus that had cut in front of his car. With one hand he steered, and with the other he pounded on the bus's metal exterior until it let him pass. His wife recounts his outbursts, and they sound cute. It is true, as she points out, that furious one minute, he is calm and collected the next. He doesn't hold grudges. "It's a quick switch in my hypothalamus" is how he thinks of it. "You couldn't go on like that all the time." After the fact, he, too, laughs. He even tells stories on himself. "At home, if the toaster doesn't work, I treat it like fucking brain surgery," he says. He goes crazy in the kitchen. His wife has to remind him, Take it easy, it's only the toaster or the car or whatever, not life or death.

In the OR, of course, it really is life or death, and there is no being talked down, no end until the drama itself concludes.

I sit at the bottom of the video screen, hastily taking notes. I am exhilarated by the spectacle, the drum roll, that brain surgery represents. This is the the call to arms I sought, suspected, hoped for; live and in color. Then, in the next moment, I feel awful. I catch myself thinking what the bastard firemen must have thought: Isn't this exciting! Let's see what he can do! I stop writing, as it seems like very bad manners. Flamm's anger is the most terrifying thing to watch. His face contorts, and he yells ugly things at people he likes. It scares me, it alarms me, for its message is suddenly unmistakable: The patient on the table is about to go out. So strongly do I sense this that my breath is taken away. My mind leaps to a larger awareness. No matter how cautiously a person proceeds, how closely he keeps account, how innocent the headache with which he awakes, another's mistake or misfortune might plunge this innocent into disaster. A person has hold of only one end of the rope! Flamm's agony is mine, too, is everyone's. I am witnessing the real core of brain surgery and the real essence of the brain surgeon, and it is a piling on of mishaps, and it is errors and a man, and maybe two, coming apart. Seeing how completely Flamm is given over to the crisis, I cannot imagine that things were ever different. Flamm's natural state, like the real state of brain surgery, I am sure, is chaos, his moments of control always in danger of slipping. I cover my masked mouth with my hand, as if I, too, have some responsibility for just having enjoyed the spectacle, for having viewed this as spectacle. All I can think is Don't let anything happen to this poor sleeping patient.

Inside the head, Flamm clears away the blood with one hand; with the other, he clips, positioning, repositioning, easing one clip after another around the deformity. How can he turn from his frustration to the careful work at hand? Under the microscope, he is methodical. Anesthesia has already fed the patient two units of blood. Flamm puts in five clips. Lined up on the stalk of skin, they look like staples. One he brings in from the opposite direction so that the blades of the clips cross. "Releasing temporary clip," he calls. All eyes focus on the video screen. Are there firemen still hoping for more?

The bleeding has stopped. He looks at the anesthesiologist, who is staring at his watch. Elapsed time: five minutes. Flamm hadn't missed a branch; the force of the blood flowing through the aneurysm was so great that not one or two clips could entirely close it. In another day or two that aneurysm surely would have blown. That man would have suffered another hemorrhage and probably died.

The excitement passes, and the room, which had fallen into a gloomy pall, reanimates. Flamm asks anesthesia to bring the pressure up to 130, the patient's normal pressure, to make sure the clips hold.

Flamm, his gown splattered with blood, turns to the scrub nurse in a new, understanding tone. Cushing's OR nurse had once fled an operation in tears, and Cushing had run after her to apologize. Flamm, like the master, tries to make amends for hurt feelings. "I guess we went through a lot of clips. I know it gets confusing," says Flamm. The operative report will take that same understated tone:

> The aneurysm was punctured and bleeding . . . ensued. It was not apparent where the bleeding was coming from since a clip was well across the base of the aneurysm. Several other clip applications were made to try to control the bleeding. A temporary clip was placed proximal to the middle cerebral artery. It was put on for five minutes while the clips were adjusted. Finally, a 10 mm Sugita clip was placed in the opposite direction to the original clip and just distal to it. This obliterated the aneurysm and stopped the bleeding, even after the temporary clip was removed.

A nurse, speaking for everyone, whispered: "If a person acted like a neursurgeon anywhere else but in the operating room, he wouldn't get away with it." The report would make no mention of the faulty suction, the histrionics.

It is five hours since the operation began. The food cart has gone. My knees are weak. Flamm had seemed like another person in there. Then, the operation over, whatever was beyond his control returned; he is calm, reflective. "You were a lot easier," he says to me. I laugh with him, but my hand inadvertently reaches for my own head, my fingers touching the ridge where two bones join. Flamm invites me to follow him.

In the locker room, Flamm lights a pipe. Blood has seeped through his gown onto his shirt. He sits on the wooden bench, shoulders sloped, back curled. He seems preoccupied. "I guess I should learn to control my temper a little better," he volunteers. This is not an apology but, I think, a way of setting the record straight, as if it were all a question of someone's having been in a bad mood, not of mortal danger. It is, I believe, a pass at mollifying my fears, and in that a warm gesture. It goes no further. I, too, am drained. Flamm seems remote, lost in other thoughts. He takes off his bloodied operating scrubs and slips on his white jacket. "I'm a little antsy until I see the patient in the recovery room," he says.

Surgery is, after all, a contract between physician and patient, which goes beyond the agreement to pay the exorbitant fees—$5,000 for an operation like this one. "If you don't have to answer to the family, then surgery is a technical exercise," says Flamm. That isn't the case. No matter how hopeless the patient's case, the surgeon who takes up the knife represents hope to the family. He offers to make a stand against disease. Flamm works in a world in which his technique can be excellent, overcoming all the hurdles, the operation technically a success, and the patient still does not come through. Flamm says he has had to learn to live with that. It is a difficult state of affairs to explain to a relative, however. "If the patient is all right, then it'll be a high," says Flamm. "If his left side is paralyzed, it'll be dammed depressing."

53

The day I learned what happened in the OR while I slept, the season's first snow was falling. It was November and, as Flamm set up the videotape player, flakes the size of half dollars were tumbling by the window. I had often mentioned to him that I someday wanted to see the video of my operation. "Whenever," he'd invariably responded; he was keeping the tape in a safe place. I know that Chalif, who'd become my friend, didn't think viewing my own operation was a very good idea. I think this was a therapeutic instinct. I suppose Chalif thought that seeing the extent of the injury in my own head might make me worry about the nature of my illness. I had no such worries, I assured him. I was just plugging a gap in the narrative. My concern was like that of the residents. I was disinterested in the personal; my fascination was in the technical. As I took a stool next to Flamm, in a narrow lab with an explosion-proof light switch, I remember thinking: How unprepared I am for this, but I meant the snow.

The two-page written report of my operation—Kricheff had sent me a copy—indicated that as soon as my dura was opened, the discoloration caused by the hemorrhage could be seen. The AVM was like a drain, sucking in enormous quantities of blood; vessels swelled to accommodate the new flow. Where vessels should be thin, they were fat. A hole was cut in the brain and about one centimeter below the surface the surgeon came upon a cavity, dug out of brain matter by the force of the hemorrhage. In AVM surgery, it turned out, a hemorrhage could actually help the surgeon, in effect, dissecting the lesion free from surrounding brain. "Old blood and liquid were easily removed, thus giving additional room to remove the malformation," said the operative report. The AVM itself was on one wall of the cavity.

Operative reports are written in a quirky, self-effacing language. Never does a person do an action to a thing. Actions simply happen to things. For instance, "a right occipital flap was created," "the dura was opened," "a small cortical incision was made." It is as if the things call forth the actions all by themselves, which made for strange reading. Not only was all the excitement suppressed; so was any sense of human skill. The operative report made surgery read like a cookbook.

Watching the video images added another dimension to my experience.

Unfortunately, the video for my operation, unlike almost all OR videos, did not have a soundtrack; it either was never recorded or had been erased. Flamm had graciously offered to narrate the tape for me. Perhaps this situation—a former patient watching his brain surgery with his brain surgeon—should have been loaded with drama. I intended to avoid the drama. There were to be no confessions, no accusations. My tone was to be inquisitive, detail oriented. I would ask what was the name of this vessel and what was the name of that tissue. That was my plan.

Yet almost as the video started, my mouth dropped rudely open. I reacted the way I would to a horror film: I pointed and gawked. The brain, *my* brain, was a luscious white, I thought, like cottage cheese, and the clot cavity, when the bipolar coagulator punctured it, poured out stagnant blood the dark hue of old crankcase oil. There is so much blood! I thought. And this is three weeks after the hemorrhage; perhaps half the volume had already been reabsorbed. The deep, wide hollow carved out by the hemorrhage seemed to me enormous. You could stick a newborn's fist in the hole in my brain!

"Boy," I said, my voice searching for tranquility, "The hemorrhage really does take out a part of brain."

"Oh, yeah, a big hole in the brain," said Flamm casually, as if commenting on the evening news.

"Kind of amazing that more damage wasn't done."

"You'd be in a pine box in Nicaragua."

To prepare for viewing the videotape, I'd gotten hold of a book on intracranial AVMs co-edited by Bennett M. Stein, chairman of neurosurgery at Columbia-Presbyterian Medical Center. In one chapter Stein described how to attack an AVM, and how not to, especially when trouble strikes.

> The AVM must not be allowed the upper hand. . . . A desperate situation must be avoided by expecting the unexpected. . . . Despite all precautions, catastrophic situations may arise during the removal of AVM's—as when turgor [swelling in blood vessels] abruptly increases within the AVM, resulting in hemorrhage from numerous sites; or when the same situation occurs in brain surrounding the AVM. Under these circumstances, the surgeon is at a point of no return. Immediate decisions will determine the outcome, and the most appropriate action must be recognized and applied quickly to avert a disaster. The situation is similar to one in which an internal carotid aneurysm tears at its neck, causing cataclysmic bleeding. . . . One must be prepared to continue operating under less than ideal circumstances despite a feeling that the operation may be out of control.

From my operative report I knew that the surgeon's maneuvering apparently led to bleeding—"some bleeding had been occurring . . ." Watching the tape it looked to me like considerably more than "some" bleeding. Perhaps there was no gush of blood as in an aneurysmal hemorrhage, but there was a slow and steady filling, an advancing red tide. Flamm, perhaps noticing my stare, said, "That's not a lot of blood in there. It looks it, but this is magnified about ten or twelve times."

I was sure that was true, and yet I had a cinematic moment. I did a double take and had to say to myself, Hey, I know how this ends. To Flamm, I said, "So you weren't worried?" But Flamm had already gone on to another thought.

On the screen, a gloved hand silently wielded a cautery cooking small vessels, which turned gray. Then the main vessel feeding the AVM was clipped. The bleeding, which had so engaged my imagination, stopped. The vessel was cut.

The wiggly strands of the malformation were interwoven with brain tissue. Because I was born with an AVM, it is presumed the malformation had grown with my brain. Flamm described the lesion as "a tuft of brain with vessels in it." Together they constituted a ball about 2 centimeters in diameter. "That big around," said Flamm, connecting thumb and forefinger into a circle the size of a quarter. Flamm worked around the AVM-encrusted lump, separating it from the rest of the brain, which I unfortunately personalized as my brain. "Although current operative techniques afford considerable precision, there are limits to the extent that the surgeon can preserve the normal brain tissue at the margin of the malformation," wrote Stein. Flamm used the suction and the bipolar coagulator until he'd isolated the chunk of my brain that contained my AVM. It was the shape of a peach pit. And then, on the screen, a forceps lifted out the skein of malformed vessels and the brain matter that hugged to it.

"I leave a little bit of the brain attached [to the tangle of vessels], because every time you try to separate just the vessels, you're going to damage the brain, anyhow, and you're more likely to get the vessels bleeding."

"We assume that was useless brain?" I said; what "we" I was using, I couldn't have said.

"Yeah, well, no brain is useless. It's not there because it's doing nothing. But it is expendable."

"Expendable?"

"Yeah, it's already been damaged by the hemorrhage. I'm sure it's not particularly functional. And that's a pretty thin layer, anyhow. We would take out as much, if not more, if we were doing a tumor."

"Oh, really?"

Flamm nodded, but I didn't know. To me it looked like a giant hand had scooped a melon ball out of my brain. We might chitchat about the wormy malformation, but suddenly I thought ominously: How large was the ball of brain that came out with the AVM!

The tape ended, and Flamm punched a button, ejecting the videocassette. My operation lasted four hours and five minutes, the tape about ten minutes. "Here's a souvenir," he said, flipping me the cassette. I thanked him, but my first thought was that this was last thing on earth I wanted on my bookshelf. It was also true, however, that I was fascinated with my operation. As my few minutes viewing this video had made plain, my concern was personal, the nature of my attention passionate. And an important element of the story still remained untold. The tape, after all, showed a landscape of wounded brain, a few surgical instruments, and the anonymous fingers of two rubber-gloved hands. But surgery was a human procedure, what one person did to another.

"This was actually a good teaching film," Flamm had said. Indeed, without the sound, the video had the feel of a textbook, a procedure demonstrated. What I still wanted to know was how steady and dependable was the human will that had stood in harm's way. I had seen Flamm in action when equipment broke. Faced with terror, he was a terrorist himself. What had the human performance been like during my surgery? To learn the answer, I asked two witnesses, both third-year medical students.

By the time I caught up with them, they were doctors, but both remembered the operation vividly. What the medical students remembered most was being terrified. In fact, Flamm had shouted from the moment he walked through the door. Perhaps Kricheff's personal stake had put Flamm under added pressure. The residents' preparations hadn't pleased him. A junior resident was in charge. The table was at a slightly wrong angle. Joe Weisstuch, who'd taken up internal medicine, remembered: "Flamm went crazy; he threw a tantrum. He screamed, 'What have you been doing here for two years?' " The chief resident was busy on another case and wouldn't arrive for half an hour. Flamm wasn't one to relax standards in the OR; nor, I knew, did he take well to perceived slights. When the chief resident entered late, the medical students recalled, he was greeted with a barrage: "You come in in the middle and you want me to show you what I'm doing because you're chief shit. You think your lousy fucking hydrocephalus is more important."

Though he terrified the medical students, Flamm was very nice to them, calling them to the microscope, explaining exactly what he was doing, urging them to ask questions. "What was fascinating was that in a millisecond Flamm went from the greatest guy in the world to the biggest monster," said Saul Stromer, who went into gynecology.

When closing the dura, a small bleeder apparently appeared, and Flamm exploded again. Stromer remembered: "You know when the mother of a six-year-old tells him he cannot have something and tells him repeatedly and he stamps with his foot and says, 'I want it.' That was what Flamm was doing."

I had a keener sense of what had gone on during my operation. I had the OR report, which read like a recipe; the tape, which looked like a how-to guide; and now I had firsthand reports, which suggested the scene of a natural disaster. What was I to make of all this? Was there a message to be gleaned about my surgery, about neurosurgery in general?

At first I was tempted to conclude, as I knew others had, Oh, Flamm, he's nuts in the OR, and disregard his behavior as an aberration. In the end, I didn't. Just the opposite. What I concluded was that Flamm's behavior was not a personality flaw, or not *only* a personality flaw; it was also an apt symbol of what brain surgery was all about. His craziness was his way of adapting to the enormous responsibilities of the job, maladapting, perhaps, but at least his behavior suggested that here was a person cognizant of the essential tragedy of brain surgery.

Often enough it might be true that brain surgeons, supple, skilled, and also lucky, make surgery seem routine. Without event, they reach the tumor or the aneurysm or the AVM, then snare or clip it. (The man whose operation I observed will turn out to be fine.) Perhaps I would have preferred to witness more mundane operations; perhaps I would have liked to consider my surgeon a cool, collected master, someone who could reassure me that brain surgery was a safe, sure vehicle, as reliable as science itself—a piece of cake, as my father had been led to believe. To have maintained this illusion I probably would have had to stay out of the OR altogether. When equipment went down, when bleeding occurred, or (maybe) just when the skull was opened, hold on to your seats, for then neurosurgery was like a bus with faulty brakes careening down a mountain road.

A surgeon, I'd learned, wasn't a scientist or even primarily a technician, though he arduously studied technique. He was the person a patient hired to stand up for him when, sleeping on the OR table, he started to die. A surgeon was an advocate. And in a field whose resources, finally, were as paltry as those of neurosurgery, the burdens of advocacy were gigantic. My own operation had been fitful and loud. Had I been awake, I would have been scared shitless. But perhaps this was an apt representation of the craft. The sad truth is that brain surgery, despite its favorable press, is not the future; it is the past, a turn-of-the-century technology that is still largely ineffective. Figures for short-stay, nonfederal hospitals indicate that probably less than a total of 35,000 brain AVMs, aneurysms, and tumors are operated on each year. (There are more operations on the eye than on the brain!) Most neurological problems still can't be attacked surgically at all, even microsurgically. A century after the first malignant tumor was removed, this lesion is still almost always a death sentence. For stroke, the biggest neurological killer—and the third leading killer of any disease—there is no worthwhile surgical intervention. Even the maladies that fall within brain surgery's purview often mock its powers. As Ransohoff once said, "Surgery is a failure of medical therapy." In one study of 1,000 brain-surgery patients, 49 percent didn't survive more than five years, even when the surgery was deemed successful. (Certainly other diseases or old age were a factor; still, the point is that brain surgery isn't the miracle cure it is sometimes cracked up to be.) And for those who survive, a substantial percentage may later develop epilepsy, trading a deadly disease for a lifelong one. After Chalif watched the tape of my operation, he praised the technique as a tour de force. Then he said to me, "Epilepsy should be the worst that happens to you." And given what I had come to understand about neurosurgery, I nodded in distracted agreement.

Part VIII

SEIZURE

He felt like someone who survives a harrowing ordeal and only afterwards begins to weaken and appreciate how precarious it all had been.
Philip Roth, *The Counterlife*

54

"Squeeze." The word is a piercing sound, like glass shattering.

"Whaaaaaaat?" My own voice is like an engine that won't start up.

"Squeeze my fingers." The imperative is there in the tone. *Do*, it says, but I can't imagine what.

"Whaaaat?" I rev.

The last I remember was trying to void into a bucket under a gown. Now a person is bent over me like an eclipse. Two fingers push into my flaccid palm. My hand is achy, bone tired, desires nothing but inaction. Can it squeeze? I try.

"Good" comes the reply, like a screech.

This is momentous news. Yet I am incapable of response. Consciousness is something that pushes past me, something I can't hold on to. Perhaps this consciousness knows: The thing is over. But the inertial mass on the bed senses nothing. It doesn't hurt, it isn't happy, until, yes, it is cold. Cold as an ice cube. That is how the precious union of mind and body returns. *I am freezing.* My teeth bump together like popping corn. "Why am I so cold?" I manage. My voice sounds like a dresser being shouldered across the floor.

The voice ignores my question. "The other hand," it insists, "the other hand." Again two fingers force their way into my reflexless palm. Like someone afraid of slipping into the tide, I grab.

"You're in the recovery room." It is Flamm's voice.

I have an instinctive response: "Ronald Reagan."

ELEVEN EAST HAS ITS OWN ICU so that neurosurgical patients can be supervised by staff with experience in neurological problems. In its beds are some of the sickest patients in the hospital. For a nurse this is a place of *real* nursing. Mindy Rothenstreich liked ICU duty. "It excites me to take care of patients right out of surgery, with forty million lines, lots of drips, all these different tubes. There is so much for me to do," she said once. Every neurosurgery patient passes through the unit. For most, it is a halfway house between the OR and the rest of the floor. For some, it is the last stop. For almost all, the ICU marks a period of limited consciousness. Nurses have to be vigilant, but when not occupied with a patient, this room of seven beds is a place of freedom. It's not as if the nurses are going to keep their drugged charges awake. The lights are usually on, and a radio, too, and in the middle of the night the staff can let off a little steam.

One slow evening a resident, dressed in bandages, climbed into a bed and had himself wheeled into the ICU. "Another patient?" groaned the nurses.

"Surprise!" shouted the resident, and popped from the bed.

Neither a patient nor his family enjoys the same perspective. "It's so scary to patients," says Rothenstreich, "I haven't seen anybody come in ready to undergo it. Everyone wonders whether you're going to come out alive. And when you wake up in the ICU, you're petrified. You can't really believe you lived through it. You don't know if you're here or in heaven." Families, too, have a dramatic reaction. "When families go into the ICU, that's when they really freak," said Rothenstreich.

At 8:00 P.M., eight hours after being wheeled off the floor, I am rolled into the ICU. By this time, the complexions of visitors who have been patrolling the halls are an exsanguinated white, their eyes lucent like liquid crystals—the ghostly uniform of the overtired relative. They are allowed a brief viewing. Julie tries to mentally block out all the other patients. But no one knows which is the right bed. They have to scan the room, which is like surveying the wreckage. Every patient looks alike, the victim of a ferocious beating. Julie wonders, which drain and which bandage is theirs? David hangs back. He isn't sure of his brother, or of himself. He feels so tenuous. He doesn't last long before rushing to the bathroom, where he pukes. And the nurses are knocking around. A container drops, and the heavy thump amid these delicate bodies is horrifying. The nurses call to one another, rowdily, like workmen moving a load. The clatter pisses Julie off. It is as if they are being disrespectful.

Kricheff had given them a pep talk. He had informed them how amazing brain surgery was. It wasn't like abdominal surgery, where great pain persisted. Soon after the operation a patient could walk. The next day, he could eat. Yet, just as a patient could look fine when he was really so ill, in the ICU, when the patient was supposed to be fine, no visitor could be completely sure how well he really was.

Erv sees the green oxygen mask, the head wrapped in a heavy white turban, worse, a tube spilling blood from under the scalp into a drain the shape of a lemon, and thinks, This is outrageously ugly; he's been violated, deformed for life. Then he thinks, How could he have let this happen? and that is a woeful thought.

Ruth had heard Flamm report, "Marvelous, everything went marvelous." The worst possibility, a surgery screwed up, was past. She expected to reassure herself in the ICU; now she couldn't believe the surgeon was telling the truth. She saw a person in a coma. Ruth took a glimpse and after a brave few minutes left, weeping.

Julie was the high functioning one. "Hey, I've been through this before, this is what intensive care is like, he'll be fine," she says, though she, too, hadn't been prepared for how bad appearances were. Julie thinks, It is important not to cry and to be cheerful and to be there and to not let on that he looks like shit. She takes hold of a limp hand; it is as lively as a plant.

Everyone else in the dismal ICU sleeps an impenetrable sleep. Someone says, "Can we wake him?"

MY EYES CRACK. Visitors stand in a half circle in a frozen light. Like a photograph, no one moves. Am I awake or in some lead-heavy dream? What if dreaming is awful and waking is, too? My will is negative will. I want not to do. I want not to be awake. If, for an instant, I let go, I will be gone. I want to let go.

"Hello." Julie holds my hand. My mouth is dry like cotton puffs.

"So thirsty," I say, but the nurse won't allow me to drink. And these adults, my allies, heel to her call. "Why am I so tired?" I manage to say, and am filled with a sense of danger. Must I fight this giant fatigue?

"It's the anesthesia that's making you so tired," says Dr. K. Irresistible chemicals. I would happily drown rather than prop open my eyes a second longer.

"Sorry I'm no fun," I say, feeling bellied up and embarrassed. My eyelids fall like broken shades.

The following morning, Erv telephones Lenore in Europe. "Everything is all right," he finally tells her. "But just get the next plane home." Lenore wants to know why. Erv, having been through so much, doesn't feel he has to, or perhaps doesn't feel he can, offer an explanation. "Just get home," he says, not authoritatively, then hands the phone to Ruth, who explains.

THE NEXT DAY, my first day of wakefulness since the operation, I am moved out of the ICU onto the floor; my bed is rolled into a two-person room. What joy! They say I am cured. I have a real skullcap. An oval leaf of bone rides unsolid on my hairless head. When I sneeze, it bucks, tugging at the silk strings that hold it in place. I am given stool softener. Don't push too hard, I am told. I am on the road out of this place. I can sense that, and as a result, I am buoyant. An end is near to the fake privacy, the drawn curtains, the individual TVs common to hospitals and bus stations.

Now to recover. I feel that this is my part. During the operation I turned my life over to the apparatus of medicine. My body wasn't corporeal. It was a machine among machines. Recovery is a human process. Recovery is mine. I am wounded, but the pain seems benign. No longer a threat, it prods me to feel, to be aware. Pain, I tell myself, is the mechanism by which I will regain control.

What is recovery? I have imagined brain surgery to be a pit stop, a place where a repair, a replacement, can be effected swiftly and efficiently. I have given myself over to the sturdy tools of modern medicine. They have come through. Now I am ready to be reinstalled in the race, right where I left off. I don't envision lasting consequences. My health has been returned. That is what recovery is: restoration. Just don't bop me on the head.

My forearms, black and blue from needles, are itchy with healing. My tubes come out one by one. Soon I will walk without trailing my pole and bag of serum. Oh, I look forward to that day, for it says that nothing is wrong and permits me the illusion that nothing ever was wrong. On this floor, health is a euphemism that applies to those who leave for good, to those who leave under their own power, or depending on your last contact, to those who can remember their own names. Certainly, on 11 East, I am not entirely incorrect in believing that if it can be fixed, then it wasn't so bad in the first place.

During morning rounds, the residents jiggle the plastic drain that dangles out of my head and stare into its blood-filled circumference, as if it is a fishbowl. One day they judge that blood has stopped seeping from under my scalp—where it might cause a troublesome clot—and remove the drain altogether, leaving nothing but the pencil-sized stab mark where its tubing pierced my skin. The kingly turban is unwound. Each day's dressing is a little less bulky, until I have only a tight gauze helmet.

I give them my symptoms: occasional headaches, fatigue, blurry vision. "As expected," I am told. I have a discomforting rash on my neck. "Referred pain," says the chief to his resident, not paying it any mind. "If you have any bedside manner when you come," resident Larry McCleary once told me, "they beat it out of you." He meant that the pressure to perform doesn't permit the kind of caring a resident might like to show. "Residents should be sensitive," he said, "but you just don't have time."

I will be glad to be rid of the residents and their high-handedness, with its suggestion that everything I say is a complaint to be dispensed with. The hospital forces on the patient a weird epistemology. You know how you feel but not what it signifies. Your powers are only descriptive, doctors are the arbiters of meaning. It is the epistemology of small children, explorers in the world who understand nothing of its dangers.

In the notebook I am keeping, I write:

> The residents' locker room nonchalance, their cockiness, their sense of camaraderie, fosters in these young doctors a notion of privilege at the same time that it reduces the patient to a state in which pain is a sign of weakness or a person's problem is interesting or not based strictly on medical criteria, just as to an auto mechanic the workings and failings of a camshaft might arouse concern. I am not being critical, not proposing change; just pointing out the differing perspectives between a patient experiencing the greatest trauma of his life and a doctor who drops in on trauma after trauma all his day long.

For a resident, a patient is, among other things, a place to practice. One resident recounted how when a patient died in the emergency room he didn't want to waste the opportunity and tried a new technique for rapidly getting a catheter into the brain by poking it in over the eye. Resident McCleary explained that doctors and patients do have different points of view. "For the patient and the patient's family the operation is the biggest day of their lives. For the neurosurgeon, if it went well, he would forget about it entirely. I mean, as soon as it was done, he stopped thinking about that. He was thinking about the next one he had to do."

The residents say I am getting better. And I agree. Nothing can set me back, even when, after a couple of days, my eyesight is still blurred. I can't read. The letters on the page look like a topiary garden, an arrangement of shaped shrubs. The residents say to wait. Perhaps Kricheff, who, in his own life, had spent so much time as a patient, understands how unnerving is the waiting game. Dr. K., champion of my cause, doesn't make me play it. He checks. The neurophthalmologist doesn't know why, but sometimes surgery causes visual disturbances that persist for a couple of weeks. Dr. K. assures me that they will go away. I am accustomed to Kricheff's optimism. I choose to believe it. Somewhere in University hospital is a bin of black eye patches. I am issued one. Wearing it will help me cope with the problem, I'm told.

I meet a young man on the floor who wears a tie without a jacket, which is a style of the residents. He stares at me a moment as if trying to remember something. "Oh, I didn't recognize you at first," he says. "I was at your operation; it was really great." How strange! As if he were there and I wasn't. Should I take umbrage that in my most vulnerable moment people shuttled into my OR and peered into my brain, as if it were spectacle? All went well, all is forgiven.

He says he enjoyed it, and I, bizarrely, respond, "Oh, thanks."

I discard the hospital blues and dress in a green T-shirt, which feels like an act of rebellion. Though I am still in gauze with a dull headache, I am ready to partake of the nurses' young sociability. Who will flirt with me? I wonder, and am quickly timid. These women in pastel tops and flouncing skirts, comely and hearty, are here to meet doctors, not patients.

One morning, my sister Lenore appears. She puts her arms around me; her black coat with its fur rim spreads behind her on the bed like a wake in the water. Her tears, her worry, are belated and hers alone. "How was Europe, Lenore?" I ask.

"Oh that," she says.

The social worker returns. The total of my hospital bill will be more than $11,000—not including doctors' fees, which will push the bill closer to $20,000—a sum so beyond my ability to pay I am not even worried by it. She suggests I apply for Medicaid, which has a provision that covers "catastrophic illness," an illness that costs more than one-quarter of a person's yearly income. For the first time, I am thankful that my previous year's income was almost nothing.

By the end of the week I am campaigning for my release. On Friday, two friends and Julie are there when Flamm arrives. He is stern, but with a soft spot, a serious man out of whom a chortle can suddenly pop. The tone of our meetings has changed. He has nothing over me anymore. Having cast an actuarial eye around this place, I know that a doctor is also pleased with each success. I have given him something, too. His worry now is that I don't gum up his admirable work. He peels the bandage off my head. The scar is dry. He wants me to stay the weekend. I can go home Monday, which will be one week after the operation. But why? I plead. He won't even be there over the weekend. Why not let me have the weekend at home? Flamm isn't against the idea. He will check, he says. In a few minutes he returns with the news: tomorrow morning.

"Take it easy. No sports. No alcohol. You can have sex," he says. In front of everybody? I think, but at least I didn't have to ask. I am to take Dilantin prophylactically for a year. It guards against seizures while the brain is healing, though I am told that really shouldn't be a worry in my case, which I assume is true.

Later, I approach one of the residents about other matters. "One surgeon," he says, "tells his patients that marijuana is okay."

On Saturday morning, my brother Dave is to pick me up. I pack my bag, including my six books, none of which I've read. My head is cold and ugly. I have taken from a nurse several of the oatmeal-colored stockinettes, which are like flesh-colored Santa Claus caps, but I have made Dave promise to bring a hat. He pulls from his side pocket a loosely knit beanie. It is a blazing purple like a clouded sunset, with shiny disco threads. A discount special. His sense of humor is back. We will take a cab to Julie's apartment, which is where I am to convalesce. It is a small one-bedroom apartment. Julie has invited me, which is really nice of her, though I wonder if, corraled by my grateful family, she felt she had a choice.

Waiting for the hospital elevator in my hat with the tinselly streaks, I feel sure my health, so rudely taken, has been given back. If there is a time when I am most at ease, it is in the moment of preparation, when I think of what I must do, what I can do, and jam my life with happy expectations. This morning, I am once again filled with the desire to do. Brain surgery will have been a process as simple as having waited in line. It will be like a place I've visited, will become part of my past, a source, like other adventures, of anecdotes. And recovery will be the taking up again of projects and deadlines, a festooning of possibilities.

The truth, as I quickly learn, is different. The mundane aspects of my life are fettered with weird obsessions. When I recount my episode, even to strangers, I feel like a child, bright-eyed with self-pity. Just talking about brain surgery makes me skittish, and in my voice there is a catch. I have been blindsided, I guess, which is taken advantage of. I encounter a patient who also had an occipital AVM excised by Flamm. In one quadrant of her vision she sees scintillating lights. They never go away. "How do you put up with that?" I blurt out.

"I *have* to, don't I?" she says in response.

Experience, which had been the movement of events from something to something better, has revealed itself to be capricious. There but for a few microns go I, a light show always playing in my head, a thought that I find nearly unbearable. Other thoughts disrupt the calm I had so fervently anticipated. One neurosurgeon tells me of a little girl he'd cured who nonetheless remained still and unspeaking. Finally, she divulged the reason. She had overheard a conversation and lay in fear that she would be a vegetable, planted in the ground like a giant turnip. Am I beset by the child's fears? I remind myself that all the risks are behind me. I am not one of the patients whose lives were returned to them, not one of the why mes that jammed 11 East like so many ransacked volumes. I had not sworn like John Corallo to change my life on leaving the hospital. I intended to pick up where I'd left off. I want only to be normal, though that seems suddenly like a state I have to earn. I don't drink alcohol; I abstain from exercise. But when the mirror of cocaine comes my way at a party of friends, I want to partake. The tug of normalcy leads me to it! I drag the long cord of the phone into the bathroom and call 11 East, a number I know by heart.

I wake the resident on call and come right to the point.

"What? Is it laid out in front of you?" he says. He sounds amused. Is it my directness or my urgency?

"Almost," I tell him.

Then his tone shifts. He is serious, doctorly. "In moderation," he says.

I emerge from the bathroom, my hands raised over my head as if the field-goal attempt has been good, and sneak around out of Julie's sight. When she eventually detects me, she is sulky and humorless, as I knew she would be, though I assure her I'd gotten permission from the highest authority. She is right, of course. It was stupid, as that same resident on later reconsideration told me. What if a subangiographic malformation remained?

I try to go to other social events. I am chipper enough but bashful about showing off my nine-inch seam, which hooks like a reverse question mark from ear to crown to nape of neck. One night, overcoming my self-consciousness, I venture to an art opening where there is hardly anybody I know. One guest has a shaved head. She zeroes in on me. We must look like two creatures from Mars. "How often do you shave?" she wants to know. I tell her my "do" isn't a style choice; then spin on my heels to reveal the scar, and, so my brother says, she nearly blows lunch. Being a freak can be fun. But this outer ugliness is also a brake on my dream of reintegration.

There are others.

Even when I am most convinced that having nearly died and then been so dramatically saved is not going to interrupt my life, evidence to the contrary abounds. I have a stock of private fears. I develop subtle, stupid inabilities, which even to myself, a sympathetic listener, seem phony. So I tell no one. Toward the end of the day, for instance, I sometimes have trouble swallowing. The more attention I pay, the more serious it grows.

I endeavor to look at this as a problem, something to be figured out.

How *do* you swallow? I stand for hours in front of the medicine chest, watching the bob of my Adam's apple and concentrating on nothing but swallowing. I am obsessed with spit. A salivaphile. This is not casual or funny. It seems at times a matter of life and death. For sometimes my throat blocks completely; no breath will pass, and real panic seizes me. Calm, I urge myself, and finally, gasping for air, figure out that if my throat locks, I can inhale through my lovely nose. This hard-earned technique provides a modicum of control.

But what is control? This seems to be the challenge my postop manias raise. Rightly or wrongly, I don't feel this is simply a matter of an un-swallowable gob of spit. Brain surgery, or its aftermath, undermines me. Not just my health but all my abilities, which are health's extensions, are called into question. It is as if, I think, not only experience betrays me but *everything* I once took for granted, every principle of action, every confidence about myself, to the least significant act. Soon I will have to *think* about walking, *think* about breathing, *think* about *thinking*, a latter-day Cartesian, doubting everything because everything is doubtful. Control, which was something I had assumed, is suddenly a quality apart from my life. Abruptly, I can only understand control in relation to some loss, or some dread of loss that I can feel but can't name. And so this strange situation develops: Even when all is working, when I have successfuly ignored my swallowing deficit or it has gone away, I sometimes have to call up fear just to be certain that I am keeping it at bay. Then I stroke my wire-brush scalp or touch the pits in my head and wonder, as the knot of anxiety grips me, how I will wrestle control back into my life.

TWO WEEKS AFTER LEAVING the hospital I run into one of the nurses from 11 East. It seems an incredible coincidence in all of Manhattan, but there she is, the white dress that reminds me of cheap paper, the milky-white shoes, and a paper cup of cherry vanilla ice cream in her hand. She recognizes me first. "Isn't it a small world," she says, which, considering where I've been recently, is a ghoulish opening.

Julie and I were on our way to a movie. When the lights are down, I don't feel like such an eyesore. Patricia Henry, R.N., has just come, she says, from church. We are all stopping for an ice cream. Actually, I am glad to see her. Just meeting her on the outside no longer tags me a patient. We speak cordially, as if we have met at boarding school.

"What is the news of the people I knew on 11 East?" I say.

"You remember Mr. Sam?" she says without hesitation.

How could I forget eighty-four-year-old Mr. Sam? Incontinent, almost always incoherent, he'd been in the hospital for eleven weeks while waiting for a nursing-home placement; we'd shared a room for two unwelcome nights.

"He died," she says. Henry lets her ice cream melt a little. The bottom of the cup fills with gooey white liquid. It looks like PhisoHex. The cherries, dark and violet, make me think of bruises. "The bad thing," she says, "was that Mr. Sam's wife wasn't called." She visited every other day, and that wasn't one of the days. When she came the next day, she didn't find him in his room. One of the nurses had to tell her he died.

Henry takes a spoonful of ice cream and picks out one of the violet cherries. Of all the nurses, I had liked Henry particularly. She was nosy, but I took her interest as a form of flattery, which every patient needs after surgery, especially from a pretty nurse.

I ask how Leonard did. When I was there, he'd fallen on his way to the bathroom once but was okay.

"Oh, he fell," says Henry, spearing a cherry on the tip of her spoon.

"Again?" I say.

"Worse," she says deadpan. "He fractured his spine. He'll be in traction now. You can't blame the hospital. You can't keep a person in restraints all the time. It's not good."

I agree.

Henry says she walks two miles to work every day, then climbs the ten flights of stairs on foot, intent on getting exercise. Henry is always upbeat; gifted in that way. This news of our mutual acquaintances stuns me, as if they are really people I know, or worse, as if my past annoyances—for both those roommates had annoyed me—had been translated into deeds. Henry seems to harbor no guilt. Later, she will transfer from 11 East. "Too much," she'll explain, and will take a job on the maternity floor. But for the moment it seems to me that the work on 11 East, and its traumas, pass her by, which makes me envious.

Given the tone of the conversation, I know I shouldn't ask, but I can't help myself.

I am going to be taking Dilantin for the next year. What does she know about the side effects?

"The gums grow," she says. She bares her teeth, which are as white as new baseballs, and touches the pink gums with the tip of the plastic spoon. "I saw one lady, it was so bad, her teeth fell out, and she couldn't even wear dentures."

Am I her straight man? Will every encounter chip away at my sense of well-being? I set them up, and Henry knocks them down. Julie is squeezing my elbow. We have to run to catch the movie. Henry has to get going, too, she says. She wants to get home to watch the soap operas from the day's television. Her sister, she says, is kind enough to videotape them so she can review the melodramas at night.

55

What does a person do after brain surgery? For one thing, I sleep a lot. Twelve to fourteen hours a night, which is well into the morning. Otherwise, I smother my head in my purple hat and ride the New York City subway, a place where a person hardly ever feels he is the strangest one. I commute to my apartment. The redecorating urge that came upon me so suddenly before I entered the hospital has subsided. I have tossed much of what was once here back into the street, but nothing so far has replaced it. The one thing that didn't go was the pine-topped table with the square chrome legs that I use for a desk. I'd picked it up on the street for five dollars, lugged it up the stairs, shimmied it sideways through the doorway, and positioned it next to a living-room window with a panoramic view of the building next door, which is where it still is. My computer arrives, an obscure brand, not long for the personal computer market, and I set it on the table's grainy surface. I have put my Nicaragua notebooks to the side, and it is here that I begin work on an article on brain surgery. My eyesight has indeed come back. Flamm's manipulations inside my brain have not hurt my vision, testimony, I know, to his surgical agility. I can read again, and I am curious as hell. Work on the magazine article will occupy most of my waking hours for three months.

At the outset, I figure that this is a story I can get into and out of quickly, which is how I'd thought of the experience itself. After all, just by surviving the operation, I'd done the bulk of the research. I believe this 3,000-word story will net me a quick $2,000, which I need.

With the hair still bristly on my head, I make appointments with each of my doctors. I want to know how they do their jobs. I have a tape recorder, a notepad, and lists of questions.

My notion of how the story will go ends during the first interview with my neurosurgeon—the first of what will turn out to be half a dozen formal interviews. We sit at a round formica-topped table in his office in Bellevue Hospital, which is affiliated with NYU. The sweet aroma of his pipe tobacco hangs in a plume of blue smoke. On one wall are photographs of his mentors, the pioneering microneurosurgeon Gazi Yasargil, barrel

chested and even in the snapshot looking barely containable; and Yasargil's
ex-boss, Hugo Krayenbuhl, whom Flamm knew well enough to call Poppie.
There is a light box for viewing X rays; shelves of books, including a set
of black-bound copies of the *Journal of Neurosurgery*; a board with the chalk
outlines of blood vessels.

When Flamm is at ease, he has a way of leaning back in his chair and
perching his chin on his chest, as if, it seems to me, he is discreetly checking
his fly. But when he wants to make a point, as he abruptly does now, his
forehead furls, and his widow's peak looks ferocious, like the front edge
of a can opener. As a good clinician, or perhaps just an inquisitive party,
he preempts my interview with his own question. "Why are you doing
this?" he wants to know. "Shouldn't you just put it behind you, forget
it?" I tell him, as I still maintained was true, that, oh, really, what happened
to me wasn't such a big deal. Personally, I am past it. What intrigues me
now is the brain, so complex, barely understood and yet reparable. I think
the topic is interesting for all the reasons other people have found brain
surgery interesting: the high risks, the exciting rewards.

Then, in answer to one of my questions, he rests his pipe on the table,
pinches his square manicured fingertips together in imitation of a blood
clot, and touches them to the back of my head. "That's about where yours
was," he says, taking up the wooden bowl of his pipe. My voice flutters
like a scolded kid's. Again, I am a patient before his doctor. I have a list
of reporter's questions, yet I only want to know one thing, which is what
every patient wants to know: Am I going to be all right?

I read that neurosurgery has among the bleakest general prognoses of
all the specialties and have a double reflection: How interesting for my
story, how ominous for me. I scan tedious medical reports. My guard finally
down, I seem to be aware for the first time of the risks.

"The 1,103 patients in this series were admitted . . . and underwent
consecutive supratentorial neurosurgical procedures for non-traumatic
conditions," said a 1981 report in *Acta Neurochirurgica* by P. M. Foy. "A
thousand cases were successfully traced, 51 percent of whom had survived
for at least five years. . . ." Nearly half of brain surgery patients aren't alive
five years after surgery! In another report, this one in *Seminars in Neurology*,
James Torner wrote, "Gudmundsson and Benedikz found that 42% of
strokes in persons under the age of 35 years were subarachonid hemorrhages, and these rates were similar to other studies of this young population." Hardly compelling prose, yet I am choked with emotion. I had a
subarachnoid hemorrhage. Did I, just as that indifferent *señora* in Nicaragua

remarked, have a stroke? I did. Weeks after the operation, I luxuriate in a kind of retrospective terror. I lie awake and fondle my wound. To the touch, my head feels strange. It *is* strange. It is bumpy and uneven, pot-holed. There is the swelling at the incision, which pushes up like a lip, and there is, at the top of my head, an indentation, like a divot, into which I can put a finger. It is where one of the holes was drilled. I think of myself as put back together.

Flamm and I pose together in the OR, a portrait of a boy and his neurosurgeon. Flamm is ruddy and nonchalant, the ho-hum countenance. I, says photographer Annie Leibovitz, "began to lose color in [my] face, to look like a patient." My research has revealed that I was lucky because of where in my brain the vascular anomaly was located, the skill of my surgeon, and the time in history when I was wheeled into the OR. Brain surgery is, like the automobile, a nineteenth-century technology. Yet re-finements have been made. I had been involved in a medical thriller. An operation that was never successful fifty years ago, never even tried sixty years ago, is now a standard element of the neurosurgical repertoire. The march of science had reached me just in time. In the article, which turned out to be 10,000 words long, I wrote that brain surgery had been a case of hardship (mine) and heroism (Flamm's). The story concluded this way: "For now, and certainly for many years to come, a person, comatose on the operating table, turns his life over to someone else—the neurosurgeon." Perhaps the conclusion wasn't terribly original. And the article ignored the doubts that had crept into my own sense of well-being. (I wasn't really going to expound on spit!) In any case, those will disappear, I am sure, as my health proves itself over time. The important part is this: Finally, brain surgery will be out of my life. Julie is sick of the subject, and maybe of me, too. She doesn't quite kick me out, but when she insists we shop for furniture for my apartment, I get the message and return home.

I haven't heard the last of brain surgery, though. Even as I am trying to put to rest my fear of chance encounters, my concern that any day my teeth will erode like beach cliffs, my worry that suddenly I will gag on my own saliva, I find that I am a lightning rod for other people's most intimate sentiments about their surgery. Some brain diseases have associations and newsletters. For instance, the Acoustic Neuroma Society, which includes people who have had a tumor of the acoustic nerve, issues a newsletter. AVMers, not as well organized, call and write to me. They are incredibly excited. My writers want to meet or correspond, as if we are all members of a club.

Kimberly Dorcy, nine, sends a photo of herself dressed in a pink Care Bears nightshirt in the hospital and a five-page letter penciled in her own handwriting. Here it is, as written.

My name is Kim. When I was 8 in Nov 1983 They found out I had AVM. For a long time I had headaches but everyone thought I just didn't want to go to school. One day I got sick and threw up and passed out. The squad took me to the hospital. My temperature was 93 degrees. After five hours they knew what I had. The operated on me a week later for 3½ hours. My aunt gave mom the paper you wrote in Science Digest and she read it to me. I hope you are ok now. I am having a hard time in school. Dr. Sayer has me still on phenobarbital and I just had another CT scan. I am doing fine. Your story explained it very well. Mom learned more from it then from the doctor. I hope you stay well and I just want you to know that your story meant alot to me and my family. If you write anymore storys about AVMs I hope you'll let us no so we can go out and by it. I think you had a real great doctor too. Tell him that for me. Please!

Hear is a picture of me when I was in the hospital. My hair is back now as you can see. I hope you have a good life ahead of you. Can you please send me a little note showing me you got this? You probably know lots of people who had this. I only know about you. I hope you have time to write me. Love Kim.

Another letter begins, "After reading your story I was very moved and couldn't believe it because the similarity to my story is very close!"

Indeed, not only our ages but the timing of our hemorrhages was very close. The letter from David Lubarsky continues:

Briefly I am 28. On October 12, 1983, I hemorrhaged in my new photo studio. My fiance took me to Lenox Hill Hospital. After CT scans and an angiogram it was clear, an AVM [was] located on the left side of my head sitting just above the speech center. On November 1, 1984, 10 hours of surgery at Columbia Presbyterian Medical Center. Nine days later I was released. Dr. James McMurtry not only saved my life, but returned me to society with no permanent effects.

Steve, I would love to speak with you any time and I hope you would like to speak with me also.

Another person my age who contacts me is Barry Milione. Milione has actually formed an AVM support group based in California, which is designed to give AVMers someone to talk to. Milione is from New York but has lived in the San Francisco area for several years. He was operated on and also underwent radiation treatment for his AVM, which, because it was located in the speech and motor centers, couldn't be entirely removed by surgery. He sends me articles about his doctor and his group and promises that he will visit when he makes his annual trip home to New York.

Frankly, these contacts make me uncomfortable. I respond when asked. And though I avoid it for a while, I meet David Lubarsky and his wife, Sarah, for coffee. She stares lovingly, almost covetously, at him when he speaks. It is a heartbreaking story. Initially, Lubarsky had not been able to remember who she was or that he intended to marry, a future erased by a few drops of blood. Gradually his memory returned, and though Lubarsky still had a reading and attention handicap, he and his courageous fiancée got married, as scheduled, five months after surgery. I also send young Kim a letter. My contacts, though, aren't enthusiastic, I admit. I've said all I have to say about my illness; I don't want to hear about other people's. I'm not organizing a club. I don't want to belong to one! I hadn't initally thought of brain surgery as a career move. In fact, when I am offered a job at a business magazine, I leap at the opportunity. My goal is to put this behind me now, just as Flamm had suggested. If Milione wants to lead a campaign, that is fine. He is the perfect person to do it. He is the type of friendly persuader that people outside of New York call pushy. He will get things done, even though he confides his memory isn't nearly as good as it used to be. I don't look down on these former AVM sufferers, but we have so little in common outside of our disease—and that we no longer even have.

If anything, over the course of my research I've come to identify, I tell myself, with the doctors, and in particular, the residents, young professionals striving, as I am, to gain skills and move ahead. David Chalif and I have become friendly. We see each other for dinner or for brunch. We always talk about brain surgery, not as doctor to patient but as two people who share an interest. It's easy to get involved in his stories of neurosurgical adventure. Chalif is intellectually and emotionally absorbed by brain surgery. Indeed, not much else holds his attention. His interests, I think, stopped evolving once his residency of twelve- to twenty-four-hour days began, which yields the odd phenomenon of someone hyperskilled in one field and also out-of-date in others. His record collection, for instance, is still heavy on Bob Dylan and Neil Young.

One Sunday, Chalif brings his new wife to brunch. Gail, five years younger than her husband, has known Chalif all her life. Their grandmothers lived across the hall from each other in an apartment building in Far Rockaway, New York. At first Gail had wondered what she was going to talk about with this person. But on their first date she leaned across the polished table of the restaurant and kissed him. After that, they were together constantly. During the day Chalif called Gail, who worked as a gemologist, and said he had an hour free and why didn't she come down. Evenings, Gail brought him dinner. They ate in the lobby of the medical school. At night, they sometimes slept in the single bed in the call room.

Chalif wears chinos and a brown-leather bomber jacket. Having just stopped by the hospital to check on a patient, his hands are smudged with dried blood. Shortly after they were married, almost as a honeymoon gesture, it seems to me, Chalif took Gail to an operation. It was July Fourth, his first solo operation.

"I was so disappointed about having to be alone that out of desperation I went with him," says Gail. "I was so nervous."

"But I was really calm, wasn't I?" says David.

"You were really calm," affirms Gail. "Sucked up that clot."

"I was scared as shit," says David.

We all laugh.

The operation went fine. After three hours, the patient, a local drunk, opened his eyes and demanded a drink.

Chalif says he really got into my article and has an idea for another: the life of a resident. "It would be sooo interesting," he says. Gail makes a little noise with her mouth; she thinks he's plugging himself. But I agree it would be fascinating. Chalif has an onion, ham, and cheese omelet and, I remember, pushes the egg onto his fork with his fingers, still soiled with the day's blood. "Who would be interested in an article like that?" Chalif says, and we are already planning its publication.

My course of treatment is over. I see Flamm every few months to check in. Visits are free, complimentary with the surgery. I like Flamm. He's smart, philosophical, not, it seems to me, a surgeon-jock. Still, trips to his office can be sobering. A woman limps out, one side of her mouth drooping as if it were caught on a fish hook. Flamm whispers to me, "AVM." I hate taking the Dilantin, even prophylactically. The daily four white capsules with the orange band are like a reminder of something I've done wrong. Flamm explains: "If a person has never had seizures [before the operation] and there wasn't a lot of extensive work in the brain in an area I would think would be the focus for a seizure, then I would take them off anti-convulsants after a year." That is my case. In the meantime, I am working. Flamm allows me to exercise, and soon enough I am at the gym. After a year it will be over. This drug regimen will have been a standard precaution, the last I will hear of brain surgery.

56 At the end of eleven months I am lowered lockstep off Dilantin. From 400 milligrams, I descend to 300 milligrams for one week. The following week, I go to 200 milligrams, and then 100 milligrams for a final week; a twenty-one-day taper to junklessness. On the last day of my last week, in other words, on the day before I am to be completely relieved of my medical duties, I am at work, when a ball of light appears in the upper left quadrant of my vision. I squeeze shut my eyes and try to clear my vision. That makes it worse: colors flare, orange and apricot. I open my eyes; it is still there, hovering like a UFO. I race to the phone and punch in the NYU hospital switchboard. No longer is it a beam of light but an area of distortion like a watery lens. It pulses. With each pulse it grows, claiming more of my vision. It is as if I am peering into a mirror that has been smashed on a pile of rocks. In a low voice I chant, "Go away, go away." I am trying not to think about the implications of these new sights, but when Flamm's office finally answers, the words rush out: "It's happening. It's happening again." Flamm's secretary tells me to get to the emergency room.

The executive editor of the magazine where I work slips on his blazer, sky blue, like those first useless pills I'd been given in Nicaragua, and takes me by the arm. "Just put me in a cab," I say, stubborn, the way stupid people are. To his credit, he will have none of it and insists on escorting me to NYU.

Lying on my back, my head propped inside the CT, I cross the fingers on both hands, tuck them into my pockets for luck, and listen to the white noise of the great pale machine as it scans my brain, I know now, for blood.

The waiting room is under construction. The ceiling tiles are gone; light fixtures dangle in midair as if abandoned. There are a few chairs pushed against the walls and fewer people: a guy in a wheelchair with a mask over his mouth, which indicates that he is dying of AIDS, and a young girl crying for her mother because she has been there all day.

"Do you want the good news or the bad news?" says Kricheff, who has come teeter-totter to my rescue once again. I can't face this all over; that would require so much more cheer than I could summon. Give me the good news.

No blood is apparent on the CT scan. Just the hole, where the clot—and before that, brain—used to be, and the metal clips, expected artifacts.

Flamm's repairs have held; no hemorrhage has occurred. My vision has indeed begun to clear. I have a headache, but nothing like the pain that accompanied my hemorrhage.

Shoving into the chair next to mine in the dilapidated waiting room, Kricheff offers the only conclusion possible. "You have a little epilepsy."

A little?

TO BE TOLD you have epilepsy is to be welcomed into a world of stigma from the very first moment. What other message can be gleaned when even doctors—people who dole out bad news for a living—are ill at ease with the term? It as if they have difficulty saying the word "epilepsy" and so qualify it, obscure it, disguise it. Medical students, in fact, are often taught to shun the term altogether. "The word *epilepsy* still has unpleasant connotations, and is probably best avoided in dealing with patients, until such time as the general public becomes more enlightened," counsels the 1985 edition of *Principles of Neurology*, a leading medical-school text. (Just how the public will be enlightened if epileptics stay hidden is not explained.) Doctors, perhaps unintentionally, can be what one sociologist calls "stigma coaches." They aren't the only ones.

Epilepsy has long brought out the worst in the public. As late as the nineteenth century, epilepsy was regarded as the result of demonic possession, and the expected outcome was idiocy. The epileptic was cast off, grouped with the insane and the deviant, and considered dangerous, folklore that is simply untrue. In 1891, the first separate institution for American epileptics was constructed at Gallipolis, Ohio, and the era of the epileptic colony began in the United States. In 1950, when my parents were twenty years old, about 50,000 people with epilepsy were still in institutions and psychiatric facilities. As recently as 1967 some states denied a person with epilepsy the right to marry. In 1971, 32 percent in a British poll said they didn't want their children playing with a child with epilepsy. A 1975 article said that one out of seven Americans believed epilepsy a form of insanity. Until recently, some epileptics, once sterilized, were stripped of the rights of motherhood. How, it was argued, could someone afflicted by fits be a fit mother? The unemployment rate for epileptics is estimated at 20 percent by the Epilepsy Foundation of America (EFA), which has eighty-seven chapters nationwide. Some epileptics are occupationally handicapped. But, says Barbara Elkin, director of EFA's legal advocacy, "people with epilepsy are far more disadvantaged by the attitudes of others than by their epilepsy."

My own father, a representative of his generation's beliefs, has been informed that I suffer seizures and will probably suffer them for the rest of my life. He seems to accept that. Yet when I use the word "epilepsy," there is real alarm in his voice.

"It's not *epilepsy*," he almost shouts, as if afraid of the term, which makes me wonder why I have heaved it at him, poor man, like a brick. Later, his cool reclaimed, he explains that epilepsy suggested to anyone who grew up in his era "uncontrollable antisocial behavior."

To me, a diagnosis of epilepsy at first means relief. At least it isn't a hemorrhage. But disappointment quickly follows. One day short of putting aside a year's worth of devices—alarms, colored glasses, plastic pinwheels with seven compartments—to remind me to ingest the two capsules in the morning and the two at night, I return to Dilantin, as if it is a habit I can't break. This news has been so unexpected; I battle waves of disappointment. I am told, and this is to hearten me, that there are people a lot worse off. It's not so bad to pop the orange-banded pills, the doctors say, speaking with the worn patience of people accustomed to tragedy. And I agree; I am not handicapped on the scale of someone confined to a wheelchair or bound by crutches, not like the AVM victim I watched limp from Flamm's office. I try to hold myself to the doctors' objective scale, to see my case as they do. Maybe an inconvenience, but not so bad, really. I repeat with the choristers that I am a lucky one.

And yet I feel so changed. I go gingerly through these days after. My hand, without my say-so, taps the wall, grips the handrail. I feel in my pocket for change. Between the time the seizure starts with a pulsing squiggle and the moment my entire visual field is lost to me, I have a few minutes. I lay plans for that time. I ask myself, Who should I call? Where will I tell them to meet me? How will I communicate urgency without signaling panic? I am not supposed to drive a car, swim alone, operate machinery, climb ladders, or because it interferes with the medication, drink alcohol. Kricheff suggests I get a necklace or a bracelet or at least a wallet-sized card identifying me as an epileptic so that if I have a seizure in the subway, I won't be mistaken for a drunk or a weirdo.

Weirdo, indeed! Is there any ailment as weird? Epilepsy is not one of those conditions whose shock fades as you learn more about it. Reading a description of seizures is like reading science fiction. Grand mal or generalized seizures—with the thrashing limbs, the rending shriek as air is forced from the lungs, the saliva pouring from the mouth as glands go into overproduction, and the brief halt in respiration that turns the epileptic a cyanotic blue—are epilepsy's trademark. But seizures come in many other forms. Almost any function the brain controls, epilepsy can take over. A seizure might be no more than a bad taste or smell. A person might recall an event or a sound (usually the same one). Objects in the environment can shrink or, just the opposite, appear gigantic. A sense of heightened reality (déjà vu) or of total unfamiliarity (jamais vu) is possible. Brief lapses of consciousness, as short as a second, or a kind of waking unconsciousness in which a person can still perform routine tasks, but clearly isn't *there*, occur. Personality might change. Even unprovoked sexual pleasure—for which a woman in a published report refused treatment—can be a seizure. At different moments, one person can have different epilepsies. (Epilepsy is really the symptom, not the disease.) One woman I knew walked around her house one morning as if in a trance. At other times, her right hand went limp, or the right side of her body stiffened. (Once she had a seizure while driving and had to use her left hand to lift her right foot onto the gas pedal.) On the phone one day, she suddenly lost her ability to talk. At other times, her jaws clenched. "I was afraid I was going to bite right through," she said. Since she was a kid, she'd suffered bouts of fear, sometimes for days at a stretch. "I just want my husband to hold me," she said. Last year she learned that these moods are also seizures.

Julie insists that the manner in which I dropped the medication was flawed. I let go of my chemical dependency too rapidly. She doesn't want to accept a little epilepsy. To me, because I, too, search for a reason, it seems like payback. I come through brain surgery. Better me than them, I thought, I can handle it. For this vanity I am to go day by day with a reminder of what is beyond my control. Without notice, I will be struck dim and sightless. I, who fashioned myself an adventurer, find my options circumscribed by four banded pills. "You'll try again in a year," Julie says. I want to believe that, to think that this is delay, not defeat. But chronic illness is a type of career. And the ID card on which I list my doctor and my next of kin—the one Kricheff suggested I get—feels like an employee ID card.

Though I go back on the medication, I have more seizures. The neurologists say my fits are under control. This is medical double-talk. Seizure control does not mean I can in any way exert control over where or when I will have one. It means that I can expect four or five or six a year, until I have more. Is this control? Compared to what? A surgeon with four or five a year would be barred from the OR; a neurologist wouldn't be able to drive to work. I felt it wrong, selfish, to complain—I didn't even have the right to be angry!—and not to my advantage. My doctors simply cannot understand the way a seizure knocks the wind out of me, catches me up short, not just for an hour every few months—the actual duration of a seizure—but every day. Epilepsy takes away my natural cockiness, which I feel is part of my charm.

The same pattern follows every seizure. I would go months with no manifestation and would think that maybe the condition is changing. It is leaving me, just as it had come, suddenly and without warning. I would believe that I was one of the 20 percent who outgrows his fits. I would, in short, puff up, go to the gym, the scene of several seizures, and play full court. Or I would skip one of my doses of medicine. Not on purpose; I would just become slightly lax. Mentally I would cakewalk. And then I would see that idiotic sphere, like a PacMan eating up my vision, forcing me to seek cover on the floor. For days after, I would see an incipient seizure in the sparkle of the silverware or a passing headlight or the inside curve of the letter O. I'd search for lapses in my abilities, a search that itself had the paroxysmal energy of a seizure. I'd compile a list of words I had misspelled. It grew, and I'd wonder if each mistake was an epileptic moment. When I knew it would be most inappropriate—in a meeting at work, say—I'd lock in on the thought that I was going to seize. Then I'd blink and look away, unable to concentrate on a conversation, unable to do anything but test my control. *Is it happening? Is it happening*? Is that the flickering spot just to the left of midline, just above the half mark? Or is this my imagination? Sometimes I would have miniseizures; the blip would appear but then disappear after a minute.

Goodgold lost patience with me. When I call, distraught, he informs me that an abbreviated seizure indicates the medication is working. For me, either by too delicate a makeup or some other fault, this is no comfort. "I'm not worried by an isolated seizure," another neurologist tells me. Oh, but I am; I am mortified by the prospect. I reach the point where I don't want to meet new people or leave my decrepit apartment but only desire to be in a place where I will feel comfortable clutching the floor as my vision begins to seethe.

What upsets me most is not the variety of symptoms, or even their course, but their timing. Other chronic diseases are predictable, even if the prediction includes the crippling or eventual death of the patient. With epilepsy, congenial you is transformed into a bat-eyed, rattling, wandering weirdo in the flip of a coin. Maybe the sniper metaphor is unavoidable. Ira Brody, who got grand mal epilepsy from a head wound in Vietnam, says: "To have epilepsy that is not controlled is like walking down a road knowing that there is a sniper there. You don't know where the sniper is. You know the sniper has this loaded gun. And you know that this sniper is going to get you. You know that you are going to be struck down somewhere, someplace, sometime. It could be in the next hour, next day, next month, or even next year." Brody, who is in public relations, is also president of the Epilepsy Institute, which has five branches in the New York area. As I interview him, he leans back in his desk chair, and my nerves tighten. How bold to be in public relations, I think. Then I think, Please don't have a seizure now.

Inevitably, none of my seizures are well-timed. At the office the executive editor again takes a few hours off to escort me to the hospital. At the gym a trainer lets me lie on the concrete floor of the equipment room; another time my brother is there and holds my hand as an ambulance takes me away. At a restaurant I crawl onto the carpet inside the coatroom. Once, when a seizure begins in a cab, I leap from the backseat and throw myself at bystanders. "Help," I manage. Julie chases me down each time, takes me home, and puts me to bed, where I wait out the migraine that always follows.

Seizures are extremely inconvenient, but they are more than that. Depression, say some researchers, is a pattern of learned helplessness. Teach a dog that he cannot escape painful electric shocks and he becomes listless, accepting the shocks without protest. In a similar way, the cooperative patient is required to learn to be helpless. But once patienthood passes, once disease recedes and health returns, so, too, is a sense of helplessness supposed to wane. I had already taken too long putting my illness behind me. As brain surgery slipped into the past I had thought to reassert control over my life. Epilepsy stopped that project in its tracks. "What epilepsy is, is you lose control," says Brody. "It is exactly the opposite of overcoming, of showing strength; it is weakness, and what you're showing the people around you is their inability to help."

This is a scandal. Medicine was supposed to be on my side. Iatrogenic is an adjective that refers to an undesired effect of treatment. My epilepsy is, most likely, iatrogenic. For the majority of the 2.5 million epilepsy sufferers in the United States—about 1 percent of the population—epilepsy shows up one day and stays, for no apparent cause. In a smaller number of cases, though in most adult epilepsy, an epileptic can point to a trauma that injured the brain and created an epileptogenic focus. Some spot in the brain, clinically trackable, sometimes visible at autopsy, is the hyperexcitable location from which the nerve cells or neurons begin to misfire. A car accident or a fall can cause a head injury that produces a focus. So can brain surgery. In one massive study of 1,000 brain surgery patients tracked for five years, 17 percent developed seizures, though the risk varied greatly, depending on the type of problem that was operated on. "The Incidence of Postoperative Seizures" by P. M. Foy, G. P. Copeland, and M. D. M. Shaw reported in 1981 that following vascular surgery, the risk was 22 percent, even in someone who had never previously suffered a seizure. Of course, a hemorrhage can cause epilepsy by itself, but the risk is not nearly so great as when surgery follows. With just a hemorrhage, the chance is 20 percent; with vascular surgery added, the risk climbs to 35 percent, according to Foy. Foy's study followed patients for five years. When they are followed longer, the results are more stark. A 1986 report, "Cerebral AVMs and Epilepsy" by P. M. Crawford, C. R. West, M. D. M Shaw, and D. W. Chadwick, tracked 343 AVM patients for up to twenty years. After two decades, 20 percent of those who hemorrhaged got epilepsy—the same as in Foy's study. But if they also had surgery, then a whopping 58 percent started seizing, almost double Foy's result!

The location of my lesion in the occipital lobe of my brain is not usually a focus for epileptic activity. Yet it would appear that in my case the scar left by the scalpel—though there is a chance the hemorrhage was a contributing or even principal cause—wounded nerve cells. Microsurgery, so delicate a maneuver, might actually be quite cloddy. I am the proof. .

Every nerve cell "fires" impulses of electrical energy to communicate with other cells, usually from twenty to fifty impulses per second. It's not understood why the nerve cells near a scar—or near any epileptogenic focus, for that matter—should suddenly start to fire abnormally and produce a seizure. Perhaps such neurons are damaged and are in a constant state of alert, ready to fire. Research shows that damaged neurons are more excitable than normal neurons and hence more reactive to even minor changes in their environment, like increased heat or decreased oxygen. Another theory is that the inhibitory processes that usually prevent random firing have been knocked out. That would explain why introducing chemical inhibitors has allowed scientists to control some seizures. Or maybe the scar, like a seizure cooker, is always producing erratic signals that, under some (still unknown) conditions, escalate and become seizures.

In my case, sensitive electrodes pasted to my skull detected abnormal firing even when I wasn't having a seizure. On an electroencephalgram, the graph showed sharp peaks or spikes. That meant that in my brain some neurons were "burst firing," firing as many as 500 impulses per second, which is the characteristic pattern of epilepsy. I was having miniseizures, most of which I didn't even know about.

In my brain, this activity occurred in the occipital lobe, where visual signals are processed. Evidently, favorable conditions occasionally permitted my miniseizures to escalate into full-blown seizures. Then the damaged, burst-firing neurons triggered adjacent normal neurons to burst fire. Normal neurons were, in effect, recruited, as if all neurons had an "epileptic mode" that could be switched on. This epileptic chain continued until hundreds of thousands of normal neurons in my occipital lobe were firing in an epileptic frenzy, as many as twenty-five times their normal rate, and not because of any visual stimulus communicated through my eyes. I can follow the progress of this chain reaction through its effect on my vision. As more neurons in my occipital lobe slip into a burst-firing mode, a larger area of my vision undulates.

Seizures don't always remain confined to one location in the brain, such as the occipital lobe. They can spread, traveling along the brain's own pathways. Thus, a seizure that starts in the occipital lobe with visual distortions might eventually trigger the frantic firing of neurons in the motor strip at the crown of the brain and, in effect, take control of the motor strip. The arms and the legs could then start to flap rhythmically. The traveling seizure might also reach the center of consciousnes at the base of the brain and the epileptic would lose consciousness. In this case, the focal seizure would be said to have become a generalized seizure, also known as a grand mal seizure.

For a long time a person's only hope of relief from seizures was barbiturates, which also sedated. An epileptic might suffer fewer seizures but in return would be chronically drowsy. In 1938, two researchers working with seizing cats—their real breakthrough was to find a way to induce seizures in animals!—discovered phenytoin, marketed in the United States as Dilantin, which was said to stabilize the electrical discharges in the brain, though it's still not known how. Thousands of epileptics, once virtual sleepwalkers, were returned to active life with Dilantin.

Neurologists today hope that with more than a dozen anticonvulsant drugs perhaps 50 percent of epileptics won't suffer seizures. Sometimes that occurs on the first prescription of a drug like Dilantin, still, half a century after its introduction, one of the drugs of choice. Perhaps another

25 percent of epileptics don't respond to drug therapy at all. As many as 200,000 Americans may have their lives devastated by frequent, uncontrollable seizures or by sometimes associated difficulties, like mental retardation. Some are so incapacitated that they become candidates for more radical therapy, like surgery. Neurosurgeons who treat epilepsy have probably done more extensive and lasting damage to the human brain than is done in any other medical circumstance. They have, for instance, severed the connection between the two hemispheres of the brain or even removed one hemisphere—the epileptic one—altogether. More often, they use electroencephalograms, implanted electrodes or recently, superconducting magnets to search for an epileptogenic focus. Then, much as brain surgeon Wilder Penfield did toward the beginning of the century, they lop it out. Yale neurosurgery chairman Dennis Spencer says that in 90 percent of the cases in which a focus is found—which happens about 65 percent of the time—seizures can be alleviated or sharply reduced. "It's the only chronic disease that can be cured overnight," he says.

Goodgold let me know that my case fell between the two extremes: My symptoms weren't completely suppressed by drugs; on the other hand, I wasn't so handicapped that I should consider surgery. I was among the 25 percent of epileptics who, as one authority explained, are "willing to take medicine every day, tolerate occasional side effects, and still run the risk of having another seizure." Goodgold also impressed on me that controlling epilepsy is a delicate business in which trial and error plays a big part. When I continued to have seizures on Dilantin, Goodgold added another medication. In my case, blood tests—the availability of which is one of the real improvements of modern therapy—showed that it never got into my system in what are normally therapeutic doses. That didn't matter. "As long as you're not having seizures, let's not play with it," Goodgold said.

VICTIMS OF SERIOUS ILLNESS inevitably prattle on about this subject: Why *me*? I remember the patient who grabbed one neurosurgeon's arm before his operation, as if he weren't going to let go, and said, "Why did this goddamned thing happen to me?" What is the point of such an interrogation? Might there really be a culprit? And then what: trade hate of the condition for hate of its cause, or causer? Would that be satisfying? Epilepsy made me think that it would.

On the day I confront Flamm we are in his Bellevue office, a brightly lit room located at the end of a dim, crowdless hall of lime-green bricks. Books are stacked on a round table; a new journal called *Theoretical Surgery* (about surgical decision making) is on top of crammed shelves. Flamm's got on his prep-school look, the one he favors, penny loafers, khaki, cuffed pants, and a hint of wildness: a tie with blue polka dots. This is a familiar routine, I with a tape recorder and a list of typed questions, Flamm with groomed hands bridged under his flat chin, going slightly double. As he kicks his feet up on a chair, it occurs to me that in past interviews I'd mostly encouraged him to talk about the perils of neurosurgery, which were also its excitement. At this session I want to ask about something different.

"I was very surprised by having a seizure," I tell Flamm, "When you were explaining the surgery to me, I don't remember your talking about the possibility of having seizures. Was that a choice you made?"

This seemed to me, then, a direct question, one in which the emotional content was clear. Yet when I listen to my tape recording to try to comprehend the nature of that emotion, I get confused. I know I felt I was being blunt, in my polite way. And yet the manner in which I expressed myself seems, in retrospect, convoluted, beside the point. I acted as if I believed that what had really troubled me was not the seizures themselves but the fact that I had not been expecting them. To Flamm I was saying: Hey, all I wanted was some warning. As if, had I been informed, I might then have comfortably planned to be an epileptic!

Flamm can be near psychotic in his style or gruff and impatient. He can also be professorial, reasoned, personable, a mood in which he relies heavily on conditional tenses. With me he chooses the latter, takes my questions literally. He responds that he hadn't intended to hide anything. He says, "When someone asks, 'Well, what do we expect after the surgery?' I tell them about seizures, and I try to remember to tell them before they go home that they're going to be on anticonvulsants for a year. And I would hasten to add that it's unlikely that they would have a seizure, but this is an added precaution."

Since we'd met in my hospital room, I'd been to Flamm's home for dinner, met his children, his wife, his dog, named Nancy, and come to admire the way he lives. Ask him how he is and he'd likely say, "Don't ask." But that was at work. At home he discoursed about the closeness of man and canine, kidded his son about the length of his hair, and showed off his new old books. His apartment was comfortable; he'd spent more on medieval books than furniture. He understood that money without culture was just money, grubby and pointless. Neurosurgery for him was an entry point into a world of historical study and scientific thought.

Recently he told me of his intent to write a biography of an eighteenth-century British surgeon. It would have been less complicated if I disliked this bottled-up man, given to fits himself, but I didn't.

In interviews my habit was not to drill Flamm; that did not make me comfortable, nor did it befit our relationship, which was amiable, if distant. Yet, as I replay the tape, I notice that for me there is an energy behind the topic of epilepsy, some heat. I pressed on, restated my question, wouldn't let it drop, and perhaps out of some chumminess Flamm allowed me to insist.

Did he generally not tell patients about the possibility of seizures? Shouldn't I have been allowed to factor epilepsy in to my consideration of whether to have brain surgery at all? "I was surprised at how high the percentage is of seizures after brain surgery," I told Flamm. "Something like twenty-five percent."

I remember that Flamm's lips buckled, a tip that he was reflecting. He pointed out that the hemorrhage could well have inflicted the brain damage that led to epilepsy. "Where your AVM was it would be somewhat unusual to expect a seizure. So I was a little surprised. Rarely, rarely in my experience do [AVM patients] have a seizure," he said.

I wasn't about to bicker over numbers, not then and not now. The statistics showed that seizures were perhaps a greater risk than Flamm indicated, although different surgeons have different experiences. What interests me is that clearly something is driving me to rephrase and repeat this question, tremulously but insistently, until, yes, it occurs to me quite clearly what motivates me. It is anger. Listening to the tape, this is clear to me now. My voice signals it. The tone is petulant; the pitch goes high. Even as Flamm sat there, his hands girding his big, expressionless face or slipping schoolboylike into his tan pockets, I had suppressed this thought: My condition has brought a load of disappointment, and why is none of it yours?

Of course I had known for a long time that epilepsy was on the line. I was, after all, taking four pills a day, day after day for a year, to prevent seizures. It is true that I couldn't know what horror a seizure was until I'd had one, couldn't imagine the experience of that neural mutiny until it had occurred. It is also true that a patient's need to understand is frequently greater than the doctor's ability to explain. Yet these considerations are probably irrelevant. Had I known with complete certainty that *I would get* epilepsy after surgery, would I then have turned down the procedure? Of course not. I still would have opted for the operation that saved my life. And if for the past year I haven't been fully conscious that epilepsy stalked me, at least I've had a time during which I could believe I was going to be my old self again.

No, the issue was elsewhere. I wasn't upset that I hadn't been informed of epilepsy's arrival; I was disappointed that it had arrived at all. I once believed I had snuck off 11 East cloaked in health. Seizures, waiting in ambush, stripped me of that belief. The result, I realize now, is that I feel like someone aggrieved. What's more, my hostility, twin of my disappointment, has a focus, if only I could bring myself to say its name. Patients bow to their surgeons as if to Buddhas. "You thought Flamm was a god," one of the medical students who followed my case had told me. This is considered appropriate patient behavior. Yet any patient who does not admit that in part he also hates his surgeon, despises his smugness, which is the ability to walk away from his mishaps, is a liar.

The conceit of the surgeon is that what he does is heroic. I've heard Flamm talk about the surgeon's courage in the OR and invoke a comparison to firemen. Chalif once explained that good neurosurgeons have "the right stuff," like test pilots. But the fireman and the pilot risk their own lives. What does the surgeon risk? Someone else's. The neurosurgical ethic is guilt without blame. These surgeons try their best, they fail, they try again. Wins are their wins, but losses aren't their losses. What a hoax this heroism is! The surgeon's ego is built on the misfortunes of others! I was cured, I had been told. But now the cure seems as reliable to me as a paper bag holding water. I don't believe that I am the victim of incompetence or evil intent, but we are really not in this together, doctor and patient. Whether epilepsy is the hemorrhage's or the surgery's glad souvenir, I am the one who seizes, and they get the credit.

In rehearing the interview, I think now there is but one line that reveals my true sentiment. I wanted to ask Flamm why so few of his patients got epilepsy. What slipped out was this: "Is it because you're such a good surgeon?" On the tape this question comes off, passes, as within the bounds of polite conversation. And though Flamm reacts with equanimity, says modestly that it reflects the types of procedures he does, I think now that this question is a question of anger. It is an accusation: If you're such a good surgeon, than why am I seizing? Owning up to anger against Flamm, a man I like, is not easy. My emotion is not pretty. For, I realize, I don't want to say to my surgeon, Why did this goddamned thing happen to me? What I really want to do is grip his arm in a steely grip and ask: Why didn't this thing happen to you?

58 My new condition carries a load of disappointment, and not just for me. Julie is terribly unhappy, which I learn one evening under strange circumstances. I am interviewing her for this book, playing journalist with another subject. Is it the impersonality of the interview situation, refereed by tape recorder, that frees her to speak her mind? Or the wine? Or just the need to have been asked?

Julie talks into the tape recorder, the one she gave me as a birthday present. Initially she is bashful, unwilling to go forward. She protests that she can't remember anything. (Her memory is notoriously poor.) We finish dinner at the round white table in the room that is both her living room and bedroom. On the tape you can hear the sounds of chewing, of glasses banging to the table, of the air filter from Julie's turtle tank. Then the tape is filled with individual notes of laughter, like musical notes, and Julie's long, airy sighs, which, on rehearing, I find heartbreaking. Julie is on her third glass of wine. Her hair has become disheveled, her voice more liquid. "This is going to be really bad," she says. "Would you hypnotize me?"

And yet once started, she is indefatigable. What had I expected? Testimony of her sadness, concern, devotion? It is quickly apparent that I have no idea what she has gone through.

After the first seizure Julie was full of emotion. She didn't know what had happened. "Then, when I found out, I was more depressed," she says. For Julie, the event raised a big question mark. It wasn't the seizure exactly or perhaps even the prospect of more. "I don't want you to be sick. I don't want you to have seizures. I'm not the mothering type. I'm not that on top of it. I'm pretty realistic about myself. Your mother works hard and doesn't expect a lot. She lives in a small apartment. She's devoted to her kids. She's pretty selfless. And I'm not. I'm selfish. I want a big place to live. I want to be comfortable. And I'm not that hard of a worker. Maybe you should be with someone who is a really-on-top-of-it woman, earning a really good living. There are plenty of people like that, but I'm not one. I don't want to have to take care of you, because I don't feel capable. I feel like I have a lot of needs, too, a lot of needs that aren't fulfilled. I want someone to take care of me. I want someone to cater to my upset stomachs and my hangnails and the holes in my shoes and the zero balance in my bank account."

At first I have the feeling that Julie isn't talking to me but that we are discussing a third person, someone outside the realm of this postprandial chat. And so, even as my behavior is excoriated, I think, This is great material. My concern is to keep her going, push her along, and focus on the subject, which is illness. Yes, but what does what you say have to do with seizures? I don't have more than a half dozen a year. I'm not handicapped. For Julie, the seizures, the surgery, and our relationship have all been rolled into one ball, which is gathering speed and mass.

"You are very demanding, and you're sick at the same time. I feel like you want someone to take care of you, answer all your needs and all your desires, all the time. You've always been demanding; maybe this plays on my sympathies more, plays on my guilt. I can't say no. Whenever there is a dispute, seizures are the trump card. For example, you get pent-up feelings." It's true; sometimes my jaw muscles ached. "Well, you kind of use it as a threat: 'I'm pent up, so we've got to do what I want to do.' It carries the weight of 'I'm going to have a seizure,' or, 'I might have a seizure,' or, 'I'm nervous about having a seizure,' and psychologically you use it. I don't know whether you know it or not, but you wield some power. You're very aggressive about things like that. If you don't want to be bugged, you don't want to be bugged. And you don't want to hear anything about it. I'm always on the alert, and I always feel on edge."

Gradually it dawns on me that my relationship of four years is ending, documented here on tape. She's wrong, I want to tell her. I can imagine how the misunderstanding started, how my actions nurtured it; yet it seems perverse that the problems have continued so long in mushroomy dark. Epilepsy, for Julie, has thrown off the balance. Why hasn't she told me any of this? Why didn't I recognize it? This is intolerable. I tell Julie I don't want to be treated special. Just argue it out. I demand nothing, I want to say. "I *do* want to be bugged," I say, which seems too little too late.

A study of 166 epileptic patients revealed that 58 percent said their social lives were restricted by their disability; 46 percent of marriageable age hadn't married according to *Epilepsy; A Handbook for Mental Health Professionals.* Is epilepsy undermining my relationship, too? I want to cock my head and say, I can take care of myself. But it's also true that I do want somebody to call when my vision drops.

Julie would like, and I would, too, to uncover a specific stress or emotional trigger. Whenever I have a seizure, we review my day, my week, my personality. Nothing—or everything—seems significant. Every epileptic frighteningly learns that seizures, outside of known causes like extreme fatigue or a failure to take medication, have a strong random component.

The truth is I can't do anything to stop the seizures. What's more, the seizures might get worse, at any time, degrading from visual to grand mal, say, which is also a phenomenon that nobody can explain. This is very upsetting to Julie. "I think you wouldn't be as needy if you didn't have seizures. I think you would feel more confident. If I feel like it's something that's going to get worse, then it scares me. Then I see that you are going to be more dependent on me, and you more dependent on me really scares me."

59 On February 20, 1985, one year and four months after surgery, I am again at work when the spot appears at the top of my vision. Once, in thinking about my visual seizures, I reasoned, If I make the room perfectly dark, then the seizure won't be visible. If I can see nothing, there'll be nothing to distort. In the comforting blackness I could wait out the seizure, then emerge as if nothing had ever happened. So as the blip enlarges, I turn off the lights, shut the blinds, close my office door, and sprawl on the carpet. I wrap one arm around my eyes, like a raccoon's mask, and wait for soothing blindness to hide my seizure. All is not cozy darkness. Just the opposite. With my eyes pressed shut, what I see is like the fireworks of my childhood, reds and oranges towering skyward from behind the bandstand. There's no escape. The hallucinations are omnipresent, eyes closed or not.

I have a double reality: There is the seizure, and then there is the consciousness of the seizure. The first, the phenomenological, is not unpleasing: seizure as source of pyrotechnics. But the second, the consciousness of the seizure, is terrifying. It is not the fit itself but the consideration of it that uncorks the fear. And so, though I have a desire to dawdle, maybe enjoy the epileptic show—is there an element of excitement in every new sensation?—my reflective side is quickly building to a panic. Call for help, it implores, while I still am able to make my way. It seems to me that the real source of suffering, and maybe even the true motor of the fit, is not the neurons going wild in my brain but the fear they generate, which is finally intolerable. I go for help. The executive editor again escorts me out. "If you could just wave your hands at the wall when we need to get out of a meeting," he jokes. This time he leads me home. There's no reason to go to the hospital. I know the course of these things now.

When I phone Julie, she insists on dropping her work and coming over. The epilepsy scares her, puts her off, and yet, strangely, the moment of seizure is a time of intense connection between us. In the instant of my need, Julie, who feared that she lacked empathy, was freed to care in a way that I think surprised and pleased her, too. By the time she arrives, the distortions are gone. My vision has almost cleared. I have a headache, but mainly I am hungry. The seizure has made me miss lunch. Julie says she'll take me around the corner to a diner.

My American cheese and onion omelet has just arrived—before Julie's fried chicken—when there it is again. The ball, the little monster that devours my vision. I'm not going to get to eat at all, I think. "We've got to go," I say, and cram my mouth with egg. I also look at my watch.

"But my chicken," says Julie.

"I'm having a seizure," I say, as if that should be the last word.

"Okay, we'll leave it," Julie says, conceding.

"Get it 'to go,' " I say, belligerently polite.

We are still waiting for Julie's damned fried chicken when I tell her to look at my watch. Four minutes have elapsed. That's how long it takes for my vision to collapse. I grip Julie's arm and tag along beside her like a feeble old man, except that I say, "Let's hurry; I'm not a feeble old man." The panic loop is feeding the seizure loop. What the fuck is Julie with her fried chicken doing, strolling? Soon, soon, every step one less step, every second one less second. Julie works the lock. I climb those bare steps, shabby even in a blur.

This will go away in ten or fifteen minutes, I tell myself, and crawl into bed to wait. The world spins. I can get no distance on this sensation. The hallucinations come as close as my eyelids. It's awful, but I am accustomed to it.

This time, though, something is different. The room presses in on me; it isn't spinning, but I think that any second it might. It has lost its stability; it's no longer *out there*, set and other, but part of some insubstantiality that I also seem to be part of. My mouth is half open, and respiration comes in short, sweaty bursts; it's as if phone books are piled on my chest. Fear will only make this worse, I think, and try to be calm. No chance. This sensation will not be placated. Fear snakes down my spine.

I am sick. I roll off the bed and run the six steps to the toilet. Kneeling, I give up my American cheese and onion omelet, like a bubble bursting. Even in the domain of this wild loss of control I had begun to have expectations. This has never happened.

Julie says she'll call the doctor. But I say not yet. Neurologists have let me know they can't be bothered every time I have a seizure. She calls, anyhow. He says there's nothing to do, ride it out. "You were right," she tells me. I don't think Julie likes that much.

I crunch my eyelids shut as if they are tinfoil and hug my stomach. I want only to go to sleep, to leave this heaving world behind. My orientation in space is gone; I can't tell distance. I only sense motion, unpleasant, kaleidoscopic motion. It feels as if I am about to tip over, although this can't be true, not here on this bed with its four planted legs. Or can it? Fear is rushing ahead, intoning, "Danger, danger." Suddenly I am sure that one by one my capacities—to walk, to talk—are about to go under.

"Am I dying?" I mutter to Julie.

WHEN I COME TO, Julie is crouched over me, her knees on the bed like a tackler's. What are you doing? I'm trying to say, which comes out, "Waaryoin?" because Julie's right hand is stuffed in my mouth up to the palm. I wonder if I have slept. I still can't see. Like everyone I know, Julie believes (falsely) that an epileptic in mid-fit can swallow his tongue. I pull her hand from my mouth.

"You were shaking," she says. "You didn't answer." My eyelids are plugged and heavy, my will gone.

"I was not. I did not. I was sleeping a little. I'm fine."

But I am an auditor in this scene, listening to my affectless tone, unable to participate. Julie is phoning the doctor. Her voice is far away. "His eyes were strange. He was jerking. No, no, he wouldn't respond."

Is this true? I can't remember and can't protest. That's all. I'm in a blank. Something is happening. Intruders are in my apartment.

"What's his name?" they say, then, "Steve, Steve, Steve, Steve." They pronounce my name at different volumes. Their voices tell me something: Am I so out of it?

"Do you know who we are?"

Why are they asking such a dumb question. "Men in blue," I say, making a joke.

"We're going to help you get dressed," they say. "Now."

"I can do it," I say, supercilious. But I can't. I have no ability to do. This is movement in a dream, where legs sink knee-deep with each running step. Everything resists, not just the outside world but my own body, as well. I'm standing, I'm walking, but these are notes I make, pure observations, not actions I've taken. Julie. Men in blue. I'm in some kind of funk. A dot on the horizon. Men in blue signal for taxi. "Ain't taking sick guy, no way." Men in blue yelling, "You wanna go to the station? You wanna go to the station? You wanna go to the station?"

I know epileptics who have been carted off (by well-meaning people) to mental wards, drunk tanks, or jail as the result of seizures. On the night of my first generalized or grand mal seizure I am escorted in a cab to the hospital. When we get there, Julie is angry because, gripped by the emergency, she tossed the unhelpful cabdriver a twenty and let him keep the change. "No," I tell the doctor, "I didn't lose consciousness, as far as I can tell." Julie says it's not so. My memory *is* spotty, I acknowledge. I have reservoirs of data, but they are not linked. And then I come back, really present, and realize for the first time that I was out, really out. At the beginning they had just been visual disturbances. This seizure involved loss of consciousness, neck arching, writhing, wandering, eye flopping. I squeeze the doctor's fingers, the old routine. Ronald Reagan. The neurologist in the NYU emergency room, of course, tells me I'm lucky: "At least it wasn't one of those piss-in-your-pants, bite-your-tongue affairs." But I am distraught. The significance of this event seems tremendous, medically and personally.

"All right," he says, "I'm going to admit you."

I know that prolonged, uninterrupted seizure states can cause permanent brain damage, including death in an hour. But I wasn't having a seizure anymore.

"Noooooo," I protest. "I'm not sick. I'm not."

"Just overnight for observation," he says.

"At least not on 11 East," I say. I can't imagine being again among those stockinged heads and those optimistic dying folk.

"It's the only place there's a bed."

Part IX

DREAMS OF RECOVERY

*The terrors of suffering, sickness and death, of losing ourselves and losing
the world are the most elemental and intense we know; and so too are our dreams
of recovery, of being wonderfully restored to ourselves and the world.*
Oliver Sacks, *Awakenings*

I think it is true that we collude with our illnesses; we invent how we live them. A person with epilepsy, for instance, embarks on strategies for cover: private denial and its public counterpart, deceit. What a double life! Consider what one remarkable study by Graham Scambler and Anthony Hopkins learned: More then half of epileptics never disclosed to a boyfriend or girlfriend that they had epilepsy. Worse, almost a third of the ninety-four epileptics studied refused to divulge their condition to a future spouse.

I, too, had dissembled. I spent my first year as an epileptic opposing the idea that this strange, incurable sequel to my AVM wasn't really a great adventure, the best yet. The seizures kept coming; I learned what to expect. At one point I even told myself that the visual distortions were fascinating. Imagine that the brain could falsify what the eye unerringly took in! This fantasy could hardly last. Okay, epilepsy is rotten, I had decided next. But as with other ailments there were prescribed countermeasures. All I had to do was heed the doctors; and swallow the pills. I'm the same as I've always been, was the attitude I assumed, I'm just taking some medication. The trouble with being unable, I knew, was that a person could also feel unworthy. Not me, I contended. I rode a bicycle and was among those epileptics who illegally drove a car. What's more I'd excitedly taken up Chalif's invitation to travel behind the lines of high-powered medicine. At the side of my resident friend, I returned to the scene of the crime, conducting hours and hours of research on 11 East. Julie said I was crazy. But, I assured her, I was hale and full of moxy just like Chalif and the other surgical wizards I tracked. Brain surgery, I continued to maintain, had been a straightforward operation from which I had recovered. Under the "catastrophic illness" clause, Medicaid had picked up my hospital fees: $11,827.35 and some doctors' bills. (Flamm had accepted $2,500—half his normal fee—which was all my insurance company would spend; my parents helped with other doctors' bills.) I hadn't even incurred grave financial debts. Neurosurgery had been a rest stop. Epilepsy was a rash, an itch, nothing to pay too much attention to. I hardly considered myself seizure ridden. And most of the time, of course, I had been right.

Two years after brain surgery my past attitudes are no longer tenable. I am returned to 11 East as a patient. My bed is a protective crib. Slate-gray cushions are tied to locked rails in case my brain again runs amok and my limbs go flippity-flop. I am a patient once more hoping a doctor will bring back his health. I realize this stay is merely overnight, only for observation. And yet it is an event that confronts me with my worst fear: my seizures are deteriorating. In the future, it will turn out, visual hallu-cinations will be a prelude to dizziness, nausea, and blackout. I will lie on a carpet or bed or whatever flat place is near, my systems shutting down: sight, balance, position sense, and, it will sometimes feel, respiration, too, until consciousness mercifully vanishes. While unconscious, I'll arch my neck, twitch, foam at the mouth, gaze opaquely at the world, and make what one witness described as "mousy sounds."

This is not the whole of it. My mother accuses me of being hypersen-sitive, of overreacting to casual comments. Julie throws in her opinion: I am hostile. If part of me passes as sociable and controlled, another part is there, too, this one less contrived, more hidden and fearful and, it seems, ready to snap. I recognize at times a kind of pan-anger. Little things set me off; I war with bank tellers. At moments, my jaws ache, and I stuff a towel in my mouth to resist grinding my teeth. Dr. K., taking my side, says I am pondering my mortality. Maybe. There is no doubt I am emotional about death. It was Tolstoy who once wrote that the "fact of the death of a near acquaintance aroused, as usual, in all who heard of it the complacent feeling that 'it is he who is dead and not I.' " I have no complacency. I am unrealistic, adamantly so. An emotional recidivist, I refuse to give up habits that are, I think, the habits of the hopeful patient. The sadness of others, even those I hardly know, makes me very sad. I am a sport-mourner seeking every occasion to exercise my grief. Opportunities abound. While my friend Chalif looks over this calamitous chamber and sees examples of surgical might, I trail behind him, picking out anguish and reduced lives, days limited by doses of medication and physical inabilities. I simply can't comprehend why everyone shouldn't be healed. When I find one of my former roommates, a nineteen-year-old with a benign but dangerously located tumor, in a coma in the ICU, I am flustered and unable to speak. I feel as if a chicken bone has caught in my throat. Chalif had told me that this boy would be cured, forever. Now, he says, in his eloquent way: "A fucking disaster." Surgery had gone badly. I sincerely wanted to get with the program, to not be a wimp sputtering about the few losses. Yet when his surgeon refers to my ex-roommate as "that boy I killed"—I am flooded with emotion.

Even the fates of patients I have never met touch me. One day Barry Milione, founder of the AVM support group, phones to say he is visiting from California. Part of his AVM had been operated on; the rest—the part the surgeon didn't dare touch—had been radiated. We leave messages but miss each other. Then one day his friend calls. She isn't familiar with the terminology, she says, but tells me that Milione has suffered a seizure. That's too bad, I think, but I'd been through enough to know he'd get over it. Where is he? "He's in the hospital," she says. Well, I know a bad seizure can land you in the hospital. At least I've caught up with him. "He can't talk," she says. "He's not conscious." Which is when it dawns on me that Milione isn't in the hospital for a seizure but for a hemorrhage.

I say, "That's awful." I mean, for me.

The import seems clear. The body is wonderfully clever and wonderfully persistent, but it also fucks up as naturally as it heals. I should have continued to identify, I know, with the young surgeons, people taking possession of their powers. The surgeons represent the gift of healing, a kind of medical virility, but I am sad to report that the dying kid with the tumor and the hapless AVM patient move me more. This is the kind of private melodrama, I realize, that, so goes the saying on 11 East, doesn't do anybody any good. But there it is. I am behind the scenes with the brilliant young residents, invited to witness the wonders of neurosurgery, and everything reminds me of medicine's awful limits. All I can think is that sickness is always sickness and deformation and loss. I am not proud of my reaction. It does not seem to me laudable or sensitive or kind but a brand of self-pity, which makes me ashamed, just as I believe I am fundamentally ashamed of my epilepsy.

A few months after being discharged from my padded hospital bed, I am asked how long I am going to live. What a silly question! I think, knowing that neither brain surgery nor epilepsy necessarily shortens one's life. Then my voice breaks, and I am tearful. Don't I *seem* normal? Added to the other breakdowns is this one, a failure to carry it off. In my mind a single image sticks, the one that Julie described, the mid-fit one, with beaded spit on my lips.

As a patient on 11 East, I had surrendered, entrusted my problems and my pain to strangers in white coats. In part I had resented the ignorance in which I had been forced to live. I had not understood why I should be so suddenly stricken or by what mechanism I should be restored to health.

But in part, it was also true, I reveled in my ignorance. Medicine makes this argument to the patient: Don't meddle and you'll be restored. I had kept my distance, and as a patient my mood had been buoyant. A lack of specific knowledge had helped keep me afloat. Had I been restored, had I been able to simply plug back into life where I had dropped out—the way I had imagined I was going to—I would not have needed to shed my ignorance. But when my cure did not hold—or only partially—I had no choice. I had a sursanure, a wound healed outwardly but not inwardly. My ignorance, part enforced, part willed, no longer protects me. I have been complicit too long. I have to confront the malaise that lingers, find a way to come to terms with my experience of recovery.

THE RETURN TO the presick world I had forlornly hoped for was not going to occur. That much was becoming clear. With epilepsy something broke for me. My notion of recovery, with its automechanical metaphors, stalled. I have not been fixed, repaired, tuned up. Recovery, for me, was not to be restoration. And I can't convince myself that this isn't awful. I can't shake the idea that in this realm there is only good and bad, only healthy and unhealthy; if you aren't one, then you are the other. The doctors told me I was healthy. I passed the tests at their offices, followed their prescriptions. And yet I feel more alone than ever and have this increasingly urgent sense that all is not well, that I am not well. Surgery entered and exited. Yet this illness, which I intended to pass through, has nested inside me.

Kricheff, benevolent force in the menacing world of medicine, could be of no help. I occassionally ran into him during the course of my research with Chalif but rarely brought up epilepsy. "Fine, fine, everything's fine," I'd say, as is my habit, and return his question. I'd come to feel that I was spying, a patient behind the lines. Admitting to an ongoing condition, I thought, would reveal me. Then I would no longer be accepted as the doctor's confidant. The one time—after my research was over—that I ventured out of role and mentioned my seizures to Kricheff, he was uncharacteristically quiet. His thick mustache, bracketed by two deep smile lines, hung immobile atop his small mouth, like the metal hood above an oven. "Maybe your seizures are settling down now," he said at one point, then joked that in any case I shouldn't be too sensitive. "In New York no one would notice." Except me. I noticed and noticed.

My parents were emotional but didn't know what to do. So they did what they did best. My mother cooked. She prepared brisket, meat loaf, two kinds of noodle pudding, Jell-O molds with canned pears, loaded them into plastic containers, and shuttled them to my door. My father tried to hem in this new condition with detail work. He followed reports from the doctors as if he were studying yesterday's box scores; he drew conclusions that I hadn't pondered and sent me out to follow them up. It's true, too, that our relations had become more strained. They felt I was less communicative, more private, almost aggressively so. I felt coddled and interfered with. One day I asked them if it wasn't the epilepsy that was at the root of their changed attitude. No, no, no, they insisted, they hadn't changed. But epilepsy was upsetting.

"How did I feel initially?" my mother said. "Devastated. I was concerned that it was going to make you feel in many ways bad, bad about yourself, distressed, discouraged, despondent, all the negatives. I think it has had a negative effect on you."

Whereas once there had been a breeziness, an amicability, in our rapport, my parents had become more conscious of my behavior.

My father joked. "I think the point she's making is she would hope it had an effect, because she would hate to think this is normal behavior."

My mother picked up. "How have you behaved differently? I don't know, sweetheart. God knows when you get down to specifics. It's the kind of thing, Stevie, when you care about somebody, you're always thinking, Gee, did that person say such and such or act in such and such a way because something is bothering him or could it be he just did it?"

Though we didn't talk about epilepsy's distress, we talked about epilepsy often enough. Every family must have such topics. Epilepsy became the topic about which I could express problems and they could respond with concern. And yet finally, because it didn't get better and might at any time get worse, epilepsy frustrated us, three people accustomed to putting our will to work against a problem, to dominating it. Perhaps it was this frustration that sabotaged the easiness that once characterized our relationship.

My mother said: "You have surgery which is totally successful, literally saves your life. The choices were life or death. You walk away from that one hundred percent. No impairment. You have all of your faculties. Everything is terrific. And then there is this which is not, as the AVM is, an aberration. It's not that kind of thing. The seizure is obviously a rather common phenomenon. And the whole neurological field says, you know: 'Big deal. So you've got a hangnail. Live with it.' And I just personally find that unbelievably frustrating."

One week I broke from my research to track down John Corallo. It took some scrambling to come up with his phone number, and when I finally did, I was afraid to dial, fearful that there would be bad news. Fortunately that wasn't the case, or didn't seem to be. His wife readily passed the phone to John, who was glad to hear from me. In part, that's just the way John is, gregarious, welcoming. He took to me as someone with whom he shared a secret past. John had collapsed in a hotel in Atlantic City, was released from one hospital with possible meningitis, and was finally operated on at NYU for a ruptured aneurysm. It had been two years and two months since we were roommates on 11 East. John was excited. "Let's get together," he said.

Our worlds never would have intersected if not for the hospital. What do we have in common but a few holes in our skulls? But he sounded great. Here, I thought, was a case to hold up as an example, maybe to emulate. I could have hugged the guy. "Let's," I said.

John said he would be wearing a gray overcoat and to look for him and his wife at the theater on Broadway where they had tickets for *Cats*. At 10:30, as the theater crowd filtered into the street, I spotted a square-shouldered man in a light gray coat. His hands were in his pockets, his elbows bumping his sides. Was that John? He was too short. Then, as he came toward me and grabbed my hand, I realized that I had never seen John standing, never met him when he wasn't in a hospital bed.

At dinner we ordered champagne and toasted our health, though neither John nor I drank. John said he brought me something, a present. He slipped from his jacket pocket stapled-together papers that, when he unfolded them, carefully, as if they were tissue paper, revealed this title: "Pterional Craniotomy and Microsurgical Clipping of Anterior Communicating Artery Aneurysm with 9 mm Curved Yasargil Clip." It was a detailed four-page summary of his operation. This was a strange gesture, but he wanted me to have it. Then John brought his head close to mine. His hair was salt and pepper—he'd stopped coloring it, he said—and fluffy, like a shoeshine brush. His head, I noticed, was lopsided from the burr hole near the right temple. "You and me," he said, "we almost died."

Yes, I thought, but that and the pterional craniotomy and the microsurgery were behind him now. He looked so healthy. He really did. He was energetic, even hyperactive, testimony to the wonders of brain surgery. That's why the tale he told was such a surprise. In the hospital, while awaiting surgery, he had sworn he was going to change his lifestyle, wasn't going to work so hard. He was going to enjoy life, take it easy. That was not exactly the way things worked out. His surgery was a success, but John said that for some reason he hadn't been able to get back on track after the operation. He still didn't understand what happened. He wasn't relaxing, though; he was traveling to the casinos in Atlantic City to gamble, and lose. His marriage, his second, was strained. I remembered how worried his wife, Lani, had been in the hospital. She grew short on patience, the constant talk of his operation, of his problems. "It wasn't my fault," she said, "I didn't do this to him." John had owned a couple of garden centers. He lost his business and declared bankruptcy, owing creditors more than $1 million. He was a person who had worked all his life, and then one day his ambition had fizzled. Sometimes surgery in the region of the anterior communicating artery affects behavior, since it is near the frontal lobe, storehouse of personality. (In one 1984 study of thirty-two patients with anterior communicating artery aneurysms, eleven showed a slackening of initiative; two demonstrated personality changes so severe they couldn't resume work.) Could this explain John's inability to readjust? Who knows? John said that both his surgeon and neurologist told him there was nothing wrong. John went on disability compensation. Lani was fed up. John was not the man she married. She left.

It wasn't until about a year and a half after surgery that John began to come out of it and start to think again about work. Lani had agreed to return. Maybe it was because his wife was pregnant, John couldn't say, but he started again to look at the world as the practical person he'd always been, a person whose life had been rooted in buying cheap and selling dear. "I'm forty-two now. That's kind of late to get started again. I just have to work at it," John said to me over dinner. "It's not too late to start over, I hope."

"I hope so, too," I said, but really I didn't know. What I do know is that disease is something different from what I had believed. Neurologists consider illness a set of specifiable biologic symptoms. For neurosurgeons, disease is a few millimeters of brain matter. Remove the sick cells and you cure the sickness! What concerned the young surgeons I hung out with was what could be done about a condition; what *they* could do about it with a drill, a forceps, a microknife. And yet, as John and I could attest, people didn't always return to their former lives, patients' hopes weren't consistently fulfilled, the promise, implied if not stated, when a surgeon lifted the scalpel was sometimes broken, and *not* because the surgery failed.

After his surgery, David Lubarsky had recovered remarkably well, but for a year he says he found it difficult to assimilate back into life. "On the streets I felt like a stranger," he said. Finally, he turned to his neurologist. "I'm really depressed here." His medication was changed, and he joined a therapy group, which helped.

How many times had my friend Chalif told me, "You're cured," and waved a hand in my direction as if all I needed was convincing. Initially, I had agreed. I had thought it unseemly to give in to self-pity, which is how the patient's emotions are stereotyped. As far as neurosurgery was concerned I *was* a success story. Like John, I had been saved from death or incapacitation. (Flamm says, "I treat diseases that kill people.")

But brain surgery and its aftermath dogged me, as it had dogged John and David. And though the neurologists ignored it and the surgeons derided it, a preempted sense of self was part and parcel of our illness as certainly as the mutant blood vessels. If what I had was the cure, then I suffered it as well as the disease. To me it became clear that illness wasn't merely a matter of some balled or ballooned-out vascular tubing. Serious disease was an attack not merely on a person's central nervous system but also on his identity. It rolled over lives, clogged them up.

61

Epilepsy was a tyrant in my life, and the doctors gave me pills! What's more, the medication took its toll. I still had seizures—though reduced in frequency and intensity—and I was drowsy. At work I locked my office door, spread out an exercise mat, and napped in the afternoons. Goodgold said, "Listen, our priority is to avoid seizures." The implication was that I should put up with the fatigue. The medical model says this: Treatment decisions are to be left to doctors; the effects of illness (and also of therapy) are to be tolerated by patients. One day I decided I'd had enough. I was too tired. I cut back on my medication. My decision wasn't unusual. In an in-depth study of eighty epileptics, fully 42 percent "self-regulated" their medications for long periods of time. The result isn't always a happy one. My first generalized seizure and hospitalization had followed my attempts at self-prescribing. So, too, had a change of doctors. My next neurologist was very tall, very thin, had a mop haircut, and agreed to adjust my medication. My seizures continued, but at least I was perkier. Still, when I talked of the tension in my jaws, he responded, "That's not pathologic," which made me wish it were, since I knew it was real and disturbing. Medicine, though, has a practical bias; it has a tendency to dismiss what it can't treat, or suggest it is "psychological," which is a way of dismissing it as well.

I am not impugning the competence of my neurologists. What I began to realize, however, was that their expertise was narrowly focused. My interest, like that of anyone trying to live with a chronic ailment, was outside their domain. To be fair, this is not a choice of an individual doctor but a collective decision foisted on the field by long tradition. Consider how neurologist John Hughlings Jackson, the nineteenth-century father of epilepsy research, reacted to seizures. He loved them! Convulsions, he said, are "an experiment made on the brain by disease." Fits were, in effect, a living laboratory for the most brilliant neurologist of his age. He watched them by the hour. Ironically, one of Jackson's study subjects was his wife, who suffered what would later be labeled Jacksonian epilepsy. (Jacksonian seizures are restricted, usually to certain groups of muscles on one side of the body due to disease of the cortex.) When I first learned about Jackson's wife, I was very excited. I thought that here no doubt was a doctor who had examined chronic illness from the point of view of the sufferer as well as of the clinician. Jackson wrote hundreds of pages about epilepsy, and I thumbed through them with glee and then gloom as the consideration of his wife's epilepsy—of its effect on her sense of competence and completeness—failed to show up. "Calm and cold scientific observation" is needed, Jackson argued, and all neurology followed his mechanistic trail. The neurology that Jackson helped create, says neurologist Oliver Sacks, is "deaf to anguish." My neurologists asked for my seizure history. How often did I suffer them? How did they start? How did they progress? they wanted to know, and I dutifully told them. More than dutifully. I was expectant. I would detail for them my seizure past; they would see its significance, then take this thing and squash it. And yet, as fitful Mrs. Jackson must surely have known and as I soon learned, it was not the seizures which disrupt a life. It was how they affected a person ontologically, how fearing a seizure beat up my confidence, subdued my jollity, forced on me the dishonesty that accompanies disability. And this no neurologist considered.

One example of the far-reaching effects of illness on my life is the way in which my relationship with Julie fell apart. It wasn't brain surgery or epilepsy that separated us; the underlying issues existed apart from these climactic events. But the aftermath of my AVM is in there;

it cast a pall from which the relationship never emerged. These are among the real products of disease: relationships under new strains. To Julie, I had become self-obsessed, and that was a clear consequence of my illness.

She said: "The fact that you've been working on this book for three years, the fact that you've been essentially writing a story and a book that is a hundred percent about you, about the most sensitive topic that it could possibly be about you, about something that deeply upsets me about you. . . . You forget that I'm putting up with it and that I would sometimes prefer to hear about a boring day of graphic design," which is what she worked at.

Julie felt I should be moving ahead. How could I live in my dump of an apartment, anyhow? she said, which I guess was a way of asking why I was returning to my computer day after day to dwell on my surgery. She felt shortchanged, and the feeling was sometimes more and sometimes less but never went away. I stayed up all night to take call with the residents. I spent evenings at the hospital. I would like to wrap up the research and the writing, but it dragged on. And she was probably right; I was obsessed with the new burdens of my health. Truly, I never thought about not continuing the project.

She said: "I think you forget what brain surgery means to me. It means a responsibility I don't want to have. I can't sweep it under the carpet. I can't say it's over and you're going to have seizures a couple of times a year and I can deal with that."

"Why do you stay?" I said to her at one point.

"I don't know; that's a good question. I keep thinking that when the book finishes you'll move on. That finally brain surgery will be over. It's essentially like you've been having brain surgery for three years."

The deadline on the book was pushed back four months, then six more months, almost an entire year. Each time the due date was postponed, our relationship sputtered.

The weight of my illness fell on Julie in a way I didn't understand and maybe didn't care to understand. Victims should get in line *behind* me, I believed. She felt as if she were owed something, some better treatment, in part no doubt for having put up with so much. I didn't feel as if I owed anybody anything. I was the victim, after all. I resented her horning in on that territory. Most of the time I didn't really care that she felt aggrieved. I was incapable of taking on her moods, which is what her feelings seemed like to me. I had my own complaints. Despite her conviction that I was self-absorbed, I felt she paid me no attention.

Here were issues that might have deepened our understanding of one another, and yet we never discussed them. Julie tiptoed around the problems, afraid to bring them up. High-handedly, I didn't think they mattered. I hadn't made myself ill, but it was my prerogative to recover at my own pace. Nobody, and that included her, understood what I had gone through.

The quality of attention we gave one another, which is what relationships thrive on, dropped off. We sniped at each other, squabbled over how much (or how little) time we spent together. She harbored a grudge. I ignored it, as I had ignored the other consequences of my changed health status, and it got worse. She burrowed deeper into her grievances, based on how she thought I felt.

Julie said, "Before the seizures I could say: 'You're being an asshole.' The fact that you've been sick and have seizures and are on medication, maybe it has some effect on me that overwhelms me. Now I wonder if you're being an asshole because of the drug."

"And if I don't get my way," I ask, "you think I'll have a seizure?"

"That's right," she said.

Up to the end I felt sure I could recapture the old connection at any moment, but this was a delusion, one of them. The goodwill was gone, the certainty of which occurred to me one evening when we were talking on the phone. There had been so much energy expended on the claims and counterclaims that there was none left for love. What had we loved in each other? From our current vantage point the question was no longer possible to answer. As we conversed, she washed dishes. I heard the clang of her cast-iron frying pan, the rush of steamy water, and I believed that she didn't really have time to devote to me. She was squeezing me in with her chores. I hated that. I was not the person she wanted. She, like me, kept waiting for the illness to lift and resolve our problems. Normalcy never returned. Recovery, of the kind we thought had been promised, never happened. "You need a break," I said at one point, as if being apart might vitiate our difficulties in being together. But there was nothing to break from. Blame had crept into her fatigue.

The water from the faucet was as loud as traffic. I felt so ill at ease; nearly unwanted. I had hoped, I think, that she would protest, say that we needed time together, not apart. But she took me up, talked about visiting California alone. The world seemed out to defeat her, and I, and my epilepsy, were part of that world. "I often feel like I'm not living up to your demands," she said, "I think that you forget that you have to woo someone or romance them." I was tired of hearing what I had to do. As we spoke on the phone, I took her photo, the one with the bow in her hair, from my mantel and stuffed it in a drawer.

Later, Julie said to me, "I think we just missed our time. We should have moved in together two years ago."

I think that it was my misfortune to come into kindness when I was not able to reciprocate. Now I wonder, with a growing terror, if someone else will accept that I've been sick, still am, and be kind to me again.

62 I had thought that the neurologists' pills would halt my epilepsy and, consequently, install control in my life. It hadn't worked out that way. At another point I had believed that by hanging out with the neurosurgeons, and in particular the residents, I could share in their sense of command, which is what seemed most lacking in my own existence. Instead, their burgeoning skills, their bluster, mocks me. One morning, I remember, Chalif had greeted me with this news. "It was the hardest thing I've done in neurosurgery," he said, "Period." Chalif had opened the skull of a young girl. He had paused to adjust the retractor when the fragile aneurysm blew. Chalif searched frantically for the source of the bleed when, after a move of his forceps, the bleeding became torrential. Is it possible to teach someone to tolerate sensational pressure? Could Chalif roll half a dozen years of training into a single correct action? "My life flashed before my eyes," he said. Flamm, who was standing by, was earnest and cool. Chalif called for the clip applicator. "I visualized the aneursym and fired the clip in," said Chalif. He waited. The bleeding stopped. "I triumphed," he told me, euphoric.

Chalif mastered the brain, and mine, flawed by hemorrhage or scalpel, made my days ungovernable. Something had to change. But how? How does the patient, even one with access to the inner workings of medicine, look out for himself? I left the tight circle of neurodoctors and fell back, as I had once before, on a flimsy referral network. I began to see a therapist. After all, some of Freud's early successes were with psychologically provoked epilepsy. A friend of Julie's sister recommended a psychiatrist whose major interest was people with seizures. Frankly,

I harbored about psychiatrists and anything psychological the same prejudices as other nonpsychological doctors. I suspected that if a problem
was labeled psychological it probably didn't exist. Or that its treatment
was endless. But I had nowhere else to turn. The dilemma was not only
that the remedy was beyond the capabilities of the neurologist and neurosurgeon; it was outside their area of interest. I'd been given the impression, not always, but often enough, that the symptoms I talked of were
vague or invalid. I'd been led to believe that I was a complainer, which
is a type of liar. The psychiatrist spoke in a voice as high and whiny as
Truman Capote's. Immediately, though, he said that he knew what I was
talking about. He'd seen epilepsy infiltrate people's lives all the time.
That felt like a victory in and of itself.

He believed—as do most clinicians—that stress is a factor in triggering
a seizure. ("What a stressful remark!" said another neurologist while acknowledging its truth.) He had developed some techniques, he said, relaxation techniques. He sat me in a plump corner chair and instructed me
to close my eyes and let my wrist "float" off the armrest and into the air.
"Your arm is getting weightless . . ." he said in that ridiculous voice. He
taught me a mantra to repeat. Whenever a seizure erupted, I was to whip
into this self-hypnosis routine and chase the seizure as if it were a dream.
I loved the idea. What control! Unfortunately, the scheme was not feasible.
Try letting your wrist sail into the air while lying on a shiny basketball
court, a dozen out-of-breath guys in shorts saying things like "He looks
weird," "Hey, get somebody," "The guy's flipping."

The psychiatrist did, however, suggest a switch in medication. I was
taking orange-banded Dilantin capsules. He favored pink tabs of Tegretol,
which, research shows, has fewer effects on subtle cognitive functions (like
memory). My neurologist was initially opposed, warning that my seizures
could get worse. But I was determined.

My first reaction to the switch was: What a mistake! For a few weeks,
every time my subway car started or stopped, I got nauseated; on the street
I'd sometimes see two people, whereas I knew there was but one. I didn't
know that I was remembering any better. Plus I still had seizures, although,
and this was important, none escalated into generalized seizures. Perhaps
the crucial implication for my well-being was this: By changing medication,
I had exerted a measure of control, which I realized not only epilepsy but
doctors, too, took away.

Next, I looked up epilepsy in the phone book. Two of the four listings
were for the Epilepsy Institute. I phoned. It is important for me, I decided,
to meet people who have epilepsy and who also lead normal lives and

aren't upset all the time. Epileptics harbor the same misconceptions about epilepsy as the rest of the world—that the condition is linked to criminality, deviancy, retardation, or more mundanely, that epileptics are all fat and unattractive. A group of half a dozen people—Yuppies with epilepsy— met weekly at the institute.

Here at last, amid the portable beige walls and mud-colored formica desks of the Epilepsy Institute, I am not cast as the moper crowding the doctor's telephone line, the manipulator trying to beat my medication regimen. My symptoms aren't dismissed because they don't appear in the neurology texts, aren't "pathological." Here the anguish that neurosurgery passed over, that neurology, according to one neurologist, had methodically suppressed, was lent credence. Hell, it was permitted to exist.

Still, I wasn't babied. We sat in a circle in a small pink room whose door had to be propped closed with a chair and people who locked in to one, negative attitude got bullied.

"I just want to stay home," I said at one point.

Why? comes the response, almost, it seemed to me, in a hostile tone.

"I don't want to have a seizure in front of everyone" was my comeback. My voice was high, which is how it gets when I'm exasperated.

The group leader was the Institute's executive director, Reina Berner. She spoke in a New York accent as heavy as a cabbie's.

"Do you have that many?" she said.

"Well, no, but I'm always afraid that I'm going to have one, and in front of strangers." Like everyone didn't understand! I thought.

Berner, a social worker, could suddenly shift her expression from a squirmy giggle to an eyes-drawn-down blank. In her blank mode she said: "What happens when you have one in front of people?"

"I'm dreadfully embarrassed."

"Is embarrassment so terrible?"

I didn't immediately have an answer. Indeed, it struck me as a bizarre question. After a brain hemorrhage and then brain surgery, I wondered, What *is* the locus of my fear, its real redoubt? I have harbored it so long, coddled it, and yet left this aspect of my personality unexamined. Why is it that a blow I suffer for half an hour half a dozen times a year lays me up day after day? Am I afraid of the seizure itself or how it makes me appear to others or how I imagine it will make me appear?

Sociologists and pyschologists make an important distinction between a "stigma," which is a condemnation by the outside world, and a "felt stigma," which is the opprobrium that a sufferer suspects awaits him. In a real stigma situation someone calls you an ugly name. In the case of a felt stigma, you tremble because you are afraid of the epithet that *may* be uttered.

The person who anticipates stigma doesn't need to be insulted. He acts as his own accuser, constantly imagining the worst. The epileptic, and maybe any person who believes himself handicapped, suffers the stigma and the felt stigma, the real prejudice and the anticipation of prejudice separately, but, in fact, it is the imagined blow that is the more ruinous.

"The anxiety caused by epilepsy is real," Berner explained, "try to deal with it. Talk about it. Stretch your limits, see what you can do. Is epilepsy going to make you stop seeing friends because you're afraid of having a seizure? Dealing with the anxiety is the way to take control of your life. Can you do something for yourself to get over that, to live? You have to. If you let epilepsy control you, you're in bad shape."

I guess so.

If I came clean, what would I admit to being afraid of: that people would put me down, laugh, cringe, steer clear? Would the surgeons really disqualify me as their interlocutor? The truth is, I don't know. I hide my condition and my fears of it, confine the precious knowledge to a few friends, and thus act as my own disciplinarian. My tendency as someone with epilepsy is to move in the markers of my own freedom. Perhaps my fears are unfounded. Indeed, polls suggest that the general population that once burned epileptics as witches and more recently refused them as playmates is increasingly accepting. "It seems on the balance that the public may well be less ignorant and more tolerant than the orthodox viewpoint implies," write Graham Scambler and Anthony Hopkins in a study funded by the British Epilepsy Association.

Finally the insight that I believe sets me on a more fruitful path is this: Recovery is not to be restoration of a prior identity, which is a version of nostalgia that pervades medicine. It is change and adjustment to a new way of being in the world. There's no denying that serious illness attacks a person's cells. The neurons misfiring in my brain are a fact from which I cannot distance myself. I can't promise to do better next time, to not make the same mistake. I don't blame anyone for my epilepsy—perhaps it was not even the surgery, but the hemorrhage that caused it—though I often feel I don't deserve such a malady. Yet more importantly, epilepsy, like any handicap, like illness itself, is not so much a question of what you can do and what you can't do but how you feel about those facts. The condition takes away control, but perhaps that is more a social and psychological issue than a neurological one. Epilepsy, as Scambler and Hopkins learned, is not nearly as restrictive as having assumed the identity of the epileptic. Recovery is adaptation. Epilepsy requires redefinitions.

I experiment.

Fortified in the belief that I'm not the weird one—or I'm only as weird as I choose to be—sometimes I tell people I have just met about my epilepsy. I give up my cover, don't try to pass. This is a big step. My voice is trembly at first, as if I've been caught doing something wrong.

Robert Murphy, an anthropologist who suffered from a crippling tumor, found that when he was in a wheelchair, he was treated differently. The largest part was an unpleasant marginalization, even by those he knew. But there were also moments when people—perhaps because they no longer found him threatening—warmed to him. Women, for example, sometimes opened to him in a more direct, more open way, catching his eye, initiating conversation.

No one hopes for such incapacities; only the naive make the argument that their advantages outweigh their misery. Yet perhaps they do reveal, more than other instances in life, how large a part of our interactions are based on learned cues. What I find is that even strangers don't run when I bring up my epilepsy. Moreover, and this is bizarre, epilepsy gives me access to people in a way I never had before, not to their masterful side, their autonomous, achieving side, which is their public front, but to the vulnerable aspect of them, their private interior.

At a party, one person tells me how his childhood dyslexia retarded his schooling, another that his first wife left him for another woman. Over lunch a colleague mentions that her son was born with cerebral palsy and that it depressed her for a year. The first time I talk with another acquaintance she says, "I never tell this to anyone, but I'm a recovering alcoholic." Perhaps we would have gotten to this eventually, but it seems to me that epilepsy can be a pipeline. By bringing it up myself, I have recast it, given it a different value. Certainly it is not a strength, nor am I convinced I want to hear the burdens of each stranger I meet. But who would have seen it as a shortcut to intimacy, as something I could employ to really get to know someone? Even Chalif's reaction when I impress on him that I continue to have seizures surprises me. He didn't realize I had ongoing fits and urges me to insist that my doctors be aggressive. "You shouldn't have to live with that," he said with concern.

Each of the group members has, in effect, taken Chalif's advice and become more demanding in behalf of his or her health. Since joining the group, everyone has changed doctors. When I say that my neurologist considers my half-dozen seizures a year "controlled," the response is a groan. I enroll with a third neurologist. He has no radical new therapy, but his attitude is different: "We're going to adjust your medication to stop your seizures." I know it might not work, but why not try? I go for further testing. Even when I am not having seizures there are epileptic spikes, which could account for the instances when I think I see a fleeting seizure blip. He increases my medication. On an increased dose of Tegretol, I go six months without a seizure.

Group meetings change. Each week, we sit on thin metal-legged chairs and, led by Berner, we crack up. We laugh—at one woman taking off her shirt during a seizure and scandalizing Broadway topless, at another traipsing around the supermarket in an epileptic haze and no one noticing, at me in a cab while my vision is falling to pieces, of all things, during rush hour. "If you don't laugh, you really go bananas," says one member. Our laughter lets off steam, but it has, I think, another purpose. This is an exercise in attitude adjustment that carries this implication: A seizure is behavior. Moreover, like most behavior, its significance is ambivalent, open to interpretation. It might be a horror, a grievous embarrassment, sure, but it also might be interpreted as something else, as, say, grist for the joke mill. Seizures might not be colossal social faux pas but antics. It's as if, by laughing, we are saying: What if we consider that we are not victims but perpetrators; that we are like Marx Brothers chortling at the world's uptight reaction to our epileptic stunts! The point is that a seizure need not be an object of derision or scorn or shame. It is an empty vessel that I can fill with whatever meaning I choose.

This is not to say that I feel great about epilepsy, that I wouldn't feel blessed if it one day evaporated. The day at the Epilepsy Institute that I saw someone else have a seizure was traumatic. The woman's neck swiveled like a tank turret, and her jaws snapped shut and clenched. Her eyes gave out a wide, blank stare but clearly took nothing in. Saliva poured out of her mouth. She stiffened and extended her arms straight in front of her, as if she were preparing for a dive. They vibrated. I turned away, then forced myself to observe, like a kid playing peekaboo. A human being was out of control. It was dreadfully ugly. I tried to think of this as behavior, maybe eccentric, but within the normal range. I couldn't. What *possessed* her? I thought, calling up the prejudices epileptics have fought for two thousand years. Then I thought, like one of my ancestors in antiquity, It is contagious. And among us who have a predisposition! We will all seize. We will link agitating arms like those plastic monkeys with curled limbs I played with as a child and form a chattering simian necklace.

No, epilepsy is not something I am tempted to put on my résumé. Hardly a week goes by that I don't go out to a diner and a blip, cruising into my vision like a spaceship, doesn't send me into a panic. I remind myself that it might just be a wayward signal from the occipital lobe of my head. I ask myself, What's the worst that could happen? I scout a place to lie down. Stress, I know, feeds the seizure. I try to talk myself down. To no avail. I feel as if a spring has uncoiled in my stomach. I pay without finishing my meal and get out of there. Once outside, I squeeze my eyes shut. Is it really there? Most often it is not.

What's more, even the small possibility that seizures can worsen is depressing. I have a four-minute warning period. That is a period of enormous distress as I witness my eyesight close down. Yet I wonder what it would be like not to have those minutes, to simply wake up from a convulsion that has sacked me without notice. Or what if I had more seizures?

"I think if I had the seizure frequency that Emily has," one group member says about another, "I would commit suicide." I, too, don't know how I'd live with that.

Emily Ranseen, thirty-eight, a landscape architect, is attractive and sweet; she uses words like "gosh" and "darn." After a bicycle accident seventeen years ago she suffered as many as ten seizures a month, an average of one every three days. At first her seizures were "a terrible sensation." Later she would stare or faint or occasionally walk around telling children they were the Second Coming or have a convulsion.

"Have you been in status?" Emily says, jolting me. She is referring to status epilepticus, a prolonged seizure state that can cause brain damage in an hour. As much as 10 percent of the time, by one published report, status epilepticus kills.

"Well, there was one time I was admitted to the hospital," I say, bonding. Then I ask the question that preoccupies me: Has she ever thought of suicide?

Emily hasn't. She says: "I got this novel out of the library. I've read it after every bad seizure, about six times. It's about a teenage girl who has epilepsy. She says, 'I'm going to go out into the world and accept what's me.' There was a point where it all clicked, and I thought, Oh, I shouldn't worry so much."

Emily's wristwatch tinkles, a reminder to take her medication.

"It's too bad," she says, "I'd rather not have seizures. I'd rather have fewer. But what can I do?"

When I complain about six a year, she says, "Oh, gosh, that's nothing."

On good days I think that Emily is right. If I had been born at the turn of the century, I might have been locked up in an epileptic colony. Before 1938, the year Dilantin was introduced, I'd have been a zombie, sedated on phenobarbital. On these same days I am glad to report I also marvel at the undaunted nurses who inch patients toward recovery and look with admiration at the residents and attendings who choose neurosurgery. That they have the nerve to go into the head, and do it so well, despite what seems nature's intent to have its own flawed way, continues to astound me. Those who have a lesion that the brain surgeon can attack are the lucky ones.

I have come a long way from the hotel lobby in Nicaragua where nearly a half cup of blood jetted into my brain and almost killed me. I have been introduced to medicine's most sophisticated diagnostic machines, benefited from its finest therapeutic skills. I had signed on as a booster of high-powered medicine, the medicine that saved my life. In the end I got epilepsy, a weird ailment with an incomplete treatment, and needed other help. Having been marked cured, I was left to cope, which changed how I viewed the cure.

Cure, I believe now, is an attitude. And that attitude begins to take hold not solely because a clot was evacuated from my brain or a congenital blood-vessel malformation was excised from my occipital lobe. If there are periods of time when I feel in control again, it is not because of the neurologists' pills or the neurosurgeons' scalpels but because I am able to accept that being subject to seizures is like any limitation, like being unemployed, or picked last on the playground. Having epilepsy is not different from life, which is a story of possibilities shutting down, details ranging a little beyond control, things failing. I had once maintained this: I am the same as I've always been, just taking medication. The shame I felt was the inability to be, in some sense, normal, the normal I had known. Medicine claimed to have done its part. Why wasn't I holding up my end? In truth, medicine could not return me to a presick state, nor could I. The surgeons learned to accept failure by putting it behind them; I had to learn to live with it. The attitude I hold to now is this: I'm different, but it's not that big a deal.

Often enough I feel ready to move on, to make new friends, my courage screwed up to "come out," as one group member described it, about my epilepsy. I can sometimes joke about my own epileptic shenanigans. I even on a first date have a seizure—about the worst scenario I could imagine.

And things were going so well, I thought. She blushed easily—"Nice venous system," I'd said—then hurried to cover her mouth, as if she were revealing too much. It was a gesture I found adorable. She ordered a beer, I went with coffee.

"You don't drink," she said.

"Teetotaler." I smiled. One does not go through the list of one's chronic conditions over appetizers. And then, as the pasta arrived, there it was, the rent in my vision! My most social moment collided with my most private fear. What to do?

"I'm sorry," I said, "but will you follow me?" She wasn't laughing now. I hustled toward the bathroom, thinking all the while about what I could possibly say. I turned to her, looked in her spinning green eyes. Her eyebrows had fallen. She looked arch. What must she expect? "You remember that I didn't drink alcohol, well, I want to tell you why," I said. She made a sound, like the creak of a lawn chair folding, as if to say, Is this the place for confessions? My words rushed out. "I have epilepsy," I said, "And right now I'm having a seizure." Her legs bowed back. She was stunned, I think, and somewhat frightened as I tried to engage her in this little caper. I told her to follow me *into* the bathroom! (Fortunately, they were individual bathrooms, not a large men's room.)

"You're shaking," she said, her voice windy, as if she were going to be hoarse.

"Hold my hand," I said shamelessly. Her arms shot straight out, as if she were holding a boat's tiller. She sandwiched my hand tightly in her two hands. Even then I think I knew what an uproarious story this would make back at the group. Something along these lines: my vision in free-fall, nausea, dizziness coming in spasms, and sitting on the toilet, my impulse? To be social. I ask my pretty date where Dolly, her interesting name, came from. Taking me entirely at my word, she answered without hesitation. Within a few minutes my vision was gone, or rather given over to my new epileptic vision, swelling and easing like turbulent waves.

My seizure lasted for maybe ten or fifteen minutes. I *was* embarrassed much longer. It seemed bad manners or just cloddy, not the image of myself I had in mind. Though she said not to worry about it, I apologized uncontrollably, as if this, too, were a seizure. "Thanks for being a good sport," I said when she finally ducked into a cab.

Is embarrassment so terrible? I felt I could answer the question with a shrill yes. Then, a few days later, she called me. Not to learn if I was all right but to say she was in the neighborhood and was I free.

Hadn't she been put off by the seizure?

"It was an ice breaker," she said.

Come on.

"It was something very real and very personal. Your way of dealing with it was kind of great. You talked to me. I felt kind of moved by it."

Oh, boy.

EPILOGUE

In 1987, Eugene Flamm left his post as vice-chairman of neurosurgery at NYU to become Charles Harrison Frazier professor of neurosurgery at the University of Pennsylvania. Perhaps he would have preferred to be chairman at NYU, but Chairman Ransohoff was still going strong, and the Penn offer was too good. "My head's in the clouds," he said when it began to unfold. He would be chairman of neurosurgery and have the opportunity to create and lead his own department.

In the few months before he was to complete the residency, David Chalif said, "This is the end of the line." He was thirty-one, had been in school or training for the past twenty-five years, and it seemed to him he had put off his future long enough. His wife was pregnant; he had a family to plan for. Some residents leave the program bitter; they don't thrive in what Ransohoff called its "hyperactive, hypercritical" atmosphere. Chalif had thrived. And he thought he had a good shot at an attending's job. "I'm going to have a meeting with Ransohoff. I'm going to lock the door. I'll tell the secretary not to disturb him unless someone is dying." At night he practiced a speech in the room with the imported skull, the brain-surgery books that Flamm had given him, and the bassinet. "I'm going to tell him he's not planning for the future."

Flamm had suggested that Chalif specialize for a year in vascular neurosurgery, the way Flamm had. Then Flamm said he could return to NYU with a real specialty, not just a pair of golden hands, which the department had a few of already. Flamm had arranged for a fellowship at the University of Virginia. But to Chalif it felt like putting his future on hold yet again. Chalif turned down the fellowship. In return, he received by mail a very upsetting cartoon of a tombstone. "RIP David Chalif, academic neurosurgeon" was the inscription.

Chalif's big meeting with Ransohoff was not decisive. There weren't any positions available at NYU. Chalif knew of a private practice on Long Island, the preeminent practice on Long Island. Chalif felt a little betrayed, but so be it. He would build an empire on Long Island.

Jacqueline Mawby left the neurosurgery service. For a while she dropped out, going to school and trying to figure out how, and if, she wanted to get back into nursing. She eventually went to work part-time on the maternity floor at University Hospital. "That (11 East) is one end of life; this is the other," she said.

Patricia Henry also transferred to maternity. "I couldn't take it up there: too many people die," she said.

Mindy Rothenstreich left as well. She got a better job offer and now works as Alejandro Berenstein's assistant in interventional neuroradiology.

Barry Milione recovered from his hemorrhage, which, the most recent tests show, destroyed what remained of his AVM. His memory was deficient, and that frustrated him, but his plans were to return to school to become a dentist. Kimberly Dorcy, now thirteen, has had some difficulties in school—it's not possible to say whether they're related to her AVM—but is working hard and doing okay. Tests of her brain show some abnormal waves in the area of her surgery, so she has remained on medication, which unfortunately makes her quite hyperactive. Sometimes she can't get to sleep at night.

For those close to John Corallo, his operation had marked a turning point. "He was never the same after that," one person said. It's no doubt impossible to know what part his brain surgery really played in his misfortunes, but his new business went under, as did his second marriage.

Sam died in the hospital, never making it to the nursing home for which he had long been waiting. Rothenstreich remembered his death well, because she wheeled him down to the morgue. "It was my first time down there. When we walked out, I let out a scream. I just got hysterical. You work so hard and get so mad at yourself and for what?" Leonard's health initially declined then made a comeback. Feisty man that he is, he slipped once when too impatient to wait for help and broke a leg. He sold his store and retired. His speech came back, though he could be incoherent sometimes. David Lubarsky was doing fine. Maybe his reading was off a bit, or he had to concentrate on conversations harder, or he got headaches, but those were minor disturbances. He and his wife had a brand-new baby girl. Sometimes, he said, he even forgot that he'd ever had brain surgery.

Bibliography

I. EXPLOSION IN MY HEAD

Adams, Raymond D., and Maurice Victor. *Principles of Neurology*. 3d ed. New York: McGraw-Hill, 1985.

Bakal, Donald A. *Psychology & Medicine: Psychobiological Dimensions of Health and Illness*. New York: Springer, 1979.

Liebeskind, J. C., and L. A. Paul. "Psychological and Physiological Mechanisms of Pain." *Annual Review of Psychology* (1977).

Melzack, Ronald. *The Puzzle of Pain*. New York: Basic Books, 1973.

Melzack, Ronald, and Patrick D. Wall. *The Challenge of Pain*. New York: Basic Books, 1983.

Melzack's books are readable and engaging, and my discussion of pain leans heavily on his inquiries.

Sacks, Oliver. *Migraine: Understanding a Common Disorder*. Berkeley: Univ. of California Press, 1985.

Toole, James F. *Cerebrovascular Disorders*. 3d ed. New York: Raven Press, 1984.

Wang, Michael, and Alan Freeman. *Neural Function*. Boston: Little, Brown, 1987.

II. PEERING INTO THE BRAIN

Cairns, H., and M. H. Jupe. *A Textbook of X-Ray Diagnosis by British Authors*, Vol. 1. London: H. K. Lewis, 1951.

Crane, A. W. "The Research Trail of the X-ray." In *Classic Descriptions in Diagnostic Roentgenology* Vol. 1. Springfield, Ill.: C. Thomas, 1964.

This is part of a wonderful two-volume set for anyone interested in browsing through original papers, most of which are eminently readable.

Hounsfield, G. N. "Historical Notes on Computerized Axial Tomography." *The Journal of the Canadian Association of Radiologists* (September 1976).

Roentgen, Wilhelm Conrad. "On a New Kind of Rays: Preliminary Communication," "On a New Kind of Rays," and "Further Observations on the Properties of X-rays." In *Classic Descriptions in Diagnostic Roentgenology*, Vol. 1. Springfield, Ill.: C. Thomas, 1964 .

Leonard, Charles Lester. "The Application of the Roentgen Rays to Medical Diagnosis." *Journal of the American Medical Association* (December 4, 1897).

Lindgren, Erik. "A History of Neuroradiology." In *Radiology of the Skull and Brain*, Vol. 1, edited by Thomas H. Newton and D. Gordon Potts. St. Louis: C. V. Mosby, 1971.

Oldendorf, W. H. *Quest for an Image of Brain*. New York: Raven Press, 1980.

III. ASSESSING THE EVIL

Ballance, Charles. "A Glimpse into the History of the Surgery of the Brain." *The Lancet* (January 21 and 28, 1922).

Horrax, G. *Neurosurgery: An Historical Sketch*. Springfield, Ill.: C. Thomas, 1952.

Hubel, David, and Torsten Wiesel. "Brain Mechanisms of Vision." In *The Brain: A Scientific American Book*. New York: W. H. Freeman, 1979.

Luria, Aleksandr Romanovich. *Higher Cortical Functions*. 2d ed. New York: Basic Books, 1980.

Penfield, Wilder. *No Man Alone: A Neurosurgeon's Life*. Boston: Little, Brown, 1977. While this book, like so many physician autobiographies, can get lost in disputes the reader cares little about, it engagingly traces parts of the history of neurosurgery.

Sacks, Oliver. *A Leg to Stand On*. New York: Summit Books, 1984.

Shorter, Edward. *Bedside Manners: Troubled History of Doctors and Patients*. Toronto: Simon and Schuster, 1985.

Spillane, John D., *The Doctrine of the Nerves*. London: Oxford Univ. Press, 1981. This book is filled with neat accessible commentary and is great reading. My discussion of neurologic history draws heavily on this source.

Van Allen, Maurice W., and Robert L. Rodnitzky. *Pictorial Manual of Neurologic Tests*. 1st and 2d eds. Chicago: Year Book Medical Publishers, 1969 and 1981.

IV. LIFE AND DEATH ON 11 EAST

Litman, Theodor J. "The Family as a Basic Unit in Health and Medical Care: A Social Behavioral Overview." *Social Science & Medicine* 8 (1974).

Parsons, Talcott, *The Social System*. New York: Free Press, 1951.

——— "Definitions of Health and Illness in the Light of American Values and Social Structure." In *Patients, Physicians and Illness*, edited by E. G. Jaco. New York: Free Press, 1972.

Parsons, Talcott, and Renee Fox. "Illness, Therapy and the Modern Urban American Family." *Journal of Social Issues* 8 (1952).

Shapiro, Johanna. "Family Reactions and Coping Strategies in Response to the Physically Ill or Handicapped Child: A Review." *Social Science & Medicine* 17 (1983).

Tagliacozzo, Daisy L., and Hans O. Mauksch. "The Patient's View of the Patient's Role." In *Patients, Physicians and Illness*, edited by E. G. Jaco. New York: Free Press, 1972.

V. FANTASTIC VOYAGE

Dandy, Walter E. "Ventriculography Following the Injection of Air into the Cerebral Ventricles." In *Classic Descriptions in Diagnostic Roentgenology*. Springfield, Ill.: C. Thomas, 1964.

Lindgren, Erik. "A History of Neuroradiology." In *Radiology of the Skull and Brain*, Vol. 1, edited by Thomas H. Newton and D. Gordon Potts. St. Louis: C. V. Mosby, 1971.

Moniz, Egas. "Arterial Encephalography: Importance in the Localization of Cerebral Tumors." In *Classic Descriptions in Diagnostic Roentgenology*. Springfield, Ill.: C. Thomas, 1964.

VI. PERILOUS BATTLE

Bakal, Donald A. *Psychology & Medicine: Psychobiological Dimensions of Health and Illness*. New York: Springer, 1979.

Bartrop, R. W. et al. "Depressed Lymphocyte Function After Bereavement." *The Lancet* 1 (1977).

Bosk, Charles. *Forgive and Remember: Managing Medical Failure*. Chicago: Univ. of Chicago Press, 1979.

Cushing, Harvey, and Percival Bailey. *Tumors Arising from the Blood Vessels of the Brain: Angiomatous Malformations and Hemangioblastomas*. Springfield, Ill.: C. Thomas, 1928.

Among his other gifts, Cushing could tell a wonderful story. Even these technical books have the benefit for the lay reader of being filled with wonderful, chilling prose.

Dandy, Walter E. "Arteriovenous Aneurysm of the Brain." *Archives of Surgery* 17 (1928).

Kornfeld, Donald S. "The Hospital Environment: Its Impact on the Patient." In *Stress and Survival: The Emotional Realities of Life Threatening Illness*, edited by Charles A. Garfield. St. Louis: C. V. Mosby, 1979.

Mechanic, David. *Medical Sociology: A Selective View*. New York: Free Press, 1968.

Ornstein, Robert, and David Sobel. *The Healing Brain*. New York: Simon and Schuster, 1987.

Pool, J. Lawrence, and D. Gordon Potts. *Aneurysms and Arteriovenous Anomalies of the Brain*. New York: Harper and Row, 1965.

Troupp, Henry. "Arteriovenous Malformations of the Brain: What Are the Indications for Operation?" In *Current Controversies in Neurosurgery*, edited by T. P. Morley. Philadelphia: W. B. Saunders, 1976.

Troupp, Henry, I. Marttila, and V. Halonen. "Arteriovenous Malformations of the Brain: Prognosis without Operation." *Acta Neurochirurgica* 22 (1970).

Selye, Hans. "Stress without Distress." In *Stress and Survival: The Emotional Realities of Life Threatening Illness*, edited by Charles A. Garfield. St. Louis: C. V. Mosby, 1979.

———. *The Stress of Life*. 2d ed. New York: McGraw-Hill, 1976.

Wong, Normund. "Psychological Aspects of Physical Illness." *Bulletin of the Menninger Clinic* 48 (1984).

VII. THE EXCITEMENT OF BRAIN SURGERY

Bucy, Paul C., ed. *Neurosurgical Giants: Feet of Clay and Iron*. New York: Elsevier, 1985.

Fulton, John F. *Harvey Cushing*. Springfield, Ill.: C. Thomas, 1946.

There are two biographies of Cushing. Fulton's is for aficionados who can't

stand not knowing what Cushing did every day of his adult life. Thomson's
is shorter and still very informative.

Jacobson, Julius H. II. "The Introduction." In *Microsurgery*, edited by Sherman J. Silber. Baltimore: Williams and Wilkins, 1979.

Paget, Stephen. *Sir Victor Horsley: A Study of His Life and Work*. London: Constable, 1919.

Penfield, Wilder. *No Man Alone: A Neurosurgeon's Life*. Boston: Little, Brown, 1977.

Pernick, Martin S. *A Calculus of Suffering: Pain, Professionalism and Anesthesia in 19th Century America*. New York: Columbia Univ. Press, 1985.

Robinson, Victor. *Victory Over Pain: A History of Anesthesia*. New York: Schuman, 1946.

Taplinger, Betty MacQuitty. *Victory Over Pain: Morton's Discovery of Anesthesia*. New York: Taplinger, 1971.

Weirdly, there are two books by same title. Both are filled with strange details about the unhappy personalities that brought anesthesia to medicine.

Thomson, Elizabeth Harriet. *Harvey Cushing: Surgeon, Author, Artist*. New York: Schuman, 1950.

Wilson, Charles B., and Bennet M. Stein, eds. *Intracranial Arteriovenous Malformations*. Baltimore: Williams and Wilkins, 1984.

VIII. SEIZURE

Afshar, F., and D. F. Scott. "Post-Operative Epilepsy." *Progress in Neurological Surgery* 11 (1984).

Crawford, P. M., C. R. West, M. D. M. Shaw, and D. W. Chadwick. "Cerebral Arteriovenous Malformations and Epilepsy: Factors in the Development of Epilepsy." *Epilepsia* 27 (1986).

Foy, P. M., G. P. Copeland, and M. D. M. Shaw. "The Incidence of Postoperative Seizures." *Acta Neurochirurgica* 55 (1981).

———. "The Natural History of Postoperative Seizures." *Acta Neurochirurgica* 57 (1981).

Sands, Harry, ed. *Epilepsy: A Handbook for the Mental Health Professional*. New York: Brunner/Mazel, 1982.

Torner, James C. "Epidemiology of Subarachnoid Hemorrhage." *Seminars in Neurology* 4 (September 1984).

IX. DREAMS OF RECOVERY

Murphy, Robert F. *The Body Silent*. New York: Henry Holt, 1987.

Scambler, Graham, and Anthony Hopkins. "Being Epileptic: Coming to Terms with Stigma." *The Sociology of Health and Illness* 8 (1986).

Schneider, Joseph, and Peter Conrad. *Having Epilepsy: The Experience and Control of Illness*. Philadelphia: Temple Univ. Press, 1983.

Teissier du Cros, J., and F. Lhermitte. "Neuropsychological Analysis of Ruptured Saccular Aneurysms of the Anterior Communicating Artery After Radical Therapy." *Surgical Neurology* 22 (1984).

Tolstoy, Leo. *The Death of Ivan Ilych*. Translated by Aylmer Maude. New York: New American Library, 1960.

Some books about the experience of illness:

FICTION

Doestoevsky, Fyodor. *The Idiot*. Translated by Constance Garnett. New York: Bantam, 1981.
Girion, Barbara. *A Handful of Stars*. New York: Scribner's, 1981.
Mann, Thomas. *Magic Mountain*. Translated by H. T. Lowe-Porter. New York: Vintage, 1969.
Roth, Philip. *The Anatomy Lesson*. New York: Farrar Straus Giroux, 1983.
———. *The Counterlife*. New York: Farrar Straus Giroux, 1987.

NONFICTION

Cousins, Norman. *Anatomy of an Illness: As Perceived by the Patient*. New York: Bantam, 1981.
Dobkin, Bruce H. *Brain Matters: Stories of a Neurologist and His Patients*. New York: Crown, 1986.
Halberstam, Michael, and Stephan Lesher. *A Coronary Event*. Philadelphia: J. B. Lippincott, 1976.
Heller, Joseph, and Speed Vogel. *No Laughing Matter*. New York: Avon, 1986.
Lax, Eric. *Life and Death on 10 West*. New York: Laurel Books, 1985.
Lear, Martha Weinman. *Heartsounds*. New York: Simon and Schuster, 1980.
Pond, Jean, *Surviving*. New York: Hill and Wang, 1978.
Rabin, Roni. *Six Parts Love: A Family's Battle with Lou Gehrig's Disease (ALS)*. New York: Scribner's, 1985.
Sacks, Oliver. *A Leg to Stand On*. New York: Summit Books, 1984.
———. *The Man Who Mistook His Wife for a Hat*. New York: Summit Books, 1986.

Some books about the surgeon experience:

Cooper, I. S. *The Vital Probe: My Life as a Brain Surgeon*. New York: Norton, 1981.
Frankling, Jon, and Alan Doelp. *Not Quite a Miracle: Brain Surgeons and Their Patients on the Frontier of Medicine*. Garden City, N.Y.: Doubleday, n.d.
Kramer, Mark. *Invasive Procedures: A Year in the World of Two Surgeons*. New York: Harper and Row, 1979.
Nolen, William A. *The Making of a Surgeon*. New York: Random House, 1968.
Rainer, J. Kenyon. *First Do No Harm: Reflections on Becoming a Brain Surgeon*. New York: Villard, 1987.
Selzer, Richard. *Confessions of a Knife*. New York: Simon and Schuster, 1979.
Shainberg, Lawrence. *Brain Surgeon: An Intimate View of His World*. New York: Fawcett/Crest, 1979.

Index

313